New Testament Commentary

New Testament Commentary

Exposition of the
Second Epistle to the Corinthians

Simon J. Kistemaker

Baker Books
A Division of Baker Book House Co
Grand Rapids, Michigan 49516

©1997 by Simon J. Kistemaker

Published by Baker Books,
a division of Baker Book House Company
P.O. Box 6287
Grand Rapids, Michigan 49516-6287

Printed in the United States of America

Library of Congress Cataloging-in-Publication Data

Hendriksen, William, 1900–82
    New Testament commentary.

    Accompanying Biblical text is author's translation.
    Vols. 14— by Simon J. Kistemaker.
    Includes bibliographical references and indexes.
    Contents: [1] John I-VI — [2] John VII–XII— [etc.] — [19] Exposition of 2 Corinthians.
    1. Bible. N.T.—Commentaries. I. Kistemaker, Simon. II. Bible. N.T. English. Hendriksen. 1953.
    BS2341.H4   1953   225.77   54-924
    ISBN 0-8010-2105-7 (v. 19)

Scripture translation of the text of 2 Corinthians is the author's own. Unless otherwise noted, Scripture quotations are from the Holy Bible: New International Version, © copyright 1978, 1984 by the International Bible Society. Used by permission.

Contents

Abbreviations

AJP	*American Journal of Philology*
ASV	American Standard Version
ATR	*Anglican Theological Review*
AusBRev	*Australian Biblical Review*
AV	Authorized Version
Barn.	The Epistle of Barnabas
Bauer	Walter Bauer, W. F. Arndt, F. W. Gingrich, and F. W. Danker, *A Greek-English Lexicon of the New Testament*, 2d ed.
BETL	*Bibilotheca ephemeridum theologicarum lovaniensium*
BF	British and Foreign Bible Society, The New Testament, 2d ed.
BFT	Biblical Foundations in Theology
BGBE	Beiträge zur Geschichte der biblischen Exegese
Bib	*Biblica*
BibArch	*Biblical Archaeologist*
BibRev	*Biblical Review*
BibSac	*Bibliotheca Sacra*
BibToday	*The Bible Today*
BibTr	*Biblical Translator*
BibZ	*Biblische Zeitschrift*
BJRUL	*Bulletin of the John Rylands University Library of Manchester*
BTB	*Biblical Theological Bulletin*
Cassirer	*A New Testament Translation*, E. Cassirer
CBQ	*Catholic Biblical Quarterly*
CD	Cairo (Genizah text of the) Damascus Document
CEV	The Contemporary English Version
I Clem.	First Epistle of Clement
Collat	*Collationes*

ConcJourn	*Concordia Journal*
CrisTheolRev	*Criswell Theological Review*
DPL	*Dictionary of Paul and His Letters*
EDNT	*Exegetical Dictionary of the New Testament*
EpworthRev	*Epworth Review*
ETR	*Études Théologiques et Religieuses*
EvQ	*Evangelical Quarterly*
ExpT	*Expository Times*
Faith Miss	*Faith and Mission*
FilolNT	*Filologia Neotestamentaria*
FRLANT	Forschungen zur Religion und Literatur des Alten und Neuen Testaments
GNB	Good News Bible
HTR	*Harvard Theological Review*
Interp	*Interpretation*
ISBE	*International Standard Bible Encyclopedia*, rev. ed.
JB	Jerusalem Bible
JBL	*Journal of Biblical Literature*
JBR	*Journal of Bible and Religion*
JETS	*Journal of the Evangelical Theological Society*
JournGrace EvangSoc	*Journal of the Grace Evangelical Society*
JSNT	*Journal for the Study of the New Testament*
JSNTSupS	Journal for the Study of the New Testament Supplement series
JSOT	*Journal for the Study of the Old Testament*
JTS	*Journal of Theological Studies*
KJV	King James Version (= Authorized Version)
LCL	Loeb Classical Library edition
LXX	Septuagint
Merk	Augustinus Merk, ed., *Novum Testamentum Graece et Latine*, 9th ed.
MLB	Modern Language Bible
Moffatt	*The Bible: A New Translation, James Moffatt*
Month	*The Month*
NAB	New American Bible
NASB	New American Standard Bible
NCV	New Century Version (The Everyday Bible)
NEB	New English Bible
Neotest	*Neotestamentica. Journal of the New Testament Society of South Africa*

Nes-Al	Eberhard Nestle; Kurt Aland, rev., *Novum Testamentum Graece*, 27th ed.
NIDNTT	*New International Dictionary of New Testament Theology*
NIV	New International Version
NJB	New Jerusalem Bible
NKJV	New King James Version
NovT	*Novum Testamentum*
NovTSup	Novum Testamentum, Supplement
NRSV	New Revised Standard Version
n.s.	new series
NTS	*New Testament Studies*
PEQ	*Palestine Exploration Quarterly*
Phillips	*The New Testament in Modern English,* J. B. Phillips
Presbyt	*Presbyterion*
PThR	*Princeton Theological Review*
1 QM	Milhāmāh or War Scroll from Qumran Cave 1
1 QS	Serek Hayyahad or Rule of the Community, Manual of Discipline from Qumran Cave 1
RB	*Revue biblique*
REB	Revised English Bible
ResQ	*Restoration Quarterly*
ResScRel	*Recherches de Science Religieuse*
RevExp	*Review and Expositor*
RevHistPhilRel	*Revue Histoire et de Philosophie Religieuses*
RevRel	*Review for Religious*
RSV	Revised Standard Version
RTR	*Reformed Theological Review*
RV	Revised Version
SB	H. L. Strack and P. Billerbeck, *Kommentar zum Neuen Testament aus Talmud und Midrasch*
SBEC	Studies in the Bible and Early Christianity
SBLDS	Society of Biblical Literature Dissertation Series
SBLSBS	Society of Biblical Literature Sources for Biblical Studies
SBT	Studies in Biblical Theology
SEB	The Simple English Bible
SJT	*Scottish Journal of Theology*
SNTSMS	Society for New Testament Studies Monograph Series
Souter	Alexander Souter, ed., *Novum Testamentum Graece*
ST	*Studia theologica*
StudBibT	*Studia Biblica et Theologica*
StudNTUmwelt	*Studien zum Neuen Testament und seiner Umwelt*

SWJourTh	*Southwestern Journal of Theology*
Talmud	The Babylonian Talmud
TC	Theological Collections
TDNT	*Theological Dictionary of the New Testament*
Thayer	Joseph H. Thayer, *Greek-English Lexicon of the New Testament*
ThBeitr	*Theologische Beiträge*
ThLZ	*Theologische Literatur Zeitung*
ThSt	*Theological Studies*
ThZeit	*Theologische Zeitschrift*
TNT	The New Translation
TR	Textus Receptus
TU	Texte und Untersuchungen
TynB	*Tyndale Bulletin*
UBS	United Bible Societies, 4th rev. ed.
Way	*The Way*
WUzNT	Wissenschaftliche Untersuchungen zum Neuen Testament
ZNTW	*Zeitschrift für die neutestamentliche Wissenschaft*

Introduction

Outline

A. Paul's Visits and Letters to Corinth

In Paul's day Corinth prospered because of its location as a crossroads for seafaring Mediterranean peoples. The city served the needs of those who transported and traded goods. With its two harbors, Lechaeum to the west and Cenchrea to the east on the Peloponnesian isthmus, Corinth occupied a central place. Immediately to the north of the city was a thoroughfare that crossed the narrow isthmus. Along this path cargoes were transported from the western harbor to its eastern counterpart and vice versa. As a commercial service center, Corinth became either a temporary or a permanent residence to an estimated population of seventy to eighty thousand inhabitants.[1]

This metropolis reflected the world of its day, and consequently the church at Corinth shared and reproduced that image. Both the Book of Acts and Paul's Corinthian correspondence list persons with Latin names (e.g., Erastus, Fortunatus). Some people were wealthy, others of moderate means, and still others slaves.

Paul arrived in Corinth during the spring of 50 and stayed there for eighteen months. During that period he proclaimed the gospel first in the local synagogue and then in the house of Titius Justus (Acts 18:4, 7). Here he founded the first Christian church in southern Greece. Leaders in this church were Crispus, Sosthenes, Gaius, Stephanas, Fortunatus, and Achaicus (I Cor. 1:1, 14; 16:17). Some time later, Paul received help in his ministry: Timothy and Silas came from the churches in Macedonia, and Christians in Ephesus sent Apollos to Corinth (Acts 18:5, 27–28). Thus, when the apostle decided to depart from southern Greece, he could leave the church in the care of capable men.

After Paul had founded the church in Corinth and took leave of the Christians there to minister in Ephesus, he remained their spiritual father (I Cor. 4:15). Removed geographically from the Corinthians, he provided spiritual care for them by his correspondence. The apostle also gave leadership by a visit and through his representatives, Timothy and Titus.

The problems that arose in the Corinthian community demanded much of Paul's time and energy. Counseling the church on their striving for sexual purity,

---

1. Ben Witherington III, *Conflict and Community in Corinth: A Socio-Rhetorical Commentary on 1 and 2 Corinthians* (Grand Rapids: Eerdmans; Carlisle: Paternoster, 1995), p. 18.

for example, was a daunting task. Paul's initial letter (I Cor. 5:9) seemed to have been misunderstood by the Corinthians and had caused confusion. Hence, in his next epistle (I Corinthians), the apostle devoted three chapters to teachings on morality (5, 6, and 7). He had received information about the church in Corinth through members of the household of Chloe, from a letter of the church requesting advice on social and religious matters, and from a three-man delegation (I Cor. 16:17).

After Paul wrote I Corinthians, problems in the church continued to smolder. Paul had sent Timothy and Erastus to Corinth via Macedonia (Acts 19:22; I Cor. 16:10); but Timothy returned (1:1), we assume, without solving any problems. When conditions worsened, Paul left Ephesus for Corinth and crossed the Aegean Sea to settle the matter of offense and offender. His second visit proved to be painful (2:1). He arrived in Corinth to give leadership in the local congregation but was rebuffed. This rebuff caused him to return to Ephesus, where he wrote his sorrowful letter (2:1–4), which probably was delivered by Titus. Thereupon Paul commissioned Titus to arbitrate and restore order in the Corinthian church and at a specified time report to him.

In the meantime, Paul left Ephesus, went to Troas, and waited for Titus's return. But when Titus failed to arrive, the apostle traveled overland to Macedonia because sailing had ceased during the winter (2:13).[2] Consequently, he would be assured that while walking to Macedonia he could meet Titus along the way. During the periods of waiting and traveling, Paul began writing II Corinthians, which appears to have been composed in several stages. Writing chapter 7, he rejoiced in the safe arrival of Titus, who delivered the news that the church in Corinth desired to implement the teaching of Scripture and submit to Paul's apostolic authority (7:15). The matter of offense and offender had been brought to a satisfactory conclusion. Hence, the spiritual atmosphere in Corinth had improved considerably, to the great satisfaction of both Titus and Paul.

The apostle still had to deal with two other problem areas: the collection (chaps. 8 and 9) and the growing opposition to his apostleship (chaps. 10–13). He again took pen in hand and started to write about the collection for the poverty-stricken saints in Jerusalem, a collection he already had mentioned in I Corinthians 16:1–4. Even though he promoted the collection among the Galatian and the Macedonian churches and in Corinth, he preferred not to be personally involved in this work, so that no one could accuse him of exploiting the Corinthians (8:20–21; 12:17–18).

The last four chapters in this epistle were occasioned by the increasing influence of Paul's opponents, whose slander centered on his apostolic authority

---

2. C. K. Barrett leaves open the possibility that Paul traveled on foot to Macedonia because of a seasonal cessation in sailing. "The land route was open and Paul could safely take it, knowing that Titus, if on the way at all, would be found there." See "Titus," in *Neotestamentica et Semitica: Studies in Honour of Matthew Black*, ed. E. Earle Ellis and Max Wilcox (Edinburgh: Clark, 1969); also in *Essays on Paul* (Philadelphia: Westminster, 1982), p. 124.

(10:1–2, 10). These chapters demonstrate that Paul knew how to counteract his opposition (12:16–18, 20). He wrote four chapters to prepare the Corinthians for his intended third visit (13:1).

B. Differences

The tone and tenor of II Corinthians differ from that of I Corinthians, in which Paul discusses practical issues in the church. Second Corinthians presents a discourse that is profoundly theological. It teaches truths that do not occur elsewhere in the New Testament. For example, these truths comprise the apostle's teaching on the new covenant (2:12–4:6), our earthly and heavenly dwellings (4:7–5:10), and the ministry of reconciliation (5:11–21). Often writing under duress as he reveals his sufferings for Christ (4:8–12; 6:4–10), Paul provides the entire church with a treasury of doctrinal truths.

Writing on a scroll rather than on individual sheets of paper, Paul was unable to alter what he had said earlier. When Titus arrived, the writer could not erase his earlier anxious remarks concerning Titus (2:13). Also, if at the beginning Paul had heard Titus's good report about the Corinthians, he would not have asked them to show him their affection (6:11–13). We receive the impression that he wrote his epistle at intervals during his travels from Ephesus to Troas and Macedonia. He also went to Illyricum (modern Albania and the former Yugoslavia [Rom. 15:19]). And we understand that from time to time he responded to news from and about the Corinthian church. A detailed discussion follows.

Admittedly, the flow in II Corinthians is disjointed in places and reveals haste; transitions are cumbersome (6:14) and grammatical breaks in the Greek text are common (e.g., 6:3; 7:5, 7; 9:11). Throughout the letter the emotional tone is at times painful (1:8–11; 2:13; 7:5), at other times enthusiastic (7:13–16; 8:2–4), and at still other times vigorous (10:7–8; 11:12; 13:2–3, 5). But these characteristics do not impugn the genuineness of the epistle. They reflect the writer's concerns and personality.

Second Corinthians can be divided into five parts: introduction (1:1–11), the apostle's ministry (1:12–7:16), the collection (8:1–9:15), a defense of Paul's apostolic authority (10:1–13:10), and a conclusion (13:11–14). The introduction and conclusion aside, the epistle has three major sections that appear to have been written at different times.

C. Form and Genuineness of the Epistle

From the Corinthian correspondence, we know that Paul composed at least four letters. Scholars conveniently label them A, B, C, and D.

Epistle A, no longer extant, is Paul's counsel not to associate with sexually immoral people (I Cor. 5:9).
Epistle B is the canonical I Corinthians.

Epistle C is the sorrowful letter (II Cor. 2:4) that some scholars consider to be II Corinthians 10–13, others I Corinthians, and still others no longer extant. A discussion follows.

Epistle D is the canonical II Corinthians. Some scholars divide this letter into Epistle D (chaps. 1–9) and Epistle E (chaps. 10–13).[3]

1. Unity and Integrity

The focal point on II Corinthians is the discussion on its unity and integrity. Scholars address some of these points:

a. The identity of Epistle C (2:4).
b. The formation of Epistle D.
c. An interpolation: chapters 2:14–7:4 without 6:14–7:1.
d. A second interpolation: chapters 6:14–7:1.
e. Three or more separate documents: chapters 1–7, chapters 8–9 or 8 and 9, chapters 10–13.
f. Two separate letters (chaps. 1–9, 10–13) combined.
g. The basic unity of the epistle.

Let us discuss these points seriatim, evaluate the arguments, and draw a conclusion. We admit that ultimately we must resort to a hypothesis, but then we occupy common ground, for no one is able to avoid the use of hypotheses in this matter.

a. The Identity of Epistle C (2:4)

Some authors aver that chapters 10–13 constitute Paul's sorrowful letter or are parts of it.[4] They base this hypothesis on references in the context of chapters 1–9 that seem to relate to chapters 10–13. But their hypothesis must be rejected because the last four chapters do not say anything about a single offender mentioned in 2:5–11 and 7:8–12. Writes Margaret E. Thrall, "The Painful Letter was concerned with *one* particular incident. In chap[ter]s 10–13 there is no such single offender."[5]

3. F. F. Bruce, *1 and 2 Corinthians,* New Century Bible (London: Oliphants, 1971), pp. 166–70; Barrett, "Titus," p. 128; Victor Paul Furnish, *II Corinthians: Translated with Introduction, Notes and Commentary,* Anchor Bible 32A (Garden City, N.Y.: Doubleday, 1984), pp. 41–48; Ralph P. Martin, *2 Corinthians,* Word Biblical Commentary 40 (Waco: Word, 1986), p. li; Colin G. Kruse, *The Second Epistle of Paul to the Corinthians: An Introduction and Commentary,* Tyndale New Testament Commentaries series (Leicester: Inter-Varsity; Grand Rapids: Eerdmans, 1987), pp. 29–35.

4. James H. Kennedy, *The Second and Third Epistles of St. Paul to the Corinthians* (London: Methuen, 1900), p. xiii; Jean Héring, *The Second Epistle of Saint Paul to the Corinthians,* trans. A. W. Heathcote and P. J. Allcock (London: Epworth, 1967), pp. xi–xiv.

5. Margaret E. Thrall, *A Critical and Exegetical Commentary on the Second Epistle to the Corinthians,* 2 vols., International Critical Commentary (Edinburgh: Clark, 1994), vol. 1, pp. 16–17.

Other scholars state that the sorrowful letter comprises Epistle B.[6] Paul instructs the Corinthian church to take disciplinary action against the man who committed incest (I Cor. 5:1–5, 13), and the context of the sorrowful letter discloses that the church had taken action against an offender (2:5–11). Although there are strong reasons for seeing a link, the hypothesis that Epistles B and C are identical cannot be sustained. True, Paul had to reprove the Corinthian congregation for failing to punish a man who had committed incest (I Cor. 5:1–5). But we cannot say that the apostle wrote all of I Corinthians out of great affliction, anguish, and grief (2:4). The greater part of I Corinthians is Paul's answer to questions raised by the Christians in Corinth on social and ecclesiastical matters and Paul's teaching on the resurrection (I Cor. 7–15).

If the Corinthian believers failed to expel the evildoer (I Cor. 5:13), Paul would have to go to Corinth and take action. Should they refuse to cooperate, he would have to write them an intermediate letter that, for both him and them, would prove to be a painful document. We reject the identification of chapters 10–13 with the intermediate letter and I Corinthians with these chapters. We think that Epistle C was a separate letter and, therefore, conclude that Epistle C, like Epistle A, is lost.[7]

b. The Formation of Epistle D

The first two parts of this epistle (chaps. 1–7 and 8–9) impart a warm and encouraging tone that differs from that in the last four chapters, which exhibit harshness and rebuke. In the last part of the epistle, Paul had to counteract the verbal attacks of his opponents, so that the tone is scathing and at times even laced with irony.

Some writers suggest that the two parts of II Corinthians ought to be reversed: chapters 10–13 should precede chapters 1–9.[8] They point out that Paul's direct speech in chapters 10–13 seems to have had its desired effect; afterward he wrote the conciliatory chapters (1–9). But this suggestion has failed to gain support, because no Greek manuscript shows a reversed sequence of these chapters. In addition, if the present sequence should be reversed, why does not Paul mention the presence of the superapostles in chapters 1–9? "Even if the problem had cleared up by the time chapters 1–9 were written, why is that fact not

---

6. Philip Edgcumbe Hughes, *Paul's Second Epistle to the Corinthians: The English Text with Introduction, Exposition and Notes,* New International Commentary on the New Testament series (Grand Rapids: Eerdmans, 1962), pp. xxviii–xxx, 52, 54–57; James Denney, *The Second Epistle to the Corinthians,* 2d ed., The Expositor's Bible series (New York: Armstrong, 1900), pp. 66–67.

7. Allan Menzies, *The Second Epistle of the Apostle Paul to the Corinthians: Introduction, Text, English Translation and Notes* (London: Macmillan, 1912), p. xix.

8. Kirsopp Lake, *The Earlier Epistles of St. Paul: Their Motive and Origin* (London: Rivington, 1911), pp. 155, 157. Rudolf Bultmann rearranges the epistle and calls 1:1–2:13; 7:5–16 Letter D, while Letter C consists of 2:14–7:4; 10:1–13:14. He adds chapter 8 to Letter C and chapter 9 to Letter C. See *The Second Letter to the Corinthians,* trans. Roy A. Harrisville (Minneapolis: Augsburg, 1985).

recorded?"[9] The available evidence points in the direction of the traditional order and not vice versa.

Next, scholars argue that Paul could not have stated that he would "preach the gospel in regions beyond [Corinth]" (10:16) when he was not in Ephesus but to the north in Macedonia. This view lacks plausibility, however, especially when we realize that Paul spoke of not his own geographic perspective but that of the Corinthians. Whenever he addressed a letter to his readers, he frequently adopted their viewpoint, as is evident from the recurring use of the so-called epistolary aorist.

Third, Paul commissioned Titus to be in charge of the collection in Corinth. But note the sequence of the missions of Titus to Corinth. Paul had sent him to begin the work of collecting money for the saints in Jerusalem (8:6) and afterward again to complete this task (8:6, 17, 18, 22). From the context of 12:18, we infer that Titus had been commissioned earlier.

Last of all, even though inverting chapters 1–9 and 10–13 may alleviate some problems, the process itself creates new problems. Is there any indication in the epistle that two separate letters have been fused? We expect that a letter has appropriate addresses, salutations, final greetings, and benedictions; thus, the last few verses of chapter 13 consist of one short clause after another. This indicates that the end of the scroll was near and Paul was running out of space. But if we reverse the two parts (10–13 followed by 1–9), we detect no traces that point to either beginnings or endings of letters.

c. An Interpolation: Chapters 2:14–7:4 Without 6:14–7:1

Among the numerous breaks in this epistle, the one in the second half of chapter 2 to the beginning of chapter 7 is conspicuous. If we were to delete chapters 2:14 to 7:4, the result would be a smooth narrative about Paul's travel to Macedonia. The last sentence (2:13) before the break reads: "However, when I had said good-by to them, I went to Macedonia," and at 7:5 Paul writes, "When we came into Macedonia, our body had no relief." These sentences and their contexts fit as smoothly as two pieces of broken porcelain. Some experts are ready to paste these pieces together and move the interpolation to another place.[10] This seems to solve a problem, but the question remains whether it is necessary and warranted to paste the two sentences together. The vocabulary of going and coming to Macedonia in these sentences seems repetitive. "They sound much more as if Paul is *resuming* a theme, knowing he has digressed."[11]

Note the following considerations. First, if this were the only digression in Paul's correspondence, we would have reason to be surprised. However, Paul

---

9. D. A. Carson, *From Triumphalism to Maturity* (Grand Rapids: Baker, 1984), p. 12. See also D. A. Carson, Douglas J. Moo, and Leon Morris, *Introduction to the New Testament* (Grand Rapids: Zondervan, 1992), pp. 268–69.

10. E.g., Bultmann, *Second Letter*, p. 52; Dieter Georgi, *The Opponents of Paul in Second Corinthians* (Philadelphia: Fortress, 1986), pp. 9–18.

11. Carson, Moo, and Morris, *Introduction to the New Testament*, p. 273.

often digresses, especially when an important thought comes to mind. Take, for instance, I Corinthians 9, which breaks his discussion in chapters 8 and 10 on food sacrificed to an idol. And Romans 5:12–19 is a classic example of a Pauline digression, in which Paul gradually returns to his earlier discourse.

Next, if there is an insertion of another document, then we would look for a break at both the beginning and the end of the insertion. But this is not the case here, because Paul uses similar Greek vocabulary in 7:4–7, a fact that is evident even in translation: words like "comfort" (vv. 4, 6, 7), "joy" and "rejoicing" (vv. 4, 7), or "affliction" and "distress" (vv. 4, 5) recur.[12] To ascribe the choice of these words to the work of an editor is unconvincing. It is more natural to ascribe the choice of words to Paul, the author of this letter. In addition, the first words in 7:5 ("for indeed") serve as a natural bridge between this verse and the preceding context.

Third, is there a break in the progression of thought at 2:14? Paul's main concern seems to be Titus, for the apostle mentions him in 2:13 but not again until 7:6. Although this point is well taken, it is better that we focus attention on Macedonia. The sequence of thought in chapter 2, which moves from Paul's travels to Macedonia (2:13) to God's leading him in triumphal procession (2:14), refers to his intended Macedonian visit (1:15–17). Earlier his plan to visit there had been thwarted, not by failure on his part but by his total commitment to God, who changed his plans. Paul was not his own master but God's subservient captive. Thus, he entrusted to God any changes in his travel plans.[13] He expressed his praise to God in jubilant tones (2:14) and made what he considered an acceptable transition.

Last, Paul's love for the Corinthians (2:4) is a factor in his decision to leave "the open door" for the gospel in Troas and to travel to Macedonia. By coming closer to them geographically, he showed them genuine concern. And the thanksgiving he expresses in 2:14 takes on a forward momentum with reference to his discourse on apostleship in the following chapter.[14]

Although there is a break at 2:14, explanations for a smooth transition cannot be ignored. In fact, they witness to the unity and integrity of II Corinthians and show that Paul indeed could have written chapters 1–7 sequentially.

d. A Second Interpolation: Chapters 6:14–7:1

Another section that is considered to be an insertion, either from a letter Paul wrote or from some other source, is the second half of chapter 6 and the first verse of the next chapter. I have fully discussed this issue in a lengthy section pre-

12. Hans Lietzmann, *An die Korinther I/II*, augmented by Werner G. Kümmel, Handbuch zum Neuen Testament 9 (Tübingen: Mohr, 1969), p. 131.
13. Frances Young and David F. Ford, *Meaning and Truth in 2 Corinthians*, BFT (London: SPCK, 1987), pp. 18, 35.
14. Thrall, *Second Corinthians*, vol. 1, p. 23; and "A Second Thanksgiving Period in II Corinthians," *JSNT* 16 (1982): 111–19.

ceding the commentary on 6:14, which should be consulted. But additional comments are in order.

Some writers assert that this segment is non-Pauline, because the vocabulary is different from that in the rest of II Corinthians. But are we able to limit Paul's rich vocabulary? Hardly. When we consider the apostle's literary skills, we follow the traditional route of accepting the feasibility and reality that Paul composed 6:14–7:1.[15]

Further, no manuscript evidence is available to support the view that this segment is an interpolation. If Paul wrote this epistle on a scroll instead of on individual papyrus leaves, then it is hard to believe that someone inserted the segment 6:14–7:1.

Finally, we cannot be certain that before the second century Christians used a codex of loose papyrus leaves. Before that time, the form of Paul's letter was set, so that when the use of codices came into vogue, the possibility of altering the letter's content with the insertion of another document hardly seems plausible.[16]

e. Three or More Separate Documents: Chapters 1–7, Chapters 8–9 or 8 and 9, Chapters 10–13

Let us discuss the suggestion that chapters 8 and 9 should be taken as two separate letters.[17] These are some of the arguments: With the Greek words *peri men gar* ("For concerning [the service to the saints]," 9:1) Paul introduces a new theme. Next, his remark about the service to the saints seems out of place immediately after chapter 8.[18] Third, the apostle's statement that there is no need to write to the Corinthians (9:1) indicates a new topic. Last, he mentions Titus in chapter 8 but not in the succeeding chapter.

First, the argument that the words *peri men gar* introduce a different topic fails to be convincing. These words function as a bridge from the preceding to the succeeding contexts. In addition, the passage "9:1–4 provides a warrant and explanation for Paul's exhortation in 8:24."[19]

---

15. Using a sociorhetorical approach to Paul's Corinthian correspondence, Witherington calls this section a digression. He states: "There is nothing un-Pauline about this passage, in the light of 1 Corinthians 8–10, though it may draw on some non-Pauline material" (*Conflict and Community in Corinth*, p. 403).

16. Consult Ernest B. Allo, *Saint Paul Seconde Épître aux Corinthiens*, 2d ed. (Paris: Gabalda, 1956), p. 191.

17. Among others, Hans Windisch, *Der Zweite Korintherbrief*, ed. Georg Strecker (1924; reprint ed., Göttingen: Vandenhoeck und Ruprecht, 1970), pp. 268–69; Hans Dieter Betz, *II Corinthians 8 and 9: A Commentary on Two Administrative Letters of the Apostle Paul*, ed. George W. MacRae, Hermeneia: A Critical and Historical Commentary on the Bible (Philadelphia: Fortress, 1985), pp. 90–91, 129–44. Günther Bornkamm even suggests a total of five distinct letters in II Corinthians. See "The History of the Origin of the So-Called Second Letter to the Corinthians," *NTS* 8 (1961–62): 258–64.

18. Consult Bultmann, *Second Letter*, p. 256.

19. Stanley K. Stowers, "*Peri men gar* and the Integrity of 2 Cor. 8 and 9," *NovT* 32 (1990): 348; Furnish, *II Corinthians*, pp. 432–33, 438–39. But Martin regards chapter 9 "as a separate composition" (*2 Corinthians*, p. 250). Thrall (*Second Corinthians*, vol. 1, p. 42) also calls this chapter "an independent letter."

Next, Paul praises the Corinthians for their service to the saints to stimulate them to greater participation in collecting funds. He is confident that they will contribute enthusiastically to the collection for the poor in Jerusalem (refer to 8:6–7, 10–12; I Cor. 16:1–4).

Third, when Paul says that there is no need to write to the Corinthians, he employs a verbal device not to begin a new topic but instead to keep the attention of his readers. He does the same thing elsewhere: "We do not need to write to you" (I Thess. 4:9; 5:1). That is, he states a negative to emphasize the positive.

And last, Titus's name occurs in chapter 8, not in chapter 9. But Paul did not need to mention Titus's name again when he already had referred to him six times, three each in chapters 7 and 8 (7:6, 13, 14; 8:6, 16, 23).

In general there is more evidence to support the basic unity of these chapters than to argue for their division. The vocabulary is similar (e.g., consider these words and phrases: Macedonians, service to the saints, the gift, generosity, needs, the brothers). Further, Paul's reference to "last year" in both chapters (8:10 and 9:2) indicates a fact known to the Corinthians. Also, the term *brothers* surfaces in 8:23 and 9:3; the term refers to "representatives of the churches" who were well known to the Corinthians. The link between the last verses of chapter 8 and the first verses of chapter 9 appears to be quite strong. Lastly, why would Paul address two short letters on the same topic to the church in Corinth when one presentation achieves his purpose?[20]

We agree that II Corinthians consists of three parts: chapters 1–7; 8–9; and 10–13. But some scholars argue that these parts were three separate letters. For example, Thrall proposes that chapters 1–8, chapter 9, and chapters 10–13 are a combination of three letters that would "produce a document more nearly comparable in length to 1 Corinthians, and so give its contents more weight, perhaps, as an apostolic letter."[21] But this arrangement creates more problems than it solves.

For one thing, when as an apostle of Jesus Christ Paul wrote his epistles, he spoke with divine authority (13:3). He told his readers to circulate his letters (Col. 4:16; I Thess. 5:27), so that the entire church could benefit from his teachings. We know that the recipients of these documents placed his epistles on the same level as the inspired writings of the Old Testament (II Peter 3:15–16). In the first century, the early church demonstrated a profound respect for Paul's letters. Thus, it is questionable indeed whether the church would permit a fusion and a reworking of some of Paul's writings to form a single epistle.[22] And if shorter epistles were combined into a longer one, other epistles could also have undergone this process. Yet in the New Testament epistolary we see no evidence

---

20. Furnish (*II Corinthians*, p. 433) concludes that these two chapters can be read "as a single, integrated discussion of the collection project."

21. Thrall, *Second Corinthians*, vol. 1, p. 46.

22. F. W. Grosheide, *De Tweede Brief van den Apostel Paulus aan de Kerk te Korinthe*, Kommentaar op het Nieuwe Testament series (Amsterdam: Van Bottenburg, 1939), p. 25.

of such a process in the letters to the Thessalonians, the prison epistles, or those addressed to Timothy.

Next, if joining separate documents into one epistle were practiced, an editor would have to delete some greetings, introductions, prayers, thanksgivings, conclusions, and final salutations.[23] But no manuscript evidence in New Testament circles has emerged to verify this possibility.

f. Two Separate Letters Combined: Chapters 1–9 and 10–13

Many commentators cite several reasons for positing that there are two separate letters in II Corinthians. First, Paul's tone is conciliatory and encouraging in the first nine chapters, but in the last four chapters his address is spiked with irony and harsh language. In addition, between these two parts there seems to be a time lapse during which the Corinthians became followers of false apostles (11:13). This caused Paul to write an additional letter, which now forms the second half of II Corinthians. Also, Paul had sent to Corinth Titus and others (8:22–24) who served as the letter carriers of chapters 1–9. These arguments are worthy of serious consideration.

In my commentary preceding 10:1, under the heading "Apostolic Authority: 10:1–13:10," I present a detailed discussion on this matter, and I refer the reader to that discussion. At the same time I add extensive comments here.

First, the change in Paul's tone can be attributed to his design in writing this letter. After settling the controversy regarding the offender (chaps. 1–7), Paul discussed the matter of the collection (chaps. 8–9). Then he realized that he had to address his opponents, for they were making inroads into the church (chaps. 10–13). He had to exert apostolic authority and in the process rebuke the Corinthians for their allegiance to these false apostles. Paul intentionally adopted an encouraging voice to stimulate the readers to action with respect to both the offender and the collection. But in the last four chapters of his epistle he speaks as their pastor about the dangers they were facing by listening to his adversaries.[24] These particular topics cause a variation in Paul's manner of address.

Second, the possibility that Paul wrote his letter in stages is a viable option indeed. After the apostle composed the first nine chapters, either travel or visits from church delegations may have interrupted his writing. Someone brought him the news about the encroachments of interlopers among the Corinthians and the worsening situation in the local church. We are aware that Paul gives no indication that he had received further news. But if we consider the points of contact he had with the Corinthians, we are not assuming too much by saying that periodically he received new information. To illustrate from I Corinthians: there was the news that prompted him to write a letter (5:9), the report from

---

23. Philipp Vielhauer, *Geschichte der urchristlichen Literatur* (Berlin and New York: de Gruyter, 1975), pp. 153–55.
24. Compare R. C. H. Lenski, *The Interpretation of St. Paul's First and Second Epistle to the Corinthians* (Columbus: Wartburg, 1946), p. 1192.

members of the household of Chloe (1:11), the letter from the Corinthians (7:1), the visit from a three-man delegation (16:17), and an account from Timothy (16:10; II Cor. 1:1). Hence, we confidently adopt the hypothesis that someone informed him about the pernicious influence of the antagonists.

Without delay, Paul wrote chapters 10–13, in which he reproved the members of the Corinthian church for their quarrels, slanderous remarks, arrogance, and disarray (12:20). Would the readers be confused by the gentle tone in the first part of the epistle and the harsh rebuke in the second? Those who had rejected Paul's authority may have been offended. But the ones who listened to his reproof would have welcomed the apostle's words that dealt with the disobedient. More, Paul customarily reserves his condemnation of certain people and practices for a place toward the end of his epistles (see, e.g., Phil. 3; Col. 3).[25]

Third, scholars interpret 12:17–18 to mean that Paul had sent Titus and the brother to Corinth to complete the work on the collection and presumably to deliver the apostle's letter (chaps. 1–9). A careful reading of 8:6, however, allows for the possibility that Paul is referring to "an *earlier* visit to Corinth in connection with the collection" (12:17–18).[26] Note that Paul writes the present tense ("we are sending," 8:18, 22) to indicate that his envoys will soon depart for Corinth to complete the collection. Because we have no proof that the gathering of the funds was completed at the time Paul wrote 12:17–18, we suggest that these men went to Corinth after Paul finished writing his epistle.

Last, there are undeniable links between the first nine chapters and the last four. In the first two chapters of his letter, Paul notes a change in his travel plans and his reluctance to make another visit to Corinth (1:15–2:1). After Titus returned from Corinth with a favorable report, the apostle wanted to go there again. Paul announces the proposed visit three times in the last four chapters (10:2; 12:14; 13:1). His candor in telling the readers about his travel plans supports the perception that the sequence of II Corinthians is continuous. Dividing this epistle into two letters appears to be "contrary to its own evidence."[27]

Paul writes that in comparison with the superapostles he displayed the marks of an apostle—signs, wonders, and miracles—among the Corinthians. We have no record of Paul performing miracles in Corinth, but he tells the readers that "the signs of an apostle were worked out among you with great perseverance" (12:12). When he founded the church in Corinth, these signs became increas-

---

25. Consult Donald Guthrie, *New Testament Introduction,* 4th rev. ed. (Leicester: Apollo; Downers Grove: InterVarsity, 1990), p. 446.

26. Carson, Moo, and Morris, *Introduction to the New Testament,* p. 270, and Carson, *From Triumphalism to Maturity,* p. 15.

27. Menzies, *Second Corinthians,* p. xxxix. See also W. H. Bates, "The Integrity of II Corinthians," *NTS* 12 (1965): 56–69; R. V. G. Tasker, *The Second Epistle of Paul to the Corinthians,* Tyndale New Testament Commentaries series (Grand Rapids: Eerdmans, 1968), pp. 23–35; A. M. G. Stephenson, "Partition Theories on II Corinthians," in *Studia Evangelica II.1: The New Testament Scriptures,* ed. F. L. Cross, TU 87 (Berlin: Akademie, 1964), pp. 639–46; and "A Defence of the Integrity of 2 Corinthians," in *The Authorship and Integrity of the New Testament,* TC 4 (London: SPCK, 1965), pp. 82–97.

ingly visible and proved that Paul was an apostle of Christ. Earlier he had written about letters of recommendation to prove the genuineness of his apostolicity (3:1). In 12:12 he again shows that his credentials came from God, who gave him the authority to be a qualified minister of the new covenant (3:5–6). With these remarks, Paul demonstrates the basic unity of this epistle.

g. The Unity of the Epistle

Numerous scholars defend the basic unity of II Corinthians and do not see a need to suppose it is a compilation of two, three, or even four letters.[28] They are unable to find Greek manuscript evidence to support a theory that the epistle had been divided into separate letters. Also, they refuse to accept the theory that an editor excised portions of Paul's writings to create a single document.[29]

Paul's writing material, the scroll, limited him in changing or editing the first nine chapters. Individual columns on a scroll provide room for changing an occasional word but not for rewriting segments. Other factors also are to be considered: Paul's instructive theological message and various admonitions throughout these chapters had to be preserved intact; rewriting some sections and copying others in these chapters was a time-consuming task; and finally, the cost of buying another scroll may have been considerable. Indeed, the length of the scroll emerges as a definitive factor in the discussion on the unity of the epistle.

The break between chapters 1–9 and 10–13 is undeniable, for Paul's tone changes from one of encouragement and gentleness to one that borders on reproof and irony. We would have expected a gradual change, but instead we read the word *bold* at the outset of the last four chapters (10:1–2). It is hard to judge the severity of Paul's message and its effect on the congregation in Corinth; that judgment varies from reader to reader. Some read the content of chapters 10–13 as a "savage reproach and sarcastic self-vindication."[30] Others argue that "the change of tone and content of the final four chapters is more imaginary than real."[31]

Explanations for the break between the first nine and the last four chapters are many. A frequently quoted remark is that of Hans Lietzmann, who attributes Paul's abruptness to a sleepless night.[32] But I suggest another reason: Paul con-

---

28. Some representatives of this view are Denney, Bachmann, Menzies, Lietzmann, Allo, Grosheide, Tasker, Guthrie, Hughes, Kümmel, Stephenson, Bates, Harris, Carson, Young and Ford.

29. Menzies (*Second Corinthians*, p. xxxiv) observes, "Marcion passes from vii.1 to xi.4 without any hint in connection with xi.4 that he is taking up a different work."

30. Jerome Murphy-O'Connor, *The Theology of the Second Letter to the Corinthians,* New Testament Theology series (Cambridge: Cambridge University Press, 1991), p. 11.

31. Hughes, *Second Epistle to the Corinthians,* p. xxx.

32. Lietzmann, *Korinther,* p. 139; Hughes (*Second Epistle to the Corinthians,* pp. xxiii–xxxv) and Guthrie (*New Testament Introduction,* p. 445) argue that the contrast between chapters 1–9 and 10–13 "must not be overstressed."

sidered himself to be an apostle of all the churches he had founded. He relates that he continually prayed for these churches, visited them whenever possible, and received delegations that asked for advice. At the conclusion of his list of suffering, Paul writes, "Besides these external things, there is the daily pressure on me: my concern for all the churches" (11:28). His responsibility to the churches increased in proportion to their growth. After advising delegates from other churches, Paul perhaps resumed his discourse to the Corinthians with a new and different emphasis. Thus, he broke with the tone and content of the preceding chapters.

There is also Paul's pastoral care for the Corinthian church. Its members had endured trouble caused by an offender, a controversy that Paul had settled by letter and by a visit from his helper Titus. Paul wanted to establish a sound and wholesome relationship with the Corinthians. After discussing the sensitive issue of the collection, he had to address the problem that stemmed from the destructive work of his opponents. Paul had to counter their opposition by showing that his own vocation was based on a genuine call to apostleship, while that of his opponents was fraudulent. Confident that he had established rapport with the Corinthians, Paul then candidly told them to fight a spiritual battle in obedience to Christ and to be aware of the pernicious influence of his adversaries (chap. 10). He was fully aware of negative reactions from some people in Corinth who were influenced by the intruders. The risk of seeing this pernicious influence grow was far greater than that of temporary negative repercussions. As the spiritual shepherd of the flock in Corinth, Paul had to ward off the attacks of his adversaries.

Could Paul have written the entire epistle on one scroll and sent it to Corinth as the canonical II Corinthians? The answer is affirmative as long as we acknowledge that the writing of this letter took place with interruptions that impeded continuity. Breaks in Paul's presentation were sometimes caused by traveling from one place to another, as is evident in 2:12–13, where the apostle states that he went from Troas to Macedonia. At other times, he entertains an important thought and temporarily suspends the subject at hand, as is evident at 6:14–7:1. Also, Paul alters his tone in the last four chapters of II Corinthians to further a pastoral purpose. We acknowledge that the flow in this epistle is at times abrupt and uneven. Yet we opt for the unity of this epistle while fully realizing that not all the difficulties have been solved. Considering the factors involved, we conclude that defending the unity of II Corinthians is a viable option.

2. Genuineness

a. Internal Evidence

The internal evidence for this epistle is solid, for Paul identifies himself at the outset as its author (1:1); he also presents himself by name in an appeal to the Corinthians (10:1). The format of the greetings and the address are Pauline; so are the vocabulary, syntax, and diction.

A close look at both I and II Corinthians reveals similarities in authorial style: repetitions (I Cor. 6:12; 10:23; II Cor. 12:14; 13:1); Old Testament quotations (I Cor. 1:31; II Cor. 10:17 [Jer. 9:24]); antitheses (I Cor. 1:22–23; II Cor. 3:7–8); superlatives (I Cor. 4:3; II Cor. 12:9, 15); and parenthetical comments (I Cor. 7:10, 12; II Cor. 11:23).

References and allusions to I Corinthians are numerous, for already in the first chapter Paul announces a change in his intended travel schedule: arriving in Corinth, departing for Macedonia, and returning to Corinth (1:15–16; I Cor. 16:3, 5–7).

Grief caused by an offender (2:5–11; 7:11) echoes Paul's comments in I Corinthians 5:1–5, 13. Paul's instruction on being clothed with a heavenly dwelling (5:2) affirms his earlier teaching on this subject (I Cor. 15:53–54). His catalog of hardships in 6:3–10 has parallels in I Corinthians 4:9–13. Both in 6:15–16 and I Corinthians 10:21, he emphasizes separating believers and unbelievers. Also, Paul fully explains the matter of the collection (chaps. 8 and 9), which he had mentioned earlier (I Cor. 16:1–4). For the Corinthians, he preaches the gospel free of charge (11:7; 12:13; I Cor. 9:18). And last, one of the basic themes is Christ's crucifixion (13:4; I Cor. 1:23).

With respect to Paul's travels and teaching, the many cross-references to the Book of Acts underscore the genuineness of this epistle. For instance, Paul refers to Timothy (1:1; Acts 16:1); Corinth and Achaia (1:1; Acts 18:1, 12); Troas (2:12; Acts 16:8; 20:6); and the Macedonians (9:2, 4; Acts 16 and 17). Paul summarily mentions that he was stoned (11:25), but Luke gives a full report (Acts 14:19).

The internal evidence for Pauline authorship of II Corinthians is indisputable. The apostle to the Gentiles is its author.

b. External Evidence

At the beginning of the second century, Polycarp quotes from II Corinthians at least three times in his epistle to the Philippians. He writes, "Among whom the blessed Paul laboured, who were his epistles in the beginning" (Polycarp *Phil.* 11.5 from II Cor. 3:2); "He who raised him" from the dead "will also raise us up" (Polycarp *Phil.* 2.3 from II Cor. 4:14); and "Ever providing for that which is good before God and man" (Polycarp *Phil.* 6.2 from II Cor. 8:21).[33]

The Muratorian Canon, about 175, states that Paul wrote twice to the Corinthians. Toward the end of the second century and the beginning of the third, Clement of Alexandria, Irenaeus, Origen, and Tertullian frequently quote from and refer to II Corinthians. Tradition overwhelmingly ascribes this epistle to the apostle Paul.

---

33. *Apostolic Fathers,* LCL. Bornkamm ("History," p. 263) notes, "There is a complete lack of quotations from II Corinthians" and qualifies this statement by saying that those "very few passages which could be referred back to II Corinthians" are references to other epistles. But he fails to prove his point by not showing another source for these references.

D. Composition

If there were one church on which Paul poured out his loving care, Corinth would be that church. This church received more letters than any other congregation or individual. The Corinthians presented him with problems that originated in the controversy that began when Paul founded Gentile churches.

The general content of II Corinthians is Paul's vindication of being an apostle to the Gentiles.[34] He condemned the false teachers who were "peddling the word of God" to fill their own pockets (2:17); proved that the Corinthian believers were his letter of recommendation (3:1–3); preached not himself but the Lord Jesus Christ (4:5; 11:4); demonstrated that his opponents were false apostles in the service of Satan (11:13–15); and despised the slander against him by these false apostles (12:16).

By means of the collection for the saints in Jerusalem, Paul tried to unify both the Jewish and the Gentile parts of the church. During the collection of the funds, Paul made it clear that he himself would not handle the money. He wanted to avoid any criticism about the administration of this gift (8:20–21; I Cor. 16:3–4).[35]

1. Time

Paul arrived in Corinth in the second half of the year 50 and left in the first part of 52. After he founded the church, he served as its pastor for a year and a half. He spent a brief period in Ephesus, sailed to Caesarea, and traveled to Jerusalem. From there he returned to Ephesus via Syrian Antioch. He stayed there for three years, from 52 to 55. During that last year, he composed I Corinthians in Ephesus and sent it on to Corinth. He promised the readers that he intended to travel through Macedonia and arrive in Corinth to spend the winter there (I Cor. 16:5–6).

Even though Paul was a man of his word and would have carried out his plan to visit the Corinthians, a festering problem in their church prompted him to sail across the Aegean Sea from Ephesus to Corinth. Paul was unable to settle the problem, for he was harassed by an offender, probably the one whom he had ordered to be expelled (I Cor. 5:13).[36] (For a detailed discussion on this point, consult the section *Additional Comments on 2:5–11* following the commentary on

---

34. Refer to Jerry L. Sumney, *Identifying Paul's Opponents: The Question of Method in 2 Corinthians* (Sheffield: JSOT, 1990), pp. 85–126.

35. Thrall advances the hypothesis that Paul had accepted some of this money "for temporary safekeeping," and the money was afterward stolen. Paul suspected that a member of the church had stolen the money and then accused the apostle. Since other members of the congregation were probably involved in the theft, Paul was unable to prove his case. He returned to Ephesus and wrote his sorrowful letter (see *Second Corinthians*, vol. 1, p. 68). But Paul's candid statement in 8:20–21 undermines Thrall's hypothesis, and nothing in the epistle provides proof for it.

36. Hans-Josef Klauck declares that a prominent member of the church who was a devotee of Paul's opponents had deeply offended him. See *1. Korintherbrief, 2. Korintherbrief* (Leipzig: St. Benno-Verlag, 1989), p. 134.

2:11.) When he returned to Ephesus, he had no desire to make another painful visit to Corinth (2:1). Instead he wrote his so-called sorrowful letter (2:3–4), which Titus delivered and interpreted to the Corinthians. Paul also gave him the responsibility of settling a disciplinary matter (2:5–11). And for a final obligation, he charged Titus with the task of collecting the monetary gift for the church in Jerusalem (8:6).

Paul and Titus agreed to meet in Troas, but Titus was unable to be there at the appointed time. We presume that during the winter of 55/56, when all sailing had stopped, Paul took the land route and walked from Troas to Macedonia. Thus, he could be sure to meet Titus along the way; indeed, Titus gave him encouraging news concerning the spiritual conditions in the Corinthian church.

Titus not only told Paul about the happy resolution of the offense in the Corinthian congregation but also informed the apostle about the restraint that the offense had placed on the matter of the collection. Hence, Paul devoted a lengthy discussion to this particular topic (chaps. 8 and 9).

There probably was either a shorter or a longer period of waiting between the writing of chapter 9 and the last four chapters of this letter. But new information concerning the insidious work of Paul's adversaries in Corinth forced him to compose the third part of II Corinthians.[37] We can be relatively certain that the entire epistle was completed in 56, probably in the second half of that year. From Macedonia Paul went to Corinth, where he spent the winter of 56/57, supervised the work of the collection, and composed his epistle to the Romans.

2. Place

On the basis of the evidence in the epistle itself, we can confidently say that Paul wrote the letter in the province of Macedonia (see 2:13; 7:5; 9:2). Some Greek manuscripts have a subscript to the epistle that reads: "The second epistle to the Corinthians written from Philippi by Titus and Luke."[38] The church in Philippi was the first one Paul founded in Macedonia and had become dear to him. However, we are not sure how much value we can attach to this subscript that appears to be added in a later century (see the commentary on 8:18).

3. Characteristics

To say that II Corinthians differs from I Corinthians is an understatement, for in many respects there is no comparison. The first canonical epistle is practical in design and orderly in composition. By contrast, the second is profound in theology but disorderly in arrangement. Its language is loose, cumbersome, and

---

37. In "The Date of 2 Corinthians 10–13" (*AusBRev* 39 [1991]: 43), Jerome Murphy-O'Connor says that Paul wrote chapters 10–13 "in anger from Illyricum (Rom 15:19)." Conjecture is implied.

38. Nes-Al[27]; see also John Wenham, *Redating Matthew, Mark and Luke: A Fresh Assault on the Synoptic Problem* (London: Hodder and Stoughton, 1991), p. 231; Hughes, *Second Epistle to the Corinthians*, p. 312.

marked by sudden breaks; there are digressions and parenthetical asides throughout the letter.

Paul wrote the first canonical epistle when he was asked to respond to some problems in the church (e.g., divisions, incest, immorality, and lawsuits). He also had to answer questions raised in a letter he received from the Corinthians (questions about marriage, food offered to idols, spiritual gifts, and the collection). His second epistle, conversely, is a defense of his divine calling. He often illustrates his defense with lists of his sufferings for the Lord. Paul presents his near-death experience in the context of comfort and hope in God (1:3–11). He writes that he is doing his work gratis (11:7; 12:12–17); he repeatedly expresses his love toward the Corinthians in direct and indirect language (2:4; 6:12; 11:11; 12:15); and he prays for their perfection (13:9). He encourages them to forgive and to love a repentant brother (2:7–11), to strive for unity in the body of Christ (6:14–18), to give generously (8:10–12; 9:2–3), and to test their commitment to Jesus Christ (13:5–6).

The epistle is exceptionally personal in presenting information about Paul's pastoral work, résumés of sufferings, and supernatural experiences. No other New Testament book depicts such a depth and extent of emotional, physical, and spiritual anguish. Throughout this letter, most markedly in the last four chapters, Paul uses the pronouns *I* and *we*, but frequently it is impossible to determine whether the plural is to be interpreted as a singular or a plural. In chapters 10–13, the first person singular is much more pronounced than the plural pronoun. And in places it is obvious that Paul uses the plural pronoun to refer to himself (see, e.g., 10:3, 7, 11, and 13).[39]

Second Corinthians has many passages that are hard to interpret. Trying to find answers, scholars have resorted to hypotheses and guesses; they confess that there are no easy solutions. We have gleaned valuable information from historical and sociological background studies, and rhetorical analyses have given us insight into writing styles.[40]

In many respects we admit that although we have the text of Paul's epistles his explanatory footnotes are missing. A list of a few difficult texts includes these examples:

a. "But thanks be to God, who in Christ always leads us in triumphal procession" (2:14).

b. "All of us with uncovered face are beholding the reflected glory of the Lord" (3:18).

---

39. Maurice Carrez, "Le 'Nous' en 2 Corinthiens. Paul parle-t-il au nom de toute la communauté, du groupe apostolique, de l'équipe ministérielle ou én son nom personnel? Contribution à l'étude de l'apostolicité dans 2 Corinthiens," *NTS* 26 (1980): 474–86. At times Paul refers to himself, at other times to his associates, and sometimes to believers in general.

40. Consult John L. White, "Ancient Greek Letters," in *Greco-Roman Literature and the New Testament: Selected Forms and Genres,* ed. David E. Aune, SBLSBS 21 (Atlanta: Scholars, 1988), pp. 85–105; Witherington, *Conflict and Community in Corinth,* pp. 327–39.

c. "While we are in this tent we groan, being burdened, because we do not wish to be unclothed but to be clothed [over]" (5:4).
d. "We are sending with [Titus] the brother who is praised by all the churches in the service of the gospel" (8:18).
e. "I know a man in Christ, who fourteen years ago (whether in the body or outside the body, I do not know, but the Lord knows) was caught up as far as the third heaven" (12:2).
f. "I was given a thorn in my flesh, a messenger of Satan, to buffet me, so that I might not be too elated" (12:7).
g. "I fear that again, when I come, my God may humiliate me before you" (12:21).

Paul's chapter about the resurrection (I Cor. 15) is a lengthy and continuous theological discourse. By comparison, II Corinthians is a study of profound theological truths on the new covenant, the gospel, the heavenly dwelling, and the ministry of reconciliation (chaps. 2–5). In fact, the second canonical epistle is much more theological in content than the first.

4. Theological Themes

Even though Paul's design in this letter is to defend himself against the assaults of his adversaries, theological themes are evident. Alfred Plummer asserts that doctrine or rules of life are incidental to II Corinthians, but he briefly considers a few doctrinal topics: apostolicity, Christology, the Trinity, the resurrection, and eschatology.[41] In addition to and in place of this list, we will consider the following themes:

a. Suffering and glory
b. Covenant and transformation
c. Dwellings on earth and in heaven
d. Reconciliation and righteousness
e. Eschatology and Christology
f. Trust and apostolicity

Taken from various chapters, these themes sound a clear theological message. We must limit ourselves, however, to some comments on each theme. An introduction to a commentary is not the place to present a full-fledged discourse on Paul's theology in this letter, for this goal is accomplished in separate volumes.[42]

---

41. Alfred Plummer, *A Critical and Exegetical Commentary on the Second Epistle of St. Paul to the Corinthians*, International Critical Commentary series (1915; Edinburgh: Clark, 1975), pp. xli–xliv.
42. See, e.g., Murphy-O'Connor's *Theology of the Second Letter to the Corinthians*.

Introduction

a. Suffering and Glory

Not so much in I Corinthians but certainly in II Corinthians, Paul describes the extent and the significance of suffering for the Lord. This is a major theme in his Corinthian correspondence (I Cor. 4:8–13; II Cor. 1:5–10; 2:14; 4:7–12; 6:4–10; 11:23–28). He portrays himself and his colleagues as prisoners condemned to die in an arena and to be a spectacle for the universe. Paul notes that he and his associates are treated with contempt, go hungry and thirsty, walk around in rags, receive beatings, belong with the homeless, and are considered to be the filth of the earth (I Cor. 4:9–13). As a servant of Christ, the apostle suffered because of the gospel. During his ministry he was often near death for the sake of Christ. "Paul thus views his suffering as the divinely orchestrated means by which the knowledge of God is revealed to the world."[43]

Using the imagery of a triumphal procession, Paul describes how a Roman general, entering the imperial city, returns victoriously from a war and leads captive a suffering slave who is condemned to death (2:14). This metaphor Paul applies to himself, and he further relates that he despaired even of life, for he was sentenced to die (1:8–9).

The catalogs of suffering appear three times in this epistle (4:7–12; 6:4–10; 11:23–28). The first list demonstrates that suffering discloses God's glory: Paul's own body shows the death of Jesus; he himself submits willingly to death for Jesus' sake; and he knows that death is at work in him (4:10–12). This means that Paul and his co-workers preached the gospel of Jesus' death everywhere and were willing to endure severe punishment for their work, as was evidenced in Philippi (Acts 16:22–24). All this occurred so that the march of the gospel might continue and God's glory might be revealed (4:15).

The apostle's second catalog of suffering (6:4–10) was written so that Paul's ministry might not be blamed (6:3) but rather that God be glorified. As a servant of God Paul quietly endured hardships and adversities knowing that he could do so in the power of God (6:7). Thus, he could report striking contrasts: "dying, and look, we live, . . . chastened and yet we are not killed" (6:9).

Last, Paul presents an extended list of sufferings (11:23–29) to tell his readers that he serves Christ as a true and faithful servant. He did not glory in having endured affliction to elevate himself above others. Nor did he regard suffering as an atonement for sin. Rather he saw that his afflictions served the glorious cause of furthering the gospel, church, and kingdom of Christ.[44] Doing God's will in a sinful world where a spiritual warfare rages inevitably incurs suffering of one kind or another.

---

43. Scott J. Hafemann, "Corinthians, Letters to the," *DPL*, p. 169; and *Paul, Moses, and the History of Israel: The Letter/Spirit Contrast and the Argument from Scripture in 2 Corinthians 3*, WUzNT 81 (Tübingen: Mohr [Siebeck], 1995), p. 92.

44. Compare Murphy-O'Connor, *Theology of the Second Letter to the Corinthians*, p. 154.

Introduction

b. Covenant and Transformation

Aside from a few references in his epistles,[45] Paul hardly discusses the concept *covenant*. But in the context of chapter 3, he fully contrasts the difference between the old and the new covenants. He speaks about letters written not on tablets of stone but on tablets of human hearts (3:3). With this comparison he points out the divergence of the two covenants. And he states that his co-workers and he are competent ministers of a new covenant (3:6). God called Moses to minister to the Israelites in the desert. This was a ministry within the context of the law that was given from Mount Sinai. And because of the law it was a ministry that brought death and condemnation (3:7, 9). But the ministry of the Spirit effects obedience and righteousness in a new covenant community. This community, the church, obeys the law of God by the power of the Holy Spirit. Paul has been appointed to minister to God's people who are transformed into the likeness of the Lord "from one degree of glory to another" (3:18).[46]

The people of Israel ratified the covenant at Sinai by responding with one voice, "We will do everything the LORD has said; we will obey" (Exod. 24:3, 7). But while God gave Moses the two tablets of stone upon which God had written the Decalogue, the Israelites were worshiping the golden calf they had made (Exod. 31:18–32:6). Breaking the covenant obligation through idolatry leads to death and destruction. When Moses reappeared with another set of stone tablets, the people were unable to look at his face because divine glory radiated from it (Exod. 34:29–35). Their sin of idolatry prevented them from viewing Moses' face. And their hardened hearts brought an end to the glory of the old covenant. In time the old covenant faded away before the new covenant that brought unfading glory to God's people.

Paul contrasts the glory of the old covenant with that of the new and intimates that there is no comparison. He served God in the ministry of righteousness (3:9) by preaching Christ's gospel and witnessing the work of the Holy Spirit. He knew that God reserved his transcending and lasting glory for this ministry. The glory of God's presence, which at one time was Israel's privilege, has now become the distinguishing mark of God's people in the new covenant.[47] They are being transformed by Christ and with unveiled face now see and reflect the glory of the Lord (3:18). Thus believers fulfill their divinely created disposition to live to the glory of God and to mirror the glory that emanates from the face of Christ.

c. Dwellings on Earth and in Heaven

In the first part of chapter 5, Paul presents theological thoughts that extend and elaborate on his discourse on the resurrection (I Cor. 15). With a series of

---

45. Rom. 9:4; 11:27; I Cor. 11:25; Gal. 3:15, 17; 4:24; Eph. 2:12.
46. For a thorough study see Hafemann, *Paul, Moses, and the History of Israel.*
47. Refer to Herman N. Ridderbos, *Paul: An Outline of His Theology,* trans. John Richard de Witt (Grand Rapids: Eerdmans, 1975), pp. 336–37.

three metaphors, Paul illustrates his teaching on death and the resurrection: a tent that is taken down (5:1); clothing after death (5:2–4); and being at home with the Lord (5:6, 8). He elucidates the first metaphor of the tent with the adjective *earthly*. With this word, he reminds the readers that the first man was taken from the dust of the earth (Gen. 2:7; I Cor. 15:47) and that the curse of death rests on Adam's race (Gen. 2:17).

The second metaphor that Paul uses refers to being clothed with a heavenly dwelling. He actually writes that we long to be clothed over with that dwelling, much as we wear an additional garment on top of other clothes.[48] That covering which the Lord supplies is in the form of heavenly glory. By being clothed in glory, we eagerly await the day when our physical bodies are raised from the dead (Rom. 8:18, 23). At the return of Christ, all those who eagerly await him will be transformed instantaneously. Their own bodies will be glorified in the twinkling of an eye (I Cor. 15:51; Phil. 3:21).

The Old Testament teaches that soul and body belong together (Gen. 2:7), but that the curse God pronounced on sin has brought about their division through death. But this separation will end at the time of Jesus' return, when our bodies will be either resurrected or transformed.[49] Paul is not interested in separation but restoration in glory. He knows that should the Lord come after Paul's departure from this earthly scene, he will be with the Lord.

Hence, with the third metaphor Paul teaches that at death the soul will be in a bodiless state in the presence of the Lord. But he fails to provide details except to give the assurance that at the moment of departure all believers will be forever with Jesus in heavenly glory. Paul's desire is to spend eternity with Christ even if this means to be in his presence without a body. Jesus is always with his people when he calls them to their heavenly home.[50] And at his return, he takes with him the saints who, reunited with glorified bodies, meet the saints whose bodies have been transformed in glory. Thus, we shall be forever with the Lord (I Thess. 4:17).

d. Reconciliation and Righteousness

When two parties are at fault, the process of reconciliation can succeed only by having both admit their wrongs. But when only one party is at fault, we ask the wrongdoer to apologize to the injured party and, if possible, to restore a harmonious relationship. No one would expect the injured party to take the initiative in the process of reconciliation. Yet this is exactly what God did when Adam and Eve fell into sin. Our first parents hid themselves from the presence of God (Gen. 3:8), but God reached out to them. He promised the coming of his Son Jesus Christ to the human race. The Messiah would achieve reconciliation. Through

---

48. Bruce, *1 and 2 Corinthians*, p. 202; Hughes, *Second Epistle to the Corinthians*, p. 168 n. 31; Albrecht Oepke, *TDNT*, 2:320–21; Horst Weigelt, *NIDNTT*, 1:316.

49. Consult Joseph Osei-Bonsu, "Does 2 Cor. 5.1–10 teach the reception of the resurrection body at the moment of death?" *JSNT* 28 (1986): 81–101.

50. See, e.g., Pss. 119:151; 145:18.

23

the atoning work of his Son, God has reconciled us to himself (5:18). Paul writes that God initiated and completed reconciliation before we would ever think of responding to God's invitation to be reconciled to him (Rom. 5:10, 11). As the offended party God did not have to seek reconciliation, yet he offered up his Son to effect it through him for the human race. Not only did God reconcile himself to us, but as Paul says, "God was in Christ reconciling the world to himself" (5:19).[51]

God established a special relationship with the human race, because all human beings are created in his likeness and image. Because of their sin they were alienated from him. As their judge, he could have condemned them. But God through his Son Jesus Christ removed the curse of sin, reconciled himself to his people, imputed to them his righteousness, and extended his friendship and peace. Because of his Son's atoning work, God acquits his people and drops all charges against them. He grants them his gift of righteousness, which is akin to holiness, for their sin breaches his holiness. Through Christ Jesus, God has declared us righteous and has sanctified us, "so that we might become God's righteousness in him" (5:21).[52]

e. Eschatology and Christology

In scattered passages, this epistle exhibits eschatological doctrine. For instance, Paul alludes to immortality and resurrection (5:1–9) and the day of the Lord and the final judgment (1:14; 5:10). The physical body is similar to a tent—a temporary dwelling (5:1). But our heavenly house is eternal and glorious; for those who enter heaven, it supplies a covering of divine glory (4:17; Rom. 8:18). When this earthly life ends, the soul enters heavenly glory. But we long for the day of consummation when our bodies shall be either raised to or transformed into eternal glory and immortality.

Paul mentions the phrase *the day of the Lord Jesus* in 1:14. The phrase points to the time of Jesus' return, but it should not be restricted to the consummation. For Christians, that day comes when they depart this earth and enter heaven, where Jesus welcomes them. In the Old Testament and in Paul's epistolary, "the day of the Lord" is a general reference to the final judgment day.[53] When the books are opened, everyone will appear before the heavenly Judge; no one is excluded. Unbelievers who have heard the gospel but willfully rejected it are consigned to eternal separation from the living God, while those who belong to Christ joyfully enter into his unending fellowship.

The difference between a human court and the court held in the judgment day is telling. On earth a court has judges, lawyers, witnesses, members of the jury, recorders, and reporters. When a verdict is read, the accused are either ac-

---

51. Refer to G. K. Beale, "The Old Testament Background of Reconciliation in 2 Corinthians 5–7 and Its Bearing on the Literary Problem of 2 Corinthians 6.14–7.1," *NTS* 35 (1989): 550–59.

52. Consult N. T. Wright, "On Becoming the Righteousness of God," in *Pauline Theology*, vol. 2, *1 and 2 Corinthians*, ed. David M. Hay (Minneapolis: Fortress, 1993), pp. 200–208.

53. See, e.g., Joel 3:14; Amos 5:18–20; I Cor. 1:8; II Cor. 5:10.

quitted or convicted and then sentenced to terms of punishment. No judge will ever reward someone for deeds the accused have done. But on the judgment day, the heavenly Judge confers rewards on the good and punishments on the bad.[54] Those who know that the judgment day will eventually come live on this earth in reverent fear for God and his Word (I Peter 1:17).

Paul describes Jesus' divinity with the term *Son of God,* for he calls God the Father of the Lord Jesus Christ (1:3, 19; 11:31). He teaches Christ's preexistence in glory when he writes that Jesus Christ left his heavenly riches. By coming to this earth Jesus became poor, yet through his poverty he made his people rich (8:9). This seemingly contradictory statement means that through his death and resurrection, Jesus grants his followers spiritual riches in this life and incomparable riches in the world to come.

Jesus entrusted his gospel to Paul, so that the apostle's message is not his own but that of his Sender (4:5). He did not commission the intruders who entered the Corinthian church; they came with a gospel that differed from Jesus' gospel (11:4; compare Gal. 1:6–7). Jesus was raised from the dead and promised his followers that also they will be raised (4:14). As an apostle of Christ, Paul carried around in his body Jesus' death and life (4:10–12). And he makes it known to his readers that Jesus Christ is living in them (13:5).

f. Trust and Apostolicity

Paul is rooted in the confidence that God is his hope and strength. God is able to raise him from the dead (1:9). It is God who leads him in triumphal procession in Christ (2:14), enables him in his apostolic mission (2:17; 3:5–6; 6:7), entrusts to him his gospel (11:7), and comforts him with abounding grace (7:6; 9:8).

That Paul is an apostle of Jesus Christ is evident from the opening remarks of this letter (1:1). When his apostleship is challenged by his adversaries, he ascribes his confidence through Christ to God who made him a minister of a new covenant (3:4, 6). He demonstrates the veracity of his apostolic calling by noting his undying love for the Corinthians (2:4; 6:12; 11:11; 12:15); his suffering for the cause of Christ (4:8–12; 6:3–10; 11:23–29); and his ability to perform signs, wonders, and miracles in the church (12:12; Rom. 15:19).

5. Purpose

Some writers see the purpose of II Corinthians to be proclaiming God's glory; they direct attention to the theological depth of the epistle and its practical application.[55] A look at the number of times the word *glory* appears in this epistle supports this observation.[56] As such, this doctrine is a golden thread in the fabric of this epistle and speaks to the day-by-day living of individual believers. Sverre

---

54. Refer to Plummer, *Second Corinthians,* p. 159.
55. Young and Ford, *Meaning and Truth in 2 Corinthians,* p. 260.
56. Of the 165 New Testament occurrences, II Corinthians has 19; John, 18; Revelation, 17; Romans, 16; Luke, 13; and I Corinthians, 12.

Aalen observes, "Glory with its transforming power is operative even now among believers."[57]

In this letter, Paul commends the readers by confirming them with words of joy and encouragement. He seeks to strengthen those members of the church who are faithful to God, the Scriptures, and apostolic teaching. But he also has words of rebuke and refutation for those who side with his opponents. Addressing a minority in the church, he firmly establishes his apostolic authority.

A last purpose is to foster unity in the churches of that day. To have these Gentile churches express their indebtedness to the Jewish Christians in Judea, Paul solicited money for the poor in Jerusalem. By sharing their material blessings with the believers in Jerusalem who had shared spiritual blessings with them, the Corinthians demonstrated that they belonged to the true church and practiced their Christianity.

E. Opponents

Scholars are not at all agreed on the identity of Paul's opponents in Corinth—at least a dozen different hypotheses have been advanced.[58] But all of these hypotheses can be grouped in three categories: Gnostics, the divine men, and the Judaizers. There is also a group of Corinthians whom some scholars portray as Spirit-people.

1. Gnostics

Some writers contend that the apostle's opponents were Gnostics whom Paul never fully understood. Champions of this view see numerous verbal similarities in I and II Corinthians to Gnostic teaching.[59] Gnosticism raised its heretical head in the Christian church of the second century, but there is no evidence that it began in the middle of the first century.

2. Divine Men

Other scholars have advanced the hypothesis that Paul's opponents were divine men in the line of Moses and Jesus, able to perform miracles in a Hellenistic-Jewish culture and rooted in either Christianity or Judaism.[60] These opponents traveled from place to place, claimed to have divine power, preached in imitation of Hellenistic-Jewish leaders, and performed miracles.

---

57. Sverre Aalen, *NIDNTT*, 2:48.

58. John J. Gunther, *Paul's Opponents and Their Background: A Study of Apocalyptic and Jewish Sectarian Teachings*, NovTSup 35 (Leiden: Brill, 1973), pp. 1–2.

59. Refer to Walter Schmithals, *Gnosticism in Corinth*, trans. John E. Steely (Nashville: Abingdon, 1971). See also his *Paul and the Gnostics*, trans. John E. Steely (Nashville: Abingdon, 1972); Bultmann, *Second Letter*.

60. Gerhard Friedrich, "Die Gegner des Paulus im 2. Korintherbrief," *Abraham unser Vater; Juden und Christen im Gespräch über die Bibel, Festschrift für Otto Michel zum 60,* ed. Otto Betz, Martin Hengel, and Peter Schmidt (Leiden: Brill, 1963), pp. 181–215.

We ask a few questions, however. If Paul's adversaries had to carry letters of commendation, did Jewish leaders write them? Would not these adversaries rather choose to be independent?[61] Was the "divine man" doctrine current in Corinth during the middle of the first century? Is there any evidence apart from Paul's correspondence to substantiate this teaching? We cannot equate the parts of one group of people with another group that existed in an earlier period. Groups or movements follow a course of development and are subject to change. Colin J. A. Hickling observes, "It is always tempting . . . to explain the unknown by the known, or by what we imagine we know."[62] A word of caution is in order whenever we try to trace a path into history and have a view of the end but not of the beginning.

3. Judaizers

Most scholars teach that Paul's opponents in Corinth were Judaizers who had Jewish roots.[63] Paul answers the question whether they are Hebrews, Israelites, and Abraham's descendants with a threefold affirmative reply, "So am I" (11:22). Everything in this passage points to the opponents' Jewish origins without specifying a precise geographic location. Yet nothing in this epistle is said about the typical Jewish teachings of circumcision, dietary laws, and the Sabbath ordinance.[64] These tenets, however, were not the issue when Paul wrote the epistle. The Judaizers came to attack his apostleship and the preaching of Christ's gospel.

Paul defended his apostolic calling by pointing to the church in Corinth as his letter of commendation (3:2–3); his suffering for the cause of Christ (11:23–29); his labors offered free of charge (12:13–14); his demonstration of the marks of an apostle—signs, wonders, and miracles (12:12); and his proof that Christ was speaking through him (13:2–4).

There are two questions relative to the identity of the superapostles (see the commentary on 11:5; 12:11). Are the Judaizers to be identified with the super-apostles? And are the superapostles and the false apostles the same people?

Some commentators argue that the Judaizers were sent by the apostles in Jerusalem and thus had a status superior to Paul's apostleship.[65] But there are objections to this argument, because the flow of thought from 11:4–5 features the phrases *if someone comes* and *superapostles*. The singular "someone" repre-

---

61. See Carson, *From Triumphalism to Maturity,* pp. 21–22; Craig Price, "Critical Issues in 2 Corinthians," *SWJourTh* 32 (1989): 16 n. 37.

62. Colin J. A. Hickling, "Is the Second Epistle to the Corinthians a Source for Early Church History?" *ZNTW* 66 (1975): 287.

63. See, e.g., C. K. Barrett, *The Second Epistle to the Corinthians,* Harper's New Testament Commentaries series (New York: Harper and Row, 1973), pp. 6–7; "Paul's Opponents in 2 Corinthians," in *Essays on Paul* (Philadelphia: Westminster, 1982), pp. 60–86.

64. Friedrich, "Die Gegner des Paulus," p. 192. Witherington prefers not the term *Judaizers* but *Jewish Christians* (see *Conflict and Community in Corinth,* p. 346 n. 49).

65. Consult, e.g., Barrett, *Second Corinthians,* pp. 31, 277–78; Héring, *Second Epistle of Paul,* p. 79.

sents a group of people, a group Paul identifies in the next verse (v. 5) with the second term.[66]

Next, in the service of the Lord, the rank of apostle is incomparable.[67] There is no higher level, because no one but Jesus appointed the Twelve and Paul to be his apostles. Jesus never commissioned superapostles. All apostles were equal in his sight.

Third, Paul's epistles and the Book of Acts nowhere hint at tensions among Paul, Peter, and other apostles. It is true that Paul opposed Peter in Antioch because of Peter's wrongful attitude toward Gentile Christians (Gal. 2:11–14). But both Paul and Peter speak well of each other in their respective epistles. Hence, we have difficulty relating the Judaizers to the apostles in Jerusalem.

We identify the Judaizers with the superapostles on the understanding that the second term refers to self-appointed messengers. Whether these Judaizers were the same as those alluded to in Galatians 1:6–7 remains an open question. We assume that Paul's adversaries had come to Corinth after he sent the church his first canonical epistle. There are no conclusive indications in I Corinthians that they were there before Paul wrote that letter.

We answer the second question, "Are the superapostles and the false apostles the same people?" in the affirmative. The contexts of these passages (11:5, 13) speak in favor of such an identification. They are the people who presented a different Jesus, brought a different spirit to Corinth, and preached a gospel different from that of Paul and his associates. Paul portrays them as deceitful workers, servants of Satan who masquerade as servants of righteousness (11:13–14). The false apostles were Judaizers.[68]

Studies on philosophical trends in the middle of the first century have proved that Sophism was a rising movement. Paul's opponents may have been influenced by the Sophists, emulating their rhetorical skills while presenting empty words for profit.[69]

4. Spirit-People

The church in Corinth included a group of people opposed to Paul. This group is known as the Spirit-people (from the appellation *pneumatics* [Greek: *pneumatikoi*]). Proponents of this theory hold that Apollos, a native of Alexandria (Acts 18:24), had been influenced by the Jewish philosopher Philo and came to Corinth to teach the Christian faith within the framework of Philo's philosophical thought. Thus, they say, the Corinthians began to use terminology

---

66. Refer to Windisch, *Der Zweite Korintherbrief,* p. 330; Lietzmann, *Korinther,* p. 148; but see Martin, *2 Corinthians,* p. 342.

67. Karl Heinrich Rengstorf, *TDNT,* 1:445.

68. Consult C. K. Barrett, "ΨΕΥΔΑΠΟΣΤΟΛΟΙ (2 Cor. 11.13)," in *Essays on Paul* (Philadelphia: Westminster, 1982), p. 103.

69. Bruce W. Winter, "Are Philo and Paul among the Sophists? A Hellenistic Jewish and a Christian Response to a First-Century Movement," Ph.D. dissertation, Macquarie University, 1988, pp. 51–53. See Witherington, *Conflict and Community in Corinth,* pp. 348–49.

akin to Philo's: they were the people of the Spirit (I Cor. 2:12, 15); they were wise, strong, and honored (I Cor. 4:10). According to the argument, these Spirit-people ridiculed the speaking ability of Paul (II Cor. 10:10), for they were enamored of the oratorical skills of Apollos. When Apollos left, the Judaizers arrived in Corinth and immediately made the Spirit-people their allies against Paul. The apostle, so the argument goes, employed language that reflects the emphasis that the Judaizers placed on the law and the covenant and that the Spirit-people put on the Spirit. Throughout II Corinthians, Paul had to oppose both the Judaizers and the Spirit-people and wean the latter from the former.[70]

Critique on this line of reasoning must come from the New Testament itself. First, even though Apollos was well educated in Alexandria, he received "the way of God more adequately" from Aquila and Priscilla in Ephesus (Acts 18:26).

Next, in neither Acts nor I Corinthians is there evidence of conflict between Paul and Apollos. Luke writes that Apollos was of great help to the believers in Corinth (Acts 18:27). In fact, Paul mentions Apollos seven times and always speaks appreciatively of him (I Cor. 1:12; 3:4, 5, 6, 22; 4:6; 16:12).

Third, the Greek adjective *pneumatikos* (spiritual) never occurs in II Corinthians. One year elapsed between the writing of Paul's two canonical epistles to Corinth (55 and 56 respectively), yet we find this adjective in its various forms only in I Corinthians. There it occurs twelve times, of which nine are in the neuter gender referring to truths, things, and bodies. The other three are in the masculine gender, either singular or plural (2:15; 3:1; 14:37). In their respective contexts, these three passages describe God's people filled with the Holy Spirit, spiritual wisdom, and a desire to obey the Lord's commands.[71] Paul chooses the term *pneumatikos* in the singular and the plural not to write about a segment of people who oppose him but to characterize persons who truly love and follow the Lord. If the apostle had meant to identify a group of Corinthians opposed to him, he would have penned a recurring term to describe them. As is obvious, *pneumatikos* is not that term.

F. Conclusion

We cannot point to a single theme in this epistle, but we are able to detect a few characteristic ones. The letter expresses Paul's personal concerns for the spiritual welfare of the believers in Corinth, as is evident in a number of places (e.g., 1:6–7, 11, 14; 4:12; 6:1, 11–13; 8:7, 10–11; 9:2, 8, 10–15; 12:19; 13:5, 11). He speaks words of encouragement and comfort, while he reveals the sufferings he has experienced in the service of the Lord (among many other places, see 1:8).

Another feature of this epistle is Paul's genuine relationship to Jesus Christ, a relationship that he commends to the Corinthians (see 4:10–15; 5:16–21; 6:14–

---

70. See Murphy-O'Connor, *Theology of the Second Letter to the Corinthians*, passim.

71. Consult Simon J. Kistemaker, *Exposition of the First Epistle to the Corinthians*, New Testament Commentary series (Grand Rapids: Baker, 1993), pp. 13–14.

18; 11:2; 12:8–10; 13:3). For Paul and his people, that relationship demonstrates the Christian aspiration to glorify God in Christ Jesus.

And a last characteristic is the defense of Paul's apostleship. "[This letter] is at once a triumphant vindication of his apostolic ministry, and a searing indictment of the pretensions of the 'super-apostles' who were attempting to overthrow his work in Corinth by basely slandering his character and his motives."[72]

G. Outline

1:1–11	I. Introduction	
1:1–2	A. Address	
1:3–7	B. Distress and Comfort	
1:8–11	C. Deliverance and Gratitude	
1:12–7:16	II. Apostolic Ministry	
1:12–2:11	A. Paul's Travel Plans	
	1. Trustworthiness	1:12–14
	2. Revised Plans	1:15–17
	3. Authenticity	1:18–22
	4. A Painful Visit	1:23–2:4
	5. Forgiving the Sinner	2:5–11
2:12–4:6	B. The New Covenant	
	1. Paul's Anxiety	2:12–13
	2. Christ's Message	2:14–17
	3. Commendation	3:1–3
	4. Confidence	3:4–6
	5. Comparison of Glory	3:7–11
	6. Unveiled Faces	3:12–18
	7. Light of the Gospel	4:1–6
4:7–5:10	C. Earthly and Heavenly Dwellings	
	1. Jars of Clay	4:7–12
	2. Resurrection	4:13–15
	3. Outward and Inward	4:16–18
	4. Home in Heaven	5:1–5
	5. With the Lord	5:6–10
5:11–21	D. Ministry of Reconciliation	
	1. Christ's Love	5:11–15
	2. Christ's Ministry	5:16–19
	3. Christ's Ambassadors	5:20–21
6:1–7:16	E. Paul's Ministry	
	1. Working Together	6:1–2
	2. Enduring Hardships	6:3–10
	3. Opening Hearts	6:11–13

---

72. Geoffrey B. Wilson, *2 Corinthians: A Digest of Reformed Comment* (Edinburgh and London: Banner of Truth Trust, 1973), p. 12.

Commentary

1

Introduction

(1:1–11)

and

Apostolic Ministry, *part 1*

(1:12–22)

Outline

1 1 Paul, an apostle of Christ Jesus through the will of God, and Timothy our brother, to the church of God that is in Corinth with all the saints who are in all of Achaia. 2 Grace to you and peace from God our Father and the Lord Jesus Christ.

3 Blessed be the God and Father of our Lord Jesus Christ, the Father of compassion and the God of all comfort. 4 He comforts us in all our affliction to enable us to comfort those in any kind of affliction through the comfort with which we ourselves are comforted by God. 5 Because just as the sufferings of Christ are abundant for us, so through Christ our comfort is also abundant. 6 And if we are afflicted, it is for your comfort and salvation. If we are comforted, it is for your comfort that is effecting in you patient endurance for the same sufferings that even we suffer. 7 And our hope for you is steadfast, for we know that as you are sharers in our sufferings, so you are sharers even in our comfort.

8 For we do not want you to be ignorant, brothers, concerning the affliction we endured in the province of Asia, because we were burdened exceedingly beyond our strength so that we despaired even of life. 9 However, we have in ourselves the sentence of death, so that we trust not in ourselves but in God who raises the dead. 10 He delivered us from such mortal danger and will rescue us. In him we put our hope. He will rescue us again, 11 as also you help us through your prayers for us. Then from many people thanks may be expressed on our behalf for the blessing granted us through the prayers of many people.

I. Introduction
1:1–11

A. Address
1:1–2

In his correspondence with the Corinthian church, Paul stresses his apostleship, the recipients of his letters, and the saints who reside elsewhere. He wants his readers to understand that he indeed is an apostle appointed and sent by Jesus Christ. They belong to the church of God that is both local and universal.

1. Paul, an apostle of Christ Jesus through the will of God, and Timothy our brother, to the church of God that is in Corinth with all the saints who are in all of Achaia.

a. "Paul." The writer introduces himself in the first word of the sentence. In all his other epistles, which are part of the New Testament canon, Paul begins with his own name and often cites it throughout his letters (see, e.g., Gal. 5:2; Eph. 3:1; Col. 1:23; 4:18; Paul refers to himself again in the second half of this epistle [10:1]). The epistolary literature of the New Testament reveals that writers commonly wrote first their name and afterward that of the addressees. In brief, the combination of both the author's identification and the recipients' names amounts to an address written on an envelope.

37

b. "An apostle of Christ Jesus through the will of God." In most of his epistles, Paul stresses his apostleship. The exceptions are his epistles to the Philippians, the Thessalonians, and Philemon. Paul says that he is an apostle despite the fact that he could not meet both requirements for apostleship: being a disciple during Jesus' ministry and being a witness of his resurrection (Acts 1:21–22). Yet Paul had met the resurrected Lord near Damascus (Acts 9:1–19; 22:6–16; 26:12–18), and Jesus called him to be an apostle to the Gentiles (I Tim. 2:7; II Tim. 1:11).

Paul signifies that he is "an apostle of Christ Jesus," which is the identification he uses repeatedly.[1] He readily confesses that his appointment is on the authority of Christ Jesus, who commissioned Paul as his ambassador. That is, he was fully aware of the charge to be Jesus' spokesman and to represent him accurately and faithfully. Paul explains his apostleship from Christ Jesus with the phrase *through the will of God.* Thus he emphasizes the origin of his apostolic status. Paul notes elsewhere that God set him apart from birth, called him in due time, caused him to know Jesus, and empowered him to preach Christ's gospel to the Gentiles (Gal. 1:15; compare Jer. 1:5). "Paul's call to Christ, his call to be an apostle to the Gentiles as a slave of Christ, and his call to be a slave of those to whom God sent him were all one in purpose and all divine in origin."[2]

Paul announces his status at the outset, so that when in the course of his epistle he discusses the superapostles and the false apostles (11:5, 13; 12:11, 12), the readers know that God through Christ called him to be an apostle. Whereas other men were commissioned by the church to serve as apostles,[3] Paul was commissioned by Jesus through the will of God.

Jesus appointed twelve men to be his apostles. After Judas betrayed him and committed suicide, the apostles placed two names before the Lord and asked Jesus to choose one of these to fill the vacancy left by Judas. When the lot was cast, the apostles saw that Jesus had named Matthias to be added to their number (Acts 1:23–26). Jesus commissioned no other people except Paul.

c. "And Timothy our brother." In the introductory sentence of his first epistle to the Corinthian church (I Cor. 1:1), Paul adds the name of Sosthenes, whom he calls "our brother." There we receive no further information concerning Sosthenes, but here we know that Timothy had served the local church in Corinth (Acts 18:5). Some years later, Paul dispatched him from Ephesus to Corinth (I Cor. 4:17; 16:10; compare Acts 19:22). We infer that Timothy had returned from his visit to the Corinthians and was now in Paul's presence. The two words *our brother* (literally, the brother) reveal the bond that existed between Paul and

---

1. Eph. 1:1; Col. 1:1; I Tim. 1:1; II Tim. 1:1; see also I Cor. 1:1; Titus 1:1.

2. The Greek text features the noun *apostoloi,* which is translated at times as "representatives" (8:23, NIV) and, in the singular, as "messenger" (Phil. 2:25). Similarly, Barnabas was not authorized by Jesus to be an apostle but was commissioned by the church at Antioch to do mission work among the Gentiles (see Acts 14:4, 14).

3. Scott J. Hafemann, "The Comfort and Power of the Gospel: The Argument of II Corinthians 1–3," *RevExp* 86 (1989): 326.

Timothy and, presumably, also between the Corinthians and Timothy (but see I Cor. 16:10–11). By placing Timothy's name in the first verse, Paul meant to strengthen the relationship between the addressees and his co-worker (I Thess. 3:2).

Paul had great respect for Timothy; he invited him to become his fellow helper (Acts 16:1–3) and sent him on several missions.[4] But he never regarded Timothy as a fellow apostle, much less as a writer of Paul's epistle. Rather, we assume that, on his return from Corinth, Timothy provided Paul with information about the local church. Thus we conclude that the letter was written not by two authors, Paul and Timothy, but only by Paul.

d. "To the church of God that is in Corinth." From the perspective of the Corinthians, the concept *church* signified the gathering of God's people for worship, praise, and fellowship. Whether they met in private homes or in the open air for a mass gathering, the Corinthians viewed themselves as the church of God locally present in Corinth. They were part of the universal church, and Paul continually reminded them of that fact (see I Cor. 4:17; 7:17; 14:33; II Cor. 8:18; 11:28). In other words, Paul is not addressing a single house church; rather, he is speaking to the church of God that is represented in the city of Corinth through many house churches.

From Paul's perspective, the expressions *assembly of the Lord* and *assembly of God* appear in the Old Testament Scriptures, and in the Septuagintal translation those expressions become "church of the Lord" and "church of God."[5] Paul used these Old Testament appellations to show that the early Christians represented the continuation of God's true people. According to Paul, the privileges and promises that God had given to Israel (Rom. 9:4–5) have now been applied through Christ to the church.[6] And out of the world at large, God continues to call forth his people and to gather a joyful assembly of those "whose names are written in heaven" (Heb. 12:23). The church belongs to God because of Jesus Christ.

e. "With all the saints who are in all of Achaia." The word *saint* conveys the idea of a people who are models of virtue, piety, and holiness. But the contents of Paul's Corinthian correspondence fail to portray the Christians in Corinth as such. Paul is addressing not individual Christians but the entire church, which he views as being sanctified through Jesus Christ. The holiness of all the believers originates in Christ's redemptive work (Heb. 2:11; 10:14). Believers are exhorted to live a life of holiness by keeping God's commands and thus to show him gratitude for their deliverance. Being declared holy in the sight of God,

---

4. Acts 17:14–15; 19:22; 20:4; I Cor. 4:17; 16:10; I Thess. 3:2.

5. The Hebrew Scriptures use the noun *qāhāl*, which in Greek becomes either *synagōgē* or *ekklēsia*. See Num. 16:3; 20:4; Deut. 23:2–4, 8 [9]; Mic. 2:5; I Chron. 28:8 and Neh. 13:1 [II Esd. 23:1] respectively. Consult SB 1:733–34; Lothar Coenen, *NIDNTT*, 1:292–93; Karl L. Schmidt, *TDNT*, 3:528.

6. Consult Herman N. Ridderbos, *Paul: An Outline of His Theology,* trans. John Richard de Witt (Grand Rapids: Eerdmans, 1975), p. 328.

however, does not guarantee that believers never fall into sin. After he taught his followers to petition for forgiveness of sins, Jesus taught them to pray the sixth petition: "And lead us not into temptation, but deliver us from the evil one" (Matt. 6:13). Sanctification is a lifelong process that increasingly renews God's people after his image. Following this earthly life they reach their goal: perfect holiness in the presence of Jesus.

The phrase *all of Achaia* includes every church that had been founded throughout the province (see 9:2; 11:10). We know about only the church in Cenchrea (Rom. 16:1) but are confident that in time the Christian faith spread to other cities and villages in Achaia (refer to I Thess. 1:7–8). In 27 B.C., the Romans had divided Greece into two provinces: Achaia in the south and Macedonia in the north. The capital of Achaia was Corinth, and it was the seat of the proconsul (Acts 18:12).

2. Grace to you and peace from God our Father and the Lord Jesus Christ.

This was the common greeting that Paul[7] and other New Testament writers extended to the early Christians who received their letters. The Greek term *charis* (grace) is related to the common greeting *chairein* (see, e.g., Acts 15:23; 23:26; James 1:1), which conveys the intent of "Good day," or "I am glad to see you."[8] The New Testament writers, however, give the term *charis* a spiritual connotation that relates to God's indispensable blessing extended to the recipient. Grace flows from God. As oil makes a machine function smoothly, so the grace that comes from God facilitates the relationship between himself and the believer.

To the noun *chairein* Paul adds the word *peace*, which is the translation of the Hebrew greeting *shalōm*, a greeting used by the Jews even today. However, *shalōm* has a deeper significance than does the greeting *good-by* or *keep well*. In context, the word intimates absence of tension between two parties and the presence of goodwill. Further, the Hebrew expression connotes completeness, prosperity, ease, health. The one who sends greetings, therefore, wishes that the recipient may enjoy both spiritual and material prosperity.

The greeting states that both grace and peace derive "from God our Father and the Lord Jesus Christ." The expression *God our Father* implies that the readers of this epistle are his children. They are members of God's family through Jesus Christ; they owe him faithful allegiance and perfect obedience because he is their Lord. From the Father and his Son, every member of the household of faith receives the blessings of grace and peace.

Greek Words, Phrases, and Constructions in 1:1

τῇ ἐκκλησίᾳ—the definite article indicates Paul's reference to the universal church, of which a part is present in Corinth.

---

7. Rom. 1:7; II Cor. 1:2; Gal. 1:3; Eph. 1:2; Phil. 1:2; II Thess. 1:2; Philem. 3; and with variations Col. 1:2; I Thess. 1:1; Titus 1:4.

8. Bauer, p. 874.

τῇ Ἀχαίᾳ—the definite article appears before names of Roman provinces but is omitted in translation.

B. Distress and Comfort
1:3–7

A quick overview of this passage reveals that Paul stresses the concept *comfort.*[9] Indeed, this is the most eloquent passage on comfort in the entire New Testament. Paul notes that all comfort comes from God the Father who, whenever his children experience sufferings and hardships, has compassion.

3. Blessed be the God and Father of our Lord Jesus Christ, the Father of compassion and the God of all comfort.

a. "Blessed be the God and Father of our Lord Jesus Christ."

After the initial greeting, Paul bursts out in joyful praise with a Jewish benediction: blessed be the God. This is a liturgical formula frequently uttered by God's people in worshipful praise and prayer. Doxologies in the five books in the Psalter, for instance, direct praises to God (Ps. 41:13 [40:14]; 72:19 [71:18]; 89:52 [88:53]; 106:48 [105:48]; 150:6). Paul voices a blessing or a eulogy that is identical to any Jewish benediction addressed to God (compare Luke 1:68). In nearly all his epistles, he utters praises and thanksgiving directed to God on behalf of the addressees. In verse 3, Paul expresses a benediction in which he urges the people to praise and to thank God (see Rom. 1:25; 9:5; II Cor. 11:31; Eph. 1:3; and I Peter 1:3). The expression *blessed be the God* is in the passive voice; the passive connotes that the agent, the Christian community, together with Paul, blesses God the Father.

Paul links the Christian formula *of our Lord Jesus Christ* to the nouns *God* and *Father.*[10] R. C. H. Lenski interprets this correlation as follows: "For Jesus in his human nature God is God, and for Jesus in his deity God is his Father; his God since the incarnation, his Father from all eternity."[11] Moreover, through Jesus Christ all believers may freely address God as God and Father. On Easter Sunday Jesus instructed Mary Magdalene to tell the disciples: "I am returning to my Father and your Father, to my God and your God" (John 20:17). Amplifying a familiar Jewish blessing with a Christian formula, Paul invites the recipients of his epistle to join him in praising God the Father.

---

9. The verb occurs four times and the noun six: 1:3, 4, 5, 6 (twice), and 7. Consult Peter T. O'Brien, *Introductory Thanksgivings in the Letters of Paul*, NovTSup 49 (Leiden: Brill, 1977), p. 242.

10. Some translators and commentators either change the conjunction *and* to *even* (KJV) or omit it. Refer to NAB, SEB, *Phillips;* C. K. Barrett, *The Second Epistle to the Corinthians*, Harper's New Testament Commentaries series (New York: Harper and Row, 1973), p. 56; Victor Paul Furnish, *II Corinthians: Translated with Introduction, Notes and Commentary*, Anchor Bible 32A (Garden City, N.Y.: Doubleday, 1984), p. 109. Other scholars present a literal translation, e.g., Ralph P. Martin, *II Corinthians*, Word Biblical Commentary 40 (Waco: Word, 1986), p. 8.

11. R. C. H. Lenski, *The Interpretation of St. Paul's First and Second Epistle to the Corinthians* (Columbus: Wartburg, 1946), p. 814.

b. "The Father of compassion and the God of all comfort." The two nouns *God* and *Father* are now reversed and supplied with descriptive modifiers. With the phrases *Father of compassion* and *God of all comfort*, Paul alludes to the Scriptures (Ps. 103:13, 17; Isa. 51:12; 66:13) and to a Jewish liturgical prayer, *Ahabah Rabbah*, offered in synagogue worship services.[12] He stresses the love of the Father, who, by granting mercy to his erring children, sets them free.

Compassion is God's love that seeks out, extends to, and transforms the sinner. Out of compassion flows God's comforting love. God has tender love for those who are hurting and he comforts them in their hour of need. Notice that Paul writes "the God of *all* comfort." This means that God is always ready to comfort those people who call on him. Whatever the hardships may be, God proves to be near to his saints and reassures them with his all-encompassing support (compare Rom. 15:5; I Cor. 10:13).

A last remark: The two phrases *the Father of compassion* and *the God of all comfort* fittingly introduce Paul's discussion on comfort, trouble, hardship, and deliverance (vv. 4–11).

4. He comforts us in all our affliction to enable us to comfort those in any kind of affliction through the comfort with which we ourselves are comforted by God.

a. "He comforts us in all our affliction." Paul notes that the God of all comfort continually comforts him and all others who are suffering. Paul uses the first person plural pronoun three times in this verse. Does he employ the pronoun editorially? Is he referring to himself and his co-workers, including the recipients of this epistle? Although scholars present arguments that support either position, the immediate context is determinative. It points to Paul's sufferings in the province of Asia (1:8–9; compare also 11:23–29). Thus we assume that the apostle is speaking primarily about himself.[13] Nonetheless, we surmise that at times the Corinthian believers, like those in Macedonia, especially Thessalonica, faced suffering for the sake of Christ (see 8:2; I Thess. 2:14; 3:3). Following Jesus Christ inevitably elicits suffering for him in some form or other. A more inclusive use of the personal pronoun, therefore, cannot be ruled out.[14] And this fact is evident from the second part of this verse.

b. "To enable us to comfort those in any kind of affliction." If anyone could empathize with Christians who had to endure affliction, it was Paul himself. He had experienced and continued to experience hardships because of his calling to proclaim Christ Jesus. He and Barnabas strengthened the churches of Derbe,

---

12. A. Marmorstein records the explanation, "God, the Father of Mercy, finds it hard to destroy men who studied Torah and Mishna and are stained by ugly conduct and unworthy deeds." *The Old Rabbinic Doctrine of God* (1927; New York: KTAV, 1968), p. 56.

13. Consult J. J. Kijne, "We, Us and Our in I and II Corinthians," *NovT* 8 (1966): 171–79; Scott J. Hafemann, *Suffering and the Spirit: An Exegetical Study of II Cor. 2:14–3:3 Within the Context of the Corinthian Correspondence,* WUzNT 2.19 (Tübingen: Mohr, 1986), pp. 12–17.

14. Refer to Alfred Plummer, *A Critical and Exegetical Commentary on the Second Epistle of St. Paul to the Corinthians,* International Critical Commentary (1915; Edinburgh: Clark, 1975), pp. 9–10.

Lystra, Iconium, and Pisidian Antioch and instructed the Christians to remain true to Christ. They said, "We must go through many hardships to enter the kingdom of God" (Acts 14:22).

With the words *in any kind of,* which translate the Greek *pas* (all), Paul uses an expression that covers any and every affliction the Corinthians may encounter. He is able to testify that affliction produces perseverance, character, and hope (Rom. 5:3). He has learned that allowing affliction in the lives of believers is part of God's design to save sinners.[15] Paul knows that God not only comforts and sustains him in his distress, but also gives him both the ability and the task to comfort others who suffer hardship.

c. "Through the comfort with which we ourselves are comforted by God." In the last part of this verse Paul draws a parallel with the love of God. That is, as recipients of God's love we are obliged to love our fellow men. Similarly, the comfort we receive in our affliction must be extended in turn to fellow believers who also endure difficulties. By being encouragers we are able to help effectively those around us when we ourselves have been recipients of God's comforting care. This text, then, speaks of the corporate responsibility we have toward our fellow men.

5. Because just as the sufferings of Christ are abundant for us, so through Christ our comfort is also abundant.

a. *Translation.* The first word in the Greek is *hoti,* which can have a causal meaning. Is verse 5 making a causal connection with the preceding verse? Numerous translators understand it in this way and translate *hoti* as "because," but others disagree and consider this verse to be a parenthetical thought. If this is the case, then the first word in this verse becomes meaningless and should be omitted.[16] However, Paul explains the concept *affliction* by referring to the sufferings he and others are enduring as Christ's representatives. Hence, verse 5 elucidates the previous verse, and the causal connotation of the first word is indeed significant.

b. *Explanation.* The phrase *sufferings of Christ* can be interpreted subjectively or objectively. Subjectively, the sufferings are the pain and agony Jesus endured in the garden of Gethsemane and on the cross at Golgotha. But the objective interpretation of the phrase is preferred. In this view, these are the sufferings that Christ's followers undergo for his church and kingdom. For instance, Saul on his way to Damascus heard Jesus ask him, "Why are you persecuting me?" (Acts 9:4; 22:7; 26:14). Saul was victimizing Christians. However, the Lord told Saul that Jesus and the church are one, so that when believers suffer for Christ, both Jesus and his followers endure the pain. Conclusively, Christians share in suffering for Christ, as Paul writes elsewhere (4:10; Gal. 6:17; Phil. 3:10; Col. 1:24).

c. *Contrast.* The comparison ("just as . . . so") that Paul draws relates to the verb *abound.* Note that with respect to the subjects of this verb he uses first the plural

---

15. Consult Reinier Schippers, *NIDNTT,* 2:809.

16. GNB, NAB, NEB, NCV, REB, SEB. Both JB and *Phillips* have the translation *indeed.*

("sufferings") and then the singular ("comfort"). The sufferings that Christians bear on behalf of Christ are numerous, yet the comfort that is channeled through Christ to them exceeds every kind of agony.[17]

In the preceding verses (vv. 3–4), Paul specified that the source of comfort is divine. Here he also emphatically states that comfort comes to us through Christ. This means that the many sufferings that Christians have to endure for their faith are outweighed by the comfort that Christ extends to us. By implication, Paul wants believers to share this abundant comfort with others who are suffering for Christ.

6. And if we are afflicted, it is for your comfort and salvation. If we are comforted, it is for your comfort that is effecting in you patient endurance for the same sufferings that even we suffer.

a. "And if we are afflicted, it is for your comfort and salvation." Here Paul continues the theme of affliction and comfort. This verse, however, links affliction to Paul and comfort and salvation to the Corinthians. Paul does not teach that his suffering, whether in Corinth or elsewhere, has earned salvation for the Corinthians. Not at all: Christ's death alone is sufficient to save sinners. The sufferings Paul endured for the sake of Christ are unable to add anything to the process of redemption, but Christ uses those sufferings to lead sinners to himself.

The conditional clause ("if we are afflicted") in the Greek indicates reality. Paul indeed suffered distress, although he fails to provide details (see v. 8). But Paul's sufferings were always to bring the gospel to both Jews and Gentiles. The hardships he experienced were for the benefit of Christ's people (compare 4:15); he purposed to assist and to encourage them in their Christian life and to show them the way of salvation. In brief, Paul's sufferings must be seen in the light of his intent to promote believers' spiritual welfare. As a servant of Christ he suffered for the benefit of Christ's people.

b. "If we are comforted, it is for your comfort . . ." Notice the parallel of the two conditional clauses in this verse. The first one speaks of being afflicted and the second of being comforted. We note that suffering and support are two components in the life of a Christian. Also, this conditional sentence reflects reality (see v. 6a).

The readers of this epistle can derive comfort from Paul's life, for Paul is an example to them as he appropriates the Lord's overarching support in times of affliction (Acts 18:9–10). They, too, should accept the comfort God extends to them during their troubles.

c. "Your comfort that is effecting in you patient endurance for the same sufferings which even we suffer." What is Paul trying to convey in the last part of this verse? The encouragement Paul received from God also reached the Corinthians in their own hardships for Christ. This encouragement is producing within them a steadfast perseverance so that they are able to bear up under the

---

17. John Albert Bengel, *Bengel's New Testament Commentary*, trans. Charlton T. Lewis and Marvin R. Vincent, 2 vols. (Grand Rapids: Kregel, 1981), vol. 2, p. 275.

strain (refer to 6:4). They undergo tribulations that differ from those Paul has sustained, but they are afflictions just the same. Some had to confront arrogant teachers in their midst (I Cor. 4:18–19); others had to live with an unbelieving spouse (I Cor. 7:15); still others had qualms of conscience because of an invitation to eat meat offered to an idol (I Cor. 10:27–29). All of them had promised to remain true to Christ and now had to suffer the consequences of this decision.

7. And our hope for you is steadfast, for we know that as you are sharers in our sufferings, so you are sharers even in our comfort.

a. "And our hope for you is steadfast." Paul now concludes this segment of his letter, which began with praising the God and Father of Jesus Christ (v. 3). Looking to the future, he expresses a hope that is steadfast. He hopes unwaveringly that the readers will be able to sustain the pressures that arise from living the Christian faith. Paul knows that they have already proven themselves and will continue to do so in the future. He echoes a sentiment that David expressed in one of his psalms: "The LORD will fulfill his purpose for me; your love, O LORD, endures forever—do not abandon the works of your hands" (Ps. 138:8). Paul realizes that the Lord, who began his work among the Corinthians, will never forsake his own (compare Phil. 1:6).

b. "For we know." Paul frequently writes the word *hope* as either a noun or a verb in his Corinthian correspondence. He intimates that hope is based on knowledge, as is evident in the present verse. Knowledge is closely connected not only with faith but also with hope; it is basic to and gives direction to these virtues.[18]

The apostle introduces the words *as* and *so* a second time (see v. 5) to feature comparison in respect to suffering and comfort. Verse 7, therefore, is a summary that restates the theme of this entire passage. The key word is *sharers*, which does not mean that the Corinthians shared Paul's suffering and comfort, but rather that they with him have a share in the distresses Christians suffer when they follow Christ. With him, they receive the sustaining comfort Christ extends to them. Here and elsewhere in this epistle, Paul expresses the communion of the saints as they together share in the affliction and consolation they endure for the sake of Christ.

Practical Considerations in 1:4–7

Comfort. The thought of agreeable temperatures comes to mind, of being in a warm home during the winter or of enjoying cool relief from the heat in summer. We think of comfortable living quarters equipped with modern appliances and conveniences. We reflect on enjoyable experiences in the past and on a feeling of contentment in the present.

However, the term *comfort*, which derives from the Latin *con* and *forte*, means "to make strong together." It shows a relational aspect that greatly overshadows the idea of individualistic comfort that prevails today. The word implies that one party strengthens another.

---

18. Compare Ridderbos, *Paul*, p. 243.

For instance, medical doctors and nurses aid their patients in recovery from physical ailments; a counselor helps a person to overcome periods of depression; and a pastor consoles those who are grieving.

New Testament writers use the concept *comfort* repeatedly, but the biblical intent of that word is nuanced. It conveys the idea of encouraging and exhorting those who cope with defeat, doubt, and depression. When Paul proclaimed the gospel in the synagogue of Corinth, the Jews opposed him so that he and his followers had to leave and establish a house church. Paul lost his initial enthusiasm and intended to go elsewhere. Then Jesus gave him words of comfort and encouragement: "Do not be afraid; keep on speaking, do not be silent. For I am with you, and no one is going to attack and harm you, because I have many people in this city" (Acts 18:9–10). Jesus kept his word by shielding Paul from harm and danger; he blessed Paul's ministry in Corinth.

At the time of Paul's conversion, the Lord told him that he would have to suffer much for the name of Jesus (Acts 9:16). Nonetheless, in all his trials the Lord stood with him with words of comfort, assurance, and exhortation. Indeed, Jesus always stands next to his people with the pledge that he will never forsake them (Matt. 28:20).

Greek Words, Phrases, and Constructions in 1:3–7

Verse 3

εὐλογητός—this is a verbal adjective that reflects the passive voice. The clause does not have a verb, so that the verb *to be* must be supplied in the indicative, imperative, or optative mood. "The omission of the verb . . . portrays the liveliness of the exclamation."[19]

ὁ θεὸς καὶ πατήρ—the one definite article fuses two aspects of the deity, God and Father. Note that in the second half of this verse the order of the two nouns is reversed.

τῶν οἰκτιρμῶν—the plural literally means "mercies." Influenced by the Hebrew plural *rah^amim*, οἰκτιρμός always appears in the plural but in meaning it often does not differ from the singular.[20]

πάσης—the significance of the singular "all" must be interpreted in the light of verse 4, where it occurs twice with "affliction."

Verses 4–5

The use of various prepositions is meaningful: ἐπί followed by the dative case signifies "over"; God's comfort encompasses the person who is afflicted. εἰς τὸ δύνασθαι expresses purpose, that is, the obligation we have to comfort others. ἐν is followed by the words πάσῃ θλίψει and points to a person being in any kind of affliction.[21] διά conveys means and ὑπό, agency.

The relative pronoun ἧς is in the genitive case because of its attraction to the preceding noun. The present passive construction παρακαλούμεθα (we are comforted) in

---

19. Robert Hanna, *A Grammatical Aid to the Greek New Testament* (Grand Rapids: Baker, 1983), p. 315; J. H. Moulton and Nigel Turner, *A Grammar of New Testament Greek* (Edinburgh: Clark, 1963), vol. 3, *Syntax*, p. 296.

20. Friedrich Blass and Albert Debrunner, *A Greek Grammar of the New Testament and other Early Christian Literature*, trans. and rev. Robert Funk (Chicago: University of Chicago Press, 1961), #142; Hans-Helmut Esser, *NIDNTT*, 2:598.

21. Blass and Debrunner, *Greek Grammar*, #275.3.

Greek can take a direct object, but in translation we are compelled to add a preposition: "*with* which."

τοῦ Χριστοῦ—this is not the subjective genitive (sufferings Christ endured on the cross) but the objective (sufferings Christians endure for Christ).

ἡμῶν—the context favors the objective interpretation: comfort that comes from Christ to us.

Verses 6–7

The Greek text adopted for these verses has the support of many and varied manuscripts. However, the Majority Text has a variant that presumably originated when a copyist accidentally omitted in verse 6 the words "and salvation. If we are comforted, it is for your comfort." These words later were inserted in verse 7 (see KJV and NKJV). The error is due to an oversight of a copyist who read the same ending of παρακλήσεως at two places in verse 6 and accidentally chose the second place to continue the copying. The omitted words were subsequently placed in the margin but in later manuscripts were included in verse 7.[22] The harmony of the adopted text supports the reading preferred by translators and textual experts.

ἐνεργουμένης—the present participle can be either middle or passive in meaning.[23] The middle, "is effecting," is preferred.

ὧν—the relative pronoun is in the genitive case because of attraction to the preceding noun.

βεβαία—in classical Greek, this adjective, which signifies "sure," "becomes a predominantly legal term, used to refer to a position or guarantee which is subject to no risk of alteration."[24]

C. Deliverance and Gratitude
1:8–11

Although Paul wrote a summary in the preceding verse (v. 7), he has more to say about his own perils from which God has rescued him. He no longer alludes to afflictions of the Corinthians but refers to personal, life-threatening experiences from which he was delivered by divine intervention. Hence, he expresses gratitude to God for his deliverance and thanks to the Corinthians for the many prayers uttered on his behalf.[25]

8. For we do not want you to be ignorant, brothers, concerning the affliction we endured in the province of Asia, because we were burdened exceedingly beyond our strength so that we despaired even of life.

22. Bruce M. Metzger, *A Textual Commentary on the Greek New Testament*, 2d ed. (Stuttgart and New York: United Bible Societies, 1994), pp. 505–6.

23. For the passive see K. W. Clark, "The Meaning of ἐνεργέω and κατεργέω in the New Testament," *JBL* 54 (1935): 93–101.

24. Hans Schönweiss, *NIDNTT*, 1:658.

25. Linda L. Belleville asserts that the body of the letter begins with verse 8. See her study, "A Letter of Apologetic Self-Commendation: II Cor. 1:8–7:16," *NovT* 31 (1989): 142–63; *Reflections of Glory: Paul's Polemical Use of the Moses-Doxa Tradition in II Corinthians 3.1–18*, JSNTSupS 52 (Sheffield: JSOT, 1991), pp. 115–18.

a. "For we do not want you to be ignorant, brothers." The first word, "for," joins verse 8 to the previous verse and paragraph by expressing cause in the form of a personal example. Paul uses a formula that occurs often in his epistles.[26] The formula affirms the negative to stress the positive. The Corinthians had heard about Paul's perils, and consequently he does not have to provide details for his initial readers, even though these features would have been helpful to subsequent readers of his epistle. He addresses the Corinthians as brothers, a term that includes all the sisters in the family of God (see 8:1; 13:11).

b. "Concerning the affliction we endured in the province of Asia." This particular part of the verse fails to convey the facts that we need to gain insight into the perils Paul endured. Because we lack further information, we can only suggest possible situations. A number of these have been proposed, such as incidents that occurred in Ephesus, the province of Asia's capital:

1. The riot instigated by Demetrius (Acts 19:23–41). But Luke writes that Paul was kept away from the theater and was relatively safe at that time.
2. Fighting wild beasts (I Cor. 15:32). Because Paul was a Roman citizen, he would not have been thrown to the lions. We conclude that the words *wild beasts* should be interpreted not literally but figuratively.
3. Imprisonment by Roman authorities (II Cor. 11:23). We have no certainty whether Paul was incarcerated in Ephesus, yet he writes that he had been in prison frequently. During his nearly three-year teaching ministry in that city (Acts 19:8, 10; 20:31) he probably spent time in prison.
4. A physical malady (II Cor. 12:7–10). The exact nature of this malady is not known, and Paul does not indicate that the "thorn in [his] flesh" was endangering his life.

All these suggestions are interesting, but they fail to explain the immediate context of verse 8. Paul writes, "[God] delivered us from such mortal danger and will rescue us. In him we put our hope. He will rescue us again" (v. 10). Indeed, Paul still faced the same danger from which he had been set free (v. 10).

It is not unthinkable that Paul had been dragged into various local synagogues to stand trial before Jewish courts. The punishments he received were the prescribed thirty-nine lashes. He reveals, "Five times I received from the Jews the forty lashes minus one" (11:24). These floggings could be perilous when administered harshly, especially if they were repeated in close succession. In addition, Roman authorities three times beat Paul with rods (11:25). Luke records only the beating Paul and Silas received in Philippi (Acts 16:22) and refrains from recording the other two incidents. The question must be raised, "How much punishment is a human body able to endure?"

If Paul was exposed to this recurring mortal danger, it is possible that the threat originated because of his directive to Jewish and Gentile Christians to

---

26. See Rom. 1:13; 11:25; I Cor. 10:1; 12:1; II Cor. 1:8; I Thess. 4:13.

gather a collection for the saints in Jerusalem. The period for collecting the money was prolonged for more than one year (8:10) and was a cause of friction to Paul's antagonists. Jewish leaders in Asia Minor, Macedonia, and Greece may have misunderstood Paul's motive. They judged that he was interfering with the collection of the temple tax that all Jews everywhere had to pay annually.[27] These Jewish leaders resisted the spread of Christianity with its challenge to Judaism. Thus they frequently attacked Paul as one of the chief proponents of Christianity. The fierce opposition that Paul had to endure from Jewish adversaries continued to be a persistent threat to his life (compare Acts 20:3, 19; 21:27–32).

c. "Because we were burdened exceedingly beyond our strength so that we despaired even of life." The danger Paul incurred was so great that he describes it as an extremely heavy load that he was unable to bear physically.[28] More than that, spiritually he lacked the necessary strength and entered into a state of despair (contrast 4:8). He expected the end of his earthly life unless God himself intervened and, as it were, brought him back from the dead.

9. However, we have in ourselves the sentence of death, so that we trust not in ourselves but in God who raises the dead.

In the Greek text, much more so than in the English translation, we find a decided emphasis on the personal pronoun *we*. Paul writes from a strictly personal point of view about an experience he has had, one that he was unable to avoid. This experience made Paul despair of life and believe that he could no longer rely on his own senses. He asked God for deliverance but instead was given the sentence of death. The word *sentence* implies that Paul had petitioned God, just as Jesus in the garden of Gethsemane pleaded with his Father to remove the cup of suffering and death from him.

Even though Paul came to the verge of death, he did not die. God wanted him to abandon his reliance on himself and instead to put all his trust in God. Being at death's door means a complete abandonment of any trace of reliance on one's self and an utter dependence on God alone. It entails that we do not deem ourselves indispensable in God's service but realize that with body and soul we belong entirely to Jesus Christ. That is the trust Paul has in mind.

During this experience, Paul emotionally experienced death and thereafter committed himself totally to God. He trusted that God was able to raise him from the dead.[29]

The deliverance that God provided for Paul was a type of resurrection that resembles the experience of Abraham and Isaac. Abraham displayed true faith

---

27. Roy Yates, "Paul's Affliction in Asia: II Corinthians 1:8," *EvQ* 53 (1981): 241–45; and consult John E. Wood, "Death at Work in Paul," *EvQ* 54 (1982): 151–55.

28. Paul employs the Greek expression *kath' hyperbolēn* (exceedingly) seven times in his epistles: Rom. 7:13; I Cor. 12:31; II Cor. 1:8; 4:7, 17; 12:7; Gal. 1:13.

29. See also Hafemann, "Comfort and Power," p. 329; Calvin J. Roetzel, "As Dying, and Behold We Live," *Interp* 46 (1992): 5–18.

A similar incident took place when the Jews stoned Paul in Lystra and left him for dead, but God rescued him so that he returned to the city (Acts 14:19–20; II Cor. 11:25; II Tim. 3:11).

when, in obedience to God's command, he was ready to sacrifice Isaac. Leaving his servants behind, he told them that he and his son would worship God and return to them (Gen. 22:5). The writer of Hebrews says, "Abraham reasoned that God could raise the dead, and figuratively speaking, he did receive Isaac back from death" (11:19).[30]

10. He delivered us from such mortal danger and will rescue us. In him we put our hope. He will rescue us again.

We are not told what this mortal danger is, but Paul's references to being burdened, to despairing of his life, and to a sentence of death in verses 8 and 9 provide clues. The apostle had in mind imprisonment, physical suffering, and injurious punishment that could result in death. Paul is not interested in providing details, because these details are known to the Corinthians. He presents the fact of being delivered from mortal danger. If his detractors in Corinth doubt Paul's zeal for the gospel and his love for the church, they should consider his suffering on behalf of Christ. Paul risked his life not for personal gain or glory, but in serving his Lord in advancing the cause of the kingdom.

Paul put his trust in God who rescued him from "so great a peril of death."[31] He thought that his earthly life had ended, but God restored him by delivering him from a crisis that he identifies as "so great." The confidence Paul displays is evident from the future tense of the verb *rescue*. His trust in God is so great that he knows God will deliver him again from seemingly fatal predicaments. He knows that attacks by the Jews will certainly recur in the future. For this reason Paul repeats himself by saying, "In [God] we put our hope. He will rescue us again."

This is the second time that Paul uses the word *hope*. The first time (v. 7) he wrote the word as a noun, but now it is a verb that in the Greek is in the perfect tense: "we have hoped and continue to hope." Similarly, in verse 9 he writes a verbal construction in the perfect tense for the word *trust* ("we have not trusted in ourselves"). Hope is not less than trust but is related to and supportive of trust. And last, Paul's hope is so firm that he believes God will rescue him again and again.

11. As also you help us through your prayers for us. Then from many people thanks may be expressed on our behalf for the blessing granted us through the prayers of many people.

This text presents a number of difficulties that are apparent from the intricate word order. First, should the first clause of verse 11 serve as the conclusion to verse 10? The context seems to favor such a linkage. Next, the verse repeats the phrase *from/of many people*. Some translators change the second occurrence to "in answer to many prayers" (RSV), "because of their many prayers" (NCV), or "through many" (NKJV). Third, is Paul accommodating himself to the Jewish cus-

---

30. Colin J. Hemer, "A Note on II Corinthians 1:9," *TynB* 23 (1972): 103–7. See also Adolf Deissmann, *Bible Studies*, trans. Alexander Grieve (1923; reprint ed., Winona Lake, Ind.: Alpha, 1979), p. 257.
31. Bauer, p. 814.

tom of avoiding the use of the divine name? His wording implies that God has granted a blessing to those who are praying (NCV, NJB, REB, SEB).

a. "As also you help us through your prayers for us." Paul commends the readers for being prayer warriors on his behalf (compare Rom. 15:30; Phil. 1:19). He alludes to the bond of fellowship they have by praying for one another. The act of helping is a continuous one and points to two parties cooperating in a certain cause, which in this case is praying. The Corinthians are asking God to rescue Paul from mortal danger and to do so continually. The Greek gives the word *prayer* in the singular, but English usage demands the plural.

b. "Then from many people thanks may be expressed on our behalf." Those people who prayed for Paul's deliverance could now with Paul thank God (4:15; 9:11–12). The Greek has a word that literally means "faces" but is translated "persons." We are not amiss, however, to see that the Greek term portrays faces lifted upward to God in prayer.

c. "For the blessing granted us through the prayers of many people." The blessing that God granted refers to Paul's rescue from lethal danger. The Greek gives the term *charisma*, which in the Corinthian correspondence usually signifies a spiritual gift. But here Paul has in mind the gift of restoring his life by rescuing him from the clutches of death. Finally, the Greek text is remarkably brief by saying "through many." This phrase can mean either "many people" or "many prayers." Of the two translations, the first one is favored because Paul wants to emphasize the involvement of his readers.

Practical Considerations in 1:8–11

From early childhood to old age we pursue, guard, and treasure our independence. We even enhance independence by linking it to personal dignity, especially with respect to the elderly in our society. We consider as praiseworthy people who are able to care for themselves.

The New Testament, however, teaches us that spiritually we are part of Christ's body, in which the individual members care for one another (I Cor. 12:25). We are dependent on each other. In addition, God wants us to depend on him by fully trusting that he will meet all our spiritual and material needs "according to his glorious riches in Christ Jesus" (Phil. 4:19). Thus, his servants must trust him without fail and, if need be, must be willing to die for him.

Two examples. First, before his scheduled execution, Peter spent the night in prison between two guards and was bound with two chains. While fellow Christians held a prayer vigil for him, he had complete trust in his Lord and slept soundly. Indeed, the angel who came to rescue him had to strike Peter on his side to wake him (Acts 12:6–7). Second, God taught Paul the lesson of trusting completely in him. When Paul faced death and saw no escape, he had no one to rely on but God. His desire for human independence was stripped away when, at death's door, he looked up into the face of the Lord.

One is truly a spiritual giant when one relies totally on God. This is a consequence of true faith, intimate communion with the Lord, and continuous prayer offered to God by oneself and fellow believers.

Jesus, Jesus, how I trust Him!
How I've proved Him o'er and o'er!
Jesus, Jesus, precious Jesus!
O for grace to trust Him more!
—Louisa M. R. Stead

Greek Words, Phrases, and Constructions in 1:8–11

Verse 8

ὑπὲρ τῆς θλίψεως—the preposition in context is equivalent to περί and signifies "concerning" or "about."[32]
ὥστε—the particle with the infinitive expresses actual result.

Verses 9–10

αὐτοὶ ἐν ἑαυτοῖς . . . ἐσχήκαμεν—in this verse notice Paul's emphasis on the pronoun *we*.[33] The verb is in the perfect tense to indicate the clear memory of the incident.

μὴ πεποιθότες ὦμεν—the periphrastic construction with the perfect participle from the verb πείθω (I convince; as a second person perfect, I trust) has a present connotation: "we should not trust."

τηλικούτου θανάτου—in the New Testament the adjective always refers to size.[34] Some manuscripts have the noun θάνατος (death) in the plural, which may be the original reading. It is possible that "the plural may have originated from a desire to heighten the intensity of the account."[35]

The Majority Text has the present tense ῥύεται (he rescues; see KJV, NKJV) instead of the future tense ῥύσεται. The present tense is the easier reading, for it provides a sequence of past, present, and future of the same verb. In view of its repetition in the next clause, the harder reading is the future tense and therefore, with the support of the better manuscripts, it is preferred. The conjunction ὅτι is omitted in a number of influential witnesses.

Verse 11

συνυπουργούντων καὶ ὑμῶν—the compound present active participle with the personal pronoun indicates the genitive absolute construction. The participle denotes not condition but attendant circumstance ("as you help"); it commends the Corinthians for their prayer support.

ἐκ πολλῶν προσώπων—"from many faces." This is a Greek idiom that is translated "from many people."

εὐχαριστηθῇ—the passive construction does not require an accusative of the thing and a dative of the person, which is the case for the active.

---

32. C. F. D. Moule, *An Idiom-Book of New Testament Greek*, 2d ed. (Cambridge: Cambridge University Press, 1960), p. 65.

33. Blass and Debrunner, *Greek Grammar*, #283.4.

34. A. T. Robertson, *A Grammar of the Greek New Testament in the Light of Historical Research* (Nashville: Broadman, 1934), p. 710.

35. Metzger, *Textual Commentary*, p. 506; G. Zuntz, *The Text of the Epistles: A Disquisition upon the Corpus Paulinum* (London: Oxford University Press, 1953), p. 104.

διὰ πολλῶν—this phrase should be taken with the preceding noun χάρισμα (blessing) and not with the succeeding verb εὐχαριστηθῇ. The adjective ("many") can be either masculine ("people") or neuter ("prayers").

---

12 For this is our boasting: it is the testimony of our conscience that with simplicity and sincerity to God, and not with worldly wisdom but with the grace of God, we have conducted ourselves in this world and especially toward you. 13 For we write you no other things than what you [can] read and understand. And I hope that you will fully understand 14—just as you have indeed understood us in part—that we are your boast inasmuch as you are our boast in the day of our Lord Jesus.

15 And because of this confidence, I was planning to come to you first, so that you might receive a double blessing. 16 I wanted to visit you on the way to Macedonia and on the way back from Macedonia to visit you again. And I wanted to be sent forth by you to Judea. 17 When I wanted to do this, did I do it lightly? Or, whatever my plans are, do I make them as the world does, so that I say first "Yes yes" and then "No no"? 18 But as surely as God is faithful, our word to you is not both Yes and No. 19 For the Son of God, Jesus Christ, who is preached among you through us—by me, Silvanus, and Timothy—was not both Yes and No, but in him it continues to be Yes. 20 For as many promises of God as there are, in him they are Yes. Wherefore also through him we say Amen to God for his glory. 21 Now it is God who confirms us with you in Christ and has anointed us. 22 He also has sealed us and given us the first installment of the Spirit in our hearts.

II. Apostolic Ministry
1:12–7:16

A. Paul's Travel Plans
1:12–2:11

Having concluded the segment about thanksgiving to God (vv. 3–11), Paul now enters into the body of his epistle. He continues the thought of the preceding verse (v. 11): the support he has received from the Corinthians. For him this support is a source of boasting. Should anyone speak negatively about Paul, the Corinthians know that he conducted himself honorably among them and in the world. He commends the readers that they are able to boast of him just as he is of them. They themselves can testify to Paul's integrity.

1. Trustworthiness
1:12–14

12. For this is our boasting: it is the testimony of our conscience that with simplicity and sincerity to God, and not with worldly wisdom but with the grace of God, we have conducted ourselves in this world and especially toward you.

a. "For this is our boasting." Throughout his epistles, but especially in his Corinthian correspondence, Paul writes the verb *to boast* and the noun *boasting* numerous times.[36] He wants the Corinthians to know that he continues to regard them as an object of boasting, and he tells them that their boasting should

---

36. In the New Testament, the verb occurs thirty-eight times, twice outside of Paul's epistles (James 1:9; 4:16), and twenty-nine times in the two Corinthian epistles.

be in the Lord (I Cor. 1:31; II Cor. 10:17; see Jer. 9:24). Boasting in the form of human arrogance is sin, for the triune God must receive all glory and honor. Human pride must be banished and God glorified. Christians, therefore, should never extol themselves but only glory in the Lord Jesus Christ (Rom. 5:11; Gal. 6:14; Phil. 3:3).[37]

What is Paul's boast? He gives God the glory for enabling him to live an exemplary life by his grace. As a recipient of God's grace, Paul expresses thanks for being the object of the Corinthians' boasting (v. 14). He describes his boast:

b. "It is the testimony of our conscience that with simplicity and sincerity to God." Paul introduces the testimony of one's conscience in the setting of a courtroom, so to speak (compare Acts 23:1). For Paul, conscience meant the faculty that gives a person "the sense of moral self-judgment."[38] A person's conscience is either clear or guilty and, thus, can either acquit or condemn. In the case of Paul, the testimony of his own conscience was unimpeachable. His conscience acquitted him in the light of his dedicated life of serving God.

Paul ministered to God's people with "simplicity and sincerity to God." He endured criticism and verbal opposition from a number of people in the Corinthian community. But his goal in life was to do his work in the presence of God with undivided attention and purity of motive. Sixteenth-century Reformer John Calvin echoed Paul's testimony with a motto: "I offer my heart to you, Lord, promptly and sincerely."

Although the Greek word *haplotēti* (simplicity) speaks for itself, a variant gives the reading *hagiotēti* (holiness), which some translators have adopted.[39] It is not easy to decide which of the two choices is better, yet the fact that Paul uses the word *haplotēti* at four additional places in this epistle seems to tip the balance in favor of the reading *simplicity* (8:2; 9:11, 13; 11:3). Also, this word fits the context better than does the term *holiness*. Fully dedicated and utterly sincere (2:17), Paul performs his work as a minister of the gospel for everyone to see. In this setting, he demonstrates his love for God's people in Corinth.

c. "And not with worldly wisdom but with the grace of God." Paul accentuates a contrast between two qualities: the wisdom of the world and the grace of God. The wisdom that Paul has in mind does not originate in God and is therefore rejected by Paul (I Cor. 2:1–5). Paul, however, receives heavenly wisdom. This wisdom comes to him by God's grace, which has enabled him to be a faithful minister of the Word (I Cor. 15:10).

d. "We have conducted ourselves in this world and especially toward you." The conduct of Paul has been impeccable, and everybody is able to observe his ac-

---

37. Consult Maurice Carrez, "La confiance en l'homme et la confiance en soi selon l' apôtre Paul," *RevHistPhilRel* 44 (1964): 191–99.

38. Ridderbos, *Paul*, p. 288.

39. E.g., NAB, NASB, RSV, *Cassirer*, and *Moffatt*. See also Margaret E. Thrall, "II Corinthians 1:2: ΑΓΙΟ-ΤΗΤΙ or ΑΠΛΟΤΗΤΙ?" in *Studies in New Testament Language and Text*, ed. J. K. Elliott, NovTSup 44 (Leiden: Brill, 1976), pp. 366–72.

tions and to hear his words. Like Jesus, who spoke openly to the world and said nothing in secret (John 18:20), Paul has nothing to hide.

The gospel message is for all people of all nationalities. But now, Paul concerns himself with the Corinthians because he is their spiritual father through the gospel (I Cor. 4:15). For eighteen months Paul labored gratis in Corinth. He never asked for material support, so that the cause of the gospel might prosper (I Cor. 9:17–18). No one in Corinth could ever say that Paul had been self-serving. His conduct had been and continued to be above reproach.

13a. For we write you no other things than what you [can] read and understand.

Not only can the Corinthians examine Paul's conduct, but also they can scrutinize his epistles—those addressed to them and those sent to other churches. His letters have taken on permanency, for they are read as part of the liturgy in worship services (see Eph. 3:4; Col. 4:16; I Thess. 5:27; also Rev. 1:3). Indeed the Corinthians are able to examine closely what he has said, and they will conclude that Paul has been perfectly honest in everything he has written.

When the wording of a written communication is not clear, the message is likely to be misunderstood. That danger apparently became real when Paul had addressed a letter, no longer extant, to the Corinthians (I Cor. 5:9) that they had misinterpreted and laid aside. Now Paul calls attention to the message he conveys and asserts that the recipients are able to comprehend what he has to say. They will have to conclude that Paul's intentions are clear. The implication is that some of his critics would like to find fault. But when they examine Paul's letters, they will be unable to find substantiating evidence to denounce him.

13b. And I hope that you will fully understand 14.—just as you have indeed understood us in part—that we are your boast inasmuch as you are our boast in the day of our Lord Jesus.

The last line in verse 13 is introductory to the following verse (v. 14). Paul hopes that when the Corinthians read the correspondence, they will heartily commend his integrity. When Paul was with them as their missionary-pastor, they understood his teachings. But when they were induced by others to cast aspersions on Paul, they were confused. Now Paul hopes that by looking at the available evidence, they "will come to their senses again."[40]

Paul's tone is free of reproach; he merely states the fact that the Corinthians have not fully understood him (see I Cor. 3:2). Their partial understanding needs to be enhanced and brought to full comprehension. He intimates that their partial knowledge must become complete in understanding his epistles. In other words, Paul encourages them to understand him fully and as quickly as possible.

The Greek sentence in verses 13b–14 is complex and cumbersome. Translators smooth the awkwardness of its style by changing the word order from the Greek to the English. Others follow the original order but consider the clause

---

40. John Calvin, *The Second Epistle of Paul the Apostle to the Corinthians and the Epistles to Timothy, Titus and Philemon*, Calvin's Commentaries series, trans. T. A. Small (Grand Rapids: Eerdmans, 1964), p. 17.

"just as you have indeed understood us in part" to be a parenthetical comment. Difficulties remain, but a modern paraphrase clearly captures the intent of these verses: "We're . . . hoping that you'll now see the whole picture as well as you've seen some of the details. We want you to be as proud of us as we are of you when we stand together before our Master Jesus."[41]

The Corinthians should thankfully acknowledge Paul and his fellow workers as persons who, because of their spiritual labors, are worthy of praise (see 5:12; 8:24; Phil. 2:16; I Tim. 5:17). Conversely, Paul and his associates boast about the church at Corinth as they do about the churches in Philippi and Thessalonica (Phil. 2:16; I Thess. 2:19–20). Christians can never boast in themselves but only in others through Jesus Christ. Paul wants the Corinthians to boast in him and he to boast in them. This is evident when Paul tells the Corinthians, "I have great confidence in you; I take great pride in you" (7:4). The basis for Paul's boasting is Jesus Christ.

What does the phrase "in the day of our Lord Jesus" convey? If Paul had written the future tense of the verb *to be* and had said, "We will be your boast . . . in the day of our Lord Jesus," the sentence would flow as we might expect. Instead he writes the present tense of this verb ("we are your boast") and places it in the context of the day of the Lord Jesus. The reference is to the judgment day at the end of time (I Cor. 1:8), but the verb tense indicates that Paul "regards himself as already involved in the eschatological event."[42] The concept *day of the Lord* should not be limited to the last day; in a sense that day is almost here, and Christians are exhorted to walk in the light of that day (see Rom. 13:12–13). For believers, that day comes at the moment of their death when Jesus welcomes them as they enter his presence.

Greek Words, Phrases, and Constructions in 1:12–14

Verse 12

καύχησις and καύχημα (v. 14) are identical in meaning and refer to the act of boasting. ἁπλότητι—"simplicity." The variant ἁγιότητι (holiness) occurs only once more in the New Testament (Heb. 12:10). It is not a word that Paul includes in his vocabulary.

Verses 13–14

γράφομεν—"we write." The present tense denotes continued action whereby the Corinthians can repeatedly return to Paul's letters to check the message he conveys in them.

---

41. Eugene H. Peterson, *The Message: The New Testament in Contemporary English* (Colorado Springs, Colo.: NavPress, 1993), p. 370.

42. Georg Braumann, *NIDNTT*, 2:894; consult F. W. Grosheide, *De Tweede Brief van den Apostel Paulus aan de Kerk te Korinthe*, Kommentaar op het Nieuwe Testament series (Amsterdam: Van Bottenburg, 1939), p. 59; Philip Edgcumbe Hughes, *Paul's Second Epistle to the Corinthians: The English Text with Introduction, Exposition and Notes*, New International Commentary on the New Testament series (Grand Rapids: Eerdmans, 1962), p. 30.

Notice the play on words with the compound verbs ἀναγινώσκετε (you read; that is, you know again) and ἐπιγινώσκετε (you understand). The present tenses are durative.

ἕως τέλους—some translators render this phrase as "to the end" and give it an eschatological meaning (I Cor. 13:12).[43] They imply that Paul expected the consummation to occur soon. Others, however, offer the translation "fully" (see NEB, NJB, REB), which refers to the readers' immediate future. Of the two, the latter is preferred.

τοῦ κυρίου ἡμῶν Ἰησοῦ—the Majority Text omits the possessive pronoun. The omission of the pronoun calls for an explanation, just as its insertion does. We prefer its inclusion on the basis of Pauline usage of the phrase *our Lord Jesus*, which is common in Paul's epistles.

---

2. Revised Plans
1:15–17

15. And because of this confidence, I was planning to come to you first, so that you might receive a double blessing. 16. I wanted to visit you on the way to Macedonia and on the way back from Macedonia to visit you again. And I wanted to be sent forth by you to Judea.

a. "And because of this confidence." In the preceding section (vv. 12–14), Paul spoke confidently of personal conduct, of the Corinthians' respect for Paul and Paul's respect for them. The Greek word *pepoithēsis* (confidence) in this verse is a summary of his earlier description of boasting. Paul seems to have a penchant for choosing the term in this epistle (see 3:4; 8:22; 10:2). It occurs nowhere else in the New Testament, except in Ephesians 3:12 and Philippians 3:4, and expresses a basic trust in God, people, or self.

b. "I was planning to come to you first, so that you might receive a double blessing." Notice that Paul writes the first person singular instead of the plural; he frequently switches from the pronoun *we* to the singular *I* and back to the plural in the first two chapters of this letter. He uses the pronoun *I* here because the Corinthians doubted the integrity of his words. Earlier Paul had written that after Pentecost he would travel from Ephesus through Macedonia to Corinth. He said that he would then stay with the Corinthians for some time and even spend the winter months (I Cor. 16:5–8), when travel by sea was impossible. But now he writes that a visit to the Corinthians was first on his itinerary.

Some translators connect the term *first* with the verb *plan*: "I made plans at first" (GNB).[44] But the context relates that Paul planned to come to Corinth first and after his visit to Macedonia to arrive there again (v. 16). The better explanation, then, is to join the adverb *first* to the verb *to come*.

Another problem in this verse is the Greek expression *charin*, which translators variously render as "benefit," "goodwill," or "blessing." But some scholars object to the use of this expression because they see it as a form of self-glorifica-

---

43. Bauer, p. 812.
44. See also Peterson, *Message*, "I had originally planned," and *Cassirer*, "My original intention."

tion by Paul. They adopt a Greek variant, *charan* (joy), which may be either a scribal error or a deliberate change; by using this variant, ancient scribes wished to remove any misunderstanding of the text.

The word *charin* may also mean "gift" or "grace of giving" in the sense of the collection destined for the saints in Jerusalem (I Cor. 16:3; II Cor. 8:4, 6, 7, 19). It is this grace of giving that the Corinthians experience when they contribute to the collection for the poor in Jerusalem.[45]

What is the meaning of the expression *double blessing?* It is the act of helping Paul twice. Paul wants the Corinthians to send him first on his way to Macedonia and upon his return to send him and his companions to Jerusalem with the monetary collection.

c. "I wanted to visit you on the way to Macedonia and on the way back from Macedonia to visit you again." Paul's initial plans had been to visit the Macedonian churches. Afterward he would travel to Corinth and spend time there (I Cor. 16:5–6). Probably because of a crisis in the Corinthian congregation, Paul changed his mind and decided to pay a brief visit to Corinth, go on to Macedonia, and then return to Corinth. However, when he arrived in that city, the visit became painful (2:1), and we have no certainty that he visited the Macedonian churches. He went back to Ephesus, where he wrote the so-called grievous letter (2:3–4) that Titus delivered to the Corinthians. Paul eventually met Titus in Macedonia, and Titus conveyed the desire of the Corinthians to see him. Paul was filled with joy (7:6–7). He decided to stay with his original plan (I Cor. 16:5–7) and travel via Macedonia to Corinth, where he would spend the winter. Traveling through Macedonia, he would ask church representatives to accompany him with the collection from these churches (8:1–7).[46] These representatives would travel with him to Corinth, add the collection of the Corinthians, and sail from there to Judea to deliver the money to the poor in Jerusalem.

d. "And I wanted to be sent forth by you to Judea." The phrase *to be sent forth by you* does not mean merely that the Corinthians said good-by to Paul. In the early church, it was a phrase that obligated Christians to supply a missionary with money, food, beverage, clothing, and protection provided by traveling companions.[47] Paul wanted the Corinthians to show their generosity by sending him on his way to Jerusalem with both the collection for the saints and the necessary supplies for the journey. When Paul eventually left Corinth and traveled via Macedonia to Jerusalem, he had no one from Corinth as his companion (Acts 20:4). Perhaps Luke and Titus were stewards whom the church in Corinth had chosen to deliver the monetary gifts to the Jerusalem saints (8:16–19).

17. When I wanted to do this, did I do it lightly? Or, whatever my plans are, do I make them as the world does, so that I say first "Yes yes" and then "No no"?

---

45. Gordon D. Fee, "ΧΑΡΙΣ in II Corinthians I.15: Apostolic Parousia and Paul-Corinth Chronology," *NTS* 24 (1977–78): 533–38.
46. Compare ibid., pp. 537–38.
47. See Acts 15:3; Rom. 15:24; I Cor. 16:6, 11; Titus 3:13; III John 6; Polycarp *Phil.* 1.1.

The Greek text shows a variant for the verb *wanted* in the form of "planned"; a number of translators have adopted this variant.[48] But the first reading is preferred; it forms a flowing transition from verse 16 to verse 17 and expresses Paul's original intention to visit Corinth. The phrase *I wanted to do this* conveys the thought that both Paul and the Corinthians were aware of his intentions.

Paul had heard that the Corinthians were accusing him of instability. What is his response to this complaint? He answers by asking a question: "Did I do it lightly?" He asks his readers a question that they can answer only in the negative. In the Greek, Paul indicates that he does not ask this question glibly. He implies that not everything in life is in our own hands, for sometimes God uses circumstances that necessitate a change of plans.

To make his point Paul asks a second question that also expects a negative reply: "Or, whatever my plans are, do I make them as the world does?" The Greek has the expression *kata sarka* (according to the flesh; I have rendered it "as the world"), which occurs often in this epistle (5:16; 10:2–3; 11:18). Paul does not live according to the flesh but according to the Spirit (Rom. 8:4).[49] No one can accuse Paul of making plans from a worldly perspective, for the apostle has always demonstrated his total dedication to the Lord. The Corinthians should have known that the responsibility for a change in Paul's plans rested not with him but with God.[50]

The last part of verse 17 parallels a saying of Jesus that is recorded in two different places: "Let your 'Yes' be 'Yes' and your 'No,' 'No'" (Matt. 5:37; James 5:12b). This utterance of Jesus was so well known in the early church that only a few words quoted from it were sufficient to recall the entire saying.[51] We assume that Paul had taught the Corinthians this particular saying of Jesus. They knew that Jesus taught them honesty in speech, but now the Corinthians denounced Paul and accused him of untrustworthiness.

Why is there a doubling of the words *yes* and *no*? A Greek variant has a shorter reading that eliminates the duplication. But this may be a misunderstanding of the Aramaic wording spoken by Jesus. Semitic languages often repeat a word for emphasis, as is evident in the repetition of a name: "Moses, Moses" (Exod. 3:4); "Samuel, Samuel" (I Sam. 3:10). Indeed, this Semitic characteristic is carried over into the New Testament in the repetition "Lord, Lord" (Matt. 7:22). Conclusively, the saying of Jesus, "Yes, yes and No, no," means "Again and again yes and again and again no."[52]

---

48. GNB, JB, KJV, NKJV, NAB, NCV, SEB.

49. Horst Seebass, *NIDNTT*, 1:675.

50. Frances Young, "Note on II Corinthians 1:17b," *JTS* n.s. 37 (1986): 404–15, who translates the text as follows: "Or do I make plans at the human level so that yes being yes and no being no rests in my hands?"

51. David Wenham, "II Corinthians 1:17, 18: Echo of a Dominical Logion," *NovT* 28 (1986): 271–79.

52. W. C. van Unnik, "Reisepläne und Amen-Sagen, Zusammenhang und Gedankenfolge in 2. Korinther i 15–24," in *Sparsa Collecta: The Collected Essays of W. C. van Unnik*, part 1, NovTSup 29 (Leiden: Brill, 1973), pp. 144–59, especially p. 147. Consult also Fritz Reinecker, *Sprachlicher Schlüssel zum Griechischen Neuen Testament* (Giessen: Brunn-Verlag, 1970), p. 398.

Greek Words, Phrases, and Constructions in 1:16–17

Note the many prepositions in verse 16: διά, εἰς, ἀπο, πρός, ὑπο, εἰς; also πρό in the compound verb *to send forth.*

βουλόμενος—"wanting." The Majority Text has the reading βουλευόμενος (planning), but earlier and better manuscripts support the first reading.

μήτι ἄρα—the first particle demands a negative answer to the rhetorical question; the second infers a conclusion from the preceding context and signifies "then."

τῇ ἐλαφρίᾳ—the noun refers to fickleness and the definite article points to the Corinthian reproach placed on Paul.

ἵνα—this clause expresses the "concerned result of an action" rather than purpose.[53]

---

3. Authenticity
1:18–22

18. But as surely as God is faithful, our word to you is not both Yes and No.
The Greek text translates as "But God is faithful," which can be either a confessional statement or an oath formula. In view of the second part of this verse, which in the Greek begins with the conjunction *hoti* (that), scholars are of the opinion that Paul probably is writing an oath formula by calling God as his witness.[54] This apparently is Paul's intent, even though he uses the phrase *God is faithful* at other places where it is not an oath (I Cor. 1:9; 10:13; compare I Thess. 5:24; II Thess. 3:3).

With the expression *word,* Paul explains the first clause. With the phrase *our word to you,* he refers to the preaching of God's Word by Paul and his colleagues (Silvanus and Timothy [v. 19]). God's Word is absolutely trustworthy because God is faithful and true. When the apostles and their associates proclaim that Word, they present the truth. "Ministers of the Word should have the same assurance of conscience when they enter the pulpit to speak in Christ's name, knowing that their doctrine can no more be overthrown than God Himself."[55]

Paul first mentions God who is faithful, and then the gospel he and his associates preach; notice the plural form *our word.* He uses the Jewish hermeneutical principle of going from the greater to the lesser. Thus, he intimates that as the Corinthians put their trust in God and the preaching of his Word, so they ought to put their trust in Paul even when his travel schedule changes.[56]

The Corinthians should know that Paul is honest and true to his word. Therefore, as he is dependable in preaching the gospel, so he is trustworthy in making known his travel plans. They should not accuse him of saying yes and no at the

---

53. Blass and Debrunner, *Greek Grammar,* #391.5.

54. Gerhard Barth, *EDNT,* 3:98; Rudolf Bultmann, *The Second Letter to the Corinthians,* trans. Roy A. Harrisville (Minneapolis: Augsburg, 1985), p. 39.

55. Calvin, *II Corinthians,* p. 20.

56. Consult van Unnik, "Reisepläne," p. 156.

same time. Paul has more to say about changing his plans to visit the Corinthians (v. 23), but first he bases the veracity of his word on Jesus Christ.

19. For the Son of God, Jesus Christ,[57] who is preached among you through us—by me, Silvanus, and Timothy—was not both Yes and No, but in him it continues to be Yes.

a. "For the Son of God, Jesus Christ." The conjunction *for* is the bridge between this verse and the preceding passage; it introduces an explanation of verse 18. The word order in the first part of this verse is unique because it stresses the concept *Son of God,* and in that concept the emphasis is on God. Paul states that God is faithful and now suggests that God's Son, too, is faithful, as is evident from God's revelation. The combination *Son of God, Jesus Christ* appears only here in Paul's epistles (compare Gal. 2:20; Eph. 4:13). In the Greek, Paul stresses the divinity of Jesus Christ by saying literally, "of God [is] the Son." The normal word order would be "the Son of God is Jesus Christ."

b. "Jesus Christ, who is preached among you through us—by me, Silvanus, and Timothy." The theme of preaching, says Paul, is Jesus Christ. As true ambassadors, he and his associates represent Jesus, who himself testified that he is truth (John 14:6). This Son of God certainly would not vacillate and say yes and no at the same time. Correspondingly, Paul and his co-workers would not preach Christ's gospel to the Corinthians and then alternate from affirmation to denial.

Both the place and the choice of pronouns in this part of the sentence are deliberate for the sake of emphasis. The phrase *among you* unites Jesus Christ with the Corinthians, who is their model of truth. The next phrase, "through us," depicts both Paul and his co-workers as channels through whom the truth reaches the Corinthians. They receive truth through the preaching of the gospel. Note both the number and the sequence of the three names, Paul, Silvanus, and Timothy. Both the Old and New Testaments teach that the testimony of three witnesses is needed to establish truth.[58] In this verse the veracity of the apostolic preaching is affirmed by Paul, Silvanus, and Timothy. The sequence of names is significant. Paul was first in proclaiming the gospel to the Corinthians (Acts 18:1–4). When he had been in Corinth for some time, Silvanus (Silas) and Timothy arrived from Macedonia (Acts 18:5). Silvanus accompanied Paul on his second missionary journey, and Timothy followed them later in Lystra (see Acts 15:40 and 16:1–3 respectively). These two men were faithful servants of Christ and with Paul preached the gospel in Corinth.

c. "[Jesus Christ] was not both Yes and No, but in him it continues to be Yes." Paul ends this verse by stressing that Jesus Christ, the personification of God's truth (Rom. 15:8), never breaks his word, and, therefore, is unchangeable. Jesus Christ was, is, and remains true to his word. The writer of the Epistle to the He-

---

57. Some editions of the New Testament Greek (Nestle[25], BF[2]) and translations (NEB, REB) have the reverse order, "Christ Jesus."
58. See Num. 35:30; Deut. 17:6; 19:15; Matt. 18:16; II Cor. 13:1; I Tim. 5:19; Heb. 10:28.

brews puts it succinctly: "Jesus Christ is the same yesterday and today and forever" (13:8).

20. For as many promises of God as there are, in him they are Yes. Wherefore also through him we say Amen to God for his glory.

a. "For as many promises of God as there are." Paul reflects on the numerous promises God has given his people. He knows that ultimately all of them have been and are being fulfilled in the Son of God. Replete with God's promises, the Old Testament points to their fulfillment in Christ. Peter mentions that the prophets were "trying to find out the time and circumstances to which the Spirit of Christ in them was pointing when he predicted the sufferings of Christ and the glories that would follow" (I Peter 1:11). The Old Testament message is that God who makes promises ultimately fulfills them through the coming of the Messiah.[59]

b. "In him they are Yes." The entire New Testament is a testimony that God's promises have been and are being fulfilled in Jesus Christ. Jesus came to fulfill the Law and the Prophets (Matt. 5:17–18), to remove the curse of the law (Gal. 3:13), to grant the gift of righteousness (Matt. 6:33), to give eternal life (John 17:3), and through the Father to send the Holy Spirit (John 14:16, 26; 15:26). In Jesus Christ God's promises have been realized, and the Corinthians will have to acknowledge the truth of this matter.

c. "Wherefore also through him we say Amen to God for his glory." The Greek construction of this part of verse 20 is cumbersome if we provide a literal translation and follow the sequence of the verse: "Wherefore also through him the Amen to God for glory through us." But the word *Amen* is uttered "through us," and this affirmation serves to glorify God. When we understand that the phrase *through us* carries the meaning of the verb *we say*, the subsequent translation is smooth. This is how, in the first few centuries, some Christians whose native tongue was Syriac, a sister dialect of Aramaic, understood the text. Writing "yes" and "Amen" in this passage, Paul is expressing a parallelism that was current in his day. Among speakers who were conversant in both Greek and Aramaic, the "yes" and the "Amen" meant the same thing.[60]

When Paul, his associates, and the Corinthians say "yes and amen" through Jesus Christ to God, no one legitimately can accuse Paul of vacillating. Those who attest to the veracity of God's Word respect one another's personal integrity. As Paul indicates, when believers say "Amen" to the promises of God in Christ, they glorify God.

21. Now it is God who confirms us with you in Christ and has anointed us. 22. He also has sealed us and given us the first installment of the Spirit in our hearts.

---

59. Refer to Ernst Hoffmann, *NIDNTT*, 3:72; Alexander Sand, *EDNT*, 2:14.

60. "'Yes' answers not a promise, but a proposed obligation," according to J. D. M. Derrett, "ναί (II Cor. 1:19–20)," *FilolNT* 4 (1991): 206. But van Unnik shows that a few Greek New Testament passages use "yes" and "Amen" as synonyms (e.g., Matt. 23:36 and Luke 11:51; Rev. 1:7; 22:20). See his "Reisepläne," pp. 150–51. The use of these synonyms should be seen not from the perspective of the audience but of the author.

First, we make a few preliminary observations:

1. With these two verses Paul concludes his remarks on justifying his trust-worthiness.
2. The apostle teaches the doctrine of the Trinity by noting that God confirms believers, anoints them in Christ, and seals them with the Spirit.
3. The wording in these verses—confirm, seal, down payment—has been borrowed from the legal sphere and has commercial implications.
4. A degree of parallelism is evident in these two verses; each has two verbs with direct objects: confirm us and anoint us (v. 21), seal us and give us (v. 22).

Next, let us look closely at the wording of the passage verse by verse.

a. "Now it is God who confirms us with you in Christ and has anointed us." God is the One who performs the act of confirming Paul and the Corinthians— an act that occurs in the present time (compare I Cor. 1:8). He creates, strengthens, and sustains the fellowship that believers have in Christ Jesus. The basis for this fellowship is God's promises given to his people through his Word. God's Word is indisputably valid and, to make it unchangeable, God even swore an oath (see Heb. 6:17–18). The Corinthians, with Paul and his co-workers, can trust the Scriptures. It is God himself who confirms their relationship to Jesus as his true disciples through the preaching of his Word.[61] God has made a contractual agreement with his people. He guarantees the covenant he has made with them in Christ, who is the mediator between God and the people. The promises of God, therefore, are in the form of a legally certified security in Christ.[62]

God is the One who anoints his people. The Greek shows an unmistakable word play (*Christos* and *chrisas*) that we can capture by saying, the anointed One and anointed ones. But what is the significance of the term *anoint*? In Old Testament times prophets, priests, and kings were anointed with oil that symbolized the gift of the Holy Spirit. They were appointed to assume an office and to fulfill a task in the service of God. Similarly, God anointed Jesus with the Holy Spirit and power (Isa. 61:1 and Luke 4:18; Acts 4:27; 10:38; Ps. 45:7 and Heb. 1:9). At Jesus' baptism, he received the Holy Spirit. Does this mean that believers at baptism likewise receive the Spirit, so that the act of anointing is equivalent to baptism? Perhaps, but the reference to anointing is broader. God anoints his people with the Holy Spirit (I John 2:20, 27). This occurs at the time of regeneration (John 3:5), at special occasions (Acts 4:31), and when believers receive spiritual gifts (I Cor. 12:7–11).

b. "He also has sealed us and given us the first installment of the Spirit in our hearts." Scholars present two divergent interpretations of verses 21 and 22.

---

61. Refer to Bauer, p. 138; Hans Schönweiss, *NIDNTT*, 1:660; Heinrich Schlier, *TDNT*, 1:603; Albert Fuchs, *EDNT*, 1:210–11.
62. Consult Deissmann, *Bible Studies*, pp. 104–9.

Some scholars see these two verses as parallels, so that the second (v. 22) explains the first (v. 21). Others take the four Greek participles (confirm, anointed, sealed, given) and declare that the last three participles explain the first one. They advance the view that Paul refers to baptism. I favor the first interpretation for the following reasons: First, these two verses depict parallelism, whereby the two participles of verse 22 strengthen the two in verse 21. Next, in the Greek text the word *Theos* (God) stands last in verse 21 and marks the end of a clause. And last, although all four Greek participles display elements that characterize baptism, Pauline usage of these words elsewhere in his epistles does not support an interpretation that implies baptism. The members of the Corinthian congregation no doubt had received the sign of baptism. But this passage (vv. 21–22) appears to reveal the entire process of a person who comes into a living relationship with the Lord: conversion, faith, baptism, and the presence of the Holy Spirit in the believer's life.[63]

"[God] also has sealed us." Seals denote ownership and authenticity. Not only in ancient times, but also today, seals are placed on legal documents to authenticate them. Moreover, logos stamped or printed on articles are marks of ownership. By analogy, God attaches a seal to his people for two reasons: to confirm that they belong to him and to shield them from harm.

"[God] has given us the first installment of the Spirit in our hearts." Verse 22 is echoed in another epistle, where Paul writes: "Having believed, you were marked in [Christ] with a seal, the promised Holy Spirit, who is a deposit guaranteeing our inheritance until the redemption of those who are God's possession—to the praise of his glory" (Eph. 1:13–14). God has given us the Holy Spirit as a deposit, a first installment. We have the assurance that after the initial deposit a subsequent installment follows. Paul uses the expression *heart* as a figurative abbreviation for the entire person. He implies that the Holy Spirit lives within us and continues to supply us with spiritual strength and vigor.

Practical Considerations in 1:18–22

Ever since Eve was seduced by the serpent in the garden of Eden, those who oppose God distort, reject, abhor, or ignore God's spoken or written Word. Yet his Word is clear, direct, earnest, and honest. God wishes to communicate with humanity by constantly addressing both believers and unbelievers.

Those who love God know that his Word is trustworthy and completely reliable. He fulfills his promises and is true to what he has said. With warnings and threats, he addresses those who willfully turn away from him. Indeed, he carries out those threats in case people do not repent. But when they return to him, he annuls the threats as if he had never uttered them.

To make his Word absolutely sure, God swore an oath that can never be revoked. When people swear an oath in court and tell a lie, they are called perjurers. When they

---

63. Barrett, *Second Corinthians*, p. 81.

maliciously attack and subvert the truth of a sworn testimony, they are equally guilty of perjury. Thus people who purposely undermine God's Word falsify the truth and imply that God is a liar. John writes that the Word of God has no place in their lives (I John 1:10). Indeed, they blaspheme God and his Word.

Believers, however, know that Jesus Christ has come as God's messenger and the manifestation of truth. When Christ's gospel is preached, his people express either verbally or silently their affirmation. They do so as Christians who bear Christ's name, belong to him because of his seal on their foreheads, and are filled with the Holy Spirit.

Greek Words, Phrases, and Constructions in 1:19–22

Verse 19

ὁ τοῦ θεοῦ—in this clause, notice the word order by which Paul places unique emphasis on the Son Jesus Christ, who belongs to God.

ὁ ἐν ὑμῖν δι' ἡμῶν κηρυχθείς—this sequence is deliberate to achieve emphasis: the definite article at the end of the clause and the aorist passive participle at the beginning. The two juxtaposed phrases of pronouns are designed to exhibit the unity of Christ, the Corinthians, and Paul with his co-workers.

Verse 20

The variant reading of the Majority Text seeks to achieve a smoother reading of the text: καὶ ἐν αὐτῷ (and in him). The more difficult reading, however, seems to be closer to the original.

ἀμήν—this word is transliterated Hebrew; it was known in Corinth through the liturgy of the local Jewish synagogue and the Christian church.

Verse 22

ἀρραβῶνα—a Semitic loanword that was used as a legal and commercial term for a down payment.

ἐν—there is an overlapping of the preposition ἐν with εἰς (into our hearts).[64]

Summary of Chapter 1

After writing his familiar identification, greeting, and blessing, the apostle thanks God for all the comfort extended to him. During severe persecution, he suffered for the sake of Christ and became an example to others. He tells the readers that as they share Paul's sufferings so they share in his comfort.

The recipients of this letter are acquainted with the severe hardship that Paul had to endure in the province of Asia. He refrains from providing details, but he does indicate that the peril he faced nearly cost him his life. He relied on God, who delivered him from mortal danger and raises the dead. He thanks the Corinthians for their prayers on his behalf.

Paul testifies that he has conducted himself honorably in the world and espe-

---

64. Consult Moule, *Idiom-Book*, p. 76.

cially toward the Corinthians. He asks them to understand him fully, so that they can boast of him and he of them in the day of the Lord.

The original travel plans of Paul were to visit the Corinthians, then go to Macedonia, and return again to visit Corinth. From there he would travel to Judea. But these plans changed, and now Paul receives criticism that his word cannot be trusted. He defends himself by pointing to God who is faithful to his Word, to Jesus Christ whose message Paul, Silvanus, and Timothy preach, and to the promises God has made in Christ. Believers affirm this truth by saying "Amen." Paul concludes this segment of the chapter by asserting that God confirms and anoints believers, who receive God's seal and the indwelling of the Holy Spirit in their hearts.

2

Apostolic Ministry, *part 2*

(1:23–2:17)

Outline (continued)

23 And I call God as a witness against me [if I fail to tell the truth], because I tried to spare you when I did not come again to Corinth. 24 We do not lord it over your faith, but we are fellow workers for your joy. For it is by faith that you stand firm.

2 1 So I decided not to pay you another sorrowful visit. 2 For if I grieve you, then who is there to cheer me except the one whom I have saddened? 3 And I wrote this very message so that by coming I might not receive grief from those who should have made me glad. I had confidence in all of you that my joy would be the joy of all of you. 4 For I wrote you out of great affliction and anguish of heart with many tears, not to make you sad but that you may know the more abundant love I have for you.

---

4. A Painful Visit
1:23–2:4

The chapter division at this point in the epistle is unfortunate: Paul continues to speak about his visit to Corinth, its effect and consequence (1:23–2:4), but the division occurs in the middle of this segment, which introduces new material. The question we face is whether the segment belongs to the preceding or the succeeding discussion. In view of the information that relates Paul's interaction with the congregation in Corinth, we add the last two verses of chapter 1 to chapter 2.

23. And I call God as a witness against me [if I fail to tell the truth], because I tried to spare you when I did not come again to Corinth.

a. "And I call God as a witness against me [if I fail to tell the truth]." Much more than the English translation, the Greek text shows remarkable force when Paul calls God as his witness. Paul stresses the personal pronoun *I* to state unequivocally that he himself, without his co-workers, appeals to God. He had just informed his readers that they belonged to God, who had put his seal of ownership on them and had given them the Holy Spirit as a deposit (1:22). Indeed the Corinthians could count on God's faithfulness. This is an echo of 1:18, where Paul also appeals to God's faithfulness in view of Paul's change in travel plans (1:15–16). The present verse is a prelude to the remark about his painful visit to the Corinthian church (2:1).

As he does repeatedly in his epistles, Paul calls upon God to be a witness to the truth.[1] Calling upon God to verify the validity of one's words and deeds implies a conditional clause ("if I fail to tell the truth") whose logical conclusion could form a curse. That is, Paul intimates that if he were not telling the truth, God

---

1. Rom. 1:9; Phil. 1:8; I Thess. 2:5, 10; compare II Cor. 11:31; 12:19; Gal. 1:20; I Sam. 12:5–6 (LXX).

would have every reason to punish him. Before God, Paul bares his soul and says literally, "I call God as a witness against my life." He is always standing in the very presence of God, who knows his inmost being. Paul knows that God is able to take his life should he speak a lie.

b. "Because I tried to spare you when I did not come again to Corinth." Paul now reveals the reason for not returning to Corinth as he has promised: he wanted to spare the Corinthians (contrast 13:2). Although he expresses his loving care for the Christians with the verb *to spare*, he fails to say from what he wished to shield them. He merely says that he did not reappear in Corinth. In his earlier correspondence he asked the Corinthians whether he should come to them with a rod or with a loving, gentle spirit (I Cor. 4:21). Paul had visited them in an attempt to take care of the trouble in their church (II Cor. 2:1). After this visit, he decided not to return, so that the Corinthians might repent and so that he might demonstrate his love for them (2:4).

24. We do not lord it over your faith, but we are fellow workers for your joy. For it is by faith that you stand firm.

a. "We do not lord it over your faith." The preceding verse (v. 23) emphasized the first person singular pronoun. In this verse, however, Paul involves his associates and uses the first person plural. But Paul returns to the first person singular in the next few verses (2:1–4) to explain his visit and his letter to the Corinthians.

The believers in Corinth could easily misunderstand Paul's motives or those of his colleagues. Paul wants to avoid any ill will on the part of the Corinthians; he does so by showing them his good will and gentleness. As a sequel to his comment on sparing his readers, he now states that neither he nor his co-workers have any desire to lord it over their faith (I Peter 5:3). The verb *to lord it over (someone)* describes power that an individual either has been given or has assumed for himself.[2] With this verb, Paul conveys the message that he, his associates, and all Christians acknowledge Jesus Christ as their Lord and Master. All are free in the Lord but are obligated to help one another. So Paul writes that he and his partners do not lord it over the faith of the Corinthians but instead minister to the believers.

b. "But we are fellow workers for your joy." Through his correspondence, Paul shows that he cares for the church in Corinth by personal visits, letters, and representatives including Timothy and Titus. The people in Corinth have to admit that Paul and his co-workers are working for them to advance their spiritual welfare and joy.

c. "For it is by faith that you stand firm." Using the plural pronoun *you* to include all the members of the Corinthian congregation, Paul briefly explains the first line in this verse, "We do not lord it over your *faith*." Faith is a spiritual bond

---

2. This verb occurs seven times in the New Testament: once in Luke (22:25) and six times in Paul's epistles (Rom. 6:9, 14; 7:1; 14:9; II Cor. 1:24; I Tim. 6:15). Consult Hans Bietenhard, *NIDNTT*, 2:518; Werner Foerster, *TDNT*, 3:1097.

between the individual believer and his or her God, and no one has authority over that relationship. A living faith is instrumental in producing genuine joy (compare Phil. 1:25; I John 1:4; II John 12). The apostle highlights the concepts *faith* and *joy* in this verse to signify that these two virtues are the infrastructure of a vibrant Christian life and a healthy relationship between himself and the Corinthians.[3] Considering the strained relations between him and the members of the Corinthian church (see 2:1–4), Paul takes extra care to point out these two virtues, faith and joy. He himself rejoices that by faith his readers are standing firm, for their developing faith will effect stability, growth, and happiness in the Lord Jesus Christ.

1. So I decided not to pay you another sorrowful visit. 2. For if I grieve you, then who is there to cheer me except the one whom I saddened?

a. "*So I decided not to pay you another sorrowful visit.*" Paul's earlier comment had been that he would not visit the Corinthians so as to spare them (1:23). Now he elaborates on the reason for not visiting them. I follow the Greek text, which in translation gives the reading *so* as the first word. Its self-evident conclusion clarifies some preceding remarks.[4] The Greek text is more descriptive than a smooth translation reveals: Paul writes that he made up his mind by himself once for all. His decision is his own; being certain of its correctness, he makes it known to the Corinthians. He had been accused of unreliability in respect to keeping his word (1:17). But having commented on his truthfulness, he declares that he had come to a firm decision not to pay the Corinthians another visit that would cause them grief. Furthermore, if we follow the Greek word order, we do well to take the expression *another* (literally, "again") with the adjective *sorrowful* and not with the noun *visit.* The emphasis, then, falls on the grief that such a visit causes and not on the visit itself.

The implication is that the visit Paul had paid the Corinthian church had been grievous. He is not interested in a recurrence. It appears that Paul refers not to his initial stay in Corinth, when he founded the church, but to a subsequent visit after he had composed I Corinthians. He had waited for a response from the recipients of this epistle. Their response caused Paul to travel to Corinth. This intermediate visit occurred between his departure from Corinth after a sojourn of eighteen months (Acts 18:11, 18) and his three-month stay there before he traveled to Jerusalem (Acts 20:3).

Some scholars assert that the painful visit took place before Paul wrote I Corinthians and that this epistle was his sorrowful letter.[5] Although much can be

---

3. Refer to F. W. Grosheide, *De Tweede Brief van den Apostel Paulus aan de Kerk te Korinthe,* Kommentaar op het Nieuwe Testament series (Amsterdam: Van Bottenburg, 1939), p. 76 n. 1.

4. Other translators prefer the Greek reading *de,* rendered as the adversative *but* or *however* (KJV, NKJV, NAB, NASB, *Cassirer*).

5. Philip Edgcumbe Hughes, *Paul's Second Epistle to the Corinthians: The English Text with Introduction, Exposition and Notes,* New International Commentary on the New Testament series (Grand Rapids: Eerdmans, 1962), pp. 52, 54–57; D. R. Hall, "Pauline Church Discipline," *TynB* 20 (1969): 3–26; Udo Borse, "'Tränenbrief' und 1. Korintherbrief," *StudNTUmwelt* 9 (1984): 175–202.

said in favor of this view, a major objection is that calling the entire epistle sorrowful is incorrect. If this were true, we would have expected the delegation from Corinth (Stephanas, Fortunatus, and Achaicus) to have supplied dreadful news (I Cor. 16:17–18). But this is not the case, for the delegation gladdens Paul's heart.

Another obstacle is the wording of II Corinthians 7:8 and 12, in which Paul expresses regrets over writing a sorrowful letter. These two verses apply more to the intermediate letter than to I Corinthians.

A third obstacle is Paul's intention to visit Corinth for the third time (12:14; 13:1). Paul notes that he was with the Corinthians a second time when he warned that he would not spare those who had sinned (13:2). The implication, then, is that during the second visit the relationship between Paul and the Corinthians (see 2:1) worsened. It is difficult to place a second visit between the founding of the church (Acts 18:1–11) and the writing of I Corinthians. We would have expected Paul to refer to that painful visit in his first canonical epistle.[6] In view of these obstacles, we prefer the view that Paul wrote a severe letter after he sent I Corinthians.

Paul provides no information concerning the occasion or the nature of his painful visit. He intimates, however, that his promised return visit would also have been painful for the Corinthians. For this reason, he decided to forego travel to Corinth. Indeed, he would spare the church heartache and then experience mutual joy while visiting them.

b. "For if I grieve you, then who is there to cheer me except the one whom I saddened?" A cursory reading of this interrogative sentence conveys absurdity. Therefore, some commentators (Bultmann, Héring, and Martin) have divided this sentence by placing the question mark after the word *me* instead of "saddened." They then make Paul answer his own question by taking the last clause as a declarative statement: "Certainly not the one whom I saddened." The Greek expression *ei mē*, however, communicates an exception with the invariable translation "except, "if not," or "but," and is part of the text.[7]

Is the commonly adopted punctuation of this sentence expressing nonsense? Hardly. Paul asserts that he and his associates were trying to make the Corinthians joyful (1:24). Paul expects that if the people see the error of their way and acknowledge his integrity, they will cheer him and rejoice with him. Paul is the spiritual father of the Corinthians (I Cor. 4:15) and, like any father, he wants his children to be joyful and content. But it saddens him when he has to grieve his spiritual children for the purpose of correcting them. He wants them to reflect on their grief, to repent, and to yearn for Paul. Then his grief will turn into joy.

---

6. Donald Guthrie, *New Testament Introduction*, 4th rev. ed. (Leicester: Apollos; Downers Grove: Inter-Varsity, 1990), p. 442. Udo Borse dismisses Paul's failure to mention the second visit in I Corinthians as insignificant. See his "Tränenbrief," p. 181.
7. Bauer, p. 220. The NCV repunctuates but has a paraphrase to make the point: "If I make you sad, who will make me glad? Only you can make me glad—particularly the person whom I made sad."

And when Titus returns eventually from Corinth to Paul, the Corinthians are sorrowful, long for Paul, and express concern for him. We read that the report of Titus made Paul extremely happy (7:6–7).

Paul had visited the Corinthian congregation and with his words had grieved the members. The conditional clause ("For if I grieve you") states a simple fact; the present tense of the verb *grieve* also indicates an enduring effect of Paul's rebuke. Addressing the congregation, Paul uses the singular *who, the one,* and *whom* to include the entire church of Corinth.[8] He fails to relate what he said to the members and the cause of his grief. The sequence of this passage, however, provides further information.

3. And I wrote this very message so that by coming I might not receive grief from those who should have made me glad. I had confidence in all of you that my joy would be the joy of all of you.

a. "And I wrote this very message." What is the message to which Paul refers? He has in mind the intermediate letter that he sent to the Corinthians after his painful visit. Perhaps he lifted a thought out of this letter when he told the readers that he would not plan another painful visit to Corinth (v. 1; see also 1:23). Verse 2 must be regarded as a parenthetical remark in which he explains the reason for not visiting them. And verse 3 is a continuation of his reference to the sorrowful letter. Scholars debate whether this letter is no longer extant or is part of the last four chapters of this epistle. If we consider to be inadequate the arguments that identify chapters 10–13 as the sorrowful letter, the alternative is to regard the sorrowful letter as lost. (For a full discussion on the unity and integrity of II Corinthians, see the Introduction.)

b. "So that by coming I might not receive grief from those who should have made me glad." We assume that the letter Paul sent to the Corinthians exhorted them to rectify the situation in their church. He wanted them to be joyful in the Lord and to eliminate any hard feelings that had arisen between them. He looked forward to a forthcoming visit during which he might share in their happiness. Paul had no intention of afflicting his readers and causing them to build up resentment. His sorrowful letter was meant to show them his love, much as a parent sternly reproves an erring son or daughter but always in the context of parental love. When the child listens and obeys, the relationship is fully restored. Paul was of the opinion that the breach between him and the Corinthians would heal in time. He anticipated that the grief he had experienced might turn into joy when the members of the church in Corinth would indeed change their minds.

c. "I had confidence in all of you that my joy would be the joy of all of you." Paul wanted to avert resentment by showing kindness and love, for he knew the proverb, "How good is a timely word" (Prov. 15:23). He knew that the congrega-

---

8. Consequently, some translators make the reference in the last clause of verse 2 plural: "but you whom I have grieved" (e.g., NIV; Eugene H. Peterson, *The Message: The New Testament in Contemporary English* [Colorado Springs, Colo.: NavPress, 1993]).

tion, apart from the person who had caused him grief, looked to him for spiritual leadership. Thus, Paul stresses his confidence in all the members of the Corinthian church. He asserts that he wants to see them to be cheerful so that he can share in their happiness (compare John 15:11). He is confident that their revived joy will result in the sharing and intensifying of his joy for them.

4. "For I wrote you out of great affliction and anguish of heart with many tears, not to make you sad but that you may know the more abundant love I have for you."

a. "For I wrote you out of great affliction and anguish of heart with many tears." Paul did not write his sorrowful letter thoughtlessly or carelessly. On the contrary, he reveals that the situation in Corinth had caused him overwhelming heartache.

Do we still have the letter in which Paul shows spiritual distress? Three answers are usually given to this question. One answer is that the letter is part of II Corinthians 10–14. But even though Paul reproves the Corinthians in the last four chapters of this epistle, he demonstrates that the earlier tension has dissipated. A second view is that the sorrowful letter is I Corinthians (see the commentary on v. 2). Granted that Paul had to rebuke the Corinthians for failing to discipline a man who had committed incest (I Cor. 5:1–5), we cannot affirm that all of I Corinthians with its detailed instruction on church and social life was composed out of great affliction, profound anguish, and grief that caused him to shed many tears. A third possibility is that if the congregation had not expelled the wicked man from its midst, then Paul would be forced to visit Corinth to rectify the situation. If the members failed to respond to him, then he would have to write an intermediate letter that, for both him and them, would be sorrowful. The third view appears to be preferable.

The spiritual condition in Corinth evidently deteriorated to such an extent that Paul had to compose a severe letter to rebuke the members of the church. As their spiritual father he was greatly distressed. Writing this epistle was extremely difficult for Paul because he knew what would be its effect on the Corinthians. The letter arose out of his anguished heart and was written through a flood of tears. In other passages Paul speaks about anguish he endured because of persecution (e.g., 1:4, 6, 8), but here his distress relates to the situation in Corinth. When Paul delivered his farewell address to the Ephesian elders, he said that he warned everyone day and night with tears (Acts 20:31; see Phil. 3:18). Now he warns the Corinthians with a letter that was bathed in tears.

b. "Not to make you sad but that you may know the more abundant love I have for you." Every word in this part of the verse is emphatic. The first word, "not," negates the verb, "to make sad," so the intermediate letter was meant to have the Corinthians see their error, acknowledge their guilt, turn from their ways, and joyfully accept Paul's corrective message. Paul balances the negative with the positive; that is, the adversative *but* introduces his love for the Corinthians. And that love is not mere affection or friendship; it is genuine love that the Christians in Corinth were able to experience during his eighteen-month ministry in their midst. Now Paul informs them that he extends his love for them even more abundantly. The Greek has a comparative structure. The sense is not that Paul loves the Corinthian church more than other congregations. Rather, Paul loves the believers in Corinth even more now than when he served them as their pastor. And they will know this by acknowledging Paul's tender care.

Greek Words, Phrases, and Constructions in 1:23–2:4

Verses 23–24

μάρτυρα—"witness." In the accusative, this noun is appositional to the following accusative, τὸν θεόν.

φειδόμενος—the participle ("sparing") is in the present tense to indicate continued action; it denotes cause and controls the genitive case ὑμῶν.

κυριεύομεν—the present tense of this verb signifies lasting action. The first person plural *we lord it over* refers to Paul and his associates, not to the Corinthians. The verb controls the genitive of πίστεως (faith).

τῆς χαρᾶς—the genitive is objective: "for your joy." The dative case of τῇ πίστει can be construed as means (by faith), place (in the sphere of), or reference (in respect to). The first choice is strengthened by the reference to Romans 11:20, "you stand by faith." The second has the support of Colossians 1:23, "if you continue in your faith." Translators are about evenly divided in regard to these three choices. Of the three, I prefer the first one, for the words and word order are the same in Romans 11:20. This cannot be said for the other choices and passages.

Verses 1–2

γάρ—manuscript support for this particle is less than for δέ. But γάρ provides the reader with an explanation of Paul's decision not to return to Corinth (1:23–24).[9]

ἐμαυτῷ τοῦτο τό—"For I decided for myself this thing, that is, not to come." The reflexive pronoun ἐμαυτῷ is a dative of advantage, the demonstrative pronoun τοῦτο is the direct object, and the definite article τό stands in apposition to the preceding pronoun and introduces the articular infinitive ἐλθεῖν.

καὶ τίς—the conjunction should be seen as the introduction of an abrupt question, "who then?"[10]

Verses 3–4

ἔγραψα τοῦτο αὐτό—the verb is not an epistolary aorist and alludes to a letter Paul had previously sent to the Corinthians. The combination of the two pronouns means "this very [point]."

---

9. Bruce M. Metzger, *A Textual Commentary on the Greek New Testament*, 2d ed. (Stuttgart and New York: United Bible Societies, 1994), p. 508. See also the commentaries of Alfred Plummer, *A Critical and Exegetical Commentary on the Second Epistle of St. Paul to the Corinthians*, International Critical Commentary (1915; Edinburgh: Clark, 1975), p. 46; and Victor Paul Furnish, *II Corinthians: Translated with Introduction, Notes and Commentary*, Anchor Bible 32A (Garden City, N.Y.: Doubleday, 1984), p. 139.

10. Bauer, p. 392; Friedrich Blass and Albert Debrunner, *A Greek Grammar of the New Testament and Other Early Christian Literature*, trans. and rev. Robert Funk (Chicago: University of Chicago Press, 1961), #442.

πεποιθώς—the perfect active participle of the verb πείθω denotes cause: "For I am confident."

ἐκ—the preposition that signifies source controls the two nouns *affliction* and *anguish*, while διά expresses attendant circumstance ("with many tears").[11]

---

5 But if someone has caused you grief, he has not grieved me, but to some extent—that I may not be too severe—all of you. 6 For this particular person, the punishment inflicted on him by most of you is enough. 7 By contrast, you should rather forgive and comfort him, that such a person might not be overcome by excessive sorrow. 8 Therefore, I exhort you to affirm your love for him. 9 For this purpose I also wrote you, so that I might test you to see if you would be obedient in all things. 10 The one you forgive, I forgive. For what I have forgiven, if indeed I had to forgive something, I did on account of you in the presence of Christ, 11 not to be outwitted by Satan. For we are not unaware of his designs.

---

5. Forgiving the Sinner
2:5–11

To protect the identity of the person concerned and to encourage the offender's readmission into the church, Paul now speaks indirectly about the disciplinary problem with which the Corinthian church had to deal. The incident itself is well known to the recipients of this letter, so Paul has no need to be specific. He uses allusions that are sufficiently clear to the initial readers but lack specificity for all others. From Paul's correspondence we know that the Corinthian church had its share of problems that have troubled the church throughout the centuries. This segment of the epistle, which deals with a disciplinary problem in the Corinthian church, has relevance for the church today. Problems that call for corrective action are sensitive, delicate, and frequently painful. Those leaders who try to solve them must be filled with wisdom to proceed tactfully. Paul gives an example in the following passage.

5. But if someone has caused you grief, he has not grieved me, but to some extent—that I may not be too severe—all of you.

a. *Parenthesis.* The verse shows emotional tension that causes Paul to hesitate momentarily. The thought Paul tries to express is that a certain man has brought grief not only on Paul but also on all the members of the Corinthian church. But he realizes that not every person in Corinth was offended and, therefore, he moderates his thoughts. In doing so, he uses a phrase that appears to say, "in order that I may not encumber [you too much with words]." I present the translation "that I may not be too severe."[12] Because of insufficient evidence, translators must decide on the basis of the context how to convey Paul's meaning.

---

11. C. F. D. Moule, *An Idiom-Book of New Testament Greek*, 2d ed. (Cambridge: Cambridge University Press, 1960), p. 57.

12. Compare Bauer, p. 290, "that I might not be a burden to any of you." Translations vary: for example, "I do not want to make it worse than it already is" (NCV); "I have no wish to press my point unduly" *(Cassirer);* and "I do not want to be too hard on him" (GNB). Many versions paraphrase the Greek text and try to approximate its exact meaning.

b. *Purpose.* The conditional clause in the first part of the verse states a simple fact. Someone in the church has brought grief to its members. The presence of this person affects the entire congregation, much as a bit of yeast leavens the entire batch of dough (I Cor. 5:6–8). Moral sins are not confined to persons immediately involved but usually affect the entire congregation. Paul's illustration of yeast and dough applies to the incestuous man, and it applies equally to the grief someone has caused the Corinthian church.[13] The Greek verb *lelypēken* (has caused grief) is in the perfect tense to indicate that some time has elapsed since the offense.

Paul does not intend to say that he himself has not experienced grief caused by the offender. Rather he is saying that he is not the only one who has been grieved; the entire Corinthian church has been touched (see 7:8–12). This sadness about a grievous sin prevents the church from reaching out effectively to others in the Corinthian community. To some extent, this paralysis influences every Christian in that church.

Nevertheless, not everyone in the congregation is affected by grief. Paul qualifies his statement and adds that he does not want to be too severe. When Paul heard about the problem in Corinth, he came to Corinth but his visit was painful. After the Corinthians received his severe letter, the majority in the church realized that all of them were adversely influenced by the conduct of the offender. Even though some members remained unconcerned, the church as a body understood the severity of the case and punished the person who had affronted God and his servant Paul. The church saw its corporate responsibility and took appropriate measures.

6. For this particular person, the punishment inflicted on him by most of you is enough. 7. By contrast, you should rather forgive and comfort him, that such a person might not be overcome by excessive sorrow.

a. "For this particular person, the punishment inflicted on him by most of you is enough." The church had to deal with a sinner who had committed an offense that affected the entire congregation and hampered its work. We assume that the church applied the rules for discipline that Jesus prescribed (Matt. 18:15–17). If Titus had delivered Paul's severe letter to the Corinthians and remained with them, he perhaps chaired the meeting in which the offender was disciplined. Paul indicates that Titus had visited the church at an earlier occasion to gather the collection for the saints in Jerusalem (II Cor. 8:6). We cannot exclude the possibility that in addition he took care of this disciplinary matter.[14]

Most of the Corinthian believers agreed to the disciplinary measures that were designed to mete out appropriate punishment. As is usually true, however, the offender seems to have had some sympathizers who defended him and ob-

---

13. Consult Colin G. Kruse, "The Offender and the Offence in II Corinthians 2:5 and 7:12," *EvQ* 60 (1988): 129–39, esp. p. 135.

14. Consult A. M. G. Stephenson, "A Defence of the Integrity of II Corinthians," *The Authorship and Integrity of the New Testament*, TC 4 (London: SPCK, 1965), p. 93.

jected to the measures decided upon by the majority. (Incidentally, the Greek expression *epitimia* [punishment] is a legal term that in this case pertains to a church court.) Paul had hoped to achieve disciplinary action through his leadership. He wanted the church to censure one of its own members. In context, Paul stresses the church's responsibility more than the repentance of the particular offender (2:5–9; 7:12).[15] His insistence on the Corinthians taking appropriate action in this matter has a parallel in Paul's efforts to expel the incestuous man from the church (I Cor. 5:1–5, 13).

The punishment is exclusion from the church when the majority of its members cast their votes to condemn the man. The majority rules, even though the minority opposes the action. The congregation realizes that in addition to censuring the sinner, it is ready to readmit him upon true repentance. The Corinthians may have asked Paul what steps they should take to readmit the man. Indeed, they have to consider that the punishment they administered is equal to the offense.

b. "By contrast, you should rather forgive and comfort him." Paul advises his readers to be merciful to the penitent sinner and not to prolong the duration of his punishment now that he has repented. With respect to the offender, the Corinthians must change their thinking from removal to acceptance, from condemnation to restoration, from judgment to forgiveness, and from indignation to encouragement (Gal. 6:1). If there is genuine repentance, there must also be full-scale reinstatement. If God forgives a sinner, the church must do no less (Col. 3:13). Although the burden of sin is cancelled, for the forgiven sinner the consequences of sin remain. What a person whom the church has censured and has reinstated needs more than anything else is daily words of encouragement from fellow Christians (see Heb. 3:12–13).

c. "That such a person might not be overcome by excessive sorrow." The shame of sin and the pain of rejection are such that the forgiven offender faces the possibility of sinking into despair and succumbing to depression. For this reason, Christians are exhorted to receive and to restore such a person as a brother or a sister in Christ. We should never allow a forgiven sinner to turn away from the body of believers and abandon the faith because of the church's lack of love.

8. Therefore, I exhort you to affirm your love for him. 9. For this purpose I also wrote you, so that I might test you to see if you would be obedient in all things.

A group or person who has been injured by an offender must overcome great difficulties to forgive a sinner from the heart, especially when one is influenced by others in the community. When people forgive one another, an uneasiness often prevents them from treating the offender as if that person is completely restored.

---

15. Refer to G. W. H. Lampe, "Church Discipline and the Epistles to the Corinthians," in *Christian History and Interpretation: Studies Presented to John Knox*, ed. W. R. Farmer, C. F. D. Moule, and R. R. Niebuhr (Cambridge: Cambridge University Press, 1967), pp. 353–54.

John Calvin correctly counsels the church, "Whenever we fail to comfort those that are moved to a sincere confession of their sin, we play into Satan's hands."[16]

Using the personal pronoun *I,* Paul is telling his readers to reaffirm their love for the sinner. He wants to see a continued outpouring of genuine love, so that the person is indeed fully restored. The verb *reaffirm* is a legal term that conveys the ethical principle of genuine love.[17]

Paul exhorts the Corinthians to love the repentant sinner from the heart. He desires that the church as a body and as individual members pay serious attention to the summary of the Decalogue: "Love the Lord your God with all your heart and . . . your neighbor as yourself" (Matt. 22:37–39).

When Paul says, "For this purpose I also wrote you," he has in mind his earlier correspondence, especially the sorrowful letter. He desires that the church administer censure to keep the church pure, but at the same time he counsels the church to restore a repentant sinner in Christian love. When a sinner repents, both reconciliation and reinstatement should follow as a matter of course. Both truth and grace should be applied in keeping a sound and balanced approach to offense and offender in the church.

The purpose of Paul's letter is to test the members of the church to find out whether they were genuine in spiritual matters. He expresses his apostolic authority to the Corinthians and expects them to demonstrate compliance in both administering discipline and embracing the repentant sinner with sincere love. But Paul writes, "obedient in all things," not just a few things. He wants obedience to the Lord Jesus Christ, and thus his probe is uniquely applicable to the problematic church of Corinth. A proper reading of the text shows that the Corinthians in fact are (present tense) obedient and are doing what Paul expects from them. Here Paul acknowledges the spiritual progress that the people of Corinth have made after he wrote and counseled them many times. He also sent Titus, who was able to induce them to obey (7:15).

10. The one you forgive, I forgive. For what I have forgiven, if indeed I had to forgive something, I did on account of you in the presence of Christ, 11. not to be outwitted by Satan. For we are not unaware of his designs.

a. "The one you forgive, I forgive." Paul speaks as the father of his spiritual children in the family of God. When the children of this family are willing to pardon the sinner, Paul also forgives. He wants the Corinthians to take the lead in forgiving the person in question. When they are ready and willing to pardon the offender, Paul also is ready to forgive him and to do so from the heart.

b. "For what I have forgiven, if indeed I had to forgive something, I did on account of you in the presence of Christ." Paul holds no grudges against the offender. The tense of the verb *to forgive* indicates that Paul had dealt with this mat-

---

16. John Calvin, *The Second Epistle of Paul the Apostle to the Corinthians and the Epistles to Timothy, Titus and Philemon,* Calvin's Commentaries series, trans. T. A. Small (Grand Rapids: Eerdmans, 1964), p. 30.

17. Johannes Behm, *TDNT,* 3:1099; see also J. I. Packer, *NIDNTT,* 1:664.

ter prior to the writing of this epistle. He put the church first and himself second with respect to the offense that was committed. Paul shows a magnanimous spirit of love toward the offender by absolving him of guilt. Paul is willing to count the affront insignificant by saying, "if indeed I had to forgive something." An offender sometimes fails to admit wrongdoing and in those instances never apologizes to the injured party. Should the offended person nurse a resentment while waiting for an apology that does not come? Paul provides an answer with his remark that he stood above the offender's affront and doubted whether he had to forgive anything.

There is another side to the matter of forgiving one another. If there happened to be any resentment in the Corinthians toward him, Paul wholeheartedly exonerates them in the presence of Christ. As their pastor, he readily pardons the congregation so that nothing hinders the cause of Christ. Ministering to the members of the church, Paul has placed the matter before the Lord Jesus Christ and now exhibits a forgiving spirit.

Grudges in the congregation are quickly exploited by Satan to undermine the church's spiritual health. He capitalizes on insults that remain unforgiven and unresolved; deluding the people, he causes them to foster a spirit of animosity that divides and scatters them. Jesus said, "He who is not with me is against me, and he who does not gather with me scatters" (Matt. 12:30). It is Satan's design to frustrate the work of Christ in his church on earth. By scattering God's people, Satan is able to block the advancement of Christ's church and kingdom.

Paul notes that he and the Corinthians are not unaware of Satan's desire to sift God's servants as wheat (Luke 22:31) and to cause them spiritual ruin. To harbor ill will toward a repentant sinner instead of showing love, mercy, and grace plays into the hands of Satan. The devil hates forgiveness and Christian love; he wants to see despondency, despair, and darkness. In that atmosphere Satan is able to reclaim a pardoned sinner. Consequently, Paul teaches the Corinthians to forgive one another in love just as Christ has forgiven them (Eph. 4:32).

Additional Comments on 2:5–11

There are at least three views on identifying the offender mentioned in this passage. I first list these three opinions, then I examine each in the light of available evidence, and last I try to avoid speculation.

Those scholars who consider I Corinthians to be the severe letter (II Cor. 2:3) have identified the man who committed incest (I Cor. 5:1–5) with the man who caused grief, received punishment, repented, and sought forgiveness (II Cor. 2:5–11). When church members expel someone for flagrant sin, they open the door of readmission to such a person after he or she shows genuine repentance.

Other scholars think that the severe letter is the one Paul wrote between 1 and II Corinthians. They are of the opinion that someone in the congregation had offended Paul when the apostle made his second visit to Corinth. They are not sure what the offense may have been, but it affected the church in such a way that most of the members had taken action to punish him (v. 6). When the man repented, Paul forgave him and urged the Corinthians to pardon and reaffirm him.

Some scholars say that after Paul wrote I Corinthians, he briefly visited Corinth but was rebuffed and offended by one person. Paul returned to Ephesus and composed the severe letter. These scholars suggest that the incestuous man (I Cor. 5:1–5) is the same person who confronted and offended Paul during his second visit to Corinth (II Cor. 2:5).[18] The man did not repent after the congregation received Paul's specific demands for his expulsion (I Cor. 5:13) but also had verbally attacked Paul during the apostle's second visit to Corinth. Then Paul wrote the severe letter, which presumably Titus delivered to the Corinthians. From Titus Paul heard the news that the church in Corinth was longing for Paul and expressed deep sorrow (II Cor. 7:6–7, 13–15).

Now let us discuss these views in detail.

1. *Traditional interpretation.* This first view has its roots in the early Christian church and is known as the traditional interpretation. During that second visit Paul encountered the man who had committed incest with his father's wife (I Cor. 5:1). The case affected the entire congregation, but Paul's confrontation with the person who offended him (II Cor. 2:5, 10; 7:12) resulted in a personal attack on Paul.

Many commentators have rejected the traditional interpretation. They say that during Paul's second visit to Corinth someone insulted and attacked Paul. The possibility is not unreal that the incestuous man could have been the person who humiliated the apostle.

We apply the tested rule to let Scripture be its own interpreter; that is, for an obscure point in a particular text we turn to other passages of Scripture that can illuminate the text. Assuming that the two passages, 2:5–11 and 7:12, refer to the same person, we learn that the offender is the same person who attacked Paul. Not the congregation but the offender is guilty, for 7:11 indicates that the Corinthians were innocent. The injured party, it appears, is Paul himself.

2. *Two different cases.* The discipline that Paul meted out for the incestuous man was to hand him over to Satan, who is given authority to punish him (I Cor. 5:5). But in the second epistle (2:5–11), Paul urges the recipients to forgive the sinner, whom they punished and who repented. Scholars believe that the two cases have hardly anything in common.[19] Although there is some truth in this observation, Scripture teaches that God always keeps open the door to forgiveness through repentance. God forgives every sin, except the sin of blasphemy against the Holy Spirit (Matt. 12:32). The church likewise must be ready to accept a repentant sinner and fully reinstate him. We have no indication what damage Satan may have inflicted on the person, but Paul's objective—to save the man's spirit— may have been realized (I Cor. 5:5). Consider that as God forgave Paul for his violence against the church, so the church ought to pardon the offender for his incestuous conduct (Gal. 6:1).[20] The argument for seeing a clear difference between the sexual offender

---

18. Colin G. Kruse, *The Second Epistle of Paul to the Corinthians: An Introduction and Commentary,* The Tyndale New Testament Commentaries series (Leicester: Inter-Varsity; Grand Rapids: Eerdmans, 1987), vol. 8, pp. 41–45.

19. Refer to C. K. Barrett, "Ὁ ᾽ΑΔΙΚΗΣΑΣ (II Cor. 7, 12)," in *Verborum Veritas,* ed. Otto Böcher and Klaus Haacker (Wuppertal: Brockhaus, 1970), pp. 153–55; also in *Essays on Paul* (Philadelphia: Westminster, 1982), pp. 111–13. Barrett thinks that the offender is not a Corinthian but a stranger. See *The Second Epistle to the Corinthians,* Harper's New Testament Commentaries series (New York: Harper and Row, 1973), pp. 89–90.

20. Compare Hughes, *Second Epistle to the Corinthians,* p. 63; James Denney, *The Second Epistle to the Corinthians,* 2d ed., The Expositor's Bible series (New York: Armstrong, 1900), p. 74.

and the person who offended Paul may be formidable,[21] yet it is not conclusive. The two passages in Paul's Corinthian correspondence may refer to the same person.[22]

3. *Two deeds by the same person.* The third view is that because the incestuous man was not expelled from the Corinthian congregation, Paul came to Corinth on his second visit. There the man assaulted him verbally by challenging his apostolic authority to exercise discipline in the Corinthian church. Paul was deeply hurt and, unable to solve the dilemma, returned to Ephesus. Upon his arrival in Ephesus, Paul wrote such a severe letter that the Corinthians could have turned completely away from him. Titus probably delivered the letter to the church in Corinth. On the basis of this letter and the persuasive influence of Titus, the congregation changed its attitude, took action, and punished the offender.[23] Titus was filled with joy and happiness (II Cor. 7:7, 13).

In the meantime, Paul had traveled from Ephesus to Macedonia, where he anxiously waited for Titus to tell him about the effect of the severe letter (7:5–16). Titus informed him that the Corinthians had punished the sinner, who as a result had repented. Paul expressed both relief and joy that the critical situation in the Corinthians church had passed. He now encouraged the congregation to reinstate the repentant sinner and to forgive him (2:6–10). Paul declares his joy (7:7), which may be compared to the joy angels express over one sinner who repents (Luke 15:7, 10).

This hypothesis has merit. When we consider the ramifications of Paul's directives to the Corinthian church to expel the immoral man from their midst, we must consider the offender's reaction (I Cor. 5:13). Note that Paul writes as if he himself were present at the congregational meeting in Corinth where he is to give leadership (I Cor. 5:3). But when the church received Paul's epistle, Paul himself was not there. Without his firm leadership, the church had to conduct its own discipline.[24] This procedure was risky, for Paul's opponents in Corinth would see this as a sign of personal weakness (compare II Cor. 10:10). The congregation met opposition from the immoral man, who had a number of friends to defend him. The church became divided over the issue and was unable to act. Paul learned about this deteriorating situation from Timothy, who had returned from Corinth (II Cor. 1:1).

Not Timothy but Titus was able to end the conflict in Corinth, and Titus could then ask the Corinthians to collect gifts from the saints in Jerusalem (II Cor. 8:6). In the midst of the turmoil, the church members were not ready to accept Paul's appeal for monetary gifts. But when the unrest had subsided, Titus could again encourage the believers to help the poverty-stricken saints elsewhere.

4. *Evaluation.* The details Paul provides are scarce, for he alludes to a situation that is well known in Corinth. As a pastor he tries to protect the person who is directly involved and thus is vague in his correspondence. Reading between the lines to gain an understanding of the entire Corinthian account, we hypothesize and deal with probabilities.

Nevertheless, a few significant facts reveal similarities between the incestuous man (I Cor. 5) and the person who abused Paul (II Cor. 2 and 7).

First, both accounts mention that a single person was involved. Next, the Corinthians have cause to be ashamed and grieved in both instances (I Cor. 5:2, 6, and II Cor. 2:5). Third, in the first account Paul demands that the church punish the wrongdoer and in

---

21. Refer to the detailed presentation of Furnish, *II Corinthians,* pp. 163–68.

22. See Frances Young and David F. Ford, *Meaning and Truth in II Corinthians,* BFT (London: SPCK, 1987), p. 53.

23. Consult Kruse, "Offender and the Offence," pp. 132–34.

24. Hall, "Pauline Church Discipline," p. 24.

the second the majority of the congregation meet that demand (I Cor. 5:5, 13, and II Cor. 2:6). Although Paul prescribes expulsion, he does not rule out the possibility of restoration (I Cor. 5:5). When this happens, Paul exhorts the Corinthians to extend to the sinner love, comfort, and pardon (II Cor. 2:7–9).[25]

Fourth, Paul refers to Jesus Christ in both passages (I Cor. 5:4 and II Cor. 2:10). The first text refers to Jesus' name and power that are present, and the second mentions the presence of Christ. In both passages, Paul acts as Christ's representative who places the matter before the face of Jesus, who "looks down with approval."[26]

And last, Satan advances his cause either by means of destructive force or with deliberate deceit. Both methods serve his purpose, as is demonstrated in delivering the incestuous man to Satan for the destruction of the person's sinful nature (I Cor. 5:5) and in his deceptive work of abducting a repentant brother (II Cor. 2:11).

Even though the similarities are striking, we have no proof that the two persons are the same individual. Conversely, there is no proof to preclude this identification.

Greek Words, Phrases, and Constructions in 2:5–11

Verse 5

εἰ δέ τις—this conditional clause denotes reality. The perfect indicative λελύπηκεν (he has grieved) shows action in the past with effect in the present. The indefinite pronoun τις is not general but specific, for it refers to a special case.

ὑμᾶς—note the emphasis placed on this pronoun at the end of the sentence and the contrast with the indefinite pronoun at the beginning of the sentence.

Verses 6–7

τῶν πλειόνων—the meaning of this particular expression is "the majority" with the implication that a minority dissented.[27]

ὥστε—the result clause introduced by the conjunction needs a complementary infinitive, δεῖν (is necessary), before the aorist middle infinitive χαρίσασθαι (to forgive).

λύπῃ—the dative case expresses means ("by sorrow"), although some grammarians designate it as a dative of cause: "because of sorrow."

Verse 9

ἔγραψα—this is not the epistolary aorist but the regular aorist active of the verb to write (see vv. 3–4).

εἰ—the textual readings vary, with εἰ having substantial manuscript support. Due to similarity in sound, ῇ (whereby) has taken the place of εἰ in some witnesses; scribal confusion is responsible for the reading of ὡς (as); and the omission of εἰ is accidental.[28]

Verses 10–11

ἐν προσώπῳ—the combination of preposition and noun means "in the presence of [Christ]."

---

25. Consult Borse, "Tränenbrief," p. 188.
26. Bauer, p. 721.
27. Compare Moule, *Idiom-Book*, p. 108.
28. Metzger, *Textual Commentary*, p. 508.

οὐ . . . ἀγνοοῦμεν—the double negative of the particle and the verb ("we are not un-aware") signifies "we know well."

B. The New Covenant
2:12–4:6

Luke's history book of Acts provides little detail about Paul's three-year min-istry in Ephesus. We assume that he was there from A.D. 52 to 55 and that he spent 56 in Macedonia and possibly Illyricum (Rom. 15:19). Titus had traveled to Corinth probably as the carrier of the severe epistle (2:3–4) and had arranged to meet Paul in Troas at a certain time. When Titus failed to come, Paul proclaimed the gospel in that harbor town. Eventually, he went around the northern Aegean Sea and entered Macedonia, where he met Titus (7:5–6, 13).

If we place the verses 5 through 11 in parentheses, we see that Paul continues in verse 12 the train of thought from verse 4. There is a decided connection be-tween his anxiety over the severe letter, probably delivered by Titus, and the re-port that Titus would bring concerning the Corinthians' reception of the letter.

---

12 When I came to Troas for the gospel of Christ and although a door was opened to me in the Lord, 13 I had no relief in my soul because I did not find Titus my brother. However, when I had said good-by to them, I went to Macedonia.

---

1. Paul's Anxiety
2:12–13

12. When I came to Troas for the gospel of Christ and although a door was opened to me in the Lord, 13. I had no relief in my soul because I did not find Titus my brother. However, when I had said good-by to them, I went to Macedonia.

a. "When I came to Troas." The city of Troas was located about ten miles south of ancient Troy in the northwest corner of Asia Minor (Turkey). During the fourth century B.C., after the death of Alexander the Great, Antigonus founded the city and called it Antigonia Troas. It later was renamed Alexander Troas. After the Romans conquered Asia Minor, the city became a Roman colony with the same privileges as other colonies (e.g., Philippi and Corinth).[29]

Paul had come to Troas during his second missionary journey (Acts 16:8). Here he received a vision of a Macedonian man who pleaded with him to come over to Macedonia to help the people there. Paul founded no church in Troas but sailed across the northeastern part of the Aegean Sea to Macedonia. There he went to Philippi and Thessalonica and established churches (Acts 16 and 17). On his third missionary journey, Paul preached in Troas, where the people were receptive to the gospel and formed a sizeable congregation. We assume that during Paul's

---

29. Refer to F. F. Bruce, *The Acts of the Apostles: Greek Text with Introduction and Commentary*, 3d rev. and enlarged ed. (Grand Rapids: Eerdmans, 1990), p. 357.

three-year residence in the province of Asia the Good News had spread from Ephesus to Troas. About a year later, Paul spent an entire week with the Christians in Troas (Acts 20:6). And near the end of his life, he instructed Timothy to bring him the cloak that he had left in the home of Carpus at Troas (II Tim. 4:13).

b. "For the gospel of Christ." Throughout his epistles, Paul repeatedly mentions the gospel of either Christ or God.[30] Verse 12 indicates that Paul went to Troas with the express purpose of preaching Christ's gospel. When he qualifies the term *gospel* with the phrase *of Christ,* Paul has in mind both the content of the gospel and the act of proclaiming it. As he proclaimed the gospel, it became relevant to the people and led them to salvation in Jesus Christ. Grammatically, the phrase *of Christ* has the genitive case that is both objective and subjective.[31] Paul preached the gospel to make Christ known objectively and to make known the gospel that belongs to Christ subjectively. In Troas he had a receptive audience, and the Lord blessed his preaching ministry.

c. "And although a door was opened to me in the Lord." The verbal imagery in this clause appears frequently in the Scriptures (Acts 14:27; I Cor. 16:9; Col. 4:3; Rev. 3:8). The image of an open door must be understood not literally, as if to stress that Paul occupied living quarters in Troas, but figuratively in the sense of opportunities. Indeed, the passive perfect tense of the form *was opened* shows that, first, God is the agent who unlocked the door; next, the action itself happened in the past; and last, the action has relevance for the present and the future. The tense, then, implies that the gospel had already come to Troas and that Paul now reinforced and expanded its influence. God opened the door to furthering the cause of Christ by having Paul evangelize the local inhabitants and strengthen the believers there.

The last part of the clause can be understood as either "in the Lord" or "by the Lord." I prefer the first reading because in his epistles Paul regularly uses the phrase *in the Lord.*[32] He intimates that the effort to evangelize the people can succeed only when the Lord blesses it. Preachers preach and listeners listen, but the effect of the spoken Word depends on the Holy Spirit to lead people into the sphere of the Lord through conversion and faith.

d. "I had no relief in my soul because I did not find Titus my brother." Paul concedes that the Lord blessed his evangelistic efforts in Troas by giving him the satisfaction of seeing tangible results: people opening their hearts to the teachings of the gospel.

The unrest Paul experienced in his soul was the continual concern for the Corinthians from and about whom he had not heard anything at all.[33] Paul min-

---

30. The gospel of Christ: Rom. 15:19; I Cor. 9:12; II Cor. 2:12; 9:13; 10:14; Gal. 1:7; Phil. 1:27; I Thess. 3:2, II Thess. 1:8. The gospel of God: Rom. 1:1; 15:16; II Cor. 11:7; I Thess. 2:2, 8–9.

31. Ulrich Becker, *NIDNTT,* 2:111; Gerhard Friedrich, *TDNT,* 2:731.

32. E.g., Rom. 16:2, 8, 11–13, 22; I Cor. 4:17.

33. Consult Scott J. Hafemann, "The Comfort and Power of the Gospel: The Argument of II Corinthians 1–3," *RevExp* 86 (1989): 333.

istered not only to one particular congregation but to all the churches he had founded (see I Cor. 4:17; 7:17; 14:33; II Cor. 11:28). He had a special interest in the Corinthian church, which he had established and pastored.

Paul knew that Titus was the right man for settling problems in the church, but the lack of information about the spiritual conditions in Corinth increased Paul's anxiety. Further, Paul and Titus had agreed to meet each other in Troas on a certain date. When the time had expired and Paul had duly exercised a measure of patience, he had to make a decision: stay in Troas and continue preaching the gospel or travel to Macedonia in search of Titus. (In passing, notice that Paul calls Titus his brother.[34] This identification refers not to a biological brother but rather to his fellow worker in the cause of Christ.)

e. "However, when I had said good-by to them, I went to Macedonia." If Paul went from one place to another in search of Titus, he might miss Titus altogether. He had no peace of mind, and this uncertainty forced Paul to take leave of the believers in Troas and travel to Macedonia. Paul's wording is repeated almost verbatim in 7:5.[35] Note the parallel:

2:12, 13	*7:5*
When I come to Troas	When we came into Macedonia
I had no relief	our bodies
in my soul	had no relief

Sailing stopped during the winter months, so that travelers had to go on foot from place to place. The time-consuming journey over the land route from Troas to Macedonia may have caused the break (2:14–7:4) in Paul's narrative.[36] Nevertheless, the text provides no evidence on the route Paul traveled.

Earlier Paul had promised the Corinthians that he would travel to Corinth via Macedonia (I Cor. 16:5), but he changed his plans when he paid them a painful visit (II Cor. 2:1). The time had come to fulfill his previous intention to visit the Macedonian churches and eventually to spend sufficient time with the Corinthians.

Practical Considerations in 2:12–13

When a pastor receives a call from a congregation, how does he know whether to stay in his present charge or to move to a new field of labor? He is told to seek the will of God

---

34. References to Titus are 2:13; 7:6, 13–14; 8:6, 23; 12:18; Gal. 2:1, 3; II Tim. 4:10; Titus 1:4. Borse ("Tränenbrief," p. 196) advances the hypothesis that Paul uses the name *Titus* as a diminutive form of Timothy, so that in this epistle he thinks of only one person: Timothy. The question is whether this hypothesis is necessary at all.

35. For the hypothesis that 2:14–7:4 is a separate unit, an interpolation, see the discussion in the Introduction.

36. Refer to C. K. Barrett, "Titus," in *Neotestamentica et Semitica: Studies in Honour of Matthew Black*, ed. E. Earle Ellis and Max Wilcox (Edinburgh: Clark, 1969), pp. 8–9; also in *Essays on Paul* (Philadelphia: Westminster, 1982).

with respect to the call he has received. The question remains, however, how does he know the will of God? One answer to this query is the evidence of an open door to the preaching of the gospel (2:12). When the Lord blesses the pastor with numerous opportunities to present Christ and gives him great satisfaction in his work, the pastor knows that he is obedient to the will of God.

But the matter is not that simple, particularly when the pastor has received a call to do mission work abroad or church planting at home. Should he stay in his present charge where the Lord has shown his favor or move to other fields? Which area has priority? The pastorate, missions, or evangelism? The church in Antioch had the services of five eminent leaders, among them Barnabas and Paul (Acts 13:1). Yet the Holy Spirit instructed the Antiochean church to send these two leaders to do mission work abroad. When Paul and Barnabas returned to the church at Antioch at the conclusion of their first missionary journey, they reported "all that God had done through them and how he had opened the door of faith to the Gentiles" (Acts 14:27).

When the Lord calls a pastor, a missionary, or an evangelist, as a rule he clearly reveals where the laborer has to work in his church. Furthermore, the Lord also gives peace of mind and inner assurance to his servants. In the words of Jesus, "As the Father has sent me, I am sending you" (John 20:21). Jesus is the sender and the worker is the one who is sent forth with God's grace, peace, and love with the assurance of the Holy Spirit.

Greek Words, Phrases, and Constructions in 2:12–13

The definitive article before the word *Troas* suggests that Paul and Titus had agreed to meet there.

εἰς—the second use of this preposition in verse 12 states the purpose for Paul's arrival in Troas: to preach the gospel.

ἀνεῳγμένης—the perfect passive participle of the verb ἀνοίγω (I open) gives the tense as lasting effect and duration, the passive in which God is the agent, the participle denoting concession, and the case as genitive absolute.

ἔσχηκα—the perfect tense in Greek is translated as a past tense in English: "I had [no rest]."

τῷ μὴ εὑρεῖν—the dative with the aorist infinitive signifies a causal sense: "because I did not find [him]."[37]

---

14 But thanks be to God, who in Christ always leads us in triumphal procession and through us God makes known the fragrance of the knowledge of himself everywhere. 15 Because we are the aroma of Christ to God among those who are being saved and among those who are perishing. 16 We are to the latter a smell of death to death and to the former an aroma of life to life. And who is competent for these things? 17 For we are not, unlike many, peddling the word of God; however, we speak it before God in Christ as men of sincerity, as men [sent] from God.

---

2. Christ's Message
2:14–17

With a lengthy digression (2:14–7:4), Paul suddenly interrupts his narrative on waiting anxiously for Titus; he continues the account in 7:5. A few observa-

---

37. Moule, *Idiom-Book*, p. 44.

tions are helpful in understanding Paul's digression. In his epistles, Paul readily switches from one topic to another, especially when an important thought comes to his mind (e.g., I Cor. 9, which is an interlude between chapters 8 and 10). Next, thinking of the Macedonian churches in Philippi and Thessalonica, Paul was filled with gratitude to God. He expresses this thankfulness in 2:14–7:4.[38] Third, traveling from Troas to Macedonia, Paul realized that God continued to bless despite Paul's departing from the "open door" in Troas. Hence, verses 13 and 14 display a deliberate contrast between a negative tone of suspense and a positive tone of thanksgiving.[39] With these considerations, we begin to understand what caused Paul to interrupt the flow of his narrative from chapters 2 through 6. (See the Introduction for a full discussion on the unity of the epistle.)

14. But thanks be to God, who in Christ always leads us in triumphal procession and through us God makes known the fragrance of the knowledge of himself everywhere.

a. "But thanks be to God." The tone of Paul's discussion changes when he expresses his thanks to God. He turns from a depressing narrative to a cheerful hymn of praise. Especially in this epistle, but also in Romans and I Corinthians, Paul often breaks forth in gratitude to God. He frequently contrasts words of praise with the immediately preceding context.[40] The emphasis is on Paul giving personal thanks to God for making him joyful and happy.

b. "Who in Christ always leads us in triumphal procession." The scene Paul portrays with this imagery is that of a victorious Roman general who leads his armies in a triumphal parade into the capital of the empire. The general parades the prisoners of war through the streets and exhibits them to all the spectators, while the sweet fragrance of burning spices fills the air. At the conclusion of the procession, these captives usually are executed as a tribute to the conqueror. For the victors, the fragrance is sweet; for the captives, the fragrance is the smell of death.

How does this imagery apply to Paul himself? And how are we to interpret the clause "Christ always leads us in triumphal procession"? Scholars propose a number of views:

First, many commentators have been unable to accept the picture of Paul being led to his death in God's victory parade. They think that the apostle himself should be celebrating the victory; and they say that portraying Paul as a defeated enemy of Christ is incongruous with the context. Why should a prisoner of war who is about to be executed express exuberant thanks to God? Hence, Paul should be depicted as a triumphant partner in Christ's procession.

---

38. See Jerome Murphy-O'Connor, "Paul and Macedonia: The Connection between II Corinthians 2.13 and 2.14," *JSNT* 25 (1985): 99–103; Margaret E. Thrall, "A Second Thanksgiving Period in II Corinthians," *JSNT* 16 (1982): 101–24.

39. Consult Andrew Perriman, "Between Troas and Macedonia: II Cor. 2:13–14," *ExpT* 101 (1989): 39–41. See also Jean Héring, *The Second Epistle of Saint Paul to the Corinthians*, trans. A. W. Heathcote and P. J. Allcock (London: Epworth, 1967), p. 18.

40. Rom. 6:17; 7:25; I Cor. 15:57; II Cor. 2:14; 8:16; 9:15.

Next, some writers are of the opinion that the Greek verb *thriambeuein* (to lead in triumph) should not be taken literally (as in Col. 2:15) but should be given a causative sense: "to cause to triumph." For instance, Calvin writes, "Paul means that he had a share in the triumph that God was celebrating."[41]

For a similar view, some commentators supply the word *soldier* as a predicate of the verb *thriambeuein* (to be a soldier in the triumphal procession). Hence, Paul depicts himself as a soldier who marches in a victory parade.[42] But support from Greek literature is lacking for this interpretation.

Third, still another suggestion is to translate the Greek verb *thriambeuein* as "making a spectacle [of us]." This reading appears in a number of ancient translations of the Greek text, including the Coptic and the Syriac, and has merit.[43]

Last, Greek literature in New Testament times lacks examples that present a figurative use of the verb in question. On the basis of Greek and Latin usage in Paul's time, the verb *to lead in triumph* should be taken literally. It refers to "the triumphal procession in which the conquered enemies were usually led as slaves to death, being spared this death only by an act of grace on the part of the one celebrating the triumph."[44] The context of the verse itself forces us to look closely at the wording: "[God] in Christ always leads us in triumphal procession." God is the subject and Paul is the object of the verb *to lead*. The verb is in the present tense and denotes not single but continued action. Moreover, the verb is strengthened by the adverb *always*. And last, the phrase *in Christ* qualifies the object *us*. God is the victor who continuously leads Paul as a captive, a prisoner "in Christ," to his death.

Taking verse 14a literally, we interpret it to mean that God leads Paul as a captive in Christ and uses him as his servant.[45] Paul's suffering as Christ's servant is a major theme in the Corinthian epistles (I Cor. 4:8–13; II Cor. 1:5–10; 2:14–16b; 4:7–12; 6:4–10; 11:23–28). The imagery that Paul conveys is that of a suffering slave who faces death. Nonetheless, in Christ Paul constantly preached and taught God's revelation. Paul's lot of being led to death is inseparably linked to his call to preach God's Word as the source of life. In the context of suffering,

---

41. Calvin, *II Corinthians*, p. 33. Compare also, "[God] makes us, in Christ, partners of his triumph" (JB). Another translation inserts the words *with him* in the clause "[God] always leads us in triumph with him in Christ" (Bauer, p. 363). And see Hans Lietzmann, *An die Korinther I/II*, augmented by Werner G. Kümmel, Handbuch zum Neuen Testament 9 (Tübingen: Mohr, 1969), p. 198.

42. Consult Barrett, *Second Corinthians*, p. 98; Paul B. Duff, "Metaphor, Motif, and Meaning: The Rhetorical Strategy behind the Image 'Led in Triumph' in II Corinthians 2:14," *CBQ* 53 (1991): 79–92.

43. Rory B. Egan, "Lexical Evidence on Two Pauline Passages," *NovT* 19 (1977): 34–62.

44. Scott J. Hafemann, *Suffering and the Spirit: An Exegetical Study of II Cor. 2:14–3:3 within the Context of the Corinthian Correspondence*, WUzNT 2.19 (Tübingen: Mohr, 1986), p. 36.

45. See Grosheide, *Tweede Brief aan Korinthe*, p. 95; Lamar Williamson, Jr., "Led in Triumph, Paul's Use of Thriambeuō," *Interp* 22 (1968): 317–32; Peter Marshall, "A Metaphor of Social Shame: *thriambeuein* in II Cor. 2:14," *NovT* 25 (1983): 302–17.

Paul's preaching is God's celebration of triumph. "God, the victorious general, always celebrates his victory over Paul. He conquered Paul and now Paul spreads his fame."[46]

c. "Through us God makes known the fragrance of the knowledge of himself everywhere." Here Paul uses still more imagery taken from his environment. Roman victory parades were both political and religious, for the conquering general would lead his captives to the temple of Jupiter where sacrifices were offered. "In no other Roman ceremony do god and man approach each other as closely as they do in the triumph."[47] Paul describes the odor of these sacrificial offerings with the words *fragrance* and *aroma* (v. 15). These two synonyms in the Old Testament characterize the sacrifices offered to God. Paul uses metaphors that depict preaching Christ's gospel as the fragrance of the knowledge about God and the aroma of Christ. But he credits God for using him as an instrument to spread the fragrance of Christ's good news everywhere.[48]

Knowledge of God is not merely an intellectual awareness of a divine being. It includes serving God obediently and loving him with heart, soul, and mind. The application of true knowledge emits a fragrance that people cannot help but notice. Wherever God's servants proclaim the gospel, its sweet-smelling savor becomes evident. Believers are God's agents to reach people everywhere with the gospel of salvation. Thus, Paul's work as Christ's apostle is on display as he marches in God's victory parade.

15. Because we are the aroma of Christ to God among those who are being saved and among those who are perishing.

a. "Because we are the aroma of Christ to God." The word *because* introduces an explanation: "We are the aroma that belongs to Christ." That is, Paul and his fellow workers are the agents who spread the fragrant odor that emanates from Christ. The terms *fragrance* (v. 14) and *aroma* (v. 15) are synonyms and occur together in a number of passages in the Greek text of both the Septuagint and the New Testament.[49] As technical terms, these terms were well established in New Testament times and appear in the context of offerings and sacrifices. For Paul, the aroma of Christ is a sacrifice that is pleasing to God. In passing, I refer to the Martyrdom of Polycarp (15.2) that describes the burning of Polycarp at the stake. This burning emitted a fragrant smell as if it were the odor of frankincense or other precious spices.

C. K. Barrett introduces the word *sacrifice* into the translation of this verse and reads, "We are the sweet savour of sacrifice that rises from Christ to God."[50] Paul,

---

46. Cilliers Breytenbach, "Paul's Proclamation and God's 'thriambos' (Notes on II Corinthians 2:14–16b)," *Neotest* 24 (1990): 269.

47. Hendrik Simon Versnel, *Triumphus: An Inquiry into the Origin, Development and Meaning of the Roman Triumph* (Leiden: Brill, 1970), p. 1.

48. Compare Hafemann, *Suffering and the Spirit*, p. 45.

49. Gen. 8:21; Exod. 29:18; Ezek. 20:41; Eph. 5:2; Phil. 4:18.

50. Barrett, *Second Corinthians*, p. 99. Refer to SB 3:497. Both Plummer and Furnish, in their respective commentaries, disagree with Barrett's interpretation.

then portrays himself and his associates as the fragrance that issues from Christ's sacrifice and ascends to honor God. Notice that in this passage (vv. 14–15a), the apostle thanks God, depicts him as the victor, and honors him for Christ's unique sacrifice.

b. "Among those who are being saved and among those who are perishing." The imagery of the victorious Roman general should not be forgotten. During this procession, religious decorum demanded the burning of spices, and their fragrance filled the air. The triumphant armies would celebrate their victories, while the captives would face execution.

Similarly, the aroma of the gospel penetrates everywhere so that both those people who are being saved and those who are perishing take notice. Preachers of the good news present to everyone Jesus Christ as the savior of the world. Their heart is filled with the knowledge of Christ so that from their mouth and by their conduct all people hear and observe Jesus.

The victorious general would determine who of the captives would be spared and who would be executed. We should not press the imagery beyond its limits; the text itself speaks of the aroma of Christ that extends to both those who are saved and those who are lost. It is this aroma that gives either life or death to those who come in contact with it. Writes Calvin, "The Gospel is preached unto salvation, for that is its real purpose, but only believers share in this salvation; for unbelievers it is an occasion of condemnation, but it is they who make it so."[51] The heralds who proclaim God's Word meet acceptance and rejection. God takes no pleasure in the death of the unbeliever, as is evident from both Old and New Testaments. In fact, God pleads with the wicked to repent and believe (see Ezek. 18:32; 33:11; and see II Peter 3:9). The responsibility for accepting or rejecting the pleasant aroma of the gospel is that of the individual, who chooses either life or death.

Paul writes the present tense for the two verbs *to save* and *to perish*. The present tense shows that the people who obediently listen to the proclamation of the Scriptures are in the process of being saved (I Cor. 1:18; II Thess. 2:10; compare II Cor. 4:3). Those who refuse to obey God's word are in the process of being lost—they perish by their own volition.

16. We are to the latter a smell of death to death and to the former an aroma of life to life. And who is competent for these things?

Because the Greek text has no verbs, for this passage we must supply forms of the verb *to be* ("we are" and "is"). In his own words, Paul and his co-workers are the aroma of Christ as they proclaim the gospel. But when they proclaim it, they see that the gospel divides mankind into two groups. Some people hear the spoken words, refuse to accept them, and turn away from the source of life. They perish because the gospel is for them a smell of death that leads to death.

This passage presents in inverted sequence two categories, "the ones being saved" and "the ones who are perishing," that are mentioned in the preceding

---

51. Calvin, *II Corinthians*, p. 35.

verse (v. 15). The inverted order stresses the concept *aroma,* which can be either good or bad.[52] Paul begins with the bad by pointing out that the smell which a corpse emits is death. When people reject the Word of God, they constantly smell this foul odor.

Others listen to God's voice and respond in faith. For them, the aroma of the gospel is a fragrance that emerges from life and produces life. As in the spring of the year nature bursts forth with new life, so the smell of newness is everywhere. By preaching the good news, Paul and his associates bring life to those who believe so that together they rejoice in the word of life.

The phrases *of death to death* and *of life to life* probably are idiomatic expressions that signify "death from beginning to end" and "life from beginning to end."[53] A similar example is recorded in Romans 1:17, where in some translations the wording "from faith to faith" reads "faith from first to last" (NIV; compare REB). Christ's gospel offers life to everyone who believes, but God's wrath rests on those who reject the message of salvation (John 3:36). Jewish rabbis saw the Law of God as medicine that gives either life to the believer or death to the unbeliever.[54]

This verse shows a transition from its first to its second part: Paul moves from a declaratory sentence (v. 16a) to an interrogative statement (v. 16b): "And who is competent for these things?" He questions his own worthiness and competence for this task. In a subsequent passage (3:4–6), he answers this question by pointing out that God enables him and others to be ministers of the gospel.

The immediate context shows that Paul places himself over against opponents who peddled the word of God for profit and whose authority and abilities were questionable (v. 17).[55] He himself proclaims the gospel with the authority that Christ has granted to him. By working with his own hands to support himself financially, he proclaims it free of charge (I Cor. 9:18). yet he strongly supports Jesus' command "that those who preach the gospel should receive their living from the gospel" (I Cor. 9:14).

17. For we are not, unlike many, peddling the word of God; however, we speak it before God in Christ as men of sincerity, as men [sent] from God.

Paul reveals that in Corinth and other places, preachers were peddling the gospel as merchandise. With all the problems that the Corinthians faced, they

---

52. Maurice Carrez translates verse 16, "For some (on the way of salvation), it is an aroma of death (of Christ) which leads to the death (of Christ); for others (on the way of perdition), it is an aroma of life (of Christ) which leads to the life (of Christ). And who is equal to such an office?" See his "Odeur de Mort, Odeur de Vie (à propos de 2 Co 2, 16)," *RevHistPhilRel* 64 (1984): 135–42. However, this version is not so much a translation as an interpretation.

53. Refer to Denney, *Second Corinthians,* p. 95.

54. SB 3:498–99; T. W. Manson, "II Cor. 2:14–17: Suggestions towards an Exegesis," in *Studia Paulina,* ed. J. N. Sevenster and W. C. van Unnik (Haarlem: Bohn, 1953), pp. 155–62.

55. Compare Dieter Georgi, *The Opponents of Paul in Second Corinthians* (Philadelphia: Fortress, 1986), p. 231; Thomas E. Provence, "'Who Is Sufficient for These Things?' An Exegesis of II Corinthians ii 15–iii 18," *NovT* 24 (1982): 54–81; Francis T. Fallon, "Self's Sufficiency or God's Sufficiency: II Corinthians 2:16," *HTR* 76 (1983): 369–74.

also had to cope with these peddlers of religion. From the business world, Paul borrowed the word *kapēleuein*, which describes the trade of a retailer or an innkeeper. But this term had gained an unfavorable connotation, namely, that of palming off something as genuine and profiting unfairly. For instance, a huckster might sell diluted wine (Isa. 1:22), pocket the money of unwary customers, and leave. Paul uses the term *huckstering* for those itinerant preachers who sold a watered-down gospel as merchandise, made a profit, and departed. He does not say how many there were, but we suggest that the word *many* indicates they were in other places besides Corinth.

In the second half of this epistle, Paul speaks of false apostles who preached a gospel that differed from the one the genuine apostles proclaimed (11:13). These false prophets were detrimental to the well-being of the Corinthian church, and their activities had to be exposed. Paul refers to both their number and their harmful influence and leaves a comprehensive discussion for the second part of this epistle.

While false teachers were defrauding the Corinthians by selling them a diluted word of God, Paul denounces this practice of distorting God's message and deceiving the people (4:2). The contrast is striking, for Paul and his associates are the men who by God's grace are competent to handle the task of preaching and teaching the Word of God (v. 16b). He writes that they bring the gospel in sincerity as men who can be fully trusted. The word *sincerity* refers to examining something in the light of the sun.[56] The term means that people of moral purity do something with laudable motives.

The structure of the Greek text is much more emphatic than the English can be. The text lists the word *however* twice, once before "men of sincerity" and once before "men [sent] from God." Paul repeats the term to distance himself and his colleagues from those who huckster the gospel. With the phrase *men of sincerity* he alludes to the human factor, and with the words *men [sent] from God* he notes the divine source of the apostle's authority and message. God granted Paul authority to speak and entrusted to him the Word of God. The peddlers, however, lacked both human sincerity and divine authority.

A final observation. Paul preached the gospel in the presence of God. As an apostle of Jesus Christ, he was an ambassador in God's service and could speak only the exact message God had given him. When an ambassador fails to represent his government and speaks his own mind, he is forthwith dismissed. Similarly, Paul was obligated to proclaim the very Word of God in full awareness that he stood in God's presence. Moreover, Paul, an apostle commissioned by Christ, proclaimed the offense of the cross, the resurrection, and the final judgment, and called people to repentance and faith in Christ (see Acts 17:31; 24:25; 26:19–29). Paul presented the whole will of God to both Jews and Gentile (Acts 20:21, 27). The Corinthians, therefore, should have noticed the difference in

---

56. Friedrich Büchsel, *TDNT*, 2:397–98.

gospel proclamation. They should have chosen to side with Paul and his apostolic helpers and not with the opponents.[57]

Practical Considerations in 2:16b

The last sentence in verse 16 is a question that demands an answer: "And who is competent for these things?" The reply appears to be: "No one in his own strength." The first words Paul writes in the Greek are "and these things." They receive emphasis, for they refer to the work of the ministry that is all-encompassing in its demands. A pastor must be ready to preach on Sundays and often during the week. In addition, there are teaching duties, leadership training, counseling sessions, visits to the sick and the elderly, weddings, funerals, youth ministry, promotion of evangelism and missions. The minister should be ready to speak a few appropriate words and to lead in prayer at various occasions in both the church and the community. For the person who devotes full time to the ministry of the Word, the work seems endless. But is there any task on earth that is more glorious and at the same time more laden with responsibility than the ministry of the Word? The answer is no. Paul knew that he could never fulfill his obligations by himself. He realized that God gave him talents, ability, and perseverance. Thus he wrote a fitting exhortation for all who work for the Lord:

> Therefore, my dear brothers, stand firm. Let nothing move you. Always give yourselves fully to work of the Lord, because you know that your labor in the Lord is not in vain. [I Cor. 15:58]

Greek Words, Phrases, and Constructions in 2:14–17

Verse 14

τῷ πάντοτε θριαμβεύοντι—note the present tense that corresponds with the present tense of φανεροῦντι (making known). The adverb strengthens the sense of continued effect.

ἡμᾶς—the plural is used to denote Paul. The use of the plural for the singular is common in this epistle. See the commentary on 1:4.

τῷ Χριστῷ—the definite article balances that of τῷ θεῷ. Note that the latter is at the beginning of the sentence and the former at the end.

Verses 15–16

τῷ θεῷ—With the dative Paul attributes credit to God. When a static verb with the dative as part of the predicate occurs, it ascribes credit (or discredit) to God.[58]

σωζομένοις—the progressive present tense of simultaneous action, "those who are being saved."

57. Georgi, *Opponents of Paul,* pp. 233–34; J.-F. Collange, *Énigmes de la deuxième épître de Paul aux Corinthiens: Étude exégétique de II Cor. 2:14–7:4,* SNTSMS 18 (New York and Cambridge: Cambridge University Press, 1972), p. 37.

58. J. H. Moulton and Nigel A. Turner, *A Grammar of New Testament Greek* (Edinburgh: Clark, 1963), vol. 3, *Syntax,* p. 239.

ἐκ . . . εἰς—note the significance of these two prepositions that denote movement from a source and motion into something—"from beginning to end." Some witnesses lack the preposition ἐκ (twice), but the harder reading with the preposition is preferred.

πρός—together with the adjective ἱκανός (able) it expresses fitness for a given task.

Verse 17

ἐσμεν . . . καπηλεύοντες—the periphrastic construction is equivalent to the present tense and conveys linear action.[59]

πολλοί—the "many" instead of the "rest" (οἱ λοιποί), which is of Western sources, is preferred.[60]

ὡς—second occurrence. The verb *to send* in the passive must be supplied to make the clause complete.

Summary of Chapter 2

Paul continues to explain the reasons for not coming to Corinth: his last visit had been painful, and he prefers that his next visit be joyful. He had written a letter out of much distress and a heavy heart.

Someone who had sinned and caused grief in the community had been punished. Paul now urges the Corinthians to forgive and comfort the sinner and to reinstate him, so that the brother would not be overcome by sorrow and fall prey to Satan. Paul himself has forgiven the man.

Apparently Paul and Titus had arranged to meet in Troas, where Paul arrived to preach the gospel. The Lord provided an open door to the gospel, but Paul had no peace of mind because Titus had not come. Thus Paul said good-by and traveled to Macedonia.

With imagery taken from a victory parade of a conqueror who leads captives in his procession, Paul portrays himself as a captured slave of God. God has conquered the apostle and is pleased with Paul's work of proclaiming the gospel. Paul describes this work as an aroma that is pleasing to those who are being saved and foul to those who are perishing. While others peddle the gospel for profit, Paul and his co-workers proclaim it out of a sincere heart and with the knowledge that God has sent them.

---

59. Moule, *Idiom-Book*, p. 17.
60. Metzger, *Textual Commentary*, p. 508.

3

Apostolic Ministry, *part 3*

(3:1–18)

Outline (continued)

3 1 Are we beginning to commend ourselves again? Or do we need, as some do, letters of recommendation for you or from you? 2 You yourselves are our epistle, written on our hearts, known and read by all men. 3 It is evident that you are a letter from Christ delivered by us, written not with ink but with the Spirit of the living God, not on tablets of stone but on tablets of human hearts.

---

3. Commendation
3:1–3

The difference between Paul's first and second canonical epistles to the Corinthians is that in the second one he has to confront intruders who have come to Corinth with letters of recommendation. By contrast, Paul came to Corinth as an apostle of Christ, but the people knew that he was not a member of the Twelve who followed Jesus. Paul had to defend himself and provide solid evidence that he needed no recommendation. He knew that Jesus had called him to be an apostle to the Gentiles and had blessed his work in Corinth. Hence, Paul's work as an apostle proved the legitimacy of his office. His sufferings for Christ and his being the spiritual father of the Corinthians serve as proof that he is indeed an apostle.[1]

The three verses in this section (vv. 1–3) constitute a bridge between the last section of the preceding chapter (2:14–17) and the rest of chapter 3. Paul's discussion about letters of recommendation fits the culture of his day, in which these letters were common (see Acts 9:2; 18:27; 22:5). Paul himself commended Phoebe to the Romans (Rom. 16:1), Timothy to the Corinthians (I Cor. 16:10–11), and Onesimus to Philemon (Philem. 10–17).

1. Are we beginning to commend ourselves again? Or do we need, as some do, letters of recommendation for you or from you?

a. "Are we beginning to commend ourselves again?" Should the adverb *again* modify the verb *to begin* (see, e.g., KJV, MLB) or the verb *commend?* Translators are divided on this point, yet the second choice is more natural. Why should Paul again begin something when the emphasis is on commending (see 5:12)?

Letters of recommendation generally come from friends of a person who applies for a position.[2] In some cases, such letters diminish or even negate the value

---

1. Scott J. Hafemann, "'Self-Commendation' and Apostolic Legitimacy in II Corinthians: A Pauline Dialectic?" *NTS* 36 (1990): 85; and see his *Suffering and the Spirit: An Exegetical Study of II Cor. 2:14–3:3 Within the Context of the Corinthian Correspondence*, WUzNT 2.19 (Tübingen: Mohr, 1986), p. 221.

2. Armin Kretzer (*EDNT*, 3:308) observes that "this commendation should in reality be issued by the church itself." For examples from the Greek world, see Clinton W. Keyes, "The Greek Letter of Introduction," *AJP* 56 (1935): 28–44.

of the written compliments. When someone commends himself, persons who evaluate this individual usually take a dim view of the matter.

Is Paul now asking the Corinthians whether he should extol himself to them? In the context of this epistle, self-commendation can be either good (4:2; 6:4) or bad (5:12; 10:12). This text indicates that such action is bad. He asks the Corinthians whether he should present another self-commendation. If they say that he should, he would put himself in a bad light with respect to his opponents. When he came to the Corinthians the first time, they considered him their spiritual father (I Cor. 4:15). For Paul, this action was, in a sense, sufficient self-commendation.

However, the religious peddlers (2:17) slandered Paul by questioning his apostolic credibility. He was acquainted with their disparaging questions and remarks and referred to them often (5:12; 10:18; 13:6).[3] Paul had to defend both himself and Christ who had commissioned him. His apostolicity, integrity, letters, words, and conduct were at stake. Meeting the issue head-on, Paul asked the people in Corinth a rhetorical question that they could answer only in the negative.

b. "Or do we need, as some do, letters of recommendation for you or from you?" Paul expects his readers to say no to his query, but the question squarely attacks the false apostles who had come to Corinth with letters of recommendation. They prided themselves on having such letters and berated Paul, behind his back, for lacking them. Elsewhere these people may have been many in number (2:17), but in Corinth there are only some of them.

The impostors entered the church with letters of recommendation that lacked the authority Paul had as an apostle. We can be sure that these letters were not written by the leaders of the church in Jerusalem and did not have the approval of the Twelve. Perhaps a group of Jews in Jerusalem and elsewhere, opposed to Paul's teaching and conduct, produced them (compare Acts 21:20–21). Further, as peddlers of God's word the imposters not only proclaimed a distorted gospel but also verbally attacked Paul. They desired to exert authority over the Christians in Corinth and make them conform to Judaistic practices in Jerusalem.[4]

Now Paul asks the Corinthians to evaluate his work as the missionary apostle who founded the church by preaching the gospel of salvation. As their pastor, Paul had kept a lively interest in the life and conduct of the people. He corresponded with them, counseled them, and even visited them. The question Paul asks is whether he needs a letter of recommendation, for he had never had such a letter when he came to Corinth. Jesus sent him as an apostle to the Gentiles

---

3. Consult Dieter Georgi, *The Opponents of Paul in Second Corinthians* (Philadelphia: Fortress, 1986), p. 243.

4. J. Knox Chamblin, *Paul and the Self: Apostolic Teaching for Personal Wholeness* (Grand Rapids: Baker, 1993), p. 184. Compare Georgi, *Opponents of Paul*, p. 244; Ralph P. Martin, *II Corinthians*, Word Biblical Commentary 40 (Waco: Word, 1986), p. 51.

and that was more than any written document could say. For him to produce a letter would be absurd, unnecessary, and an affront to Jesus Christ.

2. You yourselves are our epistle, written on our hearts, known and read by all men.

a. "You yourselves are our epistle." The age-old proverb, "The proof of the pudding is in the eating," is an apt description of Paul's challenge to the intruders. Let them see what Paul has done in Corinth through the preaching of Christ's gospel. The apostle emphatically directs attention to the Corinthians and says, "You yourselves." They themselves are living proof that Paul is their spiritual father and leader. They are an open book for all to read.

The phrase *our epistle* is graphic and informative. The pronoun refers to the spiritual work Paul and his associates have performed. And the word *epistle* occurs figuratively only in this verse and the next. Paul obviously is playing on this word and indicates that a letter does not have to be a literal document. All his epistles present Christ, and the church itself is no exception.[5] Through Paul, the fledgling church of Corinth had come into being and now proved to be a miracle of a new creation in Christ (5:17).

b. "Written on our hearts." In the Greek text, the verb *to write on* (with the figurative meaning *inscribe* or *engrave*) occurs only here (Luke 10:20 conveys the meaning *record*).[6] It was used widely in the ancient world to express the idea of inscribing something on the heart.[7] Jeremiah voiced the same thought when he recorded the divine prophecy, "I will put my law in their minds and write it on their hearts" (Jer. 31:33b; Heb. 8:10b; compare Isa. 51:7; Rom. 2:15).[8]

Most translators and commentators have the reading *written on our hearts*. The pronoun *our* instead of *your* has excellent Greek manuscript support, which is not true for the variant. Yet, a few translations prefer the reading *your hearts* (NAB, RSV, TNT). Some commentators have adopted the pronoun *your* and argue that in the next verse Paul states: "you demonstrate that you are a letter from Christ" (v. 3). Therefore, the pronoun shows that the saints in Corinth are indeed Paul's letter of recommendation.[9] The stronger reading, however, makes just as much sense as the weaker variant. Paul dearly loved the members of the Corinthian congregation and gave them a prominent place in his heart (6:11–12; 7:3).

If Paul's opponents implicitly demand that he reveal to them a letter of recommendation, he answers them by saying that this letter is written on his heart.

---

5. Karl Heinrich Rengstorf, *TDNT,* 7:1075.

6. Bauer, pp. 213–14.

7. Josephus *Antiquities* 4.210, 213; Gottlob Schrenk, *TDNT,* 1:770.

8. See Joseph A. Grassi, "The Transforming Power of Biblical Heart Imagery," *RevRel* 43 (1984): 714–23.

9. C. K. Barrett, *The Second Epistle to the Corinthians,* Harper's New Testament Commentaries series (New York: Harper and Row, 1973), p. 96 n. 3; Jean Héring, *The Second Epistle of Saint Paul to the Corinthians,* trans. A. W. Heathcote and P. J. Allcock (London: Epworth, 1967), p. 21 n. 3; Rudolf Bultmann, *The Second Letter to the Corinthians,* trans. Roy A. Harrisville (Minneapolis: Augsburg, 1985), p. 71; Martin, *II Corinthians,* p. 44.

The writer of this epistle is Christ, who recommends Paul as his faithful servant. And Paul is the courier of the epistle.[10]

c. "Known and read by all men." Wherever Paul was or went (Judea, Syria, Asia Minor, or Macedonia), he spoke about the virtues of the Corinthian congregation (7:14; 8:24; 9:2). Everyone willing to listen to Paul would learn that Christ through the gospel had effected the miracle of conversion among the Corinthians. As Christ's ambassador, Paul could boast about the work that Christ had done in their midst. Not only the congregation of Corinth, however, but all the churches were always Paul's concern (11:28). He prayed for them night and day, sent his associates to aid them, and at times corresponded with them (compare 9:2). His heart was in his work, so that anyone coming in contact with Paul would hear from him about the churches. Anyone would be able to read him like an open book, or, in this case, an eloquent letter.

In Greek, Paul writes a play on words, probably as an idiom, which in English we are unable to reproduce: *ginōskōenē* (knowing) and *anaginōskōenē* (knowing it again, by reading). Throughout the ancient world, reading aloud occurred both privately (see Acts 8:30) and in public worship services (Col. 4:16; I Thess. 5:27). Paul states that everyone who knows him will be talking about the church in Corinth.

3. It is evident that you are a letter from Christ delivered by us, written not with ink but with the Spirit of the living God, not on tablets of stone but on tablets of human hearts.

a. "It is evident that you are a letter from Christ delivered by us." Paul is not interested in talking about himself, for he does not need a personal letter of recommendation. Instead, he calls attention to the Corinthians by revealing that through the grace of God they are demonstrating their relationship to Christ. God is at work in their lives, and he makes it known that they belong to Christ Jesus. Many translators choose the reading *you show* instead of *it is evident.* The first choice is in the middle, the second in the passive construction. Both translations are equally acceptable, but I prefer the passive construction, which has God as the implied agent. The participle *is evident* appears in the present tense to demonstrate that the activity was continuous.

The imagery has a dual focus. It switches from Paul, whose heart reveals the epistle, to the Corinthians, who are the contents of the epistle. To use different wording: all people could hear Paul speak about the letter, and by observing the Corinthians they could read its message.

Paul repeats and develops the trend of thought recorded in the preceding verse (v. 2a): "You are a letter from Christ." He avers that the Christians in Corinth are a living testimony to the Lord and, thus, a living epistle. He is more specific than he was in his earlier statement, "You are our letter." Now he declares that Christ is the author; that is, not Paul but Christ founded the church

10. William Baird, "Letters of Recommendation: A Study of II Cor 3 1–3," *JBL* 80 (1961): 166–72; Hafemann, *Suffering and the Spirit,* pp. 186–88.

in Corinth. Paul ascribes all the glory and honor to Christ, and considers himself Christ's servant.

To extend the imagery, the courier of this epistle is Paul, who functions as the minister of the Corinthian church. Christ is the author and Paul the letter carrier. But some translators state that Paul is the composer and thus have the reading *drawn up by us* (JB; compare NRSV, *Moffatt*). When Christ is the author, we cannot ascribe authorship to Paul.

We do well to translate the Greek verb *diakoneō*, from which we have the derivatives *diaconate* and *deacon*, as "I deliver [and administer a message]." Here the verb signifies that Paul proclaimed the gospel message in Corinth as Christ's mouthpiece. Paul served the believers by applying the message of salvation, much as the prophets rendered advance service to the Christian community (I Peter 1:12).[11] Ministering this message to the people in Corinth, Paul was an obedient servant of Christ (Acts 18:9–11).

b. "Written not with ink but with the Spirit of the living God." The Greek text shows that the word *written* is in the perfect tense, which points to an action in the past that has consequences for the present. This action took place when Paul first brought the gospel to the Corinthians (Acts 18:1–5).

Although Paul mentions ink but not paper, he is not carelessly expressing himself. He presents the concept of writing a letter but states that the process of writing was not by ordinary means of paper and ink. The letter instead is a spiritual epistle written with the Holy Spirit. Christ is the author of the letter, Spirit is the facilitator of life, and God is the source of life. Human writing can fade and disappear, but divine writing is permanent, alive, and life-giving. The phrase *living God* recurs in both Old and New Testaments and points to God, who gives life.[12]

c. "Not on tablets of stone but on tablets of human hearts." The first contrast of writing materials is that of ink and Spirit; the second is between stone and human hearts. We would have expected Paul to indicate the dissimilarity of paper and hearts, but instead he introduces the word *stone*. He takes the second contrast from the prophecies of Ezekiel (11:19; 36:26), where God removes the people's heart of stone and gives them a new heart of flesh and a new spirit within them.

Further, through Jeremiah God tells the people of Israel that he will put his law within them and write it on their hearts (31:33). As God had written his law on tablets of stone (Exod. 31:18; 32:15; Deut. 9:10–11) in Old Testament times, so he would write his law on the hearts and minds of his New Testament people. Paul contrasts the Old Testament law, which remained external, with the New

---

11. Hermann W. Beyer, *TDNT*, 2:86; Klaus Hess, *NIDNTT*, 3:546; Richard B. Hays, *Echoes of Scripture in the Letters of Paul* (New Haven and London: Yale University Press, 1989), p. 127; Hafemann, *Suffering and the Spirit*, pp. 195–203. Bauer translates *diakoneō* as "care for by us" with the explanation "written or delivered" (p. 184).

12. II Kings 19:4, 16; Isa. 37:4, 17; Dan. 6:20; Hos. 1:10; Matt. 16:16; 26:63; Acts 14:15; Rom. 9:26; II Cor. 3:3; 6:16; I Thess. 1:9; I Tim. 3:15; 4:10; Heb. 3:12; 9:14; 10:31; 12:22; Rev. 7:2.

Testament law, which functions internally. In effect, Paul intimates that the Old Testament covenant has become obsolete and the New Testament covenant, inaugurated by Jesus and the coming of the Holy Spirit, is now operative (compare Heb. 8:13).[13]

Greek Words, Phrases, and Constructions in 3:1–3

Verses 1–2

ἤ—"or." The variant reading adopted in the Majority Text is εἰ (if, whether). Manuscript support is weak for the variant but strong for the preferred reading. The same phenomenon occurs at the conclusion of verse 1, where the Majority Text (with weak support) inserts the additional reading συστατικῶν (recommendations).

ἐγγεγραμμένη—this compound perfect passive participle (also v. 3) conveys an action in the past with enduring results. The compound is intensive and connotes the concept *to engrave*, which is applicable to stone tablets and monuments. God has engraved in his hands the names of his people (Isa. 49:16).

ταῖς καρδίαις—the plural is used to include Paul's fellow workers. Paul represents his associates.[14] For the expression *our hearts*, see 1:22; 4:6.

Verse 3

διακονηθεῖσα—the aorist passive participle shows single action referring to the time when Paul first came to Corinth, identifies the agent as Paul and later his associates, and modifies the word *letter*. The participles in the present tense appear also in 8:19, 20. But the noun διακονία (ministry) occurs twelve times in this epistle, four of which are in chapter 3.[15]

σαρκίναις—the ending of this adjective depicts the essence or substance of flesh (see I Cor. 3:3). Instead of the plural καρδίαις (hearts), Textus Receptus has the singular καρδίας (of the heart, NKJV) with weak textual support. But the more difficult reading is the plural because of its apposition to the dative plural πλαξίν (tablets).

---

4 And we have such confidence through Christ toward God. 5 Not that we are competent of ourselves to consider anything to come as from ourselves, but our competence is from God. 6 And God has enabled us to be servants of a new covenant, not of the letter but of the Spirit. For the letter kills, but the Spirit gives life.

---

13. Herman N. Ridderbos, *Paul: An Outline of His Theology,* trans. John Richard de Witt (Grand Rapids: Eerdmans, 1975), p. 285; Hafemann, *Suffering and the Spirit,* pp. 214–15; Philip Edgcumbe Hughes, *Paul's Second Epistle to the Corinthians: The English Text with Introduction, Exposition and Notes,* New International Commentary on the New Testament series (Grand Rapids: Eerdmans, 1962), p. 30.

14. Consult Linda L. Belleville, "A Letter of Apologetic Self-Commendation: II Cor. 1:8–7:16," *NovT* 31 (1989): 161–62; *Reflections of Glory: Paul's Polemical Use of the Moses-Doxa Tradition in II Corinthians 3.1–18,* JSNTSupS 52 (Sheffield: JSOT, 1991), pp. 133–34.

15. II Cor. 3:7, 8, 9 [twice]; 4:1; 5:18; 6:3; 8:4; 9:1, 12, 13; 11:8. The noun *diakonos* appears four times (II Cor. 3:6; 6:4; 11:15, 23).

4. Confidence
3:4–6

The difference between the new covenant and the old covenant is vividly described in chapter 3. A comparison of these two covenants reveals that the new supersedes the old. I list some elements of these covenants in parallel form:[16]

Old Covenant	*New Covenant*
God writes	Christ writes
the old covenant	the new covenant
on tablets of stone;	on human hearts;
Moses' ministry is of	Paul's ministry is of
transient glory that	surpassing glory that
is veiled;	is revealed;
without the Spirit	the Spirit
the letter kills,	gives life,
is condemnation and	is righteousness and
abolition.	permanence.

The differences become apparent throughout the succeeding verses, but in the following segment Paul mentions his trust and competence that are in and from God respectively.

4. And we have such confidence through Christ toward God. 5. Not that we are competent of ourselves to consider anything to come as from ourselves, but our competence is from God. 6. And God has enabled us to be servants of a new covenant, not of the letter but of the Spirit. For the letter kills, but the Spirit gives life.

a. "And we have such confidence through Christ toward God." The key word in this sentence is "confidence," which seems to lack coherence with the preceding paragraph but has affinity with 2:17. If we label verses 1–3 a parenthetical comment, as some scholars do, we have to consider the thrust of this paragraph. Even though Paul does not use the word *confidence*, he bases his confidence on the work of Christ and the Spirit of the living God. He realizes that his detractors can readily accuse him of spiritual arrogance when they are asked to consider the results of his ministry. With the term *such*, he calls attention to the quality of his confidence that comes to him through Christ in the presence of God.

In the New Testament, the Greek word *pepoithēsis* (confidence) appears six times; all of them are in Paul's correspondence, four of them in this epistle.[17] Paul uses this word to describe trust in people, trust in one's own strength by observing the law, or trust in Christ through the power of God. Here Paul refers to the confidence in Jesus that he already noted in 1:14–15, where he expressed it

---

16. Compare F. J. Pop, *De Tweede Brief van Paulus aan de Corinthiërs* (Nijkerk: Callenbach, 1980), pp. 68–69; Seyoon Kim, *The Origin of Paul's Gospel* (Tübingen: Mohr; Grand Rapids: Eerdmans, 1982), p. 237.
17. II Cor. 1:15; 3:4; 8:22; 10:2; and see Eph. 3:12; Phil. 3:4.

in terms of "the day of our Lord Jesus." He gives the word a positive connotation by linking it to God's revelatory work in Jesus Christ. Jesus brought Paul to conversion (Acts 9:4–6), called him to be an apostle to the Gentiles (Acts 9:15), repeatedly encouraged him to proclaim the Word (Acts 18:9–10; 22:18, 21; 23:11), and constantly fulfilled his promises to him. Thus Paul fully trusted Jesus because he knew that God is true.

b. "Not that we are competent of ourselves to consider anything to come as from ourselves, but our competence is from God." In this verse (5) Paul answers the question he raised earlier, "And who is competent for these things?" (2:16). When Paul writes about competence, he intimates that this distinction is based on confidence. A person endowed with poise possesses expertise: the word *competence* denotes the capability to perform a task that demands expertise. But Paul writes that his competence is not based on self-assurance, for he knows that his motives are sinful and his desires are tainted by selfishness. In the presence of God's holiness, his sinful human characteristics are worthless. He is unable to rely on his own ability to think out something that originates within himself. He has to turn to God and realize that his ability to preach the gospel, provide leadership, and counsel the people in Corinth originates with God (see Rom. 15:18; Phil. 2:13; 4:13). Paul may have had in mind the Hebrew term *shaddai,* which is used to describe God as the all-sufficient One.[18] He gives God the glory and the honor for granting him the ability to be God's servant.

c. "And God has enabled us to be servants of a new covenant." The words in this verse (6) are filled with meaning and in some instances are open to various interpretations.

First, the concept *competence* is decisive, because this attribute originates with God (2:16; 3:5, 6). In English, translators put the verb *to enable* in the perfect tense to convey both the beginning and the continuation of God's act of granting Paul the competence to be God's servant. The beginning relates to his conversion experience near Damascus (Acts 9, 22, 26) and the continuation alludes to Paul's frequent references to divine aid. For instance, Paul writes, "I can do all things through him who strengthens me" (Phil. 4:13, NRSV). Paul leans not on his own insight and understanding but looks to God for help.

Next, the personal plural pronoun *us* appears a number of times in this epistle and generally refers to Paul himself (see, e.g., 1:8; 2:14; 3:1). Is Paul speaking about himself, does the pronoun include his co-workers in Corinth, is he referring to every member of the Corinthian community who participates in Paul's ministry, or does the pronoun apply to all the apostles?[19] The last choice relates to the apostles who received authority from Christ to extend the church through

---

18. Compare the LXX text of Job 21:15; 31:2; 40:2 (Karl Heinrich Rengstorf, *TDNT*, 3:294 n. 3). However, this Hebrew term can also mean "all-knowing," "all-powerful," and "Almighty." See Christopher J. H. Wright, "God, Names of," *ISBE*, 2:508.

19. Compare Maurice Carrez, "Le 'Nous' en II Corinthiens. Paul parle-t-il au nom de toute la communauté, du groupe apostolique, de l'équipe ministérielle ou en son nom personnel? Contribution à l'étude de l'apostolicité dans II Corinthiens," *NTS* 26 (1980): 474–86.

the preaching of the gospel. Similarly, it applies to every minister who faithfully proclaims the Word of God, edifies the believers, and calls people to faith and repentance in Christ.

Third, Paul calls himself and his fellow workers "servants." The Greek word *diakonoi* is not quite the equivalent of the English term *deacons* (see v. 3). I have chosen the translation *servants;* these workers are servants of the new covenant, that is, the Christian ministry. They proclaim the gospel.

Last, Paul introduces the words *new covenant,* which Jeremiah prophesied (31:31 [38:31, LXX]), Jesus spoke at the institution of the Lord's Supper (Luke 22:20; I Cor. 11:25), and the writer of Hebrews quoted and applied to Christ (9:15). To say that Paul is speaking of the New Testament's formation in its rudimentary form is incorrect.[20] Paul stresses not the canon but the covenant that God has made with his people. And God appointed him to be a servant of this new covenant. As Moses was given the appointment to be the mediator and prophet of the old covenant in Israel (Exod. 24), so Paul has been commissioned to be the mediator and prophet of the new covenant in the Corinthian setting.[21]

Noteworthy is the parallel between Moses and Paul as servants of the old and new covenants respectively. When God called Moses to lead the Israelites out of Egypt, Moses doubted his own ability (Exod. 4:10). And when Paul reflects on his task of preaching the gospel, he questions his own competence (2:16b). Moses relied on God to grant him ability; so did Paul. Another parallel is that of Moses receiving from God the Decalogue written on two tablets of stone (Exod. 24:12; 31:18; 34:29). Paul says that his ministry is written on tablets of human hearts (v. 3).[22] But his ministry surpasses that of Moses, for he is privileged to be the mediator of Christ's new covenant.

The new covenant has come forth out of the old covenant (v. 14), and the adjective *new* indicates that this covenant has a quality that is superior to the old. Jesus inaugurated the new covenant in his blood at the time he instituted the Lord's Supper (Luke 22:20; I Cor. 11:25) and thus fulfilled the prophecy recorded by Jeremiah. More than six hundred years earlier, through Jeremiah, God announced the coming of a new covenant that he would make with Israel (31:31–34). Note that God took the initiative for making both the old and the new covenants: the old at Sinai and the new in Zion. And God made these agreements with his people for their benefit and well-being.

The benefits of the old covenant were God's daily provisions of food and water, protection from sickness, fertility and full-term pregnancies, a long life span for every Israelite. God would fight for them by driving the nations out of the

---

20. Contra Jean Carmignac, "II Corinthiens III. 6,14 et le Début de la Formulation du Nouveau Testament," *NTS* 24 (1978): 384–86.

21. See William L. Lane, "Covenant: The Key to Paul's Conflict with Corinth," *TynB* 33 (1982): 8.

22. Scott J. Hafemann, "The Comfort and Power of the Gospel: The Argument of II Corinthians 1–3," *RevExp* 86 (1989): 337–38.

promised land, so that his people could take possession from the Red Sea to the Mediterranean, from the southern border of the desert to the northern part of the Euphrates (Exod. 23:25–31). The people were obliged to obey God by keeping the laws of the Decalogue, those pertaining to protection and responsibility, and those that promoted justice and mercy in social life (Exod. 20–23). In fact, the blessings and the obligations of the old covenant are recorded in these four chapters.[23]

The new covenant is superior to and differs from the old in respect to the place of God's law, promise, knowledge, and remission of sin. In the new covenant, the laws of God are written not on stone or paper but on human hearts and minds. They are part of the people's inner being. God fulfills his promise by proving that he is their God and they are his people. Also, God's revelation becomes so universally known that it covers the earth "as the waters cover the sea" (Isa. 11:9; Hab. 2:14). Throughout the world all classes of people know the Lord. And last, God forgives sin and remembers it no more (Jer. 31:31–34; Heb. 8:10–12). He grants complete remission through his Son Jesus Christ, who shed his blood on Calvary's cross. "Without the shedding of blood there is no forgiveness" (Heb. 9:22b).

d. "Not of the letter but of the Spirit. For the letter kills, but the Spirit gives life." The last part of verse 6 has caused ample debate in scholarly and ministerial circles. Thomas E. Provence has categorized three different interpretations and evaluations.

1. The *hermeneutical view* makes a distinction between the text and the Holy Spirit, who inspires the text to give it meaning. The text is subservient to the Spirit.

But this distinction says nothing about the respective functions Paul ascribes to the letter and the Spirit: to kill and to give life. And Paul says nothing about the manner of interpreting the text. The hermeneutical view, then, is questionable.

2. The *legal view* identifies the "letter" with the "law," so that the law and the Spirit are opposites. In effect, the new covenant abolishes the law.

But elsewhere Paul writes that the law is "holy, righteous and good" and "spiritual" (Rom. 7:12, 14). We are released from the law that was without the Spirit, but we serve God by keeping the law in a new way of the Spirit (Rom. 7:6). From Paul's discussion on the law, we know that he does not view the law and the Spirit as opposites of one another.

3. The *proper interpretation* is to see a person externally observing the letter of the law but internally ignoring it.

---

23. "Since the decalogue is styled 'words' and the social code 'ordinances,' 20:1–17 is thus integral to the covenant, chap. 21–23 are subsidiary and derivative." William J. Dumbrell, "Paul's Use of Exodus 34 in II Corinthians 3," in *God Who Is Rich in Mercy: Essays Presented to Dr. D. B. Knox*, ed. Peter T. O'Brien and David G. Peterson (Homebush West, NSW, Australia: Lancer, 1986), p. 182.

But when the Holy Spirit subdues the heart of an individual, obedience to the law and fulfilling its true intention are evident (see Rom. 2:27–29). Not the letter but the Spirit changes a person's heart. We distinguish between an external conformity to the law (the letter) and an internal obedience, through the Spirit, to fulfill the express purpose of the law: to have life.[24]

The historical setting of the Israelites' disregard for the words of the old covenant gives a clear example that the letter kills. When God at the top of Mount Sinai wrote the Ten Commandments on tablets of stone, the Israelites at the bottom of the mountain fashioned the golden calf. As a consequence of not obeying the conditions of the old covenant, three thousand Israelites died (Exod. 32:28). Conversely, Caleb was blessed with long life and an inheritance in the promised land because he had a different spirit and followed the Lord wholeheartedly (Num. 32:12; 14:24; Josh. 14:9; Deut. 1:36).

Writing on the contrast between the law and the Spirit, Paul says elsewhere, "Through Christ Jesus the law of the Spirit set me free from the law of sin and death" (Rom. 8:2). The law is not set aside, for the Holy Spirit takes that law and empowers it by giving life to all God's covenant people (Ezek. 36:27). The Holy Spirit causes the believer to understand the implications of God's law in the age of the new covenant. And the age of this covenant is the age of the Holy Spirit, who gives life to God's people. Facing the letter of the law without the Holy Spirit, man is subject; but in the presence of the Holy Spirit, man is object.[25] If then the Spirit lives in the hearts of believers, they must place themselves under the authority of God's Word, not as subjects but as objects.

As I conclude this segment, the familiar words of the Nicene Creed come to mind:

> And I believe in the Holy Spirit,
> the Lord and Giver of life.

Greek Words, Phrases, and Constructions in 3:4–6

Verses 4–5

πρός—this preposition conveys the meaning "friendly toward" God.[26] It is synonymous with κατέναντι, "before [God]" (2:17).

οὐχ ὅτι—the verb *to be* must be supplied, so that the text reads, "it is not that" (see 1:24).

---

24. Thomas E. Provence, "'Who Is Sufficient for These Things?' An Exegesis of II Corinthians ii 15–ii 18," *NovT* 24 (1982): 63–66. But Thomas R. Schreiner says that it "is wrong to separate the 'letter' from the O[ld] T[estament] law"; see *The Law and Its Fulfillment: A Pauline Theology of Law* (Grand Rapids: Baker, 1993), p. 129 n. 12. Consult also Stephen Westerholm, "'Letter' and 'Spirit': The Foundation of Pauline Ethics," *NTS* 30 (1984): 229–48.

25. F. W. Grosheide, *De Tweede Brief van den Apostel Paulus aan de Kerk te Korinthe*, Kommentaar op het Nieuwe Testament series (Amsterdam: Van Bottenburg, 1939), p. 116.

26. Bauer, p. 710.

Verse 6

ὃς καί—"yes, he also." Martin H. Scharlemann observes, "In starting a new sentence a relative pronoun may be turned into a personal one."[27]

ἱκάνωσεν—"he enabled." The aorist tense is constative and comprises Paul's entire ministry.

καινῆς διαθήκης—"new covenant." Without definite articles, the term is used in the absolute sense of the word as a technical term. It refers to the celebration of the Lord's Supper. The adjective καινή means something new that comes forth out of the old and surpasses it in quality. The framework of the διαθήκη remains the same, but its substance is superior in every respect.

τὸ γράμμα—the term γραφή signifies the Holy Scripture, but τὸ γράμμα is "the written code" (see Rom. 2:27, 29, NIV).

---

7 Now if the ministry that resulted in death, chiseled in letters on stone, appeared in glory, so that the Israelites were unable to look at Moses' face because of its glory, though this glory was set aside, 8 how much more glorious will be the ministry of the Spirit? 9 If, then, glory was conferred on the ministry of condemnation, how much more abundant will be the ministry of righteousness in respect to glory? 10 For indeed, what once was glorified has not been glorified in this respect because of the glory that surpasses it. 11 For if that which is set aside appeared with glory, how much more that which remains appears in glory.

---

5. Comparison of Glory
3:7–11

Paul avails himself of some of the same vocabulary he used in the preceding verse (v. 6) and once more compares the old covenant with the new. He notes the intensity of Moses' glory, but nevertheless that glory was transient. Then he compares the glory of the two covenants and shows the surpassing splendor of the new.

7. Now if the ministry that resulted in death, chiseled in letters on stone, appeared in glory, so that the Israelites were unable to look intently at Moses' face because of its glory, though this glory was set aside.

a. "Now if the ministry that resulted in death, chiseled in letters on stone, appeared in glory." The first word, "now," as a transitional particle, marks a new paragraph, which begins with a conditional clause. This clause expresses reality that is derived from a passage in the Old Testament Scriptures. Exodus 34:29–35 relates the historical setting of Moses, who descended from Mount Sinai with the second set of tablets on which God had written the Ten Commandments. Note that this passage follows Exodus 32, which depicts the worship of the golden calf, the destruction of the first set of tablets with the Decalogue, God's anger against Israel, and the death of three thousand people.

When Moses came to the Israelites a second time, he carried the two tablets of stone on which God had engraved his law. The presentation of this second set

---

27. Martin H. Scharlemann, "Of Surpassing Splendor: An Exegetical Study of II Corinthians 3:4–18," *ConcJourn* 4 (1978): 116.

of tablets to Moses marks God's willingness to renew his covenant with Israel. By worshiping the golden calf, the people had broken the law that God had given them and abrogated the covenant. When Paul reflected on the effect the covenant had on a disobedient people, he saw the specter of death (Exod. 32:10; Deut. 9:14). Because of their unbelief and disobedience throughout the forty years in the desert, the Israelites were condemned to perish (Num. 14:21–23). Paul calls this "the ministry of condemnation" (v. 9).

The people of Israel assented to the obligations of the old covenant (Exod. 24:3, 7), but they externalized its law, which was engraved on tablets of stone. The second time that Moses came with the tablets of the Decalogue, his face radiated divine glory and proved that he had been in God's presence (Exod. 34:29). The wording of the text does not coincide with that of the Old Testament account. In that passage we read that the face of Moses radiates glory, but here the "ministry of death" is the subject of "appeared in glory." The difference, however, is not great if we see that Paul harks back to the initial proclamation of the Decalogue at Mount Sinai. Being the source of glory, God appeared to the people of Israel in the natural phenomena of thunder, lightning, and smoke (Exod. 20:18). The writer of Sirach mentions the giving of the law to the Israelites and says:

> Their eyes saw his glorious majesty;
> and their ears heard the glory of his voice.
>   [Sir. 17:13, REB]

The divine law emits glory because it is holy, righteous, good, and spiritual (Rom. 7:12, 14). Similarly, the face of Moses, having been in God's presence, reflected divine glory. Indeed, Paul points to aspects of glory that derive from God himself. This does not mean that everything is clear. Not at all. In the next part of this verse and in succeeding verses, one of the key words in the form of either noun or verb is "glory."

b. "So that the Israelites were unable to look intently at Moses' face because of its glory, though this glory was set aside." The reading in Exodus says nothing about the people's inability to look intently at the face of Moses and about glory that was removed. We read that because Moses' face was radiant, the Israelites were afraid to approach him. Moses addressed them and covered his face with a veil only after he ended his message. The Old Testament passage is silent about glory that was ineffective (see Exod. 34:29–35).

If Paul provides details that are not in the text of Exodus 34:29–35, did he rely on a rabbinic midrash (exposition) of this passage? A background study of literary material discloses that in Paul's day many traditions pertaining to this passage were circulating. These traditions throw light on the differences between II Corinthians 3:7–18 and Exodus 34. In fact, Linda L. Belleville suggests that "Paul is interweaving fragments of the latter narrative [Exodus 34] with a number of extra-biblical traditions and his own contributions, rather than making modifications to an already existing midrashic unit."[28] Paul, then, reflects the literary traditions of his day.

The Israelites were unable to stare intently at Moses because of the radiant glory that emanated from his face. (The Greek tense of the verb *atenizein* [to look at intently] conveys the sense of a single action.) The reason for the people's inability even to gaze at Moses' face lies in the sin of idolatry they committed by worshiping the golden calf. Not only then, but throughout the history of Israel, the hearts of the people were hardened (v. 14). Many times God calls the Israelites "a stiff-necked people" (Exod. 32:9; 33:3–5; 34:9).[29]

Paul writes that the glory was set aside. This terse comment does not mean that the radiance in Moses' face gradually faded, for the words of Exodus 34:29–35 contradict this interpretation. Rather, the glory of the old covenant is being set aside because neither the Decalogue chiseled in stone nor Moses' face could achieve perfection.[30] The word *glory* (see vv. 11, 13) must be understood in the setting of the old covenant that already had brought death to the Israelites. The people's hardened hearts caused the glory of the old covenant to vanish. In time, this antiquated covenant disappeared when a better covenant brought lasting glory.[31]

8. How much more glorious will be the ministry of the Spirit?

Paul frequently uses the literary device of comparing the lesser to the greater.[32] Here is the first contrast in a series of three (vv. 8, 9, 11). The dissimilarity is between the old and the new covenants, the ministry of death and that of the Spirit. At first sight, the second part of the comparison seems misplaced, for we would expect the word *life* in contrast to the term *death* in verse 7. But in verse 6, Paul said that the Spirit gives life; now he uses an abbreviated reference. Also, the text is a parallel of 2:16, in which Paul says that the gospel is the smell of death for some and the smell of life for others.

In verses 7 and 8, Paul is asking a rhetorical question that receives an affirmative answer. Yes, the ministry of the Spirit is incomparably greater in degree of glory than that which surrounded the ministry of the old covenant. Paul writes the future tense, "will be," but is not saying that the greater glory will begin at the end of cosmic time. Certainly not. This future tense begins with the ministry of Jesus and continues after the outpouring of the Holy Spirit on Pentecost until the consummation.

---

28. Belleville, *Reflections of Glory,* p. 79. See also William H. Smith, Jr., "The Function of II Corinthians 3:7–4:6 in Its Epistolary Context," Ph.D. diss., Southern Baptist Theological Seminary, 1983, pp. 44–80; SB 3:502–16.

29. Hafemann, "Comfort and Power," p. 339.

30. Grosheide, *Tweede Brief aan Korinthe,* pp. 118–19; Derk W. Oostendorp, *Another Jesus: A Gospel of Jewish-Christian Superiority in II Corinthians* (Kampen: Kok, 1967), p. 39.

31. Compare Ekkehard Stegemann, "Der Neue Bund im Alten. Zum Schriftverständnis des Paulus in II Kor 3," *ThZeit* 42 (1986): 111.

32. E.g., Rom. 5:9, 10, 15, 17; I Cor. 12:22; Phil. 2:12.

What does Paul mean with the phrase "the ministry of the Spirit"? Surely he is not overlooking the presence of the Spirit in the Old Testament era. For instance, God took of the Spirit that rested on Moses and put the Spirit on seventy elders; they began to prophesy, and so did Eldad and Medad. When Moses heard about it, he wished that the Lord would place his Spirit on all the people so that everyone might prophesy (Num. 11:25–29). What Paul has in mind is the Spirit's abiding presence, which began on the day of Pentecost and lasts forever. Paul teaches that the ministry of the Spirit pertains to the gospel with its transforming effect in the lives of God's people. We are transformed into the likeness of Christ who grants us ever greater glory (v. 18).

9. If, then, glory was conferred on the ministry of condemnation, how much more abundant will be the ministry of righteousness in respect to glory?

The Greek word *diakonia,* which I have translated "ministry," occurs twelve times in this epistle, four of them in chapter 3. Paul uses the term more than does any other New Testament writer,[33] and in this context chooses it to designate service. God appoints both people and angels to serve others (Heb. 1:14). So the collection of money by the Gentile churches for the Jerusalem saints was a ministry of love (8:4; 9:1, 12). The expression *ministry,* then, summarizes all the activities of the givers, collectors, carriers, and recipients. Likewise, in this chapter the expression summarizes the entire ministry that pertains to the old covenant, the law, and the priesthood. Paul calls it a ministry that resulted in death (v. 7) and condemnation (v. 9); it exposed sin, and sin in itself leads to death. By comparison, the totality of the ministry that pertains to the new covenant is guided by the Holy Spirit and is filled with life. But in this verse, the dissimilarity is not of death and life but of condemnation and righteousness. These two stand in opposition to one another, for the person who is condemned before God's tribunal faces death and the one who is declared righteous has life. A person who is righteous has the Spirit, for the Spirit brings about a right relationship with God.[34]

This is the second time that Paul writes the "how much more" clause (vv. 8, 9, 11), for once again Paul resorts to the literary device of comparing the lesser with the greater. In three successive verses (vv. 7–8, 9 [v. 10 is its explanation], 11), he introduces the familiar wording: "if then . . . , how much more. . . ." The first contrast is between death and the Spirit (vv. 7–8), the second between sentencing and acquittal (v. 9), and the third between glory that is put aside and glory that endures (v. 11).

The message that Paul conveys in the first clause of verse 9 ("If, then, glory was conferred on the ministry of condemnation") appears to be incongruous. There is no glory in a courtroom when the presiding judge sentences a criminal and pronounces the death penalty. But Paul looks at the totality of "the ministry

---

33. The word appears twenty-two times in Paul's epistles, eight times in Acts, and one time each in Luke, Hebrews, and Revelation.

34. J. D. G. Dunn, *Baptism in the Holy Spirit,* SBT, 2d series 15 (London: SCM, 1970), p. 136.

of condemnation" and sees that the law given by God is glorious and the sentence just (Deut. 27:26).

The ministry of righteousness is the same as the ministry of reconciliation (5:18). God declares a sinner righteous through the redeeming blood of Jesus Christ and at the same time places him or her on the path of sanctification (Rom. 1:17; 3:21–22).

10. For indeed, what once was glorified has not been glorified in this respect because of the glory that surpasses it.

The verse seems to be a paradox that is understandable only to the original readers. To put it anachronistically, Paul probably had written a lengthy footnote to explain this verse, but the notes were lost. If we focus attention on the phrase *in this respect* and link it to the preceding verse (v. 9), we begin to understand Paul's thought. The glory conferred on the ministry of condemnation is nothing compared to the glory of the ministry of righteousness.

"In this respect," Paul continues, "that which has been glorified, namely, the old covenant of the law, has not been glorified to the fullest extent because of the glory of the new covenant of Christ's gospel." The glory of the ministry of God's righteousness far outshines the glory of the ministry that led to condemnation. Certainly, God reserved his surpassing glory for the ministry of the new covenant.[35] "Paul sees the old covenant not as having been *abolished* but as having been *subsumed* or built upon, and that the essence of the Sinai covenant had been retained."[36]

According to Exodus 34:29–35, Moses' face was radiant. In the Greek text of the Old Testament the literal translation is "the color of his face was glorified" (v. 30, and see v. 35). There the perfect tense of the verb *to glorify* appears, and Paul adopts the usage in his discussion of contrast between the old and the new covenants.

The first two words in this verse introduce an explanation of verse 9, which has a characteristic comparison: "how much more." This comparison is explained by the term *hyperballein* (to surpass), which is a Greek word that in participle form appears only in Paul's letters. Paul uses it to describe the concepts *glory* (3:10), *grace* (9:14), *power* (Eph. 1:19), *riches of God's grace* (Eph. 2:7), and *knowledge* (Eph. 3:19). These five concepts derive from God and excel all temporal values.

11. For if that which is set aside appeared with glory, how much more that which remains appears in glory.

In this third contrast, Paul stresses the abiding nature of glory in the ministry of the new covenant. The process of being set aside is compared with that which remains. Paul speaks not of making the glory of Moses' face ineffective but of the ministry in its totality as it pertains to the old covenant.

---

35. Oostendorp, *Another Jesus,* p. 36.
36. Dumbrell, "Paul's Use," p. 187.

The meaning of the Greek verb *katargein* is "to put aside."[37] The verb has a variety of meanings depending on its context, but in the current passage the verb indicates that which is transitory or evanescent. The ministry of the old covenant is put aside in its passing significance. Also, the verb *to put aside* is in the passive voice and has the people as the implied agent. Hence, human beings who are rebellious make the covenant useless. Because of their persistent disobedience, the Israelites made the old covenant ineffective (see Jer. 31:32b; Ezek. 36:16–23) and caused its glory to vanish.

The glory that accompanied the old covenant ministry is nothing in comparison with the glory that is permanent. The previous verse (v. 10) described the surpassing glory of the new covenant, but this verse mentions permanency. In verse 10 Paul spoke of degree; here he notes duration.

Paul reveals himself as a person who has left the framework of the old covenant and has fully embraced the new. He skillfully points out the transitoriness of the old and the lasting significance of the new covenant. As a Jew who became a Christian, he now addresses his fellow countrymen and others. At the same time, he vigorously opposes those Jews who attack him in Corinth and elsewhere. "In this argument the Apostle has chiefly in view the Judaizers who made the Law indispensable and superior to the Gospel."[38]

Greek Words, Phrases, and Constructions in 3:7–11

Verse 7

εἰ—in this verse and in verses 9 and 11, the conditions express fact and reality.

ἐγενήθη—"came into being." C. F. D. Moule calls this aorist "strictly appropriate—of a glory which is *past.*"[39]

τὴν καταργουμένην—the present participle in the passive voice (not the middle) denotes concession: "although it is being set aside." The nearest feminine antecedent is "glory."

Verse 9

τῇ διακονίᾳ—the Majority Text has the nominative case instead of the dative. The manuscript evidence favors the reading of the dative case,[40] while the harder reading is the nominative. The difference in translation is minimal.

δόξῃ—this is the dative of reference: "with respect to glory."

---

37. The verb derives from the word *argos* (idle) and is here in the intensive form: "to render inoperative." It is used in the New Testament twenty-five times by Paul out of a total of twenty-seven. The word also occurs in Luke 13:7 and Hebrews 2:14. Gerhard Delling, *TDNT,* 1:452–54; J. I. Packer, *NIDNTT,* 1:73–74.

38. Alfred Plummer, *A Critical and Exegetical Commentary on the Second Epistle of St. Paul to the Corinthians,* International Critical Commentary (1915; Edinburgh: Clark, 1975), p. 92.

39. C. F. D. Moule, *An Idiom-Book of New Testament Greek,* 2d ed. (Cambridge: Cambridge University Press, 1960), p. 15.

40. Bruce M. Metzger, *A Textual Commentary on the Greek New Testament,* 2d ed. (Stuttgart and New York: United Bible Societies, 1994), p. 509.

Verses 10–11

οὐ δεδόξασται—the perfect tense denotes action in the past with lasting results but now terminated, as the negative particle shows.

τὸ δεδοξασμένον—the neuter perfect passive participle sums up the entire era of the old covenant.

ἐν τούτῳ τῷ μέρει—"in this matter" (see 9:3). This phrase modifies the main verb δεδόξασται, not the succeeding part of the verse.

τὸ καταργούμενον—in the neuter singular, the participle with the definite article forms the totality of the implied object. The compound participle is intensive and derives from the preposition κατά (causative) and the verb ἀργεῖν (to be idle; ἀ and ἔργον, not working). Note also that the participle is in the present tense to indicate continued action. And last, many translators and commentators understand the participle as a middle: "is fading." This translation makes good sense. But so does the passive in all three places (vv. 8, 11, 13).

διὰ δόξης—the preposition with the noun "has the sense of accompaniment."[41]

---

12 Therefore, because we have such hope, we are very bold. 13 And we are not like Moses, who used to put a veil over his face so that the Israelites could not stare at the end of what was set aside. 14 But their minds were hardened. For until this very day, the same veil remains during the reading of the old covenant. It remains covered because only in Christ the veil is removed. 15 Yes, even today, whenever the law of Moses is read, a veil covers their heart. 16 [Scripture says,] "But whenever anyone turns to the Lord, the veil is removed." 17 Now the Lord is the Spirit, and where the Spirit of the Lord is, there is freedom. 18 And all of us with uncovered face are beholding the reflected glory of the Lord and are transformed into the same likeness from one degree of glory to another just as from the Lord, that is, the Spirit.

---

6. Unveiled Faces
3:12–18

The present section is no doubt one of the most difficult to understand in all Paul's epistles. This passage has spawned numerous interpretations and views; consequently, the literature on this particular segment is vast. To offer perspective, I summarize the salient points of this chapter before giving an explanation of the current passage.

Of this chapter's four segments (vv. 1–3, 4–6, 7–11, 12–18), the last one is Paul's application of the Old Testament teaching of God's glory to the New Testament church. Next, in this concluding segment, he explains the work of the Holy Spirit in the lives of God's people. He does so by structuring parallels of the old covenant era and that of the new covenant. He points out this difference by stressing the freedom believers have through the Spirit of the Lord. And last, he begins the chapter with a reference to letters of recommendation (v. 1) and ends the chapter by proving that the glorious message of salvation transforms human lives. That proof validates his apostolicity. God is using him as a minister of the gospel. Therefore, this last segment is a fitting introduction to the next segment (4:1–6), which is part of a discussion that Paul began at 2:14.

---

41. J. H. Moulton and Nigel A. Turner, *A Grammar of New Testament Greek* (Edinburgh: Clark, 1963), vol. 3, *Syntax*, p. 267.

12. Therefore, because we have such hope, we are very bold.
The first word in this verse links the preceding paragraph to the present one.[42] With this word Paul continues his discourse by expanding on the teachings of the previous verses. Now he builds on his earlier teachings (vv. 7–11) in which he began to explain the implications of Moses' veil (Exod. 34:29–35).

The causal connotation of the first clause has its basis in the preceding paragraph. The abiding nature of the new covenant fills Paul and his associates with hope, for they know that nothing will supplant this covenant. Also, their hope is founded on the presence and power of the Holy Spirit (v. 8) and the ministry of righteousness (v. 9).[43] In the New Testament, the word *hope* never conveys a negative but always a positive expectation of that which is good. Here it points to the surpassing glory that accompanies the ministry of the gospel (Col. 1:27).

"We are very bold." This short clause is filled with meaning, for it is a summary of previous statements and an introduction to Paul's remarks about veiled and unveiled faces. The word *bold* may refer to freedom of speech that Paul and his co-workers enjoy. At this point in the text, the Syriac translation literally says, "We behave ourselves with uncovered eye." The phrase *with uncovered eye,* which means "openly," occurs frequently in the Syriac New Testament and has a variant, "with uncovered face [or head]." This variant occurs in verse 18 and thus serves as a synonym of "bold" in verse 12.[44]

The objection is raised that the original readers of Paul's epistle would be unable to understand his bilingual switch from the Syriac to the Greek.[45] If Paul were the first and only writer to introduce the words *with uncovered face [or head],* the objection would be formidable. But first- and second-century literature of Jews, Greeks, Romans, and Christians clearly shows that covering one's face or head was a sign of either shame or reverence (compare I Cor. 11:4, 7). Here the connotation is positive, so that to appear in public with uncovered face or head means to speak reverently and boldly.

Could the Corinthians understand Paul's presentation? Yes, because Paul had been their instructor for eighteen months (Acts 18:11) and they were acquainted with his teaching. Next, numerous bilingual Jewish converts to Christianity lived in Corinth. And last, the custom of covering or uncovering one's face was not limited to a particular culture.[46]

---

42. Unfortunately most translations omit the Greek conjunction οὖν (therefore, then, so). Those that provide a translation are KJV, NKJV, SEB, NIV, NRSV, *Cassirer,* and *Moffatt.*

43. Compare Bultmann, *Second Letter,* p. 84.

44. Consult W. C. van Unnik, "'With Unveiled Face,' an Exegesis of II Corinthians iii 12–18," *NovT* 6 (1963): 161; also published in *Sparsa Collecta, The Collected Essays of W. C. van Unnik,* part 1, NovTSup 29 (Leiden: Brill, 1973), p. 202.

45. Martin, *II Corinthians,* p. 66; see J.-F. Collange, *Énigmes de la deuxième épître de Paul aux Corinthiens: Étude exégétique de II Cor. 2:14–7:4,* SNTSMS 18 (New York and Cambridge: Cambridge University Press, 1972), p. 88.

46. W. C. van Unnik, "The Semitic Background of ΠΑΡΡΗΣΙΑ in the New Testament," in *Sparsa Collecta: The Collected Essays of W. C. van Unnik,* part 2, NovTSup 30 (Leiden: Brill, 1980), pp. 290–306. See Stanley B. Marrow, "*Parrhēsia* and the New Testament," *CBQ* 44 (1982): 431–46.

With the expression *bold* Paul looks ahead to the end of the chapter, where he writes the words *unveiled faces* (v. 18). He bases the use of this term on his interpretation of Exodus 34:29–35 and its application to Christianity. He intimates that his ministry of the Spirit and righteousness (vv. 8 and 9) has an openness toward both God and man.[47] With fellow believers, he possesses a boldness that is expressed while ministering with an unveiled face.

Even though in English we place a period at the conclusion of verse 12, the Greek shows a sentence that continues into the next verse with the conjunction *and*. Paul compares our respectful boldness with the veil Moses placed over his face after he had been in God's presence. But what is the implication of Moses' action?

13. And we are not like Moses, who used to put a veil over his face so that the Israelites could not stare at the end of what was set aside.

a. *Translation.* "And we are not like Moses." Translators add the words *we are* to a terse clause in Greek to construct a smooth sentence in English. The last part of the verse begs the question of what Paul means with "at the end." Some versions add "of glory" and read "at the end of glory that was being set aside" (e.g., NRSV) to transmit the sense of the verse. I am presenting a literal translation of the last part of this verse and will try to set forth its meaning.

b. *Problem.* "Moses, who used to put a veil over his face." Why did Moses cover his face? The Old Testament passage (Exod. 34:33–35) relates that Moses' face was radiant because he had spoken with God. In God's presence Moses would remove the veil, but in the presence of the Israelites he concealed his face. He did so, however, not before but after he had addressed the people: "When Moses finished speaking to them, he put a veil over his face" (v. 33). But Paul says that Moses "put a veil over his face so that the Israelites could not stare at the end of what was set aside." The word *glory* is not in the text, even though many translators supply it (see v. 7).

The problem lies not so much in Moses' veil or his radiant face but in the last part of the verse: "the end of what was set aside." What is the meaning of this enigmatic clause? Scholars interpret the end to mean either goal or termination. Some argue that the word *end* means goal in the sense of "ultimate significance"[48] and refer to Romans 10:4, "Christ is the end of the law." Although the concept *goal* has merit, the last words of the text ("what was set aside") seem to favor the idea of termination. Does termination signify that the fading glory of Moses' face was comparable to a gradually disappearing suntan? Paul does not specifically mention the term *glory* in this verse; instead he writes, "the end of what was set aside." This wording refers to not only the termination of Moses'

---

47. Heinrich Schlier, *TDNT*, 5:883.

48. Héring, *Second Epistle of Paul*, pp. 24–25; Walter C. Kaiser, Jr., *Exodus*, vol. 2 of *The Expositor's Bible Commentary*, 12 vols., ed. Frank E. Gaebelein (Grand Rapids: Zondervan, 1990), p. 487. Paul J. Du Plessis speaks of "summit, full height," *TEΛEIOΣ. The Idea of Perfection in the New Testament* (Kampen: Kok, 1959), p. 138.

ministry but also, eventually, that of the old structure of the covenant itself. In addition, we observe that Paul's wording at this point is rather redundant. The two expressions, "the end" and "what is set aside," support each other to emphasize the same message. And as a last observation we mention that in the Greek New Testament the word *telos* generally signifies termination and not intention or goal.[49]

The context of the passage in Exodus (34:29–35) teaches that the Israelites were unable to look at the glory that beamed from Moses' face because their guilty consciences accused them. They had broken the covenant that God had made with them and that they had ratified (Exod. 24:3–8). Their sin made it impossible for them to look at the glory that represented God himself. The Israelites were afraid that the brilliance that Moses displayed might result in God executing vengeance on them. How could they endure the radiance that emanated from God, whose holiness tolerates no sin? God's full glory would have destroyed the Israelites.[50] They knew that if they would see God, they would die (Gen. 32:30; Exod. 33:20; Judg. 6:22–23; 13:22). But when God spoke to the Israelites either directly from Mount Sinai or indirectly through Moses, he revealed his glory. Hence, God's glory and God's word go together.

Whenever Moses spoke God's word, he did not cover his face. When God's spoken word addressed Moses or through Moses the Israelites, Moses was unveiled so that God's glory might shine forth unhindered. The veil covered Moses' face because of Israel's sin. Instead of repenting, the Israelites asked Moses to cover his face, for they did not want to see the radiance of his face. They chose to continue to live in sin and to harden their hearts. Thus, they themselves were instrumental in setting aside Moses' ministry, God's glory, and the old structure of the covenant.

14. But their minds were hardened. For until this very day, the same veil remains during the reading of the old covenant. It remains covered because only in Christ the veil is removed.

a. "But their minds were hardened." The adversative *but* is strong and decisively points to the reason for asking Moses to cover his face. Moses placed a veil over his face not because the radiance was fading but because Aaron and all the Israelites were afraid to approach him (Exod. 34:30). Their fear arose from guilty consciences. By contrast, a clear conscience exhibits confidence that provides a boldness to enter into God's presence. Paul interprets this fear in terms of the Israelites' refusal to obey God; that is, their minds were hardened by the deceitfulness of sin (Heb. 3:13). They indeed had the gospel preached to them but did not accept it in faith (Heb. 4:2). Their thought patterns had become

---

49. Schreiner, *Law and Its Fulfillment,* p. 133; Belleville, *Reflections,* pp. 201–2. Robert Badenas, however, claims that the term *telos* normally conveys purpose or goal; see *Christ the End of the Law: Romans 10:4 in Pauline Perspective,* JSNTSupS (Sheffield: JSOT, 1985), pp. 38–30, and Hays, *Echoes of Scripture,* p. 137.

50. See Oostendorp, *Another Jesus,* p. 39; Hughes, *Second Epistle to the Corinthians,* p. 108; Scott J. Hafemann, "Corinthians, Letters to the," *DPL,* p. 169, and "Comfort and Power," p. 339.

rigid and their thinking processes were not open to the Word of God. The god of this age blinded their minds so that they could not understand the Scriptures (4:4; compare Mark 3:5; John 12:40; Acts 28:27).[51] The evil one controlled their thinking.

Through grace, God did not withdraw himself from the Israelites but remained faithful to his covenant promises. God continued his presence in the camp of Israel. "The veil of Moses thus becomes a metonomy for the hardness of Israel's hearts under the old covenant."[52] The piece of cloth that covered Moses' face represented the stiff-necked people of Israel.

b. "For until this very day." Paul now applies the passage from Exodus to his own times and people wherever he encounters hardness of heart (Rom. 11:7, 25). Even though God sent forth his Son in all his glory (John 1:14), his own people did not receive their Messiah. As Jesus' messenger, Paul testified to the hardness of heart the Jews displayed. The wording *until this very day* is idiomatic in both Greek and English (see Rom. 11:8).

c. "The same veil remains during the reading of the old covenant." What is the meaning of the first part of this sentence? Is Paul referring to the veil Moses used in the desert? Obviously not. Is it the Jewish tallith (shawl) that Jews wear over their heads and shoulders at the time of morning prayers and readings of the law?[53] Did every Jew in Paul's day cover his head with a shawl at worship? Not so, because Paul earlier wrote that a man who covers his head when he prays or prophesies dishonors his head (I Cor. 11:4).

Paul is saying that when the Jews are reading the words of the old covenant, there is a veil over their hearts. He notes that Moses, who served as mediator between God and man, placed a veil over his face to prevent the people from seeing God's glory. And he remarks that even to his day a veil over the law of Moses prevents the Jews from seeing Christ, who is able to remove this veil. Paul shifts the imagery from Moses as a person to Moses as the personification of the law (see v. 15).[54] He calls attention not to the people who are placing a veil over the reading of the law but to the fact that the veil itself remains.

The veil had the same function in both Moses' and Paul's day, for it blocked the glory of the covenant that God had made with his people. It is a symbol of hardened hearts that refuse to accept and obey God's Word. Although Moses conveyed God's commands to the Israelites, they listened to him but declined to obey the stipulations of the old covenant. When they asked Moses to cover his face, they in fact turned away from God. Similarly, the refusal of the Jews to ap-

---

51. For a thorough discussion on Isaiah 6:9–10, which is quoted in John 12:40–41, see Carol K. Stockhausen, "Moses' Veil and the Glory of the New Testament: The Exegetical and Theological Substructure of II Corinthians 3:1–4:6," Ph.D. diss., Marquette University, 1984, pp. 242–73.
52. Hafemann, "Corinthians," p. 169.
53. See the respective commentaries of Plummer, p. 99, and Adam Clarke, *The Bethany Parallel Commentary on the New Testament*, p. 1062.
54. Hays, *Echoes of Scripture*, p. 145.

propriate God's covenantal promises in faith is a veil that obstructs God's glory when his Word is read. Paul combines both the verb *to harden* and the temporal reference *to this very day* to show their relevance to his own day (see also Rom. 11:7–8).

There are two additional considerations. First, the veil that covers the old covenant is not to be understood literally as some kind of container in which a scroll was kept. Rather, Paul sees a figurative veil that covers the words of the old covenant while they are read in worship services. As these words sound forth at a sabbath worship or elsewhere, the minds of the readers and the hearers are unwilling to understand their true meaning. Metaphorically, a veil of their own making bars them from seeing the truth. Next, should the translation be "old covenant" or "Old Testament"? Translators and interpreters are divided on this point. True, the Old Testament Scriptures (Law, Writings, and Prophets) were read in the synagogues every Sabbath. But at present, Paul is not distinguishing between the Old Testament and New Testament Scriptures. In context, he is discussing the old covenant that was ratified at Sinai.[55] He intimates that his contemporaries fail to see the replacement of the old covenant by the new covenant (Jer. 31:31–34). With his associates, Paul is a minister of the new covenant (v. 6) that Jesus inaugurated at the institution of the Lord's Supper (I Cor. 11:25). Because of his emphasis on the covenant concept, I prefer the translation *old covenant.*

d. "It remains covered because only in Christ the veil is removed." Paul himself had to step out of the old covenant context in which he was raised and educated. He adopted the new covenant structure after his conversion near Damascus, and for him Christ removed the veil by opening his spiritual eyes. In turn, Paul was sent to preach the gospel and to open the eyes of both his Jewish and Gentile contemporaries (Acts 26:17).

The covenant that God made with his people remains basically the same, for the God of Israel is the same God who reveals himself in Jesus. The old covenant differs from the new in respect to God's redemptive acts in Jesus Christ, so that the new covenant is a sequel to the old. Moses as a servant in God's house was the mediator of the first covenant, but Christ as the Son over God's house is the mediator of the better covenant (Heb. 3:1–6; 7:22; 8:6; 9:15).[56]

Only a living relationship with Christ removes the figurative veil that covers the old covenant. That veil is placed aside when the glory of the new covenant illumines the hearts and minds of Christ's people. Rejecting Jesus Christ keeps the veil in place and identifies hardened sinners with recalcitrant Israelites in the desert.

---

55. Carol K. Stockhausen, "Paul the Exegete," *BibToday* 28 (1990): 196–202; P. Grelot, "Note sur II Corinthiens 3.14," *NTS* 33 (1987): 135–44; Victor Paul Furnish, *II Corinthians: Translated with Introduction, Notes and Commentary,* Anchor Bible 32A (Garden City, N.Y.: Doubleday, 1984), pp. 208–9.
56. See Wilber B. Wallis, "The Pauline Conception of the Old Covenant," *Presbyt* 4 (1978): 71–83; Gerd Theissen, *Psychological Aspects of Pauline Theology,* trans. John P. Galvin (Philadelphia: Fortress, 1987), pp. 137–38.

Throughout the centuries, Israel lived in the presence of God's glory associated with the ark of the covenant, first in the tabernacle and later in the temple. Yet this glory was always veiled because of human disobedience with respect to fulfilling God's covenant demands. Israel received the law on stone tablets that were placed inside the ark of the covenant, that is, in the presence of God. Israel regarded these tablets externally relevant but internally ineffective, for the laws were written on stone and not on human hearts and minds. During the Old Testament era, Israel had not yet received the salvation in Christ and the gift of the Holy Spirit. But when in the fullness of time (Gal. 4:4) Jesus came to his own people, the Jews refused to acknowledge him (John 1:11). Also, after the Holy Spirit was poured out, opposition from the Jerusalem hierarchy resulted in the great persecution of the church (Acts 8:1). A veil covered the hearts of the people.

The repetition of words and phrases in verses 14b–16 is significant, for Paul employs parallelism in presenting his case. Indeed, verse 15 repeats the previous verse to emphasize its message. And verse 16 is a quotation (Exod. 34:34) by which Paul affirms his discourse. Here are some of the phrases in parallel columns:

until this very day	even today
same veil remains	the veil covers
the reading of	whenever the law
the old covenant	of Moses is read
in Christ	to the Lord
the veil is removed	the veil is removed

15. Yes, even today, whenever the law of Moses is read, a veil covers their heart.

a. "Yes, even today." Many translations have the adversative *however* as the first word in this sentence. But to maintain the parallelism, the Greek term *alla* can be better understood as the intensive *yes* rather than the adversative *however.*

Paul directs attention to the reality of that day; namely, his countrymen are rejecting Christ. Without Christ, they continue to live in the context of the old covenant. For the sake of emphasis, he alerts his readers to the indisputable fact that even in his own day those Jews who reject Christ are on the same level as the Israelites who hardened their hearts. Thus, he repeats the time reference, "even today."

b. "Whenever the law of Moses is read, a veil covers their heart." Now Paul is more specific than he was in the preceding verse, when he said that the veil covered the "reading of the old covenant"; here a veil covers the "heart of the Jewish people." That is, removing the cover is a matter not merely of the intellect but also of the heart. Paul goes further than saying the minds of the Israelites were hardened; in this parallel he notes that the hearts of the Jews are darkened. The heart is the inner core and fountain of every human being.

"The veil" no longer refers to a piece of material that covered Moses' face, but figuratively describes the hardening of the heart. The veil represents a refusal to accept the fulfillment of God's revelation in Jesus Christ. Using Hebrew parallelism, Paul repeats his thoughts of verse 14a ("But their minds were hardened") and sharpens his focus by referring to hearts that were covered, that is, hardened (see Isa. 6:10). His compatriots have eyes but they refuse to see; ears, but they decline to hear; and they have hearts that are closed. Whenever the Scriptures are read and explained during the synagogue worship services, a veil covers their understanding.[57]

From our point of view, Paul's argumentation does not adhere to principles of logic. In place of the principles to which we are accustomed, his reasoning follows the principle of inference by analogy. In brief, "Paul does not proceed logically."[58] He uses key words including "letter," "heart," "covenant," "veil," "glory," "face," and "Spirit." He moves from one term to another and, in the process, considers a number of nuances. For instance, when Moses puts a veil over his face, the Israelites cannot see him and are oblivious to Moses and the law. When the law is read, the people have a veil over their minds and over their hearts. They are spiritually blind, because they are averse to accepting the full message of the Scriptures.

16. [Scripture says,] "But whenever anyone turns to the Lord, the veil is removed."

This verse is a quotation from the Old Testament passage that Paul has consulted throughout his discourse (Exod. 34:34). He omitted an introductory formula such as "Scripture says." The text in the Old Testament differs so much from Paul's quotation that we must conclude he adapted the wording to suit his argument. We read the passage from Exodus as follows:

> But whenever he entered the LORD's presence to speak with him, he removed the veil until he came out. [34:34]

The Old Testament text has Moses as subject of the sentence, but Paul provides no subject at all for the verb *to turn*. Who is the one who turns to the Lord? Next, the word *LORD* refers to God but the expression *Lord* to Jesus. Third, Paul changed two phrases: instead of "he entered the LORD's presence" he has "he turns to the Lord"; and in place of "he removed the veil" he writes "the veil is removed." Last, the other parts of the Old Testament verse he omits.

Let us take these points sequentially. First, who is the subject of the verb *to turn*? Most translations give an indefinite answer: "a man" (RSV), "he" (NAB, REB), "anyone" (NIV), "one" (NRSV), or "they" (JB, NJB). The last clause of verse 14 refers to the Jews of Paul's day, for a veil covers their heart. This plural would be the expected antecedent were it not for the singular verb in verse 15. Paul frequently switches from the plural to the singular, as is evident in the use of the personal

---

57. See "Exkurs: Der altjüdische Synagogen-gottesdienst," in SB 4.1:153–88. Belleville (*Reflections of Glory*, p. 238) asserts that Paul speaks of two different veils in verses 14b and 15. But I agree with Plummer, p. 101, who sees both an external and an internal aspect of the metaphor. It is an intensification of the figure without presenting a change.

58. Joseph A. Fitzmyer, "Glory Reflected on the Face of Christ (II Cor 3:7–4:6) and a Palestinian Jewish Motif," *ThSt* 42 (1981): 634.

pronouns *we* and *I* throughout this epistle. Here he writes the singular to stress that conversion takes place on an individual basis whether the person is male or female, Jew or Gentile. Hence, the translation *anyone* is preferred.

Next, to whom does Paul refer when he writes the word *Lord?* Addressing his contemporaries, Paul already has noted that the veil can be removed only in Christ (v. 14b). With a parallel statement, he now notes that the person who turns to the Lord experiences the removal of the veil. The Lord is Christ Jesus and not Israel's God, for the person who turns to the Lord is not Moses but Paul's compatriot, as he indicates with three time references: "this very day" (v. 14), "today" (15), and "whenever" (vv. 15–16).[59] Because Paul adapts the Old Testament text to his own argument, he speaks no longer of Moses but of Christ.

Third, another indication that Paul modifies the passage from Exodus is evident in two phrases: instead of "he entered the Lord's presence" Paul writes "he turns to the Lord." He has in mind "the hardened hearts" of his people (v. 14a), for which he uses the wording of Isaiah 6:10 (see Matt. 13:15; Mark 4:12; John 12:40; Acts 28:27). The concluding line in Isaiah 6:10 is "and turn and be healed." From this well-known passage, Paul now borrows the verb *to turn,* which signifies conversion.[60] The veil representing the hardness of heart of Paul's contemporaries is removed whenever they turn to the Lord and convert.

Paul is relying not on the Hebrew text but on that of the Septuagint (Exod. 34:34). From it, he quotes the words *whenever, Lord, remove,* and *veil.* He changes the Greek verb *periaireitai* (he removes) from the past tense to the present and from the middle to the passive. Thus, "Moses removed the veil" becomes "the veil is removed."

Last, because Paul adjusts the Old Testament text to his discourse on the veil, he does not need the extra phrases *to speak with him* and *until he came out.* He has made his point with the direct and indirect support of the Scriptures.

So Paul writes elsewhere, "And if [the Jews] do not persist in unbelief, they will be grafted in, for God is able to graft them in again" (Rom. 11:23). When they accept Christ, the veil that has kept them from seeing him is removed. Then they are saved, when God removes their sin as the result of the new covenant he has made with them (Jer. 31:34; Rom. 11:26–27). The way the Jewish people must travel to God the Father is through Jesus Christ (John 14:6b).

17. Now the Lord is the Spirit, and where the Spirit of the Lord is, there is freedom.

a. "Now the Lord is the Spirit." The clauses are short and the words are uncomplicated, but the meaning of this relatively short verse is profound. Identifying the Lord with the Holy Spirit touches the doctrine of the Trinity. Is Paul referring

---

59. Among others, J. D. G. Dunn asserts that the term *Lord* refers to Yahweh. "II Corinthians III.17—'The Lord Is the Spirit,'" *JTS* 21 (1970): 317.

60. Georg Bertram, *TDNT,* 7:727; Bauer, p. 301; G. Wagner, "Alliance de la lettre, alliance de l'esprit. Essai d'analyse de II Corinthiens 2/14 à 3/18," *ETR* 60 (1985): 64; Stockhausen, "Moses' Veil," pp. 250–55.

to God the Father or to Christ? The answers to this question are numerous and varied. Nearly all the studies on verse 17a can be placed in two categories: those that present God as the Lord, and those that understand Christ to be the Lord.[61] The close link that this verse has with the preceding one (v. 16) and its interpretation determines to a large extent the choice for the exegete. That is, one's interpretation of verse 16 has an unavoidable bearing on verse 17.[62]

If we interpret verse 16 to suggest strictly its Old Testament setting at the time of Moses, the word *Lord* means God. Whenever Moses turned to the Lord God, he removed the veil (Exod. 34:34). One translation explains verse 17 in a paraphrase, "Now the Lord of whom this passage speaks is the Spirit" (REB). God, then, is the Spirit and the word *Lord* in verse 18, as an expansion of verse 16, points to God.[63]

If we take the term *Lord* in verses 16–18 as a reference to Christ (see v. 14), we interpret the passage to mean that Paul was addressing his Jewish contemporaries. As Moses approached God, so the Jew of Paul's day is invited to turn to Christ. If the Jew responds affirmatively to this invitation, the veil that covers his heart is removed. Throughout this passage (vv. 16–18), Paul does not use the word *God* in connection with "the Lord." Next, the purpose of verse 18a appears to focus attention on Christ: "And all of us with uncovered face are reflecting the glory of the Lord" (compare 4:4, 6). It is Paul's intention to point his readers to Jesus Christ. And last, the flow of verses 16–18 calls for the identification of Christ with the Lord.

Let us briefly retrace some of Paul's emphases in chapter 3. One of these is the work of the Holy Spirit. Paul mentioned the life-giving Spirit who works in people's hearts in a ministry of glory that surpassed that of Moses (vv. 3, 6, 8). Next, in a following section he considered the difference between the old and the new covenants. Third, he does so in terms of a veil that either remained or was removed in Christ (vv. 13–15). Whenever Paul's fellow Jews turn to Christ, the veil is lifted and they are able to accept the new covenant. Now Paul has to complete his earlier discussion on the Holy Spirit. He accentuates the nuance of the Spirit who in Christ takes away the veil from the reading of the old covenant.

The Holy Spirit works in the heart of all believers who are in Christ, for only in Christ is the veil removed (v. 14b). Without identifying the Lord and the Spirit, Paul sees the Holy Spirit at work in all the people who are in Christ.[64] The Spirit is breathing life into the words of the new covenant. Without the veil that covered the old covenant, believers meet the Christ of the Scriptures. Paul views the Lord to be the Spirit at work in giving the believers the correct understand-

---

61. For a full summary of views, see Belleville, *Reflections of Glory*, pp. 256–63.

62. Refer to W. S. Vorster, "Eksegese en Toeligting," *Neotest* 3 (1971): 37–44.

63. Dunn, "II Corinthians III.17," pp. 313–18; compare the commentaries of Martin, pp. 70–74; Furnish, pp. 212–16; Kruse, pp. 98–101.

64. Ingo Herman, *Kyrios und Pneuma: Studien zur Christologie der paulinischen Hauptbriefe* (Munich: Kösel, 1961), p. 49.

ing of God's revelation.[65] Through the Word, the Spirit changes a person's heart, fosters life, and leads a believer to freedom in Christ. In slightly different wording Paul utters the same thought at another place:

> Therefore, there is now no condemnation for those who are in Christ Jesus, because through Christ Jesus the law of the Spirit of life set me free from the law of sin and death. [Rom. 8:1–2]

b. "And where the Spirit of the Lord is, there is freedom." With the second clause in verse 17, Paul makes it plain that he does not identify the Lord with the Spirit. This second clause clarifies the first, for the phrases *Spirit of the Lord, of Jesus, of Christ,* and *of Jesus Christ* occur many times in the New Testament.[66] Paul notes a close correlation between Christ and the Holy Spirit when he writes, "where the Spirit of the Lord is, there is freedom."

Some scholars attempt to revise this part of the text, but their emendations are unconvincing. Conjectures are considered viable only when a reading makes no sense at all. This is not the case here. Nevertheless, some scholars wish to change the reading of the text. For example, Jean Héring seeks perfect parallelism and with conjectures contrives the following lines:

> There where the Lord is, is the Spirit.
> There where the Spirit is, is the liberty of the Lord.

He admits that for the reading of the first line, textual support is entirely lacking.[67] Without this evidence, we must reject his emendation. And we question his proposed reading of the second line for its lack of textual witnesses. Early and old Latin versions, Syriac and Coptic translations, and manuscripts of the Western text stress the word *there* in the reading: "However, where the Spirit of the Lord is, *there* is freedom." With respect to Héring's second line, the evidence is wanting. His proposal is speculative, and we do well to stay with the biblical formula *the Spirit of the Lord.*

What is the meaning of "freedom"? The context suggests that Jews bound to the old covenant cannot fully understand God's revelation. The hardness of their heart is a veil that prevents them from understanding the Scriptures. But when they turn to the Lord, the Spirit removes that veil. Through the Spirit of the Lord believers enjoy freedom within the setting of the new covenant, because God has written his law on their hearts and minds (Jer. 31:33). In Christ,

---

65. Grosheide, *Tweede Brief aan Korinthe,* p. 132. Ridderbos (*Paul,* pp. 88, 218) views the relationship of Christ and the Spirit from a redemptive-historical point of view.

66. Luke 4:18 [Isa. 61:1]; Acts 5:9; 8:39; 16:7; Rom. 8:9; II Cor. 3:17, 18; Phil. 1:19; I Peter 1:11. Similarly, the references to the Spirit of God are numerous (Matt. 3:16; 12:28; Rom. 8:9, 14; I Cor. 2:11, 12, 14; 3:16; 6:11; 7:40; II Cor. 3:3; Eph. 4:30; Phil. 3:3; I Peter 4:14; I John 4:2).

67. Héring, *Second Epistle of Paul,* p. 27. By contrast, see David Greenwood, "The Lord Is the Spirit: Some Considerations of II Cor 3:17," *CBQ* 34 (1972): 467–72.

they have been set free from the bondage to the law (Rom. 7:3–6; 8:3; Gal. 5:1), from the enslavement of sin that leads to death (Rom. 6:18–23), and from their old nature (Rom. 6:6; Eph. 4:22; Col. 3:9). Believers are able to lead a joyful life, for the Spirit of God lives within them (I Cor. 3:16).

18. And all of us with uncovered face are beholding the reflected glory of the Lord and are transformed into the same likeness from one degree of glory to another just as from the Lord, that is, the Spirit.

Paul now summarizes the thoughts he has presented in this chapter, especially in the words that he repeats. Note these expressions: "face" (v. 13), "glory" (vv. 7–11), "Lord" (vv. 16–17), and "Spirit" (vv. 3, 6, 8, 17). He also uses the term *uncovered* as an antonym of "veil" (vv. 13–16). And he writes three new terms: "reflect," "likeness," and "transform."

a. "And all of us with uncovered face are beholding the reflected glory of the Lord." Paul begins with an introduction, "and all of us," that includes every one of his readers. He is not merely addressing the Jewish people, for the members of the new covenant are both Jews and Gentiles. For this reason, he is rather emphatic by literally saying "we *all*" to include every believer.[68]

Much has been written about the next few words in this text: "with uncovered face are reflecting the glory of the Lord." The variations in understanding these words are multiple, for every word is meaningful and open to several interpretations.

First, the contrast of Moses' covered face before the Israelites and the Christian's uncovered face before the Lord is evident. In God's presence Moses removed the veil and then before the Israelites reflected God's glory. Looking at Christ, Christians do so without a veil and then reflect the glory of the Lord, as it were, in a mirror.[69] Between Moses in God's presence and the Christians in Christ's presence we see a degree of parallelism. But between the Israelites and the Christians we see contrast. The Israelites would not look at God's glory that Moses' face reflected, for they chose to live in spiritual blindness (v. 14a). A veil covered their hearts as long as they refused to turn to the Lord (v. 15). Christians, however, live in the presence the Lord.[70] Moses was in God's presence for a limited time, but Christians have the promise of the Lord that he is always with them (Matt. 28:20). The veil of Moses represented Israel's hardness of heart; the unveiled faces of Christians portray their confidence (see v. 12), for they have fellowship with the Father and the Son (I John 1:4).

Next, the Greek verb *katoptrizein*, here given as a participle in the present middle or passive, occurs only once in the New Testament. Because of this fact, its

---

68. Belleville asserts that the context (3:2, 12; 5:11) speaks exclusively of Paul and co-workers, who are the true ministers of the new covenant (*Reflections of Glory*, pp. 275–76). But Paul alludes to all the members of the universal church (Kim, *Origin of Paul's Gospel*, p. 231).

69. Morna D. Hooker, "Beyond the Things That Are Written? St Paul's Use of Scripture," *NTS* 27 (1980–81): 301.

70. Refer to Jan Lambrecht, "Transformation in II Cor 3,18," *Bib* 64 (1983): 247.

meaning is debatable. We know that in the active voice it means "to mirror, show in a mirror, reflect." The passive means "to be mirrored" and the middle signifies "to behold something in a mirror." The question is whether this Greek participle should be interpreted as a passive or as a middle. Here are four representative translations:

1. "beholding as in a mirror the glory" (NASB)[71]
2. "beholding the glory of the Lord" (RSV)
3. "reflect the Lord's glory" (NIV)
4. "like mirrors reflecting the glory" (NJB)[72]

Every version has its own strengths and defenders, but the issue is really between the translations *beholding* and *reflecting*. Some translators omit the words *in a mirror,* for they reason that the phrase is implied in the translations *behold* or *reflect.* I have adopted the middle voice in a combination of the second and third readings: "beholding the reflected glory of the Lord." I do so for the following reasons:

1. The active and the middle are often identical in meaning; here the verse can signify "reflect."

2. Some writers in the first few centuries of our era interpreted the verb *katoptrizein* to mean "reflect."[73]

3. Even when we support the reading *beholding,* we must admit that the deeper meaning of this verb is that Christ reflects his glory in our lives. The result is that by our conduct people realize that we are followers of Jesus (compare Acts 4:13).

Third, the three apostles Peter, James, and John saw the glory of the Lord at Jesus' transfiguration (Matt. 17:1–3 and parallels). John writes, "The Word became flesh and made his dwelling among us. We have seen his glory, the glory of the One and Only, who came from the Father, full of grace and truth" (John 1:14). Peter notes, "We were eyewitnesses of his majesty. For he received honor and glory from God the Father when the voice came from the Majestic Glory" (II Peter 1:16–17). Peter urges his readers to follow in Jesus' footsteps (I Peter 2:21b). After having seen Jesus' glory near Damascus (Acts 9:3–9 and parallels), Paul reflected his glory. This reflected glory of the Lord is not something that Christians experience only passively. On the contrary, they reflect Christ's glory as an exercise that is active and coincides with the process of sanctification. Paul, therefore, stresses some well-known Christian virtues as fruit of the Spirit: "love, joy, peace, patience, kindness, goodness, faithfulness, gentleness and self-control" (Gal. 5:22–23).

Last, Moses reflected God's glory after he had been in God's presence. When he spoke to the Israelites and communicated God's message, they saw the radi-

71. Refer to Furnish, *II Corinthians,* p. 214.
72. Compare van Unnik, "With Unveiled Face," p. 167.
73. Belleville, *Reflections of Glory,* p. 280. Compare also van Unnik, "With Unveiled Face," p. 167.

ant reflection of his face (Exod. 34:34–35). Because of their hardened hearts, they asked him to cover his face. Christians, however, are forgiven through Christ's atoning sacrifice. They see and reflect the glory of their Lord with uncovered faces. In light of the second part of the text—"[we] are transformed into the same likeness"—Paul appears to have in mind God's glory revealed in Christ.

b. "And [we] are transformed into the same likeness." This is the main part of the verse that receives special emphasis. The verb is in the present tense and passive in voice, which means that transformation is a process with an implied agent doing this work in us.

The Greek verb *metamorphousthai* (to be transformed) occurs only four times in the New Testament (Matt. 17:2; Mark 9:2; Rom. 12:2; II Cor. 3:18). The first two occurrences are parallels and refer to Jesus' transfiguration in the presence of Moses and Elijah with Peter, John, and James as observers. This was an external visible change in Jesus' appearance. The third and fourth passages (Rom. 12:2; II Cor. 3:18) speak of an internal change that one cannot readily observe. Yet the transformation changes the entire person in heart, soul, and mind. The third occurrence is a positive command of Paul to the Romans to be "transformed by the renewing of your mind." The last use of the word is a descriptive statement in the current text.

What is the meaning of being transformed? How are we transformed? And, who is the agent that transforms us? Jesus, the "firstborn among many brothers" (Rom. 8:29), was glorified on the mountain of transfiguration. By being the forerunner, he assures us that we, too, shall be glorified. Already in this life we are transformed in his image, now in principle, but eventually in full glory. The transformation that occurs in the inner being of a person affects all of his or her thinking, speaking, and acting. The external consequences become immediately apparent and gradually more explicit. (Incidentally, Paul himself is an excellent example of the inner transformation from a fanatical Pharisee into an obedient servant of Christ.) The Spirit leads believers to Christ whose image they reflect, for they are a living letter that everyone can read (v. 2).

We presently see the glory of the Lord and know that we are changed in his likeness through the working of the Holy Spirit.[74] In the consummation, we shall be fully glorified like the Son of God (Rom. 8:30; I Cor. 15:49, 51–52).

c. "Into the same likeness from one degree of glory to another." Paul uses the Greek word *eikōn* (likeness, image) also in 4:4 with reference to Christ. Believers are transformed into the image of Christ, for as Christians they bear Christ's name. They are Jesus' brothers and sisters in the family of God (Heb. 2:11). The term *same likeness* does not convey the idea that all believers are identical in appearance. Rather, all those who are led by the Spirit into joyfully obeying Christ are transformed to bear his image. They are the people who gradually go from one degree of glory to another. Paul modifies an Old Testament concept that

---

74. Consult Johannes Behm, *TDNT*, 4:758–59; Johannes M. Nützel, *EDNT*, 2:415; Jan Lambrecht, "'Tot steeds groter glory' (II Kor. 3, 18)," *Collat* 29 (1983): 131–38.

appears in one of the psalms, "they go from strength to strength till each appears before God in Zion" (Ps. 84:7; LXX, 83:8). Here he applies this concept to believers who in their earthly lives progress on the path of sanctification; ultimately they are translated from earth to heaven, from partial to full glory.

d. "Just as from the Lord, that is, the Spirit." The Greek text has only four words, which are literally translated, "as from Lord Spirit." Interpreting these words is difficult and has led to many variations presented in English translations. One is straightforward: "just as from the Lord, the Spirit" (NASB), but others paraphrase the text and read, "through the power of the Lord who is the Spirit (REB; compare NEB), or "and that fittingly enough, seeing that everything is wrought by the Lord, is wrought by none other than the Spirit" *(Cassirer).* Still others reverse the nouns *Lord* and *Spirit:* "even as by the Spirit of the Lord" (KJV, NKJV).

How do we determine the meaning of these words? The first words in this clause are "just as." Paul is introducing a comparison in the sense of "just as" and "so also." With this implied correlation he wishes to say, "Just as Moses reflected God's glory and was transfigured, so also we are transformed into the Lord's image from glory to glory. As Moses turned to God, so we turn to the Lord and derive our glory from him through the working of the Spirit."[75] We know that Jesus, who changes our lives, is the wellspring of our transformed inner being. This change occurs through the working of the Holy Spirit (see v. 17). "Our whole transformation is the work of the Lord in and by and through the Spirit."[76]

Notice also that the expression *Spirit* is the last word in the verse and thus receives emphasis. Paul's stress on the Holy Spirit, therefore, summarizes all the references to the Spirit in the entire chapter (vv. 3, 6, 8, 17). The Lord Jesus, working through the Holy Spirit, brings to completion the work of salvation in our hearts and lives.

Doctrinal Considerations in 3:18

The first two chapters of Luke's Gospel teach that those people who have something to say that relates to the conception and birth of Jesus are filled with the Holy Spirit. We read that Mary, Elizabeth, Zechariah, and Simeon receive the gift of the Spirit (Luke 1:35, 41, 67; 2:25 respectively). They utter words of prophecy that await fulfillment in Jesus Christ.

The angel Gabriel told Zechariah that John the Baptist would be filled with the Holy Spirit from the time he was born (Luke 1:15). When Jesus was baptized, the Holy Spirit descended upon him in the form of a dove (Luke 3:22). Filled with the Spirit, they proclaimed God's Word and spoke with authority. Although Jesus performed numerous miracles, his work consisted primarily of preaching and teaching the Good News.

---

75. Compare Stockhausen, "Moses' Veil," p. 276; Dunn, "II Corinthians III.17," p. 314.

76. R. C. H. Lenski, *The Interpretation of St. Paul's First and Second Epistle to the Corinthians* (Columbus: Wartburg, 1946), p. 951. C. F. D. Moule understands the text to mean that we experience the Lord as Spirit: "II Cor 3:18b, καθάπερ ἀπὸ κυρίου πνεύματος," in *Neues Testament und Geschichte: Historisches Geschehen und Deutung im Neuen Testament: Oscar Cullmann zum 70. Geburtstag,* ed. Heinrich Baltensweiler and Bo Reicke (Tübingen: Mohr [Siebeck], 1972), p. 237.

On the day of Pentecost, the Holy Spirit fell upon the apostles, who immediately began to speak in the temple area (Acts 2:1–40). Paul, after Jesus called him near Damascus, also was filled with the Holy Spirit and immediately began to preach that Jesus is the Son of God (Acts 9:17, 20). Similarly, Philip and Stephen were guided by the Spirit in their ministry of the Word.

At two successive places (I Cor. 3:16; 6:19), Paul informs believers that they, too, are recipients of the Holy Spirit who dwells within them. And in II Corinthians 3, he stresses the work and influence of the Spirit in the hearts and lives of believers. In fact, this particular chapter has seven references to the Spirit (vv. 3, 6 [twice], 8, 17 [twice], 18) and is the chapter on the Spirit in II Corinthians.

The power of the Holy Spirit accompanies the preaching, hearing, and application of God's Word in the life of every true believer. Filled with the Spirit, preachers speak with authority when they proclaim the message of salvation. Listeners whose hearts the Spirit has touched are spiritually alive and accept that message in faith. And because of the working of the Holy Spirit in their hearts, they reflect the Lord's glory so that everyone can see that they are followers of Jesus.

Greek Words, Phrases, and Constructions in 3:12–18

Verses 12–13

ἔχοντες—this present participle has a causal connotation: "because" or "since."

καὶ οὐ—"we are not."[77] The negative particle negates not the main verb ἐτίθει but the supplied verb *to be*. The subject derives from the preceding verse. The imperfect tense of the main verb denotes habitual practice—"who used to put."

πρὸς τὸ μὴ ἀτενίσαι—this phrase expresses purpose with the verb negated by the particle. The aorist tense conveys single action (see the commentary on v. 7).

Verse 14

ἀλλά—this is a true adversative.

ἐπωρώθη—the ingressive aorist points to the beginning of the act of hardening one's heart.

τὰ νοήματα—notice the plural, which is often translated in the singular as "mind." The expression appears six times in the New Testament; five times are in this epistle (2:11; 3:14; 4:4; 10:5; 11:3) and one time in Philippians 4:7.

μὴ ἀνακαλυπτόμενον—either a nominative absolute or in agreement with the noun κάλυμμα. The second option is correct, because the removal refers to the veil and not the old covenant.[78]

Verses 15–16

ἡνίκα—this particle occurs twice in the New Testament (vv. 15–16). With the subjunctive in both verses, it signifies "whenever, every time that."[79]

---

77. Friedrich Blass and Albert Debrunner, *A Greek Grammar of the New Testament and Other Early Christian Literature,* trans. and rev. Robert Funk (Chicago: University of Chicago Press, 1961), #482.

78. Ibid., #424.

79. Bauer, p. 348. Also see Blass and Debrunner, *Greek Grammar,* #455.1.

τὴν καρδίαν αὐτῶν—"their heart." The Semitic preference for the use of the singular noun is evident. "Something belonging to each person in the group is placed in the singular."[80]

ἐπιστρέψῃ—the subject of the verb (*"anyone* turns") must be supplied from the context.

Verses 17–18

ὁ δὲ κύριος—many scholars are of the opinion that the definite article is anaphoric and refers to the preceding verse with the noun κύριος that lacks the definite article. The anarthrous noun usually refers to the Lord God, they say, and thus the anaphoric use of the definite article in verse 17 almost functions as a demonstrative pronoun: *this* Lord. However, the noun κύριος in the New Testament is often used as a personal name. With the definite article it signifies the Father (II Tim. 1:16, 18), and without the definite article the noun alludes to Christ (Rom. 10:13; I Cor. 4:4; 7:22). "It is very probable that Paul refers to Christ in [verse 17]."[81]

καθάπερ ἀπό—the particle καθάπερ is a combination of κατά (according to), ἅ (which), and the emphatic enclitic -περ. The word implies comparison, which in this verse must be supplied from the context. The preposition ἀπό denotes source.

Summary of Chapter 3

Opponents are pressing Paul to present letters of recommendation to the church of Corinth. He asks whether he needs a letter, because the Corinthians themselves are a living testimony to his ministry. Speaking figuratively, Paul notes that this letter is written not with ink but with the Spirit of the living God on the hearts of the Corinthians.

The apostle states that God has given him and his associates competence in the ministry of the new covenant. He posits the contrast of the letter that kills and the Spirit who gives life. The letters engraved in stone belonged to the ministry of the old covenant. As a minister of this covenant, Moses radiated God's glory. Paul asks whether the ministry of the Spirit is not even more glorious than Moses' ministry. The first ministry brings condemnation but the second righteousness. The ministry of the old covenant passes away and is obsolete, but the ministry of the new covenant is glorious and permanent.

Paul takes a passage from the Old Testament that relates Moses covering his radiant face with a veil at the request of the people of Israel. A veil covering their hearts and minds prevented them from understanding the message of the old covenant. Only when someone turns to the Lord is this veil removed. When the veil is taken away, writes Paul, there is freedom, which the Spirit of the Lord provides. He concludes by saying that all believers reflect the glory of the Lord when they are transformed in his image. They gradually increase in glory, which they derive from the Lord through the work of the Spirit.

---

80. Turner, *Grammar of New Testament Greek*, p. 23.
81. Robert Hanna, *A Grammatical Aid to the Greek New Testament* (Grand Rapids: Baker, 1983), p. 319.

4

Apostolic Ministry, *part 4*

(4:1–18)

Outline (continued)

4 1 On account of this, having this ministry just as we have received God's mercy, we do not despair. 2 However, we have renounced the secret things of shame, not resorting to trickery and not falsifying the word of God, but with the disclosure of the truth we commend ourselves to every human conscience before God. 3 And even if our gospel is veiled, it is veiled only to those who are perishing, 4 to those unbelievers whose minds the god of this age has blinded so that they cannot see the illumination of the gospel of Christ's glory, who is the image of God.

5 For we do not preach ourselves, but we preach Jesus Christ as Lord, and ourselves as your servants for Jesus' sake. 6 For God is the one who said, "Let light shine out of darkness." God has shone forth in our hearts to provide us illumination with the knowledge of his glory in the face of Jesus Christ.

---

7. Light of the Gospel
4:1–6

Chapter divisions in the New Testament are not always precise in marking the end of a certain topic. The first six verses of chapter 4 are a continuation of Paul's discussion on his ministry and self-commendation. Key words in the vocabulary in this section are the same as those in the preceding chapter (3:1–18). They include the terms *ministry, commend, veiled, minds, glory, likeness, Lord, hearts,* and *face.* In view of these concepts, we consider 4:1–6 to be part of Paul's preceding discourse. The new element in this segment is the light that shines forth from Christ's gospel. The first two verses, divided because of their length, form a unit that depicts Paul's ministry based on the truth of God's Word.

1. On account of this, having this ministry just as we have received God's mercy, we do not despair.

Paul links this passage to the preceding verse (3:18) that speaks of every believer reflecting the Lord's glory and being transformed into Christ's likeness. In that verse he revealed the work of the Holy Spirit in the Christian's life of sanctification. Paul, then, stresses the fact that the Spirit is at work in those people who belong to the new covenant.

With the demonstrative pronoun *this,* Paul looks back to the previous discussion on his new covenant ministry and his being the recipient of divine mercy. He confidently looks ahead to the future and can say to his opponents and his readers that he is full of hope and joy. Paul and his associates have received from the Lord the ministry of the gospel. On that basis, Paul can say that he does not lose hope in preaching the Good News and teaching people.

The significance of the pronoun *we* in the second part of the verse should not be interpreted in the light of the preceding context (3:18). There the words *all*

135

of us apply to every Christian, but here the subject *we* is limited to Paul and his co-workers, and especially to Paul himself.[1] Indeed, when Paul mentions indirectly or directly his apostolic authority and calling, he says that he received God's mercy (I Cor. 7:25; I Tim. 1:13, 16). He may be alluding to his own conversion experience near Damascus.

The verb *lose heart* refers not to physical fatigue but to spiritual weariness.[2] This Greek verb always appears in the New Testament with a negative particle to stress positive conduct (see v. 16; Gal. 6:9; Eph. 3:13; II Thess. 3:13). Despite the hardship and suffering Paul has had to face as an apostle of Jesus Christ, he is not disheartened. The ministry to which the Lord has called him is a spiritual challenge. Paul knows that God grants him courage and boldness to overcome the verbal and physical attacks that he has to endure. God grants Paul and his associates mercy to overcome spiritual exhaustion so that they succeed in their ministry (v. 16). Paul defends himself against his challengers by showing them a buoyant spiritual life that is unblemished, sincere, and productive (see 2:17).

2. However, we have renounced the secret things of shame, not resorting to trickery and not falsifying the word of God, but with the disclosure of the truth we commend ourselves to every human conscience before God.

a. *"However, we have renounced the secret things of shame."* Notice that Paul is not combative but positive in his defense. That is, he talks about his own walk of life, not about that of his opponents. The adversative *however* depicts not a contrast but an explanation for his ministry. He and his fellow workers have renounced once for all shameful things that are hidden from open view (compare Rom. 6:21).

Translations vary for the second part of the first clause. To illustrate:

"all shameful secrecy" (NJB)
"secret and shameful ways" (NIV)
"the hidden things of shame (NKJV)
"things hidden because of shame" (NASB)
"the shameful things that one hides" (NRSV)
"deeds that people hide for very shame" (REB)
"secret things of which people are ashamed" (SEB)
"hide from sight for the shamefulness of them" *(Cassirer)*

My translation is literal for the purpose of indicating the genitive case of the word *shame*. Should this genitive be objective ("because of shame"), subjective ("of which people are ashamed"), or descriptive ("shameful ways")? Although all three versions are equally acceptable, we have difficulty determining Paul's pre-

---

1. Seyoon Kim, *The Origin of Paul's Gospel* (Tübingen: Mohr; Grand Rapids: Eerdmans, 1982); R. C. H. Lenski, *The Interpretation of St. Paul's First and Second Epistle to the Corinthians* (Columbus: Wartburg, 1946), p. 952; F. F. Bruce, *I and II Corinthians*, New Century Bible (London: Oliphants, 1971), p. 194.
2. Ernst Achilles, *NIDNTT*, 1:563; Walter Grundmann, *TDNT*, 3:486.

cise intention.³ He does not explain the shameful deeds that he and his associates repudiate. Paul emphasizes the verb *to renounce* but refrains from delineating the things done in secret (compare I Cor. 4:5). Speaking in generalities, he points out what he and his fellow workers are not doing.

b. "Not resorting to trickery and not falsifying the word of God." These two clauses portray Paul and his co-workers in a positive light, for their conduct is impeccable. For instance, Paul himself refused to accept any remuneration from the Corinthians for his work (I Cor. 9:18). He repeatedly laid his life on the line on behalf of Christ and the church and never sought any personal advantage (I Cor. 3:10).

Trickery is an attribute of the devil, not of the apostles and their helpers. The Greek word *panourgia* (cunning) appears five times in the New Testament, where it has an exclusively negative connotation (Luke 20:23; I Cor. 3:19; II Cor. 4:2; 11:3; Eph. 4:14). Paul's reference to the serpent's cunning in Paradise is an apt illustration (11:3). Cunning does not characterize the conduct of Paul and his colleagues, for they strive for honesty and integrity. Judaizers may charge Paul with trickery (12:16), but his life demonstrates that their accusation is unfounded.

Only here in the New Testament do we read the expression *"falsifying* the word of God." Paul alludes to the criticism his opponents have leveled against him. They claim that his preaching falsifies God's revealed Word; they insinuate that he has watered down the demands of the law with respect to the Gentile Christians (Acts 21:21). Paul adamantly rejects this accusation in light of his unequivocal fidelity to the Word of God in the context of his new covenant ministry (compare 2:17; I Thess. 2:3).

Is Paul speaking of the Old Testament or the gospel? Some scholars stress the fact that the phrase *word of God* signifies the Old Testament Scriptures (Rom. 9:6). Others observe that the immediate context mentions the gospel (v. 3) and thus compels the exegete to equate the phrase with Christ's gospel. Both observations are pertinent. In effect, Paul preached the Old Testament Scriptures as fulfilled through Jesus Christ. For him, as well as for the writer of Hebrews, God's verbal revelation is gospel (see Heb. 4:2, 6). Trained in the context of the old covenant, he adopted the structure of the new covenant with reference to God's word.

c. "But with the disclosure of the truth." Throughout this epistle, Paul emphasizes an openness to his ministry and its gospel message for anyone who cares to notice.⁴ For him, the gospel is unveiled and its ministers competent (3:5–6) and sincere (2:17).

---

3. J.-F. Collange, *Énigmes de la deuxième épître de Paul aux Corinthiens: Étude exégétique de II Cor. 2:14–7:4*, SNTSMS 18 (New York and Cambridge: Cambridge University Press, 1972), p. 128.
4. Paul writes the Greek verb *phaneroō* (I reveal) nine times (2:14; 3:3; 4:10, 11; 5:10, 11 [twice]; 7:12; 11:6) and the noun *phanerōsis* (disclosure) once (4:2; see also I Cor. 12:7). Paul-Gerd Müller, *EDNT*, 3:413; see Dieter Georgi, *The Opponents of Paul in Second Corinthians* (Philadelphia: Fortress, 1986), p. 260.

Note that in the context of verses 2 and 3, Paul mentions three synonymous terms, "word of God," "truth," and "gospel," to describe his apostolic proclamation.[5] He knows that Judaizers are accusing him of doing things in a corner (Acts 26:26). They must admit that with respect to the ministry of God's truth, the apostle needs no letter of commendation other than the fruit of his ministry. His opponents are peddlers of God's word, but Paul and his fellow workers are its preachers. The word that I have translated "disclosure" can have a twofold interpretation: the act of proclaiming the truth and the results of that proclamation.[6] Both interpretations are applicable here, as is evident from the entire epistle: Paul boldly presents the gospel (3:12), works tirelessly for the benefit of the church members (7:2–3), and is a model of unselfishness. He lives the truth of the gospel that he preaches.

d. "We commend ourselves to every human conscience before God." Being a latecomer to apostleship, Paul was obliged to show his credentials. All his epistles, except for Philippians, I Thessalonians, II Thessalonians, and Philemon, begin with the assertion that he is an apostle of Christ Jesus. To prove genuine authorization is one thing, but to commend one's authority to the people is another.[7] Paul had to prove his apostolic ministry without forcing his authority onto the church.

Paul is willing to subject himself and his ministry to public scrutiny, for he has nothing to hide. In both his word and his conduct he exemplifies truth. Everyone can see that his effective ministry in Corinth and elsewhere shows honesty and integrity.[8] By implication, Paul's accusers are presenting an artificial commendation that cannot stand the light of day.

The last part of this verse is telling, for it reveals that Paul voluntarily entrusts himself to everyone's conscience provided that this conscience is fully aware of God's presence. As Paul is living his life and doing his work in God's presence, he expects everyone who investigates him to stand in that same presence (5:11). He is saying that without wavering a person's conscience must be in complete harmony with God's Word and testimony. Like the needle of a compass that invariably points north, so one's conscience must invariably point to God.

The human conscience that is guided by God's truth registers and evaluates the good and the bad, examines the moral conduct of one's self and others, and obeys authority that God has instituted. Paul thus invites everyone to appraise his work with a conscience that is accountable to God.[9] If his opponents want to ex-

5. Refer to Gerhard Delling, "'Nahe ist der das Wort': Wort-Geist-Glaube bei Paulus," *ThLZ* 99 (1974): 407.
6. F. W. Grosheide, *De Tweede Brief van den Apostel Paulus aan de Kerk te Korinthe*, Kommentaar op het Nieuwe Testament series (Amsterdam: Van Bottenburg, 1939), p. 141.
7. Consult Robert Murray, "On 'Commending Authority,'" *Month* 6 (1973): 89.
8. Refer to Anthony C. Thiselton, *NIDNTT*, 3:886.
9. Consult Hans-Christoph Hahn, *NIDNTT*, 1:350; Christian Maurer, *TDNT*, 7:916; SB 3:91–96. See also Claude A. Pierce, *Conscience in the New Testament*, SBT 15 (Naperville: Allenson, 1955).

amine him as a servant of God, let them do so with consciences attuned to the Scriptures in God's presence.

The next two verses, which form one lengthy sentence in Greek, belong together because verse 4 explains verse 3b. Although verse 4 is cast in a negative frame, it ends on a positive note. Also, the repetition of vocabulary Paul used earlier stands out in clear detail: "veiled," "gospel," "minds," "glory," and "likeness."

3. And even if our gospel is veiled, it is veiled only to those who are perishing.

Paul's adversaries accused him of presenting a gospel that was veiled and ineffective. By implication, they claimed that their gospel was open, worthy of note, and gaining numerous adherents. Theirs is not a flippant accusation leveled against Paul, for the concessive force of the first three words, "and even if," speak of fact, not fiction.[10] We assume that their accusation had been brought to Paul's attention, who in this verse reacts by stating the truth.

Throughout his epistle, Paul switches from singular to plural pronouns, and in many instances the plural signifies the singular. But here the personal pronoun *our* must be understood literally, for Paul has in mind Christ's gospel that is proclaimed by apostles and apostolic helpers. Here he refers to the gospel of Christ (2:12) that Paul and his associates preach and teach.

Many in Corinth refused to accept this gospel and thus for them it remained veiled. The cause of this veiling lay not in the gospel itself, which was sufficiently clear, nor in Christ himself, who had commissioned the apostles, but in the hearers who rejected Christ's message. Paul's opponents and their followers publicly repudiated the oral teachings of this gospel. The blame, therefore, rests squarely on those who rebuff God's tidings of good news. For them, the gospel is veiled because their blindness makes them incapable of seeing spiritual light (John 9:39–41). These people are degenerates who have hardened their hearts and are unwilling to listen to the truth.

John Calvin encourages pastors to proclaim the truth in the face of opposition: "The fact that [Paul] dares to regard as reprobates all those who reject his doctrine is evidence of great assurance, but it is right that all who wish to be counted ministers of God should possess a like assurance so that with fearless conscience they may have no hesitation in citing those who oppose their teaching to appear at the judgment seat of God that they may receive there a sure condemnation."[11]

Paul writes that the gospel is veiled only for those who are perishing. He designates the people who reject the gospel as "those who are perishing" and "unbelievers" (v. 4). They have heard the gospel but refuse to obey Jesus Christ. The term *perishing* occurs a few times in Paul's epistles (I Cor. 1:18; II Cor. 2:15; 4:3; II Thess.

---

10. Collange, *Énigmes*, p. 131; Alfred Plummer, *A Critical and Exegetical Commentary on the Second Epistle of St. Paul to the Corinthians*, International Critical Commentary (1915; Edinburgh: Clark, 1975), p. 113.

11. John Calvin, *The Second Epistle of Paul the Apostle to the Corinthians and the Epistles to Timothy, Titus and Philemon*, Calvin's Commentaries series, trans. T. A. Small (Grand Rapids: Eerdmans, 1964), p. 53.

2:10). It refers to those people who knowingly reject the gospel of Christ and by their own choice are following the way that leads to eternal death. "Perdition is the fate that awaits the man who does not come to repentance, who rejects love of the truth, who goes on the broad way 'that leads to destruction' (Matt. 7:13)."[12]

4. To those unbelievers whose minds the god of this age has blinded so that they cannot see the illumination of the gospel of Christ's glory, who is the image of God.

Who are the unbelievers Paul mentions? Are they those Jews who refuse to accept Christ as the Son of God? Or are they those Corinthians who have heard the gospel but reject it? Because the Greek grammar of this verse is infelicitous, we do well to explain the term *unbelievers* as a synonym of "those who are perishing" (v. 3).[13] The term, therefore, applies to all those who refuse to know Jesus Christ as Son of God. This term appears again in 6:14, where Paul warns believers not to be yoked with unbelievers. Faith stands in opposition to unbelief, and these two can never exist harmoniously.

Paul calls Satan the god of this age, not to place the devil on a level with God, but to show that Satan is the ruler of this world.[14] In the first few centuries of the Christian era, Gnosticism promulgated its doctrine that not God but an evil god had created and now controlled this world. Opposing this teaching, many theologians wanted to deprive Satan of the title *god* and ascribe it only to God. Thus they proposed the translation: "to those unbelievers of this age whose minds God has blinded."[15] But the Greek word order will not support this version. God does not want the death of anyone but desires that all repent and live (Ezek. 18:23, 32; II Peter 3:9). Satan is the adversary of God and his people. On this earth, he exercises the authority that has been given to him (Luke 4:6).

Jesus calls Satan the prince of this world, but Paul designates him "god." The Hebrew plural term *elohim* is translated in the singular as either "God" or "god." When the writers of Scripture refer to a god, they usually do so with a qualifying genitive; for instance, "each cried out to his own god" (Jonah 1:5; see also Exod. 20:23; II Kings 19:37). When we translate the Hebrew text of Psalm 8:5 literally, we read, "a little lower than God" (NASB). But the Septuagint renders the verse as "a little lower than the angels." Paul probably had in mind the Hebrew expression *elohim*, which he translated "god" and applied to the fallen angel, Satan.

---

12. Hans-Christoph Hahn, *NIDNTT*, 1:464; Armin Kretzer, *EDNT*, 1:135–36.

13. Bauer translates, "In their case [those who are perishing], the god of this age has blinded their unbelieving minds" (p. 85). But the Greek has the definite article preceding a substantive, *tōn apistōn* (the unbelievers). See Jean Héring, *The Second Epistle of Saint Paul to the Corinthians*, trans. A. W. Heathcote and P. J. Allcock (London: Epworth, 1967), p. 30.

14. John 12:31; 14:30; 16:11; Eph. 2:2; I John 4:4; 5:19. Rudolf Bultmann asserts that Paul uses the language of Gnosticism, but he fails to prove that Gnosticism was rampant in Corinth and that Paul borrowed gnostic terminology. See *Theology of the New Testament*, 2 vols., trans. K. Grobel (London: SCM, 1952–55), vol. 1, pp. 170–72.

15. Consult the survey by Norbert Brox, "'Non huius aevi deus' (Zu Tertullian, adv. Marc. V 11, 10)," *ZNTW* 59 (1968): 259–61.

Satan is capable of transforming himself into an angel of light (11:14) to deceive people. Through counterfeit miracles, signs, and wonders, he employs his evil schemes to deceive those who are perishing (II Thess. 2:9). He prowls around like a roaring lion searching for prey to devour (I Peter 5:8). And as the spirit (god) of the age, he has the power to blind the minds of unbelievers. The contrast is striking: preachers drive away the darkness of the world with Christ's illuminating gospel; Satan strikes the unbelievers with blindness so that their minds are unable to see the light of the gospel. A veil covers their minds, much as the Israelites refused to see Moses' face radiating God's glory and as the Jews were unable to understand the message of the Scriptures (3:13–15). Conversely, Christians send forth the light of Christ's gospel and reflect his glory.[16] Satan has no power over the believers who stand firm in their faith, even though he tries to deceive them—if that were possible (Matt. 24:24; Mark 13:22). Believers not only see the glory of Christ through the illumination of the gospel, but also reflect his glory in their daily lives.

Paul places three genitives after the noun *illumination,* namely, "of the gospel," "of the glory," "of Christ." Each genitive explains and emphasizes the noun that precedes it. Hence, we have this sequence: the illumination that the gospel emits derives from the glory that belongs to Christ.[17]

The conclusion of this verse is a statement of fact: "Christ . . . is the image of God" (I Cor. 11: 7; Col. 1:15; compare Rom. 8:29; II Cor. 3:18; Phil. 2:6; Heb. 1:3). The concept *image of God* directs our attention to God creating man in his image and likeness (Gen. 1:26–27). Here is a father-child relationship that implies resemblance of the one to the other. While Adam is God's image bearer only by analogy, Christ is "the exact representation of his being" (Heb. 1:3). More, the Son of God brilliantly reflects God's glory and so in his essence extends the Father's glory.[18] Through Jesus Christ the Father's glory is made visible to the world of mankind (John 1:14b; 14:9). And this is exactly what Paul demonstrates in the succeeding context: "God has shone forth in our hearts to provide us illumination of the knowledge of God's glory in the face of Jesus Christ" (v. 6).

Did Paul compose the phrase *the image of God?* Many theologians argue that this line was part of a confessional formula or a hymn that was in use when Paul wrote his epistles.[19] This raises the interesting question whether Paul could have been the author of this formula or hymn.[20] It remains to be seen if the evidence is sufficient to show that Paul is not the author. The research on this point goes beyond the scope of this commentary.

---

16. Derk W. Oostendorp, *Another Jesus: A Gospel of Jewish-Christian Superiority in II Corinthians* (Kampen: Kok, 1967), p. 48.

17. Compare J. H. Moulton and Nigel A. Turner, *A Grammar of New Testament Greek* (Edinburgh: Clark, 1963), vol. 3, *Syntax,* p. 218.

18. Refer to Herman Bavinck, *Gereformeerde Dogmatiek,* 4 vols. (Kampen: Kok, 1928), vol. 2, p. 241.

19. See, among others, Jacob Jervell, *Imago Dei: Gen 1,26f im Spätjudentum und in den paulinischen Briefen,* FRLANT 76 (Göttingen: Vandenhoeck und Ruprecht, 1960), pp. 198, 209, 214.

20. Kim, *Origin of Paul's Gospel,* pp. 143–45.

5. For we do not preach ourselves, but we preach Jesus Christ as Lord, and ourselves as your servants for Jesus' sake.

a. *Format.* Having mentioned the gospel (v. 4), Paul is now obliged to explain the content of his preaching. With the word *for* he provides an elucidation of this matter. In the Greek, the first word, which always receives emphasis, is the particle *not,* which negates the verb *we preach.* Note that the negative is offset by the adversative *but* that introduces two ideas: Jesus Christ as Lord and ourselves as servants. A number of Greek manuscripts reverse the order of the words *Jesus Christ,* as is evident in many versions (e.g., NAB, NKJV, REB).

Another suggestion is to place verse 5 in parentheses and consider it an interruption of Paul's thought; that is, verse 6 follows verse 4 (see *Moffatt*). But this can hardly be true if we see verses 5 and 6 as the conclusion to the section (3:1–4:6) in which Paul defends himself and his ministry. Also, the terse message of verse 5 is explained in the succeeding verse.

b. *Message.* What is the content of Paul's preaching? The apostle repeatedly stated that he preached the gospel message of the crucified Jesus (I Cor. 1:17, 23; 2:2; 12:3; 15:3–5). The partisan spirit among the Corinthians he despised, for he desired no honor for himself (I Cor. 1:13; 3:4, 22–23). Accordingly, he once more declares forcefully that he does not preach himself, nor does Peter, Apollos, or any other apostle or helper. As John the Baptist pointed to Jesus and said, "He must increase, but I must decrease" (John 3:30, NRSV), so Paul categorically states, "We do not preach ourselves, but we preach Jesus Christ as Lord." He implies, however, that his adversaries do the opposite with their domineering demeanor (10:12; 11:13–15, 20).

Paul proclaims Jesus Christ as Lord (Rom. 10:9; I Cor. 12:3; Phil. 2:10–11) and thus indicates that he and his associates are Christ's servants. Indeed, the parallel in this verse is clear: Jesus is Lord and the apostles are servants. But Paul goes a step further and states that he and his co-workers are the servants of the Corinthian church (I Cor. 3:5). This does not mean that they are working for the Corinthians in an employer-employee relationship. Not at all, for Paul refuses to receive any compensation for his ministerial services (I Cor. 9:18). Paul is a servant of Christ sent to minister to the spiritual needs of the Corinthians. And, therefore, out of love for his Lord he serves the people in Corinth.

At times, Paul uses the name *Jesus* without a qualifier (Rom. 3:26; I Cor. 12:3; II Cor. 4:5, 11, 14; Phil. 2:11; I Thess. 1:10; 4:14). When the name occurs alone, he calls attention to the historical Jesus. In this verse, Paul alludes to the example Jesus set as a servant (John 13:15–17).

Practical Considerations in 4:4

Politicians, preachers, and entertainers often demonstrate the art of effective public speaking. Many politicians deliver their speeches with skillful oratory in the halls of the legislature. Gifted preachers likewise show their talents when they draw crowds of people to Sunday worship services. And entertainers, as crowd pleasers, have mastered the art of communication.

Not every politician is known as a statesman, because some legislators exhibit glowing rhetoric that amounts to nothing more than empty words. Not every speaker is a preacher, for many orators in the pulpit present eloquence but not the Word of God. They preach themselves instead of the Lord Jesus Christ. As such, they have become entertainers who draw a crowd to tell them "what their itching ears want to hear" (II Tim. 4:3). But such orators are not endowed with the authority of the Scriptures, for they never state explicitly: "This is what the Bible says."

If preachers wish to speak with authority, then they must be filled with God's Spirit and listen closely to his Word. They should be fully aware of the fact that they are the Lord's representatives. They not only must know that Word, but also must be utterly convinced of it and live it. And last, to be effective in the pulpit, they must teach the people the language of the Bible so that everyone becomes thoroughly familiar with its content (Jer. 31:34; Heb. 8:11). In the days of the Reformation, the people obtained answers to numerous problems by asking the simple question: "What do the Scriptures say?" (compare Acts 17:11).

---

6. For God is the one who said, "Let light shine out of darkness." God has shone forth in our hearts to provide us illumination with the knowledge of his glory in the face of Jesus Christ.

a. "For God is the one who said, 'Let light shine out of darkness.'" The first word, "for," serves as a link to the preceding verse (5). Paul asserts that God spoke the words, "Let light shine out of darkness," but in Scripture no exact reference is available except a free rendering of God's creation command, "Let there be light" (Gen. 1:3). God dispels darkness at both creation and re-creation; he eliminates the darkness in the physical realm by means of the created sun and the darkness in the spiritual sphere through his uncreated Son. This interpretation was first advanced by the fourth-century church father Chrysostom, who saw in this passage a parallel between the creation of the world and the re-creation of God's people. God says that he formed light and created darkness (Isa. 45:7), which is evident in both nature and regeneration.

On the way to Damascus, Paul saw heavenly light flashing around him and was blind for three days afterward (Acts 9:3–9). But out of darkness God caused his light to shine into Paul's heart, so that he received both physical and spiritual sight. Writes Seyoon Kim, "Along with Paul's actual experience of the light on the Damascus road, the traditional idea of conversion as transference from darkness into light may have led Paul to cite Gen[esis] 1:3 here."[21] Paul recognized the parallel of creation and re-creation, the material and the spiritual domains.

---

21. Kim, *Origin of Paul's Gospel,* p. 8. Other scholars object to linking Paul's conversion to Genesis 1:3. They think that Paul alluded to the prophecy of Isaiah (9:2; 42:6, 16; 49:6, 9; 58:10; 60:1–2); see, among others, Collange, *Énigmes,* p. 139. The words Paul used could have come from still other passages: Job 37:15; Pss. 18:28; 112:4. But the fact remains that no Old Testament passage has the exact wording. Compare Ralph P. Martin, *II Corinthians,* Word Biblical Commentary 40 (Waco: Word, 1986), p. 80.

143

Moreover, when Jesus called him to be an apostle, the Lord instructed him to turn both Jews and Gentiles from darkness to light (Acts 26:17–18).

b. "God has shone forth in our hearts to provide us illumination with the knowledge of his glory." As the apostle John testifies, "God is light; in him is no darkness at all" (I John 1:5). Through Jesus Christ he lets his light shine in our hearts to bring about regeneration. Paul does not say that God shines light *into* our hearts. He states that God illumines us *in* our inner beings, so that we (all believers) may spread the light. While Satan blinds the human mind (v. 4), God illumines the heart, which is the wellspring of life (Prov. 4:23). Satan prevents illumination, but God provides it.

In verse 4, the word *illumination* had already occurred, and it has the same meaning as it does in this verse: the spreading of light (refer to I Peter 2:9). Here Paul elucidates the concept of illumination by saying that it comes to a person through the knowledge of God's glory (compare Eph. 1:18). Illumination takes place through appropriating the message of the gospel. The apostolic teaching of God's revelation in Jesus Christ is the source of light. In the words of the psalmist, "Your word is a lamp to my feet and a light for my path" (Ps. 119:105; see v. 130 and Prov. 6:23). In a previous chapter, Paul used the expression *knowledge*, which is the proclamation of Christ's gospel as a sweet-smelling savor (2:14). Here the gospel is the light by which believers behold God's glory revealed in Jesus Christ.

c. "In the face of Jesus Christ." Even though some translators support the reading *in the presence of*, a literal version is preferred. The phrase sums up Paul's discussion on the radiance of God's glory on Moses' face (3:7, 12) and the Lord's glory that believers see and reflect (3:18). The Israelites begged Moses to cover his face so that they would not have to look at its radiance. But believers enlightened by the gospel see the face of Jesus Christ and behold his glory—"the glory of the One and Only, who came from the Father, full of grace and truth" (John 1:14).

Greek Words, Phrases, and Constructions in 4:1–6

Verses 1–2

ἐγκακοῦμεν—"we lose heart." The difference in pronunciation between this verb and that of the reading ἐκκακοῦμεν is minimal and resulted in a scribal variant. Although the meaning of these two verbs is the same, we prefer the primary reading that has the support of leading Greek manuscripts.

ἀπειπάμεθα—only here in the New Testament, this indirect middle form of the verb ἀπεῖπον means that we renounced such things from ourselves.[22] The aorist is ingressive.

περιπατοῦντες—the word means "walking" in the sense of conducting one's walk of life.

---

22. A. T. Robertson, *A Grammar of the Greek New Testament in the Light of Historical Research* (Nashville: Broadman, 1934), p. 810.

Verses 3–4

κεκαλυμμένον—the periphrastic construction (twice) with the verb *to be* and the perfect passive participles show duration of an existing state in a simple-fact conditional sentence.

ἐν οἷς—the preposition with the pronoun in the dative expresses the dative of disadvantage, in the sense of "to" or "for."[23]

τῶν ἀπίστων—because the Greek sentence is convoluted, it is best to interpret this expression as a synonym of "those who are perishing" (v. 3). The definite article demands that the adjective be understood as a substantive, "the unbelievers."

εἰς τὸ μὴ αὐγάσαι—the construction expresses purpose: to prevent the unbelievers from seeing the light of the gospel.[24] The meaning of the infinitive can be either "illumine" or "see," similar to the verb κατοπτρίζομαι (3:18). The translation *see* is preferred.

φωτισμόν—Paul does not use the noun φῶς (light) but rather the action noun that signifies illumination.

Verse 6

ὁ θεός—the verb *to be* must be supplied so that the participial phrase ὁ εἰπών and the relative pronoun ὅς can be taken in apposition to one another: "God is the one who said and who. . . ."

λάμψει—"shall shine." Many translators choose the future tense because of the better reading of the Greek manuscripts. Others adopt the inferior reading λάμψαι (let it shine), which is analogous to "let there be light" (Gen. 1:3). The Majority Text and Merk (see also the Vulgate), followed by numerous translators, have adopted this reading.

ἔλαμψεν—the aorist is ingressive. Like the preceding verb, it is transitive. The object *light* must be supplied and occurs in the prepositional phrase πρὸς φωτισμόν (for illumination). Hence, it is unnecessary to change the relative pronoun ὅς to ὅ (with φῶς as antecedent) to make the verb transitive.[25]

ἐν προσώπῳ—this phrase can be understood figuratively ("in the presence of") or literally ("in the face of"). In view of the context of Moses covering his face, the suggestion of a literal meaning has some legitimacy.[26]

Ἰησοῦ Χριστοῦ—solid manuscript evidence lends support to this reading; other witnesses omit Ἰησοῦ; and the Western text reverses the order of the two names. The shorter reading, "Christ," favored by many translators, does not have the same textual support that the double names enjoy.[27]

---

7 And we have this treasure in earthenware pots, so that the extraordinary power may be of God and not out of us. 8 In every way we are afflicted, but we are not hard pressed. We are perplexed, but

---

23. Friedrich Blass and Albert Debrunner, *A Greek Grammar of the New Testament and Other Early Christian Literature,* trans. and rev. Robert Funk (Chicago: University of Chicago Press, 1961), #220.1.

24. C. F. D. Moule, *An Idiom-Book of New Testament Greek,* 2d ed. (Cambridge: Cambridge University Press, 1960), p. 143 n. 2.

25. Contra Héring (p. 31), who advocates the emendation; but manuscript evidence to support the conjecture is lacking.

26. Compare Robert Hanna, *A Grammatical Aid to the Greek New Testament* (Grand Rapids: Baker, 1983), p. 320.

27. See Bruce M. Metzger, *A Textual Commentary on the Greek New Testament,* 2d ed. (Stuttgart and New York: United Bible Societies, 1994), p. 510.

we are not thoroughly perplexed. 9 We are persecuted, but we are not abandoned. We are struck down, but we are not destroyed. 10 We always carry around in our body the death of Jesus, so that the life of Jesus may be revealed in our body. 11 For always we who are living are delivered to death because of Jesus, so that the life of Jesus may be revealed in our mortal flesh. 12 So death is active in us, but life is active in you.

C. Earthly and Heavenly Dwellings
4:7–5:10

This segment of Paul's epistle introduces topics that differ from the preceding context and mark a contrast between the body and the soul, between earthly troubles and heavenly glory, and between mortality and immortality.

Paul addresses the church universal, including the Christians in Corinth. He writes about the mortal nature of human beings, which he places over against God's sufficiency. He stresses the power of life through the resurrection of the Lord Jesus, and he notes that Jesus will present all of us in God's presence.

1. Jars of Clay
4:7–12

7. And we have this treasure in earthenware pots, so that the extraordinary power may be of God and not out of us.

This verse shows double contrast: first, the treasure of gospel light (v. 6) and worthless clay pots; next, God's supernatural power and human weakness. The first clause states a fact that in the second results in achieving purpose.

a. "And we have this treasure in earthenware pots." The phrase *and we have* refers not to Paul only but to everyone who has received and possesses the good news of salvation. This treasure consists of the gospel message that we have received from the Lord Jesus Christ. Paul tells us that this message is a priceless gift that we carry around in earthenware vessels. He uses an illustration taken from everyday life: clay pots that contained everything from wealth to worthless things, from foods to liquids. Because jars, pots, and vessels were made from clay, they were subject to breakage and, therefore, were inexpensive and discarded in short order.

Jewish rabbis used to say: "It is impossible for wine to be kept in gold or silver vessels but in the most inferior of containers, namely, in earthen vessels. Similarly, the words of the Law are kept only in the person who is most humble."[28] An analogy is the valuable Dead Sea Scrolls, which were stored for more than two millennia in ordinary clay jars that were decaying while the scrolls remained intact. E. F. F. Bishop suggests that Paul may have had in mind "earthenware lamps of different shapes and sizes."[29] Other scholars wish to link earthenware jars to

---

28. *Sifre Deut.* 11.22, #48 (84a).
29. E. F. F. Bishop, "Pots of Earthenware," *EvQ* 43 (1971): 3–5. See also William L. Lane, *NIDNTT*, 3:914.

Paul's remark about the triumphal procession in Christ (2:14). Filled with coins, grain, wine, or water, vessels were carried along in offering processions.[30]

Lamps made out of clay spread light in every home and jars filled with various commodities were part of triumphal processions. But if Paul had intended to draw attention to either a lamp or a jar in a procession, he would have been able to express this in appropriate words. For him, the contrast of the incomparable value of the gospel and the cheap, fragile clay jars is important. He emphasizes not so much the fragile pots but their content, namely, the treasure.

Assaulted and battered numerous times, Paul's own body was living proof of its frailty and impending mortality (5:1). For this reason, Paul uses the example of earthenware pottery to illustrate the bodies and minds of humans. He himself calls attention to the potter who fashions vessels for noble and common purposes (Rom. 9:21; Isa. 29:16; Jer. 18:6).[31] And Jesus describes Paul as "a chosen vessel unto me, to bear my name before the Gentiles" (Acts 9:15, KJV).

b. "So that the extraordinary power may be of God and not out of us." We hold the gospel as it were in clay jars to exhibit the phenomenal power of God, so that everyone may see that not we but God is its source. The original text reads: "the extraordinary (quality of the) power."[32] The Greek perhaps reflects Hebraic syntax that merely says "extraordinary power." What is this great power? It is God's word that created light (Gen. 1:3), that led Israel out of Egypt (Exod. 3:7–10), that raised Jesus from the dead (Rom. 1:4), and that called Paul to be a missionary to the Gentiles (Acts 26:16–18).

God's power is revealed in human beings who, in the eyes of the world, are of no account. For example, a company of uneducated fishermen follow Jesus and, filled with the Holy Spirit, spread the gospel to the ends of the earth (Acts 1:8). Jason and some fellow Christians are dragged before the city officials in Thessalonica and are accused of causing trouble all over the world (Acts 17:6). Paul is told that he is unimpressive and lacks oratorical skills (10:10), yet he proclaimed the gospel, founded congregations, strengthened the believers, and composed epistles that have brought the message of salvation to countless multitudes around the globe. Commenting on his physical weakness and Christ's power, Paul affirms that when he is weak, the divine power of Christ is resting on him (12:7–9). The authority of the gospel is not human in origin but has its source in God. "For from him and through him and to him are all things" (Rom. 11:36).

8. In every way we are afflicted, but we are not hard pressed. We are perplexed, but we are not thoroughly perplexed. 9. We are persecuted, but we are not abandoned. We are struck down, but we are not destroyed.

---

30. Paul B. Duff, "Apostolic Suffering and the Language of Processions in II Corinthians 4:7–10," *BTB* 21 (1991): 158–65. Compare Philip Edgcumbe Hughes, *Paul's Second Epistle to the Corinthians: The English Text with Introduction, Exposition and Notes,* New International Commentary on the New Testament series (Grand Rapids: Eerdmans, 1962), p. 136.

31. Consult Collange, *Énigmes,* p. 146.

32. Bauer, p. 840.

These verses echo an earlier passage in which Paul describes the hardships he experiences: "To this present time, we are hungry, thirsty, poorly clothed, beaten, and homeless. We toil with our own hands; when we are scorned, we bless; when we are persecuted, we endure; when we are slandered, we answer with kind words. We have become like the filth of the world, the offscouring of all things until now" (I Cor. 4:11–13). And this is not all, for in four other passages Paul recounts his hardships for the sake of Christ's gospel (1:8–10; 6:4–10; 11:23–27; 12:10).

Paul continues his discourse by contrasting four sets of dissimilarities in two verses. He describes four adversities that he qualifies with four negative phrases ("but we are not"), each of which is followed by a verb.

a. "In every way we are afflicted, but we are not hard pressed." I have supplied the noun *way*, which is versatile, because Paul was afflicted in many ways: physically, mentally, spiritually, and socially. The basic meaning of "afflicted" is to be in a situation in which one bears the pressures of the surrounding world. But Paul is not dismayed, for he states that he is not driven into a narrow place (6:4).

b. "We are perplexed, but we are not thoroughly perplexed." In Greek Paul writes a play on words that in transliteration is clear in form: *aporoumenoi* (being perplexed) and *exaporoumenoi* (being in despair). The second Greek participle is stronger than the first. I have tried to capture the same sounds and meaning in English with "*perplexed*, but not *thoroughly perplexed.*" In fact, when Paul says that he despairs not, he voices an optimism that he earlier lacked. When he described a severe affliction he had endured in the province of Asia, Paul wrote that he despaired even of life (1:8). That was a single incident and not a continual threat to his life.

c. "We are persecuted, but we are not abandoned." Paul portrays himself as a fugitive hunted down by his adversaries, yet at the last moment he is able to escape. Apart from the missionary work and his voyage to Rome, recorded by Luke in Acts, we know little about the frequent suffering Paul bore. But the apostle is not disheartened, for he knows that the Lord never abandons his own. Indeed, God's promise to the Israelites is true: "The LORD your God goes with you; he will never leave you nor forsake you" (Deut. 31:6). Joshua was also told that God would never leave him or forsake him (Deut. 31:8; Josh. 1:5; see Heb. 13:5).

d. "We are struck down, but we are not destroyed." The meaning of the first verb, a technical term, is plain: as a wrestler throws his opponent to the floor, so Paul is lifted up and thrown down.[33] Again his confidence is telling, for Paul states that he is not yet passing away.

The list of the eight Greek participles in verses 8 and 9 shows an increasing degree of severity from being afflicted to not being destroyed. All the participles are in the passive voice with the implication that adversaries are the agents. Yet

---

33. Plummer counsels that the word *thrown down* not be understood as "being thrown in wrestling" (*Second Corinthians*, p. 129). But whenever Paul introduces language from the arena, he does not mean that he himself participates in physical sports (see I Cor. 9:24–27). Rather, he uses figurative speech.

Paul is able to overcome all his trials because he knows that God grants him extraordinary power (v. 7).

10. We always carry around in our body the death of Jesus, so that the life of Jesus may be revealed in our body.

This verse and the next (v. 11) are both a summary of the preceding passage (vv. 8–9) and an introduction to verse 12. In this section, Paul speaks of the death of Jesus that is at work in himself and his associates and the life of Jesus that is at work in the Corinthians.

a. "We always carry around in our body the death of Jesus." Two key words in this clause are "death" and "carry around." Paul chooses not the common word for death (*thanatos*, vv. 11, 12) but a word that describes the entire process of death (*nekrōsis*, Rom. 4:19). This latter word describes the mortification of the body; the final process of weakening, dying, and decomposition.

What stage of Jesus' death does Paul have in mind? Is Paul restrictive by looking at one aspect of death or is he inclusive by considering the whole process of Jesus' dying and death? Concludes John T. Fitzgerald, "It seems preferable not to restrict the meaning of *nekrōsis* to either the 'dying' of Jesus or his 'death.' *Nekrōsis* is likely intended to include both."[34] The name *Jesus* calls attention to his life and death on earth. Paul wishes to stress not the entire span of Jesus' earthly life but his suffering and death.

Paul and his co-workers experience Jesus' suffering and death in their body. More than once Paul mentions the sufferings of Christ in relation to himself (Rom. 8:17; I Cor. 15:31; II Cor. 1:5; 4:16; 13:4; Gal. 6:17; Phil. 3:10; Col. 1:24). Therefore, in a sense there is some similarity between the suffering of Jesus and that of the apostles, for Paul himself could testify to physical suffering for the sake of Jesus. Though the difference between Jesus' suffering and that of Paul is profound, it is irrelevant in this context. Paul now makes known that he carries around in his body Jesus' suffering and death.

The second key word, "to carry around," occurs only three times in the Greek New Testament (Mark 6:55; II Cor. 4:10; Eph. 4:14). What is the significance of this key word? It hardly means that Paul is a pallbearer who carried the body of Jesus to the tomb. No, he means that he always, in season and out of season, proclaims Jesus' death. At the same time, Paul demonstrates his willingness to suffer physically for his Lord. The apostle's scars were convincing proof of his suffering. To illustrate, in Philippi the magistrates ordered that Paul and Silas be beaten with rods and placed in prison (Acts 16:22–24). These two missionaries endured unspeakable physical pain to show the people their willingness to suffer for the cause of Jesus Christ.

---

34. John T. Fitzgerald, *Cracks in an Earthen Vessel: An Examination of the Catalogues of Hardships in the Corinthian Correspondence*, SBLDS 99 (Atlanta: Scholars Press, 1988), p. 179. Consult Jan Lambrecht, "The Nekrōsis of Jesus. Ministry and Suffering in II Cor 4, 7–15," in *L'Apôtre Paul. Personalité, style et conception du ministère*, ed. A. Vanhoye, BETL 73 (Leuven: Leuven University Press, 1986), pp. 120–43.

b. "So that the life of Jesus may be revealed in our body." The lives of Stephen and James of Zebedee were cut short for preaching the good news, but Paul's life was repeatedly spared.[35] Imminent death was Paul's constant companion, but so was the life of Jesus that God revealed in the apostle. The resurrected Lord strengthened Paul by constantly renewing his life.

Notice that Paul writes the single name *Jesus* four times in this verse and the next. He sequentially speaks of Jesus' death, life, cause, and life. The singular use of Jesus' name in this chapter (see also vv. 5 and 14) shows that the relationship between Paul and Jesus was intimate. The sufferings Jesus had endured were now part of Paul's own life. As James Denney put it graphically, for Paul "even to name His human name was consolation."[36]

Appointed as apostle to the Gentiles, Paul is the forerunner of countless servants of Christ. As such he frequently endured severe bodily harm. He knew that others, too, underwent and would suffer persecution and affliction. But Paul speaks primarily of his own suffering, as is evident from the word *body*, which occurs twice in the singular. Similarly, he writes that he bears in his body the marks of Jesus (Gal. 6:17).[37]

11. For always we who are living are delivered to death because of Jesus, so that the life of Jesus may be revealed in our mortal flesh. 12. So death is active in us, but life is active in you.

The parallelism in verses 10–12 is obvious and reveals Paul's Semitic background. With some slight modifications, I list the clauses in sequence to depict contrast, repetition, rhythm, and paradox.

> We always carry around in our body the death of Jesus
> that there be revealed in our body the life of Jesus.
>
> For we always live and endure death because of Jesus
> so there be shown in our mortal body the life of Jesus.
>
> Death is active in us
> life is active in you.

Even though we live, says Paul, our life is always dedicated to the cause of Jesus Christ. During Paul's earthly life, the danger of death was always present (6:9; Rom. 8:36). Danger constantly surrounded him and came from many sources and various people (see 11:26).

35. John Albert Bengel, *Bengel's New Testament Commentary,* trans. Charlton T. Lewis and Marvin R. Vincent, 2 vols. (Grand Rapids: Kregel, 1981), vol. 2, p. 292.

36. James Denney, *The Second Epistle to the Corinthians,* 2d ed, The Expositor's Bible series (New York: Armstrong, 1900), p. 164.

37. Consult Christian Wolff, "Niedrigkeit und Verzicht im Wort und Weg Jesu und in der apostolischen Existenz des Paulus," *NTS* 34 (1988): 183–96; Lambrecht, "Nekrōsis of Jesus," pp. 86–88; Colin G. Kruse, *The Second Epistle of Paul to the Corinthians: An Introduction and Commentary,* Tyndale New Testament Commentaries series (Leicester: Inter-Varsity; Grand Rapids: Eerdmans, 1987), vol. 8, pp. 107–8.

The translation of the main verb is given in the passive voice: "we are delivered to death." But there is a sense that this verb can also be understood as middle: "we deliver ourselves to death" in the sense of doing so willingly for the sake of Jesus. As Jesus delivered himself up for Paul (Gal. 2:20; Eph. 5:2, 25), so Paul is willing to suffer for him in thankfulness.[38]

Instead of the word *body*, Paul writes the phrase *in our mortal flesh*. The concepts are synonymous, yet the difference focuses on the transitory characteristic of human flesh, especially when it is qualified with the adjective *mortal*. That word immediately calls to mind the image of death and decay. In this perishable condition of his own people, Jesus reveals the reality of his resurrected life. And believers everywhere testify to the fact that he is not dead but lives within their hearts. Throughout our earthly lives, Jesus makes his living presence known and gives us the assurance that as he was raised from the dead so we shall be raised (v. 14; I Thess. 4:14). However, we do not have to wait until we die before the life of Jesus is revealed in our body (I Cor. 15:44).[39] Paul explicitly says that Jesus' life is revealed in our mortal flesh now.

In Paul's physical weakness, God perfected Jesus' power, with the result that Paul took delight in his weakness and dependence on that power (12:9, 10). Perhaps the distinction can be made that Paul in this earthly life lived *in* Christ, and in the life hereafter he would live *with* Christ.[40]

Paul now concludes this particular paragraph by saying, "So death is active in us, but life is active in you." He sums up his discussion on the life and death of Jesus in the mortal body of human beings. Throughout his discussion he has spoken of himself and his colleagues but never about the recipients of his letter. This leads to the question why in the concluding statement Paul distinguishes between the first person plural *we* and the second person plural *you* on matters of death and life.

When Paul and Silas were beaten with rods in Philippi, they suffered for the local believers. When the next day the Roman authorities heard that Paul and Silas were Roman citizens and thus enjoyed immunity, the local magistrates were afraid and did not dare to attack or hinder the Christians in Philippi (Acts 16:22–40). Paul and Silas had placed their lives on the line by facing death, so that the believers could live.

The sufferings that brought Paul often to the brink of death were for the benefit of Christ's people (v. 15). Paul willingly confronted death to promote the spiritual life of his fellow believers. As Christ's servant he suffered so that the Corinthians might have life. In addition, Paul displayed his willingness to encounter death in true imitation of the Lord Jesus Christ. This does not mean, however, that the Corinthians would not have to suffer and even die for Jesus

---

38. Fitzgerald, *Cracks in an Earthen Vessel*, p. 180.

39. Contra Hans Lietzmann, *An die Korinther I/II*, augmented by Werner G. Kümmel, Handbuch zum Neuen Testament 9 (Tübingen: Mohr, 1969), pp. 115–16; see also pp. 201–2.

40. Consult Collange, *Énigmes*, p. 159.

(compare I Thess. 2:14–15). Numerous believers throughout the world daily experience severe persecution for the sake of Christ. Many fulfill the proverbial saying: "The blood of martyrs is the seed of the church."

Greek Words, Phrases, and Constructions in 4:8–12

Verses 8–9

ἀλλ᾽ οὐκ—the negative particle for participles is μή, but in a number of instances writers use οὐ instead.[41] In these two verses, the use of the negative οὐ is expected because of the contrast in the four sets of participles. "The usual negative employed to denote contrast with ἀλλά (or δέ) is οὐ."[42]

Verse 10

νέκρωσιν τοῦ Ἰησοῦ—instead of the more common noun θάνατος (death), Paul uses a noun that expresses action, the putting to death of Jesus. The genitive case of Ἰησοῦ is objective, for it specifies what death has done to Jesus' body.

Verse 12

ὥστε—this particle followed by the verb *to be active* in the indicative is inferential and is translated "and so."[43]

---

13 Because we have the same spirit of faith that corresponds to the one of whom it is written, "I believed, therefore I have spoken," we too believe and therefore we speak. 14 We know that he who raised the Lord Jesus will raise us also with Jesus and place us with you in his presence. 15 For all these things happen on account of you so that grace that is multiplying through more and more people may increase thanksgiving to the glory of God.

---

2. Resurrection
4:13–15

One of the themes featured in the last few verses of this chapter is that of the resurrection of Jesus and the believers. This theme is buttressed by a discussion of two virtues: faith is the essential trust of Christians not to be discouraged; and hope is their sure expectation of a state of eternal glory. God's people know both the brevity of this earthly life and the certainty of eternal life with their Lord.

13. Because we have the same spirit of faith that corresponds to the one of whom it is written, "I believed, therefore I have spoken," we too believe and therefore we speak. 14. We know that he who raised the Lord Jesus will raise us also with Jesus and place us with you in his presence.

---

41. A. T. Robertson (*Grammar*, p. 1139) lists five instances in Luke's writings (Luke 6:42; Acts 7:5; 17:27; 26:22; 28:17), twelve in Paul's epistles (Rom. 9:25; Gal. 4:27 [twice]; I Cor. 4:14; 9:26; II Cor. 4:8, 9 [four times]; Phil. 3:3; Col. 2:19; I Thess. 2:4), three in Peter's epistles (I Peter 1:8; 2:10; II Peter 1:16), two in Hebrews (11:1, 35), and one in Matthew's Gospel (22:11). See also Blass and Debrunner, *Greek Grammar*, #430.3.
42. Hanna, *Grammatical Aid*, p. 320.
43. Robertson, *Grammar*, p. 999; Moule, *Idiom-Book*, p. 144.

The main sentence of verse 13, apart from the subordinate clauses, consists of three verbs. The first one, "we have," justifies the presence of the next two, "we believe" and "we speak." All three are in the present tense to portray the continual activity of Christians.

With the first verb, Paul states that we have an enduring possession: faith. But what message does he convey with the phrase *the same spirit of faith?* Paul has not spoken at all about faith in the preceding chapters. He is not looking back but forward and has in mind a passage from one of the psalms (Ps. 116:10; LXX, Ps. 115:1), where the psalmist remarks that because of faith he has spoken. The Old Testament saint has more to say than what Paul quotes here. The Septuagint text, which Paul follows, reads: "I believed; therefore I said, 'I am greatly afflicted.'"[44] The psalmist realized his utter dependence on God for delivering him from death. He sings praises of thanksgiving for being delivered and walking in the land of the living. Facing death, he voiced a prayer for deliverance and God, in answer to the psalmist's faith, responded favorably.

Why does Paul take this Scripture passage and apply it to his discourse? Jewish rabbis never took note of this text.[45] Apart from this quotation, the New Testament has only two allusions to Psalm 116 (v. 3 in Acts 2:24, and v. 11 in Rom. 3:4). The reason for the quotation is that Paul identifies completely with the psalmist. He meditates on the thoughts on life and death expressed in this psalm. Both he and the psalmist have the same spirit of faith in God. Even though Paul is repeatedly delivered to death, his faith in God is strong and allows him to communicate Christ's gospel (I Thess. 2:2). He can say with the psalmist, "I believed, therefore I have spoken," for Paul's afflictions are similar. Paul's speaking encompasses Jesus' life, death, and resurrection, as the general context indicates.[46]

Thus, Paul writes, "we too believe and therefore we speak." Elsewhere he pointedly observes that we believe with our hearts and confess with our mouths that "Jesus is Lord," whom God raised from the dead (Rom. 10:9–10). Our internal faith comes to expression in our external testimony. By obediently confessing Christ's gospel (9:13), we give evidence of our faith and testify that we belong to God's family.

In the Greek New Testament, verses 13 and 14 form one text. This means that the act of believing and speaking is based on the knowledge of both Jesus' resurrection and our future resurrection. Hence, Paul writes: "We know that he who

---

44. The Hebrew text differs from the Septuagint, "I believed even when I said, 'I am greatly afflicted'" (NIV, margin). Consult Willem A. VanGemeren, *Psalms,* vol. 5 of *The Expositor's Bible Commentary,* 12 vols., ed. Frank E. Goebelein (Grand Rapids: Zondervan, 1991), p. 727; Murray J. Harris, *II Corinthians,* in vol. 10 of *The Expositor's Bible Commentary,* 12 vols., ed. Frank E. Goebelein (Grand Rapids: Zondervan, 1976), pp. 343–44.

45. SB 3:517.

46. Jerome Murphy-O'Connor wants to limit Paul's speaking "to something he has just *written.*" But it is hard to visualize that Paul would present only a written message and not preach the gospel (I Cor. 9:16). See "Faith and Resurrection in II Cor. 4:13–14," *RB* 95 (1988): 543–50.

raised the Lord Jesus will raise us also with Jesus and place us with you in his presence." Paul's letters frequently reveal the tenet of Christ's resurrection (e.g., Rom. 6:4, 5; 8:11; I Cor. 6:14; 15:15, 20; Eph. 2:6; Phil. 3:10, 11; Col. 2:12; 3:1). For Paul, that doctrine was the center of his proclamation.[47]

During his ministry in Corinth, Paul taught the people many scriptural doctrines, especially the teaching on the resurrection. The verb *to know* (v. 14) reminds the readers of Paul's earlier lessons and those of other teachers. For instance, in I Corinthians he poses the rhetorical question "Do you not know?" ten times and expects a positive answer (3:16; 5:6; 6:2, 3, 9, 15, 16, 19; 9:13, 24). That is, the Corinthians had been well trained in biblical truths, but periodically they needed a reminder.

Paul reassures the Corinthians that God, who raised Jesus, will also raise them from the dead with Jesus. Does the pronoun *us* in the clause "he will raise us with Jesus" refer to the Corinthians and all believers or to Paul alone? Jerome Murphy-O'Connor asserts that the pronoun *us* refers only to Paul. He depicts Paul's pending arrival at Corinth, during his third visit, as a figurative resurrection.[48] It is difficult to imagine that the Corinthians, who earlier were told that God would raise them from the dead (I Cor. 6:14), would now understand Paul to be speaking figuratively about his visit as a "resurrection" for him alone.

Paul inserts the phrase *with Jesus,* which means not that Jesus was raised again, but that Jesus as the firstfruits of all his people guarantees their resurrection (I Cor. 15:20, 51–53). Jesus will secure the glorious state of all believers and be with them in God's presence (11:2; Eph. 5:27; Col. 1:22; Jude 24). There they appear before God with Jesus as their advocate (I John 2:1), brother (Heb. 2:11–12), and friend (John 15:14).

One last remark on verse 14. The words *with you* in the clause "[God will] place us with you" allude to Paul and his co-workers, who will appear together with all their converts, both Jews and Gentiles, before God. Paul looks forward to the consummation of the age and the prospect of identifying with the multitude, that no one can number, before God's throne (Rev. 7:9–10).[49]

15. For all these things happen on account of you so that grace that is multiplying through more and more people may increase thanksgiving to the glory of God.

a. *Translation.* The grammar of the Greek text is awkward in the second and third parts of this verse. It gives rise to varied translations that present different ways of expressing the meaning of the text, as these three examples show:

---

47. Herman N. Ridderbos, *Paul: An Outline of His Theology,* trans. John Richard de Witt (Grand Rapids: Eerdmans, 1975), p. 537; J. Knox Chamblin, *Paul and the Self: Apostolic Teaching for Personal Wholeness* (Grand Rapids: Baker, 1993), p. 79.

48. Murphy-O'Connor, "Faith and Resurrection," pp. 548–49; see also *The Theology of the Second Letter to the Corinthians,* New Testament Theology series (Cambridge: Cambridge University Press, 1991), p. 48.

49. Among others, Bauer (p. 628) interprets "before him" as "before his judgment seat." But he questions the forensic meaning and concludes that the sense perhaps is "bring close to God."

"That the grace which is spreading to more and more people may cause the giving of thanks to abound to the glory of God" (NASB).

"That as grace spreads, so, to the glory of God, thanksgiving may also overflow among more and more people" (NJB).

"And as God's grace reaches more and more people, they will offer to the glory of God more prayers of thanksgiving" (GNB).[50]

The grammatical difficulties lie in the sequence of the words and in the functions of the verbs (intransitive or transitive). Also, the verse has three different terms that express expansion: "more," "increase," and "abound."

The grammar also raises other questions. First, should translators supply the word *people* or *numbers* with the adjective *more*?[51] Next, should "more and more people" be taken with the word *grace* or with the noun *thanksgiving*? Third, should the verb *increase* be with or without the direct object *prayers of thanksgiving*? These questions are discussed in the interpretation of the text.

b. *Interpretation.* "For all these things happen on account of you." As the spiritual father of the Corinthians, Paul is vitally interested in them. For this reason, he expends himself completely in their service. For them he suffers agony, endures afflictions, and imperils his life. With them he rejoices in the gospel, boasts in divine comfort, and experiences transformation in the image of Christ. Paul omits nothing from his ministry to serve the people in Corinth. In respect to his relationship as apostle to the Corinthian congregation, he states that without exception all these things take place because of them.

"So that grace that is multiplying through more and more people may increase thanksgiving." The key word *grace* refers to God, who grants undeserved love to mankind through Christ's gospel and Paul's ministry.[52]

The multiplication of grace is a feature that occurs in the greeting of Peter's epistles: "Grace unto you, and peace, be multiplied" (I Peter 1:2; II Peter 1:2; see Jude 2, KJV). The Greek verb *plēthunein* (to multiply) in these epistles differs from the Greek verb *pleonazein* (to multiply) in Paul's text, but the concept is the same. God multiplies his grace when more and more people become its recipients. In other words, when the gospel enters the hearts and lives of an ever-increasing number of people, God's grace abounds. These people are fellow believers who reach out and lead unbelievers to Christ. And as a result, all believers now live to please God and express their thanks to him. Together these masses sing praises of thanksgiving to God (compare Rev. 5:9; 7:9). In his paraphrase,

---

50. Brent Noack, in "A Note on II Cor. iv.15," *ST* 17 (1963): 131, suggests the following translation: "That grace may abound and God be praised the more, because thanksgiving for grace is coming from more and more Christians."

51. Moule, *Idiom-Book*, p. 108, translates, "the increasing numbers."

52. Consult Daniel C. Arichea, "Translating 'Grace' *(Charis)* in the New Testament," *BibTr* 29 (1978): 202; John B. Polhill, "Reconciliation at Corinth: II Corinthians 4–7," *RevExp* 86 (1989): 347–48.

Eugene H. Peterson gives this summary: "More and more grace, more and more people, more and more praise!"[53]

Because the word order in the Greek follows logically, it induces the reader to take the direct object, "thanksgiving," not with the verb *to multiply* (or *spread/reach*) but with the verb *to increase*. The subject of this verb is the key word *grace*,[54] and the phrase *through more and more people* comes after the verb form *multiplying*.

An alternate version is, "that grace may multiply thanksgiving . . . and increase to the glory of God." But this translation fails to win approval because it leaves the verb *to increase* without a direct object. In short, we reject this version because of the word order and the flow of the sentence.

"To the glory of God." The chief purpose of every believer is "to glorify God, and to enjoy him forever," according to the Westminster Shorter Catechism of 1647. Paul teaches this doctrine in several of his epistles (e.g., Rom. 15:6; I Cor. 10:31; Phil. 1:11; 2:11; I Tim. 1:11).[55] Both the Scriptures and God's people throughout the centuries echo the same message: "to God be the glory." And that message is at the end of verse 15 for purposes of emphasis.

Doctrinal Considerations in 4:13–15

Steeped in the knowledge of both the Old Testament Scriptures and Jesus' resurrection, Paul had but one mission: proclaiming the Word of God fulfilled in Jesus Christ to extend the church. The message of salvation could never stay hidden in Paul's heart, for he was compelled to preach the doctrine of Jesus' resurrection to both Jews and Gentiles. Quoting Deuteronomy 30:14, Paul wrote: "The word is near you; it is in your mouth, and in your heart" (Rom. 10:8). When Paul spoke about the resurrection before the Pisidian Antioch audience of Jews and God-fearers, he stated that Jesus had risen from the dead and fulfilled the words of the Scriptures (Acts 13:25–37). When he addressed the philosophers at the Areopagus in Athens, he mentioned creation, repentance, and the resurrection of the body (Acts 17:29–31).

Wherever Paul preached, he expected his followers to echo the gospel message (compare I Thess. 1:6–8). When they believed, they also had to speak, with the result that more and more people turned to the Lord. All these believers were recipients of God's grace and joined the innumerable multitude of all those who express thanks to the glory of God.

God expects every believer to be a witness of Christ's resurrection and to lead the unconverted to the Lord. Believers must tell the good news of salvation to everyone who is

---

53. Eugene H. Peterson, *The Message: The New Testament in Contemporary English* (Colorado Springs, Colo.: NavPress, 1993), p. 374.

54. See Rudolf Bultmann's translation: "So that grace may grow and through an ever greater number (of those converted) may increase thanksgiving to the glory of God." *The Second Letter to the Corinthians*, trans. Roy A. Harrisville (Minneapolis: Augsburg, 1985), p. 124.

55. Compare C. K. Barrett, *The Second Epistle to the Corinthians*, Harper's New Testament Commentaries series (New York: Harper and Row, 1973), p. 145; and Victor Paul Furnish, *II Corinthians: Translated with Introduction, Notes and Commentary*, Anchor Bible 32A (Garden City, N.Y.: Doubleday, 1984), p. 287.

willing and ready to listen. Hence every Christian must say with Paul: "I believed, therefore I have spoken."

Greek Words, Phrases, and Constructions in 4:13–15

Verses 13–14

ἔχοντες—first in the sentence for emphasis, this participle denotes cause and depends on the main verb πιστεύομεν.

τὸ αὐτὸ πνεῦμα—"the same spirit." Most translations have the word *spirit* with a general meaning. The terminology *the spirit of* is rather common in the New Testament: the spirit of adoption, of wisdom, of grace, and of glory (Rom. 8:15; Eph. 1:17; Heb. 10:29; I Peter 4:14 respectively).[56]

εἰδότες—this perfect participle depends on the preceding verb λαλοῦμεν, occurs at the same time, and is causal.

κύριον—"Lord." The manuscript support is divided on the reading *the Lord Jesus* or *Jesus*. The reading of Romans 8:11 may have influenced the shorter reading of the text. Conversely, the rule that the shorter text is more likely to be correct should not be dismissed.

Verse 15

τὰ πάντα—the use of the definite article with the adjective describes the totality of Paul's experience and effort.

χάρις and εὐχαριστίαν—the English language cannot reproduce the Greek play on words (see 1:11). It only has "grace" and "thanksgiving." The Spanish translation, however, is able to approach the wordplay: "la gracia . . . la acción de gracias."

πλεονάσασα—the aorist participle is both active and ingressive: "is multiplying."

---

16 Therefore, we do not lose heart. But though our outer self is being destroyed, our inner self is being renewed day by day. 17 For our affliction, which is temporary and trifling, is working in us an eternal fullness of glory that exceeds all limits, 18 because we do not look at the things that are seen but at the things that are not seen. For the things that are seen are for the moment, but the things that are not seen are eternal.

How to divide Paul's discourse is a matter that varies from scholar to scholar. One is of the opinion that 4:7–5:10 forms a unit on suffering and glory, of which verses 16–18 are a constitutive part. Another thinks that verses 16–18 are the introductory part of Paul's discussion on faith (4:16–5:10). And still another believes that "one of the most important eschatological passages of the New Testament" begins at 4:16b and ends at 5:10.[57] In view of Paul's conclusive "therefore," I am inclined to see verses 16–18 as a bridge between his reflection on the resurrection from the dead and his discussion on our dwelling either in an earthly tent or with the Lord (5:1–10).

---

56. Hughes, *Second Epistle to the Corinthians*, p. 147; Collange, *Énigmes*, p. 162.
57. The three opinions are respectively of Harris, *II Corinthians*, p. 317; Kruse, *II Corinthians*, p. 54; Hughes, *Second Epistle to the Corinthians*, p. 152.

3. Outward and Inward
4:16–18

16. Therefore, we do not lose heart. But though our outer self is being destroyed, our inner self is being renewed day by day.

a. "Therefore." The adverb *therefore* indicates that Paul now concludes his discourse on the doctrine of the resurrection. He reflects on the pain and the afflictions he has endured already because of the gospel. He should have capitulated long ago. Instead Paul displays a resilience that he derives from God's power (v. 7) residing within him and that he devotes to God's glory (v. 15).

b. "We do not lose heart." These words are not mere empty words spoken to encourage others while Paul himself is despondent (compare 1:8). Nothing could be further from the truth. The apostle has repeatedly demonstrated his resilience, as two examples taken from Paul's life will demonstrate.

First, he was beaten with rods, thrown into prison, with his legs in the stocks; yet he was praying and singing hymns in the middle of the night (Acts 16:22–25). Next, when the raging storm caused the people aboard ship to give up all hope, Paul told them to be courageous. He predicted that they would run aground on an island but everyone would be rescued (Acts 27:20–26).

Once again, Paul states that he does not lose heart (see v. 1). Although his body is weakened because of the suffering he had to endure, his spirit is sincere, strong, and buoyant. Not his physical comfort but his burning zeal for the Lord is all-important.

c. "But though our outer self is being destroyed, our inner self is being renewed day by day." Is Paul adapting his discourse to Greek philosophy, which considered the human body transitory but the soul immortal? Hardly, for the context proves that Paul teaches the tenet of the resurrection from the dead (v. 14). This doctrine was repudiated by Greek and Roman philosophers.

With his Hebraic background, Paul has a biblical view of human beings. He sees them as complete units, for body and soul belong together:

> "The LORD God formed the man from the dust of the ground and breathed into his nostrils the breath of life, and the man became a living being." [Gen. 2:7]

The expression *living being* does not mean a body and a soul, but refers to a unit. The Jews always considered body and soul to be an entity and used each term to refer to the totality of a human being.[58] The separation of body and soul by death is unnatural and contrary to God's original intention.

If verse 16 serves as a bridge between Paul's discussion about resurrection and his reflection on our present and future bodies, we notice at least three features. First, Paul addresses not only himself and his co-workers but all believers. Next, the outer being, in relation to the inner self, refers to the body as an entity.

---

58. Eduard Schweizer, *TDNT,* 7:1045–48; Edmond Jacob, *TDNT,* 9:620.

Third, the outer self and the inner self have a deeper meaning in the sense of the "old self" (Eph. 4:22) and the "new self" (Col. 3:10). The word choice Paul uses in the verses with cross references is remarkably similar. He writes:

"our outer self is being destroyed" and
"the old self, which is being corrupted" (Eph. 4:22),
"our inner self is being renewed" and
"the new self, which is being renewed" (Col. 3:10).[59]

The two terms ("outer self" and "inner self") that Paul employs are comprehensive and all-inclusive. They embrace everything that pertains to the human existence of every believer. The outer self is exposed to "temptations, dangers, and decay," while the inner self is renewed through day by day communion with Christ and is strengthened by the Holy Spirit.[60] This process of renewal has its beginning in regeneration and is complete at the consummation.

For Paul, conversion on the road to Damascus marked the beginning of his new self (compare Rom. 6:6; 7:22; Eph. 3:16). He experienced daily progress in his new life. He was made stronger to trust God, proclaim the gospel, and oppose his adversaries. Even though his body often endured piercing pain and physical abuse, his inner self triumphed through Jesus Christ.

This passage relates not only to Paul and his associates but also to every believer. Created in God's image, the new self is progressively transformed by the principles of spiritual knowledge, true righteousness, and singular holiness (Eph. 4:24; Col. 3:10).

17. For our affliction, which is temporary and trifling, is working in us an eternal fullness of glory that exceeds all limits, 18. because we do not look at the things that are seen but at the things that are not seen. For the things that are seen are for the moment, but the things that are not seen are eternal.

a. "For our affliction, which is temporary and trifling." Paul is not minimizing his hardships, as is evident from the many times he lists his sufferings (I Cor. 4:11–13; II Cor. 1:8–10; 4:8–9; 6:4–10; 11:23–27; 12:10). Of all Christians, he had his share of afflictions for the sake of Christ and the gospel. However, he is not thinking of himself alone, because his statement is applicable to every believer throughout the centuries.

The term *temporary* does not relate to a brief duration. By looking at time from the perspective of eternity, Paul considers the duration of our earthly suffering but a fleeting moment (compare I Peter 1:6; 5:10).

Paul does not say "our light affliction" but "our affliction is . . . trifling." He wants to emphasize that any hardship, whatever it may be, is a trifling thing.[61] It

---

59. Kim, *Origin of Paul's Gospel,* pp. 323–24.
60. Ridderbos, *Paul,* p. 227. See also John Gillman, "Going Home to the Lord," *BibToday* 20 (1982): 277; David Stanley, "The Glory about to Be Revealed," *Way* 22 (1982): 282.
61. Grosheide, *Tweede Brief aan Korinthe,* p. 168.

seems incongruous that the apostle who endured being stoned by the Jews in Lystra (Acts 14:19) contends that this affliction was an insignificant experience. But let us not lose sight of the point Paul is making: he contrasts

the temporary and the eternal
the trifling and the weighty
affliction and glory.

b. "[Our affliction] is working in us an eternal fullness of glory that exceeds all limits." Every word in this sentence is significant. To begin, the verb is in the present tense to indicate continued action. We cannot say that affliction by itself merits glory, for then every believer would greatly desire and even seek hardship. Not believers but God allows affliction to enter their lives and through it God produces eternal glory for them.[62] As Paul and Barnabas told the Christians in Asia Minor, "We must go through many hardships to enter the kingdom of God" (Acts 14:22).

Next, the literal translation *weight of glory* is the reading in most versions. Some have variations, including "glory that far outweighs" (NIV), "load of glory" *(Cassirer),* and "solid glory" *(Moffatt).* Back of the Greek text lies a play on words in a Hebrew idiom, for the Hebrew noun *kābōd* means both "weight" and "glory" (see Gen. 18:20; Job 6:3). However, if we translate a Hebrew idiom via the Greek into English, we fail to convey the meaning of the text. The Greek word *baros* denotes both weight and fullness; this second option, "fullness," fits the context: "an everlasting fullness of glory."[63] The idiom itself signifies a great degree of glory (see NCV), which the Syriac Peshitta renders "great glory." And for a last observation, the descriptive adjective *great* appears in the clause *God's glory is great* (variations in Pss. 21:5; 138:5).

In verse 17, Paul displays Hebrew idioms. The first one, "weight of glory," and the second, "exceeds all limits," should be interpreted not literally but in accordance with the sense they convey. That is, the glory that is ours is so great that it is immeasurable.

Should the phrase *exceeds all limits* be connected with either "weight" or "eternal"? It can even be taken with the verb *to work.*[64] This particular idiom ought not to be connected with only one word but rather should be interpreted as a qualifier of the entire sentence. It describes for us heavenly glory that is indescribable and beyond measure (see Rom. 8:18).

c. "Because we do not look at the things that are seen but at the things that are not seen." This sentence describes the cause for the preceding thought about affliction that is temporary and trifling. Paul says that when we focus our

62. Compare Georg Bertram, *TDNT*, 3:635.
63. Bauer, p. 134.
64. J. H. Bernard, *The Second Epistle to the Corinthians*, The Expositor's Greek Testament, ed. W. Robertson Nicoll (Grand Rapids: Eerdmans, n.d.), vol. 3, p. 64.

attention on things invisible, we minimize hardships and maximize eternal glory.

Paul realizes that Christians often endure painful experiences and ask God the perennial question: Why they are the ones who suffer? He observes that they are not concentrating on the earthly things that they daily see, but instead they are looking heavenward (Col. 3:1–2). They are paying attention to the things that are invisible. Paul differentiates not the material from the spiritual but the earthly from the heavenly and the temporal from the eternal things. Thus, he gives the readers some pastoral advice that also appears elsewhere (Rom. 8:24; Heb. 11:1, 3; Col. 1:16; I Peter 1:8).

d. "For the things that are seen are for the moment, but the things that are not seen are eternal." In relation to eternity time is but a moment. Similarly, earthly treasures are unstable, but heavenly possessions last forever. Therefore, the inner self that is daily being renewed does not lose heart but looks at life from God's point of view. The invisible things are those that we appropriate by faith in God. We identify with the heroes of faith who saw these things "and welcomed them from a distance" (Heb. 11:13). And we keep our eyes fixed on Jesus the author and perfecter of our faith (Heb. 12:2).

Greek Words, Phrases, and Constructions in 4:16–17

ἀλλ᾽ εἰ καί—this combination introduces a concessive clause with the word *although*.[65]

ἡμέρᾳ καὶ ἡμέρᾳ—here is a translated Hebrew idiom signifying "day by day."

τὸ ἐλαφρόν—note that this adjective preceded by a definite article actually is the subject of the verb κατεργάζεται (produces).

ἡμῶν—some textual witnesses omit this pronoun, but it is easier to explain its omission than its insertion. The nearness of ἡμῖν probably caused the deletion of the pronoun.

Summary of Chapter 4

The division of the chapters in this epistle is arbitrary at places. As is evident from the content of the first six verses, they are part of the discourse Paul developed in chapter 3. The vocabulary repeats that of the preceding chapter, yet in these six verses he inserts teaching that touches on the light of the gospel.

Paul's openness in presenting the gospel is characterized by a manner that is above reproach. His veracity diverges radically from that of his opponents. He portrays his adversaries as secretive people who live shameful lives and, as deceivers, distort God's truth. Yet he admits that his presentation of the gospel is veiled for some people: only for those who are perishing because Satan has blinded their minds. Thus they cannot see the light of the gospel. God makes his light to shine in the hearts of his people so that they may see his glory in Christ.

---

65. E. D. Burton, *Moods and Tenses of New Testament Greek* (Edinburgh: Clark, 1898), p. 284.

In the next segment, Paul contrasts body and soul, hardships and glory, death and life. He mentions human frailty and God's sufficiency, Jesus' life and Jesus' death, and the willingness of Paul and his co-workers to put their lives on the line for the church.

The apostle shows a spiritual kinship with the psalmist who composed Psalm 116. The characteristics of both faith and courage to speak are common to the psalmist and Paul. The apostle freely speaks about Jesus' resurrection, for it is basic to Paul's faith. Paul notes that the message he proclaims grants the gift of the resurrection to all who believe the gospel. He expects that an ever-increasing number of people will be recipients of God's grace, so that together with the saints they will express thanks to God.

Paul reflects on the frailty of his human body and the daily renewal of his inner self. He rejoices in the incomparable glory that outshines the earthly afflictions that are momentary and trifling. He comments on the spiritual exercise of looking not at the visible but at the invisible things, not at temporal but at eternal possessions.

5

Apostolic Ministry, *part 5*

(5:1–21)

Outline (continued)

5 1 For we know that if our earthly tent in which we live is taken down, we have a house from God, an eternal house not made with hands, in heaven. 2 For indeed in this tent we groan, while we long to be clothed [over] with our heavenly dwelling. 3 If indeed we are clothed [over], we are not found to be naked. 4 For indeed while we are in this tent we groan, being burdened, because we do not wish to be unclothed but to be clothed [over], so that what is mortal may be swallowed up by life. 5 The one who has prepared us for this very purpose is God, who has given us his Spirit as a pledge.

6 Therefore we are always confident and know that while we are at home in the body, we are away from the Lord. 7 For we walk by faith, not by sight. 8 We are confident, indeed, and prefer to be away from the body and to be at home with the Lord. 9 Therefore, we consider it our aim to please him whether we are at home or away from home. 10 For all of us must appear before the judgment seat of Christ, so that each one may receive recompense for the things which he has done in the body, whether good or bad.

---

4. Home in Heaven
5:1–5

The first ten verses in this chapter have their roots in Paul's discussion on jars of clay (4:7), the resurrection (4:13–15), and the visible and the invisible (4:18). His discourse on the believer's home with the Lord is the climax of this lengthy and involved discussion. However, this does not mean that the climax is lucid, brief, and to the point. The opposite is true if we merely look at the numerous interpretations of these ten verses. Every verse has problems that require due attention and raise many questions. Here are some of the questions that we face:

1. In Paul's letters (I Thess. 4:13–18; I Cor. 15), are we able to detect a gradual unfolding of his views on Christ's return?
2. Are there indications that Paul is opposing incipient Gnosticism in his eschatological teachings?
3. In his teachings on immortality and resurrection, how much does Paul reflect the Greek and Jewish beliefs of his day?
4. Is Paul speaking of the individual or of the corporate body of the church when he refers to the resurrection of the body?
5. Does Paul teach an intermediate state between a Christian's death and Christ's return?
6. Upon death does a believer receive a resurrection body as clothing of the soul?

7. Did Paul expect the second coming of Christ to take place during his lifetime?

8. Is the believer immediately after death forever with the Lord or does the soul sleep until the resurrection of the body?

We raise these questions as an aid to interpreting 5:1–10 and to finding our way through the various interpretations of these verses. Although scholars face several problems in every one of these verses, the individual believer turns to these verses for comfort and hope in times of bereavement. And even though Paul's words seem terse and incomplete, they have been and continue to be a source of spiritual strength to those who grieve. Pastors usually read these words at funeral and memorial services to comfort the bereaved.

Questions concerning the meaning of these verses remain, however, and we intend to answer them in the discussion on verses 1–10, but not always in the order listed. We shall carefully examine the text and seek to explain its meaning as clearly as possible. We shall analyze the significance of every word in the text and understand its relation to the rest of the verse and context.

1. For we know that if our earthly tent in which we live is taken down, we have a house from God, an eternal house not made with hands, in heaven.

a. "For we know." Paul introduces this verse with the words *for we know* (see also 1:7; 4:14; 5:11). In light of the preceding verses (4:16–18) that speak of the outward and the inward person and of looking at that which is unseen, Paul reminds his readers of his former teachings on the resurrection. He can say "we know" to remind the Corinthians of the doctrine he taught them in person and later through his correspondence. His instruction is neither at variance with nor different from that which he taught in I Thessalonians 4 and I Corinthians 15. Nothing in Paul's earlier writings conflicts with his present discourse, nor are we able to detect a gradual development of the resurrection doctrine. This chapter provides no evidence that he had to correct or change his initial teaching.[1]

Knowledge of the life hereafter does not originate in our human minds. Through the Holy Spirit, God reveals the assurance of our own immortality to us, so that we meet death cheerfully.[2] But what do we know? Paul confidently answers, "We have a house from God, an eternal house not made with hands, in heaven." Before we look closely at his answer, we must consider the conditional clause that qualifies it.

---

1. After a detailed study, Ben F. Meyer concludes: "There is a total lack of persuasive evidence that Paul's teaching on the resurrection of the dead underwent significant development either between I Thess[alonians] and I Cor[inthians] 15, or between I Cor[inthians] 15 and II Cor[inthians] 5. Allusion to 'the intermediate state' occurs at least in II Cor[inthians] 5 and Phil[ippians] 1, apparently without entailing any change in Paul's conception of resurrection of the dead and transformation of the living at the Parousia." See Meyer's article, "Did Paul's view of the resurrection of the dead undergo development?" *ThSt* 47 (1986): 382.

2. John Calvin, *The Second Epistle of Paul the Apostle to the Corinthians and the Epistles to Timothy, Titus and Philemon,* Calvin's Commentaries series, trans. T. A. Small (Grand Rapids: Eerdmans, 1964), p. 67.

b. "That if our earthly tent in which we live is taken down." Some scholars stress that Paul had to oppose Gnosticism, a religious and philosophical system that taught that matter is evil and the soul good. As such, the soul sheds its outer covering at the time of death and is set free.[3] The question, however, is not whether Paul was opposing incipient Gnosticism and thus used Gnostic terminology to be effective in his dispute. Although Greek philosophy taught that this earthly life is comparable to living in a tent, Paul exhibits an Old Testament background. A tent, as the tentmaker well knew, is a temporary dwelling that is readily taken down. He alludes to Moses' tent of meeting outside the camp of Israel; in this tent, God spoke to Moses face to face (Exod. 33:7–11). This earthly tent that subsequently became the tabernacle was a reflection of God's presence among his people as his glory covered the tabernacle. Further, even Aaron's high-priestly garments reflected God's holiness and glory. Yet both the tabernacle and the garments revealed transitoriness. The tabernacle was taken down when the Israelites moved to another place, and the garments were removed whenever Aaron's priestly duties ended.[4]

In the first eight verses, Paul uses a series of three metaphors (tent [vv. 1, 4], clothing [vv. 2–4], and home [vv. 6, 8]). The first illustration that Paul, the tentmaker, uses is that of a tent. He compares our physical body with a temporary dwelling place. And he may have thought of the Feast of Tabernacles, during which the Jews lived in temporary shelters for seven days to celebrate the end of the harvest and to commemorate the forty-year wilderness journey of the Israelites.[5] The metaphor of taking down a tent points to the approaching end of not only our physical body but also our entire earthly existence. Indeed, Peter mentions living "in the tent of this body" that would soon be put aside (II Peter 1:13–14; compare Isa. 38:12; Wisd. of Sol. 9:15). The word *earthly* is used as a contrast to *heavenly*, as a reminder of the first man taken from the dust of the earth (Gen. 2:7; I Cor. 15:47), and ethically as a place of sin.[6]

Paul literally writes, "if our earthly house of the tent is taken down." He describes the house in terms of a tent to stress its transience. The probability that this tent will be destroyed in a single action is real, for death marks the end of a person's earthly body and life. But Paul does not know when the dismantling will

---

3. Consult Rudolf Bultmann, *Exegetische Probleme des Zweiten Korintherbriefes* (Darmstadt: Wissenschaftliche Buchgesellschaft, 1963), pp. 4–6; Walter Schmithals, *Gnosticism in Corinth,* trans. John E. Steely (Nashville: Abingdon, 1971), p. 262. Compare Dieter Georgi, who thinks that Paul has adopted Gnostic terminology: *The Opponents of Paul in Second Corinthians* (Philadelphia: Fortress, 1986), pp. 230, 318.

4. Consult S. T. Lowrie, "An Exegesis of II Corinthians 5:1–5," *PThR* 1 (1903): 56–57; Meredith G. Kline, *Images of the Spirit* (Grand Rapids: Baker, 1980), pp. 35–36, 42–47.

5. Exod. 23:16b; Lev. 23:33–36a, 39–43; Num. 29:12–34; Deut. 16:13–15; Zech. 14:16–19; John 7:2. T. W. Manson, "ΙΛΑΣΤΗΡΙΟΝ," *JTS* 46 (1945): 1–10; Philip Edgcumbe Hughes, *Paul's Second Epistle to the Corinthians: The English Text with Introduction, Exposition and Notes,* New International Commentary on the New Testament series (Grand Rapids: Eerdmans, 1962), p. 162.

6. J.-F. Collange, *Énigmes de la deuxième épître de Paul aux Corinthiens: Étude exégétique de II Cor. 2:14–7:4,* SNTSMS 18 (New York and Cambridge: Cambridge University Press, 1972), p. 195.

occur. If Jesus should return during his lifetime, Paul would not have to think about death.

Earlier Paul wrote that he had endured a near-death affliction (1:8). This incident reminded him of life's brevity and the possibility of dying before Christ's return.[7] But we cannot deduce from this event that in the interval between writing I Corinthians and II Corinthians Paul changed his mind and no longer expected the return of Christ in his lifetime. Paul had survived a number of near-death experiences; the stoning in Lystra (Acts 14:19) serves as an example. And in his list of sufferings, he writes that he had been repeatedly exposed to death (11:23). Knowing firsthand the brevity of life, Paul realized that the gospel had to be preached to all nations before the Lord would return. He also knew that his missionary task had just begun and would remain unfinished at his death (compare Rom. 15:20, 24, 28).

c. "We have a house from God, an eternal house not made with hands, in heaven." The second part of this verse is a source of constant debate, because Paul's words are enigmatic and at places hard to reconcile with the entire context. If there is a contrast between the earthly tent and the house in heaven, why does Paul write the present tense ("we have")? The answer is that New Testament writers frequently penned a present tense with a future meaning that is determined by the context. One example is in the Gethsemane narrative, where prior to his arrest Jesus says, "The Son of Man is betrayed in the hands of sinners" (Matt. 26:45). Just as Jesus knew the nearness of his betrayal, so Paul knew with certainty that a heavenly home was waiting for him (see John 14:2–3).

Is a house from God a resurrection body that believers receive at the time of death?[8] If so, we must think in terms of three successive bodies: an earthly, an intermediate, and a resurrected or a transformed body. But why would the dead have to be raised at Jesus' return if they already have a resurrection body? Scripture speaks only of our physical body that either dies and is raised at Jesus' coming or that meets the Lord at his return and is transformed (I Cor. 15:42, 51; Phil. 3:20–21; I Thess. 4:15–17). The Bible fails to provide details on our house in heaven.

We admit that Scripture portrays people of the hereafter in terms of the physical form in which they left this earth. Samuel is described as an old man (I Sam. 28:14); Lazarus in heaven has a finger, and the rich man in hell has eyes and a tongue (Luke 16:23–24); the saints in heaven are dressed in white robes and hold palm branches in their hands (Rev. 6:11; 7:9). But the writers of Scripture use anthropomorphic language. That is, they depict the dead as human beings with flesh and blood, for they know of no other way to portray the departed. Scripture states unequivocally that the departed saints are spirits; their bodies

---

7. F. F. Bruce, *Paul: Apostle of the Heart Set Free* (Grand Rapids: Eerdmans, 1977), p. 310; Murray J. Harris, "II Corinthians 5:1–10: Watershed in Paul's Eschatology?" *TynB* 22 (1971): 56; T. Francis Glasson, "II Corinthians v. 1–10 *versus* Platonism," *SJT* 43 (1990): 145–55.

8. Numerous scholars hold this view. See the list presented by Murray J. Harris, *Raised Immortal: Resurrection and Immortality in the New Testament* (Grand Rapids: Eerdmans, 1983), pp. 98, 255 n. 2.

rest in the dust of the ground and their spirits have returned to God (Eccles. 12:7; Heb. 12:23).[9]

What is the meaning of the word *house?* This noun is qualified as being from God, eternal, not made by human hands, in heaven. Some scholars interpret the word to signify the corporate body of Christ, that is, the church. They point out that in the Greek, the term *oikodomē* (house) refers to the church and not to an individual body. To support their interpretation, they rely on a few passages from the Pauline epistles, especially I Corinthians 3:9 (God's building); Ephesians 2:21 (the building or holy temple; by extension, the body of Christ); Ephesians 4:12, 16 (the body of Christ).[10]

However, the context in which an expression is used always determines its meaning. Here the context for the word *house* differs from that of the passages that speak of the church. Furthermore, whenever Paul refers to the church as the body of Christ, he puts it not in a future context but in a present setting.[11] In verse 2, Paul notes our longing to be clothed with a heavenly tent in the future. This interpretation proves to be incongruous if we already belong to Christ's body (I Cor. 12:13; Gal. 3:27).

Other scholars think that the house in heaven is the temple of God that is awaiting the believer at the time of death. When Christians enter this building, they in effect enter God's presence.[12] Supporting this interpretation is the fact that the concept *not made with human hands* appears also in the description of the greater and more perfect tabernacle in heaven. That place is the very presence of God (Heb. 9:11). An objection to this interpretation is that the symmetry of verse 1 suffers, because an earthly tent and a heavenly house represent not a physical body and God's temple but a physical body and a spiritual body.

Perhaps we should think of this heavenly house as a place that supplies a covering in the form of divine glory (4:17; Rom. 8:18), a glory of immeasurable worth. Even though we enter God's presence, where we are clothed with glory, we eagerly await the redemption of our bodies, namely, the resurrection of our bodies (Rom. 8:23).

The link between the preceding paragraph (4:16–18) and this verse is undeniable. Earlier Paul spoke of the outer and inner person, temporary troubles and lasting glory, the visible and the invisible things. In verse 1, he speaks of an earthly tent, that is, our physical bodies brought into the world through human

---

9. Herman Bavinck, *Gereformeerde Dogmatiek,* 4 vols. (Kampen: Kok, 1930), vol. 4, p. 595.

10. J. A. T. Robinson, *The Body,* SBT 5 (London: SCM, 1952); A. Feuillet, "La demeure céleste et la destinée des chrétiens. Exégèse de II Cor. 5:1–10 et contribution à l'étude des fondements de l'eschatologie paulienne," *ResScRel* 44 (1956): 161–92, 360–402; E. Earle Ellis, "II Corinthians v.1–10 in Pauline Eschatology," *NTS* 6 (1959–60): 211–24; F. G. Lang, *II Korinther 2, 1–10 in der neueren Forschung,* BGBE 16 (Tübingen: Mohr, 1973), pp. 179–82; Nigel M. Watson, "II Cor 5:1–10 in recent research," *AusBRev* 23 (1975): 33–36.

11. See F. F. Bruce, "Paul on Immortality," *SJT* 24 (1971): 270.

12. Karl Hanhart, "Paul's Hope in the Face of Death," *JBL* 88 (1969): 445–57; Charles Hodge, *An Exposition of the Second Epistle to the Corinthians* (1891; Edinburgh: Banner of Truth, 1959), pp. 109–14.

effort. He contrasts this temporary tent with a permanent house that originates with God and belongs to an entirely different order. The house is God's very presence that at the portals of heaven envelops the believer with eternal glory. Paul teaches that if he should die before Jesus' return, then his soul would enter and be in heaven without his body until its resurrection at the consummation.

2. For indeed in this tent we groan, while we long to be clothed [over] with our heavenly dwelling.

Notice that verse 4 has the same beginning as verse 2, "for indeed." Thus, Paul stresses the fact that we are presently groaning in our physical bodies, while we express a longing to be clothed with clothing that God provides. In these two verses (vv. 2 and 4), he reiterates this thought as an explanation of the preceding passage (v. 1).

If Paul had supplied a noun with the literal phrase *in this,* scholars would be able to give only one translation. As it is, the noun is lacking and the many variations range from "in this present state" to "because," "here," "now," and "meanwhile." But the context of the first four verses, especially the repetition *in this tent* (v. 4), appears to indicate that Paul has in mind our physical body, which he characterizes as "this tent."

The verb *to groan* usually communicates pain and discomfort; but here the dark clouds of our earthly life appear with the gilded edge of hope and eager expectation. Indeed, the text imparts an affirmative message with the verb *to long* in the last half of the verse. Paul writes that we groan while longing to be clothed, for this intense longing is the basis for our groaning. In his epistle to the Romans, Paul mentions the groans of creation, the redeemed, and the Spirit. Both creation and the redeemed endure distress and long for the day when God's children will be liberated, that is, when they experience the redemption of their bodies. In the meantime, the Holy Spirit himself groans while interceding on behalf of God's people (Rom. 8:22–23, 26 respectively).

Paul's second illustration in verses 1–8 is that of clothing (vv. 2–4). He writes that "we long to be clothed [over] with our heavenly dwelling," and uses the Greek verb *ependysasthai* (to be covered over). This verb conveys the idea of putting on an additional garment, rather like wearing an overcoat.[13] Here Paul is considering not the resurrection of the dead but the transformation at the coming of Christ. He is saying that we eagerly await Christ's return. Then our present bodies will be transformed instantaneously when they receive the additional clothing of our heavenly dwelling in the form of a glorified body (I Cor. 15:51; Phil. 3:21).

Not every scholar agrees with the traditional interpretation of this text. Some writers argue that the verb *ependysasthai* does not necessarily mean that Paul dis-

---

13. Albrecht Oepke, *TDNT,* 2:320–21; Horst Weigelt, *NIDNTT,* 1:316; F. F. Bruce, *I and II Corinthians,* New Century Bible (London: Oliphants, 1971), p. 202; Hughes, *Second Epistle to the Corinthians,* p. 168 n. 31; Herman N. Ridderbos, *Paul: An Outline of His Theology,* trans. John Richard de Witt (Grand Rapids: Eerdmans, 1975), p. 501.

tinguishes between those who die before the return of Christ and those who are alive at his coming. They say that believers at their death immediately don a resurrection body over their physical body. And this happens also to those believers who are alive when Christ returns.[14]

These scholars explain the Greek verb in question only from a temporal point of view.[15] But the verb also connotes a dimensional aspect, with the preposition *over*, that should not be neglected. Paul is saying that the heavenly body is put on over the earthly body. Reality teaches us, however, that physical bodies at death decay and are not immediately donning resurrection bodies.[16] Paul applies the imagery of clothing to the believers who are alive at Christ's coming but not to those whose bodies descend into the grave. Only those who do not experience death and the grave have physical bodies that receive an additional garment.

3. If indeed we are clothed [over], we are not found to be naked.

a. *Variant reading.* This brief verse, which is intimately connected to the preceding passage, has at least one variant that has given commentators some difficulty. To illustrate, here are two versions:

> "If so be that being clothed
> we shall not be found naked" (KJV).

> "If indeed, when we have taken it off
> we will not be found naked" (NRSV).

The question is, "Are we dressed or undressed?" The Alexandrian manuscripts support the reading *having been clothed,* while the Western witnesses have the reading *having taken it off.* Scribes either changed the wording to help the reader understand the text or committed a scribal error. In the Greek text the difference between the words in question is a matter of only one letter: *endysamenoi* (having been clothed) and *ekdysamenoi* (having been unclothed). Of the two choices, most translators and many commentators favor the reading of the major witnesses: "having been clothed."[17]

b. *Meaning.* Either version presents problems. The first reading, "having been clothed," followed by "we shall not be found naked," is a trite statement that pro-

---

14. Harris writes, "Paul viewed himself as donning the resurrection body without having first doffed the earthly body." "II Corinthians 5:1–10: Watershed in Paul's Eschatology?" 44; *Raised Immortal,* p. 99.

15. Compare Hans Windisch, *Der Zweite Korintherbrief,* ed. Georg Strecker (1924; reprint ed., Göttingen: Vandenhoeck und Ruprecht, 1970), pp. 161, 163.

16. John W. Cooper, *Body, Soul, and Life Everlasting: Biblical Anthropology and the Monism-Dualism Debate* (Grand Rapids: Eerdmans, 1989), p. 158.

17. Nes-Al[27] and United Bible Societies[4] have the reading ἐκδυσάμενοι, but all other Greek New Testament editions have ἐνδυσάμενοι. And of the translations, only the NRSV has "have taken it off." Alfred Plummer calls the first reading "an early alteration to avoid apparent tautology." See *A Critical and Exegetical Commentary on the Second Epistle of St Paul to the Corinthians,* International Critical Commentary (1915; Edinburgh: Clark, 1975), p. 147.

vides no new information. And the second reading, "having taken it off," forces the scholar to assert that the believer at death receives an intermediate body as a covering for the naked soul. But if the believer receives a body at the time of death, why is there a need for the resurrection of the physical body?

In addition, the reading of the major manuscripts can be supported with the observation that Paul writes the verb *to clothe over* in verse 2. This necessitates that the apostle mention the verb *to clothe* in the next verse.[18]

Verse 3 is an extension of verse 2 and as such is connected and in full agreement with it. The emphasis in Paul's discourse continues from verse 2 to verse 4, so that verse 3 becomes a supportive parenthetical comment. Paul longs for Christ's return when in the twinkling of an eye his physical body will put on a heavenly body (compare I Cor. 15:53–55). He shudders at the thought of death, for then his soul will be without covering and will be found to be naked. This thought is repugnant to him because soul and body belong together (Gen. 2:7). He understands the separation of body and soul to be the result of sin and death, but he knows that this separation will end. He would not have feared the separation of body and soul and longed for the clothing of a heavenly body "if he had held the view that the resurrection body was received at the moment of death."[19]

If Paul refers to Christ's return and the resurrection, is he so distraught at the prospect of disembodiment that he fails to look forward to an intermediate state? He longs to be with the Lord (v. 8; Phil. 1:23), but he would rather meet him at Christ's return and be transformed than to die and have to wait for the resurrection.[20] Paul teaches that Christ will take our physical bodies that are subject to disability, deterioration, and death and make them like his glorious body (Phil. 3:21). Hence, Paul's aversion to an undressed soul should be interpreted within the framework of his desire for an immediate transformation of his physical body.[21] Nevertheless, when death does occur, he will always be with the Lord. Thus he writes elsewhere, "If we live, we live to the Lord; and if we die, we die to the Lord. So, whether we live or die, we belong to the Lord" (Rom. 14:8). In short, Paul does not teach that the soul sleeps until the day of resurrection; upon death, the believer is forever with the Lord.

---

18. Margaret E. Thrall, "'Putting On' or 'Stripping Off' in II Corinthians 5:3," in *New Testament Textual Criticism: Its Significance for Exegesis, Essays in Honour of Bruce M. Metzger,* ed. Eldon Jay Epp and Gordon D. Fee (Oxford: Clarendon, 1981), pp. 221–38. Also see her *Critical and Exegetical Commentary on the Second Epistle to the Corinthians,* 2 vols., International Critical Commentary (Edinburgh: Clark, 1994), vol. 1, pp. 379–80.

19. Joseph Osei-Bonsu, "Does II Cor. 5.1–10 teach the reception of the resurrection body at the moment of death?" *JSNT* 28 (1986): 91.

20. Refer to C. K. Barrett, *The Second Epistle to the Corinthians,* Harper's New Testament Commentaries series (New York: Harper and Row, 1973), p. 156; John Yates, "Immediate or Intermediate? The State of the Believer upon Death," *Churchman* 101 (1987): 310–22.

21. Refer to Raymond O. Zorn, "II Corinthians 5:1–10: Individual Eschatology or Corporate Solidarity, Which?" *RTR* 48 (1989): 100.

Additional Notes on 5:3

Paul writes two conditional sentences, one in verse 1 and the other in verse 3. The first one, with the Greek particle ἐάν (if), expresses a degree of uncertainty because we as human beings do not know the hour of our death. We *are* certain that our earthly life will end, for we are destined to die (Gen. 3:19; Heb. 9:27). The second conditional sentence, introduced by the Greek particle εἰ (if), expresses an assurance that for Paul is based on his knowledge of the general resurrection of the dead: "For if the dead are not raised, then Christ has not been raised either" (I Cor. 15:16). Thus, Paul knows that if he is still living at Christ's return, the transformation of his body will preclude the exposure of his unclad soul. But this assurance jars with Paul's comment on the probability of death and a disembodied state before Christ's return (vv. 1, 8–10). Although this observation is valid, Paul's ardent longing for a glorified body without an intervening period of disembodiment removes much of the confusion that is inherent in these verses.[22]

Another view is that Paul thinks that he receives a resurrection body immediately upon death. This body, then, is the clothing that protects him from being naked. However, we must test this view with an accepted rule of exegesis: We look at the whole of Scripture from the perspective of the text, and we look at the text from the perspective of the whole of Scripture.

Hence, what do the Scriptures say? The New Testament teaches that the resurrection occurs at the time of Christ's return, a doctrine that Paul consistently writes throughout his epistles. It appears in one of his early letters (I Thess. 4:13–18), in all of his major epistles (I Cor. 15:22–28, 52–55; II Cor. 1:9; 4:4; Rom. 8:22–24), in one of his prison epistles (Phil. 3:11, 20–21), and even in his last letter (II Tim. 2:18). We conclude that if we are unable to find support from New Testament writers for the view that Christians receive their resurrection body immediately at death, then this interpretation is weak and seriously undermined.[23]

What does Paul mean in the last clause of verse 3, "we are not found to be naked"? Both Plato and Philo taught that the body as a shell imprisons the soul, which yearns to be set free from this body.[24] These philosophers stress the desirability of the soul's release, but Paul teaches the opposite by expressing his aversion to this separation.[25]

E. Earle Ellis avers that the concept *naked* must be seen in the context of shame, guilt, and judgment,[26] an interpretation that presents the concept in an ethical setting and that anticipates Paul's reference to the judgment seat of Christ (v. 10). It is difficult to understand that Paul in verse 3 connects the concept of nakedness to the certainty of judgment.

Instead, Paul teaches that the soul, being found naked, exists without the body in the presence of Christ. But he fails to provide further information on the bodiless state of the

---

22. Compare Geerhardus Vos, *The Pauline Eschatology* (1930; reprint ed., Grand Rapids: Baker, 1979), pp. 194–95.

23. See the list of objections provided by Harris, *Raised Immortal,* p. 255 n. 4; and see George Eldon Ladd, *A Theology of the New Testament,* ed. Donald A. Hagner, rev. ed. (Grand Rapids: Eerdmans, 1993), p. 599.

24. Plato *Phaedrus* 250C; Philo *De virtute* 76–77.

25. J. Sevenster, "Einige Bemerkungen über den 'Zwischenzustand' bei Paulus," *NTS* 1 (1955): 291–96; "Some Remarks on the ΓΥΜΝΟΣ in II Cor. v.3," in *Studia Paulina,* Festschrift J. de Zwaan (Haarlem: Bohn, 1953), pp. 202–14.

26. Ellis, "II Corinthians v. 1–10 in Pauline Eschatology," 211–24.

soul. After death, he says confidently, he waits for the resurrection of the body. The apostle addresses the reality of death in the lives of his fellow believers and himself. When death occurs, they as well as he are forever with the Lord in glory.

---

4. For indeed while we are in this tent we groan, being burdened, because we do not wish to be unclothed but to be clothed [over], so that what is mortal may be swallowed up by life.

a. "For indeed while we are in this tent we groan, being burdened." The parallel between verse 2 and verse 4a is striking and repetitious. The phrases are presented side by side:

Verse 2	*Verse 4a*
For indeed	For indeed
[being] in this tent	being in this tent
we groan	we groan
	being burdened
while we long	because we do not wish
	to be unclothed but
to be clothed [over]	to be clothed [over]
with our heavenly dwelling	

The differences consist primarily of additions in verse 4, with verse 2 having the extra words *with our heavenly dwelling*. Paul is groaning because he is burdened with the apprehension of an impending rift between body and soul at the time of death. In verse 2, he links his groaning with positive longing for extra covering; in verse 4, he negatively repeats this thought with the wish not to be without clothing but rather to have a heavenly body superimposed on his physical body.

b. "Because we do not wish to be unclothed but to be clothed [over]." Much more here than in verse 2 we notice that Paul conveys his dislike for putting aside his body. He uses the word *unclothed* as a synonym of "naked" in the preceding verse (v. 3). Paul desires to be covered with a resurrected body and the future glory that God already has prepared for him. He fails to disclose details concerning our future existence; the absence of these details must caution us not to view the transformation of our bodies too literally.[27]

Purposely Paul alludes to his discourse on the resurrection (I Cor. 15:53–54), for transformation entails the clothing of the perishable with the imperishable and the mortal with immortality. The verb *to clothe over* connotes that resurrection transforms the body and adds to it. That is, when the earthly body is destroyed (v. 1), the soul enters a state of being unclothed. But our desire is to see the resurrection of our bodies covered with everlasting glory and immortality.

c. "So that what is mortal may be swallowed up by life." Paul adapts an Old Testament passage that he quoted earlier: "Death has been swallowed up in victory" (Isa. 25:8; I Cor. 15:54b). For him and for his readers, the victory over death is of prime importance. John testifies of Jesus and says, "In him was life, and that life

---

27. Consult John Gillman, "Going Home to the Lord," *BibToday* 20 (1982): 275–81.

was the light of men" (John 1:4; see also 14:6). Jesus who is life conquered death, for by dying on the cross he destroyed the power of death. Jesus set his people free from the fear of death (Heb. 2:14–15). And God granted them the gift of eternal life through his Son (I John 5:11–13).

Although both death and grave insatiably devour mortal humanity, they will ultimately surrender to the power of Christ's eternal life that swallows up mortality. Notice, for example, that on the waves of human depravity that threaten to engulf and shipwreck everyone, moral standards continuously beckon and guide us to a safe haven. And in the midst of lies and deceit, truth eventually triumphs. Similarly, death has power but will come to an end. Says Paul, "[For] the last enemy to be destroyed is death" (I Cor. 15:26).

At death, our physical body descends into the grave, because the body cannot be held in bondage. It will come forth renewed and glorified through Christ at his coming; he triumphs over the power of death and the grave. Conversely, those believers who are alive at Christ's return are instantly transformed and do not experience death and the grave. We conclude that, with every believer, Paul longs for the Lord's coming and hopes that it may occur in his lifetime.

5. The one who has prepared us for this very purpose is God, who has given us his Spirit as a pledge.

Paul completes the first paragraph of this chapter with a sentence that stresses God's prominence. At the same time, this verse serves as an introduction to the next paragraph (vv. 6–10) that speaks of confidence, faith, and purpose.

The subject of verse 5 is God, whom Paul described with two clauses: he has prepared us, and he has given us his Spirit. First, then, God's work in preparing us. The verb *to prepare* can mean diligently working with and in someone, much as an instructor trains a student in anticipation of graduation and service. Paul's life is a case in point: God prepared him for missionary service by giving him an education, a conversion experience, faith in Christ, and numerous hardships and trials.

Paul writes that God has prepared us "for this very purpose," but what is that purpose? It is to be covered with a resurrected body and the future glory that God already has prepared for us. To put it differently, God has in store for us an existence of which the pristine life of Adam and Eve in paradise is a reflection. This existence is what God had originally designed before sin entered the world and now has planned for us. At the close of the age, Christians will be reclothed with either transformed or resurrected bodies.[28]

---

28. C. F. D. Moule in "St. Paul and Dualism: The Pauline Conception of Resurrection," *NTS* 12 (1965–66): 118, argues that the conjunction δέ is contrastive and means "but." And the phrase *for this very purpose* refers to stripping off the old clothing (our physical bodies) and receiving new clothing. Thus, God made us for the process of exchange. Ralph P. Martin notes that this "sounds perilously close to affirming that God has made us for the purpose of dying," a conclusion that cannot be confirmed in Scripture. See Martin's "The Spirit in II Corinthians in Light of the 'Fellowship of the Holy Spirit' in II Corinthians 13:14," in *Eschatology and the New Testament, Essays in Honor of G. R. Beasley-Murray,* ed. W. H. Gloer, Festschrift for G. R. Beasley-Murray (Peabody, Mass.: Hendrickson, 1988), p. 120.

God has given us the Holy Spirit as a pledge concerning matters that will be revealed in the future. He has made a contract with us with a down payment that obliges him to continue to make additional payments. Now we are receiving a foretaste of the Spirit but in the hereafter we will receive the full allotment that God has in store for us.[29]

Paul writes the Greek word *arrabōn* (pledge), which is a transliteration of the Hebrew (see Gen. 38:17, 18, 20) and a technical term used in commercial and legal circles. He also writes this term elsewhere with reference to the Holy Spirit (1:22; Eph. 1:14). Moreover, when God gives us a pledge in the person of the Holy Spirit, then he will also give us rest in due time. God's Word cannot be broken (John 10:35), for it is entirely trustworthy and true. We have the assurance that the Spirit, who is with us, will lead us safely into God's presence at the time of death.

Greek Words, Phrases, and Constructions in 5:1–5

Verse 1

ἔχομεν—the present tense is future in meaning. The protasis with the subjunctive has a futuristic propensity, and the apodosis expresses Paul's confidence of future bliss with a present tense.[30]

ἀχειροποίητον—this is a verbal adjective that is a compound with a negative ἀ, and a passive voice with the implication that God is the agent. It occurs only three times in the New Testament (Mark 14:58; II Cor. 5:1; Col. 2:11; and compare Heb. 9:11, 24).

τοῖς οὐρανοῖς—the plural form reflects the Hebrew *shammayim*, but see also 12:3.

Verses 2–3

ἐπενδύσασθαι—here and in verse 4, this aorist passive infinitive is a compound with two prepositions. Therefore, it does not have the same meaning as the compound ἐνδύσασθαι (to be clothed).[31] It is not perfective but directive: "to be clothed over."

εἴ γε καί—this combination conveys assurance in a conditional sentence and means "if indeed," "inasmuch as," or "since." The variant reading εἴπερ καί has solid manuscript support and is even more emphatic; nonetheless, internal considerations rule against its acceptance.[32]

ἐκδυσάμενοι—"being unclothed." Supported only by Western witnesses (D* a f^c; Tert Spec), the reading ἐνδυσάμενοι (being clothed) with better manuscript evidence is preferred, even though it contributes to tautology. For this reason, the preferred text is the more difficult reading. Furthermore, the aorist tense is constative and describes the state and not the action of being clothed.

---

29. Consult C. L. Mitton, "Paul's Certainties. V. The Gift of the Spirit and Life beyond Death—II Corinthians v. 1–5," *ExpT* 69 (1958): 260–63.

30. Consult Robert H. Gundry, *Sōma in Biblical Theology with Emphasis on Pauline Anthropology* (Grand Rapids: Zondervan, Academie Books 1987), p. 150.

31. Contra R. F. Hettlinger, "II Corinthians 5:1–10," *SJT* 10 (1957): 178–79.

32. Consult Margaret E. Thrall, *Greek Particles in the New Testament* (Leiden: Brill; Grand Rapids: Eerdmans, 1962), pp. 86–91; and "'Putting On' or 'Stripping Off,'" pp. 222–29.

Verses 4–5

ἐφ᾿ ᾧ—this combination is a contraction of ἐπὶ τούτῳ ὅτι (with respect to this matter that) and expresses cause.

τὸ θνητόν—the adjective *mortal* appears in the neuter with the definite article and is the counterpart of ἡ ζωή.

---

5. With the Lord
5:6–10

Thus far, Paul has resorted to the use of two metaphors: a tent (v. 1) and clothing (vv. 2–4). Now he introduces a third, that is, a home (vv. 6, 8). He writes two Greek verbs that do not occur elsewhere in the New Testament or in the Septuagint. With variations in verses 6–9, they are *endēmountes* (being at home) and *ekdēmountes* (being away from home). The words themselves present no problems but their use raises a few questions. Is Paul coining new words or is he borrowing them from another context? Is he addressing the believers or is he attacking his opponents and employing their terminology?

Paul's opponents in Corinth were apt to use a number of slogans, of which "Everything is permissible for me" and "Food for the stomach and the stomach for food" are the most prominent (I Cor. 6:12–13).[33] Paul usually states the slogan and then, taking some of its words, rejects its teaching. Perhaps also in verse 6b we encounter a slogan used by some of his opponents: "While being at home in the body, we are away from the Lord."[34] Paul uses this slogan to his advantage by presenting his view on death and the life hereafter in the succeeding verses (vv. 8–9). A detailed study of this paragraph aids us in understanding Paul's teaching.

6. Therefore we are always confident and know that while we are at home in the body, we are away from the Lord. 7. For we walk by faith, not by sight.

a. "Therefore we are always confident." I take the conjunction *therefore* to refer to the preceding verse (v. 5). There Paul mentions God's gift of the Holy Spirit to us in the form of a down payment with the pledge of greater gifts to come. The very presence of the Spirit in the lives of believers gives Paul and the Corinthians reason to be confident with respect to the future. Paul tells his readers that they can always be of good courage in view of God's pledge to them. The Greek verb *tharrein* or *tharsein* (to be confident, of good cheer) is a word that only Jesus utters in the Gospels and Acts, and that Paul writes in his letters.[35] The verb connotes fear that vanishes upon the reassurance that God is in control.

---

33. See John C. Hurd, Jr., *The Origin of I Corinthians* (Macon, Ga.: Mercer University Press, 1983), p. 68.

34. Refer to Jerome Murphy-O'Connor, "Being at home in the body we are in exile from the Lord: II Corinthians 5:6b," *RB* 93 (1986): 214–21. Presumably Paul's remark is a slogan uttered by some Corinthians who denied the doctrine of the resurrection (I Cor. 15:12).

35. Only Jesus uses *tharsein* in Matt. 9:2, 22; 14:27; Mark 6:50; 10:49; John 16:33; Acts 23:11; Paul writes *tharrein* in II Cor. 5:6, 8; 7:16; 10:1, 2, and nowhere else; and the author of Hebrews uses it in 13:6.

b. "And know that while we are at home in the body, we are away from the Lord." This is the second time in chapter 5 that Paul says "we know" (v. 1; see also vv. 11, 16). What is the sure knowledge that Paul and his readers have? The answer is: While we are at home in the body, we are away from the Lord. The expressions *being at home* and *being away from home* refer respectively to being in one's own country and being a stranger living abroad.[36] And, for some Corinthians, being a stranger living abroad meant being separated from the Lord. For Paul, however, it signified that he is in the world, but not of the world (John 17:14, 16).

> I am a stranger here, within a foreign land;
> My home is far away, upon a golden strand;
> Ambassador to be of realms beyond the sea,
> I'm here on business for my King.
> —E. T. Cassel

But note also that the expression *being at home* applies to the physical body, an expression which in this discourse is used for the first time and has a metaphoric meaning. A logical conclusion is then that when we die, we are at home with the Lord—precisely the doctrine that Paul's opponents deny. By itself, verse 6b contradicts what Paul has been saying about God's gift of the Holy Spirit as a pledge (v. 5). But the words of verse 6b should be interpreted with verse 7, where Paul gives them a distinctively Christian connotation.

c. "For we walk by faith, not by sight." With these two clauses Paul removes the inherent contradiction that the context presents. He tells his opponents to look at life with their eyes of faith, not through physical observation. Faith in God, not reliance on appearance, is all-important in this discussion.

Throughout this entire discourse (vv. 1–10), Paul contrasts the physical with the spiritual. Here are the parallels (the numbers indicate the verse):[37]

Physical	Spiritual
1. earthly tent	2. heavenly dwelling
4. unclothed	4. clothed
4. mortality	4. life
6. away from the Lord	8. with the Lord
6. in the body	8. away from the body
7. sight	7. faith
10. bad	10. good

Physical appearance stands in stark contrast to daily walking by faith and complete trust in Jesus Christ. In other words, the external image that we observe is

---

36. Consult Walter Grundmann, *TDNT*, 2:63; Hans Bietenhard, *NIDNTT*, 2:789; Collange, *Énigmes*, p. 228.

37. Compare Ellis, "Pauline Eschatology," p. 223. His conclusion, "The passage simply does not deal with the intermediate state" (p. 224), must be rejected. Paul reveals that the believer awaiting the resurrection of the body has a close relationship to the Lord. See Zorn, "II Corinthians 5:1–10," pp. 101–3.

passive and passing, while the internal quality of faith is active and abiding. We focus our attention not on visible things that are temporal but on those that are invisible and timeless (4:18; Rom. 8:23–25; I Cor. 13:12; I Peter 1:8). We live by faith and not by sight.

8. We are confident, indeed, and prefer to be away from the body and to be at home with the Lord.

Paul reinforces the beginning of verse 6 by repeating the same clause, "we are confident," and by adding the word *indeed*. But what he is saying sequentially is the opposite of the presumed Corinthian slogan: "While we are at home in the body, we are away from the Lord" (v. 6). He reverses the words of this slogan and communicates his longing to be with the Lord. He writes the same teaching elsewhere: "I desire to depart and be with Christ, which is better by far" (Phil. 1:23). Paul wants to leave his physical body and enter heaven in the presence of the Lord.

These words would not have caused any difficulty if Paul had not written that he did not wish to be unclothed but to be clothed (vv. 3–4). How can Paul, who abhorred the thought of a separation of body and soul, say that he prefers to be away from the body? Paul's overriding desire is to be with Christ, which for him is life, and to die, gain (Phil. 1:21). He has to choose one of three different states:

1. to be alive at Christ's return and to receive a transformed and glorified body;
2. to die, to leave the body, and to be at home with the Lord with an unclad soul;
3. to remain in the body because of obligations to serve the church (Phil. 1:24–26).

Of these three choices, Paul opts for the first one. But if the Lord tarries and death overtakes Paul, he would opt for the second choice. Nonetheless, because of the progress of the gospel in the church, he has to choose the last option. In summary, if there is a delay in Christ's coming, Paul prefers the second state.[38]

How do we interpret the apparent conflict in Paul's presentation? Perhaps a parallel can be drawn by pointing to Paul's commission as an apostle to the Gentiles and his readiness to die for the Lord (Acts 20:24; 21:13). He asked the church at Rome to pray for him that he might visit them on his way to Spain (Rom. 15:23–25, 30–32), yet at the same time he was willing to face death in Jerusalem. The conflict is resolved when we understand that Paul lived by faith and trusted in the Lord. He was ready to serve the Lord but also to die for him and then "to be at home with the Lord." The Greek is more descriptive, however,

---

38. Consult William L. Craig, "Paul's dilemma in II Corinthians 5. 1–10: a 'Catch-22'?" *NTS* 34 (1988): 145–47. Refer also to Lorin Cranford, "A New Look at II Corinthians 5:1–10," *SWJourTh* 19 (1976): 95–100; Ronald Berry, "Death and Life in Christ: The Meaning of II Corinthians 5:1–10," *SJT* 14 (1961): 60–76.

than English translations convey, for it expresses movement and rest: "to go on home to [and be with] the Lord" (compare NEB, "go to live with the Lord").[39]

The Lord is always near his people (Ps. 119:151; 145:18), and when he calls them to glory, that relationship continues (Rev. 22:7, 12, 20). They leave the body and are forever in the Lord's presence. The verb *to be at home* describes a state that begins at the moment of death.

9. Therefore, we consider it our aim to please him whether we are at home or away from home. 10. For all of us must appear before the judgment seat of Christ, so that each one may receive recompense for the things which he has done in the body, whether good or bad.

a. "Therefore, we consider it our aim to please him." Paul is writing his concluding remarks on this topic, and on the basis of the preceding verses he says "therefore." He now reverses the order of "away from home" and "at home" (v. 8) and returns to the original sequence (v. 6). The reversals make no difference in the understanding of this passage. Whether believers are in or out of the body does not matter, for their aim is to please the Lord. Does this mean that in the intermediate state, Christians are not able to please him? The answer is no. Paul is not addressing those who have died and are with the Lord. He is speaking to the readers who are alive. He is exhorting us to serve the Lord in such a manner that both God and our fellow men always take pleasure in our conduct (Rom. 14:18; Heb. 13:21).

b. "For all of us must appear before the judgment seat of Christ." When Paul writes "all of us," is he referring to all people? The New Testament teaches that everyone must appear before the judgment seat of God or Christ (Acts 10:42; 17:31; Rom. 14:10; II Tim. 4:1; I Peter 4:5). But here the Greek construction shows that he addresses the Corinthian Christians and presumably his opponents in that church. No one is exempt from being summoned to appear in court, for the word that Paul uses is "must"; the command to stand trial has a divine origin, for God through Christ issues the summons. The accused must answer to God (Rom. 14:10) and will receive the verdict from Christ.

c. "So that each one may receive recompense for the things which he has done in the body, whether good or bad." Each individual appears in court and hears the verdict based on one's conduct on earth. When the Lord returns (I Cor. 4:5), all works, whether good or bad, will be revealed. At that time, he assigns recompense to each individual for deeds performed through the instrumentality of the body while one is on earth. Jesus says, "Behold, I am coming soon! My reward is with me, and I will give to everyone according to what he has done" (Rev. 22:12).

Paul is not teaching a doctrine of earning one's salvation by doing good works. God accepts us not because of works that in themselves are stained by sin, but because of the meritorious work of Jesus Christ. Calvin notes, "Having thus

---

39. Here is a combination of "going to the Lord ('linear' motion) and that of being in His presence thereafter ('punctiliar' rest)." Hughes, *Second Epistle to the Corinthians*, p. 178 n. 53.

received us in His favour, He graciously accepts our works also, and it is upon this undeserved acceptance that the reward depends."[40]

Practical Considerations in 5:6–10

Through the news media, we become familiar with court cases on an almost daily basis. We are acquainted with many legal terms that are part of reporting the news of these cases: litigant, plaintiff, prosecution, defense, plea bargain, jury, and verdict. The outcome of a trial is the verdict *guilty* or *not guilty,* and in case of a guilty verdict, appropriate punishment.

When at death we enter the portals of heaven, we are accepted on the merits of Christ and declared innocent. On the judgment day, we appear before the Judge and the books will be opened (compare I Cor. 3:13; Rev. 20:12). Then our conduct will be evaluated and we shall be either rewarded or punished in accord with our deeds.

What a difference between a court on earth and the judgment seat in heaven! In human courts, lawyers, witnesses, members of the jury, and judges deal with matters of crime. The innocent are set free and the guilty serve terms of punishment and often must pay restitution. But no human court rewards a person according to deeds he or she has performed. By contrast, the divine Judge metes out rewards for good conduct and punishment for unacceptable behavior.[41]

Greek Words, Phrases, and Constructions in 5:6–10

Verses 6–7

καί—this is a conjunction that links two participles: "being confident" and "knowing." Most translators omit the conjunction, while others give the second participle a causal connotation ("since"; TNT, Barrett) or a concessive meaning ("even though"; NRSV, Héring). The conjunction should be kept, for it connects the import of the two participles.[42]

διὰ πίστεως—the preposition denotes manner, not means; it characterizes our daily conduct: "we walk by faith." The noun can mean either the beliefs and practices of the church or one's personal trust in God. Here it refers to trust.

εἴδους—this word refers to either external appearance or the act of seeing. I favor the interpretation that it means sight as an object of sight and not as an exercise.[43] True, with this interpretation the balance within the sentence is broken, because faith is active and sight passive. But such balance may not have been Paul's intent.

---

40. Calvin, *II Corinthians,* p. 72.

41. Refer to Plummer, *Second Corinthians,* p. 159.

42. Ralph P. Martin, *II Corinthians,* Word Biblical Commentary 40 (Waco: Word, 1986), p. 109. See Jean Héring, *The Second Epistle of Saint Paul to the Corinthians,* trans. A. W. Heathcote and P. J. Allcock (London: Epworth, 1967), p. 37.

43. Hodge, *Second Epistle to the Corinthians,* p. 122; Hughes, *Second Epistle to the Corinthians,* p. 176 n. 52; Gerhard Kittel, *TDNT,* 2:374. Others understand the noun in the active sense: Bauer, p. 221; Hans Lietzmann, *An die Korinther I/II,* augmented by Werner G. Kümmel, Handbuch zum Neuen Testament 9 (Tübingen: Mohr, 1969), pp. 121, 203.

Verse 8

ἐνδημῆσαι—"to be at home." The aorist is ingressive, while the related forms in verses 6 and 9 are in the present tense.

πρὸς τὸν κύριον—the context of this verse suggests that the preposition denotes movement toward and residence with the Lord.

Verse 10

τοὺς γὰρ πάντας ἡμᾶς—notice the position of the adjective, which is placed between the definite article and the personal pronoun. Paul is addressing the readers in Corinth and not every human being. The phrase means "the sum total of us."[44]

πρὸς ἅ—the preposition with the accusative in awkward Greek indicates a transferred sense: "in proportion to his deeds."[45]

---

11 Therefore, because we know the fear of the Lord, we attempt to persuade men. We are revealed to God. And I hope we also are revealed in your consciences. 12 We do not again commend ourselves to you but [we say this] by giving you an occasion to boast concerning us, so that you may have something to answer those who boast about what is observable, not about what is in the heart. 13 For if we are out of our minds, it is for God; if we are in our right mind, it is for you. 14 For the love of Christ controls us, because we are convinced that one died for all. Thus all died. 15 And he died for all, so that those who live might no longer live for themselves but for him who died for them and was raised.

16 Hence, from now on we know no one from a worldly perspective. For though we knew Christ from a worldly perspective, we do so no longer now. 17 So, if anyone is in Christ, there is a new creation. The old things passed away, and look—the new things have come. 18 And all things are from God, who reconciled us to himself through Christ and has given us the ministry of reconciliation. 19 That is, God was in Christ reconciling the world to himself, not counting their sins against them, and having entrusted to us the message of reconciliation.

20 Therefore, we are ambassadors for Christ, as God is making his appeal through us. We plead with you on behalf of Christ, be reconciled to God. 21 He made him who knew no sin to be sin on our behalf, so that we might become God's righteousness in him.

D. Ministry of Reconciliation
5:11–21

After Paul discourses on the intermediate state, he returns to a defense against some charges his opponents leveled. These opponents questioned his apostleship, requested proof of commendation, and discredited his motives and teachings. But he refuses to engage in self-commendation, because his task of proclaiming Christ's gospel is his authentication of apostleship. He is driven by the love of Christ that lies at the heart of the gospel. Paul summarizes the content of this gospel in two brief sentences: "One died for all. Thus all died." He adds the explanation that, for Christ, death signifies resurrection, and for the Christian, death signifies living for Christ. In summary form, verses 11–21 appear to

---

44. J. H. Moulton and Nigel A. Turner, *A Grammar of New Testament Greek* (Edinburgh: Clark, 1963), vol. 3, *Syntax*, p. 210.

45. C. F. D. Moule, *An Idiom-Book of New Testament Greek*, 2d ed. (Cambridge: Cambridge University Press, 1960), p. 53.

have a relatively straightforward message, yet they occupy a place among the most intriguing and difficult passages in all of Paul's epistles.[46]

1. Christ's Love
5:11–15

A superficial look at this paragraph would tell us that Paul presents a complete break with the preceding context. But this is not quite true, as is evident from at least three links in verse 11.

1. He mentions the fear of the Lord, a concept that relates to the previous verse (v. 10).
2. He twice uses the Greek verb *phaneroun* (to reveal), which also appears in verse 10.
3. He refers to the conscience of the Corinthians (see 4:2).

In addition, Paul returns to the topic *commendation* in verse 12 (refer to 3:1; 4:2).

11. Therefore, because we know the fear of the Lord, we attempt to persuade men. We are revealed to God. And I hope we also are revealed in your consciences.

a. "Therefore, because we know the fear of the Lord, we attempt to persuade men." Paul frequently employs the Greek conjunction *oun* (therefore) in this epistle,[47] and here it should not be omitted. The connection with verse 10 is obvious in light of the clause "we know the fear of the Lord." Paul speaks of an innate knowledge of fear that he and his readers have. He does not have in mind a reverence for the Lord—that is taken for granted (I Peter 1:17)—but a holy fear that relates to the judgment seat of Christ (v. 10). He is not speaking about overwhelming dread but rather about reverent fear of divine judgment.

Paul subjects himself and his associates to an introspective examination. He desires a thorough examination to see whether their preaching has advanced the cause of the gospel and whether their conduct has been exemplary (compare 2:17; 4:2). They had to examine their lives as if they were standing before Christ's judgment seat. That realization caused Paul to know the fear of the Lord, and he urged all his readers to submit to self-examination before the Lord's tribunal. During our brief sojourn on earth, we are scrutinized not only by the world but also by the Lord, who judges us (I Cor. 4:4). We know that "everything is uncovered and laid bare before the eyes of him to whom we must give account" (Heb. 4:13).

This verse appears to be a defense of Paul's personal integrity and in a related sense an effort to witness for Christ. First, Paul is trying to persuade people of his sincerity as Christ's apostle. He tells them that they should have no qualms about

---

46. Barrett, *Second Corinthians*, p. 163.
47. II Cor. 1:17; 3:12; 5:6, 11, 20; 7:1; 8:24; 9:5; 11:15; 12:9.

his honesty. Next, in word and deed Paul proved his love for the cause of Christ and the church by preaching the gospel free of charge (I Cor. 9:18). At all times he demonstrates his integrity and responsibility as God's servant.[48]

b. "We are revealed to God. And I hope we also are revealed in your consciences." If we read between the lines, we receive the impression that Paul was experiencing stress when he composed this segment of his epistle. Many of the clauses are short, compact, and sometimes open to more than one interpretation (e.g., vv. 13–14). The clause "we are revealed to God" can mean either "we are revealed" or "we have been revealed." The verb denotes either the situation or the activity. In this instance, both meanings are blended into one, for Paul's works are known to God while he constantly communes with God. And Paul expects that the same thing is true with reference to the Corinthians; that is, Paul's words and deeds have been and are an open book to the readers of this epistle.[49] The readers, too, have to acknowledge the apostle's integrity. Paul appeals to their individual consciences (compare 4:2). He knows that their consciences invariably point to God in whose presence they continually stand. Further, he uses the noun *consciences* in the plural to include everyone in the Corinthian church. The plural form occurs only here in the New Testament, a fact that suggests that Paul is asking everyone to attest to the veracity of his words and conduct.[50]

12. We do not again commend ourselves to you but [we say this] by giving you an occasion to boast concerning us, so that you may have something to answer those who boast about what is observable, not about what is in the heart.

The first clause states the obvious. When the Corinthians let their consciences speak about Paul's fidelity, there is no need for him to repeat what he has been saying earlier (3:1–3). There Paul stated that he did not need letters of recommendation because the Corinthians themselves were his endorsement. Similarly here, he is not interested in promoting his own cause. He would prefer to see that the members of the church in Corinth tell his opponents about their appreciation for the ministers of the gospel. Even though Paul's reasoning sounds paradoxical, he seeks no glory for himself. Instead he wants the Corinthians to take a firm stand against his adversaries and to glory in the gospel of Christ.

The natural flow between the first clause and the following one is broken, but we can adjust it with an additional verb and pronoun: "but [we say this] by giving you an occasion to boast concerning us." The word *occasion* does not necessarily mean a single opportunity to do something. Rather, it implies a solid basis for boasting about the apostle and his co-workers.[51] The Corinthians need reasons

---

48. Compare the comments of Malcolm Tolbert, "Theology and Ministry: II Corinthians 5:11–21," *Faith Miss* 1 (1983): 64; David L. Turner, "Paul and the Ministry of Reconciliation in II Cor. 5:11–6:2," *CrisTheolRev* 4 (1989): 80; Rudolf Bultmann, *TDNT*, 6:2.

49. Calvin writes, "It is as if he [Paul] had said, 'My mouth speaks to men, but my heart speaks to God'" (*II Corinthians*, p. 72).

50. Martin, *II Corinthians*, p. 124.

51. Georg Bertram, *TDNT*, 5:473.

to boast about Paul's faithfulness in his service of the gospel and enunciate these reasons clearly in the hearing of the adversaries. When they do so, they indeed are Paul's letter of recommendation that is known and read by everyone (3:2). Conclusively, Paul's apostolic ministry of the gospel is the object of their boasting (compare 1:14 and 9:3).[52]

Paul is fully aware of his opponents and their unwholesome influence in the Corinthian community. He perceives that they are boasting of their credentials and preach a gospel of Israel's superiority (11:4).[53] They are led by sight and not by faith; they present "a powerless message [that] encourages an achievement-centered ministry."[54] What Paul is giving the members of the Corinthian church is verbal ammunition to oppose these false apostles (11:13). He writes, "that you may have something to answer those who boast about what is observable, not about what is in the heart."

The boasting of Paul's opponents rings hollow, for their message touches only the externals. In their conduct, they exemplify the opposite of what God told Samuel: "The LORD does not look at the things man looks at. Man looks at the outward appearance, but the LORD looks at the heart" (I Sam. 16:7). Paul's opponents valued letters of commendation (3:1), eloquence (10:10; 11:6), Jewish birth and heritage (11:22), visions and revelations (12:1), and the performance of miracles (12:12). They boasted of possessing these externals and mocked Paul for lacking them. Their objectives were to boast about appearances, skills, and lineage, but they failed to see that true religion (James 1:27) is a matter of the heart that must be right with God. According to Paul, boasting must always be boasting in the Lord (I Cor. 1:31).

Practical Considerations in 5:12

Approval ratings are part of society; they are applied to all of us and especially to leaders. We strive for positive scores that reflect the good will of our peers, family, friends, associates, and the public. Preachers, greeting church members at the conclusion of a worship service, receive verbal and often nonverbal approval ratings. Praise for their ministry, especially on the delivery of sermons, is pleasant. At the same time, they know that not they but God should receive the glory and honor. The temptation to cultivate praise for themselves is enticing but in reality is dishonoring to God. The words of Jesus offer a fitting antidote: "So you also, when you have done everything you were told to do, should say, 'We are unworthy servants; we have only done our duty'" (Luke 17:10).

---

52. Consult Josef Zmijewski, *EDNT*, 2:276–79. Together the verb *kauchasthai* (to boast) and the two nouns for boast (*kauchēma* and *kauchēsis*) occur about sixty times in the New Testament. Fifty-three or fifty-four (see the reading of I Cor. 13:3) are in Paul's epistles. The word *boast* as either verb or noun plays a significant role in II Corinthians (it is used twenty-five times).

53. Derk Oostendorp, *Another Jesus: A Gospel of Jewish-Christian Superiority in II Corinthians* (Kampen: Kok, 1967), pp. 12, 80.

54. J. Knox Chamblin, *Paul and the Self: Apostolic Teaching for Personal Wholeness* (Grand Rapids: Baker, 1993), p. 192.

13. For if we are out of our minds, it is for God; if we are in our right mind, it is for you.

Once again, the brevity of these clauses indicates that Paul must have been emotionally agitated. In Greek, the clauses are much shorter than they are in translation: the first clause has three words and the second only one; the third clause consists of two words and the fourth of one.

> *eite gar exestēmen, theō*
> *eite sōphronoumen, hymin*

The two conditional sentences display balance and contrast; they appear to be a rhetorical device.[55] With these lines Paul is launching an attack against his opponents by taking the sting out of their boast. He had a divine revelation when he was caught up to the third heaven (12:2), but this vision did nothing for his ministry to God's people (12:5–6). When he was in ecstasy, Paul was cut off from humanity and could relate only to God. He knew that to be able to serve the Christian church, he had to be in full control of all his senses (compare I Cor. 14:2, 14).[56]

During his missionary career, Paul had at least one other ecstatic experience. It occurred when he returned from Damascus to Jerusalem and was praying at the temple. At that time, Jesus told him to leave the city immediately because of unbelieving Jews (Acts 22:17–18). This experience involved only Paul and Jesus, not the church.[57]

Visions and revelations were part of Paul's life, but he never displayed these experiences as badges of apostolic authority. Paul was interested not in promoting himself but in advancing the church that he served without allowing any distraction. Thus, by serving Jesus he followed in the footsteps of the Lord (John 13:15–16). This, then, is the lesson Paul teaches the readers of his epistle. Calvin adds some pastoral advice: "This passage deserves not just passing notice but constant meditation, for unless we are as resolute as Paul is here, the smallest causes of offence will again and again distract us from our duty."[58]

14. For the love of Christ controls us, because we are convinced that one died for all. Thus all died.

The brevity of this verse need not diminish its pertinent message. These few words present the gospel that must be understood in the context of this chapter. Paul opposes the intruders and reminds the members of the Corinthian church of his faithfulness toward them as a minister of that gospel. Fully aware of the dis-

---

55. Moule, *Idiom-Book*, p. 195.

56. Refer to Jerome Murphy-O'Connor, *The Theology of the Second Letter to the Corinthians*, New Testament Theology series (Cambridge: Cambridge University Press, 1991), p. 56.

57. Albrecht Oepke, *TDNT*, 2:460, notes that Paul was hardly out of his mind during ecstatic experiences. This is true, but ecstasy is a state "in which consciousness is wholly or partially suspended" (Bauer, p. 245). The words Paul heard were meant for him and not for others (compare Acts 22:9).

58. Calvin, *II Corinthians*, p. 74.

cord the intruders cause, he seeks to remove the conflict by reminding his readers of the gospel of Christ.

a. *"For the love of Christ controls us."* The connection between the preceding verse and this one is clear. Paul is in his right mind as he preaches the gospel of salvation. That gospel demonstrates the indescribable love of Christ toward his people.

The New Testament employs the expression *the love of Christ* only three times: Paul asks the rhetorical question, "Who shall separate us from the love of Christ?" (Rom. 8:35); he refers to the dimensions of Christ's love and states that it surpasses human knowledge (Eph. 3:18–19); and he notes that the love of Christ controls us (v. 14). God originates this love, for he sent his one and only Son to redeem sinners (John 3:16; Rom. 5:8). He elects his people in love and makes them more than conquerors through Jesus Christ (Rom. 1:7; 8:37).[59]

Some translators supply an objective genitive in this sentence: "our love for Christ."[60] But most scholars understand the phrase as a subjective genitive: the love that Christ has for us. We are not saying that Christ's love for us does not elicit our love for him, but the intent of this verse is to reveal Christ's death as evidence of his love.

The Greek verb *synechei,* which I have translated "controls," reveals some variations. Here are a few representative versions:

1. "The love of Christ impels us" (NAB)
2. "For Christ's love compels us" (NIV)
3. "For the love of Christ urges us on" (NRSV)
4. "For the love of Christ overwhelms us" (NJB)
5. "For the love of Christ lays hold of us" (MLB)

The significance of this Greek verb is that Paul and all believers are completely dominated by the love of Christ, so that they live for him.[61] As Paul writes elsewhere, "I have been crucified with Christ and I no longer live, but Christ lives in me. The life I live in the body, I live by faith in the Son of God, who loved me and gave himself for me" (Gal. 2:20). As for Paul himself, he states that Christ controls him. And this claim his opponents can never utter, for they are governed not by Christ but by their own ambitions.

b. *"Because we are convinced that one died for all. Thus all died."* The clause *one died for all,* which eloquently expresses Christ's love, is the gospel in summary—perhaps a creedal statement of the early church. We acclaim the truth of

---

59. Consult Ethelbert Stauffer, *TDNT,* 1:49.

60. TNT; Héring, *Second Epistle of Paul,* pp. 41–42; Armin Kretzer, *EDNT,* 3:306; Windisch, *Der Zweite Korintherbrief,* p. 181. Both interpretations are suggested by Ernest B. Allo, *Saint Paul Seconde Épître aux Corinthiens,* 2d ed. (Paris: Gabalda, 1956), p. 165.

61. Helmut Köster, *TDNT,* 7:883.

this statement, because all Scripture testifies to it (refer to I Cor. 15:3). It is by reading God's Word that we come to this conclusion.

That Christ died on Calvary's cross is fact; that he died for all is gospel. But how do we explain the two terms *for* and *all?*

First, let us take the preposition *for* (Greek, *hyper*). It occurs in John 11:50, where the high priest Caiaphas suggests to the Sanhedrin that he would rather see one man die *for* the people than to see the whole nation perish. The preposition *hyper* with reference to Christ's death means substitution, as for example in the words of the institution of the Lord's Supper, "This is my blood of the covenant, which is poured out for many" (Mark 14:24; Luke 22:20). Christ gave his body for his followers (Luke 22:19; I Cor. 11:24; and see John 6:51). He suffered and died for sinners (I Peter 2:21; 3:18); and he laid down his life for his own (I John 3:16). In the statement, "Christ died for our sins" (I Cor. 15:3), the term *hyper* conveys the meaning that Jesus is both our representative and substitute. Christ represents us by pleading our cause before the Father (I John 2:1), and he is our substitute by taking our place and being the bearer of our sins (v. 21).[62] Similarly, "Christ redeemed us from the curse of the law, by becoming a curse for us" (Gal. 3:13). When the preposition *hyper* occurs in the context of Christ's death, it signifies substitution.[63] Hence, the fact that Christ lifted the curse from humanity through his death is indeed a summary of the gospel.

Next, the adjective *all* occurs twice in this verse and once in verse 15. Does Paul have in mind that Christ died for every human being? Or is he referring to every believer? We can say that the atoning death of Christ is sufficient for all people but efficient for all true believers. Jesus elected Judas Iscariot to be one of the twelve disciples, yet he calls him "a devil" and describes him as "the one doomed to destruction" (John 6:70; 17:12). Only those who appropriate Christ's death in faith are included in the word *all*. We must examine, therefore, the usage of the word first in Paul's epistles and then in verses 14 and 15. Thereafter we can fully appreciate the meaning of this passage.

The use of "all" in Paul's letters does not always mean universality. The apostle refuted the Corinthian motto "All things are permissible" (I Cor. 6:12; 10:23) in the contexts of sexual immorality and of food offered to idols. And Paul's statement "For all things are yours" (I Cor. 3:21) appears in his discussion about earthly and heavenly wisdom. As always, the context determines the sense of a given expression.

If we look closely at the wording of verses 14 and 15, we notice that the expression *all* is modified by three persons or qualities: the governing love of Christ, the pronoun *us,* and those who live for him. Christ died for all who believe in him, for faith is an essential element in the believer's redemption. To all true believers Christ extends his redeeming love. Although the pronoun *us*

---

62. Contra Richard T. Mead, "Exegesis of II Corinthians 5:14–21," in *Interpreting II Corinthians 5:14–21. An Exercise in Hermeneutics,* ed. Jack P. Lewis, SBEC 17 (Lewiston, N.Y.: Edwin Mellen, 1989), p. 147.

63. Hughes, *Second Epistle to the Corinthians,* p. 193; Ridderbos, *Paul,* p. 190.

often refers to Paul and his co-workers, here it is broad enough to embrace all Christ's followers.

In addition, this text must be explained in harmony with similar passages (Rom. 5:18; I Cor. 15:22). Only those who have true faith in Christ Jesus receive eternal life, are reconciled to God, and are justified. Those who have died with Christ are recipients of eternal life (Rom. 6:8). They are the ones who are united with him in his death and resurrection and are alive to God.

"Thus all died" is a brief statement that appears self-evident, if not superfluous. But the statement is a continuation of the preceding clause: "one died for all." There the verb *to die* has a literal meaning that alludes to Christ's physical death on the cross. Here that same verb may be taken in a *figurative* sense, namely, the removal of the curse of death (Gen. 2:17; 3:17–19; Gal. 3:13). Hence, the death of all who died points to the death that Christ, as both their representative and substitute, experienced for all his people. I make three observations: Paul draws a consequence from the previous clause by saying *thus* in "thus all died"; next, the Greek literally says "the all" to specify a particular group; and last, the verb *died* in this short clause shows the past tense and single action. The action occurred at Calvary but its significance is for the present.[64]

In other places, Paul pointedly states that God delivered his Son for us all (Rom. 8:32); now he also seems to say, "Christ died for us all." All who have died *metaphorically* at the cross died with him,[65] for Christ and his people are one body (I Cor. 12:27; Eph. 1:23; Col. 1:18, 24). On the cross of Calvary, Christ Jesus delivered the deathblow to death and set his people free from the bondage of sin (Rom. 6:6–7).

15. And he died for all, so that those who live might no longer live for themselves but for him who died for them and was raised.

a. "And he died for all." With the conjunction *and,* Paul repeats the words of verse 14. He returns to the literal use of the verb *to die* to indicate the death of Christ at Golgotha. But the short clause that features the word *all* is explained by a lengthy sentence.

b. "So that those who live might no longer live for themselves." The purpose of Christ's redemptive work is that his people, set free from the curse of sin, now enjoy life in fellowship with him. They are no longer spiritually dead but are the recipients of new life in Christ. Selfish goals and ambitions are set aside, because believers' purpose now is to live for the One who died for them. Says Paul, "For none of us lives to himself alone and none of us dies to himself alone. If we live, we live to the Lord; and if we die, we die to the Lord. So, whether we live or die, we belong to the Lord" (Rom. 14:7–8).

---

64. John O'Neill conjectures that the clause "thus all died" is a theological explanatory note that a scribe incorporated into the body of the text. But he lacks textual evidence to support his theory. "The Absence of the 'in Christ' Theology in II Corinthians 5," *AusBRev* 35 (1987): 103.

65. Jack P. Lewis, "Exegesis of II Corinthians 5:14–21," in *Interpreting II Corinthians 5:14–21. An Exercise in Hermeneutics,* ed. Jack P. Lewis, SBEC 17 (Lewiston, N.Y.: Edwin Mellen, 1989), pp. 133–34.

c. "But for him who died for them and was raised." In Greek, the stress is on the phrase *for them*, a phrase that is placed emphatically between "for him who" and "died and was raised." Paul calls attention to this phrase and intends it as an explanation of the preceding clause ("and he died for all"). He states that Christ died and was raised for those people who now live for him and produce spiritual fruit (Rom. 6:11; 7:4). Through his death, Christ set them free from the power of this world. And through his resurrection, he places them under his dominion to have them serve him as citizens in his kingdom.

Lastly, the two concepts *died* and *raised* are intimately related to the phrase *for them* and govern it. It is one thing to say that Christ died as our substitute, but to say that he was raised as our substitute is inexact. Accordingly, with respect to his resurrection, Christ is our forerunner (Phil. 3:21). God raised him from the dead with the intent that we too shall be like him. Christ is the firstfruits of the resurrection harvest (I Cor. 15:20, 49).

Greek Words, Phrases, and Constructions in 5:11–14

Verses 11–12

τοῦ κυρίου—the objective genitive is preferred to the subjective genitive.

πείθομεν—the present tense denotes an action begun but not completed: "we continue to persuade."

ἐλπίζω—this verb in the present tense is followed by the perfect passive infinitive πεφανερῶσθαι (are revealed), which needs the implied subject *we*. The verb may mean "I think."[66]

οὐ—the negative stands first in the sentence for emphasis, and the verb *we commend* occupies a place between the pronouns *ourselves* and *you* (plural).

ὑπὲρ ἡμῶν—Paul is asking the Corinthians to testify to his integrity, not vice versa. The reading ὑπὲρ ὑμῶν must be rejected.

Verses 13–14

ἐξέστημεν—this is the aorist active: "we are out of our minds." Even though the aorist is translated in the present, the single action of an ecstatic experience for Paul was temporary.[67]

συνέχει—some scholars present the translation *embraces us*. But the sense *holds tight* corresponds with divine love that controls all our religious decisions.[68]

ὑπέρ—"in the place of," not "in the interest of." Scholars remark that the preposition ἀντί more accurately describes substitution. This is true, but as Murray J. Harris observes,

---

66. Friedrich Blass and Albert Debrunner understand the verb *to hope* as "to think." See *A Greek Grammar of the New Testament and Other Early Christian Literature,* trans. and rev. Robert Funk (Chicago: University of Chicago Press, 1961), #350.

67. Jan Lambrecht, *EDNT,* 2:7.

68. George S. Hendry, "ἡ γὰρ ἀγάπη τοῦ Χριστοῦ συνέχει ἡμᾶς—II Corinthians v.14," *ExpT* 59 (1947–48): 82; Ceslaus Spicq, "L'entreinte de la charité (II Cor. V:14)," *ST* 8 (1955): 123–32. Victor Paul Furnish favors "lays claim to" (*II Corinthians: Translation with Introduction, Notes and Commentary,* Anchor Bible 32A [Garden City, N.Y.: Doubleday, 1984], pp. 307–9); Windisch, *Der Zweite Korintherbrief,* p. 181.

"We may conclude that the *emphasis* in *hyper* is on representation, in *anti* on substitution; yet a substitute represents and a representative may be a substitute. That is, *hyper* sometimes implies *anti*."[69]

οἱ πάντες—the definite article with the adjective must be explained as "these all."

---

2. Christ's Ministry
5:16–19

From a discussion on Christ's love that is demonstrated by his death on the cross, Paul now continues and looks at the consequence of this event. He ponders what our perspective on the death of Christ should be. As believers we ought to see Christ in regard to our redemption, because he transformed us into a new creation. In Christ, a new community has come into being, a community whose its members are reconciled to God and to one another.

16. Hence, from now on we know no one from a worldly perspective. For though we knew Christ from a worldly perspective, we do so no longer now.

a. "Hence, from now on we know no one from a worldly perspective." Some commentators see little or no connection between the word *hence* and the two foregoing verses (vv. 14–15). They take this verse to be parenthetical.[70] But this is not quite the case if we link the teaching on Christ's death to the change of thinking that has taken place since that historic moment. The effect of his death has been that we know people not from a worldly point of view but from the perspective of Christ's love.

The phrase *from now on* refers not so much to the moment Paul wrote the letter or to the time of his conversion.[71] It instead points to the transformation that took place when Christ died on the cross. From that moment, he and his followers could no longer view the world from a worldly point of view. (The phrase *from a worldly perspective* modifies the verb *we know*, not the object *no one*. To connect the modifier with the verb preserves the writer's balance here and in the second part of the verse.) Thus, Paul's perspective on life changed completely when Jesus called him on the way to Damascus. And all Christians must demonstrate this new viewpoint in their lives when they acknowledge Christ as their Lord and Savior.

There is a difference between knowing a person and understanding a fact. The verb *to know* in verse 16a means "being (intimately) acquainted with [or] stand[ing] in a (close) relation to" someone.[72] Paul is saying that when we interact closely with others, we do so as followers of Christ. It is possible that the first part of this verse may be Paul's reaction to his opponents, who stressed external

---

69. Murray J. Harris, *NIDNTT*, 3:1197.

70. Consult the commentaries of Plummer (p. 177) and Lietzmann (p. 127).

71. Compare Seyoon Kim, *The Origin of Paul's Gospel* (Tübingen: Mohr; Grand Rapids: Eerdmans, 1982), p. 16.

72. Bauer, p. 556.

appearances such as Jewish identity (see the commentary on v. 12). Yet the application of Paul's words is universal.

b. "For though we knew Christ from a worldly perspective, we do so no longer now." The first part of this sentence is best translated as a concessive clause that expresses reality. In fact, the Greek verb *egnōkamen* (we have known) is in the perfect tense but is translated in English as a simple past ("we knew"). Probably Paul had heard and seen Jesus in Jerusalem, where he studied under Gamaliel for many years (Acts 22:3). It would have been unlikely that Paul had never heard Jesus or heard of him during his student years. But whether or not he had heard Christ is not the point that Paul is trying to make. He viewed Jesus in those days with an unspiritual and worldly mindset (compare 11:18).[73] He refused to accept Christ in faith and repudiated his teachings to such an extent that he persecuted Christians.

As in the first part of this verse, the phrase *from a worldly perspective* must be connected here with the verb *to know* and not with the noun *Christ*. If we make the phrase modify the noun, the words could be interpreted to mean that Paul had no interest in the earthly Jesus but only in the exalted Christ. Writes Rudolf Bultmann, "For Paul, Christ has lost his identity as an individual human person."[74] This explanation suggests a division between the historical Jesus and the Christ of faith. But Paul teaches that he has a decided interest in the earthly, historical Jesus (e.g., Acts 13:38–39; Rom. 1:2–4; 9:5; I Cor. 15:3–8), whom he continually identifies as Jesus Christ or Christ Jesus.

Despite his interest in the earthly, historical Jesus, Paul here is not alluding to a time when he had seen Christ in human appearance. Rather, he refers to the time during which he was still unconverted and became acquainted with Christ's teachings. At that time, he refused to acknowledge Jesus as God's Son and honor him as the Messiah. From the moment of his conversion, however, Paul saw Jesus Christ through spiritual eyes and understood that Christ's death and resurrection occurred for the benefit of all believers. At the time of writing, he expected the Corinthians to imitate him by following Jesus. Thus, they are not to judge others from a worldly point of view; instead, they must regard one another, including Paul, from a spiritual perspective.

17. So, if anyone is in Christ, there is a new creation. The old things passed away, and look—the new things have come.

Verses 16 and 17 are the logical conclusion of the preceding passage (vv. 14–15), are analogous, and show both a negative and a positive contrast (vv. 16 and 17 respectively). Because these two verses convey a parallel message, the last one

---

73. Consult Otto Betz, "Fleischliche und 'geistliche' Christuserkenntnis nach 2. Korinther 5,16," *ThBeit* 14 (1983): 167–79.

74. Rudolf Bultmann, *Primitive Christianity in Its Contemporary Setting,* trans. R. H. Fuller (New York: Meridian, 1956), p. 197. And see his *Theology of the New Testament,* trans. K. Grobel, 2 vols. (London: SCM, 1952–55), vol. 1, pp. 238–39. Compare D. E. H. Whiteley, *The Theology of St. Paul* (Oxford: Blackwell, 1964), p. 100; Henry Beach Carré, *Paul's Doctrine of Redemption* (New York: Macmillan, 1914), p. 140.

depends on and is influenced by the first. The Greek clauses are short and in translation have to be augmented with the verb *to be* in the first sentence.

Let us look first at the word *so,* which introduces a summary of what Paul has been saying earlier about the unity believers have with Christ. He died for them and was raised, and they in turn live for him (v. 15). When Paul writes, "If anyone is in Christ," he expresses the fact that numerous people in Corinth and elsewhere are true believers.

Next, the phrase *in Christ* occurs some twenty-five times in Paul's epistles and signifies the intimate fellowship believers enjoy with their Lord and Savior.[75] To be in Christ connotes being part of Christ's body (I Cor. 12:27), and Christ brings about a radical transformation in the believer's life.[76] Instead of serving the ego, the Christian follows Christ and responds to the law of love for God and the neighbor.

Some translators want to see balance in this sentence and thus link the word *anyone* in the first clause with the pronoun *he* ("he is a new creation") in the second.[77] But most expositors, rightly so, see the new creation not as being limited to a person but as extending to the total environment of this individual (compare Gal. 6:15; Rev. 21:5). That is, when people become part of the body of Christ at conversion, their lives take a complete reversal. They now abhor the world of sin and former friends are hostile to them. Their preconversion lifestyle is history, and "the old things have passed away" (see the parallel in Isa. 43:18–19). For converts, the life in Christ is a constant source of daily joys and blessings; the body of believers provides them with ready support and help; and self-assurance and trust certify the genuineness of their composure.

Scholars debate whether Paul borrowed the phrase *a new creation* from the rabbis of his day. Even if he did, these Jewish teachers never associated this phrase with moral renewal and regeneration. According to them, renewal occurred with respect to remission of sins,[78] but not in the sense of the transformation that Jesus Christ brings about in the life of believers. For converts to the Christian faith, the old things no longer attract, for new things have taken their place through Christ. Although temptations always surround them, believers pray the sixth petition of the Lord's Prayer, "And lead us not into temptation,

---

75. J. H. Bernard (*The Second Epistle to the Corinthians,* The Expositor's Greek Testament, ed. W. Robertson Nicoll [Grand Rapids: Eerdmans, n.d.], vol. 3, p. 71), is of the opinion that the words *in Christ* refer to the Christ-party (10:7; I Cor. 1:12). But this opinion can hardly be applied to an idiom that occurs throughout the New Testament epistolary literature and Revelation.

76. Compare Furnish, *II Corinthians,* p. 332; Michael Parsons, "The New Creation," *ExpT* 99 (1987–88): 3–4.

77. GNB, NAB, NASB, KJV, NIV, NKJV, MLB, SEB. The Vulgate disregards balance and translates, "If, then, there is any new creation in Christ, the old things have passed away"; similarly, Héring, *Second Epistle of Paul,* pp. 42–43. But Collange points out that the phrase *in Christ* relates to "a new creation" and not to "anyone" (*Énigmes,* p. 264).

78. Consult SB 2:321; 3:519; Barrett, *Second Corinthians,* pp. 173–73. See the comment of Johannes Behm, "New creation is the glorious end of the revelation of God's salvation" (*TDNT,* 3:350).

but deliver us from the evil one" (Matt. 6:13), and they know that God supplies strength to resist evil.

18. And all things are from God, who reconciled us to himself through Christ and has given us the ministry of reconciliation.

a. "And all things are from God." No one can ever say that renewal has its origin in human beings, for Paul clearly teaches that God is the originator and source of renewal. God created all things through Christ Jesus (John 1:3; Col. 1:15–18; Heb. 1:2) and *re*creates all things for his children. They are in Christ Jesus, for God is the cause of their membership in the body of Christ (refer to I Cor. 1:30).

b. "Who reconciled us to himself through Christ." This astounding statement reveals God's infinite love. We offended God by breaking his commands and sinning against him. Therefore, the initiative for reconciliation should have come from us, for we are the offending party. Instead we read that God, as the offended party, reached out to us to achieve restoration of relationships. God took the initiative and completed the work of reconciliation before we, as sinners, began to respond to God's gracious invitation to be reconciled to him (Rom. 5:10–11). In brief, God restored the relationship between himself and us, so that his new creation for us could be fully realized.

In apostolic times, the Jews believed that man had to initiate reconciliation with God, chiefly by prayer and confession of sin. For instance, the writer of II Maccabees uses the verb *to reconcile* four times, but all of them are in the passive voice. They disclose that human beings petition God to be reconciled to them.[79]

By contrast, the New Testament teaches that God restores us to himself by "putting us in right relations with himself."[80] God is the subject and we are the object whenever the verb *to reconcile* is in the active voice. But when in the same context this verb is in the passive voice, we are the subject (see v. 20). God did not cause alienation between himself and us and, therefore, did not have to reconcile himself to us. Yet in love God reconciles us to himself through the atoning work of his Son Jesus Christ. For this reason, Paul says that God brings about restoration through Christ, that is, through Jesus' redemptive work. The phrase *through Christ* alludes to his death and resurrection (vv. 14–15), which bring about both a new creation (v. 17) and a reconciliation (vv. 18–20).[81]

c. "[God] has given us the ministry of reconciliation." God himself commissioned Paul and his co-workers to acquaint the readers of this epistle with his

---

79. II Macc. 1:5; 5:20; 7:33; 8:29. See I Clem. 48.1. According to Josephus, God is reconciled to people who confess their sin and repent (*War* 5.415; *Antiquities* 3.315; 6.144–56; 7.184). See also SB 3:519, "To initiate reconciliation is the duty of the offender, yet there is the instance in which reconciliation is initiated by the offended party" (author's translation).

80. Martin, *II Corinthians,* p. 148; also in his *Reconciliation: A Study of Paul's Theology* (Atlanta: John Knox, 1981), p. 106. Thrall (*Second Corinthians,* p. 430) notes, "Paul's own use of the verb is in the active, with the sense 'reconcile (someone) to oneself', has no parallel."

81. G. K. Beale, "The Old Testament Background of Reconciliation in II Corinthians 5–7 and Its Bearing on the Literary Problem of II Corinthians 6.14–7.1," *NTS* 35 (1989): 559.

work. God wants his servants to be engaged in a restorative ministry by preaching, teaching, and applying the gospel. For Paul, this is ministry of the Spirit of the living God (3:3, 8), and is glorious in bringing forth righteousness (3:9). Also, this ministry secures peace between God and human beings (Rom. 5:1, 10; Col. 1:20; see Acts 20:24). Peace is the result of restoring personal relations that were broken and is "a denotation of the all-embracing gift of salvation."[82]

19. That is, God was in Christ reconciling the world to himself, not counting their sins against them, and having entrusted to us the message of reconciliation.

a. *Preliminary observations.* This verse explicates the content of the message of reconciliation that Paul mentioned in the preceding clause. Paul's explanation clarifies God's intention to achieve a reconciliation that spans the entire world. In different words, Paul repeats his reference to Christ's love that extends to the whole world (v. 14): in Christ God reconciles the world to himself.

There is a degree of repetition in the vocabulary of verses 18 and 19, especially these words: God, reconcile, Christ, himself, us, reconciliation. With these words Paul achieves a parallelism by which he stresses the extent of God's reconciling work.

Differences in grammar, an explanatory clause, and synonymous expressions amplify Paul's teaching. Instead of the past tense ("reconciled," v. 18), Paul now writes "was reconciling." He adds the clause "not counting their sins against them." And he makes the following changes: "through Christ" to "in Christ," the pronoun "us" to the object "the world," and "ministry of reconciliation" to "message of reconciliation."

b. *Interpretation.* "That is, God was in Christ reconciling the world to himself." The first two words in this sentence are explanatory and form the bridge between Paul's reference to the "ministry of reconciliation" (v. 18) and his explanation of the content of this ministry.

The variations of word order in English versions are many, as some representative translations show:

"God was reconciling the world to himself in Christ" (NIV)
"In Christ God was reconciling the world" (NRSV)
"God, in Christ, was reconciling the world" (NAB)
"God was in Christ reconciling the world" (NASB, NJB, REB)
"God was in Christ, reconciling the world" (KJV)

A few points favor the last reading. First, with the Greek word order Paul wanted to stress the position of the phrase *in Christ* and thus placed it after the words *God was.* Next, Jesus repeatedly teaches that the Father is in him and he in the Father (John 10:38; 14:10, 11, 20; 17:21). Third, by placing a comma after

---

82. Ridderbos, *Paul,* p. 184; see Frederick W. Danker, "Exegesis of II Corinthians 5:14–21," in *Interpreting II Corinthians 5:14–21: An Exercise in Hermeneutics,* ed. Jack P. Lewis, SBEC 17 (Lewiston, N.Y.: Edwin Mellen, 1989), p. 118.

the phrase *in Christ,* we see that Paul divides the remainder of the sentence into three parts, each of which contains a participle: reconciling, counting, having entrusted. The first two participles are in the present tense, and the last one in the past. Finally, the three participles can be interpreted to denote complement. That is, on the basis of Jesus' redemptive ministry, God reconciled the world to himself, forgave sin, and entrusted the preaching of the gospel to his servants.[83]

Every translation has its reasons for existence, but it is noteworthy that scholars prefer the next to the last reading mentioned above: "God was in Christ reconciling the world." The reason is that this version shows continued action with the past tense of the verb *to be* and the participle in the present tense. This is the so-called periphrastic construction, which is common in the Greek New Testament.[84]

The phrase *in Christ* refers to Jesus' death and resurrection (see vv. 14–15). Because of Christ's atoning work, God continues to reconcile people to himself, as Paul indicates by using the present tense of the participle *reconciling.* In other words, reconciling the world takes place in and through Christ as a continuing activity. In the Greek, the term *world* lacks the definite article and thus expresses the comprehensive meaning of the word. Paul is not espousing universalism; rather, he is saying that God's love in Christ extends to both Jews and Gentiles worldwide (compare Rom. 1:16).

"Not counting their sins against them." Note the present tense of the participle, which indicates that God continues to release believers from their guilt.[85] God does so in answer to the repeated cries of repentance from those who have fallen into sin and have been amiss. Through Christ's redemptive work, God forgives sinners who repent and whose faith is fixed on Jesus, the author and perfecter of their faith (Heb. 2:10; 12:2).

"And having entrusted to us the message of reconciliation." Once for all, God commissioned Paul, his associates, and all others to make God's message of reconciliation known to the world. This commission may be compared to that of a manager who is entrusted with a treasure for which he must give periodic accounts to his employer. The manager is expected to increase the owner's assets with the treasure and not to put it in a hiding place.

Doctrinal Considerations in 5:17–19

Reconciliation takes place when two parties, estranged from each other, are brought back into a harmonious relationship through the efforts of a mediator. For us, that mediator is Jesus Christ, God's Son. We readily admit that estrangement from God was our fault, for our sins grieved him and our animosity toward him aroused his anger.

---

83. Compare Allo, *Seconde Épître aux Corinthiens,* p. 170.
84. A. T. Robertson points out that not all the New Testament entries are periphrastic: for instance, Luke 2:8. *A Grammar of the Greek New Testament in the Light of Historical Research* (Nashville: Broadman, 1934), p. 376.
85. Ps. 32:1–2, 5; Ezek. 18:23, 27–28, 32; 33:14–16; Rom. 4:7–8.

Now notice all the things that God has done for us: He did not abandon us; instead, he took the initiative to restore the relationship. He gave his one and only Son to die on the cross for the remission of our sins. He permitted us entrance into his presence, and he granted us everlasting life. He made all things new by restoring them to their original design, glory, and purpose. He reconciled us to himself by

> having Christ pay the penalty for sin,
> appeasing God's wrath and removing our enmity,
> and demonstrating his divine love and grace to us.

Because of all these gifts, God empowered us to tell his message of reconciliation to our fellow human beings.

We are accountable to God for our sins, yet through Christ he has forgiven us. We had alienated ourselves from God, yet God through Christ reinstated us as his sons and daughters and welcomed us into his family. We were isolated without fellowship, but he invited us to joyful communion with both the Father and the Son (I John 1:3). With respect to reconciliation, God inaugurated it in the coming of his Son. He continues it by daily forgiving sin, and he will complete it at the consummation. To him be eternal praise, honor, glory, and power (Rev. 5:13).

Greek Words, Phrases, and Constructions in 5:16–19

Verse 16

εἰ καὶ ἐγνώκαμεν—as a concessive clause, the protasis conveys reality, not necessarily something that is "hypothetically real."[86] The two particles εἰ καί mean "even though." The perfect tense relates to a past event that has significance for the present. To say that Paul uses the perfect tense of γινώσκω because οἶδα does not have this tense is true.[87] But this observation must respond to two queries: Why does Paul write the present tense γινώσκομεν instead of οἴδαμεν in verse 16c? And why does Paul need the perfect tense in verse 16b if the sentence is an unreal condition? Paul's intent is to use these two Greek verbs as synonyms in this verse.

Verse 17

παρῆλθεν–the aorist tense ("passed away") points to the past event of conversion, and the perfect tense γέγονεν (has come) refers to something that happened in the past but has lasting significance for the present and future.

καινά—"new things." Two variants add the words τὰ πάντα either preceding or following the adjective. They are the first words in verse 18 and thus may have influenced copyists to include them in this verse.[88] The shorter text is preferred.

---

86. Rudolf Bultmann, *The Second Letter to the Corinthians,* trans. Roy A. Harrisville (Minneapolis: Augsburg, 1985), p. 157; Georgi, *Opponents of Paul,* pp. 256 n. 5 and 257; Lietzmann, *Korinther,* p. 125.

87. Rudolf Bultmann, *TDNT,* 1:703. See the commentaries of Barrett (p. 17), and Plummer (pp. 176–77).

88. Bruce M. Metzger, *A Textual Commentary on the Greek New Testament,* 2d ed. (Stuttgart and New York: United Bible Societies, 1994), p. 511.

Verses 18–19

τὰ πάντα—the definite article preceding the adjective signifies that the concept *all things* is all inclusive.

ἡμᾶς—the context (see ἡμῖν, vv. 18b, 19b) appears to allude to Paul and his associates but does not exclude the readers of this epistle.

τὴν διακονίαν τῆς καταλλαγῆς—"the ministry of reconciliation." Notice the definite articles before each noun, a usage that indicates that both the ministry and the reconciliation originate with God. Paul repeats the phrase with a slight change (τὸν λόγον τῆς καταλλαγῆς) to convey the idea of good news. Indeed, P[46] and the Western text (D*, F, G, [a]) feature the reading *the gospel.*

αὐτοῖς—the pronoun in the plural points to all those individuals in the world who are and will become the beneficiaries of Christ's atonement. Hence, the word *world* in the singular is interpreted with plural connotation.

---

3. Christ's Ambassadors
5:20–21

20. Therefore, we are ambassadors for Christ, as God is making his appeal through us. We plead with you on behalf of Christ, be reconciled to God.

a. "Therefore, we are ambassadors for Christ." Paul is now ready to draw a conclusion from the foregoing context (vv. 18–19). In view of what God through Christ has done for sinners, Paul takes most seriously the divine charge to preach and teach the good news of reconciliation. He considers himself and his co-workers ambassadors for Christ, because God commissioned them to be his representatives. God charged them to be faithful preachers of God's message of redeeming love.

Paul purposely chose the meaningful word *ambassador,* which in the Greek is a verb ("to be an ambassador"). The word implies that an older person or the eldest person in a group was appointed as a spokesman to represent a king, a ruler, or a community. In Jewish circles, this person was called a *šālîaḥ,* one who would speak the exact words of his sender. Similarly, today an ambassador represents his government by conveying to the host country messages of either the president or the prime minister who has appointed him. As soon as an ambassador utters his own opinion and speaks contrary to the intent of his government, he is relieved of his post.

A tremendous responsibility, then, rests on a minister of the Word of God. He has been commissioned by God to represent the Lord of lords and King of kings before the people to whom he has been sent. He must speak only the words that God has revealed to him, must not utter opinions that conflict with God's message, and must never misrepresent or deny his sender. Should he fail in his task, he will have to face his Lord and give an account.

Paul writes that he and his colleagues are ambassadors for Christ. They represent him, so that all the people of Corinth and elsewhere may see, hear, and come to know Jesus Christ in the apostle and his associates.

b. "As God is making his appeal through us." The first word clarifies the first clause in the verse: "We are ambassadors for Christ." This word expresses certainty and signifies, "In fact, God is speaking to you through us." The present tense of the participle *speaking* dispels the notion that God's Word is frozen in history. His Word is living and active, says the writer of Hebrews, and sharper than a two-edged sword (4:12). Through his servants, God is communicating to the people the message of reconciliation and pleading with them to accept his word in faith. And this appeal goes forth from day to day but especially on the Lord's Day, when God's Word is proclaimed.

c. "We plead with you on behalf of Christ." Paul appears to say that although he and his fellow workers are faithful mouthpieces, God himself is pleading with the people to obey his voice. And this divine appeal comes to all people, for God does not want "anyone to perish, but everyone to come to repentance" (II Peter 3:9). Once again Paul writes that the plea is on behalf of Christ. On the basis of Christ's redeeming work, God entreats all people everywhere to listen obediently to his word of appeasement. And this is the message of reconciliation:

d. "Be reconciled to God." Here is God's communication to all human beings without exception; it is valid for all people of all ages and places; and it is applicable in every era. But if God has reconciled the world to himself (vv. 18, 19), and if he effects conversion and repentance,[89] then why does he now appeal to human beings and urge them to be reconciled? God made the first move, and we must make the second move. God calls us, but he expects us to answer. God provides reconciliation, but he wants us to accept it. Scripture teaches that human beings play an active role in their conversion and repentance (see Isa. 55:7; Jer. 18:11; Ezek. 18:23, 32; 33:11; Luke 24:47; Acts 2:38; 17:30; Titus 2:11, 12).[90]

God's plea uttered through Paul as his official spokesman is, "Be reconciled to God." The verb is a command to do something once for all; and it is in the passive voice, with the question of agent left unanswered. Paul has used the verb *to reconcile* twice in the active voice with God as the subject (vv. 18, 19). God then is the initiator of this process and, with respect to the passive, is the agent. However, there is an analogy in Paul's instruction to the wife who separated from her husband to be reconciled to him (I Cor. 7:11). "Were she to be regarded as purely passive, there would be no point in Paul's exhortation."[91] Likewise, God has initiated reconciliation through Jesus Christ, and now he expects man to respond.

---

89. See Ps. 85:4; Jer. 31:18; Lam. 5:21; Acts 11:18; II Tim. 2:25.

90. The Old Testament mentions conversion seventy-four times as a deed of man and fifteen times as a deed of God. The New Testament records it twenty-six times referring to man and two or three times alluding to God. Consult Louis Berkhof, *Systematic Theology* (Grand Rapids: Eerdmans, 1941), p. 490.

91. Margaret E. Thrall, "Salvation Proclaimed. V. II Corinthians 5.18–21: Reconciliation with God," *ExpT* 93 (1982): 228. Consult also Friedrich Büchsel, *TDNT*, 1:255–56.

Paul wants his readers to accept and acknowledge once for all God's outstretched hand of reconciliation. But also whenever they fall into sin and seek forgiveness, they can turn to him and find that God's hand remains extended to them.

Is Paul addressing only the members of the Corinthian church or does the apostle have in mind all the people in the world? The answer to this question is found in the preceding verses, where Paul first says that God reconciles *us* to himself (v. 18) and then that God reconciles *the world* to himself (v. 19). The imperative *be reconciled* is directed to both the Corinthians and the world.[92]

21. He made him who knew no sin to be sin on our behalf, so that we might become God's righteousness in him.

This is one of the epistle's outstanding verses that summarizes God's good news to sinners. It discloses the meaning of the word *reconciliation,* a word that until now Paul has not fully explained. In his discussion, the question always remained as to why God was willing to overcome his anger toward sin as he reached out to us in love and peace. Now the apostle explains that God took his sinless Son and made him the sinbearer in our place. God had his Son pay the death penalty for our sins, so that we might be set free and declared righteous in his sight. Christ redeemed us by taking upon himself the curse that rested on us (Gal. 3:13).[93]

a. *Contrast.* A cursory reading of this verse reveals that Paul writes a number of opposites. Viewing the verse in two parallel columns, we immediately see a comparison.

He made	so that
him	we
who knew no sin	might become
to be sin	God's righteousness
on our behalf	in him

The differences between Christ and us are obvious: sinlessness and sinfulness (implicit), sin and righteousness, substitution and source. Having created perfect human beings, God established a special relationship with Adam and Eve. When they fell into sin, they offended their creator God and caused alienation. As their judge, God called them to account for their disobedience and sentenced them (Gen. 3:8–19). An earthly judge does not bear any personal animosity toward a person who is accused, proven guilty, and sentenced. Nor does the judge establish a friendship with an offender. This is not so between God and the sinner, because at the dawn of human history God established a personal relationship with human beings. True, Adam and Eve and their descendants have

---

92. Some commentators stress the world instead of believers (Hughes, p. 211; Lietzmann, p. 127); others doubt whether it is a question of either/or (Bultmann, p. 164; Windisch, p. 196).

93. See Morna D. Hooker, "Interchange in Christ," *JTS* 22 (1971): 349–61; "Interchange and Atonement," *BJRUL* 60 (1978): 462–81.

offended God by their sins, but God continued his relationship with them by removing the curse of sin through his Son Jesus Christ. Through him, God imputed to his people righteousness, extended to them his friendship, and effected peace between himself and them.[94]

b. *Significance.* "[God] made him who knew no sin to be sin on our behalf." Paul designates Christ as "him who knew no sin." Even though Jesus' sinlessness is implied throughout the New Testament, in only a few places do writers specifically refer to his purity. For instance, disputing with the religious establishment of his day, Jesus challenged the Jews to prove him guilty of sin (John 8:46; compare 7:18). The writer of Hebrews states that Jesus was identical to us but without sin (4:15; refer to 7:26; 9:14). Quoting Isaiah 53:9, Peter writes, "He committed no sin, and no deceit was found in his mouth" (I Peter 2:22; see 3:18). And John confesses that Jesus "appeared so that he might take away our sins. And in him is no sin" (I John 3:5).

"[Jesus] knew no sin," Paul writes. Yet Jesus must have been gravely offended and deeply grieved when he observed and continually experienced in himself the effects of human sin. He was "a man of sorrows, and familiar with suffering" (Isa. 53:3). During his earthly ministry, he was frequently confronted by Satan and his evil cohorts, yet he never succumbed to sin. Even though he appeared "in the likeness of sinful man" (Rom. 8:3), he kept himself free from sin by showing his constant love to God and humankind.

Although Jesus was tempted by Satan, he did not become a sinner. When God made him sin by imputing to him our sin, he regarded him as the sinbearer, not as a sinner. True, as the Lamb of God, Christ removed the sin of the world by his sacrificial death on the cross (John 1:29; 3:14–15). But presently Paul portrays not a sacrificial offering but rather a courtroom scene in which a judge either sentences the guilty or releases the innocent. By imputing sin to Jesus Christ, God imputes righteousness to his people. Christ took our place as the head of redeemed humanity; he is our representative speaking to God in our defense (I John 2:1).[95]

Also, Christ became our substitute by taking our place before God to receive the punishment that was due us. Standing before God, Jesus bore the greatest burden of sin ever. He paid for sin when he was spiritually severed from God and was physically dying on the cross (Matt. 27:46, 50). Jesus took upon himself our sins and through his atonement made us recipients of God's righteousness.[96]

c. *Effect.* "So that we might become God's righteousness in him." The good news of Christ's death is that our sin, which separated us from God, has been removed; he accepts us as if we had never sinned at all. Because of Christ's death,

---

94. Refer to C. E. B. Cranfield, *The Epistle to the Romans*, 2 vols., International Critical Commentary (Edinburgh: Clark, 1979), vol. 1, p. 259.

95. Compare Paul Ellingworth, "'For our sake God made him share our sin'? (II Corinthians 5.21, GNB)," *BibTr* 38 (1987): 237–41.

96. Collange, *Énigmes,* p. 276.

God declares us innocent. He acquits us, drops all charges against us, and grants us the gift of righteousness. Sixteenth-century German theologian Zacharius Ursinus put this truth succinctly in these words:

> God grants and credits to me
> the perfect satisfaction, righteousness,
>   and holiness of Christ,
> as if I had never sinned nor been a sinner,
> as if I had been perfectly obedient
>   as Christ was obedient for me.[97]

Let us briefly discuss the meaning of the phrase *God's righteousness*. Is it righteousness that belongs to God (subjective genitive)? Or is it righteousness that he receives from us (objective genitive)? Or does righteousness originate with God and then is granted to us (genitive of origin)?[98]

The second of these three questions describes a circumstance that is improbable if not impossible. And the third question would expect the answer that we have received complete righteousness, but we can say only that our righteousness is in Christ. His righteousness is imputed to us in justification, which is a declaratory act of God. We do well to answer the first question and say that righteousness, akin to holiness, is an inherent characteristic that belongs to God. He expresses this attribute by judging sin as a violation of his holiness. The righteousness that God possesses must be understood in terms of judgment, justice, and grace. Through Christ Jesus, God has placed us within the context of that righteousness and has reconciled us to himself. Hence, reconciliation and righteousness are the proverbial two sides of the same coin.

Greek Words, Phrases, and Constructions in 5:20–21

ὑπὲρ Χριστοῦ—"on behalf of Christ." See also ὑπὲρ ἡμῶν, "in our place." Jesus Christ is both our representative and substitute. Compare verse 14.

ὡς τοῦ θεοῦ παρακαλοῦντος—while the particle stresses actuality, the genitive absolute denotes concession with the present participle disclosing continued activity: "as, in fact, God is appealing."

τὸν μὴ γνόντα ἁμαρτίαν—"the one who did not know sin." The aorist participle has either a causal or a concessive connotation. The negative particle precedes the participle, not the noun.

ἡμεῖς γενώμεθα—the personal pronoun adds emphasis to the verb in the aorist (single action).

δικαιοσύνη θεοῦ—the genitive is subjective. Note that the noun without the definite article must be seen in an absolute sense, namely, righteousness that belongs to God.

---

97. Heidelberg Catechism, answer 60.

98. Rudolf Bultmann, *Theology of the New Testament*, 1:270–72; *Second Letter to the Corinthians*, p. 165; "ΔΙΚΑΙΟΣΥΝΗ ΘΕΟΥ," *JBL* 83 (1964): 12–16.

Summary of Chapter 5

Paul has been fixing his sight on eternal verities and now is considering the transition from our frail physical bodies to our eternal house with God. This earthly body is like a tent that serves as a temporary dwelling and is quickly taken down. We long for the clothing of our heavenly dwelling, says Paul. He has in mind God's sacred presence that covers believers with eternal glory when they enter heaven.

During our time on earth, Paul continues, we reside in our physical bodies, but we are away from the Lord. Nevertheless, we live by faith with the purpose of pleasing him. At the end of time, all of us have to appear before Christ's judgment seat to give an account of our deeds. All our works, whether good or bad, will be revealed at the consummation. And Christ assigns recompense to each individual for deeds performed through the instrumentality of the body while that person was on earth.

Paul and his associates desire to examine themselves to see whether they have advanced the cause of the gospel in their preaching and conduct. Paul's opponents questioned his claim to apostolicity and asked for proof. He blunted the attacks of his adversaries with conduct that was above reproach in every respect. Paul writes that he and his co-workers did not commend themselves, but instead received their commendation from the sincerity of the believers' hearts. They are driven by the love of Christ and have the sure knowledge that one, namely, Christ, died for all.

Everyone who appropriates Christ's death in faith is included in the number of people who make up the totality of the word *all*. And all these people live not for themselves but for the resurrected Christ.

At the moment of Paul's conversion, he encountered Jesus Christ and then began to understand that Christ's death and resurrection happened for the benefit of all believers. Every person who comes to faith in Christ is a new creation; former things belong to the past and everything is new.

Paul explains that God is the originator of all that is new, of reconciling sinful people to himself, of forgiving sin, and of appointing his servants to proclaim the message of reconciliation.

He exhorts everyone to be reconciled to God. Having made Christ the sin-bearer, God grants to all his people the gift of righteousness.

6

Apostolic Ministry, *part 6*

(6:1–7:1)

Outline

6

1 Working together [with him], then, we exhort you not to receive the grace of God in vain. 2 For he says,

> "At a favorable moment I heard you
> And in the day of salvation I helped you."

Look, now is the acceptable time, look, now is the time of salvation. 3 We do not give anyone an opportunity to take offense, so that our ministry may not be faulted. 4 However, as servants of God we commend ourselves in every way: in great endurance, in afflictions, in anguish, in distresses, 5 in beatings, in imprisonments, in civil disorders, in hard work, in times of sleeplessness, in hunger, 6 in purity, in knowledge, in patience, in kindness, in the Holy Spirit, in genuine love, 7 in the word of truth, in the power of God; with the weapons of righteousness in the right hand and in the left, 8 through glory and dishonor, through bad report and good report, as impostors yet true men, 9 as unknown yet well known, as dying, and look, we live, as chastened and yet we are not killed, 10 as sorrowful yet always rejoicing, as poor yet making many rich, as having nothing and yet possessing everything.

11 We have spoken freely to you, Corinthians, and opened our hearts wide. 12 We are not restricting our love to you, but you restrict your love toward us. 13 Yes, even you, widen your hearts in the same way in return—I speak as to my children.

14 Do not be unevenly yoked with unbelievers. For what do righteousness and lawlessness have in common? What fellowship has light with darkness? 15 And what harmony is there between Christ and Belial? Or what does a believer have in common with an unbeliever? 16 Or what agreement does the temple of God have with idols? For we are the temple of the living God. Just as God said,

> "I will dwell with them and walk among them
>   And I will be their God
> and they will be my people."
> 17 "Therefore, come out from their midst
>   And be separate," says the Lord.
> "Touch nothing unclean
> And I will receive you.
> 18 And I will be a father to you
>   And you will be my sons and daughters,"
> says the Lord Almighty.

7 1 Having, therefore, these promises, my dear friends, let us cleanse ourselves from every defilement of flesh and spirit, and perfect [our] holiness in the fear of God.

E. Paul's Ministry
6:1–7:16

The first two verses of this chapter are closely linked to the last paragraph in the preceding chapter.[1] Some translations include these verses, therefore, in the last part of chapter 5. But the alternative of treating verses 1–2 as a separate section in the current chapter, or of making it an introduction to the rest of the chapter, is equally valid.

Paul has returned to his earlier discussion of the work God has assigned to him and his associates (5:11). And this work places them in positions where they have to be engaged in spiritual warfare as they face dangerous and undesirable situations.

1. Working Together
6:1–2

1. Working together [with him], then, we exhort you not to receive the grace of God in vain.

a. "Working together [with him], then." Most translations expand this clause by adding "with God" or "with him." The Greek lacks the words in brackets, and these words must be supplied on the basis of the preceding context. The last few verses of the previous chapter do not describe a working relationship between Paul and the Corinthians or Paul and his co-workers.[2] At the moment, that is not the point the apostle is emphasizing. Instead, Paul stresses the fact that he and his associates are ambassadors for Christ and speak on his behalf (5:20–21). Also, Paul writes that through him and his fellow workers, God is making his appeal to the people. Throughout his epistles, Paul often fails to distinguish clearly between God and Christ. Thus, we affirm that the apostolic workers served Christ as ambassadors and as mouthpieces for God. Perhaps it is best to see that God is the subject in the last verses of chapter 5 and that the words *with him* in this verse designate God.

The translation *working together with him* is acceptable as long as we interpret it to mean that God uses his servants as instruments (I Cor. 3:9; I Thess. 3:2). Further, messengers can never be on the same level as their sender (compare John 13:16; 15:20).

b. "We exhort you not to receive the grace of God in vain." The work that God has entrusted to his servants is that of urging the people to be reconciled to him (5:20). When Paul writes, "As God is making his appeal through us" (5:20), he indicates that God works through his servants to make the message of reconcili-

---

1. E.g., J.-F. Collange, *Énigmes de la deuxième épître de Paul aux Corinthiens: Étude exégétique de II Cor. 2:14–7:4,* SNTSMS 18 (New York and Cambridge: Cambridge University Press, 1972), pp. 283–84; Victor Paul Furnish, *II Corinthians: Translated with Introduction, Notes and Commentary,* Anchor Bible 32A (Garden City, N.Y.: Doubleday, 1984), pp. 338, 341.

2. F. W. Grosheide proposes that the phrase *working together* should be applied to Paul and his associates. *De Tweede Brief van den Apostel Paulus aan de Kerk te Korinthe,* Kommentaar op het Nieuwe Testament series (Amsterdam: Van Bottenburg, 1939), p. 217. John Calvin understands the phrase to mean "working together with God." *The Second Epistle of Paul the Apostle to the Corinthians and the Epistles to Timothy, Titus and Philemon,* Calvin's Commentaries series, trans. T. A. Small (Grand Rapids: Eerdmans, 1964), p. 83. Compare Ernest B. Allo, *Saint Paul Seconde Épître aux Corinthiens,* 2d ed. (Paris: Gabalda, 1956), p. 173.

ation known to the people. Now Paul with his co-workers is exhorting the readers in Corinth to heed God's appeal. (Incidentally, the Greek verb *parakalein* is translated "appeal" in 5:20 and "exhort" in 6:1.)

The exhortation is directed to the readers and the hearers in Corinth. By placing the pronoun *you* at the end of the Greek sentence, Paul emphasizes it. As it were, he points directly at the Corinthians and tells them that God gives them the message of his grace, a message that they accept and approve.[3] The good news of God's grace includes Jesus' death and resurrection, God's reconciliation with mankind because of Christ's atoning work, peace with God and forgiveness of sin, and God's fathomless love toward his people. This love is demonstrated in the charge to have the message of reconciliation proclaimed to the whole world (5:20).

Translators must decide whether to render the Greek infinitive *dexasthai* as either the past ("to have received"[4]) or the present ("to receive"[5]). Did the Corinthians accept the gospel and then put it aside when Paul preached it during his first visit? Is this the reason the apostle now exhorts them not to let God's grace be unproductive? This conclusion is unlikely, for they showed signs of spiritual growth (see, e.g., 1:11; 3:2–3, 18; 4:15; 7:12–16; 9:2; 10:15). And Paul writes that "it is God who confirms us with you in Christ" (1:21). True, God never fails his people, but his spiritual sons and daughters must exercise human responsibility in accepting and obeying his message of salvation. This message was not given once for all; it was proclaimed, heard, and read repeatedly in Corinth. After Paul left, his associates (Timothy, Silas, Apollos, and even Peter) continued to preach the gospel there. The Greek infinitive *dexasthai* (to receive) should be translated not as a past tense that refers to a single occurrence but as a present tense that shows that its action comprises the entire extent and duration of preaching and receiving God's message of grace. Writes John Calvin, "Here ministers are taught that it is not enough merely to propound doctrine. They must labour that those who hear it should also accept it, and not once but continually."[6]

What is the significance of the phrase *in vain?* Throughout the preceding chapter, Paul opposed his adversaries who tried to influence the Corinthians with selfish ambitions rather than the cause of Christ. Thus he exhorted the believers in Corinth to not live for themselves but for Christ, who died for them and rose from the dead (5:15). This exhortation had to be repeated numerous times, for the human heart is prone to serve self instead of Christ.[7] An inactive response to God's word is worthless and unprofitable.

---

3. Refer to Walter Grundmann, *TDNT,* 3:54; Hans-Georg Link, *NIDNTT,* 3:746; Gerd Petzke, *EDNT,* 1:292.

4. E.g., GNB, JB, NCV, NEB, NEB, REB, SEB, TNT.

5. E.g., KJV, NKJV, MLB, NAB, NASB, NIV, NRSV, RSV, *Cassirer, Moffatt.*

6. Calvin, *II Corinthians,* p. 83.

7. Compare C. K. Barrett, *The Second Epistle to the Corinthians,* Harper's New Testament Commentaries series (New York: Harper and Row, 1973), p. 183; Ralph P. Martin, *II Corinthians,* Word Biblical Commentary 40 (Waco: Word, 1986), p. 166.

2. For he says,

> **"At a favorable moment I heard you**
> **And in the day of salvation I helped you."**

Look, now is the acceptable time, look, now is the time of salvation.

a. *Quotation.* When God is making his appeal through his messengers, and they are God's fellow workers, then it follows that God himself is speaking through the words of the Old Testament messianic prophecy of Isaiah 49:8. Paul quotes the Isaianic passage verbatim from the Septuagint and introduces it with the formula, "For he says." Isaiah also has an introductory formula, "This is what the LORD says." These formulas disclose that God speaks with divine authority both through the prophet Isaiah and through the apostle Paul as he addresses the people of Israel and Corinth.

The Old Testament prophecy may have come to Paul's mind when he wrote the Greek infinitive *dexasthai* (to accept, receive; v. 1) and thought of the Greek adjective *dektos* (acceptable, favorable; v. 2) in Isaiah 49:8.[8] The context of this prophecy is that of the humiliation and the exaltation of the Lord's Servant, the Messiah (49:7). Through him, God restores the people of Israel politically by setting them free from captivity in exile and spiritually by sending them the Messiah.

The messianic era commenced with the coming of Jesus Christ who inaugurated the new era. The old things passed away, and through him all things became new (5:17). God reconciled the world to himself at the acceptable time and in the day of salvation. Nevertheless, as God sent his Servant to his own people, they did not receive him (John 1:11). Similarly, he sends Paul to the Corinthians with the message of reconciliation. As Jesus during his earthly ministry constantly prayed to God the Father, so Paul and his co-workers ask for help. And God's affirmative reply is: "At a favorable moment I heard you and in the day of salvation I helped you."

b. *Affirmation.* Paul applies the Old Testament prophecy to the Corinthians. He notes that its fulfillment has come by telling his readers: "Look, now is the acceptable time, look, now is the time of salvation." He provides a one-sentence commentary on Isaiah's prophecy and twice says, "Look!" His readers are able to understand that the Messiah was indeed humiliated by suffering, death, and burial. But after rising from the dead and ascending to heaven, he completed his mediatorial work and took his place of honor at God's right hand. Therefore, the Corinthians should see that for them the time of reconciliation has arrived; the era of God's good pleasure has come (compare Luke 4:19, 21; Isa. 61:2). And this era continues until the consummation of all things occurs.

Paul is not talking about chronological time, but about the new era in which God is favorably disposed to his people. He describes this era as "a specially welcome time" (MLB). The Greek word he uses, *euprosdektos,* is the compound form

---

8. Charles Hodge, *An Exposition of the Second Epistle to the Corinthians* (1891; Edinburgh: Banner of Truth, 1959), p. 155.

of the term *dektos* (acceptable). Although it is commonly translated as a synonym,[9] it conveys nonetheless the meaning *welcome*.[10] Its parallel is the phrase *day of salvation,* which correspondingly refers to the new era. The gift of salvation that God makes available to mankind is the restoration of peace with him. Now is the day of salvation, says Paul, and by implication, "Do not let it pass by."

If New Testament believers receive the gift of salvation in this era, what happened to the Old Testament saints who lived in a time when God had not yet reconciled the world to himself? These people received adoption as sons and daughters, divine glory, the covenants, the law, and God's promises (Rom. 9:4). By faith, these people longed for a heavenly home, and God was "not ashamed to be called their God" (Heb. 11:16). Together with believers from New Testament times and beyond, they are made perfect in Jesus Christ.

Practical Considerations in 6:2

The last few verses of chapter 5 and the first two of this chapter reveal urgency. Paul pleads with his readers to be reconciled to God and exhorts them to accept God's message of salvation now. Paul uttered the same appeal to the Athenian philosophers when he said, "In the past God overlooked such ignorance, but now he commands all people everywhere to repent" (Acts 17:30).

The urgency of repentance is due to the time limit that God has set. For us, that limit begins at the time the good news of salvation is heard and ends when we die. We know the time when we first heard the gospel, but we do not know when we will leave this earthly scene. God has set the date of our departure, for "man is destined to die once, and after that to face judgment" (Heb. 9:27). The call to repentance goes forth within the limits God has set for us. Beyond death there is no salvation.

Paul's brief commentary on the time of God's favor alerts the readers to its immediacy. Pay attention, he says twice; now is the moment to accept God's love in Christ Jesus. By implication, he warns that tomorrow may be too late.

> Only one life, 'twill soon be past;
> Only what is done for Christ will last.

Greek Words, Phrases, and Constructions in 6:1–2

δέξασθαι—the aorist infinitive (deponent) does not necessarily denote single action. It can also be comprehensive in scope to include all occurrences of accepting God's message of salvation. Here it should be translated in the present tense, "to receive."

λέγει—the subject must be supplied from the context, namely, God the speaker through his servants (5:20). Similar omissions occur elsewhere (Rom. 9:15; Heb. 1:5, 6, 7, 13), and in these instances translators must supply a noun ("God") as the subject.

---

9. See 8:12; Rom. 15:16, 31.

10. Jean Héring notes that this is "a nuance which translation must not lose." *The Second Epistle of Saint Paul to the Corinthians,* trans. A. W. Heathcote and P. J. Allcock (London: Epworth, 1967), p. 46.

ἰδού—"look." Apart from an Old Testament quotation (Rom. 9:33; Isa. 28:16), Paul uses this demonstrative particle only eight times, six times in this epistle (I Cor. 15:51; II Cor. 5:17; 6:2 [twice], 9; 7:11; 12:14; Gal. 1:20).

---

2. Enduring Hardships
6:3–10

In this section, Paul presents a catalogue of his sufferings on behalf of Christ. He already had written a preliminary list of hardships (4:8–11) and will tabulate all his afflictions and experiences later (11:23–33). The suggestion that Paul has borrowed words from an existing list remains to be proven. He is relating his personal experiences and may have had no need to rely on an outside source.[11] Indeed, the frequent references to Paul's sufferings are illustrative of the trials and adversities preachers in the first century endured.

The passage is neatly divided into three parts. The first section (vv. 4b–7a) has a list in which the preposition *in* occurs eighteen times to introduce an equal number of phrases. The second segment (vv. 7b–8a) features three sets of words or phrases, each preceded by the preposition *with* or *by*. And the third section (vv. 8b–10) consists of seven contrasts, all prefaced by the particle *as*. Each group is subdivided and shows parallelism (see the commentary on vv. 4b–10).[12]

3. We do not give anyone an opportunity to take offense, so that our ministry may not be faulted.

In the preceding verse (v. 2) Paul inserted an Old Testament quotation to lend scriptural support to God's appeal for and Paul's ministry of reconciliation (5:20; 6:1). Now he discusses the conduct of God's servants by reverting to the familiar theme that he and his fellow workers must be above reproach (compare 1:12; 2:17; 4:1–2; 12:19).

Ministers of Christ's gospel must exert themselves to be blameless in their conduct so that no one who observes them can take offense. If they proclaim the Word of God but fail to follow its teaching, they deny the truth, destroy the church, and insult their Lord and Master. Paul himself sets an example by providing no one an occasion to criticize his conduct (e.g., see I Cor. 9:18). Writes James Denney, "If it is not the chief end of the evangelist to give no occasion of stumbling, it is one of his chief rules."[13]

---

11. Contra Collange, *Énigmes*, p. 290; and compare Robert Hodgson, "Paul the Apostle and First Century Tribulation Lists," *ZNTW* 74 (1983): 59–80.

12. Rudolf Bultmann divides the series into four groups. He considers the entry "in great endurance" (v. 4b) to be introductory and then lists the first cluster of nine phrases with the Greek preposition ἐν (vv. 4b–5), followed by another eight with the same preposition (vv. 6–7a). The third group has three phrases with the preposition διά (vv. 7b–8a), and the last collection has seven parts with the particle ὡς (vv. 8b–10). *The Second Letter to the Corinthians*, trans. Roy A. Harrisville (Minneapolis: Augsburg, 1985), p. 168.

13. James Denney, *The Second Epistle to the Corinthians*, 2d ed., The Expositor's Bible series (New York: Armstrong, 1900), p. 229.

In the first clause of verse 3, the Greek strengthens the negative by duplicating it. Paul literally says, "We give no one no opportunity to take offense." Most translators render the text as "no offense to anyone," but others prefer the translation "no offense in anything" (compare KJV, NKJV, NASB, NEB, REB, *Cassirer*). The context is used to support either version, for it can be argued that in verse 3 Paul calls attention to a person (anyone) and then, by contrast, presents a list of adversities (anything) in the succeeding verses (4–10). Conversely, it can also be said that the phrases *in anything* (v. 3) and *in every way* (v. 4) strengthen each other. Nevertheless, the first translation carries more weight because of its personal nature. Whenever anyone can find an opportunity to take offense, he or she will not fail to respond to it. Thus, Paul wants to remove any reason that may provide a cause for someone to take offense.[14]

Why is Paul so interested in avoiding offense to anyone? His answer is, "So that our ministry may not be faulted." Above all else, Paul wants to safeguard the ministry of the gospel that he has received from the Lord.[15] He knows that he is a minister of the new covenant (3:6), serves in a ministry of righteousness (3:9), and is charged with a ministry of reconciliation (5:18).

In Paul's letters, the word *ministry* or *service* occurs twenty-three times, twelve of which are in this epistle.[16] The emphasis on this one word shows the importance Paul attaches to the ministry and how he treats it with utmost respect. "His ministry, not his person, is what matters."[17]

The conduct of a pastor ought never to impede the work of the gospel ministry. A pastor is always first a minister of the Word and then a servant of the Lord to his people. In earlier centuries, the initials *V.D.M.* (Minister of the Word of the Lord) were often placed after the name of a pastor to indicate his calling to the ministry of God's Word. When a minister of the gospel breaks God's moral law, the church can no longer witness effectively to the world. The church becomes a laughingstock, for the blemish of sin exhibits the contradiction of deed and words. The sinful deed cancels the message of the gospel. For the minister and for every member of the church, all things in every way should serve the cause of Christ's good news of salvation. Thus Paul commends himself and his associates as God's servants.

4a. However, as servants of God we commend ourselves in every way.

The adversative *however* contrasts the negative of verse 3 with the positive of verse 4. Positively stated, Paul and his fellow workers are servants of God who have received delegated authority to present themselves in his name. They have been set aside and called by God to serve him in the ministry of the Word (Gal. 1:15; and see Isa. 49:1, 5; Jer. 1:5).

---

14. Joachim Guhrt, *NIDNTT*, 2:705; Gustav Stählin, *TDNT*, 6:747.

15. Even though the better Greek manuscripts read "the ministry," translators prefer the reading *our ministry*. Exceptions are KJV, NASB, SEB, *Cassirer*.

16. The Greek word *diakonia* occurs in II Cor. 3:7, 8, 9 [twice]; 4:1; 5:18; 6:3; 8:4; 9:1, 12, 13; 11:8. The noun *diakonos* appears four times (II Cor. 3:6; 6:4; 11:15, 23).

17. Barrett, *Second Corinthians*, p. 184.

As a servant of God, Paul with his co-workers is commending himself in regard to not his person but his ministry. Hence, there is no incongruity between his earlier comments on recommending himself (see 3:1–3; 5:12), for he never stresses himself but always his ministry. Paul risked everything to serve his God, and God supplied him in his needs during all the adversities he encountered.

4b. In great endurance, in afflictions, in anguish, in distresses.
The first of these four phrases that describe Paul's ministry, "in great endurance," differs from the others in that it denotes a virtue that Paul must exercise throughout his ministry. To be able to persist he had to rely on his Sender for physical, mental, and spiritual strength. The virtue of endurance is fundamental to the three sets of hardships Paul has to bear passively at some times and actively at other times (vv. 4b–5).

1. afflictions, anguish, distresses
2. beatings, imprisonments, civil disorders
3. hard work, times of sleeplessness, hunger

The first set of triplets illustrates general hardships; the second has to do with Paul facing law enforcement and judicial authority; and the third relates to physical matters.

a. "In great endurance." Notice that Paul describes his endurance as great. In a passive sense, the word points to the sufferings he had to endure for the sake of Christ (compare 1:6). And in an active sense the word refers to good works that were prompted by signs, wonders, and miracles (12:12).[18]

b. "In afflictions." From personal experiences Paul could recite a number of afflictions. Wherever he brought the gospel, he had to endure afflictions (in Pisidian Antioch, Iconium, Lystra, Philippi, Thessalonica, Berea, Corinth, and Jerusalem). He knew that affliction would be his lot, especially in Jerusalem (Acts 20:23).

c. "In anguish." We use the singular collectively for the plural word that in the Greek text often conveys the concept *calamities*.[19] These calamities occurred through the forces of nature (being shipwrecked three times, and spending a night and a day on the open sea; 11:25) or because of human force. At times Paul was exposed to mortal danger.

d. "In distresses." This noun is a synonym of the preceding phrase. It indicates a narrow squeeze from which there is no escape, unless that escape is providentially provided. Again, Paul could easily recount a number of near-death experiences from which God had miraculously delivered him (compare 12:10).

5. In beatings, in imprisonments, in civil disorders, in hard work, in times of sleeplessness, in hunger.
These six phrases are the second and the third sets of triplets that Paul presents as either sufferings or hardships he has had to endure for the sake of the

---

18. Compare Friedrich Hauck, *TDNT*, 4:587.
19. Bauer, p. 52.

ministry. These can be corroborated with references from Luke's Book of Acts and Paul's epistles.

a. "In beatings." Luke describes how Paul and Silas were beaten with rods before the Roman magistrates in Philippi (Acts 16:22). And Paul reveals that in total the Jews flogged him five times and the Romans beat him with rods three times (11:24–25). Before the Roman authorities, Paul could have demanded legal protection on the basis of his Roman citizenship. Such was not so before the Jewish synagogue officials, who ordered an offender to be flogged "forty lashes minus one." So Paul could claim that he had been flogged more severely than anyone else.

b. "In imprisonments." Luke relates details on Paul's and Silas's imprisonment in Philippi (Acts 16:23–40). We have no further information on other incarcerations, yet Paul writes that he has been jailed frequently (11:23).[20]

c. "In civil disorders." Opposition to Paul's ministry often degenerated into riots that had to be quelled by the authorities. These disorders limited Paul's effectiveness as a missionary (see Acts 19:29). The worst case of civil unrest occurred in Jerusalem in the court of the Gentiles. There the mob tried to kill Paul, but a Roman commander with two hundred soldiers prevented them from murdering him (Acts 21:30–32).

d. "In hard work." The singular in English represents the plural in Greek. If we think of Paul's intent to be financially independent by working as a tentmaker in addition to being a missionary, we know that he toiled (Acts 18:3; 20:34–35). In Ephesus, he worked to defray expenses and to help the poor, lectured daily in the hall of Tyrannus, and went from house to house to exhort both Jews and Gentiles to repent and believe (Acts 19:9–10; 20:20–21).[21] Mental toils are much harder to endure than physical labors. Hence Paul writes that he never stopped warning the Ephesians night and day with tears (Acts 20:31). And from his own testimony, we know that he worked harder than all the other apostles (I Cor. 15:10). Here, then, is an indication that hard work refers to Paul's missionary task.

e. "In times of sleeplessness." Time spent in prayer was often taken from the hours of much-needed nightly rest. Paul followed Jesus' example (see Mark 1:35; Luke 6:12) by spending nighttime and early morning hours in prayer. Paul proved to be a prayer warrior who sought the Lord in the quiet hours of the night.

f. "In hunger." Paul writes that often he lacked the basic necessities of food and drink (11:27). Elsewhere he discloses that he knew what it was to be hungry at one time and to have abundance at another (Phil. 4:12; I Cor. 4:11). He also observed periods of fasting (11:27).

---

20. I Clem. 5.6 states that Paul was confined seven times.

21. Philip Edgcumbe Hughes suggests, rightly, that manual toil can be included only secondarily. *Paul's Second Epistle to the Corinthians: The English Text with Introduction, Exposition and Notes,* New International Commentary on the New Testament series (Grand Rapids: Eerdmans, 1962), p. 225.

6. In purity, in knowledge, in patience, in kindness, in the Holy Spirit, in genuine love, 7a. in the word of truth, in the power of God.

The preceding verses conveyed nine hardships in Paul's life: three sets of threes (vv. 4b–5). Paul continues with a listing of eight gifts of God, a list that can be subdivided into four sets of two qualities each:

purity, knowledge	patience, kindness
Holy Spirit, genuine love	word of truth, power of God

The first four gifts complement each other; so do the next four. The first four gifts come implicitly from God, but the next four are explicitly linked to the Holy Spirit. Next, the first four gifts are described by single words, but the next four gifts are named in four sets of double words in the Greek. And last, the second category features the Holy Spirit as the first gift to God's servants.

a. "In purity." The word *purity* occurs only here in the New Testament and for some translations in 11:3. Yet the concept is not unfamiliar, because the adjective *hagnos* (pure, sincere) appears eight times in the New Testament.[22] The noun refers to purity in respect to sexual and moral relations and also to one's conscience. A person who is pure exhibits innocence and integrity (see 7:11; 11:2; Phil. 4:8).

b. "In knowledge." This is not intellectual knowledge "that puffs up" (I Cor. 8:1). Paul is thinking instead of knowledge concerning God and salvation through Jesus Christ. Earlier Paul wrote, "God has shone forth in our hearts to provide us illumination with the knowledge of his glory in the face of Jesus Christ" (4:6). The spiritual knowledge we have of God is that which he has mediated to us through revealing Jesus' life and work.[23] Paul was blessed with the gift of knowledge so that he could share his insight into the gospel of Christ with the Corinthians (11:4–6).

c. "In patience." The gift of patience can best be described as "self-restraint which does not hastily retaliate wrong."[24] It is forbearance to endure wrongs without becoming angry. Old Testament writers describe God as "slow to anger, abounding in love" (Exod. 34:6; Num. 14:18; Ps. 103:8). One of the characteristics of love is patience, says Paul (I Cor. 13:4). Patience, together with love and kindness, is one of the fruits of the Holy Spirit (Gal. 5:22).

d. "In kindness." God shows kindness, tolerance, and patience toward us to lead us to repentance (Rom. 2:4; compare 11:22). The Greek word *chrēstotēs*

---

22. For the adjective *hagnos,* see II Cor. 7:11; 11:2; Phil. 4:8; I Tim. 5:22; Titus 2:5; James 3:17; I Peter 3:2; I John 3:3. The adverb *hagnōs* appears once, in Phil. 1:17.

23. Consult Ernst Dieter Schmitz, *NIDNTT,* 2:402. John Albert Bengel wants to link knowledge and patience. Thus he comments, "*Knowledge* often means *leniency,* which inclines to and admits favorable constructions of harsh things; an interpretation according with *in long-suffering*" (*Bengel's New Testament Commentary,* trans. Charlton T. Lewis and Marvin R. Vincent, 2 vols. [Grand Rapids: Kregel, 1981], vol. 2, p. 303). However, this interpretation is skewed to accommodate two concepts without doing justice to both.

24. Thayer, p. 387. See also R. C. Trench, *Synonyms of the New Testament* (Grand Rapids: Eerdmans, 1953), p. 195.

(kindness) includes the qualities of ease, pleasantness, and goodness. It corresponds to something that fits, is easy to wear, and pleasing. To illustrate, Jesus invites us to take up his yoke, because it fits, is easy on our shoulders, and is pleasing (Matt. 11:30). In our daily lives, we exercise the gift of kindness so that people immediately are at ease with us and are attracted to our pleasant disposition.[25] Paul exhorts us to clothe ourselves "with compassion, kindness, humility, gentleness, and patience" (Col. 3:12).

e. "In the Holy Spirit." Some commentators are of the opinion that Paul is thinking not of the Holy Spirit but of "a spirit that is holy."[26] But this interpretation runs into difficulties. In the New Testament, the noun *spirit* refers to the Holy Spirit whenever it is qualified by the adjective *holy* (ninety-two times). True, the Holy Spirit does not seem to fit the category of gifts that Paul lists in verses 6 and 7a. So, two translations try to alleviate the problem by expanding the text: "by gifts of the Holy Spirit" (NEB, REB). This is not quite necessary. Luke writes an almost verbatim parallel to Matthew 7:11, but he substitutes the words *good gifts* by "the Holy Spirit" (Luke 11:13). The Holy Spirit, then, is the source of all good gifts (see I Cor. 12:11). By mentioning some fruits of the Spirit he has listed elsewhere (love, patience, kindness; see Gal. 5:22–23), Paul also mentions the Spirit himself.[27] He knows that the Spirit of God directs him in the work of his apostolic ministry (Acts 16:6; 20:22; I Thess. 1:5).

f. "In genuine love." Paul ranks love as the preeminent spiritual fruit that the Holy Spirit gives to the believers (Gal. 5:22). He describes this fruit as genuine to reveal the true quality of love (Rom. 12:9; see I Peter 1:22). Love must always be genuine; so must faith (I Tim. 1:5). When genuineness is lacking, virtues such as love and faith are worthless and contradict what they are intended to be. Genuine love toward our fellow man is the fulfillment of the royal law (James 2:8).

g. "In the word of truth." Translators understand the phrase to mean either "speaking the truth" or "proclaiming the truth." Is Paul defending his veracity to reassure his readers that he is trustworthy? Or is he referring to his ministry which for him consists of preaching Christ's gospel? Paul sometimes uses the concept *truth* in this epistle to offset the distortions set forth by his opponents. Hence he speaks the truth at all times (4:2; 7:14; 12:6; 13:8).

No doubt Paul calls attention to the term *truth,* but he probably employs the coined phrase *the word of truth* to mean proclamation of the gospel. First, this phrase occurs in four other places (Eph. 1:13; Col. 1:5; II Tim. 2:15; James 1:18) with reference to preaching. Next, Christians in the early church knew that this well-known expression stood for the ministry of the Word. And third, the immediate context of Paul's discourse is that of his ministry (5:18–20; 6:3).

---

25. F. J. Pop, *De Tweede Brief van Paulus aan de Corinthiërs* (Nijkerk: Callenbach, 1980), p. 194.

26. Alfred Plummer, *A Critical and Exegetical Commentary on the Second Epistle of St Paul to the Corinthians,* International Critical Commentary (1915; Edinburgh: Clark, 1975), p. 196; Barrett, *Second Corinthians,* pp. 186–87; compare Bultmann, *Second Letter,* p. 171; JB.

27. Martin, *II Corinthians,* p. 177.

h. "In the power of God." It is interesting to note that the concepts *word* (of the gospel) and *power* at times appear together in Paul's epistles (I Cor. 2:4; I Thess. 1:5; see also Rom. 1:16). The phrase *in the power of God* stands at the end of the list of four gifts and the phrase *the Holy Spirit* at its beginning. In effect, these two phrases form a pair and complement each other. The power of the Holy Spirit is especially evident in the preaching of the gospel and its consequences as he extends Christ's church and kingdom (Rom. 15:13). God is manifesting his power in Paul's ministry by using a man who is unimpressive, not a fluent speaker, and physically weak (I Cor. 2:3–5; II Cor. 4:7; 10:10; 11:6; 12:9–10). "Of all men in the world he was the weakest to look at, the most battered, burdened, and depressed, yet no one else had in him such a fountain as he of the most powerful and gracious life."[28]

7b. With the weapons of righteousness in the right hand and in the left, 8a. through glory and dishonor, through bad report and good report.

After writing eighteen phrases that begin with the Greek preposition *en* (in), Paul now writes three clauses, one lengthy and one short, with the preposition *dia,* which signifies going through something. We have translated the preposition first as "with" to express means and next as "through" to depict circumstances. The first clause represents balance: an armed soldier with weapons in the right and left hand. The next two clauses delineate contrast: glory and dishonor, bad report and good report, in reverse order. As a soldier stands between weapons on his right and left so Paul and his associates are between glory and dishonor, bad report and good report.[29]

a. "With the weapons of righteousness." Engaged in spiritual warfare, the soldier in Christ's army is armed with spiritual weapons to do battle against the forces of the evil one.[30] Paul does not specify the kinds of weapons that are used, but there is no doubt that the sword or the spear is for the right hand and the shield for the left hand. A soldier is fully equipped to fight both offensively and defensively.

What is the meaning of "weapons of righteousness"? The phrase can mean either the weapons that righteousness supplies or the weapons that promote righteousness. Each position has its own defenders: some understand righteousness as "uprightness of conscience and holiness of life."[31] Others say that the weapons of righteousness are for both defense and offense: the shield in the left hand is for defense and the sword in the right for offense.[32]

---

28. Denney, *Second Corinthians*, p. 232.

29. Consult R. C. H. Lenski, *The Interpretation of St. Paul's First and Second Epistle to the Corinthians* (Columbus: Wartburg, 1946), p. 1070.

30. Rom. 13:12; II Cor. 6:7; 10:4; Eph. 6:13–18; I Thess. 5:8.

31. Calvin, *II Corinthians*, p. 87; Grosheide, *Tweede Brief aan Korinthe*, p. 226.

32. Among others, Hans Lietzmann, *An die Korinther I/II*, augmented by Werner G. Kümmel, Handbuch zum Neuen Testament 9 (Tübingen: Mohr, 1969), p. 128; Furnish, *II Corinthians*, p. 346.

Instead of taking sides, we accept both interpretations. Paul is upright in character and does not want to give anyone an opportunity to take offense (v. 3). But he is also on the defense against the attackers of the cause of Christ (11:13–14) and is on the offense by destroying their strongholds and capturing every thought for Christ (10:4–5). An upright soldier of Christ is flanked on the left and the right with weapons to defend and attack.

b. "Through glory and dishonor, through bad report and good report." Just as Paul moves through spiritual battles with weapons in the left and the right hand, so he moves through circumstances in which he receives honor and good reports on the one hand and slander on the other. The apostle stays unswervingly devoted to the ministry of the Word.

Paul was the spiritual father of the Corinthian congregation (I Cor. 4:15) and the founder of numerous churches throughout the Mediterranean world. These churches were his joy and crown (Phil. 4:1), yet at the same time he had to endure physical and verbal abuse from both Gentiles and Jews (e.g., Acts 16:19–24; 17:5–9).

When diligence and faithfulness are recognized and appreciated, honor and a good report result. But undeserved dishonor and slander come from malevolent and uninformed people. "A man's disgrace or infamy is proportioned to his glory or good report."[33] Although Paul and his ministry were recognized by many Corinthians (I Cor. 16:15–18), others dishonored him and talked behind his back (I Cor. 4:10–13, 19; II Cor. 10:10; 11:7).

8b. As impostors yet true men, 9. as unknown yet well known, as dying, and look, we live, as chastened and yet we are not killed, 10. as sorrowful yet always rejoicing, as poor yet making many rich, as having nothing and yet possessing everything.

This is the third and last part of Paul's list of hardships, and it includes seven sets of contrasts; he presents them in a form similar to those in 4:8–9. With these contrasts, he portrays himself as one who may be pushed down but rises again without fail.

a. "As impostors yet true men." The slanderers call the apostle and his associates deceivers, just as the chief priests and the Pharisees labeled Jesus a deceiver (Matt. 27:63; see also I Tim. 4:1). But in reality, the impeccable character of both the apostle and his helpers stands in poignant contrast to the slanderous accusation. They are not shifty vagrants but honest men.

Some translators do not present the clauses of verses 8b–10 as contrasts but rather as ironic statements: "We are the impostors who speak the truth."[34] Although both translations are accurate, vivid contrast suits better in this context.

b. "As unknown yet well known." The opponents consider Paul to be a nobody who lacks apostolic authority and whom they can degrade at will. Peter and the

---

33. Bengel, *New Testament Commentary,* vol. 2, p. 303.

34. NEB, REB; see MLB, *Cassirer.*

other apostles followed Jesus, but Paul himself admitted that he did not "even deserve to be called an apostle" (I Cor. 15:9).

Yet Paul is a well-known and recognized figure. He is an acknowledged leader during his missionary journeys, a knowledgeable speaker at various gatherings, and a learned teacher of God's Word. Paul was *well known* first by God (I Cor. 13:12), but then by the church in Corinth and the other churches that Paul had founded.

c. "As dying, and look, we live." Paul's life appears to be one long series of actions in which he stays one step ahead of death: in Lystra nearly killed by stoning (Acts 14:19), in Philippi beaten with rods and placed in stocks (Acts 16:22–24), in Jerusalem being attacked by a mob (Acts 21:31). He was flogged eight times; one flogging probably brought him to the point of despairing even of his life (1:8). Paul was repeatedly struck down but not crushed, exposed to death but given life, in constant danger but always given an avenue of escape (4:9; 11:23, 26). His association with Jesus' death and resurrection was so close that the life of Jesus constantly heartened and strengthened him (4:10–12). The divine power that raised Jesus from the dead kept Paul from dying a premature death.

Filled with enthusiasm, Paul called attention to the fact that he was alive. Look, he said calling attention to a miracle, we live and keep on living (see v. 2). He strove to fulfill the words of the psalmist, "I will not die but live, and I will proclaim what the Lord has done" (Ps. 118:17). His life was completely dedicated to preaching the message of Jesus' life, death, resurrection, and return.

d. "As chastened and yet we are not killed." Once more Paul alludes to the words of the psalmist, "The Lord has chastened me severely, but he has not given me over to death" (Ps. 118:18). The word *chastened* actually means "disciplined," with the implication that God is the agent who metes out discipline. God does not punish his own people for whom Christ has died, for our punishment for sin was laid on Christ. His Son suffered in our place so that we might be acquitted. Therefore, it is incorrect to say that believers suffer God's wrath and do so in addition to Christ's suffering on our behalf. Our own weaknessess and character flaws often cause us difficulties and troubles, but no believer may ever say that these adversities are punishments. Rather, they are God's corrective measures designed to bring us closer to himself.

Consider Paul's fiery nature that had to be subdued because it caused him numerous difficulties. He had to flee from the city of Damascus, where he was let down in a basket over the wall in the middle of the night (11:32–33; Acts 9:23–25). He had to be taken from Jerusalem to Caesarea, where he was put aboard a ship bound for Tarsus (Acts 9:30). He remained in his birthplace, Tarsus, for many years before Barnabas invited him to teach in the church of Antioch (Acts 11:25–26). By chastening Paul, God showed Paul divine love as a Father correcting his son (compare Heb. 12:4–11).

Severely chastened, Paul always experienced God's protective power so that he was kept safe. So Paul writes, "yet we are not killed." This play on words connects with the preceding line, "as dying . . . yet we are not killed." God does not allow death to be the outcome, for repeatedly he rescues Paul from mortal danger. Throughout the difficulties Paul encounters, God's loving care is evident.

e. "As sorrowful yet always rejoicing." Paul's opponents and some members of the Corinthian church caused him untold grief and sorrow. As a result he had to endure persecution; also, night and day with tears he warned the believers to be on guard against those who distort the truth (Acts 20:23, 29–31). Yet Paul could take comfort and encouragement from Jesus' words: "Blessed are you when people insult you, persecute you and falsely say all kinds of evil against you because of me. Rejoice and be glad, because great is your reward in heaven, for in the same way they persecuted the prophets who were before you" (Matt. 5:11–12). Paul's emphasis on rejoicing and happiness in this epistle is noteworthy. It is similar to his letter of joy to the Philippians with respect to the number of times he emphasizes rejoicing and joy.[35] This emphasis in II Corinthians is offset by a greater number of times in which he writes about sorrowing and sorrow.[36] Yet Paul is not overcome by sorrow; he is filled with joy and cheerfully writes, "always rejoicing."

f. "As poor yet making many rich." The difficulty we meet in this clause is the question whether Paul has in mind spiritual or material riches. Jesus' beatitude in Matthew 5:3 reads, "Blessed are the poor in spirit," but in Luke 6:20, "Blessed are you who are poor." We know that Paul performed manual labor to provide for his material needs (Acts 18:3; 20:34–35; I Thess. 2:9) and belonged to the poor, so we cannot conclude that he made many economically rich. Paul is talking about making people rich spiritually, while he portrays himself as poor in a material sense. He explains this point elsewhere in this epistle as he depicts the poverty and riches of Jesus Christ: "Though he was rich he became poor on account of you, so that you might become rich through his poverty" (8:9). As it is with the Sender, so it is with the messenger; Paul with his associates enriches the people with the message of Christ's gospel (I Cor. 1:5; see James 2:5).

g. "As having nothing and yet possessing everything." This is a parallel to the preceding set of contrasts. Earthly poverty is compared to heavenly riches; material scarcity is distinct from spiritual wealth; and temporal gains are differentiated from eternal treasures.[37] With body and soul believers, who in themselves have nothing, belong to Jesus Christ (Rom. 14:7–8; I Cor. 6:19b). In him, they own everything. Thus Paul tells the Corinthians, "You will be made rich in every way to be altogether generous, and through us your generosity will produce thanksgiving to God" (9:11; see Rom. 8:32; I Cor. 3:21).

Paul does not teach that Christians must live in material poverty to gain abundant spiritual riches. His teaching is in harmony with that of Jesus, who said: "No

---

35. The verb *chairein* (rejoice) occurs eight times: II Cor. 2:3; 6:10; 7:7, 9, 13, 16; 13:9, 11; and the noun *chara* (joy) five times: II Cor. 1:24; 2:3; 7:4, 13; 8:2.

36. As verb and participle *lypein* (to sorrow) occurs nine times: II Cor. 2:2 [twice], 4, 5; 6:10; 7:8 [twice], 9, 11; the noun *lypē* (sorrow), six times: II Cor. 2:1, 3, 7; 7:10 [twice]; 9:7.

37. Compare Martin, *II Corinthians*, p. 184. See also David L. Mealand, "As having nothing and yet possessing everything," *ZNTW* 67 (1976): 277–79.

one who has left home or brothers or sisters or mother or father or children or fields for me and the gospel will fail to receive a hundred times as much in this present age (homes, brothers, sisters, mothers, children and fields—and with them, persecutions) and in the age to come, eternal life" (Mark 10:29–31). The Lord keeps his word and grants both material and spiritual possessions to his people and also invites them to full fellowship in the household of faith (Eph. 3:15). Nonetheless, Jesus instructs his followers not to lay up treasures on earth but in heaven, for "you cannot serve both God and Money" (Matt. 6:24; Luke 16:13).

Greek Words, Phrases, and Constructions in 6:3–10

Verses 3–4

ἐν μηδενί—this adjective can be understood as either the masculine ("in no one") or the neuter ("in no way").

διδόντες—the present active participle should not be connected with the main verb παρακαλοῦμεν (we exhort) of verse 1, because the participle has nothing in common with a verb of persuading. We do well to treat the participle as a finite verb, "we give," a usage that occurs more often in Paul's epistles (see, e.g., Rom. 5:11; 12:6; II Cor. 8:20).

διάκονοι—not the accusative but the nominative plural is used to stress the fact that they, in the capacity of workers for God, commend themselves. The accusative would require the translation, "We commend ourselves as servants of God."[38]

Verses 8c–10

ὡς—this particle expresses manner, that is, "We are treated as" (GNB, SEB).

Notice that all the participles in verses 9 and 10 are in the present tense. So is the one and only finite verb, ζῶμεν (we live). The tense indicates continued action, as is evident especially in ἀποθνῄσκοντες (dying), which an aorist would depict as single action; here it signifies repeated occurrences of Paul's near-death experiences.

κατέχοντες—the compound is not directive but perfective; it means possessing all things to the fullest extent.

---

3. Opening Hearts
6:11–13

The apparent similarity in the content of verses 6:11–13 and 7:2–4 has elicited this hypothesis: preceding these passages are two documents that Paul used; they are the catalogue of hardships (6:3–10) and the warning not to be yoked with unbelievers (6:14–7:1).

We grant that Paul's segmented discourse has rough transitions. But the apostle may have been interrupted in the process of writing his letter, perhaps due to travel or dictation schedules. It is hard to accept the contention that the apostle

---

38. Similar is the translation of Lietzmann, *Korinther I/II*, pp. 126–28. See also A. T. Robertson, *A Grammar of the Greek New Testament in the Light of Historical Research* (Nashville: Broadman, 1934), p. 454.

could not have composed these passages, for both passages reveal his style. Also, in his other letters Paul often digresses from his theme and thus causes breaks in his discourses. Nonetheless, he always continues to develop the main point of his arguments.

There is no need to hypothesize that this letter consisted of two editions sent to two different groups of people, and that one of these was directed to the Corinthians (v. 11).[39] Neither do we have to conjecture that single leaves of a manuscript were interchanged; in Paul's day not individual pages but scrolls were used as writing material. About half a century later "the codex, or leaf-form of book, began to come into extensive use in the Church."[40] In the second century, the church at large acknowledged Paul's epistle as an inspired document that was kept secure and guarded.

The tone of verses 11–13 differs from that of the catalogue of hardships, for Paul now addresses the readers in a forthright manner by first calling them Corinthians (v. 11) and then children (v. 13). Paul begins the paragraph (vv. 11–13) in the indicative mood to describe his love towards them and then writes the imperative mood to order them to follow his example. And last, he returns to the train of thought he was developing in chapter 5 and the first two verses of this chapter. Briefly interrupted by a recital of his distresses, Paul's exhortation to the Corinthians (v. 1) continues in verse 11, where he notes that he has spoken freely to his readers.

11. We have spoken freely to you, Corinthians, and opened our hearts wide.

Paul addresses his readers with the appellation *Corinthians,* an appellation that is akin to Paul calling the Galatians (Gal. 3:1) and the Philippians (Phil. 4:15) by name. The term is only an address, which he augments with a word of tender love, "children" (I Cor. 4:14; Gal. 4:19; Eph. 5:1).

The Greek text reveals a typically Semitic idiom, that of opening one's mouth to say something. For instance, "he opened his mouth, and taught them" (Matt. 5:2, KJV) actually means "he began to teach them" (NIV; see also Acts 8:35; 10:34; 18:14). Paul literally writes, "Our mouth has been open to you," which I have translated as "We have spoken freely to you."

Note the use of the perfect tense in this sentence, for it relates to the past and has significance for the present and the future. At the beginning of this chapter, Paul urged the readers not to receive God's grace in vain (v. 1). They received God's revelation Lord's Day after Lord's Day, so that Paul with his fellow workers could truthfully say, "From the beginning of our ministry, we have proclaimed Christ's gospel to you and have done so openly and will continue to do so."

---

39. Contra Collange, *Énigmes,* p. 301. However, he is not sure of the destination of the other letter; the recipients could be a group in Corinth (p. 284 n. 1). See Margaret E. Thrall, "The Problem of II Cor. VI. 14–VII.1 in Some Recent Discussion," *NTS* 24 (1978): 142.

40. Bruce M. Metzger, *The Text of the New Testament: Its Transmission, Corruption, and Restoration,* 2d ed. (New York and Oxford: Oxford University Press, 1968), p. 6. Allo notes that in the second century the text of Paul's epistle was fixed (*Seconde Épître aux Corinthiens,* p. 191).

Paul's desire to teach them the truth of God remained steady and uninterrupted.

The second idiom is "Our heart has been enlarged," which means "We have opened our hearts wide." The words derive from the Greek translation of Psalm 119:32, "For you enlarge my understanding" (NRSV; see Ps. 118:32, LXX). Though the Septuagint wording relates to knowledge and insight,[41] Paul talks about the affection he and his colleagues have for the Corinthians. Also, this clause has nothing to do with openheartedness, even though Paul has been quite frank with his readers. Nor does it refer to magnanimity, in spite of Paul's noble and forgiving spirit (2:10). Here he expresses his love to his readers and tells them there is plenty of room for them in his heart (compare 7:3).

12. We are not restricting our love to you, but you restrict your love toward us.

If Paul and his co-workers open their hearts in love to the Corinthians, they do expect reciprocal action from these believers. The text is parallel to the previous verse except that it presents its converse, namely, the negative. In fact, the Greek term conveys a sense of narrow-mindedness that would limit his tenderness for the Corinthians. Restrictions exhibit a lack of love and an excess of suspicions.[42] The apostle says, however, that there is sufficient room for the Corinthians in his heart because he loves them all. There are no restrictions to his love for them. Paul declares that he and his companions have no such constraints, even if the Corinthians have them. Hence, Paul invites the believers to follow his example of love and open their hearts wide for him and his helpers.

Translators use the word *love,* but the Greek word *splanchna* signifies intestines, which for the ancients were the seat of affections, compassion, sympathy, and mercy. In Pauline literature, the word refers to love that persons extend to and receive from one another.[43] Usually it is understood as a synonym of "heart" and thus is a parallel to verse 11.

13. Yes, even you, widen your hearts in the same way in return—I speak as to my children.

The language in this verse is forceful and stresses the second person plural pronoun *you,* which in Greek stands at the end of the verse for emphasis. Then there is the verb *to widen* as an imperative in the middle voice to command the Corinthians: "enlarge your own hearts."

The sentence in Greek is incomplete because the clause "in the same way in return" lacks a verb. Therefore, looking at the entire sentence, which features a break at "I speak as to my children," we have to render the clause as a preposi-

---

41. The Hebrew text reads, "You have set my heart free" (NIV) as an expression of either joy (Isa. 60:5) or understanding.

42. "Surprisingly, a heart full of love and affection expands, while one filled with selfishness and suspicion has a strong tendency to shrink" (Martin, *II Corinthians,* p. 186).

43. Helmut Köster avers that "σπλάγχνα concerns and expresses the total personality at the deepest level," *TDNT* 7:555; Hans-Helmut Esser, *NIDNTT,* 2:600; E. C. B. MacLaurin, "The Semitic Background of Use of 'en splanchnois,'" *PEQ* 103 (1971): 42–45; Hans Windisch, *Der Zweite Korintherbrief,* ed. Georg Strecker (1924; reprint ed., Göttingen: Vandenhoeck und Ruprecht, 1970), p. 211.

tional phrase that stands by itself. With the words *in return,* Paul is clear and to the point, because he expects the Corinthians to accept him in love just as he has accepted them.

The Corinthians must rid themselves of all the negative thoughts they hold against Paul and fill their hearts with love for him. Then they will be able to pay back the reciprocal love they owe him, for since they first met him Paul has proved to be their devoted father (I Cor. 4:14–15). In turn, they as his children should now demonstrate how much they care for their spiritual father.

Greek Words, Phrases, and Constructions in 6:11–13

ἀνέῳγεν—this is the perfect active from ἀνοίγω (I open), and here the tense is durative. Paul's mouth remains open, for he has talked and continues to talk.

ἡμῶν—leading manuscripts (P[46], a, B) have the reading ὑμῶν, which must be attributed to a scribal error. The context militates against it.

τὴν δὲ αὐτὴν ἀντιμισθίαν—the accusative case can be explained best as "an accusative in apposition to the whole sentence which follows it."[44] The noun ἀντιμισθίαν appears twice in the New Testament: here in the positive, and in Romans 1:27 with a negative connotation. In this compound word, the noun μισθός (recompense) is preceded by the preposition ἀντί (in return), which intensifies the idea of repayment of that which is owed. And the pronoun αὐτήν (same) strengthens support for the concept of returning something in kind.

Preliminary Comments on 6:14–7:1

Scholarly debate on the composition of 6:14–7:1 has been both prolonged and ample. The debate centers primarily on whether this composition is anti-Pauline, a non-Pauline Qumran fragment, an Essene document reworked by Paul, or Pauline. Of these four approaches, the first two lack convincing arguments; while the third is plausible, the fourth is possible.

1. *Composition.*

a. The view that this segment in II Corinthians is not from the hand of Paul has few proponents. Hans Dieter Betz asserts that on the basis of theology, the passage "is not only non-Pauline, but anti-Pauline."[45] But his view lacks support.

b. Joachim Gnilka thinks that a member of the local church in Corinth collected an accumulation of Pauline letters or fragments of letters. Somehow the fragment of 6:14–7:1 happened to be among them; and this church member, functioning as an editor and thinking that the fragment was Pauline, included it in II Corinthians. Thus not Paul but

---

44. C. F. D. Moule, *An Idiom-Book of New Testament Greek,* 2d ed. (Cambridge: Cambridge University Press, 1960), pp. 160–61; Friedrich Blass and Albert Debrunner suggest τὸν αὐτὸν πλατυσμὸν ὡς ἀντιμισθίαν (the same enlargement as recompense). *A Greek Grammar of the New Testament and Other Early Christian Literature,* trans. and rev. Robert Funk (Chicago: University of Chicago Press, 1961), #154.

45. Hans Dieter Betz, "II Cor. 6:14–7:1: An Anti-Pauline Fragment?" *JBL* 92 (1973): 108.

the editor was responsible for incorporating an independent segment into the epistle.[46] This view is only a guess.

Joseph A. Fitzmyer asserts that the passage in question is non-Pauline, because of its resemblance to Qumran documents. The contrasting phrases such as "righteousness and lawlessness," "light and darkness," "Christ and Belial," he notes, illustrate that Paul could not have written this particular section.[47] However, there is no reason to believe that Paul could not have used the same expressions that are found in the Qumran documents. Margaret E. Thrall observes, "The similar terms and ideas are found as widely scattered in the Dead Sea Scrolls as they are in the Pauline epistles. It is just as likely that Paul brought them together in short compass as that an Essene or Jewish-Christian author should have done."[48]

c. Other scholars are of the opinion that 6:14–7:1 is an Essene document that Paul modified and inserted into the epistle; that is, Paul is the redactor of an Essene piece of literature.[49]

Six words in this segment that are peculiar (hapax legomena) to Paul and the New Testament are used to support the hypothesis. These Greek words are heterozygountes (mismated), metochē (participation), symphōnēsis (agreement), Beliar (Belial), synkatathesis (agreement), and molysmou (defilement). In addition, there is a seventh expression, pantokratōr (Almighty), but this term occurs nine times in Revelation (1:8; 4:8; 11:17; 15:3; 16:7, 14; 19:6, 15; 21:22). Except for Beliar, all the other expressions belong to word families that in one form or another appear frequently throughout the New Testament. The example of symphōnēsis is a case in point; it is part of the extended family symphōnein (to agree with).

The hypothesis that Paul made use of an existing document is plausible, for in his letters he incorporates a creedal statement (I Cor. 15:3–5) and a Christian hymn (Phil. 2:6–11).

d. Proponents of the view that 6:14–7:1 is authentically Pauline point out that peculiar terms in this segment occur in Greek literature other than the New Testament. The literature includes the Septuagint, apocrypha, pseudepigrapha, and the works of Josephus. For example, the expression Beliar surfaces in Jewish apocryphal and pseudepigraphical writings and in the Qumran literature. Even though the expression occurs in Qumran documents, we have no proof that it originated in Qumran.[50] Words peculiar to Paul are so numerous in his epistles that similar concentrations can be found in many places not

46. Joachim Gnilka, "II Kor 6, 14–7, 1 im Lichte der Qumranschriften und der Zwölf-Patriarchen-Testamente," in Neutestamentliche Aufsätze, Festschrift Joseph Schmidt, zum 70 ed. J. Blinzler, O. Kuss, and F. Mussner (Regensburg: Pustet, 1963), p. 99; English translation in Paul and the Dead Sea Scrolls, ed. Jerome Murphy-O'Connor and J. H. Charlesworth (New York: Crossroad, 1990), pp. 67–68. Compare Hans-Josef Klauck, II Korintherbrief (Würzburg: Echter, 1986), pp. 60–61.

47. Joseph A. Fitzmyer, "Qumran and the interpolated paragraph in II Cor. 6:14–7:1," CBQ 23 (1961): 271–80, reprinted in Essays on the Semitic Background of the New Testament (London: Chapman, 1971), pp. 205–17; reprinted from CBQ 23 (1961): 271–80.

48. Thrall, "The Problem of II Cor. vi. 14–vii. 1," p. 138; and see Gordon D. Fee, "II Corinthians vi. 14–vii. 1 and Food Offered to Idols," NTS 23 (1977): 146–47; Barrett, Second Corinthians, p. 198; F. F. Bruce, I and II Corinthians, New Century Bible (London: Oliphants, 1971), p. 214.

49. David Rensberger, "II Corinthians 6:14–7:1—A Fresh Examination," StudBibT 8 (1978): 25–49; Martin, II Corinthians, pp. 193–94; Furnish, II Corinthians, pp. 382–83. Compare John J. Gunther, St. Paul's Opponents and Their Background. A Study of Apocalyptic and Jewish Sectarian Teachings, NovTSup 35 (Leiden: Brill, 1973), pp. 308–13.

50. Fee, "II Corinthians," p. 146; Thrall, "The Problem of II Cor. V.14–VII.1," p. 137; Barrett, Second Corinthians, p. 198. See also Otto Böcher, EDNT, 1:212.

only in II Corinthians but also in I Corinthians and in Romans.[51] The possibility that Paul composed 6:14–7:1 is both plausible and real. Writes Jerome Murphy-O'Connor, "In sum, therefore, nothing in the language and style of 6:14–7:1 constitutes a convincing argument against Pauline authenticity."[52]

2. *Context.* First, in quick succession Paul asks five rhetorical questions that all begin with the interrogative pronoun *what* and require a negative answer (vv. 14–16). For instance, "What do righteousness and lawlessness have in common?" The answer is, nothing.

Next, educated as an expert in the Old Testament, the apostle looks at issues through the spectacles of Scripture. Even before he quotes a series of Scripture passages (vv. 16–18), he alludes to an Old Testament text (Deut. 11:16). He writes, "We . . . opened our hearts wide" (v. 11).[53] The Septuagintal Greek verb *platynein* (to open wide) translates the Hebrew word *patah*, which can mean either "to open wide" or "to deceive someone with words." Now notice that the Hebrew verb occurs in a negative command with the secondary meaning, "Beware, lest your hearts be deceived" (Deut. 11:16, NASB; the Septuagint has the verb *platynein*). We assume that Paul was thinking about this text in the Greek, deleted the negative particle *mē* (lest), and adopted the translation, "We opened our hearts wide." The emphasis in the passage from Deuteronomy is on the words *heart* and on either *deceive* or *open wide*. This is also true of Paul's passage in II Corinthians.

Furthermore, the context of Deuteronomy 11:16 details God's command to the Israelites: "love the LORD your God and . . . serve him with all your heart and with all your soul" (11:13; see also Deut. 6:5). If the Israelites obey God, he will provide food and drink for man and beast. But if his people break the covenant that God has made with them and worship other gods, then his anger will burn against them and ensue in a curse of drought and famine (11:16–17). Note that the reading "Beware, lest your hearts be deceived" (Deut. 11:16) is the variant Septuagint reading in the Alexandrian text of Deuteronomy 6:12.

Paul relied on Deuteronomy 11:16 for instructing the Corinthians to open wide their hearts to him (II Cor. 6:13). He continued the teaching of that same text by warning his readers not to be unequally yoked with unbelievers who worship other gods. Thus, against the background of the passage from Deuteronomy, Paul forms a bridge between 6:13 and 14. Yet he continues the trend of thought he is developing. "The central thrust of II Cor[inthians] 6 is contained in [verses] 1–2, 11, and 14ff."[54]

Paul's mind is focused on the Scriptures when he warns the believers not to be "unevenly yoked with unbelievers" (v. 14). This is an echo of "Do not plow with an ox and a donkey yoked together" (Deut. 22:10; consult also Lev. 19:19). The apostle teaches that from a religious point of view the believer and the unbeliever are opposites and have nothing in common. He strengthens his argument by quoting various texts from the Old Testament that express a similar theme: God's people are covenant people (Lev. 26:12) who must separate themselves from the religious practices of unbelievers, must not touch any unclean thing (Isa. 52:11), and must know that God is a Father to his spiritual sons and daughters (II Sam. 7:14).

---

51. Thayer (p. 706) lists a total of 99 entries for II Corinthians, 110 for I Corinthians, and 113 for Romans. See also Plummer, *Second Corinthians,* pp. xlix–l.

52. Jerome Murphy-O'Connor, "Philo and II Cor 6:14–7:1," *RB* 95 (1988): 62.

53. Consult Thrall, "The Problem of II Cor. V.14–VII.1," p. 146.

54. Jerome Murphy-O'Connor, "Relating II Corinthians 6. 14–7. 1 to Its Context," *NTS* 33 (1987): 275.

4. Calling Holy Ones
6:14–7:1

14. Do not be unevenly yoked with unbelievers. For what do righteousness and lawlessness have in common? What fellowship has light with darkness?

a. "Do not be unevenly yoked with unbelievers." At first glance, this directive seems to refer to the marriage of a believer and an unbeliever or to two such partners in business. But the context indicates that this interpretation is implicit, not explicit. To be sure, at another place Paul explicitly advises a widow to marry only in the Lord (I Cor. 7:39). This context, however, speaks about a separation of the Christian religion from pagan religions. "For to be yoked with unbelievers means nothing less than to have fellowship with the unfruitful works of darkness and to hold out a hand to unbelievers to signify fellowship with them."[55] The passage (vv. 14–18) conveys the message not to form any covenant relationships with unbelievers that violate the covenant obligations a Christian has with God.[56] The Greek text reveals that being unevenly yoked means having a connection with a person who is entirely different. In this text, it relates to an individual who is not a member of the household of faith and who can cause a believer to break covenant with God.

Who are these people who lead Christians astray? The pagans who invited the Corinthians to meals in temples were idol worshipers. Just as eating at the Lord's table is participating in the Lord, so dining at the table of an idol is participating in a false religion. Such behavior is an affront to the Lord.[57] The unbelievers, then, are pagans who do not serve the Lord. They are the ones whose eyes Satan has blinded (4:4). They are non-Christians who have influenced the Christian community of Corinth.[58]

b. "For what do righteousness and lawlessness have in common?" Believers who have been justified by God (5:21) must be quick to discern deception that they encounter either in word or in deed. They must refuse to be partners with those who practice deceit. Theirs is the task to expose deception as works of the evil one (Eph. 5:6–12). They must follow joyfully in Jesus' footsteps and pursue righteousness by keeping his law, for they know that Jesus loves righteousness and hates lawlessness (Heb. 1:9; Ps. 45:7). They affirm that righteousness is the rule of Christ's kingdom and observe that lawlessness characterizes Satan's work. Indeed, Paul calls the antichrist "the man of lawlessness" and remarks that "the secret power of lawlessness is already at work" (II Thess. 2:3, 6). Conclusively,

---

55. Calvin, *II Corinthians*, p. 89.

56. William J. Webb, "Unequally Yoked with Unbelievers. Part 2 [of 2 parts]: What Is the Unequal Yoke in (ἑτεροζυγοῦντες) II Corinthians 6:14?" *BS* 149 (1992): 164, 179.

57. Refer to Fee, "II Corinthians," p. 153.

58. William J. Webb, "Unequally Yoked Together with Unbelievers. Part 1 [of 2 parts]: Who Are the Unbelievers (ἄπιστοι) in II Corinthians 6:14?" *BS* 149 (1992): 27–44. See J. D. M. Derrett, "II Cor 6,14ff. a Midrash on Dt. 22,10," *Bib* 59 (1978): 231–50.

then, the answer to Paul's rhetorical question at the beginning of this paragraph is a resounding no.

c. "What fellowship has light with darkness?" This question features three key words, the first two of which describe the Christian community: fellowship, light. The third word, *darkness,* does not describe the Christian community.

To see believers having fellowship with God the Father and his Son Jesus Christ is the greatest joy for the apostle John (I John 1:4). Christian fellowship comes to expression especially in worshiping God and in extending support and encouragement to one another.

Jesus is the light of the world (John 8:12), and through the gospel that true light enlightens mankind (John 1:9). Light and fellowship go together, but light and darkness belong to two different spheres. Spiritual darkness is devoid not only of light but also of love. John writes that anyone who hates his brother is blind and stumbles around in darkness (I John 2:11; John 11:10; 12:35). Just as light and righteousness are closely related, so darkness and lawlessness are twins. The first set belongs to Christ, the second to Satan, and these two are diametrically opposed to each other.

Satan transforms himself into an angel of light (11:14) to deceive people. He blinds the minds of unbelievers so that they are unable to see the light of the gospel. Consequently, they live in complete spiritual darkness. But God causes his light to shine in the hearts of the believers by giving them, through Christ, spiritual knowledge of himself (4:4–6).

15. And what harmony is there between Christ and Belial? Or what does a believer have in common with an unbeliever?

To ask these two rhetorical and antithetical questions is to answer them in the negative. Paul continues his sequence of contrasts by noting the utter impossibility of expecting harmony between Christ and Belial. He uses the Greek noun *symphōnēsis* to convey the meaning *harmony* or *accord.* The noun is parallel to the expressions *have in common* and *fellowship* in the preceding verse (v. 14).

The choice of the word *Belial,* which in the Greek is spelled Beliar, has caused much discussion. One thing is sure: Paul did not borrow it from the Old Testament, where the term is never personified and means someone or something wicked or perverted (e.g., Deut. 13:14; 17:4; I Sam. 1:16; 10:27; 25:25; 30:22). Unless the term is personified, a balanced contrast in this verse is lacking.[59]

Jewish writings personify Belial/Beliar as Satan, the devil, the highest demon, and the antichrist. These writings include The Testaments of the Twelve Patriarchs,[60] apocalyptic books (Jubilees, Ascension of Isaiah, and the Sibylline Ora-

---

59. Some commentators (Barrett, p. 198; Martin, p. 200) suggest that the Hebrew term בְלִי עֹל (*b'li 'ol*) means "having no yoke," that is, living without God's yoke (refer to 6:14). See the Babylonian Talmud *Sifre Deut.* 117 and *Sanhedrin* 111b. Although this solution is ingenious, the objection remains that the verse lacks balance.

60. Joseph 7:4; Judah 25:3; Issachar 6:1; 7:7; Levi 18:12–13.

cles),[61] and the Dead Sea Scrolls.[62] Paul stresses the contrast of Christ and Belial as the chief rulers in their respective realms of righteousness and wickedness, light and darkness, holiness and profanity. We do not know why Paul chose the word *Belial* instead of Satan, devil, highest demon, or antichrist. Belial/Beliar[63] should be seen, perhaps, as a comprehensive term that includes all these names.

What is Paul trying to convey to the Corinthians? He had told them that Christ had died for them, that God had reconciled the world to himself, and that Paul had endured hardships to further the cause of the gospel (5:14–15, 20; 6:3–10). Now he wanted them to choose for Christ and follow him but to reject Belial and everything that he represents. In parallel terms, the Corinthians must choose faith instead of unbelief, the Christian life instead of worldly ways.

Thus Paul asks the question, "Or what does a believer have in common with an unbeliever?" The repetition of verse 14a is clear, but now Paul uses singular nouns. He says that the believer has no share in the life of the unbeliever. With these words he is not saying that believers may have no contact at all with unbelievers, for then Christians would have to leave this world (I Cor. 5:10). He instructs believers not to share in the lifestyle of unbelievers. Writes Denney, "For the believer the one supremely important thing in the world is that which the unbeliever denies, and therefore the more he is in earnest the less can he afford the unbeliever's friendship."[64]

16a. Or what agreement does the temple of God have with idols? For we are the temple of the living God.

Here is the last of the five rhetorical questions that call for a negative answer. Paul asks whether there is any agreement between God's temple and idols. The temple is the place where God chooses to dwell, although God cannot be confined to a house built by human hands (I Kings 8:27; II Chron. 6:18; Isa. 66:1, 2; Acts 7:49–50). He is everywhere and reveals his power against an idol, be it Dagon of the Philistines or Baal of the Canaanites (I Sam. 5:1–5; I Kings 18:21–40). But how would the Gentile Christians in Corinth understand the phrase *temple of God?* The Jews said that God dwelled in the Most Holy Place in the temple at Jerusalem, but Paul taught the Corinthians that God dwelled within their hearts and made their body his temple (I Cor. 3:16; 6:19; see Rom. 8:9).

The Most Holy Place in Jerusalem was devoid of a statue and therefore became the laughingstock of the Gentiles who had temples with idols. We expect that Jewish Christians would consider pagan temples an abomination, and for them to enter these premises would be a transgression of God's law. But Gentiles who had converted to the Christian faith needed to understand that they could no longer go to these shrines and participate in the sacrifices. They had to know

---

61. Jub. 1:20; 15:33; Vit. Proph. 17:9–10; 21; Sib. Or. 2:167.
62. 1QS 3:20–21, 23–24; 1QM 4:2; 13:2, 4; CD 12:2; 5:18.
63. The interchange of the letters *l* and *r* is common in numerous languages, especially oriental tongues.
64. Denney, *Second Corinthians*, p. 244.

that such sacrifices were offered to demons and not to God (I Cor. 10:20). Participation in these worship services would make them partakers of demons. Being God's people, the Corinthians had to break with their pagan culture and serve God with heart, soul, and mind. Paul had taught the people that they were God's temple, had reminded them of this truth (I Cor. 3:16; 6:19), and now once more states it. Paul implies that the idols in pagan temples are dead and says emphatically, "we are the temple of the *living* God."

Throughout his epistles Paul strengthens his discourse with quotations from the Old Testament Scriptures. At times he takes passages from various places to form a series of verses that are linked by key words (e.g., Rom. 3:10–18; 9:25–29, 33; 10:18–21; 11:26–27, 34–35; 15:9–12). In II Corinthians, he cites at least six Old Testament references; they appear to be linked together by the thought that God is a Father to his people, who are asked to keep themselves pure.

The passages are conflated and adapted to the train of thought Paul is developing. We cannot expect that Paul always had ready access to the scrolls; he often had to rely on memory.

16b. Just as God said,

> **"I will dwell with them and walk among them,**
> **and I will be their God**
> **and they will be my people."**

God addresses his people through the Scriptures and gives them promises and instructions. This promise is fourfold: He will dwell with his people, walk with them, be their God, and make them his people. The words of this text are a conflation of two passages from the Scriptures:

1. "I will dwell with them" derives from the Hebrew text of Exodus 25:8 and 29:45, where God tells the Israelites that he will dwell among them.[65] A literal translation says, "I will dwell within them," which confirms Paul's remark, "We are the temple of the living God."

2. "[I will] walk among them, and I will be their God and they will be my people." With minor modifications—for instance, a change from the second person plural to the third person plural—these words are from the Greek text of Leviticus 26:12. God's promise is that his dwelling with his people signifies peaceful relations, and his walking among them indicates benevolent activity. He pays full attention to all people and every detail (Matt. 10:30).

The second part of this sentence, "I will be their God and they will be my people," is a golden thread that God has woven into his Word from beginning to end. To mention only four out of many references: in embryo form God begins with the covenant blessing of Genesis 17:7, consolidates it in the wording of his covenant with Israel in Exodus 6:7, continues it in the prophecy of Ezekiel 37:26–27, and concludes it with Revelation 21:3. Philip Edgcumbe Hughes de-

---

65. Furnish asserts that this statement is not found in the Old Testament. He calls it "an interpretive comment on Lev[iticus] 26:12" (*II Corinthians*, pp. 363, 374).

lineates three stages for the continuation of God's covenant through Christ among his people: the incarnation (John 1:14), the indwelling of Christ in the hearts of believers (Eph. 3:17), and God's dwelling with his people on the new earth (Rev. 21:3).[66]

But Scripture does not limit the indwelling power to Christ. It teaches that the triune God dwells in the hearts of the believers. With Christ, the Holy Spirit and God the Father make their abode with believers (e.g., John 14:17; I John 4:12). God is always with his people from the time of creation in the garden of Eden to the restored garden after the renewal of all things.

> **17. "Therefore, come out from their midst**
> **And be separate," says the Lord.**
> **"Touch nothing unclean**
> **And I will receive you."**

God requires full allegiance from his covenant people and therefore instructs them to strive for purity. As he is holy, so he expects his people to be holy (Lev. 11:44–45; 19:2; 20:7; I Peter 1:15–16). With variations, this theme appears throughout the Scriptures. God has not separated himself from his people, yet his sons and daughters repeatedly have turned away from him and adopted the ways of the world. God is a faithful covenant God who fulfills the promises that he has given to his people. And he expects his covenant partners to keep their promises to him and to fulfill the obligations of his Word.

Paul quotes a passage from the Greek text of Isaiah: "Depart, depart, go out from there! Touch no unclean thing! Come out from it and be pure" (52:11; compare Jer. 51:45). The last part, "I will receive you," is taken from the Greek text of Ezekiel 20:34, 41, and Zephaniah 3:20.

The Old Testament context is the time when the Jewish exiles were permitted to leave Babylon by a decree of Cyrus. They could carry with them the vessels that belonged to the temple in Jerusalem. God exhorted them to depart from Babylon but not to take along anything unclean that pertained to idol worship. His people, chastened by the exile but now set free, had to be pure and spotless. Likewise the Corinthians who had come out of the world of pagan idolatry now had to be a people fully dedicated to their Lord and Savior Jesus Christ.

"I will receive you." The promise is stated in future terms to indicate that God's reception of his children depends on their obedience. The Old Testament prophets looked forward to the coming of the Messiah, but the readers of Paul's epistle already lived in fellowship with Christ (I Cor. 1:9; II Cor. 5:17). The clause is preceded by the command not to touch anything spiritually unclean. Hence, if followers of Jesus keep themselves unsullied by worldly influences, God approves of them and takes them in. God requires obedience that is expressed in total commitment to him.

---

66. Hughes, *Second Epistle to the Corinthians*, p. 254.

**18. "And I will be a father to you
And you will be my sons and daughters,"
says the Lord Almighty.**

The quotation comes from an Old Testament passage, II Samuel 7:14, that Paul adapts. (Adaptation is evident in changing "his father" to "a father," and "son" to the plural "sons and daughters." The verb *to be* is altered accordingly.) In that passage God speaks to David through the prophet Nathan. About David's successor to the throne God says, "I will be his father and he will be my son." Solomon is the king of Israel about whom Nathan prophesied, but Jesus Christ is the King of kings who ultimately fulfilled Nathan's prophecy.

The apostles inaugurated a new era with the inclusion of women as spiritual equals to men to take their places in God's kingdom (Joel 2:28–29; Acts 2:17–18). God is a father to all his children as Jesus is a brother to all his spiritual brothers and sisters. God desires that his children consecrate themselves to live a life of holiness and dedication, "for what an affront it is to God for us to call Him our Father and then to defile ourselves with the abominations of idolatry."[67]

These promises are given by no one other than the Lord Almighty. The title *Almighty* is awe-inspiring, because it reveals God as the omnipotent One to whom no one in either heaven or on earth can be compared. The Hebrew text of the Old Testament uses the word *Sabaoth,* which means Lord of the armies, or Lord of hosts, and the word occurs in the Greek text of James 5:4. Martin Luther incorporated the term in his well-known hymn "A Mighty Fortress" in the line "Lord Sabaoth his name." As God's title is great, so is his promise.[68]

7:1. Having, therefore, these promises, my dear friends, let us cleanse ourselves from every defilement of flesh and spirit, and perfect [our] holiness in the fear of God.

a. ". . . Therefore, . . . my dear friends." The content of this verse matches that of the entire preceding passage (vv. 14–18) and is its fitting conclusion, as is evident from the term *therefore*. The verse relates well to verses 11 through 13, where Paul speaks of his love for the Corinthians and is asking for their love in return. For this reason he addresses his readers with the endearing term *my dear children,* which in older translations is given as "beloved," meaning they are loved by him (see 12:19).

b. "Having . . . these promises." Paul states that he and his readers are the recipients of God's promises (compare II Peter 1:4). In the Greek text, he emphasizes these promises by placing the word *these* first in the sentence. That is, the assurances that he has mentioned in the previous verses are from God. And God's word is absolutely sure and true. He will perform what he has promised.

---

67. Calvin, *II Corinthians,* p. 92.

68. Compare Bengel, *New Testament Commentary,* vol. 2, p. 305. The title occurs in the Septuagint of II Sam. 7:8; Job 5:17; Hos. 12:6; Amos 3:13; 4:13; 5:14; in Rev. 1:8; 4:8; 11:17; 15:3; 16:7, 14; 19:6, 15; 21:22; in II Macc. 8:18; III Macc. 2:2; 6:2; and in other extrabiblical literature.

c. "Let us cleanse ourselves." If the promises are real, and they are, then it stands to reason that their recipients strive to please the Giver of these promises as much as possible. Consequently, Paul issues an exhortation in which he includes himself and his colleagues to show that they are not above the readers: "Let us cleanse ourselves." These words are Paul's free admission of having been contaminated by the surrounding environment of sin.

The exhortation means not that one cleansing keeps us clean forever, but that we constantly must purify ourselves. The Reformers spoke of daily repentance as a way of making progress in our sanctification. Elsewhere Paul writes that the Corinthians were washed, sanctified, and justified (I Cor. 6:11), but the process of sanctification is continuous because human nature is prone to sin.

Jewish people who were ceremonially unclean had to wash themselves every time they touched something that was impure, and no priest or Levite was permitted to enter the tabernacle or temple unless he washed himself (Exod. 30:20–21). The same principle is true for God's people when they enter his sacred presence: they must purify themselves by confessing their sins. Paul admits that he is no better than the Corinthians; he also needs to cleanse himself and be pure (compare I Thess. 4:7; I John 3:3).

d. "From every defilement of flesh and spirit." Paul wishes to include the entire range of defilement and thus writes the adjective *every*. Although the noun *defilement* occurs only here in the New Testament, the verb *to defile* appears three times (I Cor. 8:7; Rev. 3:4; 14:4). Paul stresses that pollution affects both flesh and spirit, that is, the entire person. If defilement refers to idol worship,[69] then worshipers at pagan temples risked being unclean in body and spirit, for some rites involved cult prostitutes. "The one who cleaves to a prostitute is one body with her" (I Cor. 6:16).

What does this have to do with the church in Corinth? Much, because Paul wrote earlier in this segment, "What agreement does the temple of God have with idols? For we are the temple of the living God" (6:16). The Corinthian believers are God's temple; God dwells with them and makes his presence real by walking among them. Thus, the word choice in verse 1 (let us cleanse ourselves, defilement, holiness) "derives directly from the temple imagery."[70] God is a jealous God who tolerates no other gods before him (Exod. 20:3–5; Deut. 5:7–9). Paul's reference to flesh and spirit must be interpreted to signify a complete person in God's service (see the parallel in I Cor. 7:34).[71] The words convey the meaning that a person who is cleansed outwardly with respect to flesh and inwardly in regard to spirit walks with God.

---

69. See the context in the Septuagint of I Esd. 8:80; II Macc. 5:27; Jer. 23:15 (Martin, *II Corinthians*, p. 209).

70. Fee, "II Corinthians," p. 160.

71. Barrett remarks that Paul uses the terms "*flesh* and *spirit* without giving them their full theological meaning. Both are used in a loose popular way in this epistle" (*Second Corinthians*, p. 202).

e. "And perfect [our] holiness in the fear of God." This clause echoes Paul's exhortation, "Let us cleanse ourselves from every defilement." He uses the Greek present participle *epitelountes* (perfecting) as an exhortation to his readers: "Let us strive for perfect holiness." Paul described the Corinthian believers as "sanctified in Christ Jesus" (I Cor. 1:2; compare I Thess. 3:13) and indicates that God made them holy through the work of his Son. But sanctification remains a continuous process in which believers must assiduously apply themselves to fostering complete holiness. Paul even delineates how this must be done: "in the fear of God." Fear and reverence for God provide the motivation for perfecting one's holiness. In the presence of God the Father, his children should live on this earth as aliens "in reverent fear" (I Peter 1:17). Our relationship to God should be one of genuine respect and profound reverence. As the Father is holy, so we as his children should reflect his holiness in our lives.

Concluding Comments on 6:14–7:1

Admittedly, the transition between 6:13 and 14 and between 7:1 and 2 is abrupt. But there are indications that Paul consistently pursues his own trend of thought throughout the larger passage. He begins in the second half of chapter 5 with an exhortation to the readers to live for Christ, who died and rose again (v. 15). He commands them to be reconciled to God (v. 20) and continues to urge the Corinthians not to receive God's grace in vain (6:1). After supplying a list of his own hardships (6:3–10), he pleads with them to open their hearts for him (6:13). Paul realizes that their hearts are indifferent and influenced by unbelievers. He tells them to separate themselves from those who do not love the Lord. A corresponding injunction occurs in I Corinthians 5:9–13, where Paul instructs the Christians to detach themselves from sexually immoral people even though they called themselves believers. There Paul calls for complete separation by forbidding table fellowship.[72] And here he commands them to cleanse themselves, not to touch anything unclean, and to strive for perfect holiness.

The train of thought Paul develops in this segment is consistent, although we frankly admit that the transition between 6:13 and 14 and 7:1 and 2 is not smooth. Still, the view that Paul himself composed 6:14–7:1 is a distinct possibility that cannot be ruled out.

Practical Considerations in 6:14–18

Christians are in this world to be salt, to influence a decadent, anti-Christian society with Christ's gospel, and to work and pray for the coming of God's kingdom. They are not to yield to the surrounding culture and permit it to govern their lives, for then worldly influences will govern them.

In many parts of the world, however, Christians display an apathy that results in and contributes to a decline of Christianity. Countries that for centuries were influential in promoting the cause of Christ now count the percentage of Christians who attend church

---

72. Consult B. C. Lategan, "'Moenie met ongelowiges in dieselfde juk trek nie' ('Do not be yoked together with unbelievers')," *Scriptura* 12 (1984): 22–23.

on a given Sunday in the low single digits. No longer do they regard the Christian faith as a force; in this post-Christian era they relegate it to history.

Yet true Christians believe in the sovereignty of God and see the Christian faith circling the globe. God is at work in many parts of the world where people by droves turn to Christ in faith. If parts of the Middle East are virtually devoid of Christians, and if the West is in a spiritual recession, the growth of the Christian church is evident in Africa, in Latin America, and in Asia. In these parts of the world, Christians influence their surrounding society with the message of salvation. Believers who separate themselves from a society of unbelief are its salt; they prove to be lights that shine ever brightly in a world of gloom and darkness.

Jesus told his followers, "Because of the increase of wickedness, the love of most will grow cold, but he who stands firm to the end will be saved" (Matt. 24:12–13).

Greek Words, Phrases, and Constructions in 6:14–18

Verse 14

μὴ γίνεσθε—the negative command with the present imperative reveals that some Corinthians in fact were unequally yoked with unbelievers. Paul tells the Corinthians to avoid these associations.

δικαιοσύνη καὶ ἀνομία—the dative of possession stresses more the object that is possessed than the possessor.[73] The privative ἀ of the noun ἀνομία indicates either the absence of the νόμος (law) or its nonobservance.

πρός—the preposition denotes an intimate relationship between light and darkness, which is not the case.

Verses 15–16

Χριστοῦ—the Western readings and the Majority Text have the dative, which appears to be an accommodation to the datives in the preceding and the following verses.

μετά—the root meaning of this preposition signifies "in the midst of," thus indicating that the believer occupies a central position in the life of the unbeliever.

ναῷ—the word refers to the inner sanctuary, the Most Holy Place, not the entire temple complex.

ἡμεῖς—manuscript evidence for this reading is strong, while the variant ὑμεῖς . . . ἐστε (KJV, NKJV, NAB, Vulgate) possibly conforms to the text in I Corinthians 3:16.[74]

Verse 17

ἐξέλθατε—the aorist active imperative signifies that the Corinthians must come out of the world of idolatry once for all. Similarly, the aorist passive imperative of ἀφορίσθητε conveys the same message: "be separate [once for all]." But the negative command μὴ ἅπτεσθε is in the present tense and indicates that the people were indeed being defiled by touching unclean things.

---

73. Blass and Debrunner, *Greek Grammar*, #345.

74. Bruce M. Metzger, *A Textual Commentary on the Greek New Testament*, 2d ed. (Stuttgart and New York: United Bible Societies, 1994), p. 512.

Verse 18

εἰς—"as." This preposition, here used twice, expresses equivalence (see Mark 10:8; Acts 7:53; 13:22; Heb. 1:5).

Summary of Chapter 6

The apostle with his fellow helpers exhorts the Corinthians not to squander God's grace. He desires that they be reconciled to God, who extended his grace to them. The present time for them, Paul teaches, is their day of salvation.

As a minister of Christ's gospel, Paul must exert himself to be blameless in conduct so that no one will be able to discredit his lifestyle. For this reason he lists a catalogue of hardships he has endured for the sake of preaching and teaching Christ's gospel. He has proven to be a true servant of God as he selflessly endured physical, mental, and verbal abuse. Yet he always experienced the presence of the Holy Spirit and the power of God in his life.

The Corinthians had to admit that Paul showed them tender love, which he never withheld from them. They now are urged to open wide their hearts to him as a fair, reciprocal demonstration of their love for him.

Next, Paul feels obliged to instruct the readers that their allegiance to God must be unconditional, for they cannot be yoked unequally to the world of unbelievers. They can no longer have anything to do with idolatry in their pagan environment. Christians are God's temple, says Paul, for God lives in them and walks among them. The apostle strengthens his admonition by quoting from a number of Old Testament passages that teach complete separation of faith and unbelief. God has given his people the promise that he is their Father and they are his sons and daughters. Belonging to God's family means pursuing moral purity and striving for perfect holiness.

7

Apostolic Ministry, *part 8*

(7:2–16)

Outline (continued)

7

2 Make room for us in your hearts. We have wronged no one, we have corrupted no one, we have defrauded no one.

3 I do not say this to condemn you, because, as I have said earlier, you are in our hearts that we would die together and live together with you. 4 I have great confidence in you; I take great pride in you. I am filled with comfort; in all our affliction I am overflowing with joy.

5 For indeed when we came into Macedonia, our body had no rest, but we were distressed in every respect. Fights on the outside, fears on the inside. 6 But God, who comforts the downcast, comforted us with the coming of Titus. 7 And not only with his coming, but also with the comfort that you imparted to him. He reported to us your longing [for me], your mourning, your zeal for me, so that I rejoiced even more.

8 For even if my letter grieved you, I do not regret it. Although I did regret it—for I see that my letter hurt you but for a little while— 9 I now rejoice, not that you were grieved, but that you were grieved that led to repentance. For your grief was according to God's will, so that you suffered no loss because of us. 10 For sorrow that is according to God's will produces repentance that effects salvation, which cannot be regretted. But worldly sorrow produces death. 11 For look, what earnestness this very thing has produced in you, namely, that you were grieved according to God's will, also what eagerness to clear yourselves, what indignation, what fear, what longing, what zeal, what punishment. At every point you have shown that you were innocent in this matter. 12 So, although I wrote to you, it was neither on account of the offender nor on account of the offended, but so that your good will concerning us might be revealed to you before God. 13 Through this we are encouraged.

And in addition to our comfort, we rejoiced exceedingly at the joy of Titus, because his spirit has been refreshed by all of you. 14 For if indeed I boasted somewhat to him about you, you did not embarrass me. However, as we have spoken to you the truth in all things, so also our boasting about you to Titus has come true. 15 His affection toward you is all the more significant when he remembers the obedience of all of you, for you received him with fear and trembling. 16 I rejoice that I can depend completely on you.

---

5. Loving Deeply
7:2–4

After admonishing the Corinthians to pursue righteousness, purity, and holiness, Paul now resumes his expression of deep love and care for them. In 6:11–13, he told his readers that he had not withheld affection from them and expected that they would indeed reciprocate. He concluded by asking them to open their hearts for him. With this saying in mind, he now continues his discourse.

2. Make room for us in your hearts. We have wronged no one, we have corrupted no one, we have defrauded no one.

a. "Make room for us in your hearts." Earlier Paul wrote, "Widen your hearts" (6:13), inviting the Corinthians to show him the same love he had shown them. The charge is now repeated in the light of the immediately preceding discussion

241

on their separation from unbelief, idolatry, and pollution (6:14–7:1). When God lives with them and walks among them, Satan ought to have no place in their hearts. They should warmly welcome God's appointed messengers, Paul and his associates, as ambassadors for Christ and as bearers of the gospel. More than that, belonging to God's family as sons and daughters, they should make room in their hearts for Paul (6:13), who was their spiritual father (I Cor. 4:15). And they must oust Paul's opponents who proclaim an entirely different gospel (11:4).

b. "We have wronged no one, we have corrupted no one, we have defrauded no one." These three short statements repudiate accusations that his opponents might have hurled at Paul and his colleagues. In a sense, the three verbs in these statements are synonymous; they are not presented in either a descending or an ascending order but were written as they came to the author's mind. Paul defends his ministry among the Corinthians by using phrases his adversaries might have employed. We venture to say that the readers were fully familiar with these words.

The verb *to do wrong* occurs a number of times in the New Testament: it refers to an injustice, as in a financial agreement (Matt. 20:13) or a physical harm inflicted upon someone by creatures or fellow human beings (Luke 10:19; Acts 7:24, 26, 27). From Paul's point of view, he had not wronged anyone while he was in Corinth during both his eighteen-month stay (Acts 18:11) and his painful visit (2:1). While he served the Corinthians as their pastor, he had refused to receive monetary payments (11:7; I Cor. 9:18). In fact, no one was able to accuse him of preaching for financial gain. His record in Corinth was above reproach.

The second accusation against Paul was that he and his companions had corrupted the Corinthians. If we understand the verb *to corrupt* in this verse as a synonym of the preceding verb *to do wrong*, then it can mean either financial ruin or moral and religious ruin. Whatever the interpretation may be, such an accusation was preposterous. Paul had done everything he could to build up the believers in Corinth.

Thirdly, Paul had never been guilty of defrauding anyone. His adversaries might have spread this rumor, but his life as Christ's faithful representative in Corinth and elsewhere had been exemplary. Paul candidly asks the Corinthians whether he or Titus ever exploited them (12:17–18). The answer was a resounding no, for the apostle and his helpers never sought to enrich themselves financially. The concept *defraud* always points to material increase (except 2:11) that has been unjustly obtained at the expense of someone else.[1] The one who defrauds is breaking the tenth commandment of the Decalogue: "You shall not covet."

The people in Corinth may have misunderstood Paul's instruction about his gathering money for the saints in Jerusalem (I Cor. 16:1–3). Even though Paul himself purposely distanced himself from the collecting and the eventual deliv-

---

1. Refer to Günter Finkenrath, *NIDNTT*, 1:138.

ery of the money, the seeds of suspicion germinated and took root. Misinterpretation of Paul's motives provided the basis for an attack on his integrity.

In addition, the discipline of the man who had committed incest (I Cor. 5:1–5) still rankled some people in Corinth. Among them, Paul's painful visit and sorrowful letter (2:1–3) had been the cause of deep bitterness against Paul.

With the repetitious use of the pronoun *no one* in the three statements (wronged no one, corrupted no one, defrauded no one), Paul sought to clear himself of all allegations. These negative statements, then, must be understood in the light of his request to the Corinthians to make room for him in their hearts.[2]

3. I do not say this to condemn you, because, as I have said earlier, you are in our hearts that we would die together and live together with you.

a. *Sensitivity.* Whenever Paul admonishes his readers or touches a painful subject in their mutual relations, he takes measures to demonstrate his deep love for them. He frequently resorts to calling them dear friends, brothers, or children. In this case, attempting to put behind him the false accusations that have been leveled against him, he says that the Corinthians have a special place in his heart. That is, his life and that of his colleagues are so intimately interwoven with those of the Corinthians that they are together in life and death. "Greater love has no one than this, that he lay down his life for his friends" (John 15:13).

Notice that Paul switches from writing the first person plural *we* (v. 2) to the first person singular *I* (vv. 3–4). He speaks openly, directly, and personally to the Corinthians to strengthen the bond he has with them. The interplay of pronouns in this verse is striking. The verse begins with the first person singular *I*, is followed by the pronouns *you* and *our,* and concludes with *we.* Paul wishes to say that his personal love for the Corinthians is so great that he overlooks insults from some of them. He broadens his scope by reminding the readers of his earlier remark (6:11) and ends by assuring them that he and his colleagues love them so much that they will die and live with them.

b. *Message.* "I do not say this to condemn you." The readers could easily interpret Paul's three short statements (v. 2) as a rebuke for having uttered these remarks behind his back. This impression could lead to alienation, which Paul seeks to avoid at all costs. "Paul knows how to change his tone in an astonishing way and uses a subsequent correction of a previous impression when he feels that he has offended, still maintaining the most sensitive contact with his readers."[3] He skillfully applies pastoral tact and states that he is not denouncing the Corinthians for negative comments made in his absence. He wants them to realize that they are indeed his dear brothers and sisters in Christ.

---

2. Compare Philip Edgcumbe Hughes, *Paul's Second Epistle to the Corinthians: The English Text with Introduction, Exposition and Notes,* New International Commentary on the New Testament series (Grand Rapids: Eerdmans, 1962), p. 260; Ralph P. Martin, *II Corinthians,* Word Biblical Commentary 40 (Waco: Word, 1986), p. 218.

3. Friedrich Blass and Albert Debrunner, *A Greek Grammar of the New Testament and Other Early Christian Literature,* trans. and rev. Robert Funk (Chicago: University of Chicago Press, 1961), #495.3.

Having assured his readers that he is not rebuking them, Paul now elaborates by recalling an earlier statement. This statement he introduces with the words, "as I have said earlier." The question is, where did he make the comment, "you are in our hearts"? The perfect tense of the Greek verb *legein* (to say) compels us not to look for it in the immediate context, but two other places come to mind: "You yourselves are our epistle, written on our hearts" (3:2), and "We have . . . opened wide our hearts [to you]" (6:11). The second reference is preferred because of its context (6:11–13), in which the apostle tells the Corinthians that he does not withhold his affection from them. Paul is seeking to convince his readers that he has no intention of rebuking them but that he and his associates treasure them. The phrase *you are in our hearts* means that—to paraphrase Paul's words—"these people are not only at the center of our lives but we also honor them and seek their physical and spiritual well-being (see Phil. 1:7)."[4] Here indeed is an example of fulfilling God's royal law, "Love your neighbor as yourself" (James 2:8), and of the highest friendship one can show.[5]

"That we would die together and live together with you." How deep is Paul's love for the Corinthians? For them, he had risked his life over and over. The catalogues of hardships (4:8–9; 6:4–10; 11:23–29) eloquently testify to his love for the church. Paul would rather die with the Corinthians than renounce his love for them. John Calvin observes, "Notice that this is how all pastors ought to feel."[6]

Jerome Murphy-O'Connor asserts that Paul inverts the word order ("die . . . and live") as "a subtle invitation to die to Sin and to live for Christ," making verse 3 a reference to 5:15: "And [Christ] died for all, so that those who live might no longer live for themselves but for him who died for them and was raised."[7] But this parallel hardly fits the present context, in which Paul seeks to prove his love for the believers in Corinth. It is better to say that the apostle spoke of death before life instead of life followed by death because he constantly faced death—and God miraculously delivered him (1:8–9).

Of such loyalty and devotion the Old Testament provides a vivid illustration. Ittai swore an oath to King David, who was fleeing before Absalom: "As surely as the Lord lives, and as my lord the king lives, wherever my lord the king may be, whether it means life or death, there will your servant be" (II Sam. 15:21). Similarly, Paul tells the Corinthians that in case they die, he will die with them

---

4. Consult F. W. Grosheide, *De Tweede Brief van den Apostel Paulus aan de Kerk te Korinthe*, Kommentaar op het Nieuwe Testament series (Amsterdam: Van Bottenburg, 1939), p. 248.

5. John Albert Bengel, *Bengel's New Testament Commentary*, trans. Charlton T. Lewis and Marvin R. Vincent, 2 vols. (Grand Rapids: Kregel, 1981), vol. 2, p. 307.

6. John Calvin, *The Second Epistle of Paul the Apostle to the Corinthians and the Epistles to Timothy, Titus and Philemon*, Calvin's Commentaries series, trans. T. A. Small (Grand Rapids: Eerdmans, 1964), p. 95. Compare Jan Lambrecht, "'Om samen te sterven en samen te leven.' Uitleg van II Kor. 7,3," *Bijdragen* 37 (1976): 234–51.

7. Jerome Murphy-O'Connor, *The Theology of the Second Letter to the Corinthians*, New Testament Theology series (Cambridge: Cambridge University Press, 1991), p. 70.

and as they live, he will live with them. He does not ask them to die with him when his life comes to an end. In short, Paul expresses his love for them, not they for him.

4. I have great confidence in you; I take great pride in you. I am filled with comfort; in all our affliction I am overflowing with joy.

After Titus returned from Corinth, Paul received detailed information from him about the attitude of the Corinthians toward Paul (vv. 6–7). He now demonstrates that he loves them by praising their change of attitude. Their loyalty and love for him lie back of his words that speak of assurance, pride, and comfort. They receive the apostle's tribute and commendation.

a. "I have great confidence in you." Some translations have a different reading: "I am speaking to you with great frankness" (REB), or "Great is my boldness of speech toward you" (NKJV). The difference stems from the Greek noun *parrhēsia*, which signifies frankness or boldness. Of its occurrences in the New Testament, half denote frankness of speech and the other half show confidence demonstrated in a trusting relationship.[8] Openness in speech reveals a basic trust that one has with another, so that in actuality frankness and confidence are two complementary virtues. Paul was able to speak openly to the Corinthians because he had complete faith and trust in them. In other words, frankness of speech assumes confidence to exercise it.[9] The apostle even intensifies the sense of the noun with the adjective *great*.

In this verse we hear the language of a spiritual father who expresses his deep affection toward his children. Paul does so in full assurance that their mutual relationship is free from suspicion or strain. His words are characterized by unrestricted open-mindedness as he assures his children of a large place in his heart (compare 6:11).

b. "I take great pride in you." As their spiritual father, Paul is justifiably proud of the Corinthian believers. He is able to boast about them to anyone who wishes to listen to him. For him, the believers in Corinth are an immense source of thankfulness, because they responded to his appeal for reciprocal love (6:13). Father and children are united in mutual love, and the father is taking honest pride in his offspring (see 7:14; 8:24; 9:3; compare II Thess. 1:4).

c. "I am filled with comfort." The Corinthians have given the apostle cause to be thankful. They have supplied the necessary encouragement so that his heart is continually filled with comfort. The clause is brief, but in the next paragraph Paul fully explains its context (vv. 6–7).

d. "In all our affliction I am overflowing with joy." The news Paul received from Titus makes him leap with joy; his heart cannot contain the happiness he is experiencing in spite of all the difficulties he is facing. Certainly, Paul is not unaware of the pressure he must endure as an apostle of Jesus Christ. In an ear-

---

8. Horst Balz, *EDNT*, 3:45–47.

9. Stanley N. Olson ("Pauline Expressions of Confidence in His Addressees," *CBQ* 47 [1985]: 295) suggests that we interpret the word *confidence* "as a persuasive technique."

lier chapter he had revealed a tremendous strain he had to bear, and he spoke of comfort that he had received to strengthen him (1:6–11).

The phrase *in all our affliction* is identical to the one in 1:4. What the exact nature of the affliction has been is not known. Whether it was physical or mental agony, the point is that God's comfort was sufficient for every hardship Paul suffered. He received more than comfort, for joy was filling his heart to overflowing.

Greek Words, Phrases, and Constructions in 7:2–4

Verses 2–3

χωρήσατε—the aorist imperative implies that this is a single action that has lasting significance. Although the broader context (6:12–13) uses different verbs in Greek, nevertheless the meaning of χωρεῖν is "to make room" and "to understand."[10]

εἰς τὸ συναποθανεῖν καὶ συζῆν—the preposition and the definite article preceding two infinitives denote result. Note that the first infinitive has to be aorist and the second present tense.

Verse 4

This verse provides an example of alliteration with the Greek letter π in adjectives, nouns, verbs, and prepositions.

παρρησία—Paul writes this noun eight times in his epistles (II Cor. 3:12; 7:4; Eph. 3:12; 6:19; Phil. 1:20; Col. 2:15; I Tim. 3:13; Philem. 8). Here only the noun is followed by the preposition πρός (toward), which indicates direction.[11]

πάσῃ τῇ θλίψει—the singular "affliction" instead of the plural, preceded by the adjective πάσῃ and the definite article, indicates that Paul refers to a specific hardship, namely, his anxiety over Titus's mission to Corinth and his return.

---

6. Rejoicing Greatly
7:5–7

This letter appears to have been written in several stages. Paul moved from Ephesus to Troas, then to Macedonia, and on to Illyricum (modern Albania and Yugoslavia [Rom. 15:19]). During his travels he intermittently penned his second epistle to the church in Corinth. Whenever he heard news from or about the Corinthians, Paul responded to it. At other times, lack of news is reflected in the epistle. For example, if Paul had known about the arrival of Titus earlier, he would not have mentioned his anxiety (2:13). Nor would he have pleaded with the Corinthians for reciprocal affection (6:11–13).

We should also understand that Paul's writing material was not a collection of individual pages but a scroll, and writing on a scroll makes major revisions difficult. And last, the style of this epistle is choppy, as if the writer is in a hurry. Here

---

10. Contra Jean Héring, *The Second Epistle of Saint Paul to the Corinthians,* trans. A. W. Heathcote and P. J. Allcock (London: Epworth, 1967), p. 53.

11. Refer to W. C. van Unnik, "The Christian's Freedom of Speech in the New Testament," *BJRUL* 44 (1961–62): 473 n. 1.

and there are awkward transitions (6:14) and breaks in Greek grammar (e.g., 5:12; 6:3; 7:5, 7; 9:11), but all this confirms that Paul is genuinely human in expressing his emotions. As he writes, so he is.

5. For indeed when we came into Macedonia, our body had no rest, but we were distressed in every respect. Fights on the outside, fears on the inside.

a. "For indeed when we came into Macedonia, our body had no rest." Paul had left Ephesus and traveled to Troas in northwest Asia Minor. There he had agreed to meet Titus, whom he had sent to Corinth to deliver Paul's letter addressed to the Corinthian church (2:3–4) and to organize the ingathering of the monetary gifts for the saints in Jerusalem (8:6, 19–21).

After an absence of about four years (52–56), Paul probably visited the Macedonian churches of Philippi, Thessalonica, and Berea, which he had founded during his second missionary journey (Acts 16–17). He had longed to do so earlier but was hindered by Satan (I Thess. 2:18).

The apostle constantly worried that he and Titus had missed each other on their journeys, for by traveling to Macedonia he had taken the risk of having Titus voyaging from Macedonia to Troas at that same time. Self-accusation must have worn Paul down. He states that his flesh (in the Greek "our flesh"; see also 7:1) had no respite.

Without doubt, this text (v. 5) is a continuation of an earlier verse in which Paul speaks of his concern for Titus: "When I came to Troas, . . . I had no relief in my soul because I did not find Titus, my brother. However, when I had said good-by to them, I went to Macedonia" (2:12–13). The parallel wording is obvious even in translation.[12]

I came	we came
to Troas	into Macedonia
I had no rest	no rest
in my spirit	had our body

The intervening segment, 2:14–7:4, is a lengthy interlude in which Paul teaches a number of theological truths: the ministry of the new covenant (3); the glorious light of Christ's gospel (4); the meaning of our earthly and heavenly dwellings and Paul's ministry of reconciliation (5); his sufferings for Christ and his call to separation (6). He wrote on all these topics while traveling and waiting for the arrival of Titus.

b. "But we were distressed in every respect. Fights on the outside, fears on the inside." Restlessness had taken hold of Paul and drained his energy. He encountered adversaries in Macedonia, as is evident from his remark about "fights on the outside." He fails to elaborate what his difficulties were, but in the New Testament the Greek word *machai* refers to arguments and quarrels that disturb the peace of

---

12. C. K. Barrett, "Titus," in *Neotestamentica et Semitica: Studies in Honour of Matthew Black*, ed. E. Earle Ellis and Max Wilcox (Edinburgh: Clark, 1969), p. 9; also in *Essays on Paul* (Philadelphia: Westminster, 1982).

the church (II Tim. 2:23; Titus 3:9; James 4:1). We surmise that the developing Macedonian churches suffered numerous conflicts from both within and without.

We know that Paul's internal fears were his worries about the absence of Titus and the spiritual well-being of the Corinthian church. From his emissary, Titus, he wished to learn how the congregation had responded to his painful letter (2:3–4). The apostle, who later from his prison cell joyfully encouraged his readers, "Do not be anxious about anything" (Phil. 4:6), is himself torn apart by intense worry.

The saying, "Fights on the outside, fears on the inside," may have originated with Paul but could also have been an epigram that was current in Corinth and elsewhere. Two considerations lend support to this latter suggestion: first, the saying stands grammatically disconnected at the end of the verse; next, the assonance in the Greek text, carried over even into translations, is striking. Nonetheless, Paul fittingly applies these words to his own life as he must defend the cause of Christ in the face of controversy. In this saying we hear the echo of the lists of hardships Paul has to endure for Christ and the church (4:7–8; 6:3–10).

6. But God, who comforts the downcast, comforted us with the coming of Titus.

God never forsakes his own people, but at the right time sends them deliverance. His eye is on his children as they undergo physical and mental hardships for the sake of his kingdom. He hears their prayers and responds to their need when they are discouraged and humiliated. God comes to them in their time of need with words of encouragement and comfort. Paul, for instance, had experienced discouragement when he founded the church in Corinth. But in a vision, the Lord spoke to him and said: "Do not be afraid; keep on speaking, do not be silent. For I am with you, and no one is going to attack you, because I have many people in this city" (Acts 18:9–10).[13]

Writing his epistles, Paul always has in mind passages from the Old Testament Scriptures. Here he is thinking of the words God spoke to Israel: "For the LORD comforts his people and will have compassion on his afflicted ones" (Isa. 49:13). Paul follows not the Hebrew but the Greek text and loosely cites its wording from memory.[14]

The coming of Titus as the bearer of good news is God's way to comfort Paul. We have no knowledge of why Titus was delayed, but his arrival and the news about Corinth lifted Paul's spirit and gave him unspeakable joy.

7. And not only with his coming, but also with the comfort that you imparted to him. He reported to us your longing [for me], your mourning, your zeal for me, so that I rejoiced even more.

a. "And not only with his coming, but also with the comfort that you imparted to him." This verse is closely linked to the preceding verse (v. 6) with its emphasis

---

13. In perilous situations, the Lord invariably counseled and encouraged Paul. See Acts 22:18; 23:11; 27:23–26.

14. Consult Hans Windisch, *Der Zweite Korintherbrief,* ed. Georg Strecker (1924; reprint ed., Göttingen: Vandenhoeck und Ruprecht, 1970), p. 227.

on the concept *comfort*. Indeed, the Greek text features words for "comfort" four times in these two verses. Comfort derived first from God to Paul through the arrival of Titus. Thereupon Titus reported to Paul that the church in Corinth had comforted, encouraged, and strengthened him in his ministry to it. Indeed, Titus came to Paul to comfort him with an encouraging report.

The words and actions of the Corinthians displayed their love for God, the Word, and the servants of that Word. We would expect Titus to say that he had encouraged and strengthened the Corinthians. He certainly exhorted them, but in his report Titus mentioned not his work but the fact that the church in Corinth had comforted him. The uncertainties that Paul had concerning the Corinthians were also those of Titus, who served as his emissary.

Titus had been sent to Corinth, probably to deliver Paul's sorrowful letter and certainly to interpret it (2:3–4). He also faced the responsibility of settling a disciplinary matter (2:5–11). And he had to arrange the task of collecting the monetary gift for the church in Jerusalem (8:6).

Prior to the arrival of Titus, the tension in the Corinthian church had risen. Paul had paid a painful visit and had quickly departed (2:1). Titus had shared Paul's trepidation concerning the people in Corinth. His objective was to have them change their attitude toward Paul, to bring them to repentance, and to make them work harmoniously for the benefit of the Christian community. And this task Titus fulfilled.

b. "He reported to us your longing [for me], your mourning, your zeal for me, so that I rejoiced even more." We can understand Paul's anxiety concerning Titus in Corinth, for Titus was there as his representative. One of Titus's responsibilities, the spiritual development of the Corinthian community, was part of the work of extending Christ's church on earth. A breakdown of relations in this community would negate the church's effectiveness and would have disastrous repercussions for the missionary labors of Paul and his associates. But this was not the case. Titus's report was bright and cheerful and gave a point-by-point description of what happened in Corinth.

Titus's report shows that the Corinthians had a complete change of heart, as the emphasis and the repetition of the plural personal pronoun *your* shows. In three short phrases Paul says, "Corinthians, your longing to see me, your shedding tears of remorse, and your enthusiasm for our ministry—all this has made me very happy."

The response to Paul's desire to receive reciprocal love from the Corinthians was overwhelming; they were indeed opening their hearts to him and were not withholding their affection from him (6:11–13). The verb *to long* has a positive connotation and needs the prepositional phrase *for me* to complete the sentence. Also, the mourning of the Corinthians can possibly be described as "violent expressions of bitter remorse."[15] The people repented of the grief they had caused Paul during his brief and painful visit (2:1–2).

---

15. Consult Friedrich Hauck, *TDNT*, 5:116.

That the Corinthians had a genuine change of heart was proved by their zeal for the cause of Christ. Paul praises the Corinthians for their interest in him; he intimates that they were expending their zeal on his behalf—to be precise, in place of himself but for the benefit of Christ. In a succeeding verse he again commends their zeal: "Look what earnestness this [godly sorrow] has produced in you, . . . what indignation, what fear, what longing, what zeal, what punishment" (v. 11).

The result of Titus's report is evident in the overwhelming joy Paul experienced. God provided encouragement by having Titus return to the apostle with a good report, and that encouragement was translated into immense joy. The comfort Paul received turned into joy that was shared with one another. He says, "And in addition to our comfort, we rejoiced exceedingly at the joy of Titus" (v. 13).

Practical Considerations in 7:5–7

"Absence makes the heart grow fonder" is a proverbial saying that fails to include patience as a necessary ingredient. Being separated geographically from another without adequate and frequent communication indeed tests one's patience. When we pass this test, however, our hearts are filled with happiness that enlivens our true personality.

Sometimes God puts us to the test when he creates distances and withholds the means of communication. He places us before uncertainties, gives us periods of waiting, tests our patience, and makes us cope with discouragement.

But at the very moment when everyone seems to have lost hope, God intervenes by removing the walls of separation and by providing the necessary information. An apt illustration is found in Luke's report on the voyage to and shipwreck at Malta. The crew and passengers aboard ship had lost all hope of survival, but an angel of God spoke to Paul and brought good news to them by saying that all would survive and the ship would run aground on an island (Acts 27:13–26).

God suddenly ends our periods of desperation and changes them into seasons of joy. He then fills our hearts with contentment and thankfulness toward him. God teaches us to be patient in afflictions and thankful for accomplishments, but above all he wants us to put our trust in him. Spiritual growth is his objective for us as he continues to work out his plan of salvation in our lives. Moreover, he gives us his assurance that absolutely nothing "in all creation will be able to separate us from the love of God that is in Christ Jesus our Lord" (Rom. 8:39).

Greek Words, Phrases, and Constructions in 7:5, 7

Verse 5

ἔσχηκεν—Greek New Testaments feature the perfect tense, even though a number of leading manuscripts have the aorist ἔσχεν of the verb ἔχω (I have, hold). The aorist may be an unintentional error of a scribe who dropped two letters (η and κ) from the verb in the perfect. It could also be an intentional "error" at the hand of a scribe who thought that the perfect tense had to be replaced by the aorist.[16] But the more difficult reading is probably the correct text.

---

16. Alfred Plummer, *A Critical and Exegetical Commentary on the Second Epistle of St. Paul to the Corinthians,* International Critical Commentary (1915; Edinburgh: Clark, 1975), p. 218.

θλιβόμενοι—"being distressed." This present passive participle is an anacoluthon. It has no grammatical antecedent, for the participle ἐχόντων (v. 1) is part of the genitive absolute construction.

Verse 7

ἀναγγέλλων—"reporting." Loosely connected to the subject of the verb παρεκλήθη (he was comforted), this participle is almost another anacoluthon.

ὑμῶν—for emphasis, Paul places this pronoun three times as a subjective genitive between the definite articles and the nouns.

ὑπὲρ ἐμοῦ ὥστε με—the sequence of two personal pronouns is significant. The prepositional phrase discloses personal benefit for Paul with the result that he is the one who greatly rejoices.

---

7. Expressing Sorrow
7:8–13a

Overcome by emotion, Paul is unable to write his letter smoothly. He writes in the first person singular throughout this section to indicate that the matter at hand touches him deeply and disturbs his equilibrium. The next two verses (8–9) reveal his emotional frame of mind as he refers to the intermediate letter he has sent to the church in Corinth. The grammatical break in verse 8 can be ameliorated with punctuation that helps to make the transition to verse 9.

8. For even if my letter grieved you, I do not regret it. Although I did regret it—for I see that my letter hurt you but for a little while— 9. I now rejoice, not that you were grieved, but that you were grieved that led to repentance. For your grief was according to God's will, so that you suffered no loss because of us.

a. "For even if my letter grieved you, I do not regret it." We presume that one of the first questions Paul asked Titus concerned the reaction the Corinthians had to the painful letter he had written them (2:3–4).[17] The letter is no longer extant, so we are unable to say anything about its content. But we expect that Paul dealt with a sensitive issue that involved one of the members of the Corinthian congregation. The possibility is not remote that the letter dealt with a disciplinary problem (see the commentary on 2:5–11). And we surmise that Titus had to provide leadership in this delicate matter.

The vocabulary in 2:1–7 is similar to that of 7:8–11. In both passages, "grief" or "grieve" occurs in the form of a verb, a participle, or a noun.[18] In addition, the concept *joy* appears in the context of these passages (2:3; 7:4, 7, 9, 13). Last, Paul uses the word *comfort* or *encourage* in both contexts.[19] The conclusion we

---

17. The letter to which Paul refers can hardly be I Corinthians, because that epistle in general is not sorrowful but practical and instructive. For a discussion of this point see the Introduction and the commentary on 2:1–2.

18. The verb and participle occur four times in chapter 2 (vv. 2 [twice], 4, 5) and six times in chapter 7 (vv. 8 [twice], 9 [three times], 11). The noun appears three times in chapter 2 (vv. 1, 3, 7) and twice in chapter 7 (v. 10).

19. As a verb (2:7, 8; 7:6, 7, 13) and as a noun (7:4, 7, 13).

draw is that Paul returns to the same subject he had discussed in the second chapter of this epistle.

What is new in this text is Paul's emphasis on regret. He writes that the letter caused sorrow for the Corinthians, but he does not regret their sorrow. Then, seeming to contradict himself, he says that he does regret it. To explain this anomaly I make a few observations. First, Paul is in an emotional state of mind that prevents him from writing a smooth sentence. Next, verses 8 and 9 must be read in the light of 2:1–4, where Paul stresses the fact that he wants to make the Corinthians happy even if he has to grieve them with a stern letter. He desires that they come to repentance after they see their error, and that then they will rejoice. Third, as their spiritual father he corrects them with painful words, but he writes to them in love (2:4). Last, for a while he regretted having written this letter,[20] but he hoped that it would result in joy. This is exactly what happened, as Titus confirmed.

b. "Although I did regret it—for I see that my letter hurt you but for a little while." The first clause is concessive and has its complement in verse 9, "I now rejoice." Why did Paul rue the fact that he composed the sorrowful letter? He knew full well that its content would grieve the Corinthians. When a parent has to correct an erring child, the correction hurts the parent much more than it hurts the offspring. A father who takes his role of parenting seriously will discipline his child in love. Thereby he promotes health and happiness in his family, even though the procedure itself is painful.[21] The same thing is true of Paul, who served the Corinthians as a spiritual father. His regret for having to discipline them would last only until the people in Corinth came to their senses, repented, and admitted their wrong.

By using the word *regret* a number of times, the writers of the New Testament shed light on its meaning. It can mean a change of mind, as in the parable of the two sons who were asked to work in the vineyard. Jesus relates that one son refused to go but then was sorry and went to work after all (Matt. 21:29). Conversely, the writer of Hebrews quotes Psalm 110:4 and writes that God swore an oath and did not change his mind (Heb. 7:21). The word can also mean "repent." Judas was filled with remorse after he betrayed Jesus; his remorse, however, resulted not in repentance but in suicide (Matt. 27:3–5). Similarly, the Jewish clergy and the elders who heard and saw John the Baptist refused to repent (Matt. 21:32).[22]

Paul writes the word *regret* twice in this passage. He clearly points out that his regret was positive, for it effected repentance in the recipients of his letter. Notice that Paul transfers to himself the regret that belonged to the readers; he hurts with them and speaks of his regret, not theirs. Yet their regret resulted in repentance (v. 9).

---

20. The tense of the Greek verb *metemelōēn* (regretted) is imperfect and indicates continued action for a period in the past.

21. Compare Prov. 13:24; 19:18; 22:15; 23:13–14; 29:17.

22. Otto Michel, *TDNT*, 4:629; Fritz Laubach, *NIDNTT*, 1:356–57.

The hurt that Paul's letter caused lasted for only a little while. The literal translation of the Greek is "for an hour," which in common parlance means a brief period that is not measured in hours or days.

The pleasures of sin are momentary, but its wages are grief and destruction that lead to death (compare Rom. 6:23). Conversely, even though correction is painful, it results in repentance and forgiveness. Then the pain that is caused by not only discipline but also repentance is replaced by joy that lasts forever. The psalmist states that God does not despise a broken and contrite heart (Ps. 51:17).

c. "I now rejoice, not that you were grieved, but that you were grieved that led to repentance." The clause "I do not regret it" (v. 8a) must be seen as parallel to the clause "I now rejoice." Both clauses are both in the present tense, but one is negative and the other is positive.[23] They follow each other in conveying the message that Paul has no regrets and is filled with joy.

With the words *I now rejoice,* Paul fills in the second part of the concessive statement that began with the words, "Although I did regret it." Why is Paul rejoicing? Now that Titus has arrived with the good news that the Corinthians have reacted positively to Paul's letter, regret has vanished and joy has taken its place.

At first glance, Paul seems to be repetitive and contradictory when he writes, "not that you were grieved, but that you were grieved." Note, however, that Paul seeks to eliminate possible misunderstanding. He writes in the passive voice: "you [the Corinthians] were grieved" by his letter. This is a fact that Paul wishes to make known. But he clarifies the statement by repeating the verb ("you were grieved") and then adds that their grief "led to repentance." The ultimate objective of Paul's severe letter was to have the Corinthians repent. This could be done only by hurting them through his corrective words.

The parable of the prodigal son illustrates the deprivation and rejection a Jewish young man had to suffer while tending the pigs of his Gentile employer. But these very hardships brought the young man to his senses and made him say: "How many of my father's hired men have food to spare, and here I am starving to death! I will set out and go back to my father and say to him: Father, I have sinned against heaven and against you. I am no longer worthy to be called your son; make me like one of your hired men" (Luke 15:17–19). Here we have a picture of true repentance that turned into abundant joy for both father and son. Grief that originates from awareness of sin leads to genuine repentance, and repentance alters one's will, intellect, and emotions. Repentance turns one away from evil and toward God; it involves asking God for remission of sin.[24]

d. "For your grief was according to God's will." A literal translation of the Greek is confusing because of its compact construction: "you were grieved ac-

---

23. R. C. H. Lenski, *The Interpretation of St. Paul's First and Second Epistle to the Corinthians* (Columbus: Wartburg, 1946), p. 1107.

24. Consult Johannes Behm, *TDNT*, 4:1004; Byron H. DeMent and Edgar W. Smith, *ISBE*, 4:136. Consult also Robert N. Wilkin, "Repentance and Salvation. Part 5: New Testament Repentance: Repentance in the Epistles and Revelation," *JournGraceEvangSoc* 3 (1990): 24–26.

cording to God." The grieving of the Corinthians was a process that began when they read the sorrowful letter. That process led them to God, for they realized that they had offended him by their conduct (see Rom. 8:27; I Peter 4:6). Through his Word, God made known his law to the people in Corinth, and through his Spirit he led them to repentance. As a result of their repentance, the Corinthians desired to do God's will in obedience to his Word. Note that Paul telescopes this entire process of repentance in the phrase *according to God's will*.[25]

f. "So that you suffered no loss because of us." The result of God's leading the Corinthians to repentance was that they would not suffer any spiritual damage. It was Paul's duty to write a painful letter, to admonish its recipients, and to express his love to them (2:4). If the apostle had neglected this duty, he would have been responsible for their spiritual degradation. He trusted God to use the letter to effect contrition in the hearts of the Corinthians. Nonetheless, Paul had to endure an anxious period of waiting before he would know the impact of and reaction to his writing. He fully realized that should the readers react negatively, they would suffer untold harm. When Titus came with his encouraging report, Paul's anxiety turned into boundless joy. Then he knew that the Corinthians because of their repentance suffered no loss in any respect. Everything happened as he had expected. His letter served the spiritual well-being of the believers in Corinth.

10. For sorrow that is according to God's will produces repentance that effects salvation, which cannot be regretted. But worldly sorrow produces death.

The contrast in this text is plain: true repentance versus remorse, and salvation versus death. The one side of the proverbial coin is positive and elaborate; the other side is negative and brief. The dissimilarity is so striking that no one can fail to see it.

a. *Godly sorrow.* "For sorrow that is according to God's will produces repentance that effects salvation, which cannot be regretted." Once again, Paul condenses his teaching on God's law, will, and guidance in the expression *according to God* (see the comments on verse 9). He means to say that sorrow for sin must be seen in the context of our God who gives us his commandments, makes known his will, and guides his people to obedience.

The sorrow that Paul mentions refers to sadness for sin that has been committed; such sorrow can cause the repentant sinner to shed tears of bitterness. For instance, when Peter disowned Jesus by swearing that he did not know him, he heard the rooster crow. Thereupon he remembered Jesus' words, went outside, and wept bitterly (Matt. 26:74–75).

Paul writes that godly sorrow produces repentance, but in all his epistles he uses the Greek noun *metanoia* (repentance) only four times (Rom. 2:4; II Cor. 7:9, 10; II Tim. 2:25). And the related verb *to repent* occurs only once in his letters (II Cor. 12:21). Although the Synoptic Gospels repeatedly record the noun and

---

25. Compare Hans Lietzmann, *An die Korinther I/II*, augmented by Werner G. Kümmel, Handbuch zum Neuen Testament 9 (Tübingen: Mohr, 1969), pp. 131–32.

the verb, John's Gospel and Epistles lack both of them. But Paul and John express this concept with two substitutes, the noun *faith* and the verb *to believe*. These two words occur numerous times in the writings of both John and Paul and indicate the action of a sinner turning to God in full dependence on him. The Old Testament teaches that God wants his people to turn away from sin and toward God. This teaching appears graphically in the prophecy of Ezekiel: "But if a wicked man turns away from all the sins he has committed and does what is just and right, he will surely live" (18:21, 27).

Repentance leads to salvation, says Paul, that cannot be regretted. No one can ever say that he or she has made a mistake by having repented and thus receiving salvation. Salvation means restoration to the fullness of life. It means to be whole again, to live in harmony with God and his people. Perhaps Paul's statement, "Repentance that effects salvation cannot be regretted," was a well-known axiom in the early church.[26] Whether the clause *which cannot be regretted* is connected with repentance or salvation is inconsequential. It is a fact that genuine repentance results in salvation, which then can be described as something that is not to be regretted.

b. *Worldly sorrow.* "But worldly sorrow produces death." What a contrast! Now we see the opposite of the preceding pronouncement. Genuine contrition is a turning away from sin and a going toward God, but worldly sorrow is remorse that expresses itself in self-accusation. Peter repented and returned to the apostles and afterward met Jesus (Matt. 26:75; Luke 24:33–34). Judas was filled with remorse, but returned to the chief priests who rejected him (Matt. 27:3–5). Peter was restored and became the head of the apostles (John 21:15–19). Judas committed suicide and was doomed to destruction (Acts 1:18–19).

The Corinthians had chosen life by repenting and turning to God. They received salvation full and free and were completely restored in their relationship to God and Paul. When a sinner repents, says Jesus, the angels in heaven rejoice (Luke 15:7, 10). Paul also exulted at the news that the people in Corinth had a change of heart. His letter and Titus's visit had not been in vain. The people in Corinth had abandoned their evil ways and had turned to the living God, the author of salvation. Hence, Paul's joy knew no bounds when Titus brought him the news concerning the Corinthian church.

11. For look, what earnestness this very thing has produced in you, namely, that you were grieved according to God's will, also what eagerness to clear yourselves, what indignation, what fear, what longing, what zeal, what punishment. At every point you have shown that you were innocent in this matter.

a. "For look, what earnestness this very thing has produced in you, namely, that you were grieved according to God's will." Filled with deep emotion, Paul has difficulty writing a smooth and balanced sentence. He wants the people to know that their sorrow for sin, which turned them to do God's will, is of utmost importance to him.

---

26. Compare Grosheide, *De Tweede Brief aan Korinthe,* p. 260.

Utterly amazed by the diligence of the Corinthians, Paul calls attention to it by exclaiming, "Look, what earnestness," a synonym for "eagerness."[27] Their sorrow for sin, which Paul here describes as "this very thing," has brought about a comprehensive reversal. The dedication of the Corinthians is so overwhelming that Paul places it first in a series of seven characteristics listed in this verse. "This very thing" is nothing other than their conversion experience that led them from genuine repentance to salvation, and from sorrow to an obedience to do God's will.

Conversion leads to a diligence to keep God's law, and this diligence is attributed to human effort. Conversely, praise and thanks must be attributed to God, who calls sinners away from the road that leads to death and into a life of joyful service (see v. 10). Although the apostle fails to say so, the opposite of diligence is lethargy, a behavior that had characterized the church in Corinth. Instead of listening to Paul's instructions, they had succumbed to idleness and had failed to obey him (see the implicit reference in 2:9). They should have removed sin from their midst (compare I Cor. 5:9–13).

How did the Corinthians exhibit their diligence? Paul writes six short phrases that are added to the repetitive "also." As if the apostle repeatedly says, "Look at this one," he introduces each phrase separately. Every individual phrase demonstrates the Corinthians' diligence.

b. "Also what eagerness to clear yourselves." "Eagerness to clear yourselves" is a translation of the Greek word *apologia,* from which we have the derivative *apology.* Are the Corinthians apologizing to Paul for their disregard of his instructions? If this were so, we would have expected more detailed information. Rather, Paul means to say that the readers sought to mend their ways and clear themselves before God. Indeed, their sorrow led them "to seek correction in the sight of God."[28]

c. "What indignation." This phrase describes a human attitude that reveals righteous anger about sin that affronts our sense of decency. Elsewhere Paul speaks of putting aside the old self and putting on the new self (Eph. 4:22–24; Col. 3:9–10). A sixteenth-century catechism asks, "What is the dying-away of the old self?" The answer is:

> It is to be genuinely sorry for sin,
> to hate it more and more,
> and to run away from it.[29]

The Corinthians abhorred themselves because of sin, but at the same time they were indignant with the false teachers who had led them astray.

---

27. The Greek word *spoudē* (diligence, eagerness, earnestness) occurs five times in this epistle (7:11, 12; 8:7, 8, 16) and only twice more in his epistolary literature (Rom. 12:8, 11). See also the two adjectives *spoudaioteros* and *spoudaion* (II Cor. 8:17 and 22 respectively).

28. Martin, *II Corinthians,* p. 234. Calvin (*II Corinthians,* p. 100) interprets the phrase as "a kind of defence that has more to do with seeking for pardon than with rebutting charges."

29. Heidelberg Catechism, question and answer 89.

d. "What fear, what longing." Does "fear" signify reverence or fright? Does the word refer to a person or a thing? We do well to look at the context and see that Paul uses the word *fear* five times in this epistle, of which four are in this chapter (vv. 1, 5, 11, 15; 5:11). He uses "fear" in the sense of reverence and respect for God and man, so that we may conclude that the word signifies reverence for God and respect for Paul. That is, the Corinthians respect Paul as God's representative and bringer of divine revelation. This interpretation agrees with the intent of the next word, "longing," which Paul mentioned earlier (7:7). The Christians in Corinth desire to see the apostle and to receive personal instruction from him.

e. "What zeal." In his letters Paul writes the Greek term *zēlos* (zeal) ten times, and five uses are in this epistle.[30] The word conveys either a bad sense (jealousy, 12:20) or a good sense (as the other instances in this epistle impart). In verse 7, it alludes to expending one's energy for the cause of Christ. Thus, it is synonymous with the word *earnestness* at the beginning of verse 11.

f. "What punishment." This noun is best understood as God's justice applied and evidenced when the Corinthians were morally aroused to see "that sin ought to be punished."[31] The reference is to the sexually immoral man (I Cor. 5:1–5, 13). And this interpretation harmonizes with the wording of the following clause.

g. "At every point you have shown that you were innocent in this matter." The matter Paul alludes to is a particular sin committed by one of the Corinthians (I Cor. 5:1). The church members had been remiss in administering discipline, but after Paul's visit and painful letter they punished the evildoer (2:1–6). Except for the Corinthians' initial laxity and lack of support for Paul, they themselves were without guilt in this offense.

12. So, although I wrote to you, it was neither on account of the offender nor on account of the offended, but so that your good will concerning us might be revealed to you before God. 13a. Through this we are encouraged.

Once again Paul pens a lengthy sentence in which he reveals that his emotions affect his writing (see v. 11). The issue he discusses has been a sensitive one for him and for the Corinthian church (see the *Additional Comments on 2:5–11*).

The paragraph division at verse 13 is infelicitous, for the first sentence of the verse belongs to the preceding text (v. 12) and the rest is part of the remarks about Titus (vv. 14–15). Most translations, therefore, divide the text accordingly.[32]

a. "So, although I wrote to you, it was neither on account of the offender nor on account of the offended." The first item we notice is that Paul employs legal

---

30. II Cor. 7:7, 11; 9:2; 11:2; 12:20; and Rom. 10:2; 13:13; I Cor. 3:3; Gal. 5:20; Phil. 3:6.

31. Charles Hodge, *An Exposition of the Second Epistle to the Corinthians* (1891; Edinburgh: Banner of Truth, 1959), p. 186. See also Hughes, *Second Epistle to the Corinthians*, p. 275.

32. Exceptions are KJV, NKJV, TNT, *Cassirer;* see also the commentaries of Hughes, p. 278; Héring, p. 57; and Alford, p. 678.

language with the terms *offender* and *offended*.[33] In the previous passage, he also used legal terminology: *eagerness to clear yourselves* and *punishment*. All these expressions are commonplace in a court of law, presumably in this case a church court.

Next, the letter Paul addressed to the Christians in Corinth is most likely not our canonical I Corinthians but the sorrowful letter (see the commentary on 2:2–3 and 7:8). He wrote it after he had paid the Corinthians a brief visit that proved to be for him a distressing experience.

Third, with the words "so, although" Paul is not writing a conclusion based on the previous text (v. 11). This could be true on the basis of the first word, "so." But the ensuing clause that begins with "although" is not a conclusion but a recollection of earlier remarks about the sorrowful letter.

Fourth, who are the offender and the offended? Paul purposely omits personal references now that the entire issue has been resolved. Both he and his readers are fully familiar with the details. In a strict sense, the offended party is the one who has been unjustly treated.[34] The legal term *offended* (plaintiff) is in the singular to denote the party, not necessarily an individual, who has endured the offense. This interpretation thwarts the suggestion that the offended party is the father of the man who committed incest (I Cor. 5:1).[35] Not only Paul but all the faithful believers in Corinth were offended by what the offender had done (see the commentary on 2:5).

The interpretation that the offender was the man who committed incest (I Cor. 5:1) should not be dismissed. It is possible that the man whom Paul wanted expelled from the Christian community also insulted the apostle during his painful visit (2:1).[36] The offender had a following in the congregation and affronted both Paul and those in the church who supported the apostle. This person was expelled at Paul's request (I Cor. 5:13). Subsequently he repented, sought remission, and was reaffirmed in love by the Corinthians (2:6–8).

Last, Paul is indicating neither vindictiveness toward the offender nor defensiveness for the offended. He wants to lift the members of the Corinthian church to a higher level and tries to do so by stressing the positive instead of the negative. Hence, the two negatives, "it was neither on account of the offender nor on account of the offended," should not be taken literally, because he did write the letter. Paul contrasts the negative and positive without canceling the negative. The positive is more important than its converse, and thus he stresses the one

---

33. Rudolf Bultmann states that the verb *adikein* means "to do someone an injustice, to injure someone" (*The Second Letter to the Corinthians,* trans. Roy A. Harrisville [Minneapolis: Augsburg, 1985]), p. 58. Compare Windisch, *Der Zweite Korintherbrief,* p. 238.

34. Bauer, p. 17.

35. Contra Bengel, *New Testament Commentary,* vol. 2, p. 310.

36. C. K. Barrett suggests that the offender was an outsider, but this need not be so. If the offending person was a member, he had insider support. "Ὁ ἈΔΙΚΗΣΑΣ (II Cor 7,12)," in *Verborum Veritas,* ed. Otto Böcher and Klaus Haacker (Wuppertal: Brockhaus, 1970); also in *Essays on Paul* (Philadelphia: Westminster, 1982), pp. 108–17.

but not the other. The reference to the offender and the offended must be interpreted in the light of the positive part of this verse.

b. "But so that your good will concerning us might be revealed to you before God." The positive in this part of the text is Paul's aim to advance the unity of the church (see I Cor. 12:12, 27). He desires harmony between himself and the people in Corinth, and his sorrowful letter was written to make the readers repent and turn to him again. This purpose is exactly what the letter achieved. But now he wants the readers to see that the effect of their good will toward him strengthens the oneness of the body of Christ.

The Greek word *spoudē*, which I have translated "good will,"[37] is rendered "earnestness" in verse 11. The diligent care of the Corinthians is important, especially when the church must see its unity with Paul and with the forgiven sinner (2:7–11). The believers' actions toward Paul and his associates must be genuine and sound. Such actions must also become visible to the Corinthians themselves, for Paul writes that their good will might be revealed to them. The agent who does the revealing is not identified. It stands to reason that if Paul had written the active instead of the passive voice, he would have named as agent the Corinthian church. The Christians in Corinth should be cognizant of their own zeal for the cause of Christ and see themselves always in God's presence. In other words, they must ever see their actions from a divine perspective. When believers perform their works and are aware of God's sacred presence, then their zeal is genuine, their attitude praiseworthy, and their unity secure.

c. "Through this we are encouraged." With this sentence Paul concludes a lengthy segment (vv. 8–13a) of his epistle. The apostle is greatly encouraged by the genuine zeal the Corinthians have demonstrated on behalf of him and his co-workers. The phrase *through this* points to the zeal of the Christians in Corinth.

Paul alludes to a thought he expressed earlier in verses 6 and 7. There he mentioned that God had comforted him with the arrival and good news of Titus. But now he summarizes his feelings by saying that the favorable response of the church in Corinth to his admonitions has been a lasting source of comfort to him. He has been and continues to be greatly encouraged.

Greek Words, Phrases, and Constructions in 7:8–12

Verses 8–9

βλέπω γάρ—here are two textual problems. First, the indicative verb βλέπω has solid manuscript support, but so does the present participle βλέπων. Although Greek New Testaments feature the former, the choice is difficult indeed.[38] Next, the particle γάρ is omit-

---

37. Bauer, p. 763.

38. Hughes (*Second Epistle to the Corinthians,* p. 269 n. 6) pleads for the reading of the present participle by appealing to the Westcott-Hort edition of the Greek New Testament. Except for the Vulgate and a marginal note in *Moffatt,* translators have not adopted this reading.

ted in many manuscripts; it may have been added to relieve the syntax of the anacolu-thon.[39] Again, there is no easy decision, yet most texts leave it in.

ἐλυπήθητε—the aorist passive construction is inceptive; that is, the grieving began as a result of Paul's letter.

κατὰ θεόν—this phrase, which occurs three times (vv. 9, 10, 11), means "in a godly way"[40] or "according to God's will, pleasure, or manner."[41]

ἐξ ἡμῶν—the preposition conveys the notion of cause or occasion.

Verses 10–11

ἀμεταμέλητον—this is a verbal adjective with the privative ἀ, to negate the adjective, and with a passive connotation, to suggest that the Corinthians are the agents: "they are unable to regret it."

ἰδού—see the note on 6:2.

τό with the aorist passive infinitive λυπηθῆναι (to be grieved) is in apposition to the pronoun τοῦτο.[42]

ἀλλά—used five times in succession, this conjunction is not adversative but rather as-censive.[43] It means, "yes, and in addition."

Verse 12

ἄρα εἰ—"although."

ἔγραψα—the aorist is not epistolary but refers to a previous letter (2:3–4).

ἕνεκεν τοῦ—this combination introduces purpose, as is the case when it precedes the infinitive ἕνεκεν τοῦ φανερωθῆναι (in order to be revealed). But the first two instances with participles are causal.[44]

ὑμῶν . . . ἡμῶν—these two pronouns should not be interchanged as in some manu-scripts. The reading ὑμῶν . . . ὑμῶν or ἡμῶν . . . ἡμῶν distorts Paul's intent in the text. He is not stressing the care he and his fellow workers are expending on the Corinthians but the opposite. Of importance is the care that the Christians show toward him and toward each other.

---

8. Meeting with Titus
7:13b–16

The conclusion to this chapter consists of further details concerning the mis-sion and the reception of Titus in Corinth. Earlier Paul mentioned his anxiety about Titus's delay (2:13; 7:5), then he reported his associate's arrival in Mace-

---

39. Consult Bruce M. Metzger, *A Textual Commentary on the Greek New Testament,* 2d ed. (Stuttgart and New York: United Bible Societies, 1994), p. 512.

40. C. F. D. Moule, *An Idiom-Book of New Testament Greek,* 2d ed. (Cambridge: Cambridge University Press, 1960), p. 59.

41. Bauer, p. 407.

42. Blass and Debrunner, *Greek Grammar,* 399.1.

43. Bauer, p. 38.

44. Compare A. T. Robertson, *A Grammar of the Greek New Testament in the Light of Historical Research* (Nashville: Broadman, 1934), p. 1037; Richard A. Young, *Intermediate New Testament Greek: A Linguistic and Exegetical Approach* (Nashville: Broadman and Holman, 1994), p. 167; and Moule, *Idiom-Book,* p. 140.

donia and the comfort and joy this had given him (vv. 6–7), and now he provides additional information about his co-worker.

13b. And in addition to our comfort, we rejoiced exceedingly at the joy of Titus, because his spirit has been refreshed by all of you.

a. *Abundant joy.* The tone of this verse shows explicitly Paul's great joy and implicitly his earlier anxiety. What made the apostle so concerned about the church in Corinth? We answer that Satan infiltrated this fledgling congregation (I Cor. 5:1) and sought to destroy its witness in the community. Just as the devil used Ananias and Sapphira to discredit the church in Jerusalem (Acts 5:1–11), so he sought to wreck the congregation in Corinth.

Paul's letters and visit were designed to expel the immoral man from the midst of God's people (I Cor. 5:13), but he had not seen any results. He sent Titus to solve the problem, yet in the meantime he himself was filled with uncertainty whether the people in Corinth would heed the words of Titus.

When Paul's emissary returned from Corinth with good news, Paul was not only comforted but also filled with exceedingly great joy. The pendulum swung from despair to delight, so to speak. It is not difficult to picture Paul and Titus talking together about the spiritual climate in Corinth, the offender and his supporters, and the people's repentance. We can imagine Paul's exuberance when, in addition to the initial encouragement he had received, he heard in detail how the Corinthians had come to repentance.

b. *Buoyant spirit.* Titus demonstrated his happiness about the church in Corinth by telling Paul that the people there had been a blessing to him. We know very little of Titus, for in Acts his name never appears. Apart from frequent references to him in II Corinthians, Paul mentions his name in Galatians 2:1 and 3, where he notes that Titus accompanied him and Barnabas to Jerusalem but that he did not have to be circumcised. He addresses Titus as his true son in their common faith (Titus 1:4), and at the end of his life he notes that Titus has gone to Dalmatia (II Tim. 4:10).

Perhaps the first major task Titus faced was to settle the problems in Corinth. Because Paul himself had been unsuccessful in Corinth, the achievement of Titus takes on impressive proportions. By God's grace he had done more than Paul and Timothy combined.

All the people in Corinth had refreshed Titus's spirit, Paul writes. The verb *to refresh* means that conflicts have ceased and peace has returned. The Corinthian community, now at rest, restored the good relations Paul enjoyed when he first founded the church. The members did everything in their power to help Titus in his work and thus refreshed his spirit (compare I Cor. 16:18).

14. For if indeed I boasted somewhat to him about you, you did not embarrass me. However, as we have spoken to you the truth in all things, so also our boasting about you to Titus has come true.

a. "For if indeed I boasted somewhat to him about you, you did not embarrass me." In a simple-fact conditional sentence, Paul reveals his genuine love for the Corinthian believers. Apart from the difficulties he had encountered, he never-

261

theless had praised them somewhat in the presence of Titus (v. 4). This is not so much a favorable reflection on the Corinthians as it is on the attitude of Paul. Commenting on this verse and the next, James Denney describes Paul's demeanor toward the members of the church in Corinth: "[Paul] not only tells the truth *about* them (as Titus has seen), but he always told the truth *to* them. These verses present the character of Paul in an admirable light: not only his sympathy with Titus, but his attitude to the Corinthians, is beautifully Christian."[45]

What an embarrassment it would have been for Paul if the people in Corinth had not followed his apostolic counsel! What a letdown it would have been for Titus if he, too, would have failed. But this was not the case, for the Corinthians indeed had listened to Titus and obeyed Paul's instructions. Therefore, Titus was able to compliment the Corinthians and thank Paul for commending them.

b. "However, as we have spoken to you the truth in all things, so also our boasting about you to Titus has come true." We notice two features in this last part of the text. First, Paul states that he, a servant of Jesus Christ, who is truth (John 14:6), speaks the truth, and that he does so always and in every respect. Next, the Corinthians themselves have proven to be true. As their pastor, Paul knew the spiritual condition of his people. He trusted that they would be true to form: as in the past, so in the present and future. Hence, Paul could boast of them in the presence of Titus before he sent Titus to Corinth. What a joy these words must have been to Titus when he realized that Paul's evaluation of the people in Corinth proved to be accurate. The Corinthians demonstrated their love and faithfulness to Paul and Titus, who were able to praise them in the presence of other churches (8:24).

15. His affection toward you is all the more significant when he remembers the obedience of all of you, for you received him with fear and trembling.

I have translated the Greek word *splanchna* (entrails) "affection," because the Greek-speaking population of Paul's day considered human internal organs to be "the seat and source of love."[46] The word denotes the deepest love that one can express for a fellow human being. Paul puts the degree of Titus's affection to the level that equals the superlative: "all the more significant." He is not making a comparison of a supposedly earlier visit of Titus and the one just completed.[47] There is no evidence of such an earlier visit. Instead we consider Paul's penchant for using superlatives in his epistles and look at a few examples:

"All the more gladly" (12:9)
"I will very gladly" (12:15)
"For I am the least" (I Cor. 15:9)
"I am less than the least" (Eph. 3:8)

---

45. James Denney, *The Second Epistle to the Corinthians,* 2d ed., The Expositor's Bible series (New York: Armstrong, 1900), p. 259.

46. Bauer, p. 763; Helmut Köster, *TDNT,* 7:555; Hans-Helmut Esser, *NIDNTT,* 2:600.

47. Contra Hughes, *Second Epistle to the Corinthians,* p. 294.

Paul frequently enhances his statements by expanding them. Here he thinks about Titus's ministry to the Corinthians that resulted in a bond of mutual love and care. Speaking with him about the church in Corinth, Paul notes that Titus, remembering the people's obedience, speaks all the more fondly of his affection for them.

Titus reports that all the members of the Corinthian church showed their obedience to the teaching of the Scriptures and Paul's apostolic authority. This means that everyone was included in the turnabout of the church. The members had accepted Titus as Paul's representative and had listened attentively to the message of the Scriptures.

The clause "for you received him with fear and trembling" seems out of place in this text. Why would Paul's opponents be afraid of Titus? They had forced Paul to leave Corinth after his painful visit and they could do the same with his representative.

The words *fear and trembling* occur four times in the New Testament and all are in Paul's epistles (I Cor. 2:3; II Cor. 7:15; Eph. 6:5; Phil. 2:12). They convey not the fear and trembling of alarm but rather the apprehension of attempting to do the best one is able to accomplish. When Paul entered Corinth the first time, he was filled with anxiety about whether he would be able to establish a church (I Cor. 2:3). He instructed the Philippians to exert themselves exceedingly with respect to their salvation (Phil. 2:12). And he told slaves to obey their masters as they would obey Christ (Eph. 6:5). In every case, the phrase *fear and trembling* describes the believer's attitude in God's sacred presence. The Christians in Corinth received Titus as God's ambassador who spoke the words God had given him. Their repentance, then, exhibited fear and trembling in the presence of the Almighty and a desire to do his will.

16. I rejoice that I can depend completely on you.

At last, Paul concludes the lengthy discourse that he began at 6:11. He pleaded with the Corinthians to open their hearts to him just as he had shown his love to them (6:13; 7:2). And now at the end of this section, the apostle rejoices with Titus about the news that the members of the Corinthian church have done what he asked them to do.

Notice the many times that Paul writes the words *joy* or *rejoice* in this chapter (vv. 4 and 13 for the noun and vv. 7, 9, 13, 16 for the verb). He expresses his exuberance in joyful tones that without doubt were uplifting to his readers in Corinth. His letter brought them joy and happiness to strengthen their unity in Christ.

The Corinthians demonstrated to Titus their readiness to live obediently in harmony with God's Word proclaimed to them by the apostle and his helpers. For this reason, Paul has confidence in them (v. 4), not in the sense of blind trust in people[48] but in their relation to Christ. As expressed in this concluding verse, Paul's confidence extends through the following two chapters, in which he pleads for monetary gifts for the saints in Jerusalem. He is confident that the

---

48. Héring, *Second Epistle of Paul*, p. 57.

Corinthians, who already have begun to give for this purpose, will bring this work to completion (8:6).[49]

Greek Words, Phrases, and Constructions in 7:13b–15

Verses 7:13b–14

ἐπὶ δέ—with the dative of παρακλήσει (comfort), the preposition signifies "in addition to."

ἐπὶ τῇ χαρᾷ—the preposition with the object *joy* means "on" or "about."

ἀναπέπαυται—note the passive form in the perfect tense ("has been refreshed"). The Corinthians are the agents, and the action of giving Titus peace of mind continues into the present.

ἀπό—agency in Greek grammar is usually expressed with the preposition ὑπό. Writers often interchange these two prepositions.[50]

κεκαύχημαι—the perfect tense denotes that Paul has boasted of the Corinthians and continues to boast.

Verse 15

περισσοτέρως—the comparative as the elative superlative can be expressed as "far greater" or "very great."

ἀναμιμνησκομένου—this present tense participle in the passive voice ("remembering") depends on the genitive case of αὐτοῦ.

μετά—the preposition conveys the idea of accompaniment. That is, the reception Titus received in Corinth was accompanied by fear and trembling.

Summary of Chapter 7

After a brief interlude in which Paul warned the readers not to be yoked to unbelievers, the apostle continues the thought he had expressed in the preceding chapter. There he challenged the Corinthians to a mutual opening of hearts and to demonstrations of love (6:13). Now he repeats this sentiment and tells his readers that he is willing to live or die with them. His confidence in them is so great that there are no limits to his joy.

In the second chapter Paul had mentioned Macedonia and his eagerness to see Titus (v. 13). Here he informs his readers that Titus indeed arrived in Macedonia. This meeting was a source of encouragement to Paul, who heard about the Corinthians' desire to see him, their change of heart, and their concern for him. From the depths of anxiety he reached the heights of joy when he heard Titus's report.

Paul reflects on the letter that caused the Corinthians grief. But he knew that he had to write it, so that they might turn from the error of their way. He was not

---

49. Consult Victor Paul Furnish, *II Corinthians: Translated with Introduction, Notes and Commentary,* Anchor Bible 32A (Garden City, N.Y.: Doubleday, 1984), p. 398.

50. Robertson, *Grammar,* p. 579.

sorry for writing the letter, for its effect became evident when they repented with godly sorrow. The result of their turnabout was that they were eager to mend their ways and prove themselves in God's sight. Their attitude and actions greatly encouraged Paul.

Titus reported that the Corinthians gave him peace of mind. His report filled Paul with joy. The apostle openly admitted that he had boasted about the Corinthians in the presence of Titus. Indeed, his boasts had proven to be true. Their affection for Titus was genuine, as the Christians in Corinth confirmed with their obedience. Paul concludes this chapter by saying that he has great confidence in the Corinthians.

8

The Collection, *part 1*

(8:1–24)

Outline

8

1 And we make known to you, brothers, the grace of God given to the churches of Macedonia, 2 that in much testing due to affliction, their abundant joy and their extreme poverty overflowed into their wealth of generosity. 3 Because I testify that they gave according to their means and beyond their means—on their own accord—4 they begged us earnestly for the privilege of sharing in the service [of helping] the saints. 5 And not just as we had expected [did they do this], but they gave themselves first to the Lord and then to us through the will of God. 6 So we urged Titus that just as he had earlier begun this work of grace, so he might even bring it to completion for you.

7 However, as you excel in everything—in faith, in speech, in knowledge, in all diligence, and in our love for you—see that you excel in this work of grace as well. 8 I do not say this as a command, but I am testing the genuineness of your love even by the diligence of other people. 9 For you know the grace of our Lord Jesus Christ, that though he was rich he became poor on account of you, so that you might become rich through his poverty.

10 And so I am giving you my opinion in this matter, for this is beneficial to you. Since last year you were not only the first to do so but even expressed the desire to do so. 11 But now also complete the work, so that your readiness to desire it may be matched by your completion of it, as your means allow. 12 For if the readiness is there, the gift is acceptable insofar as a person has it, not insofar as he does not have it. 13 For not that others should have relief and you be burdened, but that there be equality. 14 For the present time your surplus is for their deficiency, so that also their surplus is for your deficiency, that there may be equality. 15 Just as it is written, "He who has increased much does not have too much, and he who has less does not have too little."

16 But I thank God who put into the heart of Titus the same eagerness that I have for you. 17 Because he not only accepted our appeal, but being very eager, he also is going out toward you on his own accord. 18 We are sending with him the brother who is praised by all the churches in the service of the gospel. 19 But not only this, he also has been appointed by the churches to be our traveling companion as we administer this gracious work to the glory of the Lord himself and to show our readiness to help. 20 I am trying to avoid this, namely, that anyone might blame us in the way we administer this lavish gift. 21 For we aim to do the right things not only before the Lord but also before men.

22 We are also sending with them our brother whom we often have tested and found eager in many ways, but now much more eager because of his great confidence in you. 23 As for Titus, he is my partner and fellow worker for you. As for our brothers, they are delegates of the churches, [and] the glory of Christ. 24 Therefore, to these men in the presence of the churches, present proof of your love and our pride in you.

III. The Collection
8:1–9:15

Many scholars regard this chapter and the next as two separate letters,[1] and they do so on the basis of content: the ingathering of the gifts for the poor in

---

1. Among others, see Dieter Georgi, *The Opponents of Paul in Second Corinthians* (Philadelphia: Fortress, 1986), p. 17; Hans Dieter Betz, *II Corinthians 8 and 9: A Commentary on Two Administrative Letters of the Apostle Paul*, ed. George W. MacRae, Hermeneia: A Critical and Historical Commentary on the Bible (Philadelphia: Fortress, 1985), pp. 35–36.

Jerusalem. The one letter is addressed specifically to the church in Corinth, the other to Christians at large.

In the opinion of these scholars, the break between chapters 7 and 8 introduces an entirely new subject not discussed earlier. The link between chapter 8 and the preceding one, however, consists of similar vocabulary and theme. For instance, in both chapters Paul mentions

abundant joy (7:4, 7, 13; 8:2);
privilege, comfort, appeal (7:4, 7, 13; 8:4, 17);
earnestness, good will, readiness (7:11, 12; 8:7, 8, 16).

In both chapters, he refers to Titus (7:6, 13, 14; 8:6, 16, 23) and Macedonia (7:5; 8:1) and writes about encouraging one another (7:6, 7, 13; 8:6 [urged]).[2] In addition, chapter 7 contains a number of allusions to the collection for the saints. Although they are not explicit, they are always near the surface (see the commentary on vv. 4, 5, 7, 16). For a full discussion on the unity of II Corinthians, see the Introduction.

Paul had to deal with two sensitive issues: the matter of the offender and the donations to the church in Jerusalem. He wrote about the first issue in chapter 7 and the second one in chapter 8. Before he composed chapter 8, he judiciously laid the groundwork for it in the last segment of the preceding chapter. There Paul expressed his praise for the Corinthians in affectionate wording.[3] The link between these two chapters, therefore, is undeniable as Paul moves from one related subject to another.

A. Generosity Shown
8:1–6

1. And we make known to you, brothers, the grace of God given to the churches of Macedonia.

a. "And we make known to you, brothers." Whenever Paul discusses a sensitive issue with the Corinthians, he writes the word *brothers,* which in those days included the sisters in the congregation. The topic he wishes to discuss has to do with money. Apart from his remarks about the collection for the poor in Jerusalem in his first epistle (I Cor. 16:1–4), Paul has not yet mentioned this matter again. No wonder! Matthew Henry rightfully observes, "How cautious ministers should be, especially in money-matters, not to give occasion to those who seek occasion to speak reproachfully!"[4]

---

2. Compare Nils A. Dahl, *Studies in Paul: Theology for the Early Christian Message* (Minneapolis: Augsburg, 1977), pp. 38–39.

3. Refer to Hans Lietzmann, *An die Korinther I/II,* augmented by Werner G. Kümmel, Handbuch zum Neuen Testament 9 (Tübingen: Mohr, 1969), p. 133.

4. Matthew Henry, *Matthew Henry's Commentary on the Whole Bible,* 6 vols., *Acts to Revelation* (New York: Revell, n.d.), vol. 6, p. 629.

The act of making something known to the Corinthians in this instance is not a divine revelation but rather a report presented by the apostle. Elsewhere in the Old and New Testaments, the verb *to make known* discloses a proclamation of God's will (e.g., Ps. 16:11; Rom. 9:23). But here Paul is about to begin a discussion on the matter of raising funds for the mother church in Jerusalem. The Corinthians were not unfamiliar with the issue, so the apostle reminds them of his earlier instructions and gives them further details.

Paul's instructions for the ingathering of money for the church in Jerusalem were not confined to a certain locale. They were made known to all the churches in Asia Minor, Macedonia, and Greece. For example, Paul gave the churches in Galatia the same directions that he gave in Corinth (I Cor. 16:1). He informed the church in Rome that the churches in Macedonia and Achaia had donated money for the poor among the saints in Jerusalem (Rom. 15:25–26). And last, Paul revealed that he indeed delivered these gifts to the poor in that city (Acts 24:17).

When Paul received Titus's positive report concerning the Corinthians' attitude toward the apostle, he also heard that the church had not progressed at all in the matter of collecting gifts for the saints in Jerusalem. Time had slipped away because of the controversy about the offender. Also, false teachers were spreading rumors that Paul was using the collection for himself (2:17; 11:7; 12:14). The time had come to set the record straight, and thus Paul depicts the Macedonian churches as a model and an incentive for the Corinthians.

b. "The grace of God given to the churches of Macedonia." In his letters to the church in Corinth, Paul frequently pens the phrase *the grace of God* (with variations).[5] The phrase has various meanings that depend on the context in which it is used, and the setting here indicates that Paul is referring not to God's saving grace but to the consequence of that grace. To be precise, he has in mind the willingness of the recipients of God's grace to give generously to alleviate the physical needs of fellow saints (vv. 2–9). Grace is God's gift that makes participation in the collection possible and real; and it results in a demonstration of Christian love as a response to Paul's ministry.[6] Although helping the poor is commendable, not everyone is ready to do so, as John Calvin observes: "All men do not consider it a gain to give, nor do they ascribe it to God's grace."[7]

The three churches Paul founded in Macedonia were those in Philippi, Thessalonica, and Berea (Acts 16:12–40; 17:1–12). Of these congregations, the one in Philippi repeatedly sent financial aid to Paul while he was in Thessalonica and later when he was under house arrest in Rome (Phil. 4:16–18). Notice that Paul

5. I Cor. 1:4; 3:10; 15:10 [three times]; 16:23; II Cor. 1:12; 6:1; 8:1, 9; 9:14; 12:9; 13:13.

6. Consult Keith F. Nickle, *The Collection: A Study in Paul's Strategy*, SBT 48 (Naperville: Allenson, 1966), pp. 109–10.

7. John Calvin, *The Second Epistle of Paul the Apostle to the Corinthians and the Epistles to Timothy, Titus and Philemon*, Calvin's Commentaries series, trans. T. A. Small (Grand Rapids: Eerdmans, 1964), p. 106.

states that God had given his grace to the Macedonian churches to make them willing to help others in need. That is, not the churches but God receives the honor and praise. The churches merely do the work God requires of them. Through the apostolic preaching of the gospel, believers were exhorted to show Christian love to all people, especially to the members of God's household (Gal. 6:10). By making God the implied agent for the giving of grace, Paul skillfully avoids arousing intense competition between the churches in Macedonia and in Corinth. Yet he stirs them to action.

In the epistolary literature of the New Testament, writers never refer to money as a source of income for themselves. They mention gifts, but never in the form of silver or gold (vv. 12, 20; Phil. 4:17; James 1:17). They comply with Jesus' command: "Do not take along any gold or silver or copper in your belts; . . . for the worker is worth his keep" (Matt. 10:9–10).

2. That in much testing due to affliction, their abundant joy and their extreme poverty overflowed into their wealth of generosity.

a. *Trials.* "In much testing due to affliction." The emphasis in this clause is on the word *affliction,* and the New Testament relates some of the afflictions the churches in Macedonia had to endure. For example, Paul's preaching the gospel in Thessalonica stirred up the Jews against those who converted to Christianity. The Jews then dragged Jason and his fellow Christians before the city officials, who told the Christians to post bond (Acts 17:1–9). In a subsequent letter to the believers in Thessalonica, Paul observes that they suffered from their own people, just as the churches in Judea suffered from the Jews (I Thess. 2:14; 3:3–4; II Thess. 1:4). But apart from Paul being dragged before the tribunal of Proconsul Gallio in Corinth (Acts 18:12), persecution of the Corinthians was unknown. Paul's words, therefore, convey a hint of comparison that should not have escaped the observant Corinthian readers.

Even though persecution had not been the lot of the people in Corinth, they nonetheless had experienced a degree of testing. They were tested when an offender had insulted Paul and when the apostle's opponents were disseminating false rumors concerning his instructions. In an earlier chapter, Paul wanted to test the members of the church in Corinth to see whether they would be obedient in spiritual matters (2:9). Yet the affliction they endured derived more from moral problems than from brute force.

b. *Contrast.* "Their abundant joy and their extreme poverty overflowed into their wealth of generosity." The Macedonians knew that during their severe suffering the Lord never failed them; as a result, their joy in him was boundless (I Thess. 1:6). Suffering produces abundant joy, as the apostles were able to testify when they were flogged by order of the Sanhedrin (Acts 5:41; see also Matt. 5:12).

The contrast that Paul introduces is not one of riches and poverty but rather one of abundant joy and extreme poverty. Affliction results in joy, and joy and poverty result in a wealth of generosity.

Two centuries before Paul came to Macedonia, gold mines in that province provided a measure of wealth for its population. But during the first century of the

Christian era, the economy had deteriorated, and the province was brought to the depths of poverty. Wars, barbarian invasions, Roman settlement, and the restructuring of the province had contributed to a dismal financial status. Not only the countryside but also the urban centers, including "the Romanized cities of Philippi, Thessalonica, and Beroea," were impoverished.[8] Conversely, the city of Corinth flourished financially because of the volume of trade that its two harbors, Cenchrea and Lechaeum, generated. In brief, there was a distinct difference between Macedonia and Corinth in economic terms. Paul alludes to this contrast.

Despite their poverty, the Macedonians were lavish in their giving. To describe their giving, Paul uses the Greek word *haplotēs*, which is best translated "generosity" in the sense of reflecting the unity of the body of Christ (see 9:11, 13; Rom. 12:8).[9] The word portrays singleness of heart and undivided simplicity. In this context it expresses an overarching unity of the church: the churches in Macedonia are sending their gifts to the poverty-stricken saints in Jerusalem. With this Greek word, Paul verbalizes his joy in seeing the unity of the universal church in which Gentile Christians show their loving care to their Jewish counterparts in Jerusalem.

When Paul writes "the wealth of their generosity," he is not thinking of material riches. The word *wealth* should be understood spiritually, as a few verses taken from the Pauline epistolary show:

"the riches of his kindness" (Rom. 2:4)
"the riches of his glory" (Rom. 9:23)
"the riches of God's grace" (Eph. 1:7)
"the full riches of complete understanding" (Col. 2:2)

Paul sees riches in relation to Jesus Christ and the work of redemption. He rejoices when the word of Christ dwells richly in the hearts and the lives of believers (Col. 3:16).[10] And this is what he observed in the Macedonian churches.

3. Because I testify that they gave according to their means and beyond their means—on their own accord.

This short verse is incomplete because it lacks the main verb *they gave;* the verb must be taken from verse 5 to complement the clauses *according to their means* and *beyond their means.*

As is evident in many translations, the verse division is infelicitous. The phrase *on their own accord* stands between verses 3 and 4 as an aside, and the reader has the option to connect it with what precedes or follows. The words *I testify* are a parenthetical remark and make the sentence itself concise.

Paul indicates that he had observed the overwhelming generosity of the Macedonian Christians. He had acquainted them with the material needs of the

---

8. Betz, *II Corinthians 8 and 9,* p. 50.

9. Otto Bauernfeind, *TDNT,* 1:387; Burkhard Gärtner, *NIDNTT,* 3:572.

10. Refer to Friedrich Hauck and Wilhelm Kasch, *TDNT,* 6:328–29; Friedel Selter, *NIDNTT,* 2:844.

believers in Jerusalem and they had responded enthusiastically to his report. As an eyewitness, he noticed their readiness to contribute to the funds set aside for the needs of the poor. Even though they themselves belonged to the impoverished class of society, they gave as much as they were able, and even beyond. In his further instructions on this point, Paul writes: "Let each one give as he has decided in his mind to give, not reluctantly or out of necessity. For God loves a cheerful giver" (9:7).

Without any prompting by Paul or his associates, the Macedonians were ready to give. Spontaneity sparked both their desire to give and their plea to share in the service to the saints in Jerusalem. In a succeeding verse, Paul writes that what they did was in harmony with God's will (v. 5). By his Word and Spirit, God opened their hearts so that they reacted magnanimously.

4. They begged us earnestly for the privilege of sharing in the service [of helping] the saints. 5. And not just as we had expected [did they do this], but they gave themselves first to the Lord and then to us through the will of God.

a. "They begged us earnestly for the privilege of sharing in the service [of helping] the saints." We presume that Paul, knowing the poverty of the Macedonians, mentioned to them the dire needs of the church in Jerusalem. He also taught them that the saints in that city had shared spiritual blessings with them in the form of Christ's gospel. They were indebted to those saints who had sent Paul and others to them with the Good News (see Rom. 15:26–27).[11] Their reaction—an ardent plea to be allowed to share their material blessings with the needy people in Jerusalem—touched Paul deeply. As recent converts to the Christian faith, the Macedonians responded beyond everyone's expectation.

Note that verse 4 is composed of four theological concepts: privilege, sharing, service, and saints. These four concepts promote the unity of Christ's universal church in both the first century and our modern times. We shall examine and comment on each concept.

1. *Privilege.* Spiritual life in Christ motivated the churches in Macedonia to implore Paul and his associates for the privilege of giving from their material resources to the church in Jerusalem. The Greek word *charis* (privilege) refers to the act of giving, not to the gift itself.[12] Just as God gives good gifts to his children (Matt. 7:11; Luke 11:13), so the Macedonians freely give of their possessions to the needy and consider their giving a privilege.

2. *Sharing.* The act of giving is closely connected with sharing one's possessions, except for differences in nuance: sharing is the consequence of the privilege; sharing implies fellowship with Christ and one another; and sharing denotes unity and mutuality.[13] Commenting on the collection that took place

---

11. Compare Simon J. Kistemaker, *Exposition of the First Epistle to the Corinthians*, New Testament Commentary series (Grand Rapids: Baker, 1993), p. 593.

12. Consult Gordon D. Fee, "ΧΑΡΙΣ in II Corinthians I.15: Apostolic Parousia and Paul-Corinth Chronology," *NTS* 24 (1977–78): 536.

13. Among others, consult Nickle, *The Collection*, pp. 105–6, 122–25.

among the believers in Macedonia and Achaia, Paul writes that "they owe it to the Jews [in Jerusalem] to share with them their material blessings" (Rom. 15:27). Sharing material and spiritual blessings is a mark of the true church and a vivid demonstration of living Christianity.

3. *Service.* Paul uses the familiar Greek term *diakonia* for "service." Being part of the church is neither having one's name on the roll nor attaining a perfect attendance record. It is participation by reaching out to others in Christian love and by helping each other in humble service to the Lord (John 13:14–17). Helping a fellow human being promotes the unity of the church and illustrates the application of one of the Spirit's gifts (I Cor. 12:28).[14]

4. *Saints.* The New Testament is replete with the expression *saints;* especially in Paul's epistles this word occurs frequently and applies to all Christians of both Jewish and Gentile origin. Here it applies to those Christians in Jerusalem who were living in abject poverty. They had endured persecution (Acts 8:1), years of famine (Acts 11:27–30), social turmoil, and political instability. All these factors had contributed directly and indirectly to the poverty of the saints in the mother church. Earlier Paul had explicitly noted that the collection was meant for Jerusalem (I Cor. 16:1–3), so that at present he has no need to mention the name of the city again.[15] Also, caring for the poor, including those in Jerusalem, was an apostolic directive (Gal. 2:10).

b. "And not just as we had expected [did they do this]." In this text we see a role reversal. We normally expect the person who solicits funds to plead with a prospective donor to support a cause. But here the donors were petitioning Paul to allow them to help the poor. This plea from the Macedonians demonstrates a genuine desire to help.

c. "But they gave themselves first to the Lord and then to us through the will of God." Had the Macedonians responded by donating a certain amount, Paul would have been thankful. But they went beyond all expectations. The enthusiasm that they displayed in their giving was directed first to the Lord. He was the recipient of their gratitude for the spiritual gifts they had received from him. Realizing that Paul and his co-workers had brought them Christ's gospel, the Macedonians directed their fervor also toward them. They yielded themselves to the Lord and his servants. The apostle and his aides gave themselves completely to the Macedonians to present a perfect model of mutual service: the members dedicate themselves to serving the apostle, and he also gives himself to them without reserve.[16]

Paul writes, "through the will of God." With this phrase, he expresses the thought that the Macedonians submitted themselves completely to the Lord and to the apostles.[17] Nothing happens apart from God's will, so that the giving of

---

14. SB 3:316–18.

15. Compare Hans Windisch, *Der Zweite Korintherbrief,* ed. Georg Strecker (1924; reprint ed., Göttingen: Vandenhoeck und Ruprecht, 1970), p. 246.

16. F. J. Pop, *De Tweede Brief van Paulus aan de Corinthiërs* (Nijkerk: Callenbach, 1980), p. 241.

17. Refer to Gottlob Schrenk, *TDNT,* 3:59.

gifts by the Macedonians was through his divine will. We know that God reveals his will through the Scriptures and the preaching of the gospel (compare 1:1). He is in full control as he leads and guides his people to live a life of thankfulness.

The closer in fellowship Christians are to the Lord, the more they show their love toward each other. They must make Jesus Christ central in their lives, so that he may receive honor, praise, and glory. But is it correct for Paul to place himself and his colleagues on a level equal to that of the Lord? In a sense the apostle is correct. Christ performs his work through his servants who proclaim the gospel, and he does so by delegating his authority to them.

6. So we urged Titus that just as he had earlier begun this work of grace, so he might even bring it to completion for you.

In the Greek, Paul writes one long sentence that comprises verses 3 through 6. For translation purposes, we divide the sentence into separate verses and are forced to add a word here and there (vv. 4 and 5) to achieve a smooth rendering.[18]

Translators also differ on paragraph divisions within this section. Older translations have no divisions at all; others place the break at the end of verse 7. Still others begin a new paragraph at either verse 6 or verse 7. Because Paul ends his lengthy sentence at verse 6, I have chosen to bring the paragraph to a close at this text.

The information Paul provides is revealing. He tells his readers that when Titus visited them in Corinth, he had begun the work of the collection. And in a subsequent passage, the apostle notes that a year earlier the Corinthians were willing to give to this cause (v. 10). This information suggests that Titus had visited Corinth more than once. Prior to his peace-keeping mission, Titus must have been in Corinth to promote the cause of the collection. In the interim, the matter of collecting money for the poverty-stricken saints in Jerusalem had come to a standstill (see the comments on v. 1).

Nowhere else do we read about the labors of Titus, yet we know that he was a long-time associate of Paul (see Gal. 2:1) and an able assistant. He probably delivered I Corinthians and other letters to Corinth.[19]

a. "So we urged Titus." The verb *to urge* at times conveys a negative idea, which in this verse would mean that Titus was disheartened and needed to be prodded to action. But this is not the case, for Paul was greatly encouraged by Titus's report (7:4–7). Here the verb in question has a positive connotation. When Paul and Titus talked about the Corinthian church, they also touched on the collection for the saints. Titus remarked that this matter had been shelved because of the turmoil in the congregation. But when peace had returned, Paul encouraged Titus to return to Corinth and advance the matter of giving. Pointing to the

---

18. For a syntactical study of these verses, see Norbert Baumert, "Brüche im paulinischen Satzbau," *FilolNT* 4 (1991): 5–7.

19. Refer to Philip Edgcumbe Hughes, *Paul's Second Epistle to the Corinthians: The English Text with Introduction, Exposition and Notes,* New International Commentary on the New Testament series (Grand Rapids: Eerdmans, 1962), pp. xvii, 293–94.

splendid example of the Macedonians, the apostle urged his colleague to take up the matter again with the Corinthians when he returned.

b. "Just as he had earlier begun this work of grace." We assume that the reference to an earlier occasion pertains to the time when the Corinthians read Paul's first major epistle, in which he instructs the people to set aside weekly their gifts for the poor (I Cor. 16:1–3).

What is "this work of grace"? Ralph P. Martin gives a succinct description by saying, "'Grace' is the activity inspired by God's grace that leads to giving."[20] In this chapter, the act of giving is mentioned repeatedly (vv. 4, 6, 7, 19) and alludes to the collection.

c. "So he might even bring it to completion for you." Paul encourages not only Titus but also the Corinthians to complete the task of giving. Paul writes literally, "so he might also complete for you also this grace," a construction that is awkward in our parlance. Even if we eliminate one "also" to achieve a smooth translation, we still have to provide an explanation for this word. In view of the word order in the Greek, we see that the emphasis is on "this grace." Hence, the conjunction *also* is assensive and means "even." That is, in addition to all the work Titus has performed in Corinth, he will *even* complete the task of gathering the gifts.

The wording *for you* does not mean that Titus will do all the work for the Corinthians, for they themselves are personally involved. Perhaps we should say, "with reference to you," which then includes the people in Corinth.

One last remark. The Jewish religious hierarchy in Jerusalem levied a temple tax on all the Jews living in dispersion. This tax was collected annually and sent to the holy city. But we cannot equate the collection for the poor in Jerusalem with a temple tax, for we lack confirmation that the mother church initiated this collection. It was Paul's idea to raise the funds for the poor and thus strengthen and promote the unity of the Jewish and Gentile churches.

Practical Considerations in 8:3–5

Paul writes that the Christians in Macedonia were so generous that, even though they were extremely poor, they gave "even beyond their ability" (8:3). But elsewhere Paul says, "Owe no one anything, except to love one another" (Rom. 13:8, NRSV). Are his instructions to the Christians contradictory? No, not really, for the sentiment expressed harmonizes with what Jesus told the rich young ruler: "If you want to be perfect, go, sell your possessions and give to the poor, and you will have treasure in heaven. Then come, follow me" (Matt. 19:21). The words of Jesus do not mean that Christians are urged to give of their resources until they go into debt. The rich young ruler coveted material wealth more than spiritual riches. Thus, he went away sad because he chose money above following the Lord.

The New Testament fails to mention tithing in Christian communities. No percentages are ever cited, for the Lord wants his people to show him their love and faithfulness.

---

20. Ralph P. Martin, *II Corinthians*, Word Biblical Commentary 40 (Waco: Word, 1986), p. 255.

Giving must be an act of joyful gratitude to him, "for God loves a cheerful giver" (9:7). Our giving must be free from mechanical or obligatory rules. Instead, it should be characterized by generosity that emanates from our joy in the Lord. This is how the Christians in Macedonia demonstrated their love: by giving beyond their ability.

Greek Words, Phrases, and Constructions in 8:1–6

Verses 1–2

ἐν ταῖς ἐκκλησίαις—the preposition literally means "in," but here it has the force of an indirect object with the translation to the churches.[21]

θλίψεως—this is the subjective genitive with a causal connotation: "testing because of affliction."

κατὰ βάθους—the preposition signifies "down to the depth," that is, "extreme poverty."

Verses 3–4

αὐθαίρετοι—"on their own accord." The compound consists of the intensive pronoun αὐτός (self) and αἱρέω (I choose); that is, I myself choose. The verbal adjective occurs only here in the New Testament and many times in other literature.

εἰς τοὺς ἁγίους—this phrase, "to the saints," is supplemented with the words δέξασθαι ἡμᾶς (that we might receive) in some minuscule manuscripts. The supplement is a gloss,[22] yet it is part of two translations (KJV, NKJV).

Verses 5–6

ἑαυτούς—note the emphatic position of this personal pronoun in the setting of the sentence.

πρῶτον—"first" followed by καί should be interpreted to mean "first and foremost to the Lord and also to us."

εἰς τὸ παρακαλέσαι—the preposition with the articular infinitive conveys result instead of purpose.[23]

B. Advice Given
8:7–15

Refusing even to be remunerated for his pastoral work in Corinth, Paul wanted to be free from any financial bonds. Being free, he was able to advise the Corinthians to give generously. Thus, he exhorted them to excel in giving spontaneously and to look to Jesus, who became poor so that they might become rich

---

21. Consult C. F. D. Moule, *An Idiom-Book of New Testament Greek*, 2d ed. (Cambridge: Cambridge University Press, 1960), p. 76.

22. See Bruce M. Metzger, *The Text of the New Testament: Its Transmission, Corruption, and Restoration* (New York and London: Oxford University Press, 1964), p. 194.

23. Richard A. Young, *Intermediate New Testament Greek: A Linguistic and Exegetical Approach* (Nashville: Broadman and Holman, 1994), p. 171; A. T. Robertson, *A Grammar of the Greek New Testament in the Light of Historical Research* (Nashville: Broadman, 1934), pp. 1003, 1072, 1090; Moule, *Idiom-Book*, p. 141.

1. Excel in Giving
8:7–9

7. However, as you excel in everything—in faith, in speech, in knowledge, in all diligence, and in our love for you—see that you excel in this work of grace as well.

a. "However, as you excel in everything." Pastoral care must be based on wisdom and tact, which Paul relies on as he seeks to encourage the recipients of this letter in their giving. He refrains from giving the impression that the Macedonians are superior to the Corinthians. He avoids commanding his readers to participate in the collection. Instead, he praises them for their record of excellence in many areas—in fact, Paul purposely writes that they excelled in everything, so that also with respect to the collection they might excel. He demonstrates the art of motivating people by addressing them positively and by pointing out their virtues (compare I Cor. 1:4–7). He lists five areas in which the readers surpass others.

b. "In faith, in speech, in knowledge." What comes to mind immediately is the list of spiritual gifts in Paul's first canonical letter to the Corinthians (I Cor. 12:8–10). In this verse, however, faith is not a creedal statement but trust in God whereby proverbial mountains can be moved (Matt. 17:20). Faith that works miracles seems to have been more evident in Corinth than elsewhere.[24]

The Corinthians were also blessed with the gifts of speech and knowledge (I Cor. 1:5) by which they demonstrated their faith. Indeed, the gifts of faith, speech, and knowledge form a triad. The Corinthians excelled in communicating the message of salvation as spiritual knowledge. With their mouths they proclaimed the spiritual knowledge that they believed in their hearts (see Rom. 10:10).

c. "In all diligence, and in our love for you." The Greek word is *spoudē*, which I have translated "diligence," occurs twice in Romans (12:8, 11) and five times in II Corinthians (7:11, 12; 8:7, 8, 16). With respect to this verse, Paul accentuates the word by modifying it with the adjective *all*.

The gifts of faith, speech, knowledge, and diligence are nothing without love, as Paul teaches in his letter of love (I Cor. 13:1–3). For this reason, love appears last in this series of five strengths. This, then, is a subtle reminder of the indispensability of love.

The Greek text of verse 7 shows two readings, either "in your love for us" or "in our love for you." Most translators adopt the first reading in view of the thought sequence within the verse. It is difficult to accept the second reading, for Paul cannot praise the Corinthians for love they have received from him. However, the second reading is the more difficult and is probably the original text. Some scholars, therefore, add a verb to the clause to clarify its meaning. For instance, one translation reads, "in the love you learned from us" (NCV).

---

24. Compare Hughes, *Second Epistle to the Corinthians*, p. 296.

d. "See that you excel in this work of grace as well." As a tactful pastor, Paul adds to the five qualities in which the readers excel the matter of the collection. He calls it "this work of grace." And he wants his readers to remember that the Macedonians begged him for the privilege of participating in this work of grace (v. 4). So, the Corinthians also should see it as a privilege. The repetition of the verb *to excel* was not accidental; it was written for the purpose of stimulating the Corinthians to act.

8. I do not say this as a command, but I am testing the genuineness of your love even by the diligence of other people.

Apostolic authority, for Paul, was embodied in the Scriptures and Christ's gospel but was never exercised on the basis of his own opinion. Whenever the topic under discussion demands his personal response, he offers advice but never a command. To illustrate, I note Paul's discussion of the sensitive topic of conjugal relations. He writes that he makes a concession but does not command (I Cor. 7:6, and see 25). Similarly, he now addresses the sensitive matter of the readers donating some of their resources. Thus he calls them to relinquish part of their earthly possessions. But he puts the Corinthians at ease when he openly states that he is not issuing a command. Nonetheless, Paul acts in accordance with a request of the apostles in Jerusalem to remember the poor (Gal. 2:10).

In response to a question the Corinthians earlier asked in a letter to him, Paul instructed them how to arrange a schedule for the collection (I Cor. 16:1–3). But even then he refused to command the Corinthians to donate money. "He nowhere lays it down how much we ought to give, . . . but simply bids us be guided by the rule of love."[25]

The apostle wants to ascertain that the readers' conduct proves the genuineness of their love.[26] He desires to be proud of the Corinthians, so that he can boast about them to the other churches. This genuine love is for Paul the norm that he sets for all the churches and that he expects the congregation in Corinth to follow. Although Paul deems comparison necessary, he excludes rivalry among the churches by adopting the genuineness of love as a norm. His letter of love speaks eloquently of love that bans all envy, boasting, pride, and self-seeking (I Cor. 13:4–5). Love is always positive and serves as a model to be emulated. Here Paul wants to give his approval to the Corinthians as they express their love not to him but to the needy saints in Jerusalem.

There is a comparison in the phrases *the genuineness of your love* and *the diligence of other people*. Genuineness and diligence are the two sides of a coin that represent excellence; the first one is the norm and the second a striving to reach that norm. In addition, Paul's emphatic use of the pronoun *your* is contrasted with the term *other*. With this comparison, Paul is exhorting the Corinthians to prove genuine love by giving generously, just as others have demonstrated their love for poverty-stricken Christians.

---

25. Calvin, *II Corinthians*, p. 110.
26. Bauer, p. 202; Walter Grundmann, *TDNT*, 2:259.

9. For you know the grace of our Lord Jesus Christ, that though he was rich he became poor on account of you, so that you might become rich through his poverty.

Note the following points:

a. *Knowledge.* "For you know the grace of our Lord Jesus Christ." The first word, "for," links this verse to the preceding text and provides a clarification. Paul points his readers not to the churches in Macedonia but to Jesus Christ. He does so by saying, "you know," which means that they had personally experienced and had come to know the grace that Jesus grants. Indeed, they were able to talk from experience and testify to that knowledge. They belonged to Jesus Christ and received from him untold spiritual and material blessings.

"The grace of our Lord Jesus Christ" is a liturgical formula that concludes many of Paul's epistles.[27] Here the focus is on the word *grace,* which encompasses the full implication of our salvation (see 6:1) proclaimed in the Good News. Grace includes the message of Jesus' death and resurrection, Christ's atoning work, peace with God, remission of sin, and the Lord's abiding presence (Matt. 28:20). Grace means that we can fully rely on Jesus Christ as our redeemer, brother, friend, and intercessor.

As the Corinthians receive divine grace, so they ought to demonstrate grace to others. They must be a channel through which God's grace reaches others. They do so with respect to the grace of giving from their material resources to help the needy.

With the possessive personal pronoun *our,* Paul indicates that he and the readers are one in the Lord. Together they acknowledge him as their Lord and master in all areas of life. The divine names in the liturgical formula point, first, to Jesus' earthly ministry and, next, to Christ's title and office in his redemptive task of prophet, priest, and king. The Lord Jesus Christ freely grants his grace to all his people, and he expects them to reflect his grace in their daily lives.

b. *Cause.* "That though he was rich he became poor on account of you." Paul gives an explanation of the grace that the Lord Jesus Christ grants to his people. He presents this explanation as a creedal statement that belonged to the liturgy in a worship service. It also echoes Paul's wording of an early Christian hymn on the status and work of Christ Jesus:

> Who, being in very nature God,
> did not consider equality with God
> something to be grasped,
> but made himself nothing,
> taking the very nature of a servant,
> being made in human likeness.
> [Phil. 2:6–7]

---

27. See Rom. 16:20, 24; I Cor. 16:23; II Cor. 13:14; Gal. 6:18; Phil. 4:23; I Thess. 5:28; II Thess. 3:18; Philem. 25.

With other New Testament writers, Paul teaches the pre-existence of Jesus Christ with the statement *though he was rich*. The riches of Christ point not to his earthly existence but to his pre-existent state: God's Son radiates divine glory, for he is the exact representation of God himself (Heb. 1:3). In his high-priestly prayer, Jesus asked his Father to glorify him with the glory he had before the creation of the world (John 17:5). Even in human form Jesus revealed his glory as the unique Son of God (John 1:14, 18).

Jesus Christ became poor because of you, writes Paul to the Corinthians. But what is the meaning of the expression *he became poor?* Did he identify with those who are economically deprived? Yes, he did with his statement, "Foxes have holes and birds of the air have nests, but the Son of Man has no place to lay his head" (Matt. 8:20). But during his earthly ministry Jesus did not shun the rich. He dined in their homes, counseled the rich young ruler, and was "with the rich in his death" (Isa. 53:9). Did he relate only to the poor in spirit, the meek who are called the blessed ones? No, because his disciples John and James, whom he called "sons of thunder," were far from meek and lowly (Luke 9:54). They wanted to sit at his left and right in the kingdom (Matt. 20:21).

Paul contrasts the riches of Christ before Jesus' birth with the poverty of human existence during his earthly life. It is the dissimilarity of leaving the holiness and glory of heaven to enter the profanity and poverty of earth. It is God's indescribable gift (9:15) to send his Son to be born, suffer, and die for sinners.

> Mild he lays his glory by,
> Born that man no more may die,
> Born to raise the sons of earth,
> Born to give them second birth.
> —Charles Wesley

The writer of the Epistle to the Hebrews teaches that Jesus Christ partook of our humanity to destroy the devil and to deliver his people who were held in the bondage by the fear of death (2:14–15). Paul applies this same teaching directly to the Corinthians and states that Jesus became poor for them. Because of their sins and ours, Jesus voluntarily laid aside his heavenly glory. He became a human being while remaining divine (Rom. 1:3–4). He became materially poor while he remained spiritually rich. He became a debtor to God by being our sinbearer (5:21; Isa. 53:6), yet he himself remained sinless.[28] He assumed our humanity to conquer death for us, and by his resurrection he promises us that we, too, will rise from the dead (I Cor. 15:21–22).

c. *Result.* "So that you might become rich through his poverty." Paul's teaching is not meant to induce Christians to try to emulate Christ by giving up material possessions to gain spiritual riches. The redemptive work of Christ can never

---

28. William Hendriksen, *Exposition of Philippians,* New Testament Commentary series (Grand Rapids: Baker, 1962), p. 108; Jerome Murphy-O'Connor, *The Theology of the Second Letter to the Corinthians,* New Testament Theology series (Cambridge: Cambridge University Press, 1991), p. 83.

be duplicated, for if this were possible, Jesus would no longer be our Lord and Savior (Luke 2:11). Through his suffering, death, and resurrection, we are heirs and co-heirs with him (Rom. 8:17). We are children of the light, filled with joy and happiness, and partakers of his glory. Through Christ's death on the cross, we have "become the righteousness of God" (5:21). We already are spiritually rich in this life and rich beyond comparison in the world to come.

If, then, the Corinthians are rich in Christ, they should express their love and thankfulness to him by helping the needy saints in Judea. Paul's theological message should inspire all believers everywhere to be generous in their giving to alleviate the needs of the poor.[29]

Practical Considerations in 8:7–9

The Gospels depict Jesus entering the world in abject poverty: in a stable because there was no room in the inn (Luke 2:7). During his ministry he had no place to lay his head (Matt. 8:20). He had to borrow material possessions for his own purposes: a boat, a donkey, and an upper room. Soldiers disrobed him at his crucifixion and divided his clothes by casting lots (Luke 23:34).

Conversely, wise men brought expensive gifts of gold, incense, and myrrh to Jesus (Matt. 2:11). During his ministry, he received support from prominent women (Luke 8:3), and he wore a seamless coat woven from top to bottom. At his death, he was embalmed with seventy-five pounds of spices and was buried in a new tomb (John 19:23, 39–40, 41).

Does Jesus teach that if we endure poverty, we are blessed, and if we possess riches, we are cursed? On the one hand, we answer this question in the affirmative. If we set our heart on earthly riches, our desires cause us to promote our ruin and destruction (I Tim. 6:9). Luke stresses poverty instead of earthly riches. In the song of Mary we read that God "has filled the hungry with good things, but has sent the rich away empty" (Luke 1:53). Jesus teaches a beatitude on the poor and, by contrast, a curse on the rich (Luke 6:20, 24). And he portrays poor Lazarus at the side of Abraham in heaven and the rich man agonizing in hell (Luke 16:19–31).

On the other hand, the gospel is for all people: the rich and the poor alike. Joseph of Arimathea and Nicodemus, both prosperous, were among Jesus' followers. Well-to-do tax collectors, Matthew and Zaccheus, were converted (Luke 5:27–29; 19:1–9), for Jesus came not to call the righteous but sinners to repentance. With the parable of the two debtors, he characterized Simon the Pharisee and the sinful woman as being indebted to God (Luke 7:36–50). Both the rich and the poor must accept Jesus Christ in repentance and faith and submit themselves to him in lifelong obedience.

Greek Words, Phrases, and Constructions in 8:7–9

Verse 7

ἡμῶν ἐν ὑμῖν—"from us in you." This reading has a {C} rating in UBS[4] and the support of manuscripts including P[46], B, 1739, and others. The variant ὑμῶν ἐν ἡμῖν (from you

---

29. Refer to Fred B. Craddock, "The Poverty of Christ: An Investigation of II Corinthians 8:9," *Interp* 22 (1968): 158–70; Eduard Lohse, "Das Evangelium für die Armen," *ZNTW* 72 (1981): 51–64; David Murchie, "The New Testament View of Wealth Accumulation," *JETS* 21 (1978): 335–44.

in us) has these witnesses: ℵ, C, D, and others. Writes Bruce M. Metzger, "the reading . . . had very wide circulation in the early church."[30]

ἵνα . . . περισσεύητε—this purpose clause with ἵνα and the present subjunctive is equivalent to an imperative, "see that you excel."[31]

Verses 8–9

δοκιμάζων—the present participle denotes progressive action. The verb to test signifies proving or approving someone.

γινώσκετε—this verb form at the beginning of a sentence could be either indicative or imperative. The context calls for the indicative. Also, the verb γινώσκειν (to know) conveys experiential, not innate, knowledge.

ἐπτώχευσεν—the ingressive aorist points to Jesus' humble birth: "he became poor." Likewise, the aorist in πλουτήσητε (that you may become rich) is ingressive.

ὑμεῖς . . . ἐκείνου—the use of these two pronouns means emphasis and contrast.

---

2. Finish the Work
8:10–12

10. And so I am giving you my opinion in this matter, for this is beneficial to you. Since last year you were not only the first to do so but even expressed the desire to do so.

a. "And so I am giving you my opinion in this matter." Dealing with the sensitive matter of giving, Paul refrains from issuing a command (see v. 8) but instead offers his own opinion while he is guided by the Holy Spirit. He does the same thing when he advises virgins and widows (I Cor. 7:25, 40). No one is able to accuse Paul of lacking tact, for on this topic his words are well chosen and wise.

b. "For this is beneficial to you." The question is whether Paul's opinion or the Corinthians' participation in the collection is beneficial. The second option is preferred: When the people in Corinth take part in the ingathering, they will receive a rich blessing. Paul's advice is the means to the end, and the end is of greater importance than the means. Not the form of the advice but its content is significant.[32]

c. "Since last year you were not only the first to do so but even expressed the desire to do so." The grammar of the Greek text is involved, but its meaning is transparent. Paul mentions an indication of time (last year), an initial response (you were the first), a matter of involvement (to do), and a willingness to act (the desire to do so).

The reference to time presents a number of problems, because the words *last year* can mean no more than a few months. For instance, we use the term in the months of January or February of a given year for the month of December of the previous year. But we can use it also in December to refer to February

---

30. Bruce M. Metzger, *A Textual Commentary on the Greek New Testament*, 2d ed. (Stuttgart and New York: United Bible Societies, 1994), pp. 512–13.

31. Consult Moule, *Idiom-Book*, p. 144.

32. See Windisch, *Der Zweite Korintherbrief*, p. 254.

of a year earlier. The time lapse, then, varies from a few months to nearly two years.

We are unable to determine what calendar both Paul and the Corinthians employed. Ernest B. Allo has tabulated the various calendars and their beginnings that were in use at the time of Paul's writing: the Jewish cultic year (spring); the Olympiadic year (summer); the Macedonian year (autumn); the Jewish civil year (autumn); the Roman year (1 January).[33] Because Corinth was a Roman colony, the assumption is tenable that the Roman calendar was in vogue and was used by Paul. Moreover, Paul was a Roman citizen and may have composed this letter in the Roman colony of Philippi.[34]

After his initial instructions for the ingathering of funds for the saints in Jerusalem, Paul told the Corinthians that he would travel from Ephesus to Macedonia and then go to Corinth to spend the winter (I Cor. 16:1–8). A change of plans caused a delay; Paul made a hasty visit to Corinth and wrote a painful letter (2:1–4); and Titus, who had been sent to Corinth with this letter, met Paul in Macedonia after some time had elapsed (2:13; 7:5–7). If Paul wrote his first canonical letter in the second half of 55, then we may infer that the second epistle was composed a year later, probably in the autumn of 56.

When Paul mentioned to the Corinthians the matter of the collection, they responded favorably and were ready to give. They were among the first to do so. But after their initial response, which was exemplary and praiseworthy, the conflict with an offender in the church (2:5–11; 7:8–9) dampened their enthusiasm. Because of their difficulties they lagged, and others took the lead (vv. 1–2; Rom. 15:26–27). They had begun and "even expressed the desire to do so." Therefore, the project in Corinth had to be reinitiated. Whenever a congregation exemplifies love, harmony, and unity, its giving to various causes increases. But discord hampers and even quells a desire to give.

Although the concepts *to do* and *to will* appear to be reversed (compare Phil. 2:13), Paul wants to remind his readers of their initial start and to rekindle within them their earlier desire to give.

11. But now also complete the work, so that your readiness to desire it may be matched by your completion of it, as your means allow.

The expanded repetition of verse 6 is evident at first sight. Paul again urges the Corinthian church to finish the task it once set out to do. He uses a compound verb in the imperative: "fully complete it once for all." The contrast is between what happened the previous year and what should happen now.

The Corinthians have the desire to give, but fulfillment is lacking. Thus, they need encouragement to take up where they left off and finish the work without delay. Paul juxtaposes the verbs *to desire* and *to complete* and tells the readers: "what you desire in your hearts should also be completed with your hands." He

---

33. Ernest B. Allo, *Saint Paul Seconde Épître aux Corinthiens*, 2d ed. (Paris: Gabalda, 1956), p. 218.

34. Victor Paul Furnish, *II Corinthians: Translated with Introduction, Notes and Commentary*, Anchor Bible 32A (Garden City, N.Y.: Doubleday, 1984), p. 406.

does not use the verb *to do*, because at one time the Corinthians were collecting funds to support the needy but never finished what they had begun. The time has come to complete the work, for the people show their readiness (see vv. 9, 12; 9:2).

To avoid any undue pressure in this matter Paul adds the phrase *as your means allow*. People should not be able to say that their resources are too scant. Calvin pertinently notes, "If you offer a small gift from your slender resources, your intention is just as valuable in God's eyes as if a rich man had made a large gift out of his abundance."[35] Paul does not say that the Corinthians should give all they have to enrich the people in Jerusalem. Such advice would sow discord. Nor does he challenge the church in Corinth to follow the example of the churches in Macedonia: to give beyond their ability. That action would create unwanted rivalry. Instead, he advises them to give as much as their means allow.

At the temple treasury, rich people threw in large amounts of money, but the poor widow put in two copper coins. Jesus said to his disciples, "I tell you the truth, this poor widow has put more into the treasury than all the others. They gave out of their wealth, but she, out of her poverty, put in everything—all she had to live on" (Mark 12:43–44).

12. For if the readiness is there, the gift is acceptable insofar as a person has it, not insofar as he does not have it.

This verse is incomplete when it is literally translated: "For if the readiness is present, it is acceptable insofar as he has, not insofar as he does not have." Is the readiness of the Corinthians acceptable? Who is the subject of the verb *to have*? And what is the direct object of this verb?

The Corinthians demonstrated their continued readiness, and this fact pleased Paul. But their lack of action was unacceptable to him and to God (compare 6:2; Rom. 15:16, 31, where Paul uses the expression *euprosdektos* [acceptable, favor] with reference to God). It is not the readiness to give that is acceptable, for that is understood. The gift itself is the implied subject of the term *acceptable* and the direct object of the verb *to have*. We must also supply a subject for this verb in the singular, and do so with the word *person*. Hans Dieter Betz comments, "Though willingness is basic to the act of gift-giving, even more important is the matter of the gift's acceptability to the recipient."[36]

Conclusively, Paul writes an abbreviated conditional sentence: "For if indeed the readiness is there, the gift is acceptable." He continues and adds a stipulation: "Insofar as a person has the resources to give a gift, not insofar as he does not have any assets." In the Apocrypha we find similar advice. Tobit instructs his son Tobias to be generous in giving alms, but to do so in accord with his means. Then he adds: "If you have little, do not be ashamed to give the little you can afford" (Tob. 4:8).

---

35. Calvin, *II Corinthians*, p. 112.

36. Betz, *II Corinthians 8 and 9*, p. 66.

Greek Words, Phrases, and Constructions in 8:10–12

Verses 10–11

τοῦτο—this neuter demonstrative pronoun has its antecedent not in the form but in the content of the noun γνώμην (advice).

οἵτινες—as subject of the main verb προενήρξασθε, it means "you who began beforehand." The indefinite pronoun appears to function as a relative pronoun.[37] The verb occurs once in the New Testament.

ὅπως—as a conjunction ὅπως needs the implied present subjunctive ᾖ (so that it may be).[38]

ἐκ τοῦ ἔχειν—here is the only occurrence of this formation ("out of your means") in the New Testament. The phrase is equivalent to καθὸ ἂν ἔχῃ (inasmuch as he has) of verse 12.[39]

Verse 12

εὐπρόσδεκτος—with the implied subject of this adjective, the word gift (the gift is acceptable), the clause is the apodosis in a true conditional sentence that begins with εἰ γάρ.

---

3. Strive for Equality
8:13–15

13. For not that others should have relief and you be burdened, but that there be equality.

Paul counsels moderation in giving. He is not displeased with the Macedonians, who gave more than they could afford, but he seeks to regulate the process. The recipients of gifts should not be living in luxury at the expense of the giver who, bereft of his possessions, faces severe poverty. This type of giving moves resources from giver to recipient and needs from recipient to giver. But in the process nothing is solved.

This text and the next one teach a fundamental rule to abolish poverty. The rule was applied in the church of Jerusalem during the time following Pentecost. "All the believers were together and had everything in common. Selling their possessions and goods, they gave to anyone as he had need" (Acts 2:44–45; and see 4:32, 34). Paul seeks to apply this same rule in the universal church by asking the Gentile Christians abroad to help the needy Jewish Christians in Jerusalem. He stresses material equality, so that those believers who have been blessed with a surplus willingly share their goods with others who lack the necessities of life.[40]

Paul is not advocating that the rich divest themselves of all their possessions, that the poor be made rich by receiving gifts, and that economic equality be

---

37. Moule (*Idiom-Book*, p. 124) argues that "a distinction certainly improves the sense and may have been intended."

38. Robertson, *Grammar*, p. 395.

39. Friedrich Blass and Albert Debrunner, *A Greek Grammar of the New Testament and Other Early Christian Literature*, trans. and rev. Robert Funk (Chicago: University of Chicago Press, 1961), #403.

40. Compare Erich Beyreuther, *NIDNTT*, 2:499.

achieved. Indeed, he is not advocating abolition of ownership but abolition of poverty.[41] He is mindful of the Old Testament instruction not to have any poor people in the land of Israel (Deut. 15:4). The principle for Paul is voluntary giving to strengthen the mutual fellowship of Christian churches.

God is pleased when we love our neighbor by relieving his or her monetary distress.[42] The saints in Jerusalem will be able to acquire goods they have lacked but are unable to reciprocate except by means of spiritual blessings (Rom. 15:27). Yet Paul's efforts to unite the churches abroad with the mother church in Jerusalem fell short of expectations. With the help of fellow travelers, he delivered the gift to the poor in Jerusalem (Acts 24:17), but the effect was less than favorable. Luke's account in Acts fails to inform us whether Paul was able to unify the Jewish and Gentile churches during the time of his two-year imprisonment in Caesarea.

14. For the present time your surplus is for their deficiency, so that also their surplus is for your deficiency, that there may be equality.

This text further elaborates on the previous one (v. 13). Paul encourages mutual concern among the Christian churches, so that the believers who have received material blessings may help those who are destitute. A decade earlier, when a severe famine struck many parts of the Roman Empire including Judea, the believers in Syrian Antioch sent Barnabas and Paul to alleviate the hunger of the Christians in Judea. These two carried a monetary gift to the Judean elders (Acts 11:29–30). With their gift, the Antiochean believers showed their love to the Judean Christians, responded to a genuine need, and sought to break down the wall that separated Jews and Gentiles. The initiative came from the Gentile believers. In the case of the collection for the saints in Judea, the initiative came from Paul as leader of the Gentile churches. We have no indication that the elders in Jerusalem asked for financial support. Paul acted in obedience to the apostolic injunction to remember the poor (Gal. 2:10).

a. "For the present time your surplus is for their deficiency." The collection for the poor in Jerusalem appears to be a one-time gift. At the moment, Paul is not asking the churches in Macedonia and Achaia to give continued support to the people in Jerusalem. He specifies that the giving is for the present time when the Corinthians have an abundance.[43] Corinth prospered because of trade, commerce, and agriculture.

---

41. Consult Simon J. Kistemaker, *Exposition of the Acts of the Apostles,* New Testament Commentary series (Grand Rapids: Baker, 1990), pp. 112–13, 173–74.

42. Dieter Georgi wants to equate the terms *equality* and *God,* but it is doubtful whether the Corinthians understood that Paul wanted to convey this equation to them. *Der Armen zu Gedenken: Die Geschichte der Kollekte des Paulus für Jerusalem,* 2d rev. and expanded ed. (Neukirchen-Vluyn: Neukirchener Verlag, 1994), p. 64; English translation, *Remembering the Poor: The History of Paul's Collection for Jerusalem* (Nashville: Abingdon, 1992), pp. 88–89.

43. By contrast, Jean Héring asserts that the church in Corinth endured "relative poverty." *The Second Epistle of Saint Paul to the Corinthians,* trans. A. W. Heathcote and P. J. Allcock (London: Epworth, 1967), p. 59 n. 4.

b. "So that also their surplus is for your deficiency." This clause lacks clarity. The contrast between Corinth and Jerusalem is plain, but the words *surplus* and *deficiency* probably do not carry the same meaning here as they do in the preceding clause. It is hard to believe that a prosperous commercial center would be poor at a time when Jerusalem is rich. Paul is not interested in supporting people, be they fellow Christians, if they are unwilling to work. He himself labored with his own hands to meet his own needs and even those of others. He gave the Thessalonians this rule: "If a man will not work, he shall not eat" (II Thess. 3:10). God's kingdom has no room for drones, only for bees that gather nectar and produce honey. Writes Charles Hodge, "[The Scriptures] inculcate on the poor the duty of self-support to the extent of their ability."[44]

c. "That there may be equality." The Christian church has the sacred duty to care for the poor and to help them improve their lives. Those who have been blessed must thank the Lord for his bounties but at the same time must provide aid to the underprivileged people that they, too, may enjoy greater blessings. Paul places the term *equality* within the framework of reciprocity. He does not advocate undermining productivity. Instead he seeks to raise the quality of life through reciprocal activity of both rich and poor. "Brotherhood cannot be one-sided; it must be mutual, and in the interchange of services equality is the result."[45]

15. Just as it is written, "He who has increased much does not have too much, and he who has less does not have too little."

Throughout the epistle, Paul supports his discourses with quotations from the Old Testament. For him, the Scriptures are useful for teaching (II Tim. 3:16). Nevertheless, he often takes a quote for the sake of its words and not its context. This is true here. Paul quotes Exodus 16:18 from the Septuagint and uses the words as an illustration. This text may have been used more often,[46] perhaps as a proverb.

With this reference, the apostle directs attention to God, who amply fulfilled the needs of everyone during the forty-year desert journey of the Israelites. Similarly, God still provides adequately for everyone by asking those who have abundance to share gladly with those who have need. The Christian church is characterized by liberality toward all people but "especially to those who belong to the family of believers" (Gal. 6:10).

---

44. Charles Hodge, *An Exposition of the Second Epistle to the Corinthians* (1891; Edinburgh: Banner of Truth, 1959), p. 206.

45. James Denney, *The Second Epistle to the Corinthians,* 2d ed., The Expositor's Bible series (New York: Armstrong, 1900), p. 272.

46. F. W. Grosheide, *De Tweede Brief van den Apostel Paulus aan de Kerk te Korinthe,* Kommentaar op het Nieuwe Testament series (Amsterdam: Van Bottenburg, 1939), p. 300.

Greek Words, Phrases, and Constructions in 8:13–15

Verse 13

ἵνα—with the present subjunctive ᾖ, which has been omitted, the clause expresses more result than purpose.[47]

Verses 14–15

Paul writes two purpose clauses, one with ἵνα and the other with ὅπως as a linguistic variation.

τὸ πολύ . . . τὸ ὀλίγον—the neuter expresses an act performed by an individual. The Septuagint has the comparative adjective τὸ ὀλαττον (lesser) for the positive τὸ ὀλίγον.

C. Visit of Titus
8:16–24

After an intermission in which Paul exhorted the Corinthians to contribute voluntarily to the fund for the poor in Jerusalem (vv. 7–15), the apostle turns his attention again to Titus. He knows that his helper has the ability to persuade the people in Corinth to return to their earlier zeal in giving to this cause (vv. 10–12). He now stresses the manner in which collection of the money is to be administered. Also, Titus is not going alone but in the company of others who are well known in the churches and even are chosen by them.

1. Avoiding Criticism
8:16–21

16. But I thank God who put into the heart of Titus the same eagerness that I have for you.

At the beginning of this chapter (vv. 1–5), Paul described his appreciation for the Macedonians, who demonstrated their generosity in the service to the saints. Now he expresses his thanks to God for Titus, who has labored and will continue to labor among the Corinthians. He mentioned Titus in verse 6 (refer also to 2:13), but here he presents further details. Before he continues he brings thanks to God, which in a literal rendering reads, "But thanks be to God." This clause appears to have been a religious saying that often appears in Paul's major epistles.[48]

The apostle always recognizes God's hand in the lives of his people. God gave the Macedonians grace to give (v. 1) and he put in Titus's heart an eagerness to serve the Corinthians (v. 16). This eagerness of Titus to return to Corinth and complete the task of giving can be favorably compared with the dedication of the Macedonians in their giving. Not only that, but also the Corinthians possessed

---

47. To interpret the ἵνα construction as an imperative is questionable. Contra Moule, *Idiom-Book*, p. 145.
48. See the Greek text of Rom. 6:17; 7:25; I Cor. 15:57; II Cor. 2:14; 9:15.

such zeal a year earlier (vv. 11–12). The reason for their enthusiasm lies in their desire to please God and to devote their gifts to him. For Titus, this matter concerns not so much the recipients as the donors of these gifts. He longs to return to Corinth to complete the task of collecting the funds. This task may prove to be rather arduous and troublesome in view of the opposition from the false apostles (see 12:14–18).

Last, Paul himself had a decided interest in the spiritual growth of the Corinthians. He indicates that he possessed the same eagerness that was present in Titus. Yet he himself remains behind in Macedonia while Titus travels to Achaia. He wants to remove himself from the handling of the gifts so that no one can say that he gained personal advantage.

17. Because he not only accepted our appeal, but being very eager he also is going out toward you on his own accord.

With this verse Paul explains the preceding text, so that Titus's eagerness is revealed in both his welcoming Paul's appeal and his readiness to go to Corinth. Paul now resumes his urgent appeal to Titus to complete the matter of the collection (v. 6).[49] After a slight digression, he uses similar wording that confirms continuity. He appeals to Titus, who welcomes the challenge to do so, to finish the task. In fact, an appeal is not necessary, for God has put into Titus's heart the desire to travel to Corinth and to take the raising of funds in hand.

No one can accuse Paul of issuing highhanded commands, for the expression *on his own accord* speaks volumes. Paul has the same concern for the Corinthians as Titus has, so that there is no command but only advice. At the time when Paul writes this sentence, Titus is still with him, is ready to journey to Corinth, and is serving the apostle as letter carrier.[50] In a way, Paul is sending Titus to the Corinthians with a letter of recommendation. Yet he and his workers are not in need of such letters, for the result of their ministry is written on the hearts of the people in Corinth (3:2–3).

18. We are sending with him the brother who is praised by all the churches in the service of the gospel.

Since the days of the early church, the intriguing question has been: "Who is this brother?"[51] Numerous candidates have been mentioned, among whom are

---

49. Betz (*II Corinthians 8 and 9*, p. 70) comments that "the commendation of Titus in v[erses] 16–17 is formulated without regard to v[erse] 6, as if v[erse] 6 had not been written." But Paul uses the same Greek vocabulary in verses 1–6 and verses 16–17: χάρις, δίδωμι, αὐθαίρετοι, παράκλησις, Τίτος. The link between the two segments is undeniable. Windisch (p. 260) thinks that verses 16–24 may have been interchanged with verses 7–15 in a mix-up of pages. We have difficulty believing that Paul wrote on separate pages; rather, he used a continuous scroll. Also, interruptions and digressions are part of Paul's epistolary style.

50. C. K. Barrett, "Titus," in *Neotestamentica et Semitica: Studies in Honour of Matthew Black*, ed. E. Earle Ellis and Max Wilcox (Edinburgh; Clark, 1969); also in *Essays on Paul* (Philadelphia: Westminster, 1982), p. 126.

51. In their commentaries, Lietzmann (pp. 136–37), Windisch (p. 262), and Héring (p. 62) suggest that Paul originally supplied the names of the brothers (vv. 18, 22), but that someone erased them. The "hypothesis is purely imaginative," according to Allo (p. 224).

Luke, Barnabas, Timothy, Silas, Mark, Aristarchus, and Apollos, to mention no more. Any one of these people will have to match the description Paul gives in this text and elsewhere. The interpretation of these verses also plays a significant role in identifying the names. I briefly list some positive and negative aspects for the names that have been mentioned.

1. *Luke.* Throughout Acts, Luke never mentions Titus; and in this epistle Paul refers to Titus repeatedly but never to Luke. Is it possible that in the first century, writers would refrain from identifying close relatives?[52] True, Paul, not Titus, is the author of II Corinthians. In the company of Titus, Paul may have been obliged not to mention the name of a near relative of his companion. But this line of reasoning runs into the objection that the expression *brother* should refer to a brother in Christ rather than to a blood relative. The word *brother* here and in verse 22 appears to mean a spiritual brother.

Next, most writers understand the words "the brother who is praised by all the churches in the service of the gospel" to mean that this person proclaimed the gospel.[53] The suggestion that Luke's Gospel circulated in the churches of the 50s cannot be proved.[54]

Last, in the list of fellow travelers who are in charge of safeguarding the collection, no one represents the church in Corinth. Yet, Luke accompanied Paul from Philippi to Jerusalem. Because nothing is said in Acts 20:4 about a representative of Corinth, may we assume that Luke is the brother who carried the Corinthians' gift? Could Luke have been present with Paul at the writing of II Corinthians in Macedonia? Many Byzantine manuscripts feature an explanatory note at the end of this epistle that says: "The second epistle to the Corinthians was written from Philippi through *(dia)* Titus and Luke."[55] This means that Luke visited Corinth and perhaps stayed there for some time. From Scripture and early Christian documents, we are unable to verify where Luke spent his time from 50 to 56 (Acts 16:16–17; 20:5). Yet many ancient and modern writers favorably support identifying the brother mentioned by Paul as Luke.[56]

2. *Barnabas.* The relationship between Paul and Barnabas was intimate, for Barnabas introduced Paul to the apostles in Jerusalem (Acts 9:27). But after the first missionary journey and the Jerusalem Council, the disagreement between

---

52. Consult Alexander Souter, "A Suggested Relationship between Titus and Luke," *ExpT* 18 (1906–1907): 285; and "The Relationship between Titus and Luke," *ExpT* 18 (1906–7): 335–36.

53. Representatives are Michael Wilcock, *The Saviour of the World: The Message of Luke's Gospel,* The Bible Speaks Today series (Leicester and Downers Grove: InterVarsity, 1979), p. 20; John E. Morgan-Wynne, "II Corinthians VIII. 18f. and the Question of a Traditionsgrundlage for Acts," *JTS* 30 (1979): 172–73; and the commentaries of Martin, p. 274; Furnish, p. 422; and Hughes, p. 312.

54. Nevertheless, consult John Wenham, *Redating Matthew, Mark and Luke: A Fresh Assault on the Synoptic Problem* (London: Hodder and Stoughton, 1991), pp. 234–38.

55. Nes-Al[27]; see also Wenham, *Redating Matthew, Mark and Luke,* p. 231; Hughes, *Second Epistle to the Corinthians,* p. 312.

56. Among ancient writers are Origen, Ephraem, Eusebius, Jerome, Ambrose, and Anselm; modern writers are Olshausen, Wordworth, Plummer, Bachmann, Strachan, Rendall, Hughes, and Wenham.

these two was so sharp that they went their separate ways. Yet in I Corinthians, Paul mentions Barnabas and implies that a cordial relationship was restored between these two men (9:6).[57] There is no evidence, however, that Barnabas was with Paul in Macedonia and was sent to Corinth. Why would Paul not use his name but allude to him as "the brother"?

3. *Timothy.* Paul writes the name of Timothy in the beginning of this epistle and identifies him as "our brother," which in the original is "the brother" (1:1). He had sent Timothy to Corinth (I Cor. 4:17; 16:10) but had counseled the Corinthians to receive him graciously so that Timothy would not have to be afraid of them. Although the identification ("the brother") fits, we lack certainty that Timothy was sent once again to Corinth.

4. *Silas.* The names of Silas and Timothy occur in the context of preaching the gospel message in Corinth (1:19). This happened when Paul first began his labors there and these two men came from Macedonia to assist him in founding the church (Acts 18:5). We have no further information about the ministry of Silas in Corinth.

5. *Mark.* The altercation between Paul and Barnabas resulted from Mark's departure for Jerusalem (Acts 13:13; 15:37, 39). His name does not appear in the Corinthian correspondence. Later, Paul again notes his name in other contexts (Col. 4:10; II Tim. 4:11; Philem. 24), but Mark is not known in Corinth.

6. *Aristarchus.* Luke relates that Aristarchus was Paul's traveling companion together with Gaius in Ephesus, to Jerusalem, and to Rome (Acts 19:29; 20:4; 27:2). Calling him "my fellow prisoner" (Col. 4:10) and his fellow worker (Philem. 24), Paul must have highly regarded his friendship. But there is no evidence that the Corinthians knew him as their spiritual brother: Aristarchus represented the church of Thessalonica (Acts 20:4). The presence of a Macedonian in Corinth would cause dissatisfaction and hurtful rivalry in the matter of the collection. Also, his presence would be at odds with Paul's statement that he hoped he would not have to be ashamed of the Corinthians if Macedonians would accompany the apostle (9:4).

7. *Apollos.* A faithful servant in the Corinthian church, Apollos was highly respected as an eloquent preacher.[58] Paul calls him "our [the] brother" and states that Apollos was reluctant to return to Corinth. "Now about our brother Apollos: I strongly urged him to go to you with the brothers. He was quite unwilling to go now, but he will go when he has the opportunity" (I Cor. 16:12). Indeed, Paul had to persuade him to go to Corinth, but he was confident that Apollos would go when possible. We have no knowledge about where Apollos may have served the churches after he left Corinth, but we conjecture that this skilled orator did visit the Corinthians again in the company of Titus. His name occurs often in I Corinthians but never in this epistle; he was away from Corinth for some time.

---

57. Refer to Kistemaker, *I Corinthians,* p. 289.
58. Acts 19:1; I Cor. I:12; 3:4, 5, 6, 22; 4:6; 16:12.

After this brief survey, we suggest that either Luke or Apollos are likely candidates.[59] But even Apollos is too well known to the Corinthians to be introduced without a name, which then leaves only Luke. Moreover, of these two persons, only Luke traveled with Paul to Jerusalem.

Although we wonder why Paul omits a name and merely says "the brother," we know that the apostle often omits identifying details concerning people he discusses. They were known to the original readers but not to others; for instance, the offender (2:5–11; 7:12); our brother (8:22; 12:18); and a loyal yokefellow (Phil. 4:3).

19. But not only this, he also has been appointed by the churches to be our traveling companion as we administer this gracious work to the glory of the Lord himself and to show our readiness to help.

a. "He also has been appointed by the churches." This is the second time in as many verses that Paul speaks of the churches (vv. 18, 19). These churches are widely representative, including those in Macedonia, because Paul speaks of "all the churches." Not he but the congregations have taken the initiative, perhaps at Paul's suggestion, to appoint a person to accompany Titus. The Greek text shows that the term *appoint* means the raising of hands in a congregational meeting. The people understood that not Paul but the churches should be involved in naming a person suitable to the task of collecting funds for the saints in Jerusalem. They chose a man who was well known by his preaching of the gospel in their churches. He had the confidence of the churches to fulfill the task to which they appointed him.

b. "To be our traveling companion as we administer this gracious work." The words *our traveling companion* signify not only that this brother accompanies Titus to Corinth, but also that he is a member of the group that accompanies Paul to Jerusalem. Thus, the possessive pronoun *our* receives full recognition. The man who is praised by all the churches is commissioned to go to Corinth for the collection of the gifts. Paul calls it "gracious work," in the sense that giving to the Lord for the poor in Jerusalem is an act of grace (v. 6).

c. "To the glory of the Lord himself and to show our readiness to help." The mandate to gather funds has a twofold purpose. First, Paul points to the glory of the Lord and then adds the pronoun *himself.* C. K. Barrett proposes that with the addition of this intensive pronoun Paul actually is saying, "his glory—I mean, the Lord's."[60] Throughout his epistles, Paul teaches the Old Testament tenet that all things must be done to the glory and honor of the Lord God. Next, he stresses human responsibility by noting the willingness of himself and others

---

59. Nickle (*The Collection,* pp. 21–22) identifies the two "brothers" as Judas (v. 18) and Silas (v. 22) because they were appointed by the Jerusalem Council (Acts 15:22). The council's mandate, however, is entirely different from that of the churches at hand.

60. C. K. Barrett, *The Second Epistle to the Corinthians,* Harper's New Testament Commentaries series (New York: Harper and Row, 1973), p. 217 n. 2.

to help in this task that he initiated earlier. Paul, however, did not go to Corinth with Titus and his companions but arrived there much later. He did not involve himself in the actual handling of the funds. Initially, he wanted the men who had been approved for this task to travel to Jerusalem by themselves. But if they deemed that his presence was needed, he would be willing to accompany them (I Cor. 16:3–4).

20. I am trying to avoid this, namely, that anyone might blame us in the way we administer this lavish gift.

Paul often warns his readers to avoid even the appearance of evil (see I Thess. 5:22), and he applies this teaching to himself also. He is fully aware of his opponents in the church at Corinth who are ready to attack him. The gathering of gifts would give them an excellent opportunity to spread the rumor that Paul is using the funds for himself. The apostle is doing everything possible to circumvent any criticism that may reflect negatively on him and hinder his ministry. In both canonical epistles to the Corinthians, he repeatedly tells his readers that his labors among them are free of charge (I Cor. 9:18; II Cor. 2:17; 11:7, 9; 12:13). He wants to avoid any and all criticism about finances.

Even though the gifts in Corinth still must be collected, Paul is confident that the total will amount to a lavish donation. In addition to the Corinthian donation, the amount of the gifts collected by the Macedonian churches and by the ones in Asia Minor must have been substantial. The delegation carrying and protecting this gift consisted of seven men in addition to Luke and Paul (Acts 20:4–5).

Twice in succession, Paul writes the words *we administer* (vv. 19, 20) to mark the importance of this work. Certainly, Paul had delegated this administrative task to his associates, but as their leader he is in charge and wants everything done properly. Karl Heinrich Rengstorf writes that Paul "was concerned not merely to demonstrate his integrity but also so to act that no suspicion might even arise concerning it."[61]

21. For we aim to do the right things not only before the Lord but also before men.

As he does elsewhere, Paul strengthens his argument with a quotation from, and in this case an allusion to, the Old Testament. With a number of adaptations, this verse derives from the Greek text of Proverbs 3:4, to which Paul also alludes in Romans 12:17.

Paul's words are not spoken merely for the sake of himself or his co-workers; they are directed to every Christian. All of us are required to lead lives that are morally upright, praiseworthy, and contributing to a good reputation. The Old Testament wording is "before God," and Paul writes, "before the Lord." The difference is of no account, for the follower of the Lord must be honest and right before God and before men.

---

61. Karl Heinrich Rengstorf, *TDNT*, 7:590.

Practical Considerations in 8:20–21

The Bible has much to say about material possessions, for they belong to God, who entrusts them to us, his stewards. He blesses us with good things so that we may use them to glorify him and to extend the cause of his church and kingdom. Yet possessions are a snare when they possess us. Then they, instead of God, are the object of our devotion. Hence, Jesus teaches that we cannot serve both God and money (Matt. 6:24; Luke 16:13).

Pastors are particularly vulnerable, for they are leaders of God's people whom the Lord has entrusted to their care. They teach spiritual truths, but they are also asked to teach the people in their giving to the causes of the Lord. In this matter, they must exercise utmost caution.

Taking advantage of someone's trust is a lurking danger for any leader. As a rule, most people have great confidence in their own integrity; but in some cases, misplaced confidence has resulted in the downfall of great men. From Scripture we know that Satan is always looking for weaknesses to destroy our reputation (2:11). He aims for those who fill the highest positions in the church.

The apostle Paul was fully aware of Satan's cunning. He realized that even a mere semblance of dishonesty would destroy his ministry, so he protected himself by asking others to collect, carry, and distribute the funds.[62] Calvin concludes, "Thus the higher the position we occupy, the greater is our need to imitate carefully Paul's circumspection and modesty."[63]

Greek Words, Phrases, and Constructions in 8:16–20

Verses 16–17

χάρις—this word means "thanks," but elsewhere "gracious work" (v. 19).

δόντι—the aorist active participle denotes single action, but many manuscripts and Greek New Testament editions have the present participle διδόντι (giving). The harder reading is the aorist, and it is thus preferred.

ἐν—the preposition has the sense of εἰς (into the heart of Titus).[64]

μέν . . . δέ—note the contrast in this sentence: "not only . . . , but he also is setting out to you." The aorist tense of ἐξῆλθεν is epistolary and must be seen not from the writer's point of view but from the reader's.

σπουδαιότερος—this comparative adjective is an elative superlative and signifies "very eager."[65]

Verses 18–19

συνεπέμψαμεν—once again the aorist is epistolary and must be understood from the recipients' point of view (see vv. 17, 22).

---

62. The Roman author Cicero (*De officiis* 2.21.75) wrote: "But the chief thing in all public administration and public service is to avoid even the slightest suspicion of self-seeking." Refer to the commentaries of Betz, p. 77 n. 308; Martin, p. 279; Plummer, p. 250; Windisch, p. 266.

63. Calvin, *II Corinthians*, p. 116.

64. Moule, *Idiom-Book*, pp. 75–76.

65. Blass and Debrunner, *Greek Grammar*, #244.2.

ἐν τῷ εὐαγγελίῳ—this expression means "in the sphere of the gospel."[66]

χειροτονηθείς—the aorist passive participle in the nominative ("having been appointed") is an anacoluthon. It relates to "the brother," which is accusative. Compare Acts 14:23.

σύν—the reading of this preposition possibly is due to its association with the noun συνέκδημος (traveling companion); many manuscripts read ἐν, which may prove to be correct.[67]

αὐτοῦ—the inclusion of this intensive pronoun is questionable. For this reason, editors have placed it in brackets. Its presence shows redundance.

Verse 20

στελλόμενοι—the participle is too far removed from the main verb συνεπέμψαμεν (v. 18) and thus is an anacoluthon. The present middle participle needs the verb ἐσμέν for a periphrastic construction: "we are trying to avoid."

---

2. Sending Representatives
8:22–24

22. We are also sending with them our brother whom we often have tested and found eager in many ways, but now much more eager because of his great confidence in you.

If we were able to guess at the identity of the brother in verse 18, we admit we have no idea who this brother may have been. Paul sends him along with Titus and the travel companion, but we surmise that the Corinthians are not acquainted with this person. The descriptive phrases relate that he had been in Paul's presence, for the apostle had often put him to the test and had done so in many ways. In contrast to the brother mentioned in verse 18, this man had not been appointed by the churches but had been under the tutelage of Paul. Yet the apostle writes that the brothers are sent out by the churches as their representatives (v. 23).

The list of Paul's co-workers is quite extensive; all these associates were given assignments and had to pass tests, but this person apparently was unknown to the Corinthians. If this is so, all Paul's associates who had labored in the church of Corinth are ruled out. We doubt whether this brother was one of the seven representatives who accompanied Paul to Jerusalem. In short, we do not know.

The Greek text stresses the concept *great,* a concept that cannot be conveyed adequately in translation. Notice that we have four expressions that embellish this concept: often, in many ways, much more, great. Paul had worked with this brother for a long period, with the result that his co-worker displayed a great eagerness. The apostle had spoken positively about the Corinthians (7:14; 9:2), so

---

66. J. H. Moulton, *A Grammar of New Testament Greek,* 3d ed. (Edinburgh: Clark, 1908), vol. 1, *Prolegomena,* p. 68.

67. Consult Metzger, *Textual Commentary,* p. 513, for the reasons pro and con.

that this person had gained great confidence in the believers there. He was ready to travel to and work in Corinth.

23. As for Titus, he is my partner and fellow worker for you. As for our brothers, they are delegates of the churches, [and] the glory of Christ.

a. "As for Titus, he is my partner and fellow worker for you." At the end of this part of his discourse, Paul singles out Titus. The two other men are representatives of the churches that commissioned them to go to Corinth, but Titus is Paul's delegate. For this reason, Paul calls him "my partner and fellow worker for you." In the Pauline letters, no other person receives the honor of being called "my partner" (in the singular; compare Philem. 17). The expression implies that Titus completely shared Paul's life and mission. His life was the same as that of Paul—being a servant of Christ for the benefit of the church. He also is described as fellow worker, which is a general term that Paul uses a number of times.[68] Here it means that Titus has been the apostle's fellow helper in the Corinthian church, which cannot be said of the two brothers who are to accompany him to Corinth.

b. "As for our brothers, they are delegates of the churches, [and] the glory of Christ." We make subtle distinctions with respect to the word *brother*. In this context it cannot mean blood relatives, so it must have a spiritual connotation, that of fellow believer. But this interpretation is too general. Here we interpret the expression to mean a person who has received a special mandate by leaders of local churches.[69]

A literal translation of the Greek text reads, "they are apostles of the churches." It is obvious that the word *apostle* has shades of meaning, for these brothers are not on the same level as Paul, who was appointed by Jesus. The Twelve and Paul served the entire church, wherever the Lord sent them. By contrast, the brothers were delegated by local churches to go to Corinth on a mission for a relatively brief period (compare Phil. 2:25).[70]

The brothers commissioned by the churches were a credit to Christ. These men had a sound reputation in their daily walk of life and would prove to be an asset to the Corinthian church. They reflected the Lord's glory in their lives and lived to please him. In fact, their commission through the churches came from Jesus Christ. There is one more consideration. As they honor their Lord, so the Corinthians ought to honor the brothers for their work.

24. Therefore, to these men in the presence of the churches, present proof of your love and our pride in you.

---

68. Rom. 16:3, 9; I Cor. 3:9; II Cor. 1:24; 8:23; Phil. 2:25; 4:3; Col. 4:11; I Thess. 3:2; Philem. 1, 24.

69. Consult E. Earle Ellis, "Paul and His Co-Workers," in *Prophecy and Hermeneutics in Early Christianity: New Testament Essays* (Grand Rapids: Eerdmans, 1978), p. 16.

70. Refer to C. K. Barrett, *The Signs of an Apostle* (Philadelphia: Fortress, 1972), p. 73; F. Agnew, "On the Origin of the Term *Apostolos*," *CBQ* 38 (1976): 49–53; J. E. Young, "That some should be Apostles," *EvQ* 48 (1976): 96–104.

As this part of the discourse nears completion, Paul now directs his attention not so much to the delegates as to the Corinthians themselves. It is one thing for Paul to boast about liberality in giving; it is another thing for the church in Corinth to make this boasting a fact. It is one thing for the Christians in Corinth to receive a trio of helpers sent by Paul and the churches; it is another to work harmoniously with these men. Paul's time for testing their sincerity has now come (v. 8).

Paul, too, is being tested. He had expressed great confidence in the Corinthians and had boasted to Titus about them (7:4, 14). And when Titus returned from Corinth and reported to the apostle his positive experiences there, Paul was filled with great joy. But now he hoped once more that the Corinthians would not turn his boasting into any embarrassment for him and the churches that sent the delegates.

The Corinthians need to understand that the brothers who are sent to them represent churches vitally interested in how the believers in Corinth respond to the collection for Jerusalem. Every eye, so to speak, is fixed on Corinth, because the universal church of Jesus Christ is one body. In both Old and New Testament the rule obtained of establishing proof on the testimony of two or three witnesses.[71] Titus and the two brothers must be able to give a favorable report to Paul and the churches. Will the mother church of Achaia provide leadership in the matter of giving?

Last, giving ought never to be done under compulsion but always out of love (see 9:7). The Macedonian churches had demonstrated their love in "a wealth of generosity" (v. 2). Thus, Paul wants to see proof of the Corinthians' love in "concrete action, first by the reception of envoys, then by the collection for Jerusalem."[72] And Paul's second request is that the Corinthians authenticate his pride in them, so that neither he nor the churches at large would be disappointed.

Greek Words, Phrases, and Constructions in 8:22–24

Verse 22

The alliteration of the Greek letter π is evident in this verse, especially in the declined forms of the adjective πολύ. This accusative adjective is used adverbially: "much more."

πεποιθήσει—because this noun lacks a possessive pronoun, the interpretation could be either the confidence that Paul has in the Corinthians (KJV, NKJV) or the brother's confidence in them. The context favors the second option.

Verses 23–24

εἴτε—this particle occurs twice, once followed by ὑπέρ and the accusative case (Titus) and once by the nominative case (brothers). The meaning is, "Whether anyone asks about Titus, whether . . . the brothers."

---

71. Num. 35:30; Deut. 17:6; 19:15; John 8:17; II Cor. 13:1; I Tim. 5:19; Heb. 10:28.
72. Betz, *II Corinthians 8 and 9*, p. 85.

δόξα Χριστοῦ—although the objective genitive ("honor for Christ") is favored, the subjective genitive cannot be ruled out.

ἔνδειξιν . . . ἐνδεικνύμενοι—this is tautology in our usage ("proving the proof") but not in Semitic writing. Also, the Semitic custom of substituting the participle for the imperative is common.[73]

πρόσωπον—this is a legal term that should be interpreted literally: "before the face of."

Summary of Chapter 8

The churches in Macedonia have shown an extraordinary measure of generosity by donating gifts for the poverty-stricken saints in Jerusalem. They gave even beyond what their resources allowed. Also, they pleaded with Paul to permit them to participate in the raising of funds to help the poor. These people devoted themselves to serving the Lord by yielding themselves completely to Paul and his associates. While Titus was visiting the Corinthians, he implemented a similar undertaking, but it stagnated. Now Paul gives him the mandate to return and complete that project in Corinth. The apostle is not encouraging rivalry between the Macedonians and the Corinthians. Instead he directs attention to the Lord Jesus Christ, who, being rich in heavenly glory, became poor on earth to make poor sinners spiritually rich.

Paul counsels the Corinthians not only to give to the collection but also to have the desire to do so. He encourages them to complete the task and to demonstrate a willingness to help. He is not asking them to give more than they are able to afford, but to give of their abundance. He is interested in sufficiency for all, much as the Israelites in the desert received sufficient food.

God gave Titus the desire to return to Corinth, and now on his own accord Paul's associate shows eagerness to go. Paul informs the Corinthians that a brother, known to the churches because of the gospel, will accompany Titus. Also, this brother, chosen by the churches, will be Paul's fellow traveler to Jerusalem. The apostle protects himself from any criticism that may arise because of the collection.

Paul sends one other brother with Titus to Corinth. This person has often been tested, is enthusiastic, and has a large measure of trust in the Corinthians. Paul commends this trio to the believers in Corinth and pleads with the recipients of his letter to accept them in love and to prove to all the churches their eagerness to help.

---

73. Metzger, *Textual Commentary,* pp. 513–14.

9

The Collection, *part 2*

(9:1–15)

Outline (continued)

9 1 For it is not necessary for me to write to you concerning the service to the saints. 2 For I know your eagerness about which I boasted to the Macedonians, saying Achaia had been ready since last year, and your zeal aroused many people. 3 But I am sending the brothers, so that our boasting concerning you might not prove to be hollow in this case, and that you might be prepared, just as I said you would be. 4 For if any Macedonians come with me and find you unprepared, we are—not to mention you—put to shame in this situation. 5 Thus I thought it necessary to urge the brothers to go on to you ahead of me and to prepare in advance the generous gift you promised beforehand. So it will be ready as a generous gift and not as one that is torn away from greed.

6 The point is this: he who sows sparingly will also reap sparingly, and he who sows generously will also reap generously. 7 Let each one give as he has decided in his mind to give, not reluctantly or out of necessity. For God loves a cheerful giver. 8 For God is able to make all grace abound toward you, so that in everything you may always have enough of everything and you may abound in every good work. 9 Just as it is written,

> He has scattered, he has given to the poor,
> his righteousness endures forever.

10 Now he who provides seed to the sower and bread to the eater will provide and multiply your seed and will increase the harvest of your righteousness. 11 You will be made rich in every way to be altogether generous, and through us your generosity will produce thanksgiving to God. 12 For the ministry of this service not only is supplying the needs of the saints but also is overflowing through many expressions of thanks to God. 13 Through the testing of this service they will be glorifying God because of your submission to the confession that acknowledges the gospel of Christ and the generosity of your [proof of] partnership with them and everyone. 14 And in their prayers for you they will long for you because of the surpassing grace of God upon you. 15 Thanks be to God for his indescribable gift.

D. Help for the Saints
9:1–5

Some commentators allege that chapters 8 and 9 are two separate letters, because in 9:1 the apostle "seems to introduce a fresh topic not yet dealt with."[1] In

---

1. Jean Héring adds, "One cannot get rid of the impression that 9 does not form the natural sequence to 8" (*The Second Epistle of Saint Paul to the Corinthians,* trans. A. W. Heathcote and P. J. Allcock [London: Epworth, 1967], p. 65). See also the commentaries of Rudolf Bultmann, *The Second Letter to the Corinthians,* trans. Roy A. Harrisville (Minneapolis: Augsburg, 1985), p. 256; Hans Windisch, *Der Zweite Korintherbrief,* ed. Georg Strecker (1924; reprint ed., Göttingen: Vandenhoeck und Ruprecht, 1970), pp. 268–69; Hans Dieter Betz, *II Corinthians 8 and 9: A Commentary on Two Administrative Letters of the Apostle Paul,* ed. George W. MacRae, Hermeneia: A Critical and Historical Commentary on the Bible (Philadelphia: Fortress, 1985); pp. 90–91, 129–44.

a sense this is true, but the evidence for the continuity and unity of these two chapters is solid. For instance, the assertion that the Greek introductory phrase *peri men gar* (for concerning) marks the beginning of a new letter at 9:1 lacks the evidence to make a convincing case. This phrase serves as a bridge that connects the preceding and the succeeding contexts. In addition, "9:4 provides a warrant and explanation for Paul's exhortation in 8:24."[2]

The vocabulary in both chapters is similar; for example, an acceptable explanation for the term *the brothers* (v. 3) can come only from the preceding chapter (8:18, 22, including Titus). The content of these chapters reveals undeniable parallels and features similar circumstances.

Furthermore, if chapters 8 and 9 were separate letters, we would expect some manuscript evidence and a possible discussion in the literature of the early church. But such sources are nonexistent, so that we do well to stay with the tradition and accept the basic unity of this epistle. When Paul wrote his letter, he did not indicate chapter divisions but continued a discussion to its conclusion. In fact, the New Testament appeared without chapter divisions until 1228, when Stephen Langton provided them and gave them to the church as a legacy.[3] What would have happened if he had combined chapters 8 and 9 into a single unit? (See the Introduction for a discussion on the relationship between chapters 8 and 9.)

Nevertheless, the differences between these two chapters are pronounced. In chapter 8, the name of Titus occurs, but it does not in chapter 9. Paul stresses thankfulness in the one chapter and generosity in the other. In passing, he introduces the administration of the collection in the eighth chapter. But in the next chapter he returns to this topic and addresses it in greater detail. And last, the tenor of chapter 9 differs from chapter 8. In the first one Paul is terse, but in the second he discusses the collection in a relaxed manner and provides rules that are valid for all churches everywhere. These two chapters definitely form a coherent unit; they follow the sections in which Paul expresses his great joy of meeting Titus in Macedonia (7:6–7, 13–16).

1. For it is not necessary for me to write to you concerning the service to the saints. 2. For I know your eagerness about which I boasted to the Macedonians, saying Achaia had been ready since last year, and your zeal aroused many people.

a. "For it is not necessary for me to write to you concerning the service to the saints." A few items stand out and demand our attention in the first part of this sentence: the word *for* is the link between the last segment of the preceding chapter and this verse; verses 1 and 2 form the first point Paul wishes to discuss,

---

2. Stanley K. Stowers, "*Peri men gar* and the Integrity of II Cor. 8 and 9," *NovT* 32 (1990): 348. Victor Paul Furnish also defends the interpretation of a close relationship between 8:16–24 and 9:1–5 in *II Corinthians: Translation with Introduction, Notes and Commentary,* Anchor Bible 32A (Garden City, N.Y:. Doubleday, 1984), pp. 432–33, 438–39. But Ralph P. Martin sees the chapters as separate compositions (*II Corinthians*, Word Biblical Commentary 40 [Waco: Word, 1986], p. 250).

3. William Hendriksen, *Bible Survey: A Treasury of Bible Information* (Grand Rapids: Baker, 1953), p. 16.

namely, his boasting about the Corinthians; verses 3 and 4 deal with the effect this boasting may have on him and the Macedonians.

At first sight, the apostle's unwillingness to write about "the service to the saints [in Jerusalem]" seems to form a break with his earlier discussion. But this is not the case if we understand Paul to say that he is fully confident of the Corinthians' desire to contribute to the collection for the poor in Jerusalem (refer to 8:6–7, 10–12; I Cor. 16:1–4). It is noteworthy that Paul mentions Jerusalem only once in his Corinthian correspondence (I Cor. 16:3). This leaves the distinct impression that no additional references to this city are needed.

Paul does not doubt the sincerity of the Corinthians, and therefore he is not interested in writing about their response to his call for giving to the collection. He wants to avoid the prospect of diminishing his readers' eagerness if he should stress this matter once more. Because the three emissaries (Titus, who is called "my brother" [2:13], and the two brothers [v. 3]) will explain all the details to them, there is no need for Paul to be specific in print (see similar passages in Phil. 3:1; I Thess. 4:9; 5:1).[4]

b. "For I know your eagerness about which I boasted to the Macedonians." Paul's admiration for their enthusiastic response to the collection is so great that he boasted about the Corinthians to the Macedonians. He compliments them and says, "I know your eagerness." His tone of voice is much the same as that of Jesus, who uses similar words when he encouragingly addresses the seven churches in Asia Minor and says, "I know your deeds."[5] Paul is not interested in exerting force; instead, he stimulates voluntary obedience to his call for action.[6]

The apostle is a man of word and deed, and he teaches his followers to imitate him (I Cor. 4:16; 11:1). Thus, he wants not merely words from the Corinthians but also deeds. Paul had used the members of the church in Corinth as an example for the churches in Macedonia: Philippi, Thessalonica, and Berea. He had been boasting repeatedly about the Corinthians during his stay in Macedonia and had praised them for their willingness to give.

The Corinthian enthusiasm for the collection inspired the Macedonians to contribute generously to this cause (8:2). Paul attributes this not to his boasting but to the grace of God that worked in the hearts of the people in Macedonia (8:1). These people imitated the eagerness of the Corinthians and went further by translating words into deeds. Now these deeds have become an example to the Corinthians, so that the circle that Paul started is nearly complete.

c. "[I was] saying Achaia had been ready since last year, and your zeal aroused many people." Paul is open and honest with his readers and reports the very words he has spoken to the Macedonians. Achaia was the Roman province that com-

---

4. Translating verse 1, James Denney correctly expands on the meaning of the verb *to write*, "For as for the ministering to the saints, it is superfluous for me to be writing to you as I do." *The Second Epistle to the Corinthians*, 2d ed., The Expositor's Bible series (New York: Armstrong, 1900), p. 280.

5. Rev. 2:2, 9, 13, 19; 3:1, 8, 15.

6. Consult Karl Heinrich Rengstorf, *TDNT*, 6:700.

prised all of southern Greece. The capital of this province was Corinth, which served as the mother church for the congregations in the surrounding area (see Rom. 16:1). To be more inclusive, Paul mentions the province instead of the city.

The people in the church of Corinth and area congregations had been ready to give to the collection since the previous year (8:10). We should be careful not to say that more than a year had elapsed, for we do not know the month in which Paul wrote this chapter. The delay caused by the controversy with the offender (2:5–11; 7:8–9) had repressed the church's eagerness. The apostle who wrote his letter of love to these Corinthians (I Cor. 13) was averse to ascribe even a hint of laxity to the recipients. He applies the words of his letter to himself: "Love does not delight in evil but rejoices with the truth. It always protects, always trusts, always hopes, always perseveres" (I Cor. 13:6–7).

The positive note in Paul's words is that the Corinthians induced many people in Macedonia (Philippi, Thessalonica, and Berea) to donate funds to the collection. This project included all the Gentile churches that Paul had founded. When he first broached the subject to the church in Corinth, the Galatian churches (Derbe, Lystra) had already been approached and had been given instructions (I Cor. 16:1). The churches in the province of Asia, including Ephesus, represented by Tychicus and Trophimus, are also mentioned (Acts 20:4). And last, Paul writes that Macedonia and Achaia were pleased to contribute to the collection for the saints in Jerusalem (Rom. 15:26).[7] Hence, Paul's confidence in the Corinthians had not been shaken, and he was gratified by the outcome of this undertaking.

3. But I am sending the brothers, so that our boasting concerning you might not prove to be hollow in this case, and that you might be prepared, just as I said you would be.

This verse and the next one appear to contradict everything Paul stated in the previous two verses. Why is he sending the brothers if he is boasting about the Corinthians' eagerness? Why does he fear that the Corinthians will fail him? Why is he casting doubts on their readiness?

The answers to these questions must be seen in the light of Paul's integrity and his honesty with the people in Corinth. He is sending the brothers to Corinth not to be administrators or controllers of the gifts that are to be collected, but rather to glorify God. Paul writes that his boasting about the Corinthians might not be in vain. For Paul, the word *boast* implies boasting in the Lord (I Cor. 1:31; II Cor. 10:17). He boasted of the eagerness the Corinthians have shown, just as he rejoiced in the generosity of the Macedonians. His boasting is directed first toward God to express his thankfulness and then toward the churches for their mutual edification. The brothers who are being sent to Corinth have heard Paul boasting about the Corinthians and rejoicing in the Macedonians. They now travel to Corinth to continue this boasting and rejoicing

---

7. Refer to Keith F. Nickle, *The Collection: A Study in Paul's Strategy*, SBT 48 (Naperville: Allenson, 1966), pp. 68–69.

in the Lord. By sending the brothers, Paul wants them to see that the Corinthians are true to the words he has spoken.[8] Therefore, delegates go to Corinth to bolster the eagerness of the Corinthians.

Does Paul fear that the Corinthians will fail him? The apostle knows that all the other churches are also involved in the collection. But he does not want to see the Corinthians falling behind the others and failing to give leadership. He wants the Corinthians to take action and demonstrate their love to the church in Jerusalem and to the brothers sent by the Macedonian churches. Paul's words, then, should be understood positively as words of encouragement. He is not doubting the readiness of the Corinthians but wants their zeal translated into deeds. Paul intimates that if they only show eagerness and nothing more, their words will be hollow sounds. Words and deeds must go together, and the apostle is confident that the recipients of his epistle will demonstrate this sequence to the churches. (Incidentally, Paul's message uttered in 8:24 is echoed in 9:3 and confirms the basic unity and continuity of chapters 8 and 9.)

Paul is using administrative language when he says "in this case."[9] The case refers to his boasting, which in the Greek shows that he did so frequently. Also, with the use of the Greek present tense the writer indicates that the Corinthians were faithful and ready to give to the collection. Paul does not doubt their willingness. As with all the churches, he encourages the people with a negative word to elicit a positive response. He is asking them not to let his boasting be vain words (compare Phil. 2:16; I Thess. 3:5).

4. For if any Macedonians come with me and find you unprepared, we are—not to mention you—put to shame in this situation.

a. *Company.* "For if any Macedonians come with me and find you unprepared." This verse is a continuation of verse 3 and begins with words that express uncertainty. That is, at the moment of his writing, Paul is not certain who will accompany him on his journey from Macedonia to Corinth. Among the travel companions who eventually accompanied Paul, the Macedonians were Sopater from Berea and Aristarchus and Secundus from Thessalonica (Acts 20:4).

If Macedonians escort Paul and find the Corinthians unprepared, blame would attach to that church. We infer from Paul's statement that the brothers Paul was sending to Corinth did not represent Macedonia (8:18, 22). If so, the apostle's escorts would have to place the blame, or at least part of it, on fellow Macedonians.[10]

---

8. Compare F. W. Grosheide, *De Tweede Brief van den Apostel Paulus aan de Kerk te Korinthe*, Kommentaar op het Nieuwe Testament series (Amsterdam: Van Bottenburg, 1939), p. 315.

9. Bauer, p. 506; Betz, *II Corinthians 8 and 9*, p. 94 n. 35.

10. Compare Philip Edgcumbe Hughes, *Paul's Second Epistle to the Corinthians: The English Text with Introduction, Exposition and Notes*, New International Commentary on the New Testament series (Grand Rapids: Eerdmans, 1962), p. 326; Alfred Plummer, *A Critical and Exegetical Commentary on the Second Epistle of St Paul to the Corinthians*, International Critical Commentary (1915; Edinburgh: Clark, 1975), p. 255; Henry Alford, *Alford's Greek Testament: An Exegetical and Critical Commentary*, 7th ed., 4 vols. (1852; reprint ed., Grand Rapids: Guardian, 1976), vol. 2, p. 686.

Paul is striving to consolidate the unity and harmony of the church, so that the collection made by the Gentile churches for the saints in Jerusalem is a unified effort. He wanted the Corinthian and the Macedonian churches to give leadership in this project (see Rom. 15:26). If the church that he fathered (I Cor. 4:15) should lag behind by being unprepared, he would be greatly embarrassed. He wanted them to have the project completely finished by the time he and the Macedonians planned to arrive.

b. *Diplomacy.* "We are—not to mention you—put to shame in this situation." This is an example of dealing tactfully with a congregation when a sensitive matter is discussed. Should the people in Corinth be unprepared when Paul arrived, they would have to suffer blame and humiliation. But note, Paul himself is willing to be held accountable and, as an afterthought, he refers to the Corinthians as if they are guiltless. The original readers would know that not Paul but they would be blameworthy.

There are two different translations of the last phrase that depend on the Greek word *hypostasis.* Nearly all the versions have the reading *confident, sure,* or *trust.* But the word can also mean "situation," "condition," or "undertaking."[11] And this interpretation fits the context in which Paul is discussing his project of collecting funds for the poor in Jerusalem. He stresses not his confidence in the Corinthians, which he already did in the preceding verses, but their readiness for this undertaking.

5. Thus I thought it necessary to urge the brothers to go on to you ahead of me and to prepare in advance the generous gift you promised beforehand. So it will be ready as a generous gift and not as one that is torn away from greed.

a. "Thus I thought it necessary to urge the brothers to go on to you ahead of me." On the basis of the preceding two verses (vv. 3 and 4), Paul writes that he had carefully thought about this matter and concluded that everything pointed to the necessity of sending the brothers (8:18, 20). He chooses his words carefully and says that he urges them to visit Corinth. The two unnamed brothers were commissioned not by Paul but by the churches and were to accompany Titus.

But why does the apostle send the threesome in advance of himself and others? Their task was to help the Corinthians in the joyous task of completing the collection, so that when Paul and the delegation from Macedonia were to arrive, everything would be ready.

b. "And to prepare in advance the generous gift promised beforehand." Paul not only had full confidence in the readers of his epistle, but also reminded them of their earlier enthusiasm and promise. Note the apostle's emphasis on the concept *before* that occurs three times in this verse: ahead of me, in advance, and beforehand. He places the burden on the Corinthians and is fully assured that they will complete what they had promised. He reminds them of a prover-

---

11. Bauer adds, "The sense of 'confidence,' 'assurance' must be eliminated, since examples of it cannot be found" (p. 846). See Helmut Köster, *TDNT*, 8:584–85; Betz, *II Corinthians 8 and 9*, p. 95. The NRSV has "undertaking." Consult Harm W. Hollander, *EDNT*, 3:407. Compare also 11:17; Heb. 3:14.

bial truth: "A promise made is a debt unpaid." Paul seems to indicate that the people in Corinth were not unwilling to give but needed help in organizing the work of collecting the funds.[12]

The promise the Corinthians had made earlier related to a substantial gift that Paul describes with the Greek word *eulogia*. This term occurs twice in two successive clauses of this verse. We have the derivative *eulogy*, referring to praise, but in the Bible the word usually means "blessing" or "the act of blessing."[13] The act of blessing signifies that the Corinthians through their generous gift to the church in Jerusalem will experience God's grace extended to both giver and receiver (compare Acts 20:35).[14]

c. "So it will be ready as a generous gift and not as one that is torn away from greed." The purpose for the preliminary work of collecting the funds is that all will be ready when Paul and fellow travelers arrive in Corinth. And the result of this work will be the joyful experience of giving generously. Once more Paul writes the Greek word *eulogia*, now in contrast with greed. Giving that originates in a heart dedicated to God always results in a blessing, for the gift will bless the recipient and God will grant his favor to the giver. But giving with a heart ensnared by greed can never receive God's approval, for greed, which is idolatry, has taken God's rightful place (Col. 3:5). This is the contrast that Paul places before his readers, and he trusts that their financial gift may come forth from generosity rather than greed. Love for one's neighbor is an act of blessing, while greed motivates one to take advantage of one's neighbor.[15]

Paul is not implying that the members of the Corinthian church were short on generosity and long on greed. On the contrary, he had commended them for their eagerness to help (8:11; 9:2), and he is confident that the people will respond well. In the last clause of this verse, Paul puts the emphasis on the grace of giving and thus his remark is positive, not negative.

Greek Words, Phrases, and Constructions in 9:1–5

Verses 1–2

περὶ μὲν γάρ—this expression differs from the repetitive περὶ δέ in I Corinthians (7:1; 8:1; 12:1; 16:1, 12), which refers to a letter addressed to Paul. Here the phrase is a continuation and an explanation of the preceding context, as is indicated by the particle γάρ. Also, the particle μέν is balanced by δέ in verse 3, so that verses 1 and 2 are contrasted with verses 3 and 4.

---

12. Refer to Hughes, *Second Epistle to the Corinthians*, p. 327 n. 58.

13. Bauer, p. 322.

14. Consult Hans-Georg Link, *NIDNTT*, 1:214. John Calvin relates the word *blessing* to God, and from God it is transferred to human beings without losing its divine connection. *The Second Epistle of Paul the Apostle to the Corinthians and the Epistles to Timothy, Titus and Philemon*, Calvin's Commentaries series, trans. T. A. Small (Grand Rapids: Eerdmans, 1964), p. 121. Refer also to SB 3:524.

15. Compare Gerhard Delling, *TDNT*, 6:273.

τὸ γράφειν—the present tense indicates continued action with the implication that Paul had written about the collection earlier.[16]

τὸ ὑμῶν ζῆλος—instead of the masculine gender (7:7, 11), Paul uses the neuter and places the possessive pronoun between the article and the noun for emphasis.

Verses 3–4

ἔπεμψα—as in 8:17, 18, 22, this is the epistolary aorist that is translated as a present: "I am sending."

τὸ ὑπὲρ ὑμῶν—the definite article with the prepositional phrase on your behalf is used to avoid any misunderstanding.

ἵνα μὴ λέγω ὑμεῖς—this clause has two nominatives, "I" and "you." Paul meant to say, "that you might not be put to shame," but that statement would be too direct. He tactfully calls attention to himself by saying, "I am not saying that you [would do this]" and leaves the opposite impression. The singular λέγω is preferred to the plural λέγωμεν.

Verse 5

προέλθωσιν—the repetition of the preposition πρό occurs three times in compound verbs. Also note the use of the Greek letter π in this verse for alliteration.

ταύτην ἑτοίμην εἶναι—after the ἵνα clause, these words express purpose or result. Perhaps both are meant.[17]

E. Cheerful Giving
9:6–11

God takes great delight in giving gifts to his people. He favors them with spiritual and material blessings that cannot even be enumerated. He challenges his people to follow his example and wants them to realize that "every good and perfect gift is from above, coming down from the Father of the heavenly lights, who does not change like shifting shadows" (James 1:17). As the Father shows his generosity, so he expects his sons and daughters to be generous. And children of the heavenly Father should remember that they will never be able to rival God in his giving. No matter how charitable they are, much to their surprise they will experience that God is still more beneficent toward them.

The next segment is closely connected with the preceding one, for Paul continues to expand the discussion on giving. He now features a proverbial saying, self-evident truths, and Scripture citations.

1. The Generous Giver
9:6–9

6. The point is this: he who sows sparingly will also reap sparingly, and he who sows generously will also reap generously.

Translations of the first clause vary because Paul's statement is brief. It literally

---

16. Friedrich Blass and Albert Debrunner, *A Greek Grammar of the New Testament and Other Early Christian Literature,* trans. and rev. Robert Funk (Chicago: University of Chicago Press, 1961), #399.2.

17. Robert Hanna, *A Grammatical Aid to the Greek New Testament* (Grand Rapids: Baker, 1983), p. 327.

says, "And this," so that we have to supply a word or phrase to complete the thought. Here are a few examples:

"Remember" or "Remember this" (NEB, REB, NCV)
"But this I say" (KJV, NKJV, NASB)
"Let me say this much" (NAB)
"Do not forget" (JB)

Although we do not doubt that Paul could have taught the truth of this verse at an earlier occasion, the present context suggests that we should state either "this I say" or "the point is this" (RSV, NRSV). The stress falls on the following saying, of which the first part may have been an agricultural proverb in that day: "He who sows sparingly will also reap sparingly, and he who sows generously will also reap generously." We do not know whether Paul was thinking of a verse in the Old Testament Book of Proverbs, "One man gives freely, yet gains even more; another withholds unduly, but comes to poverty" (11:24).

In the agricultural society of the first century, the activities of sowing and reaping lay close to the hearts of the people. The sower in Jesus' parable (Matt. 13:3–9 and parallels) did not close his hand when he saw that some kernels would fall on the beaten path, the rocky soil, and the briar patch. He sowed generously as with rhythmic walk he strode across the field. And just as the parable of the sower has a spiritual application, so the words of Paul are analogous to a spiritual truth. He writes elsewhere, "A man reaps what he sows" (Gal. 6:7; see also Luke 6:38), which is a law inherent in both physical and spiritual spheres.

When seed falls to the ground, it decays while it germinates. In a sense, the farmer loses the seed he has scattered; he takes the risk of weather conditions, disease, or insects destroying much of the seed. But as he sows, he trusts that God will grant him the satisfaction of reaping a harvest. This is also true spiritually. Missionary James Elliot put it succinctly: "He is no fool who gives up what he cannot keep to gain what he cannot lose."[18] Elliot was slain in an effort to evangelize the Auca Indians of Ecuador, but his death was instrumental in leading them to Christ.

The words of the proverbial saying reveal an inner symmetry that is striking:

> he who sows sparingly,
> > sparingly he will also reap
> he who sows blessings,
> > blessings he will also reap

The Greek text is more precise than our translations. Although the adverb *sparingly* occurs only here in the New Testament and is self-explanatory, the word *blessings* has spiritual overtones and without doubt was written by Paul. The second half of the proverbial saying literally reads: "he who sows on the basis of blessings, on the basis of blessings he will also reap." That is, he who gives by

---

18. Elisabeth Elliot, *Shadow of the Almighty* (New York: Harper and Brothers, 1958), p. 15.

praising God will in turn reap a harvest for which he thanks the Lord.[19] The generous giver responds with thanks and praises to God for the numerous material and spiritual blessings he receives (see Deut. 15:10).

7. Let each one give as he has decided in his mind to give, not reluctantly or out of necessity. For God loves a cheerful giver.

a. "Let each one give as he has decided in his mind to give, not reluctantly or out of necessity." Paul issues no command, enacts no rule or regulation, and exercises no coercion. He gives the Corinthians complete freedom and tells them to decide in their own hearts what to give. He specifies, however, that the responsibility rests on the individual and not on the church as such. Each person must ponder this matter in his or her own heart and then decide, so that the entire congregation may be united in contributing to the collection.

Paul says that the act of giving must be accomplished neither reluctantly nor grudgingly. Reluctance implies a clinging to possessions that one hardly wants to give; and when they have been given, the giver grieves. Giving grudgingly denotes that external pressures compel one to conform to the rules of society; that is, necessity forces one to comply with the community's objective. Giving, however, must be voluntary and individually motivated (see 8:3; Philem. 14).

By participating voluntarily, each person testifies to true faith in Jesus. Indeed, by voluntarily giving to the collection, Gentile Christians in Corinth demonstrate equality with the Jewish Christians in Jerusalem. They also authenticate their legitimate membership in Christ's universal church.[20]

b. "For God loves a cheerful giver." Within the Christian community, this verse is most often quoted in connection with giving. The verse comes from the Greek text of Proverbs 22:8a, "God blesses a cheerful man and giver," from which Paul has deleted the words *man and* and has changed the verb *blesses* to "loves." The Hebrew text lacks this verse; it is found only in the Greek text of the Septuagint. This saying probably circulated orally as a proverb that Paul quotes from memory.

Why did the apostle write "loves" instead of "blesses"? Did his memory fail him? While writing, could he have had access to a scroll of Proverbs? There are no specific answers, but there are at least two suggestions to explain the substitution. First, in Paul's epistle the concept *love* is much more prominent than the family of the word *bless*.[21] Next, the force of the verb *to love* is all-encompassing, while that of the verb *to bless* connotes a beneficent act.[22]

---

19. Consult R. C. H. Lenski, *The Interpretation of St. Paul's First and Second Epistle to the Corinthians* (Columbus: Wartburg, 1946), p. 1170. Compare Betz, *II Corinthians 8 and 9*, p. 103.

20. Nickle, *The Collection*, p. 127.

21. The word group *love* occurs 136 times in Paul's epistles (consult Gerhard Schneider, *EDNT*, 1:9), and that of *bless* 20 times. God's love is the "atmosphere" in which the giver lives. See Dieter Georgi, *Der Armen zu Gedenken: Die Geschichte der Kollekte des Paulus für Jerusalem*, 2d rev. and expanded ed. (Neukirchen-Vluyn: Neukirchener Verlag, 1994), p. 70; the English translation is *Remembering the Poor: The History of Paul's Collection for Jerusalem* (Nashville: Abingdon, 1992), p. 96.

22. In their respective commentaries, Plummer (p. 259) remarks that Paul "would not deliberately have changed" the text. But Paul's quotations often show changes. And Hughes (p. 331 n. 65) asserts that the reading *loves* was in the manuscript Paul knew. This is a guess.

From a theological perspective, Paul discerns the indescribable love that God the Father imparts to his children. Just as he loves them, they must love one another. For this reason, Paul told the Corinthians that he wanted to test the genuineness of their love by considering the grace of Jesus Christ (8:8–9).

8. For God is able to make all grace abound toward you, so that in everything you may always have enough of everything and you may abound in every good work.

a. *Power.* "For God is able to make all grace abound toward you." Here are two preliminary observations:

First, in the preceding verse Paul teaches that God is love, and in the present verse that God is all-powerful. That is, God expresses his love to his people through his power.

Next, throughout this verse the concept *all* appears five times: all, everything, always, everything, and every. With this concept, Paul attempts to describe God's infinite goodness and greatness.

The first item Paul discusses is that God has power "to make all grace abound toward you." God is involved in all the intricacies of a person's life, even in the decision one makes to give for a certain cause. Paul wrote that the Macedonians received God's grace so that their decision to give resulted in a wealth of generosity (8:2). In the service of the Lord grace begets grace, although the believer's grace in joyful giving can hardly be compared with God's abounding grace to the believer. God showers his love on the joyful donor, who is unable to match God's grace. He grants the gift of salvation, spiritual gifts, the fruits of the Spirit, and innumerable material blessings. In conclusion, all the spiritual and physical gifts are included in the word *grace.* The Corinthians were fully aware of Paul's teaching on this point (see, e.g., I Cor. 1:4–7; 12; II Cor. 4:15; 6:1).

b. *Sufficiency.* "So that in everything you may always have enough of everything." If we take these words literally, they appear too good to be true. Does God give the joyful Christian everything to meet all his or her material needs (compare Phil. 4:19)? True, God's grace is all-sufficient to meet our every need any time. But when he grants us his grace, it is always meant to glorify him in his church and kingdom on earth:

> It is given to us and we have it, not that we may have, but that we may do well therefore. All things in this life, even rewards, are seeds to believers for the future harvest.[23]

A Christian who because of God's grace always has enough of everything (compare I Tim. 6:6–8) must give within the framework of loving God and neighbor (Matt. 22:37–40). The spiritual and material flow of gifts coming from God to the believer may never stop with the recipient. It must be passed on to alleviate

23. John Albert Bengel, *New Testament Commentary,* trans. Charlton T. Lewis and Marvin R. Vincent, 2 vols. (Grand Rapids: Kregel, 1981), vol. 2, p. 316.

the needs of others in church and society (Gal. 6:10; I Tim. 6:17–18; II Tim. 3:17). The believer must always be a human channel through which divine grace flows to enrich others.

Paul writes the word *autarkeia*, which in this context means "sufficiency."[24] This cannot be interpreted as self-sufficiency or self-reliance, for we are completely dependent on God to supply us in every need. God provides us sufficiency for the purpose of our dependence on him and the support of fellow human beings.

c. *Service.* "And you may abound in every good work." Twice in this verse Paul relates the verb *to abound* to God and to us. God makes his grace abound so that we may abound in performing good deeds.[25] Fully trusting God to provide the necessary means, we may support the causes that promote his message at worship on Sundays. We support missions and evangelism, and in society we apply his divine message. God's grace (singular noun) appears in varied forms; similarly, our good work (also a singular noun) includes all our activities.[26]

9. Just as it is written,

> **He has scattered, he has given to the poor,**
> **his righteousness endures forever.**

As he has done all along, Paul strengthens his discourse by citing an Old Testament passage.[27] He turns to the Psalter, and from its Greek translation he quotes Psalm 112:9 (111:9, LXX) with a slight omission. He wants to portray God's boundless goodness toward the poor and his everlasting righteousness.

The subject in Psalm 112 is "the man who fears the LORD" (v. 1). Paul omits any reference to man when he quotes this verse, yet in his discourse the preceding and the succeeding verses (9:8, 10) feature God as subject. This apparent inconsistency dissipates when we look at Psalms 111 and 112 as one unit. Note that God is the subject in the first psalm (Ps. 111) and man in the second (Ps. 112). Also, both psalms have similar words and identical phrases, for example, "his righteousness endures forever" (Pss. 111:3; 112:3, 9).[28] And last, man is encouraged to live in conformity to God's commands. As God is gracious and compassionate (Ps. 111:4) so the righteous man should be (Ps. 112:4).

The first line of the quotation states that a person liberally scatters his gifts to the poor, for he has been blessed with wealth and riches. Because he is generous and lends freely, he is the recipient of good will and high honor (Ps. 112:3, 5, 9).

---

24. Gerhard Kittel, *TDNT*, 1:467; Burghard Siede, *NIDNTT*, 3:728.

25. Refer to Eph. 2:10; Col. 1:10; II Thess. 2:17; II Tim. 3:17; Titus 2:14.

26. Georgi (*Remembering the Poor*, p. 97) notes, "Only when the rule of divine grace is not given recognition does Paul feel justified in speaking of 'works' in the plural."

27. Second Corinthians has eleven quotations: Ps. 116:10 (4:13); Isa. 49:8 (6:2); Lev. 26:12 and Ezek. 37:27 (6:16); Isa. 52:11 (6:17a); Ezek. 20:34 [LXX] (6:17b); II Sam. 7:8, 14 (6:18); Exod. 16:18 (8:15); Ps. 112:9 (9:9); Jer. 9:24 (10:17); Deut. 19:15 (13:1).

28. Willem A. VanGemeren, *Psalms*, in vol. 5 of *The Expositor's Bible Commentary*, 12 vols., ed. Frank E. Gaebelein (Grand Rapids: Zondervan, 1991), p. 706.

The second line repeats words that describe God; here they are applied to his child. The clause "his righteousness endures forever" depicts one of God's characteristics but hardly fits a mortal being in a sinful world. Nonetheless, both the Hebrew and the Greek word for righteousness may also mean kindness or mercy in the sense of charitable giving.[29] And that connotation fits the psalm and Paul's context.

Doctrinal Considerations in 9:6

According to Jesus, giving should be done in secret and ought never to become a cause of boasting. When you give in secret, he says, your Father who sees in secret will reward you (Matt. 6:3–4). But does our giving obligate God to reward us? Is giving the same as investing our money to gain high returns? Certainly not, because God is not a bank. God wants giving to come out of hearts filled with love. Love keeps no record of good deeds that must be rewarded. On the judgment day, the righteous will ask: "Lord, when did we see you hungry and feed you, or thirsty and give you something to drink?" And then the King answers, "Whatever you did for one of the least of these brothers of mine, you did for me" (Matt. 25:37, 40).

The cheerful giver opens his or her hand and freely gives to the needy. Certainly this does not mean that a person must give away everything. If Christians were to donate all their belongings to help the poor, their resources to generate additional income would be gone and they themselves would be poor. The members of the early church helped the poor by selling parcels of land or houses, but they did this only from time to time (Acts 4:34). The apostles never coerced the rich to sell their property, but they expected that each person would give voluntarily from a cheerful heart.

By distributing blessing upon blessing to our fellow human beings, we in turn will receive multitudes of unexpected blessings from God. Whatever one distributes bountifully will be returned eventually in even greater measure. Calvin paraphrases rightly the words of Paul and says, "The more liberal you are to your neighbours, the more liberal you will find the blessing that God pours forth on you."[30]

Greek Words, Phrases, and Constructions in 9:7–8

προῄρηται—the perfect from προαιρέω, which in the middle means "I choose (for myself), decide." Once again (see v. 5), Paul uses a compound verb that features the preposition πρό (beforehand). The Majority Text has the present tense προαιρεῖται (see KJV, NKJV).

ἱλαρόν—"cheerful." Although we have the derivative *hilarious,* here the meaning of this word "might easily pass over into *kind, gracious.*"[31]

ἀγαπᾷ—the present tense is timeless and states a self-evident truth. It is gnomic.[32]

---

29. Bauer, p. 196.

30. Calvin, *II Corinthians*, p. 121.

31. Bauer, p. 375.

32. C. F. D. Moule, *An Idiom-Book of New Testament Greek,* 2d ed. (Cambridge: Cambridge University Press, 1960), p. 8.

δυνατεῖ—occurring only three times in the New Testament (Rom. 14:4; II Cor. 9:8; 13:3), all referring to divinity, this verb signifies that God and Christ have power.

Note the alliteration of πᾶς (four times), πάντοτε, and περισσεύω (twice). The noun αὐτάρκειαν can mean either "sufficiency" or "contentment." The first meaning is preferred.

---

2. The Grateful Giver
9:10–11

10. Now he who provides seed to the sower and bread to the eater will provide and multiply your seed and will increase the harvest of your righteousness.

a. *Scripture.* Here is still another quotation from the Old Testament Scriptures, this time from Isaiah 55:10: "The rain and the snow come down from heaven, and do not return to it without watering the earth and making it bud and flourish, so that it yields seed for the sower and bread for the eater." The context of Isaiah's prophecy shows that God is the subject who provides the rain and the snow to function as his instruments to germinate the grain that was sown. Without even mentioning him, Paul makes God the subject of this prophecy.

This verse reveals still more Old Testament Scripture, for the phrase *the harvest of your righteousness* is an allusion that comes from Hosea 10:12. "Plant righteousness, and reap the blessings that your devotion to me will produce" (GNB). The prophet exhorts the people of Israel to abandon evil, repent, plant righteousness, and reap a harvest of blessings. Although Paul does not quote the prophet verbatim, his allusion is clear and fits the context of his discourse.

b. *Significance.* After a devastating drought is over, the basic requirement of farmers is seed. When the task of plowing and sowing is completed, they wait for rain to germinate the seed and for growth to produce a harvest. They realize their inability to make the seed germinate and the plants grow. That is God's work. But Paul says that God provides even the seed that is to be sown, so that farmers are dependent on God from beginning to end. If there is no seed, there is no crop.

The Corinthians had to understand that as seed and harvests come from God, so all their material and spiritual blessings originate in him and are multiplied by him. God dispenses seed for the benefit of his people. His people likewise should give of their possessions to benefit the poor, for then they will understand that the seed that they have sown God will turn into a harvest of righteousness. Notice that Paul does not say that God will bless the giver with a harvest of material good. Alluding to the prophecy of Hosea, Paul writes that for the giver God will increase a harvest of righteousness.

The kernels of seed that are sown are only a fraction, in comparison, of the seed the farmer reaps at harvest time. The farmer sows the seed and leaves the growing and maturing process to God. Similarly, from God the believers receive material and spiritual gifts from which they must pass on gifts to those who are in need. But the increase and expansion of these gifts they leave to God, who will give them an abundant harvest of righteousness. Indeed, God will do this, and God's people can fully depend on him to keep his word.[33] In turn, they become fountains of generosity and as such they reflect God's benevolence in their lives.

In this context, the term *righteousness* is another word for openhandedness (see the commentary on v. 9). It includes feeding and clothing the poor, lending money, showing kindness and mercy, and defending the rights of those who are disadvantaged. Paul chooses his words carefully and writes, "your righteousness," to specify that it is personal. Wherever righteousness flourishes, there blessings abound as God causes the increase of more and more gifts on his people. "He who is kind to the poor lends to the LORD, and he will reward him for what he has done" (Prov. 19:17).

11. You will be made rich in every way to be altogether generous, and through us your generosity will produce thanksgiving to God.

a. *"You will be made rich in every way to be altogether generous."* When Paul writes about giving, he features the Greek adjective *pas* (all), as in verse 8 (where it occurs five times). The word *pas* appears here twice, "in every way" and "altogether." This means that God's hand is never closed to persons who joyfully pass some of their resources to those who are impoverished, as in the case of the Macedonians (8:2).

The verb form *to be made rich* is in the passive and alludes to God as the agent who enriches the Corinthians. God blesses the cheerful giver with riches in every respect: materially, economically, spiritually, intellectually, socially, temporally, and eternally. His blessings are imparted to the giver in various forms and often at different times. The verb also can be read as a middle, which then means "enriching others."[34] However, the passive voice suits the context better and is preferred.

Let no one think that God makes people rich materially because they are Christians, for the contrary is frequently true. The concept *to make rich* does not signify that God showers us with material goods to satisfy our selfish desires. This verse clearly states that the enrichment is meant that we may be immeasurably generous. Most translators put the verb in the future to conform to the future tense in the preceding verse (v. 10). But the Greek text has it in the present tense as an indication that God already is enriching the Corinthians to become extremely generous in their giving. They are a channel through which God's blessings flow to people in need.

b. *"And through us your generosity will produce thanksgiving to God."* What an insightful comment! Paul is saying that he and his colleagues brought the gospel to the Corinthians so that they could be thankful believers not only in words but also in deeds. The Lord Jesus Christ sent to Corinth missionaries who sought to exalt God in their ministry. God inspired Paul to speak and write about the collection for the poverty-stricken saints in Jerusalem. The result will be that the recipients of these gifts will express their thanks to God, and the givers in all the

---

33. Compare Lenski, *Second Corinthians*, p. 1179.
34. Héring, *Second Epistle of Paul*, p. 67.

churches will be joyful and happy in the Lord (4:14). In short, the entire church rejoices and gives God the glory.

Practical Considerations in 9:10–11

Only twice in all of Scripture do we find times in which there were no poor among God's people. First, the Old Testament teaches that when the Israelites traveled through the desert from Egypt to Canaan, everybody had sufficient food, clothing, and the basic necessities of life. God provided for the daily needs of his people and there were neither rich nor poor in the camp of Israel. Next, in the early years of the Christian church in Jerusalem, the rich from time to time would sell a piece of property and present the revenue to the apostles for distribution among the poor. Luke writes this startling statement, "There were no needy persons among them" (Acts 4:34a). During the springtime of the church, love for one another eliminated poverty.

In later years, Paul set the example of helping others. He said that he worked with his own hands to meet his needs and those of his companions. Then he instructed the Ephesian elders to help the weak, to be generous, and to remember Jesus's words: "It is more blessed to give than to receive" (Acts 20:34–35).

And last, the apostolic command to take care of the poor remains a lasting imperative for the church (Gal. 2:10; 6:10). When Christians obey this command, they experience the love of Christ revealed in both the giving and the receiving of their gifts. And they reap a harvest of righteousness.

Greek Words, Phrases, and Constructions in 9:10–11

σπόρον—following the Septuagint, most editions of the Greek New Testament have the word σπέρμα. The two terms have the same meaning. The harder reading is σπόρον, which has the support of some early witnesses (P[46], B, D[*]).

τὰ γενήματα—"fruits." This noun derives from the verb γίνομαι (I am, become), not from γεννάω (I beget).[35] The plural is translated as a singular: "harvest."

πλουτιζόμενοι—Paul frequently writes a participle that is not connected with a main verb and in translation becomes a finite verb.[36] The imperatival sense of the participle must be dismissed,[37] for the context pleads for the future tense even though Paul writes the present tense.

F. Surpassing Grace
9:12–15

12. For the ministry of this service not only is supplying the needs of the saints but also is overflowing through many expressions of thanks to God.

---

35. Bauer, p. 155.

36. See the Greek text of II Cor. 1:7; 7:5; 8:19, 20.

37. Moule (*Idiom-Book*, pp. 31, 179) suggests the possibility of an imperatival interpretation. C. K. Barrett favors the present tense; see *The Second Epistle to the Corinthians*, Harper's New Testament Commentaries series (New York: Harper and Row, 1973), p. 237.

a. "For the ministry of this service." In this epistle, Paul makes use of the word group *diakonia* more than in any other letter.[38] The word relates to Paul's ministry, especially where it pertained to the Corinthians. Here, however, the focus is on the Jewish Christians in Jerusalem, who now will be served by the Gentile churches. Not the word *ministry* but the phrase *of this service* needs a lucid interpretation.

There are three different explanations: First, the two words *ministry* and *service* are synonyms. But if this is true, why would Paul indulge in redundancy and why would he use the demonstrative pronoun *this* to modify "ministry"? Next, secular usage of the word *ministry* connotes public distribution of funds to the people in Jerusalem. But it is unlikely that in this setting Paul had in mind strictly public service. Last, "ministry" is a word that describes the religious service of Gentile Christians to the Jewish Christians in the capital of Israel. And this interpretation seems to fit the context and does justice to those terms, including "gift," "grace of giving," and "blessing." It refers to the harvest of righteousness that the Gentile churches reap.[39]

This last interpretation describes the people who obey God, give thanks to him for Christian fellowship, and help one another by participating in the collection.[40] Their offerings should be interpreted as sacrifices, and the distribution of these gifts is a true ministry to the saints.

b. "[This ministry] not only is supplying the needs of the saints but also is overflowing through many expressions of thanks to God." In the second part of this verse, Paul stresses two verbs that are written in the progressive tense: "is supplying" and "is overflowing." In view of the protracted time during which the giving and the receiving occurred, Paul appropriately writes the progressive tense.

Believers throughout Achaia, Macedonia, and Asia Minor contributed monetary gifts that delegates carried to Judea and distributed to the needy in Jerusalem. In all these places, both Jewish and Gentile Christians, united in heart and soul, were expressing joyful praises to God. As the needs of the poor in Jerusalem were met, God was glorified through the many words of thanks that were uttered.

Some forty years after Paul penned this epistle, Clement of Rome uttered a faint echo of verse 12, "Let the rich man bestow help on the poor and let the poor give thanks to God, that he gave him one to supply his needs."[41] The vocabulary (rich, supply, need, thanks, God) is similar in both documents. Both writers teach the truth of alleviating the needs of the poor, who return thanks to God for the giver and the gift (see 1:11; 4:15). The characteristics of genuine love toward the needy are revealed in words of praise to God.[42]

38. The noun *diakonia* occurs twelve times: 3:7, 8, 9 [twice]; 4:1; 5:18; 6:3; 8:4; 9:1, 12, 13; 11:8. The noun *diakonos* appears four times: 3:6; 6:4; 11:15, 23. And the participial forms of the verb *diakonein* occurs three times: 3:3; 8:19, 20.

39. Compare Klaus Hess, *NIDNTT*, 3:552–53. The word *ministry* can refer also to priestly ceremonies at religious temples. But this meaning is unsuitable in Paul's discussion.

40. Georgi, *Remembering the Poor*, p. 103; Horst Balz, *EDNT*, 2:349.

41. I Clem. 38.2 (LCL). See also the commentaries of Windisch, p. 281; Furnish, p. 451.

42. Consult Denney, *Second Corinthians*, pp. 284–85.

13. Through the testing of this service they will be glorifying God because of your submission to the confession that acknowledges the gospel of Christ and the generosity of your [proof of] partnership with them and everyone.

a. "Through the testing of this service they will be glorifying God." Who are the people that are being tested? Who is doing the testing? And who are those that will glorify God? The service of the ministry is performed by the donors; in this text, the Corinthians. The recipients of their gifts are the saints in Jerusalem, who will test the genuine love of the Gentile churches. As a result of this testing, the people in Jerusalem will magnify God's name.

Paul knew the mind and heart of the believers in Macedonia and Achaia. He had positive proof of the genuine love demonstrated by the Macedonian churches: their collection. He also was confident that the Corinthians would not disappoint him in showing their tangible love. But with respect to the Jewish Christians in Jerusalem, he had to have complete trust. Would they respond positively and spiritually to the lavish donation from the Gentile churches? The translation *will be glorifying God* looks confidently to the future and is more appropriate than the present tense, "they are glorifying." Incidentally, the Greek text has only the reading *glorifying* and does not provide a subject.

Another translation is "you glorify God."[43] Proponents of this reading assert that because of the lack of a subject in the Greek, the second person pronoun *you* fits the preceding and the succeeding contexts. But if we put the pronoun *you* in this clause, the verse applies only to the Corinthians. Paul, however, intends to underscore the unity of the churches in Judea and Achaia. Hence, scholars prefer the translation "they will be [are] glorifying God" and apply it to the saints in Jerusalem.

b. "Because of your submission to the confession that acknowledges the gospel of Christ." Among the believers in the mother church of Jerusalem were some who prayerfully supported Paul, his fellow workers, and the Gentile believers. Yet many others were distrustfully awaiting the results of Paul's missionary work among the Gentiles (see Acts 21:17–25). Now Paul wants the Corinthians to know that the Judean churches will be praising God for the confession of faith coming from the lips of the Corinthians. Admittedly, not everyone in the Christian community of Corinth is fully submissive to Christ's gospel. These words of Paul, then, serve as a stimulus for the Corinthians to attain a higher degree of obedience to Christ. Nevertheless, Paul is confident that the saints in Jerusalem glorify God because the Gentiles believe and are obeying the gospel proclamation.

The good news came to the Corinthians not in written form but as an oral proclamation. It was delivered by human messengers: the apostles Paul and Peter, with the apostolic helpers Silas, Timothy, Apollos, and Titus. The response to the preaching of the gospel came in both the words and the deeds of the Corinthians. When Paul writes the term *confession*, then, we ought not to think in terms of a creedal statement (compare I Cor. 12:3). Rather, he has in mind

---

43. RSV, NRSV; F. F. Bruce, *1 and 2 Corinthians,* New Century Bible (London: Oliphants, 1971), p. 228.

actions by which believers exhibit daily obedience to Christ's gospel. The Corinthians acknowledge the truths of that message when they hear and obey the voice of Christ.

c. "And the generosity of your [proof of] partnership with them and everyone." Paul has complete confidence that the collection in the Christian community at Corinth will be an indication of generosity toward the people in Jerusalem (v. 11). According to Paul, this deed of charity will strengthen the bond of fellowship between the Jewish and the Gentile churches. He wants to see the unity of all the churches as they share possessions with one another (compare 8:2–4).

The Gentile believers generously shared their material resources with the Jewish saints in Jerusalem as a demonstration of a bond of mutual fellowship.[44] Their act of sharing resulted in God being praised by the recipients of these gifts (Acts 21:19–20a). And Paul does not limit the proof of partnership to Corinth and Jerusalem but includes all Christians everywhere. We assume that whenever the need arose, the Gentile churches would help others. They knew that the church of Jesus Christ is one body with many members (I Cor. 12:27).

14. And in their prayers for you they will long for you because of the surpassing grace of God upon you.

Paul knew that the church in Jerusalem, and especially James and the elders, supported him in prayer. These saints also prayed fervently for the Corinthian congregation. Paul could confidently write to the church in Corinth that the saints in Jerusalem expressed unity with them in Christ by praying for their spiritual needs. Christians fervently intercede for one another because of the bond of fellowship they have in common.[45]

The members of the church in Jerusalem voice to God their heartfelt yearning for the Corinthians. This does not mean that they would travel to Achaia—the extreme poverty of the saints in Judea made it financially impossible to travel long distances. Rather, they had a spiritual longing for both the Gentile and the Jewish Christians in Corinth. They wished to edify them in their faith (Rom. 15:27). They could satisfy their longing for the Corinthians only through intercessory prayer to God and beseech him to strengthen the unity of the universal church.

Why do the believers in Jerusalem pray earnestly for the Corinthians? Paul answers, "Because of the surpassing grace of God upon you." Throughout chapters 8 and 9, the apostle has written about the collection, which he often described with the Greek word *charis* (grace, favor, gracious deed or gift). Here the word points to God and thus must be understood in an all-embracing sense. That is, Paul adorns the noun *grace* with the adjective *surpassing* to indicate that God dispenses his grace to numerous people.

In the middle of the first century, would Jewish people ever have predicted that a predominantly Gentile church in Corinth would voluntarily gather gifts

---

44. Josef Hainz, *EDNT,* 2:305.
45. Hans Schönweiss, *NIDNTT,* 2:861; Ulrich Schoenborn, *EDNT,* 1:287.

for the poor in Jerusalem?[46] Hardly, for although gifts from well-to-do Jews in dispersion were frequently sent to relatives and friends in Judea, donations from Greeks to "barbarians" would never be collected and sent. But now Gentile believers show their loving concern for the poor in another country and city. This is God's grace at work in the hearts of both the donors and recipients to bring them together as one united and universal body of Christ.

Three brief comments. First, Paul ascribes to God the glory and honor for putting in the hearts of the Corinthians a desire to contribute to the collection. Next, his faith in God is unwavering, because he knows that God's grace will surpass all expectations to bring the collection to its destined and multiple end. Last, Paul puts complete confidence in the church at Corinth and trusts that the members will respond enthusiastically to his appeal. And he counts on the church at Jerusalem for sustained prayer support.

15. Thanks be to God for his indescribable gift.

This text often appears on Christmas cards with the message that God has given us the gift of his Son. No one questions the truth of this message, but those readers who take the time to look at the context of this verse immediately notice that Paul says nothing about Jesus' birth.

What is Paul trying to convey? With the words of a prayer, "Thanks be to God,"[47] he introduces a doxology, which is a fitting conclusion to the preceding reference to God's surpassing grace. God receives the tribute that is due him for his providence to make the collection a blessing to the entire church.

Paul expresses his gratitude to God "for his indescribable gift" of Jesus Christ. The apostle John writes about the unfathomable love of God (John 3:16; I John 4:9), but Paul notes the gift of God. This gift of God to the world is the birth, ministry, suffering, death, resurrection, ascension, and eventual return of his Son. For Paul, the thought of God giving his Son to mankind is astounding. He sees the glorious results in the faith both Jew and Gentile place in Jesus Christ, in the breaking down of racial barriers, and in the unity of the Christian church. Presently the church of Jesus Christ is spanning the globe, so that everywhere Christians gather and worship the Lord. Believers meet in cathedrals, churches, chapels, private homes, a variety of other buildings, forests, caves, and hidden places. By means of the airwaves, the printed page, and the spoken word, the gospel goes forth throughout the world and accomplishes the purpose for which God has sent it (Isa. 55:11).

We see God's indescribable gift, namely, his Son Jesus Christ, in the development and progress of the church. In his lifetime, Paul saw God's kingdom advancing from Jerusalem to Rome and parts of the Roman Empire. In our times we witness its worldwide growth, power, and influence. Paul called attention to God's inexpressible gift of salvation and gave thanks. With him, we too express our gratitude to God for the coming of his Son. On this earth we will never be

---

46. Compare Grosheide, *Tweede Brief aan Korinthe*, p. 333.
47. See also Rom. 6:17; 7:25; I Cor. 15:57; II Cor. 8:16.

able to fathom the depth of God's love for us, the infinite value of our salvation, and the gift of eternal life. God's gift indeed is indescribable!

Greek Words, Phrases, and Constructions in 9:12–15

Verse 12

ὅτι—most translations make this conjunction causal (NASB, NRSV), while others omit it for stylistic reasons (NAB, NCV, NIV).

λειτουργίας—this noun appears six times in the New Testament, of which three are in Paul's epistles (here and in Phil. 2:17, 30). It describes services rendered to God or to his people, such as acts of Christian love and mercy.

The related verb λειτουργέω appears in Romans 15:27 in the context of the collection for the saints in Jerusalem.

Verses 13–14

δοξάζοντες—this participle must be interpreted as a finite verb similar to πλουτιζό-μενοι in verse 11. Note the present tense that has a future connotation, because of the eventual delivery of the collection.[48]

ἐπί—translations of this preposition vary: for, by, because. The causal interpretation has merit as it relates to verbs that express feelings and opinions, which in this case is the verb to glorify.[49]

ἐπιποθούντων—the present tense of this participle denotes continued activity; the case is the genitive absolute. The participle should be construed with the pronoun αὐτῶν as its subject: "they are longing."

Verse 15

ἐπί—the preposition imparts a causal connotation, "for" or "because of."[50]

ἀνεκδιηγήτῳ—a compound, this verbal adjective expresses both a passive sense and an inability: the privative ἀ, the preposition ἐκ, and the verb διηγέομαι (I describe), "it cannot be described."

Summary of Chapter 9

The chapter begins with a positive note of assurance. Paul is sure of the zeal the Corinthians have demonstrated with regard to the collection. He has even boasted to the Macedonians about this zeal and enthusiasm of the Corinthians. He also explains the reason for sending the brothers to Corinth: to have everything ready and complete by the time he arrives there.

The apostle teaches that a gift should always be generous. He uses a proverbial saying current in an agricultural setting: "Sow sparingly, reap sparingly; sow

---

48. Interpreting the participle as an imperative, "glorify God," hardly fits the context. Moule (*Idiom-Book,* pp. 31, 179) suggests the possibility of a Semitic idiom.

49. Bauer, p. 287.

50. A. T. Robertson, *A Grammar of the Greek New Testament in the Light of Historical Research* (Nashville: Broadman, 1934), p. 605.

generously, reap generously." Giving should never be done reluctantly or under duress. When giving stems from a cheerful heart, the giver becomes the recipient of God's bountiful blessings. Paul quotes from the Psalter and from the prophecy of Isaiah to prove that God provides gifts and causes their increase. He notes that God provides seed that, when it is sown, returns to the sower a harvest of righteousness. Generosity results in thanksgiving to God.

Supplying the needs of God's people generates gratitude to God. The name of God is praised and prayers are offered to him for the donors of the material gifts. These prayers unify the giver and the recipient as they experience God's surpassing grace. Paul concludes with a doxology in which he utters thanks to God for his indescribable gift.

10

Apostolic Authority, *part 1*

(10:1–18)

Outline

10 1 I, Paul, personally appeal to you by the meekness and gentleness of Christ—I who am subservient among you when present in person but bold toward you when away—2 I ask that when I come I need not be bold and have confidence with which I expect to be courageous against some who think that we conduct ourselves in a worldly manner. 3 For even though we are living in the world, we do not wage war in a worldly manner. 4 For the weapons we use in our warfare are not of the world but have divine power to destroy strongholds. 5 We destroy arguments and every elevated structure that rises up against the knowledge of God. And we lead captive every thought to obey Christ. 6 And we are ready to punish every disobedience as soon as your obedience is complete.

7 Look at the things that are before you. If anyone is confident that he belongs to Christ, let him consider this: that just as he belongs to Christ so do we, too. 8 For even if I boast somewhat excessively about our authority that the Lord gave for your edification and not for your destruction, I will not be ashamed. 9 [I forbid you to think] that I appear to frighten you with my letters. 10 Because it is said, "His letters are weighty and powerful, but his physical appearance is weak and his speech of no account." 11 Let such a person consider this: what we say by means of letters while absent, we will also do when present.

IV. Apostolic Authority
10:1–13:10

The tone in the last four chapters of this epistle differs from that of the first nine chapters. Now Paul is much more personal than in the first part, where he uses both the plural and the singular personal pronouns: *we* and *I; us* and *me; ours* and *mine*. In chapters 10–13 the first person singular is much more prominent than the plural pronoun. Even when Paul uses the plural pronoun in 10:1–11:6, he refers to himself, as is evident from, for instance, 10:3, 7, 11, and 13.[1]

The reason for the difference in tone between the first nine and the last four chapters probably lies in Paul's administration of pastoral care. The church had experienced some disturbances that had been settled by the time Paul wrote the epistle. He desired to establish rapport with the members of the congregation and after accomplishing that objective to write more specifically about his opponents. Paul had to point out to his people the difference between his genuine call to apostleship and his opponents' fraudulent credentials. He realized that as long as his opponents remained in Corinth peace and harmony would vanish.

---

1. A. T. Robertson, *A Grammar of the Greek New Testament in the Light of Historical Research* (Nashville: Broadman, 1934), p. 407.

Thus, Paul repeatedly has to call attention to his forthcoming visit (10:1–2; 12:14, 21; 13:1); these comments provide a connection with the previous chapter (9:4–5). But there are many other links between the first and second parts of this epistle.[2] For instance, in 2:9 Paul writes about the obedience of the Corinthians, a concept that he reiterates in 10:6. He refers to the god of this age, who has blinded the minds of unbelievers so that they cannot see the light of the gospel (4:4). And he portrays Satan as one who masquerades as an angel of light (11:14). Paul speaks of commendation in 5:12 and again in 12:11. He sends Titus and a companion to Corinth (8:17–18) and later refers to them again (12:18). The apostle does not plan to spare the Corinthians on his arrival, as he states at the beginning and the end of his letter (1:23; 13:2). And last, before he arrives in Corinth, he writes different letters to avoid receiving grief (2:3) and having to act harshly toward the Corinthians (13:10).

Next, Paul alludes to his opponents early in his epistle when he notes that they peddled the Word of God for profit and did not preach Christ (2:16–17; 3:1–4). In a later chapter, he gives a vivid description of his opponents who preach another Jesus, proclaim a different gospel, and masquerade as apostles of Christ (11:4–5, 13).

Third, Paul was forced to counteract the work of the false apostles, for they were undermining his authority in Corinth. They invaded the church he had founded and sought to destroy his work. "They were Judaists at work, impugning his authority and corrupting his Gospel; there was at least a minority of the Church under their influence; there were large numbers living, apparently, in the grossest sins (chap. xii. 20 f.); there was something, we cannot but think, approaching spiritual anarchy."[3] Paul had to change his tone when he addressed these issues in the last chapters.

Throughout his epistle, but especially in chapters 10–13, Paul defends his apostleship. The variations in tone are all part of this defense. He wrote his epistle "according to the norms of the day," so that the entire letter is apologetic and its text a unity.[4]

And last, the influx of Judaizers must have occurred after Paul had written and dispatched I Corinthians.[5] That epistle does not explicitly counteract these people. If then the teachings of Paul's opponents had just begun, the apostle was

---

2. Ernest B. Allo (*Saint Paul Seconde Épître aux Corinthiens*, 2d ed. [Paris: Gabalda, 1956], p. 240) is correct in noting links between chapters 1–7 and 10–13. But he overstates their number by saying that one can hardly count the number of correlations. Their number is limited to only a few more than a dozen allusions. See also Philip Edgcumbe Hughes, *Paul's Second Epistle to the Corinthians: The English Text with Introduction, Exposition and Notes,* New International Commentary on the New Testament series (Grand Rapids: Eerdmans, 1962), p. 343.

3. James Denney, *The Second Epistle to the Corinthians*, 2d ed., The Expositor's Bible series (New York: Armstrong, 1900), p. 290.

4. Frances Young and David F. Ford, *Meaning and Truth in II Corinthians,* BFT (London: SPCK, 1987), pp. 43–44.

5. F. W. Grosheide, *De Tweede Brief van den Apostel Paulus aan de Kerk te Korinthe,* Kommentaar op het Nieuwe Testament series (Amsterdam: Van Bottenburg, 1939), pp. 336–38.

obliged to offset their influence with a sharp rebuke in the concluding segment of his epistle. At the onset of the opponents' effort to undermine his apostolic authority, he wants to arrest their control over some members of the church in Corinth. Their subversion is a two-pronged attack against his apostolicity and his gospel message. Notice, therefore, that Paul does not address the opponents as such but rather alerts the members of the Corinthian church to be aware of their pernicious influence.

Concluding this brief survey (see the Introduction for more details), we note that Paul strengthened his relationship with the members of the church in chapters 1–9. With the membership firmly on his side, he now completes his epistle by alerting them to the spiritual dangers they face from the false apostles. Together, as apostle and members of the church, they must act.

A. Paul's Ministry and Opponents
10:1–11:33

The difference in form between the preceding chapters (8 and 9) and the next four (10–13) is readily apparent. For example, Paul delighted in the Corinthians' qualities of faith, speech, knowledge, earnestness, and love (8:7); he praised them for their obedience to the gospel, their generosity toward others, and their reception of God's surpassing grace (9:13). But in the next four chapters the emphasis changes. He hopes that he does not have to be bold (10:2); he mentions that their obedience is incomplete (10:6); he chides them for tolerating someone who enslaves them (11:20); and he tells them to examine themselves as to their own faith in Christ (13:5).

Somewhat abruptly the apostle defends his ministry to the Corinthians. He waits until the last part of his epistle to confront the undermining influence of the false teachers. He informs the Corinthians that these assaults are spiritual onslaughts that must be overcome by making every thought obedient to Christ. In the power of Christ's gospel, Paul and his fellow workers go forth exercising the authority the Lord has given them. Hence, he pleads with the Corinthians for faithfulness to Jesus and to the gospel that the apostles have proclaimed. Paul himself is able to demonstrate his faithfulness to Jesus by listing the sufferings he has endured for his Lord.

1. Defense and Power
10:1–11

a. Spiritual Weapons
10:1–6

1. I, Paul, personally appeal to you by the meekness and gentleness of Christ—I who am subservient among you when present in person but bold toward you when away.

a. "I, Paul, personally appeal to you by the meekness and gentleness of Christ." In all of his epistles, Paul speaks only three times in such an intense and personal manner (10:1; Gal. 5:2; I Thess. 2:18).[6] He demands the Corinthians' full attention, for the matter of false teachers touches all of them. He wants them to listen to him and says, "Now I, Paul, myself urge you" (NASB). And so in this verse, Paul shows his warm feelings toward these problem children in Corinth.[7] His words cannot be spoken to them by anyone but the apostle himself. Appealing to his spiritual offspring, he speaks to them as a father to his children.

The apostle personally addresses his readers, because at stake is his apostolic authority. Neither Timothy nor Titus had been maligned by the interlopers, but these interlopers had freely slandered Paul. In his absence from Corinth, all kinds of accusations had been leveled against him. Paul lists one of them: "His letters are weighty and powerful, but his physical appearance is weak and his speech of no account" (v. 10). Does he shrink from these accusations? No, he meets them directly but, as always, in the spirit of Christ.

After the phrase *I, Paul, appeal to you* he pens a reference to Christ's meekness and gentleness. Although this phrase is abrupt, Paul tempers his language by pointing to Jesus. If Jesus displayed the virtues of meekness and gentleness, so should his followers (Matt. 11:29). Paul seeks to imitate Christ, and he encourages his readers to do the same (I Cor. 11:1; see also I Peter 2:21). Asking for his readers' attention, he appeals to Christ's virtues.

Meekness is often considered to be weakness, but the Bible teaches that these two qualities are not identical. Moses is portrayed as "a very humble man, more humble than anyone else on the face of the earth" (Num. 12:3), but no one is able to ascribe weakness to him. Jesus calls the meek blessed, "for they will inherit the earth" (Matt. 5:5).

Meekness refers to enduring disgrace, maltreatment, and death at the hands of evildoers. The noun also "denotes the humble and gentle attitude which expresses itself in particular in a patient submissiveness to offence, free from malice and desire for revenge."[8] Meekness is a messianic virtue that Jesus displayed when he rode toward and into Jerusalem at his triumphal entry. He thus fulfilled the messianic prophecy that the Savior would be "gentle and riding on a donkey" (Zech. 9:9; Matt. 21:5).

Gentleness is a term that denotes graciousness, leniency, and fairness. This trait is closely related to meekness and flows forth from it (Phil. 4:5). The two terms, "meekness" and "gentleness," must describe every Christian who strives to follow Christ's example. They refer to possessing authority that is exercised without force or friction. Standing before Pontius Pilate, Jesus answered the governor with quiet dignity. And as a result Pilate sensed that he faced royalty: "You are a king, then!" (John 18:37). Jesus could have summoned legions of angels but instead he exhibited passive strength. Rulers often hide their weakness behind brute force, but Christ as King of kings and Lord of lords rules with meek humility.

---

6. D. A. Carson, *From Triumphalism to Maturity* (Grand Rapids: Baker, 1984), p. 32.
7. Hans Windisch, *Der Zweite Korintherbrief,* ed. Georg Strecker (1924; reprint ed., Göttingen: Vandenhoeck und Ruprecht, 1970), p. 290.
8. Ragnar Leivestad, "'The Meekness and Gentleness of Christ' II Cor. X.1," *NTS* 12 (1966): 159.

If the Corinthians acknowledge Jesus as Lord, they should also acknowledge and adopt for themselves his virtues of meekness and gentleness. Paul has learned to apply these two virtues to his own life, and he implies that the Corinthians should follow in his steps. The verbal and physical abuse he has endured with quiet dignity mark him as a true follower of Christ. He teaches that the world spurns a lifestyle of meekness and gentleness, but God deems it a way of life.[9]

b. "I who am subservient among you when present in person but bold toward you when away." As is his custom, Paul often quotes the very words of his antagonists, which in this case are "subservient" and "bold." Paul deliberately chooses this taunt of his detractors, for in his vocabulary the word *subservient* has a positive meaning and is akin to meekness. But his opponents use it negatively to present him as weak, miserable, and unimportant.[10] He has been accused of being a weakling when he is present in the Corinthian church, but as soon as he is away from there he is bold.

Paul's opponents could accuse him with impunity; since the founding of the Corinthian church, he had made only a brief visit that was painful (2:1). The adversaries faulted him for delegating the responsibility of caring for the church to Timothy, Silas, Titus, and Apollos. And they criticized him for communicating by letters. The word *bold* means that his adversaries called him insolent.

These two allegations should not be understood as merely personal attacks but rather as attempts to subvert his apostleship. The intruders intend to nullify his ministry by asserting that it is of human origin. Paul can endure attacks on his character, for he knows that he is far from perfect. But he cannot allow assaults on the Spirit's work through him in the churches. Indeed, these attackers touch his God-ordained calling to be an apostle and servant of the Lord Jesus Christ.

Paul takes advantage of their accusations by turning weakness into a virtue. He sees himself as an instrument in God's hand, so that in lowliness and weakness God's power becomes evident (11:30; 12:9).[11]

2. I ask that when I come I need not be bold and have confidence with which I expect to be courageous against some who think that we conduct ourselves in a worldly manner.

a. *Coming.* "I ask that when I come I need not be bold." In the Greek, the pronoun *you* as direct object of the verb *to ask* is lacking but should be understood, and it refers to the Corinthians. Paul is not appealing to them but is expressing his own preferences.

The apostle is asking three things: that he need not come to deliver a stern address; that upon his coming he may have the confidence and courage to en-

---

9. F. J. Pop, *De Tweede Brief van Paulus aan de Corinthiërs* (Nijkerk: Callenbach, 1980), p. 279.
10. Compare Ragnar Leivestad, "ΤΑΠΕΙΝΟΣ—ΤΑΠΕΙΝΟΦΡΩΝ," *NovT* 8 (1966): 45; Walter Grundmann, *TDNT,* 8:19.
11. Heinz Giesen, *EDNT,* 3:333.

counter his slanderers; and that he can show that his conduct has been above reproach.

The time for Paul's departure for Corinth is coming closer, but he hopes that opposition to his teaching may have disappeared before he arrives. Paul would rather be welcomed by the Corinthians in mutual love and respect than face hostility. He anticipates that he does not have to be bold in the sense of coming to discipline them (I Cor. 4:21). Discipline should be applied only as a last resort and then as a corrective measure designed to draw people closer together. When it arises out of anger and is administered in haste, the results inevitably are disastrous and lead to lasting separation.

b. *Confidence.* "And have confidence with which I expect to be courageous against some [people]." Note that Paul is not saying that he hopes to avoid a confrontation with the church at Corinth. Rather, he opposes the intruders who have come into the church and are leading some of its members astray. He is specific and speaks about some people, whom he later identifies as superapostles or false apostles (11:5, 13; 12:11). His is the task of nullifying the teachings and claims of these Judaizers.[12] Philip Edgcumbe Hughes correctly observes that earlier in his epistle Paul had alluded to these people who accused the apostle of conducting himself in a worldly manner (1:17). He adds that this reference is "yet another link between the earlier part and the concluding chapters of the letter."[13]

Paul explains what he means by being bold toward some people: He had to disprove the slanders of his detractors, who accused him of being a weakling in Corinth but bold at a distance. And he does this effectively by stating, "What we say by means of letters while absent, we will also do when present" (v. 11). The apostle turns their slander on its head by writing the verb *to be courageous,* a word choice that highlights his convictions.[14] He mentions that he needs both confidence and courage to void his detractors' influence.

c. *Conduct.* "Against some who think that we conduct ourselves in a worldly manner." The apostle is in combat with some false teachers, few in number, who methodically plot their course of action and use slander and misrepresentation to gain their ends. The longer they stay in Corinth, the more followers they will gain.

These false teachers cut Paul at the core of his spiritual existence: his conduct. His adversaries claim that he is seeking self-gratification and is guided by a desire

---

12. Consult R. C. H. Lenski, *The Interpretation of St. Paul's First and Second Epistle to the Corinthians* (Columbus: Wartburg, 1946), p. 1192.

13. Hughes, *Second Epistle to the Corinthians,* p. 348. Allo (*Seconde Épître aux Corinthiens,* p. 218) calls attention to 3:1; 5:12; 11:21.

14. John Motyer, *NIDNTT,* 1:365. Jean Héring says that "the words from 'τῇ πεποιθήσει' to τολμῆσαι' seem superfluous." To his surprise "no exegete has been bold enough to omit them" (see *The Second Epistle of Saint Paul to the Corinthians,* trans. A. W. Heathcote and P. J. Allcock [London: Epworth, 1967], pp. 69–70). One is reminded of Martin Luther's dictum, "Man soll das Wort stehen lassen" (Let the word stand as is).

to dominate.[15] They say that Paul conducts himself as an unbeliever; literally, that "he walks according to the flesh." This particular saying is a phrase Paul himself uses to describe unbelievers.[16] The phrase, however, is a reflection on his enemies rather than on the apostle. They themselves exhibit arrogance, egotism, disdain, and self-commendation. Yet they ascribe all this to Paul in a deliberate attempt to discredit his relationship to Jesus Christ, his call to be the apostle to the Gentiles, his ministry in the church, and his faithful preaching of Christ's gospel. It is no wonder that Paul devotes chapters 10–12 to combatting the pernicious influence of the Judaizers.

Paul's opponents also accuse him of being an inept leader, one whose timidity makes him an ineffective preacher and one who lacks basic spiritual qualities to edify the Corinthians (v. 10).

Paul does not speak to his foes directly, for this letter is addressed not to them but to the church in Corinth. He writes about these people and instructs the Corinthians how to oppose the infiltrators. Paul is not standing alone but next to and, in a sense, in the midst of the believers. He counts on his spiritual offspring to form a united front against the enemy. He does not wish to see them fall into apathy and yield to the forces of deceit and falsehood.

Practical Considerations in 10:1

The world demands competitiveness. Stressing individualism, it tells us to care for ourselves at the expense of others. The virtues of kindness, gentleness, and meekness have no place in the context of competition. The world consigns these virtues to the so-called do-gooders who, so they say, are living on the fringes of society. Such people are considered to be weaklings.

Christians face the influences of the world and, consequently, adopt a defensive posture. As soon as someone deprives them of any honor, rank, possession, or goods they react vigorously. But this defensive attitude reveals an inner weakness of character and a lack of understanding of the full teachings of Christ.

Jesus teaches the golden rule, "Do to others as you would have them do to you" (Luke 6:31); the two precepts to love God and one's neighbor (Matt. 22:37–40); and the abiding truth of fully trusting in God.

Whenever sincere Christians live by these teachings, meekness, gentleness, and kindness abound. Those followers of Christ who practice his teachings are heroes of faith, pillars of righteousness, defenders of the truth. Indeed, God places his people at strategic places in this world to promote his rule on earth.

---

3. For even though we are living in the world, we do not wage war in a worldly manner.

---

15. Compare Adolf Schlatter, *Paulus, der Bote Jesu: Eine Deutung an die Korinther* (Stuttgart: Calwer, 1934), p. 614.

16. The expression "to live according to the sinful nature" appears often in Paul's epistles: Rom. 8:4, 5, 12, 13; II Cor. 10:2, 3.

a. *Versions.* Translations of this verse vary because Paul uses two phrases that are similar but present a play on words. The literal wording is, "For though we walk in the flesh, we do not war according to the flesh" (NKJV). We face a question of interpretation, for the phrases *walk in the flesh* and *war according to the flesh* are confusing.

Walking is the Greek idiom for living and describes our conduct in life or in the world. The word *flesh* may mean our human existence, as is evident from another translation: "Indeed, we live as human beings, but we do not wage war according to human standards" (NRSV). Although the term *flesh* means "life here on earth,"[17] the immediate context suggests a slightly broader perspective, so that we understand the term to refer to the world around us. In fact, "it characterizes human behavior as a purely worldly activity and perspective."[18]

The verb *to walk* (to live) calls for a concessive conjunction, although or though. That is, Paul readily admits that he lives in the world, but he does not conform to its standards. To apply Jesus' words to Paul, he was in the world but not of the world (John 17:14–16).

b. *Intent.* In an earlier verse Paul appealed to his readers "by the meekness and gentleness of Christ" (v. 1). Because he has the mind of Christ (see Gal. 2:20; Phil. 2:5), he does not fight the world of sin by applying worldly standards; he fights according to the standards God has set.

God has rules for his kingdom (e.g., the Decalogue), has citizens in his kingdom, and has an army with generals and soldiers to fight the devil and his cohorts. The apostle is a general who serves in the army of the Lord and opposes Satan, the prince of this world. Paul wages a war of liberation by preaching Christ's gospel that sets people free from the bondage of sin and the fear of death (Heb. 2:14–15). Even though the battle is ferocious, Christ's victory is sure. All enemies shall be placed under his foot; also the last enemy, death, shall be destroyed (I Cor. 15:26).

Satan knows that his time is coming to an end, and so he uses every available weapon to resist defeat. In his arsenal he has the weapons of deceit, lies, subterfuge, guile, intimidation, compulsion, and force.

Followers of Jesus Christ, having been redeemed by Christ and set free from Satan's bondage, fight the evil that the devil and his followers perpetrate. In opposing the forces of evil, God's soldiers must use his armaments, not those of Satan. Among God's armaments are truth, honesty, integrity, justice, holiness, and faithfulness. From his people God requires faithfulness to his precepts, commands, and purposes. Dedication and wholehearted commitment to the Lord are the hallmarks of true believers. The kingdom of God knows only few people who completely trust God, and that is why they are called great.

4. For the weapons we use in our warfare are not of the world but have divine power to destroy strongholds.

---

17. Bauer, p. 744.
18. Alexander Sand, *EDNT,* 3:231.

a. "For the weapons we use in our warfare are not of the world." The conflict between God's forces and those of Satan is spiritual and must be fought with spiritual weapons. Christians are able to arm themselves against the onslaughts of Satan by putting on the full armor of God, which consists of peace, truth, righteousness, faith, love, light, the sword of the Spirit, and salvation (Rom. 13:12; II Cor. 6:7; Eph. 6:11, 13–17; I Thess. 5:8). In addition, they must prayerfully communicate with God, must hold on to the message of God's Word, and must ask God's Spirit to dwell in their hearts.

The weapons of the world embody the converse of God's rules: the lie in place of the truth, darkness instead of light, grief rather than joy, and death as a substitute for life. In his opposition to God and his people, Satan resorts to both deception (Adam and Eve in Eden, Ananias and Sapphira in the early church) and cruel force (Abel as the first victim in the Old Testament and Stephen as the first martyr in the New Testament).

With these weapons, Satan attempts to impede the power of the gospel and fights God, the church, and the believers. John Calvin observes that the believer "must learn to think of the Gospel as a fire at which the wrath of Satan is enkindled, and so he cannot but arm himself to the fight whenever he sees an opportunity for advancing the Gospel."[19]

b. "[We] have divine power to destroy strongholds." Sixteenth-century Scottish Reformer John Knox lived by this motto: "With God, man is always in the majority." And with this majority, Christians indeed can destroy Satan's strongholds (compare Prov. 21:22). These strongholds appear in many forms but are essentially the same; they are the systems, schemes, structures, and strategies that Satan designs to frustrate and obstruct the progress of Christ's gospel.

In prison, Paul penned his last epistle and wrote, "This is my gospel, for which I am suffering even to the point of being chained like a criminal. But God's word is not chained" (II Tim. 2:8b–9). The message of the gospel penetrates manmade walls by means of men and women armed with wisdom, courage, dedication, and faith. Through many means of communication (among them are the airwaves, computers, and the printed page), God's Word enters Satan's strongholds and demolishes his opposition. No one on earth is able to stop the march of the gospel, for "we are more than conquerors through him who loved us" (Rom. 8:37).

5. We destroy arguments and every elevated structure that rises up against the knowledge of God. And we lead captive every thought to obey Christ.

The punctuation of this text differs from that of other versions. I have incorporated the clause "we destroy arguments" into verse 5, whereas other translators put it with the preceding one. The flow of Paul's reasoning, however, favors its inclusion in the present text.

a. "We destroy arguments and every elevated structure that rises up against the knowledge of God." Paul describes the conflict in terms of spiritual warfare

---

19. John Calvin, *The Second Epistle of Paul the Apostle to the Corinthians and the Epistles to Timothy, Titus and Philemon*, Calvin's Commentaries series, trans. T. A. Small (Grand Rapids: Eerdmans, 1964), p. 129.

that is not against people as such but against thought patterns, philosophies, theories, views, and tactics. We see here the image of the beast that comes up out of the earth, according to the apostle John, to control the thinking and activities of all human beings. Those who do not have the mark of the beast on their foreheads (symbolizing thought) and right hands (symbolizing work) are unable to buy or sell (Rev. 13:16–17).

The present tense of the verb *destroy* indicates that in this warfare God's people continually demolish the citadels of their enemies. To do so, they must enter these forts, which the apostle describes with the expression *arguments*. The intruders in Corinth employ verbal weapons in their onslaughts against the truth. They resort to arguments with which they seek to persuade the members of the church. Paul has to destroy their false doctrine and break down their reasonings. With their theories removed, the gospel is able to advance and flourish and sinners are set free. This is true not only in Corinth, but also at every place where preachers, evangelists, and missionaries proclaim God's Word.

The language Paul adopts is borrowed from the battlefield.[20] He writes the term *hypsōma,* which I have translated as "elevated structure," literally "elevated thing." The picture is that of a wall or a tower from which defenders discharge their ammunition, and which becomes an immediate target of advancing forces.

Translated into the area of philosophy, this figurative speech relates to any human theory raised up against the knowledge of the truth. It is earthly wisdom originating with the devil (James 3:15) and, therefore, must be shattered by the knowledge of God (I Cor. 1:19). This divine knowledge is synonymous with the gospel of Jesus Christ. It is the knowledge of creation, sin, redemption, restoration, and resurrection. Paul taught and proclaimed the Good News but he also discussed the teachings of the gospel with both the Jews and the Gentiles. He demolished their human arguments to liberate human beings from the clutches of the evil one. His objective was to bring salvation to the people.

As a general in the armed forces, Paul works out his strategy for attack as he faces the forces of unbelief. He observes the line of battle and takes note of strongholds and ramparts. His diction reveals parallelism: strongholds and arguments, elevated structure and the knowledge of God, and the act of making captives with both an object (every thought) and a goal (obedience to Christ).[21]

b. "And we lead captive every thought to obey Christ." If one text in this epistle spells out Paul's battle triumphs in spiritual warfare, it is this one. The verb *to lead captive* in the present tense indicates that the act of taking prisoners is in progress, the battle is being won, and victory is inclusive (*every* thought; emphasis added).

The apostle continues with his imagery, for the conquest is to subdue not people but thoughts. There is no mention of bloodshed and killing on this battle-

---

20. Refer to Abraham J. Malherbe, "Antisthenes and Odysseus, and Paul at War," *HTR* 76 (1983): 143–73.

21. Windisch, *Der Zweite Korintherbrief,* p. 297.

field. Rather, all the theories are captured and brought into obedience to Christ. The culture that is conquered for Christ remains intact, but its components are transformed to serve him. These are the captive thought patterns that are brought into conformity with the teachings of the Lord.

The key word in the last phrase of this text is "obey." When people repent, they experience a complete reversal in their thinking that directs their actions to obey Christ. Their former beliefs are now reshaped to serve not the evil one but Christ.[22] These captives swear allegiance not to Paul the general but to Jesus the commander-in-chief. And every captive thought displays obedience to Christ as an acknowledgment of his supreme rule.

6. And we are ready to punish every disobedience as soon as your obedience is complete.

a. "And we are ready to punish every disobedience." Paul continues to speak in military terms, for enemies who face defeat suffer its consequences. The infiltrators in the Corinthian church will have to face a general in Christ's army who is ready to mete out punishment. Paul is not revealing what measures he will take when he arrives in Corinth. But everyone who has shown disobedience to Christ's gospel will face punishment. The readers are given an indirect warning not to fall into disobedience but to continue in their obedience to the teachings of Christ.

b. "As soon as your obedience is complete." Vengeance belongs to the Lord, who will punish his enemies in due time (Deut. 32:35; Rom. 12:19; Heb. 10:30). Thus, Christ controls the Corinthian situation; when the time comes, he will execute judgment and use Paul as his agent.

What is Paul trying to say in the last clause of verse 6? Although he addresses the readers as a group, the apostle distinguishes between the many who are faithful and the few who are not, namely, those who are led astray by intruders. He desires that all the members of the congregation dedicate themselves wholeheartedly to Jesus Christ by obeying his precepts.

Some scholars teach that Paul has in mind disobedience with respect to the collection.[23] But this is hardly the case, because in this chapter Paul says nothing about the ingathering of funds.

Others scholars look ahead to the next chapter (11:4) and think that Paul is referring to another gospel preached by the superapostles.[24] This interpretation has merit in view of his earlier remark in verses 1 and 2, where he confronted the readers with the slander uttered by the intruders. They and their followers will

---

22. Consult Victor Paul Furnish, *II Corinthians: Translated with Introduction, Notes and Commentary*, Anchor Bible 32A (Garden City, N.Y.: Doubleday, 1984), p. 463; C. K. Barrett, *The Second Epistle to the Corinthians*, Harper's New Testament Commentaries series (New York: Harper and Row, 1973), p. 253.

23. Grosheide (p. 350) and Pop (p. 295) in their respective commentaries.

24. Colin G. Kruse, *The Second Epistle of Paul to the Corinthians: An Introduction and Commentary*, Tyndale New Testament Commentaries series (Leicester: Inter-Varsity; Grand Rapids: Eerdmans, 1987), p. 175; Furnish, *II Corinthians*, p. 464.

be punished. The matter of false teachers touches every member of the Corinthian church, for the invaders are preaching a gospel other than that of Christ. Therefore, the entire church must eradicate the false teachings of the intruders and obey only Christ's gospel. The church must exercise discipline to maintain its purity and power.

Through the working of the Holy Spirit, Christ's gospel is an overpowering force that calls people to repentance. Then in time, the gospel changes the structure of society so that it becomes a city of God. Christ's kingdom is not a matter of talk but of power, as Paul says in another place (I Cor. 4:20). The citizens of this kingdom in Corinth and elsewhere must wholeheartedly serve Jesus in obedience to his Word.

Greek Words, Phrases, and Constructions in 10:1–6

Verses 1–2

αὐτὸς δὲ ἐγὼ Παῦλος—the intensive pronoun receives emphasis and is followed by the personal pronoun for additional emphasis.

διά—here the line between accompaniment and instrumentality is very thin,[25] yet the first choice, "accompaniment," is favored.

Notice the balance of μέν and δέ in the last two clauses; the contrast of κατὰ πρόσωπον (being present in person) and ἀπών (being away); the dissimilarity of ταπεινός (meek) and θαρρῶ (bold); and the divergence of ἐν (with, among) and εἰς (toward).

τὸ μὴ παρὼν θαρρῆσαι—this construction takes the place of a purpose clause with ἵνα μή and the aorist subjunctive. The participle is temporal ("when I am present"). And the particle negates the infinitive.

κατὰ σάρκα, ἐν σάρκι, κατὰ σάρκα—Paul repeats the noun in verses 2 and 3 for the sake of contrast and tact.[26]

Verses 3–4

κατὰ σάρκα—"in accordance with worldly standards." This phrase can also signify "as to his human nature" (Rom. 1:3) and "human ancestry" (Rom. 9:5).[27]

περιπατοῦντες—the present participle denotes continued action and is part of a concessive clause introduced by "although."

δυνατὰ τῷ θεῷ—the adjective modifying the word ὅπλα (weapons) depicts power, and the noun can be a dative of respect, "powerful in respect to God"; a dative of advantage, "for God, in whose service the weapons are used";[28] a dative of means, "powerful by God"; or a dative that represents a Semitism, "divine power."[29]

---

25. C. F. D. Moule, *An Idiom-Book of New Testament Greek,* 2d ed. (Cambridge: Cambridge University Press, 1960), p. 58.

26. Friedrich Blass and Albert Debrunner, *A Greek Grammar of the New Testament and Other Early Christian Literature,* trans. and rev. Robert Funk (Chicago: University of Chicago Press, 1961), #488.1b.

27. Moule, *Idiom-Book,* p. 59.

28. J. H. Moulton and Wilbert F. Howard, *A Grammar of New Testament Greek,* vol. 2, *Accidence and Word-Formation* (Edinburgh: Clark, 1929), p. 443.

29. Hughes, *Second Epistle to the Corinthians,* p. 351 n. 6.

πρὸς καθαίρεσιν—the preposition expresses purpose and the noun can be interpreted as an activity, "for destroying strongholds."

καθαιροῦντες—the present tense of the participle signifies continued action, and the participle itself is the equivalent of a finite verb, "we destroy."[30]

Verses 5–6

ἐπαιρόμενον—the present participle can be either passive ("is raised") or middle ("rises up"). The passive is preferred. Notice the play on words of this participle and the preceding καθαιροῦντες.

τὴν ὑπακοὴν τοῦ Χριστοῦ—the genitive following the noun *obedience* is not subjective (of Christ) but objective (for Christ). See also the contrast of obedience and disobedience.

πᾶσαν—three times in two verses (vv. 5–6) Paul writes the word *every* to emphasize the totality of Christ's victory.

πληρωθῇ—this verb is an ingressive aorist that refers to a progressive action and is passive, with the readers as implied agents.

---

b. Delegated Authority
10:7–11

The whole church of Corinth is asked to become involved in evaluating the problem at hand. To be fully informed, the Corinthians must look at the facts. Paul makes it plain that they should consider and weigh the claims that an individual makes. For this reason Paul writes "anyone" (v. 7) and "such a person" (v. 11). The congregation as a body is encouraged to affirm Paul's apostolic authority over against the claims of the individual.

7. Look at the things that are before you. If anyone is confident that he belongs to Christ, let him consider this: that just as he belongs to Christ so do we, too.

a. *Translations.* "Look at the things that are before you." The Greek can be translated as a command, as given above, or as a declarative statement, "You are looking only on the surface of things" (NIV). Others make the sentence interrogative: "Do you look at things according to outward appearance?" (KJV, NKJV).

The interrogative does not fit a context that is devoid of questions. Hence, the choice must be either the first or the second translation. There are weaknesses in both. The declarative statement reflects a weakness because it is a paraphrase. Also, this translation allows for subtle shifts in meaning: "the surface of things" is less forceful language than "obvious facts" (NIV margin). A flaw in translating the Greek as an imperative is that in the New Testament the verb *blepete* (Look!) normally stands first in the sentence, which is not the case here. But throughout the New Testament, the second person plural of this verb is always an imperative (with the exception of Heb. 10:25). Also, the verse includes one more command, "let him consider this" (v. 7b; see also vv. 11, 17). These particulars make the choice of an imperative attractive and preferable.

---

30. J. H. Moulton and Nigel A. Turner, *A Grammar of the Greek New Testament* (Edinburgh: Clark, 1965), vol. 3, *Syntax*, p. 343.

b. *Confidence.* "If anyone is confident that he belongs to Christ, let him consider this." The conditional sentence discloses reality: someone in the Corinthian church is assured that he belongs to Christ. This assurance is so intense that Paul has strengthened the sentence with extra words ("in himself") that we omit for stylistic reasons. The literal reading is: "If anyone is confident in himself that he is Christ's, let him consider this again within himself" (NASB). The person who claims to belong to Christ has a high opinion of himself, as is evident from the repetition of the pronoun *himself.*

What is the meaning of the phrase *he belongs to Christ?* We are unable to reconstruct the setting of this remark and can only surmise its origin. Some scholars who declare that the phrase is a Gnostic saying[31] must conjecture that Gnosticism was rampant in Corinth during the middle of the first century. And this can hardly be proved.

Next, the phrase brings to mind the report from Chloe's household that there were four factions in the church at Corinth, one of which belonged to Christ (I Cor. 1:12). We are not certain that the person who used this phrase was alluding to a faction, if indeed such a group existed in Corinth. Apart from the beginning of I Corinthians, we read nothing about factions.

C. K. Barrett comments that the phrase "more probably refers to a particular person who claims to be [of Christ] in a special way."[32]

Third, perhaps someone who had been an earlier disciple of Jesus boasted of possessing special knowledge of Christ and a privileged status with him. But this claim is self-glorifying speech and is not worthy of a true disciple.

Last, on the basis of the context, in which Paul defends his apostleship, we suggest that the phrase *he belongs to Christ* embodies a direct attack on him and his calling. Paul implicitly reminds his readers that he had received authority from Christ to be his apostle to the Gentiles—an office no one else could claim. Hence he tells the Corinthians to look at the obvious facts.[33] Not the intruders but Paul has a claim to apostolic authority.

c. *Consideration.* "Let him consider this: that just as he belongs to Christ so do we, too." Paul is not questioning believers who put their faith in Jesus, but he offsets their claim to Christ by stating that he, too, confesses him as Lord. This is a subtle way of negating the assertions of those opponents who apparently questioned Paul's claim to apostolicity and divine authority. His calling and confirmation indeed were unique, for after his departure from this life the Lord did not extend Paul's apostleship to someone else. If these opponents acknowledge him as an apostle of Christ, then they should work together with him in the task of strengthening the church.

---

31. Among others, see the commentary of Héring, p. 72; compare also Dieter Georgi, *The Opponents of Paul in Second Corinthians* (Philadelphia: Fortress, 1986), pp. 230, 273, 307 n. 264.

32. C. K. Barrett, "Cephas and Corinth," in *Essays on Paul* (Philadelphia: Westminster, 1982), p. 35.

33. See the respective commentaries of Windisch, p. 301; Martin, p. 308; Hughes, pp. 356–58; Kruse, p. 176.

8. For even if I boast somewhat excessively about our authority that the Lord gave for your edification and not for your destruction, I will not be ashamed.

a. "For even if I boast somewhat excessively about our authority that the Lord gave." This verse is closely linked to the preceding text (v. 7), as the word *for* indicates. Verse 7 refers to the confidence of Paul's opponents and suggests that this confidence led them to attack Paul's apostolic authority.

When Paul mentions boasting, he relates it directly to the Lord (see I Cor. 1:31; 15:31; II Cor. 10:17; compare Ps. 34:2; 44:8; Jer. 9:24). Furthermore, Paul writes about the possibility of boasting excessively. He does not say that he customarily boasts (compare 11:16; 12:6). And he does not boast by comparing his work with that of others.[34] Indeed, he devotes the last part of this chapter to boasting and its limits (vv. 12–18).

Why does Paul boast somewhat excessively, when at the beginning of this chapter he stresses the virtue of meekness? Note that he connects the two phrases *somewhat excessively* and *authority that the Lord gave* (see 13:10). Because of the authority that Jesus conferred on Paul, the apostle could unduly boast. He is saying, "Let no one of my adversaries or anyone in the Corinthian church underestimate the delegated power I possess in Christ." His apostolic authority is for him a cause of boasting.[35]

The apostle uses the first person singular ("I boast") to make this fact known. This does not mean that he indulges in self-glorification because of his calling. Far from it! He remains completely subordinate to his Sender, who has endowed him with divine authority. "But by the grace of God I am what I am, and his grace to me was not without effect. No, I worked harder than all of them—yet not I, but the grace of God that was with me" (I Cor. 15:10).

Christ's authority is so great that no one is able to thwart the power of his gospel. Every person who has been converted is a living testimony to the power of God's Word and Spirit.[36] Paul has seen the effect of this divine authority in his life and he knows that behind him stands Christ himself. Anyone who resists Paul resists the Lord (Luke 10:16). Thus, the apostle is able to boast excessively about the authority he has received but which belongs to Jesus Christ. Ministers of the Word must apply this authority properly for the spiritual well-being of the church.[37]

b. "That the Lord gave for your edification and not for your destruction." Jesus grants power never for personal use but always for the advancement of his cause. So Paul observes that his authority derives from the Lord (compare Gal. 1:1) and that he uses it not for destroying the church but for edifying and strengthening it.

---

34. Rudolf Bultmann, *TDNT*, 3:651.

35. The verb *to boast* appears twenty times in this epistle, seventeen of them in chapters 10, 11, and 12. The noun *boast* occurs nine times in II Corinthians.

36. Consult Pop, *De Tweede Brief van Paulus,* p. 300.

37. Compare Calvin, *II Corinthians,* p. 133.

The expressions *edification* and *destruction* echo the words of Jeremiah 1:10, when God tells the prophet that he appointed him "over nations and kingdoms to uproot and tear down, to destroy and overthrow, to build and to plant."[38] But the difference between Jeremiah and Paul is immense. God pronounced judgment on Jerusalem and Judea. He commanded the prophet to announce the destruction of the nation, city, and temple. Restoration came many years later with spiritual blessings culminating in the coming of the Messiah. Conversely, Paul preaches Christ's gospel and seeks not to destroy but to edify the believers (13:10). The apostle is planting churches in territory that Satan once ruled but now has ceded to Christ Jesus. With the authority given to him, Paul goes forth triumphantly to extend God's kingdom. Although Satan continues to slow the march of the gospel, he is unable to stop it. The building process of the kingdom carries on to the end of time.

The possibility is not remote that Paul's opponents have accused him of destroying the Corinthian church. True to form, Satan takes the evils that describe the adversaries of Paul and applies them to the apostle. But the good news of Jesus Christ

> restores this broken creation,
> rebuilds its ruined structures,
> and reforms sinners into saints.

c. "I will not be ashamed." Once again in this verse Paul writes the first person singular to express his involvement in the life of the Corinthians. He is confident that his boasting about the power that Christ has granted will not embarrass him or lead to public disgrace. Paul trusts that God will protect him from shame and confirm the work that he performs as an ambassador for Christ and as his apostle to the Gentiles (5:20; Gal. 2:7–9).

9. [I forbid you to think] that I appear to frighten you with my letters.

a. *Stylistic problems.* The Greek text unfortunately lacks precision in syntax. Translators are forced to modify the wording to convey the meaning of this sentence. A literal translation is "that I may not seem as if to terrify you by letters." How does this text fit into the flow of Paul's discourse? Is verse 9 a continuation of the preceding passage (v. 8) or does it introduce the next verse (v. 10)? Some scholars even suggest that verse 9 should be taken together with verse 11 and that verse 10 be seen as a parenthetical comment.

Ancient manuscripts lacked punctuation, so that editors have to decide where to place commas and periods. A helpful consideration is the fact that Paul's letters were read to the churches. Readers and listeners would understand the text in the sequence in which it was presented. This verse, then, is a follow-up of the preceding one, a fact that precludes a connection between verses 9 and 11.

---

38. Jer. 1:10; 24:6; 31:28; 42:10; 45:4. Consult the commentaries of Furnish, p. 467; Hughes, pp. 360–61; Pop, p. 300; and Windisch, p. 303.

Nonetheless, there is an undeniable break in the flow of Paul's discourse. But this break can be bridged if we assume the presence of a negative command, "Do not think that. . . ."[39] The apostle is not interested in embarrassing or frightening his readers. In effect, he has told them that his task is not to destroy but to build.

b. *Prelude*. Paul's remark anticipates the charges of his adversaries who allege that his letters cause fear but his physical presence does not. In a sense, these charges were understandable. For some time Paul had been absent from the church in Corinth. He had sent his helpers, first Timothy and then Titus, to Corinth. He had paid the Corinthians a short visit that was painful. His absence provided Paul's critics with ammunition. His letters were filled with directives and displayed Paul's apostolic authority. But they were addressed to the Corinthians from a distance, from Ephesus across the Aegean Sea.

Before the apostle addresses the charges of his opponents, he assures the Corinthians that he does not wish to intimidate them. He does not intend to frighten them with his epistles. However, when he eventually arrives in Corinth, he will show the intruders that he is a person to be feared.

10. Because it is said, "His letters are weighty and powerful, but his physical appearance is weak and his speech of no account."

a. "Because it is said." From either Titus or someone else who has come to Paul with information from Corinth, the apostle has heard of a rumor spreading throughout the congregation. Perhaps one of his opponents is the spokesman, as the wording in verse 7 ("anyone") and in verse 11 ("such a person") implies. Paul's foes seek out an apparent weak point and exploit it to their advantage.

b. "'His letters are weighty and powerful.'" This remark should not be interpreted as a compliment. His assailants are disparaging the apostle's work by insinuating that the letters Paul addressed to the Corinthians are heavy on teaching and forceful in rebuke. We surmise that the pejorative comment includes Paul's preliminary letter (I Cor. 5:9), his first canonical epistle (I Cor.), and his sorrowful letter (2:4). We are unable to say whether his critics were familiar with earlier letters Paul had written to be read elsewhere (I Thess. 5:27; compare also Col. 4:16).

Epistles are permanent, can be read by anyone, and are open to various interpretations. They lack the inflection of the spoken word to which hearers can react either positively or negatively. "An epistle is, so to speak, the man's words without the man; and such is human weakness, that they are often stronger than the man speaking in bodily presence, that is, than the man and his words together."[40]

c. "'But his physical appearance is weak and his speech of no account.'" The contrast in this saying is pronounced: letters and physical appearance are meta-

---

39. The NJB connects verses 8c and 9 as follows: "And I am not going to be shamed into letting you think that I can put fear into you only by letter." Inclusion of the adverb *only* is not needed. Consult Ralph P. Martin, *II Corinthians*, Word Biblical Commentary 40 (Waco: Word, 1986), pp. 310–11; Moule, *Idiom-Book*, pp. 144–45.

40. Denney, *Second Corinthians*, p. 306.

phors, opposites that denote absence and presence. Also, the terms *weighty* and *powerful* are the converse of *weak* and *no account.*

The Greek text reads "the presence of his body," but this is to be understood as neither Paul's physical arrival in Corinth nor his outward appearance.[41] Instead, his opponents considered him to be a man without stamina or eloquence. They implied that from a distance he roars like a lion but when he is present he is meek as a lamb. This conclusion, however, is not true to fact. Consider Paul's dedication to his task of preaching and teaching Christ's gospel. He endured beatings from Romans and Jews (11:23–25); he nearly died when the mob stoned him outside the city of Lystra (Acts 14:19–20). He addressed synagogue audiences in many places, with the result that he was forced either to leave or to flee for his life (Acts 13:50–51; 14:6). He stood in the midst of Athenian philosophers at the Areopagus and tactfully acquainted these learned men with God's revelation (Acts 17:22–31). In Ephesus he called both Jews and Gentiles to repentance and faith in Christ (Acts 20:21). He proved that he was a man of moral integrity and physical stamina.

Furthermore, the intruders' attack on Paul touches not so much his personality as his apostolic office (see the commentary on v. 1). They intimate that he is not much of an apostle because he declines to give direct leadership. And they accuse him of being a second-rate speaker, a flaw that Paul frankly admits (11:6; I Cor. 2:1). But the words "his speech is of no account" can also suggest that the effect of his apostolic message "makes no great impact" (NAB), a cutting accusation. As Jesus' ambassador he has been truthful in proclaiming the message of his Sender (John 20:21; Acts 9:15; 26:15–18). Throughout his ministry, he proves to be a worthy apostle of Jesus Christ, who faithfully preaches the gospel "in season and out of season" (II Tim. 4:2).

The readers should not forget that Paul steadfastly taught the churches everywhere and laid down rules for them (I Cor. 4:17; 7:17). He was an apostle to all the churches he had founded and exercised his authority over them.

In addition, no one should slight Paul's eloquence in addressing, for example, Governor Festus and King Agrippa (Acts 26:2–29). Indeed, God empowered him and blessed his ministry.

Next, the apostle not only reproved his readers but also urged them to obey Christ. Even though he was physically far from them, he expressed his genuine love for them in numerous ways as if he were near. His task in Corinth was not to destroy but to build (v. 8); not to alienate people but to acquaint them with Christ; not to wield power but to demonstrate grace; not to come with force but to be gentle.

---

41. An apocryphal account describes his physical features: "A man small of stature, with a bald head and crooked legs, in a good state of the body, with eyebrows meeting and nose somewhat hooked, full of friendliness." See The Acts of Paul and Thecla 3.3, in Edgar Hennecke, *New Testament Apocrypha*, ed. Wilhelm Schneemelcher, trans. R. McL. Wilson, 2 vols. (Philadelphia: Westminster, 1963–64), vol. 2, p. 354.

The critics of the apostle failed to understand the bond between the Corinthians and Paul, their spiritual father. And they failed to see that Paul's strength resided in his meekness.

11. Let such a person consider this: what we say by means of letters while absent, we will also do when present.

Paul refrains from naming his opponent, whom he identifies as "anyone" and "such a person." This person is the representative of the infiltrators in the Corinthian church. And this spokesman circulated the rumor concerning Paul's inability to lead the church and preach the gospel. The apostle has a word for him: "Let him take note that my letters are true to fact, whether I am absent now or will be present in the near future."

At the beginning of this chapter (v. 2), Paul wrote that he wished he would not have to be bold upon his arrival in Corinth. If his letter would bring about a change, he would not need to come with a whip (I Cor. 4:21). But if there is no response to his admonitions, he will have to exercise discipline (12:20; 13:2, 10).

Also, the apostle is not addressing his opponents but the church in Corinth. He expects the Corinthians to heed his warnings, to oppose the influence of the intruders, and to welcome him into their midst.

Doctrinal Considerations in 10:8–11

Jesus appointed twelve apostles (Luke 6:13–16), chose the successor of Judas Iscariot (Acts 1:23–26), and called Paul to be the apostle to the Gentiles (Acts 9:4–6, 15–16). He gave them authority to preach the gospel; he filled them with the Holy Spirit; and he endowed them with spiritual gifts to heal the sick, drive out demons, and raise the dead. He appointed no other apostle after the death of James, the son of Zebedee (Acts 12:2).[42] The New Testament indicates that the apostolic office came to an end with the death of the last apostle, presumably John.

The authority of the Word passed from the apostles to pastors and teachers in the churches. When they proclaim the gospel, they speak in the name of the Lord. They are ministers of the Word of God, ambassadors for Jesus Christ, and bearers of the Good News. Their task is to strengthen believers in the faith, to call sinners to repentance, to administer the sacraments, to oppose doctrine that is contrary to God's Word, and to exercise discipline.

Pastors can claim authority only when God has given it to them and when they live and work in obedience to his Word. If they fail to apply that Word to their own lives, their authority no longer derives from God. Consequently, when pastors exercise their own authority, the church suffers, diminishes in numbers and influence, and faces termination. Instead they must be shepherds and overseers of God's flock, "not greedy for money, but eager to serve, not lording it over those entrusted to [them], but being examples to the flock" (I Peter 5:2–3). Pastors must set the example of true obedience to the gospel of

---

42. Herman N. Ridderbos (*Paul: An Outline of His Theology*, trans. John Richard de Witt [Grand Rapids: Eerdmans, 1975], p. 449) states, "Through this special position with respect to Christ as well as to the church, the apostolate according to its nature is unrepeatable and untransferable."

Christ and walk in the footsteps of Jesus, their Chief Shepherd. By magnifying Christ's name, they reinforce the spiritual authority they have received from him.

Greek Words, Phrases, and Constructions in 10:7–11

Verses 7–8

τὰ κατὰ πρόσωπον—literally, "the things before your face," which means that which is obvious.

ἐάν τε γάρ—the enclitic should be taken with ἐάν and not with γάρ, "for even if."

ἧς—the relative pronoun is a genitive by attraction to the preceding noun and serves as a direct object of the verb ἔδωκεν (he gave).

Verses 9–10

ὡς ἂν ἐκφοβεῖν—the present infinitive is intensive ("thoroughly frighten") and occurs only here in the New Testament. The particle ἄν signals possibility and hesitancy.

φησίν—this is the singular ("he says"), but Codex Vaticanus and some Latin and Syriac translations have the plural φασίν (they say). The singular is indefinite in the sense of "it is said," "they say," or "some say."[43]

---

12 For we do not dare to count ourselves among or compare ourselves with some of those who commend themselves. But because they measure themselves with themselves and compare themselves with themselves, they fail to understand. 13 We, however, will not boast beyond limits, but we boast according to the measure of the sphere that God has assigned to us and that reaches even you. 14 For not as though by not reaching out to you we overextended ourselves, for we came even as far as you with the gospel of Christ. 15 We do not boast beyond limits in the labors performed by others. But we hope that, as your faith increases, our sphere of influence among you may be greatly enlarged, 16 so that we may preach the gospel in regions beyond you. We do not boast of work that is done in someone else's sphere. 17 "Let him who boasts, boast in the Lord." 18 For it is not the one who commends himself who is approved, but the one whom the Lord commends.

---

2. Boasting and Limits
10:12–18

In the first part of this chapter, Paul defends his ministry in Corinth against attacks from his opponents. In the chapter's last segment, he sets the standards for the ministry to which God has called him. He delineates the difference between himself and the false teachers. With a number of clauses in the negative—seven times a negative particle ("not") appears in Greek—he defines the limits of boasting about his mission work. He receives his approval and commendation from the Lord.

12. For we do not dare to count ourselves among or compare ourselves with some of those who commend themselves. But because they measure themselves with themselves and compare themselves with themselves, they fail to understand.

---

43. Compare Moule, *Idiom-Book*, p. 29; Blass and Debrunner, *Greek Grammar*, #130.3.

a. *Negative.* "For we do not dare to count ourselves among or compare ourselves with some of those who commend themselves." The first word in this sentence ("for") hardly connects with the immediately preceding verse (v. 11). Perhaps Paul had interrupted his discourse and now begins with a new perspective on his defense.

Paul continues to address the congregation at Corinth and obliquely notes the presence of the intruders. The use of the verb *to dare* makes the irony in this sentence obvious. No one can miss Paul's intention of ridiculing his opponents. The apostle sarcastically places them on a level he himself will never be able to reach. Extending his irony a little later, he calls these people "superapostles" (11:5).

With a play on Greek words *enkrinai* and *synkrinai,* which we can approximate with the translation "*count* ourselves among and *compare* ourselves with,"[44] Paul continues to deride his opponents. He dares not call them his peers (compare 11:21), for they surpass him in their ease of speaking and their use of power. He portrays them as eminent leaders whom the Lord should be pleased to have in his church. He himself does not presume to be worthy of their company, in view of the low ratings they have given him (v. 10).

The impostors have come to Corinth with letters of commendations that their close friends had written for them. These documents lack authenticity. Paul is not interested in repeating what he said earlier in his epistle (see the commentary on 3:1 and 5:12). As an apostle, he was sent not from men nor by man (Gal. 1:1), but he was called and commissioned by Jesus Christ. More, the churches he had founded were his living letters of recommendation (3:2–3). The intruders, however, lacked divine authority and did not have the compliments of caring churches.

The word *some* is an indication that the invaders are few in number. Nevertheless, their continued presence in Corinth warps the spiritual development of the church as they gain followers among those who are like-minded. Calvin comments that people who commend themselves are "starving for true praise . . . and falsely give themselves out to be what they are not."[45]

b. *Flawed comparison.* "But because they measure themselves with themselves and compare themselves with themselves, they fail to understand." The repetition of the expression *themselves* clues the reader that something is wrong. The verbs are in the present tense and indicate that the interlopers continually measure and compare themselves with themselves. They do so without objective standards: complete obedience to God's Word, a definitive call to serve God in a given area, and a commitment to endure hardship in advancing the cause of Christ's gospel. When the restraints of objective standards are removed, society yields to immorality. "Where there is less virtue, there will be more vice; and more vice inevitably leads to the destruction of society and the loss of freedom."[46]

---

44. With thanks to the translators of the MLB.
45. Calvin, *II Corinthians,* p. 135.
46. Carson, *From Triumphalism to Maturity,* p. 74.

I have given the last part of this verse a causal connotation. This means that the intruders' failure to apply objective standards makes them fools compared with true followers of Christ. These people fail because they rely on their own understanding. They are indescribably dense by not seeing the power of God at work in the spread of the gospel. And they refuse to accept Paul as Christ's representative who proclaims "Christ crucified: a stumbling block to Jews and foolishness to Gentiles" (I Cor. 1:23).

13. We, however, will not boast beyond limits, but we boast according to the measure of the sphere that God has assigned to us and that reaches even you.

a. "We, however, will not boast beyond limits." The comparison with the adversaries is pronounced. The Greek word Paul uses is *ametra,* which means "that which cannot be measured." He tells the readers that he will not boast to levels that no one can measure, even though his antagonists do so. These assailants are not guided by any objective standards; their boasting centers on themselves. They measure themselves by a standard that is invalid.[47] Paul, however, employs the standard that God has given him in his divine revelation: to boast only in the Lord.

The future tense ("we will not boast") does not mean that sometime in the future Paul is willing not to boast. Rather, Paul is saying that he does not permit that this will ever happen.[48]

b. "But we boast according to the measure of the sphere that God has assigned to us." The apostle is a true ambassador sent to an assigned area over which he has complete authority. He glories in the territory that God has apportioned to him, which includes Corinth as the farthest point on his missionary journeys. The pillars of the church (Peter, James, and John) saw that God had sent Paul to preach the gospel to the Gentiles and Peter to the Jews (Gal. 2:7–9).

I have translated the Greek word *canōn* as "sphere." The primary rendering of this word is measuring stick, rule, or regulation.[49] This is Paul's intent in Galatians 6:16, where he writes: "Peace and mercy to all who follow this rule, even to the Israel of God." But a secondary interpretation is the sphere in which a rule is observed. Paul's choice of this term reflects a combination of both the meanings *rule* and *sphere* in language that he has borrowed from public service.[50]

God gave the apostle a measured area in which he had to work, so Paul can boast about the church in Corinth as he does elsewhere in this epistle (7:4, 11, 14). He expresses his care not to have entered a sphere of activity that was not assigned to him and not to build "on someone else's foundation" (Rom. 15:20).

---

47. Compare Moule, *Idiom-Book,* p. 71; Robert Hanna, *A Grammatical Aid to the Greek New Testament* (Grand Rapids: Baker, 1983), p. 329.

48. The tense is the volitive future. Consult Robertson, *Grammar,* p. 874.

49. JB has "yardstick" and NJB "standard." See also I Clem. 1.3; 7.2; 41.1; Josephus *Antiquities* 10.49; *Apion* 2.174. See Arthur J. Dewey, "A Matter of Honor: A Social-Historical Analysis of II Corinthians 10," *HTR* 78 (1985): 209–17.

50. Consult James F. Strange, "II Corinthians 10:13–16 Illuminated by a Recently Published Inscription," *BibArch* 46 (1983): 167–68. See also C. K. Barrett, "Christianity at Corinth," in *Essays on Paul* (Philadelphia: Westminster, 1982), pp. 18–19.

Conclusively, if the intruders enter Paul's field of labor, they are trespassers held accountable to God. Theirs is not to invade someone's God-ordained area of spiritual work, but to stay away.

Also, Paul had been faithful in his work among the Corinthians with visits, letters, and capable co-workers (Timothy, Silas, Apollos, and Titus). No one in Corinth would ever be able to accuse Paul of neglecting his pastoral duties.

c. "And that reaches even you." Paul's standard was to bring the gospel of salvation to the Corinthians and to set them free from the slavery of sin. He lived by the rule the Lord had given him in a vision: "Do not be afraid; keep on speaking, do not be silent . . . because I have many people in this city" (Acts 18:9–10).

14. For not as though by not reaching out to you we overextended ourselves, for we came even as far as you with the gospel of Christ.

This verse is to be understood not as an explanation of the preceding passage (v. 13) but as its continuation. Indeed, editors of the Greek text present verses 14–16 as one lengthy sentence; because Paul dictated it and became involved in his thought, the sentence has become longer than expected.[51]

In this verse, the emphasis falls on the verb *to overextend,* to which everything else is subordinate. Paul was guided by the Holy Spirit on his missionary journeys and did not leave a field of work unless he was led to another place (e.g., Acts 16:6–7; 20:22). The apostle did not go beyond the boundaries that God through his Spirit had made known to him.

The Corinthians have to realize that Paul has a personal interest in them, is on his way to Corinth, and in the near future hopes to see them. As yet God has not informed him about any additional mission fields, for only after he arrived in Corinth did Paul mention Spain (Rom. 15:24, 28). And from Macedonia, he seemed to have traveled to Illyricum (modern Albania [Rom. 15:19]).

Paul makes it known that his work for the present is among the Corinthians, whom he expects he will soon see. The fact that he is reaching out to them should be proof that Corinth is not outside the limits of his field of labor.

Although the apostle avoids boasting, his readers understand that he was the first to teach them Christ's gospel. He planted the seed, then his associates nourished the people spiritually, and consequently God gave the increase (I Cor. 3:6). Paul reached the Corinthians with the Good News and thus has reason to glory in the Lord because of God's surpassing grace (9:14).

15. We do not boast beyond limits in the labors performed by others. But we hope that, as your faith increases, our sphere of influence among you may be greatly enlarged.

a. "We do not boast beyond limits in the labors performed by others." The repetition of verse 13 in the first line is evident, and its reiteration refers directly to the interlopers in Corinth. They are the people who seek to harvest the fruits

---

51. Refer to Alfred Plummer, *A Critical and Exegetical Commentary on the Second Epistle of St. Paul to the Corinthians,* International Critical Commentary (1915; Edinburgh: Clark, 1975), p. 289.

of Paul's labors and then accuse him of having no interest in the local church. Hardened sinners, these people are in Corinth without any God-given commendation. They do not enter by the gate but climb in over the wall; they are thieves and robbers (compare John 10:1).

The apostle states emphatically that he does not seek glory for himself from the labors of others. He has in mind not manual work to maintain himself and others but the work of teaching and preaching Christ's gospel. The Greek word *kopos* (work) in Paul's epistles describes missionary labor,[52] which is here in the plural to indicate multifaceted mission work.

Paul would rather go to regions where people have not yet heard the gospel than to enter territories where others are working. Writing to the Romans, he tells them that he hopes to visit them while passing through on his way to Spain (Acts 19:21; Rom. 15:24). But he does not intend to make Rome or Italy his mission field.

Even though both Paul and Peter brought the gospel to Jews and Greeks— and Peter apparently visited Corinth—they did not work at cross-purposes (see I Cor. 1:12; 3:22; 9:5).[53] Indeed, Paul voiced no objections if someone wanted to build on the foundation he had laid (I Cor. 3:10). But he denounces the practices of the false teachers who assert that everything the Corinthians have learned has been the result of their labors.

b. "But we hope that, as your faith increases, our sphere of influence among you may be greatly enlarged." The Greek text of this sentence is complex and incomplete because it lacks a subject for the verb *to be enlarged*. Literally the text says, "and having hope, while your faith is increasing, to be enlarged among you according to our rule [sphere] superabundantly." The implied subject is Paul's work among the Corinthians. So he hopes that his missionary labor relating to the rule (his sphere of influence) may be greatly enlarged.

Paul is saying to the Corinthians: "Increase your faith, advance beyond the initial development of the church, and enlarge our sphere of influence." He hopes that the faith of the Corinthians will be so strong that they send missionaries to areas where the gospel has not yet been preached. But his vision can become reality only when unity, harmony, and dedication show the effectiveness of his teaching. As Paul's influence continues to increase among the Corinthians and their faith becomes strong, the influence of the intruders will end.

16. So that we may preach the gospel in regions beyond you. We do not boast of work that is done in someone else's sphere.

Directed by the Holy Spirit, the church in Syrian Antioch commissioned Barnabas and Paul to proclaim the gospel to the world and organize churches (Acts 13:2). The Spirit sent Paul and his associates to both Jews and Gentiles. Many who heard the Word believed, were baptized, and formed congregations, among which was the church of Corinth.

---

52. Consult Herbert Fendrich, *EDNT*, 2:307.

53. Compare Barrett, "Cephas and Corinth," pp. 35–36.

Now Paul is telling the Corinthians that as their faith increases, they must become a mission-minded church. They should send missionaries, including Paul and his co-workers, to regions that lie beyond Corinth. The apostle is a man of vision: he brought the gospel to many cities in the Mediterranean world, opened a training school in Ephesus (Acts 19:8–10), and wanted to extend the church to the ends of the world (Acts 1:8).[54]

The work of a missionary is to proclaim the gospel to the world, and this is exactly what Paul did. Spending time in Macedonia, he mentioned the words "in regions beyond you" to the people of Corinth. Paul reasoned from the geographical perspective of his readers. He looked westward to Italy and Spain. Should the Spirit send him there, he would need prayerful support from the Corinthian church to preach in regions unknown to him. With this support, his preaching would not be in vain.

The second half of this verse repeats the wording in verse 15a, "We do not boast beyond limits in the labors performed by others." The repetition serves to summarize what Paul has been saying in this paragraph. He realizes that "visitors from Rome" (Acts 2:10) later founded a church in the imperial city. The work in Rome has been completed by someone else. By visiting the church there, Paul cannot claim any credit. Instead, he plans to travel further, to Spain. On the way he hopes to see the Christians in Rome who may assist him on his journey westward (Rom. 15:24, 28).

17. "Let him who boasts, boast in the Lord." 18. For it is not the one who commends himself who is approved, but the one whom the Lord commends.

a. *To boast.* Paul is coming to the end of this part of his discourse in which he has discussed boasting and its limits. He now presents a general principle that he has scrupulously applied to himself. His boasting is in the Lord, for whom he waits to commend him.

As he does in numerous other places in his epistles, the apostle supports his teachings with references to and quotations from the Old Testament Scriptures. Here he quotes freely from Jeremiah 9:24a, "But let him who boasts boast about this: that he understands and knows me, that I am the LORD." Paul presents a one-line summary of this verse, which he had quoted earlier (I Cor. 1:31): "Let him who boasts, boast in the Lord."

In Paul's teaching everything is directed toward the Lord. He does not distinguish between the title LORD in the Old Testament and the appellation *Lord* for Jesus in the New Testament. He depends not on himself but on his Savior to whom he ascribes glory and honor. Thus Paul writes elsewhere, "May I never boast except in the cross of our Lord Jesus Christ" (Gal. 6:14).

With his reliance on the Lord, Paul effectively defines the difference between himself and his opponents. He wants no glory for himself but devotes everything

---

54. Clement of Rome (I Clem. 5.6–7) writes: "[Paul] was a herald both in the East and in the West, he gained the noble fame of his faith, he taught righteousness to all the world, and when he had reached the limits of the West he gave his testimony before the rulers, and thus passed from the world."

to Jesus, while his adversaries want everything for themselves and present commendations that are void of divine approval.

b. *To commend.* The intruders should have consulted Solomon's writing, "Let another praise you, and not your own mouth; someone else, and not your own lips" (Prov. 27:2). Instead they rate one another by their own standards and not by God's Word. They praise themselves and are not sent by God.

If there is anything that God detests, it is self-commendation. Jesus teaches the parable of the Pharisee and the tax collector to delineate the difference between arrogance and utter dependence on God (Luke 18:10–14). God turns the self-exultation of the Pharisee into debasement but the humility of the tax collector into exhilaration. The social outcast went home justified.

Throughout this epistle, Paul has made it known repeatedly that he has no need of self-promotion. He distances himself from his antagonists who trumpet their own commendations and brag about their own achievements. Devoid of divine approval, they fail to receive God's blessings. Indeed, the words of the psalmist apply to them: "Unless the LORD builds the house, its builders labor in vain. Unless the LORD watches over the city, the watchmen stand guard in vain" (Ps. 127:1).

Paul is saying to the Corinthians that only when God ordains people to work for him can there be praise and thanksgiving. The readers of this epistle should look at the results of Paul's ministry in Corinth and elsewhere. They should note that the apostle was sent by God and blessed by him. However, Paul does not glory in his accomplishments; he received his talents, tact, wisdom, insight, and strength from the Lord. To him he ascribes honor and glory. Thus, he boasts in the Lord and in him alone.

Greek Words, Phrases, and Constructions in 10:12–18

Verses 12–13

Assonance in two verbs ἐγκρῖναι (to classify) and συγκρῖναι (to compare) is a deliberate play on words to express irony.

αὐτοί—this personal pronoun refers to Paul's opponents and not to Paul. Some manuscripts of the Western text (D* G, it^d,g,ar, and others) omit the words οὐ συνιᾶσιν. ἡμεῖς δέ (are without understanding. We, however). Then verses 12 and 13 refer to Paul and do not contrast the opponents (v. 12) and Paul (v. 13). Many scholars (Bultmann, Lietzmann, Héring, Georgi, Windisch, and the *Greek Grammar* of Blass, Debrunner, and Funk) and at least one translator (*Moffatt*) have adopted the shorter reading.

Numerous scholars, editors of the Greek New Testament, and the overwhelming majority of translators adopt the longer reading. They point out that the pronoun αὐτοί introduces a new subject that refers to Paul's opponents and not to Paul himself. Also, the better manuscripts support the longer reading. Next, it is easier to explain the omission of the intervening words than their insertion.[55] And last, why would Paul want to compare

---

55. Bruce M. Metzger, *A Textual Commentary on the Greek New Testament* (Stuttgart and New York: United Bible Societies, 1994), p. 514.

himself with himself when he is critical of such vaunting (see especially v. 18)?[56] Therefore, the longer reading is preferred.

εἰς τὰ ἄμετρα—the preposition signifies "with." The definite article in the neuter plural points to "things." These two verses reveal a recurrence of the root μετρ- (measure) in the form of participle, adjective, and noun.

οὗ—the relative pronoun relates to the genitive case not of τοῦ κανόνος but μέτρου, which Paul supplies for clarification.

Verses 14–15

οὐ . . . ὑπερεκτείνομεν—the particle negates the verb which, as a compound, is directive: "we do not reach beyond [the limit]."

ὡς μή—the negative μή controls the participle ἐφικνούμενοι, which is the present middle and denotes concession: "as though not reaching."

ἐν τῷ εὐαγγελίῳ τοῦ Χριστοῦ—"in the interest of Christ's gospel." The genitive is both objective and subjective, "for and of Christ."

The first two participles καυχώμενοι (boasting) and ἔχοντες (having) serve as finite verbs: we boast and we have.

Verse 16

ὑπερέκεινα—this is a compound from the preposition ὑπέρ (beyond) and the pronoun ἐκεῖνα (those). This adverb occurs only here in Greek literature.

τὰ ἕτοιμα—the neuter plural adjective connotes "a field that has already been cultivated."[57]

Summary of Chapter 10

In Paul's absence, his opponents accuse him of timidity when he is present in Corinth but of writing harsh letters from a distance. They portray him as a barking dog that never bites. With their accusations they seek to undercut his ministry and question his apostolic authority. The apostle states that he does not live by worldly standards. He has been endowed with power to subdue those who have decided to follow the opponents.

Paul writes that he fights with weapons that have divine power. He is engaged in a spiritual warfare and thus destroys the worldly arguments and pretexts that have been raised against God. Paul and his associates are ready to tear down everything that is in opposition to Christ and to make every thought captive to the Lord.

If the opponents state that they belong to Christ, then the Corinthians should understand that Paul also belongs to him. Unlike the intruders, the apostle uses his God-given authority to edify the believers. In the church, Paul is not a destroyer but a builder. His design is not to frighten his readers but to encourage them. He wants them to understand that he opposes the false apostles who demean him as a person by saying that his physical appearance is puny and his or-

---

56. See Furnish, *II Corinthians,* pp. 470–71; Kümmel, "Anhang," in Lietzmann, *Korinther,* pp. 208–9.
57. Walter Radl, *EDNT,* 2:68.

atory poor. Whatever Paul wrote in his letters will be enacted when he appears in Corinth to oppose his adversaries.

Paul knows that God has commissioned him and assigned to him a field of labor that includes Corinth. He was the apostle who brought them the gospel of salvation. The difference between him and the false apostles is that he works in the areas that God has specified. These infiltrators enter regions where someone else has been working; they seek to reap glory from the work performed by others.

The Corinthians need to grow in faith so that they can become a church that commissions, sends, and supports missionaries to other regions. The glory of this work is not for themselves but for the Lord. Paul concludes the chapter by saying that only the person who is commissioned by the Lord to go forth as a missionary receives God's approval.

11

Apostolic Authority, *part 2*

(11:1–33)

Outline (continued)

11

1 I wish that you would put up with a little of my foolishness. Indeed, do put up with me; 2 for I am jealous for you with a jealousy that originates in God. I gave you in marriage to one man, to Christ, to present you as a pure virgin to him. 3 But I am afraid that as the serpent with his craftiness deceived Eve, your thoughts may somehow be corrupted [to drift away] from the sincerity and the purity that is toward Christ. 4 For if someone comes and proclaims a Jesus other than the one we proclaimed, or you receive a spirit different from the one you received, or a gospel different from the one you accepted, you put up with it well enough.

---

3. Devotion to Christ
11:1–4

The moment has come for Paul to confront his opponents. He has made it known that he detests the manner in which they commend themselves. To convey his message, he continues to mock them (see 10:12–13) and applies increasingly pointed sarcasm. He portrays his opponents as superapostles (v. 5; 12:11) who masquerade as apostles of Christ (v. 13). These men are rivals intent on undermining Paul's calling and mission.[1] To counteract their strategy, Paul asks the Corinthians to play along with his jests. However, he expects the readers to acknowledge that he is a true apostle and the intruders are false. Everything that Paul conveys to the people in Corinth can be verified—see his catalogs of sufferings in this epistle (1:8–10; 6:4–10; 11:23–27; 12:10). He is free from self-promotion, but with God-given eagerness he promotes the spiritual well-being of the Corinthians.[2]

1. I wish that you would put up with a little of my foolishness. Indeed, do put up with me.

Throughout this chapter Paul almost exclusively uses the first person singular *I,* seldom the pronoun *we,* and even then he refers to himself (vv. 4, 6, 21). He clearly indicates that the attacks the opponents have launched against him are personal. He realizes that if they are able to destroy the founder of the Corinthian congregation, they will have a free hand in teaching their false doctrine (v. 4).

---

1. Dieter Georgi, *Paul's Opponents in Second Corinthians* (Philadelphia: Fortress, 1986), pp. 32–33; E. Earle Ellis, "Paul and His Opponents," in *Prophecy and Hermeneutics in Early Christianity: New Testaments Essays,* WUzNT 18 (Tübingen: Mohr-Siebeck; Grand Rapids: Eerdmans, 1978), p. 108.

2. See F. W. Grosheide, *De Tweede Brief van den Apostel Paulus aan de Kerk te Korinthe,* Kommentaar op het Nieuwe Testament series (Amsterdam: Van Bottenburg, 1939), p. 374; Ernest B. Allo, *Saint Paul Seconde Épître aux Corinthiens,* 2d ed. (Paris: Gabalda, 1956), p. 276.

The wish that Paul expresses is an invitation to the readers to join him in a little display of folly (compare vv. 16–17, 19, 23; 12:6, 11). In doing so, he wants them to bear with him in this foolishness but at the same time to see the truthfulness of his record of sufferings for Christ and the church. The apostle invites the Corinthians to examine his record of service as a recommendation of his divine calling (see especially vv. 16–29). Paul speaks the truth and declares, "I repeat: let no one take me for a fool" (v. 16). He can truthfully say that he worked harder than all the other apostles (I Cor. 15:10).

The Greek verb *anechein* (to put up with) is a key word in this chapter, for it occurs five times (vv. 1 [twice], 4, 19, 20).[3] In prose laced with irony, Paul asks the Corinthians to put up with him as he lowers himself to the level of his opponents. In fact, he acts against his own principle not to commend himself. The apostle deems this foolishness necessary not for personal glory but for the advancement of the church in Corinth.

We note two translation matters. First, the Greek can be rendered as either "put up with me" or "put up with my foolishness." Although translators are divided, the point of difference is negligible. Next, the last clause is of greater importance. The verb in this clause is translated either in the indicative ("and indeed you do bear with me," NKJV) or in the imperative ("and indeed bear with me," KJV). A solid case can be made for either translation, yet the imperative fits better into the flow of the discourse. The next clause (v. 2) seems to lend support to Paul's appeal for tolerance.

2. For I am jealous for you with a jealousy that originates in God. I gave you in marriage to one man, to Christ, to present you as a pure virgin to him.

a. "For I am jealous for you with a jealousy that originates in God." Stylistic reasons force many translators to omit the Greek word *gar* (for) in this sentence. But it points to the reason for Paul's encouragement to the readers to put up with his pretense. He guards his people with divine jealousy.

Murray J. Harris astutely observes, "Human jealousy is a vice, but to share divine jealousy is a virtue."[4] Jealousy is recorded in the Decalogue: "I, the LORD your God, am a jealous God," as a command to the Israelites that idolatry is not tolerated (Exod. 20:5; Deut. 5:9). God's zeal for his people results in blessings when they obey and curses when they disobey (Deut. 28).

God imparted to Paul a jealousy for the well-being of his people. The word *jealousy* summarizes Paul's ardor for the Corinthians and his readiness to keep them safe from the advances of his rivals. The apostle showed his ardent love for them in his teaching, visits, correspondence, and intercessions. As their spiritual father (I Cor. 4:15), he has a personal interest in the Christians at Corinth. He

---

3. Other uses refer to exasperation (Matt. 17:17; Mark 9:19; Luke 9:41), forbearance in love (Eph. 4:2; Col. 3:13), and permission (Acts 18:14). See Horst Balz, *EDNT*, 1:98.

4. Murray J. Harris, *II Corinthians*, in vol. 10 of *The Expositor's Bible Commentary*, ed. Frank E. Gaebelein, 12 vols. (Grand Rapids: Zondervan, 1976), p. 385.

guards them like a father who watches protectively over his daughter before she is given in marriage to her future husband.

b. "I gave you in marriage to one man, to Christ, to present you as a pure virgin to him." Every word in this illustration is filled with meaning and has been chosen carefully. Paul presents himself as a parent who has sought and found a suitable husband for his marriageable daughter. He is responsible for the spiritual purity of the Corinthian congregation, which he wants to present to Christ. The Old Testament depicts the betrothal of Israel as bride and God as bridegroom (e.g., Isa. 50:1; Ezek. 16:23–33; Hos. 2:19). Also, the New Testament often mentions the spiritual relationship of the bride, which is the church, and the bridegroom, who is Christ (Matt. 9:15; Mark 2:19; Luke 5:34–35; John 3:29; Eph. 5:25–32; Rev. 19:7–9).

Notice that Paul says "I gave you in marriage," a translation of the Greek word *hērmosamēn*. The basic meaning of this verb is "to fit together" (we have the derivative *harmony*) and, next, "to join or give in marriage, betroth."[5] The church in Corinth is engaged to be married, while Paul serves as friend of the bridegroom and guardian of the bride. He wants the bride to be faithful to her future husband.

The phrase *to one man* illustrates divinely intended monogamy in which one man and one woman pledge faithfulness to one another. The man is Christ and the woman the Corinthian church. Christ's loyalty to the church is faultless and need not be mentioned; but the fidelity of the Corinthians demands Paul's protective care and watchfulness.

In the oriental culture of that day, an engagement was equivalent to marriage without consummation. The betrothal period lasted for one year, during which bride and bridegroom prepared for the wedding ceremony. From the day of her betrothal, the woman legally was the wife of her future husband but she remained a virgin until the wedding day. In addition, the engagement might not be broken. If this happened, it was considered a divorce. Only death might end an engagement. Unfaithfulness of either party was regarded as adultery and had to be disciplined accordingly.[6] The bride had to remain a virgin to be presented to her husband. So Paul exerts himself to keep the church pure from doctrine contrary to the gospel as he strives to present her to Christ.

The last part of this verse augurs a bright future in which Christ as bridegroom and the church as bride will be together in full communion. To borrow a thought, God's people see "only a shadow of the good things that are coming" (see Heb. 10:1). Nonetheless, while on earth the church must be ready to appear before Christ without wrinkle or blemish in holiness and purity (Eph. 5:27).

3. But I am afraid that as the serpent with his craftiness deceived Eve, your thoughts may somehow be corrupted [to drift away] from the sincerity and the purity that is toward Christ.

---

5. Bauer, p. 107.
6. Richard Batey, "Paul's Bride Image: A Symbol of Realistic Eschatology," *Interp* 17 (1963): 178.

a. *Variation.* The Greek text presents variant readings that concern the exclusion or the inclusion of the words *and the purity.* Many versions (e.g., KJV, NKJV, NJB, JB) and numerous commentators (among them Barrett, Calvin, Lietzmann, Martin, Pop, and Windisch) omit these words. They contend that because of similar endings of the two nouns in Greek, the word *purity* first appeared in the margin and later was inserted into the text. However, the Greek manuscripts that include the expression *and the purity* are early and solid.[7] Even though the arguments for both positions are convincing, the one for the expanded version appears to be stronger.

b. *Illustration.* "But I am afraid that as the serpent with his craftiness deceived Eve, your thoughts may somehow be corrupted." What blame would have fallen on Paul if through his neglect the Corinthian church had fallen away from Christ. As a shepherd of the flock that is entrusted to his care, the apostle watches over the church to preserve Christ's honor.

By mentioning the serpent and Eve, Paul calls to mind the scene in Paradise where Satan deceived Eve and led her into sin (Gen. 3:13). He seems to discontinue his illustration about marriage and introduce one of deception and sin. Some commentators have tried to explain this sudden change of topics by alluding to a Jewish legend of Eve being sexually seduced by the serpent. This legend was probably current in the first century and presumably Paul was acquainted with it.[8]

Even if Paul knew about this Jewish tale, he selected the reference to Eve's deception only because of its contextual relevance. With Adam, Eve broke her dedication to God by transgressing the command not to eat of the fruit of the tree of good and evil (Gen. 2:17; 3:11, 17; compare also I Tim. 2:14). Similarly, the Corinthian church faced the danger of deserting Christ by listening to another gospel (v. 4).

Three considerations bear upon the interpretation of this verse. First, the Genesis account fails to disclose anything sexually immoral between Eve and the serpent.[9] To suggest that fallen angels can have sexual relations with women is an unfounded assertion, because angels do not marry (Mark 12:25). Next, Paul's objective is not to speak about something sensual but about the corruption of the mind. Just as Satan attacked the thinking of Eve, so the intruders are trying to change the thought patterns of the Corinthians. And last, Paul links the serpent's deception to the superapostles (vv. 4–5) and the masquerading Satan to

7. Refer to Bruce M. Metzger, *A Textual Commentary on the Greek New Testament* (Stuttgart and New York: United Bible Societies, 1994), pp. 514–15.

8. Rudolf Bultmann, *The Second Letter to the Corinthians,* trans. Roy A. Harrisville (Minneapolis: Augsburg, 1985), p. 201; Hans Lietzmann, *An die Korinther I/II,* augmented by Werner G. Kümmel, Handbuch zum Neuen Testament 9 (Tübingen: Mohr, 1969), pp. 145, 209–10; Hans Windisch, *Der Zweite Korintherbrief,* ed. Georg Strecker (1924; reprint ed., Göttingen: Vandenhoeck und Ruprecht, 1970), pp. 323–24.

9. R. C. H. Lenski (*The Interpretation of St. Paul's First and Second Epistle to the Corinthians* [Columbus: Wartburg, 1946], p. 1239) notes that "Eve was a married woman and not a virgin."

the masquerading false apostles (vv. 13–14). In short, these intruders are Satan's servants who attempt to subvert the thinking pattern of the Corinthians.

c. *Devotion.* "[To drift away] from the sincerity and the purity that is toward Christ." Paul's purpose in supplying the illustration about Eve's deception is to emphasize the necessity of unblemished spiritual fidelity to God. As Satan perverted Eve's guileless faith in God, so the false apostles attempt to persuade the Corinthians to abandon their single-hearted faithfulness to Christ. Seeing the servants of Satan at work among the members of the Corinthian church, Paul sounds the alarm and seeks to preserve their spiritual sincerity and purity. The word *sincerity* means simplicity, which effectively rules out every trace of duplicity. It signifies being exclusively devoted to one person or cause with respect to thinking, speaking, and doing. The term *purity* refers to moral blamelessness.

Acting as the friend of the bridegroom (Christ), Paul keeps the bride (the church) pure and blameless. He is unable to do this unless the entire membership of the local church is alerted to the impending danger. Not only for the Christians in Corinth, but for every believer, the watchword is alertness. The attacks of the evil one occur relentlessly to the end of time. Philip Edgcumbe Hughes notes, "The enmity between the seed of the serpent and the Seed of the woman continues unremittingly until the day of judgment, and mankind will continue to suffer from and be threatened by the evil effects of the first sin of the first woman until, at Christ's coming, the new creation is fully realized and the former things are passed away."[10]

4. For if someone comes and proclaims a Jesus other than the one we proclaimed, or you receive a spirit different from the one you received, or a gospel different from the one you accepted, you put up with it well enough.

a. *Parallelism.* The first word, "for," is the bridge between the preceding verse (v. 3) and this one; and it explains Paul's previous statement about an external corrupting influence on the Corinthians. Paul now speaks about the reality of someone who has come to Corinth to proclaim another Jesus, a different spirit, and a different gospel. But before we discuss the details of this text, we look at its symmetry:

someone proclaims a Jesus	*other* than the one we proclaimed
you receive a spirit	*different* from the one you received
[you accept] a gospel	*different* from the one you accepted

Notice the triad: Jesus, spirit, gospel; and note the three verbs: proclaimed, received, accepted. Also, the Greek adjective *allos* (other), which usually means another of the same kind, has the same meaning as the Greek word *heteros* (other, in the sense of different). Their correlation here is based on the parallel of proclaiming Jesus and accepting the gospel, for both activities are similar.

---

10. Philip Edgcumbe Hughes, *Paul's Second Epistle to the Corinthians: The English Text with Introduction, Exposition and Notes,* New International Commentary on the New Testament series (Grand Rapids: Eerdmans, 1962), p. 376.

In the first part of this epistle, Paul discusses the above-mentioned triad, although not in the same sequence. He relates that the Spirit of the living God is instrumental in giving life, while the letter kills (3:3, 6). Next, he writes repeatedly about Jesus' gospel, death, and resurrection (4:5, 10, 11, 14). And last, Paul speaks about "our gospel," which he compares implicitly to another gospel (4:3).[11] We are not surprised, therefore, to find the same triad in the present context.

b. *Exposition.* "For if someone comes and proclaims a Jesus other than the one we proclaimed." The "someone" is the representative of a group of meddlers, as is evident from the preceding chapter (10:7, 10, 11; see also 11:21). This person presents another Jesus to the members of the Corinthian church. Because Paul seldom uses only the single name *Jesus* instead of Christ Jesus or Jesus Christ, we assume that he calls attention to the ministry of Jesus without preaching him as crucified Lord.[12] The intruding Judaizers would refrain from depicting Jesus as the Christ, even if they called themselves "servants of Christ."[13]

Paul's opponents came to Corinth with self-commendations, were not commissioned by Jesus Christ as apostles, presented themselves on their own authority, and had never suffered for the sake of Jesus and his gospel. Refusing to listen obediently to the Scriptures, these people avoided the inevitability of enduring hardship for Christ. Instead they probably talked about a victorious Jesus who performed miracles, preached good news, and inspired multitudes. But they failed to mention Jesus' suffering, humiliation, and death on a cruel cross (compare Rom. 15:3 [Ps. 69:9]). They proclaimed a Jesus who was entirely different from the one Paul had taught the Corinthians.

"Or you receive a spirit different from the one you received." Should the word *spirit* be capitalized, referring to the Holy Spirit? No, because the spirit that the intruders propose is not the Spirit of God but a human spirit. When the Corinthians accepted Christ, God gave them his Holy Spirit.[14] In the last four chapters of this epistle, Paul says little about the Holy Spirit. But he already had spoken on this topic and did not have to repeat himself (3:3, 6, 17).

The interlopers wanted to give the Corinthians a worldly spirit in place of the Holy Spirit. But a worldly spirit enslaves people and fills their hearts with fear. Such a spirit is devoid of power, love, joy, peace, patience, kindness, goodness, faithfulness, gentleness, and self-control (I Cor. 2:4–5; Gal. 5:22–23).

11. Derk W. Oostendorp, *Another Jesus: A Gospel of Jewish-Christian Superiority in II Corinthians* (Kampen: Kok, 1967), p. 11.

12. C. K. Barrett, *The Second Epistle to the Corinthians,* Harper's New Testament Commentaries series (New York: Harper and Row, 1973), p. 277; see also "Paul's Opponents in II Corinthians," in *Essays on Paul* (Philadelphia: Westminster, 1982), pp. 68–70. Compare Georgi, *Opponents of Paul,* p. 273.

13. Alfred Plummer (*A Critical and Exegetical Commentary on the Second Epistle of St. Paul to the Corinthians,* International Critical Commentary [1915; Edinburgh: Clark, 1975], p. 296) observes that "Judaizers would not use Χριστός as a proper name."

14. See I Cor. 2:12; 3:16; 6:19; II Cor. 1:22; 5:5.

"Or a gospel different from the one you accepted." Paul preached Christ's gospel, which the Corinthians accepted in faith. When the Corinthians believed Jesus, they received from God the gift of the Holy Spirit. Note, then, that believers accept the gospel but receive the Spirit. Guided by the Holy Spirit, they were to follow Christ steadfastly.

Now the people are in danger of accepting a different gospel. They can hear the echo of Galatians 1:6–7, where Paul writes: "I am astonished that you are so quickly . . . turning to a different gospel—which is really no gospel at all." There is but one gospel of Jesus Christ, which we have in the four versions of Matthew, Mark, Luke, and John. There is no other gospel than the gospel of Jesus; all others are apocryphal.[15]

Paul wrote that he had received the tradition from the Lord and passed it on to the Corinthians (I Cor. 15:3). Afterward he wrote to them about the light of the gospel. With that light, believers are able to see Christ's glory, but those who are lost cannot see it because it is hidden from them (4:3–4; contrast 9:13). The apostle remarks that he and his colleagues never distort the word of God (4:2). But, by implication, this is exactly what his adversaries did (2:17).

"You put up with it well enough." The changes in doctrine were presented gradually so that the members of the Corinthian church hardly noticed the difference. Paul himself has to call their attention to the spiritual threat in their midst. For this reason, he must be direct in confronting the readers.

Doctrinal Considerations in 11:4

What are the scriptural consequences of presenting a Jesus void of suffering, humiliation, and death on the cross? What is the effect of proclaiming a Jesus who did not humble himself and did not become obedient to death (Phil. 2:8)? What is the result of preaching a Jesus without mentioning the shedding of his blood? The writer of Hebrews puts it squarely before the reader: "Without the shedding of blood there is no forgiveness" (Heb. 9:22). Further, through the sacrifice of Christ's body on the cross, we have been and are being made holy (Heb. 10:10, 14).

Paul is saying the same thing. He writes that if the resurrection of Jesus is nullified, then our faith is useless and forgiveness of sins nonexistent (I Cor. 15:17). Also, there is then no eternal life for the human race.

When another Jesus is preached, not according to the gospel, the biblical teaching of atonement, reconciliation, removal of the curse, and adoption is eliminated. If Jesus is merely a man whom we must use as a model, "we are to be pitied more than all men" (I Cor. 15:19). However, on the basis of Scripture we joyfully confess with the church of all ages

> the forgiveness of sins;
> the resurrection of the body;
> and the life everlasting.

---

15. Gerhard Friedrich, *TDNT*, 2:727–36.

Greek Words, Phrases, and Constructions in 11:1–4

Verses 1–2

ἀλλὰ καὶ ἀνέχεσθε—the adversative ἀλλά with καί can be interpreted as an emphatic "yes, indeed" followed by the imperative "bear with me!"[16]

ἀφροσύνης—"folly." This word occurs four times in the New Testament, of which three are in this chapter (vv. 1, 17, 21; see also Mark 7:22). The term is more moderate than μωρία (foolishness), a term that occurs only in I Corinthians 1:18, 21, 23; 2:14; 3:19. Foolishness is the opposite of wisdom and folly is the converse of moderation.[17]

θεοῦ ζήλῳ—these words can be interpreted as "divine [i.e., supernaturally great] eagerness," "God's own eagerness," or "an eagerness which springs from God Himself."[18] Of the three interpretations, the last one is preferred. That is, Paul displays an eagerness for the Corinthians that originates in God.

ἡρμοσάμην γὰρ ὑμᾶς—"for I betrothed you." The middle voice is reflexive to indicate that Paul himself had an interest in this marriage.

Verses 3–4

φθαρῇ—the aorist passive subjunctive of φθείρειν (to ruin; passive: to be led astray) does not refer to seduction but to corruption of one's mind.

καὶ τῆς ἁγνότητος—the difficulty we face at this point is whether these words were added because of the similarity to the preceding phrase ἀπὸ τῆς ἁπλότητος. The endings of these two nouns are the same. Yet there is strong attestation for the longer reading.[19]

ὁ ἐρχόμενος—except for John 6:35, 37, where Jesus calls the individual believer to come to him in faith, this term describes the Messiah throughout the New Testament.[20] The term is applied, interestingly, to someone who preaches another Jesus and whom Paul calls a false apostle (v. 13).

ἀνέχεσθε—a number of manuscripts have the reading ἀνείχεσθε, which is in the imperfect tense and introduces probability: "you would put up with someone who preaches a different gospel." But the context confirms reality, not contingency. Hence, the present tense is preferred.

---

5 For I do not think that I am in the least inferior to those superapostles. 6 I may be unskilled in respect to speech but I am not so in respect to knowledge. Certainly, in every respect and in all things we made this known to you.

---

16. A. T. Robertson, *A Grammar of the Greek New Testament in the Light of Historical Research* (Nashville: Broadman, 1934), p. 1186; Friedrich Blass and Albert Debrunner, *A Greek Grammar of the New Testament and Other Early Christian Literature*, trans. and rev. Robert Funk (Chicago: University of Chicago Press, 1961), #448.6.

17. Consult Victor Paul Furnish, *II Corinthians: Translated with Introduction, Notes and Commentary*, Anchor Bible 32A (Garden City, N.Y.: Doubleday, 1984), p. 485; Bultmann, *Second Letter*, p. 200.

18. C. F. D. Moule, *An Idiom-Book of New Testament Greek*, 2d ed. (Cambridge: Cambridge University Press, 1960), p. 184. Compare also Robert Hanna, *A Grammatical Aid to the New Testament* (Grand Rapids: Baker, 1983), p. 329.

19. Metzger, *Textual Commentary*, pp. 514–15.

20. Refer to Matt. 11:3; 21:9; 23:39; Mark 11:9; Luke 7:19; 13:35; 19:38; John 1:15, 27; 11:27; 12:13; Rev. 1:4, 8; 4:8.

4. Superapostles
11:5–6

5. For I do not think that I am in the least inferior to those superapostles.
Scholars differ on the paragraph division of the first part of this chapter. Some include verses 5 and 6 with the preceding four verses (NIV, NRSV, REB);[21] others make them part of the following segment (vv. 7–12; e.g., MLB); and still others present the two verses as a separate paragraph and prefer this division in view of the context (GNB, NCV, TNT).

Paul continues to use the first person singular (see vv. 1, 2, 3) and states his own opinion about the infiltrators. He compares himself with them and facetiously calls them superapostles. He repeats this name in the next chapter, where he again states that he is not inferior to these people (12:11; see also 11:23). By resorting to derision, Paul implicitly indicates that the Corinthians already should have evaluated the intruders as impostors. Indeed, they needed to come to Paul's defense and dismiss his rivals.

Who are these so-called superapostles? Are they Jesus' twelve disciples and others who followed him from the time of his baptism to that of his ascension (Acts 1:21–22)? This interpretation fails to do justice to the immediate context, in which Paul speaks of an opponent who preaches a different Jesus (see v. 4).[22] Moreover, the three pillars of the church (Peter, James, and John) had come to an agreement with Paul on a division of labors between Peter and Paul (Gal. 2:6–9). Apart from a confrontation at Antioch, we do not read of any tension between these two apostles (Gal. 2:11–14) or the rest of them. Hence, we cannot infer that Paul considers himself inferior to the Jerusalem apostles. Rather, he employs irony when he labels the Judaizing interlopers as superapostles.

The expression *superapostles* "even linguistically brings out the impossible nature of such apostles," because being an apostle of Jesus is in itself incomparable.[23] The list of spiritual gifts indicates no higher position than that of apostle (I Cor. 12:28; Eph. 4:11).

No one but Jesus appointed the twelve apostles, chose Matthias to succeed Judas Iscariot, and called Paul as an apostle to the Gentiles. Jesus commissioned no successors to these men, with the result that apostleship never became an established and continuing church office. The apostolate is therefore "unrepeatable and untransferable."[24]

---

21. Barrett links verse 5 directly to verse 1. The particle γάρ, occurring three times (vv. 2, 4, 5) presents three reasons for verse 1. See "Paul's Opponents," p. 71; Bultmann, *Second Letter,* pp. 200–203.

22. Contra C. K. Barrett, "Christianity at Corinth," in *Essays on Paul* (Philadelphia: Westminster, 1982), p. 20; Margaret E. Thrall, "Super-apostles, Servants of Christ, and Servants of Satan," *JSNT* 6 (1980): 42–57. See Scott E. McClelland, "Super-apostles, Servants of Christ, Servants of Satan: A Response," *JSNT* 14 (1982): 82–87; Doyle Kee, "Who Were the 'Super-Apostles' of II Corinthians 10–13," *ResQ* 23 (1980): 65–76; Oostendorp, *Another Jesus,* p. 11 n. 16.

23. Karl Heinrich Rengstorf, *TDNT,* 1:445.

24. Herman N. Ridderbos, *Paul: An Outline of His Theology,* trans. John Richard de Witt (Grand Rapids: Eerdmans, 1975), p. 449. See note 42 in chapter 10.

If the superapostles are not identified with the apostles in Jerusalem, we must associate them with the false apostles whom Paul mentions in verse 13. These men came to Corinth on their own accord, adopted the name *apostles* to gain entry into the church, and gave the impression of possessing more authority than Paul. These people probably had Judean roots. For a comprehensive discussion, see the Introduction.

6. I may be unskilled in respect to speech but I am not so in respect to knowledge. Certainly, in every respect and in all things we made this known to you.

a. *Admission.* "I may be unskilled in respect to speech but I am not so in respect to knowledge." The emphasis is on the first person singular pronoun *I*, which occurs twice in the first sentence. The plural *we* in the second half of the verse refers to Paul himself.

Verse 6a is Paul's frank acknowledgment that he was no orator. He lacked the oratorical skills of Apollos and was unable to compete with the Greeks, who favored eloquent speakers. The Greeks considered anyone who floundered in speech an amateur. Apollos was the favorite preacher in Corinth, and Paul was regarded as second best (I Cor. 2:1).

Even though Paul acknowledges his lack of eloquence, at times he was able to articulate and speak effectively. Luke recorded Paul's address before Governor Festus, King Agrippa, high-ranking Roman army officers, and prominent leaders in Caesarea (Acts 25:23; 26:2–29). This last speech is the best of Paul's addresses, for its style borders on that of classical Greek. Yet Paul knew his limitations and freely admitted his deficiency in rhetoric. He realized that his accusers had spread the word that his speaking was less than mediocre (10:10). According to the standards of the Greeks, they were correct.[25]

The apostle was an amateur in oratory but a genius in factual and spiritual knowledge. He especially knew the Scriptures and had profound insight into the mystery of Christ's gospel (see Eph. 3:4). In this text and others he associates the term *knowledge* with both the preaching of the Good News and spiritual knowledge (4:6; 6:6; 8:7; 10:5). This word directs attention to God's redemptive revelation in Jesus Christ.

b. *Difficulty.* "Certainly, in every respect and in all things we made this known to you." This sentence presents a number of difficulties that affect its interpretation. Paul has left out three expressions. With elisions, and following the Greek word order, the sentence reads: "However, in every . . . having made known . . . in all . . . to you [plural]." In sequence, I have supplied the words *respect, this,* and *things.* Other translators have inserted different terms, so that few versions are identical.

The plural form of the participle *having made known* points to Paul, who is the subject, and the supplied object is "this." We infer from the context that the object is spiritual knowledge of the gospel that Paul had imparted to the Corinthians in person and by letter.

---

25. Consult Augustine *De sacerdotio* 4.5–6; E. A. Judge, "Paul's Boasting in Relation to Contemporary Professional Practice," *AusBRev* 16 (1968): 37–50, especially 41.

Next, the verb *we made known* has the support of the better Greek manuscripts. It is definitely preferred to the passive construction, "we have been thoroughly made manifest," which makes an object unnecessary.[26] The rule that the shorter reading is probably original fails in this text, because without additions the sentence is unintelligible.

Third, if indeed Paul emphasizes spiritual knowledge in the form of Christ's gospel, then one of his earlier statements truly illuminates this text. He wrote, "But thanks be to God, who in Christ always leads us in triumphal procession and through us God makes known the fragrance of the knowledge of himself everywhere" (2:14; see the commentary). Wherever Paul comes or goes, he spreads the knowledge of his Sender. This knowledge emits a sweet fragrance that becomes evident to anyone who approaches the apostle. Paul's message of spiritual truth is received by believers but is rejected by unbelievers. The gospel is relevant in all situations and germane to all things in every respect. In Christ Jesus "are hidden all the treasures of wisdom and knowledge" (Col. 2:3).

There is no need to state that the Greek text in this sentence is corrupt. Rather, here is an instance of Paul's "clipped speech" that is rather frequent in his epistles.[27] The prepositional phrases *in every respect* and *in all things* are commonplace for Paul, as is evident from their frequency. Although many translators favor the masculine ("among all men") to the neuter ("in all things"), the translation we prefer provides balance and emphasis (see Phil. 4:12).

We conclude that because of the frequent occurrence of the phrases in question, we have no reason to doubt the authenticity of the text. What we find here is a familiar example of Paul's penchant to abbreviate his sentences whenever possible.

Greek Words, Phrases, and Constructions in 11:5–6

ὑπερλίαν—a composite adverb used adjectivally, it occurs only here and in 12:11 in the New Testament and in the writings of the Greek author Eustathius.[28] It signifies that which is beyond measure.

The case of τῶν ἀποστόλων is the genitive of comparison following the verb ὑστερεῖν (to be less than), which calls for a contrast.

---

26. KJV, NKJV. This sentence has seven variants; six are attempts to improve the text. Consult Lietzmann, *Korinther,* pp. 146–47; Bultmann, *Second Letter,* p. 204.

27. Ralph P. Martin, *II Corinthians,* Word Biblical Commentary 40 (Waco: Word, 1986), p. 343. Of the fourteen times that Paul uses the phrase ἐν παντί without a noun, ten are in II Corinthians (2:14; 4:8; 6:4; 7:5, 11, 16; 8:7; 9:8, 11; 11:6, 9); two in Ephesians (5:24) and I Thessalonians (5:18); and one in I Corinthians (1:5). Similarly, he writes the phrase ἐν πᾶσιν without a noun twelve times throughout his letters. And twice he features the combination ἐν παντί and ἐν πᾶσιν, here and in Philippians 4:12. We conclude that abbreviated speech is not at all uncommon for Paul in II Corinthians.

28. Bauer, p. 841.

εἰ δέ [εἰμι]—the first person singular of the verb *to be* must be supplied. The plural form φανερώσαντες refers to Paul himself.

---

7 Or did I sin by lowering myself to exalt you because free of charge I proclaimed to you the gospel of God? 8 I robbed other churches by accepting support from them to serve you. 9 And while I was with you and needed money, I did not become a burden to anyone, for the brothers who came from Macedonia supplied me in my need. And in everything I have kept and will keep myself from being a burden to you. 10 As surely as Christ's truth is in me, this boast of mine will not be stopped in the regions of Achaia. 11 And why? Because I do not love you? God knows I do.

---

5. Free Service
11:7–11

The flow of Paul's discourse centers on the intruders, whom he has described as superapostles. These people were spreading the word that Paul's service in Corinth was worthless because he did not accept any payments from the church. By implication, the accusers were charging the church for the preaching of their gospel (compare 2:17; 11:20). They lived comfortably by following the rule that the teacher should be paid for his work. By breaking this basic rule, so they intimated, Paul demonstrated that his work was below par and his love for the church in Corinth questionable (v. 11).

7. Or did I sin by lowering myself to exalt you because free of charge I proclaimed to you the gospel of God?

a. "Or did I sin by lowering myself to exalt you?" The transition between this verse and the preceding one (v. 6) appears to be abrupt. But the introductory word *or* links the two verses. Paul had to face the discrediting attacks of his opponents, who preached another gospel, questioned his apostleship, and ridiculed his lack of eloquence (vv. 4–6). Now he encounters the veiled assertion that his gospel was not worthy of its name because he offered it free of charge.[29]

Paul wanted to offer the gospel free of charge, so that no one would be able to accuse him of any financial dependence on the church. But whether the Corinthians understood his rationale remains an open question. When the intruders came to Corinth and heard that Paul did not accept remuneration for his spiritual work, they gained an immediate following by casting doubts on his motives.

To counteract the insidious implications that his adversaries spread, Paul addresses the readers in an unusual manner. He asks them a rhetorical question that expects a negative answer: "Did I sin by lowering myself to exalt you?" Donning the clothes of a worker, he manufactured tents to support himself. Daily he taught the gospel, admonished them as their spiritual father, and demonstrated his enduring love for the Corinthians. By doing all this free of charge, did he commit a sin? To ask this question is to answer it. Paul met his expenses by working as a tentmaker in Thessalonica (I Thess. 2:9), Corinth (Acts 18:3), and Ephe-

---

29. The Sophists in the days of Socrates and Aristotle declared that teachers who taught free of charge knew their teaching to be worthless. Plummer, *Second Corinthians*, p. 302.

sus (Acts 20:34).[30] He refused to accept remuneration when he was working in a local church as a teacher of Christ's gospel (I Cor. 9:18; II Cor. 12:14). But when he was away from a certain church, he gratefully accepted support, which he considered a fragrant offering to God. We read that the Philippians, for example, repeatedly sent him monetary gifts (Phil. 4:15–18).

Certainly Paul lowered himself in the eyes of others, but he did so to elevate the Corinthians to a spiritual level they had never had or known, namely, to be members of God's family. He is not speaking ironically when he says that he lowered himself. Rather, he presents his lowliness as a virtue, for through his weakness God's power is revealed (v. 30; 12:9). The intended contrast is that the gospel is instrumental in elevating the Corinthians to a position of honor in God's presence. Paul stresses that he personally abases himself for the sake of the Corinthians, so that they might be exalted.

b. "Because free of charge I proclaimed to you the gospel of God?" In Paul's view, nothing should hinder the proclamation of Christ's gospel (I Cor. 9:12). He preaches the Good News without charge, but does not expect others to do the same (I Cor. 9:13–14, 18; see also Luke 10:7; I Tim. 5:18). Paul wanted to be free from all obligations to anyone in Corinth and proclaimed the gospel in harmony with Jesus' dictum, "Freely you have received, freely give" (Matt. 10:8). Did Paul commit a sin by working with his hands and bringing the gospel gratuitously to the Corinthians? Not at all.

Last, Paul writes the phrase *the gospel of God,* which he does at a few other places also.[31] First, the word *gospel* means both the act of preaching the gospel and the Good News itself. Next, the genitive case ("of God") is both subjective and objective: that is, the gospel belongs to God and is proclaimed for God. Third, Paul does not differentiate between the phrases *gospel of God* and *gospel of Christ.*[32] For him, they are the same. The gospel is the power of God that exalts the members of the Corinthian church.

8. I robbed other churches by accepting support from them to serve you.

This is strong language and vivid imagery! Paul uses military terms, as he does elsewhere in his epistles (e.g., I Cor. 9:7; Eph. 6:11–17; Col. 2:8; II Tim. 2:3–4). The verb *to rob* refers to a conqueror on the battlefield who strips fallen enemies of their belongings. And the Greek word *opsōnion,* which I have translated support, signifies a soldier's pay or wages (compare Luke 3:14; Rom. 6:23).[33] In the

---

30. Jewish boys learned a trade from their father: James and John, fishing; Jesus, carpentry; and Paul, tentmaking. Rabbis had to learn to work with their own hands for their support. Consult Ronald F. Hock, "The Workshop as a Social Setting for Paul's Missionary Preaching," *CBQ* 41 (1979): 438–50; "Paul's Tentmaking and the Problem of His Social Class," *JBL* 97 (1978): 555–64; *The Social Context of Paul's Ministry: Tentmaking and Apostleship* (Philadelphia: Fortress, 1980), p. 25.

31. Rom. 1:1; 15:16; I Thess. 2:2, 8, 9; 3:2; and see Mark 1:14; I Peter 4:17.

32. Consult Oswald Becker, *NIDNTT,* 2:111.

33. "'Wages' is unfit as a translation because . . . no one can pay oneself wages." Chrys C. Caragounis, "ΟΨΩΝΙΟΝ: A Reconsideration of Its Meaning," *NovT* 16 (1974): 52; see also Hans Wolfgang Heidland, *TDNT,* 5:592.

present context, the word can also mean the missionary support in the form of a stipend.

Paul's verb choice ("robbed") appears to be harsh language, yet we must understand that the churches in Macedonia were desperately poor in comparison with the bustling trading center of Corinth. Paul speaks of the extreme poverty the people in Macedonia had to endure (8:2; see the commentary). Yet these churches were known for their lavish generosity. Paul mentions only the church in Philippi, which sent him monetary gifts (Phil. 4:15), but now he uses the plural term *churches*. This term may refer to several house churches in that city. The point Paul makes, however, touches on the disparity between the poverty in Macedonia and the prosperity in Corinth. The one counts it a privilege to help (8:4), while the other needs gentle prodding to take responsibility (8:7).

Furthermore, these poverty-stricken churches in Macedonia sent financial support to Paul so that he was able to minister to the members of the church in Corinth. While Paul served the Corinthians for eighteen months, Silas and Timothy brought him a monetary gift from the Macedonian churches (Acts 18:5, 11; Phil. 4:16). As a consequence, Paul could devote himself completely to the ministry in Corinth.

9. And while I was with you and needed money, I did not become a burden to anyone, for the brothers who came from Macedonia supplied me in my need. And in everything I have kept and will keep myself from being a burden to you.

a. "And while I was with you and needed money, I did not become a burden to anyone." The apostle does not have in mind a tourist visit to the city of Corinth. He intimates that he was there for the specific purpose of founding and developing a church. His objective was to serve the people in Corinth as their spiritual father, pastor, and proclaimer of the gospel.

During his ministry there, Paul at times was in need of money, but he did not become a burden to the people in Corinth. He refused to weigh them down with any requests for his own support.[34] He asked them to contribute to the fund for the saints in Jerusalem, but he made it plain that the money was not for himself (8:20; 12:14).

Even when the apostle accepted money from the Macedonians, his principle not to accept any remuneration for his spiritual work remained intact. He was not dependent on them but received their gift to meet his temporary need. These donors provided funds for the furtherance of the gospel among people who were more prosperous than themselves. John Calvin remarks, ""How few Macedonians there are today, but how many Corinthians everywhere!"[35]

b. "For the brothers who came from Macedonia supplied me in my need." Paul reminds the Corinthians that when he was with them the Macedonian

---

34. Compare John G. Strelan, "Burden-Bearing and the Law of Christ: A Re-examination of Galatians 6:2," *JBL* 94 (1975): 266–76.

35. John Calvin, *The Second Epistle of Paul the Apostle to the Corinthians and the Epistles to Timothy, Titus and Philemon,* Calvin's Commentaries series, trans. T. A. Small (Grand Rapids: Eerdmans, 1964), p. 144.

churches sent him a donation. These people providentially supplied him exactly at the moment he was short of funds.

They came voluntarily to him with a gift to alleviate his needs. They knew that without the necessary funds, the missionary was unable to continue the task to which Jesus had called him. Again and again, these churches sent delegations to Paul with money to further his mission work (Phil. 4:16).

c. "And in everything I have kept and will keep myself from being a burden to you." Firmly convinced of the principle he has adopted, Paul stresses the verb *to keep* in both the past and future tenses. In different wording, Paul repeats in 12:13 the same thought: that he refused to be a burden to the Corinthians (compare I Thess. 2:6). The march of the gospel continues when those who have been liberated by it cheerfully contribute to its progress and see its results.

10. As surely as Christ's truth is in me, this boast of mine will not be stopped in the regions of Achaia.

The first clause carries overtones of an oath, as most commentators aver (compare Rom. 9:1). But Paul may have in mind no more than a solemn statement that he expresses in the hearing of Christ himself. He speaks on the basis that the truth of Christ is in him, as in a vessel. This truth fills him to overflowing, as Paul says elsewhere: "It is with your mouth that you confess and are saved" (Rom. 10:10).

The phrase *Christ's truth* can be interpreted in at least two ways. First, Jesus' words "I am . . . the truth" (John 14:6) reveal truth as one of his divine attributes. Next, truth originates in Jesus Christ and is disseminated through the gospel to his people.[36] Even though both interpretations are applicable, the second is preferred. Paul has been Christ's messenger to bring the Corinthians his truth. If the Corinthians believe the accusations that the false teachers level against Paul, they sever their tie with the apostle and with the truth of Christ. For this reason, Paul appeals to this truth. He realizes that the progress of the gospel is at stake.[37]

The clause *this boast of mine* must be interpreted in the context of Paul's principle to work gratuitously. Notice that he specifies his boasting with the modifiers *this* and *of mine* (or *for me*).[38] Whenever he writes of boasting, he boasts of others through Jesus Christ. He desires that the Corinthians will boast of him just as he is boasting of them (1:14). Paul indicates that he wants the Corinthians to boast of him, for they are his beloved people (v. 11). They are his letter, so to speak, that is known and read by everybody (3:2). Even though they do not support him financially, yet they continue to be a living testimony of God's grace at work in them. Hence, Paul knows that they have boasted of him, and he will continue to boast of them.

---

36. Moule (*Idiom-Book*, p. 112) notes that the clause "presumably means *I am speaking Christian truth when I say that . . .* : if so, it is a much smaller and more particularized sense of ἀλήθεια as associated with Christ."

37. Consult Grosheide, *Tweede Brief aan Korinthe*, p. 395.

38. It is possible to contend that the Greek phrase εἰς ἐμέ should be interpreted to mean "for myself alone" (Josef Zmijewski, *EDNT*, 2:277). We do well to say that the phrase refers primarily to Paul's own boasting (Furnish, *II Corinthians*, p. 493) and secondarily to the boasting of the Corinthians.

Confidently he states that no one in the areas of southern Greece, known as the Roman province of Achaia, can stop this boasting. No intruder will be able to restrain the enthusiasm that he has shown for the Corinthians (7:4, 14; 9:2). Paul employs the Greek word *phrassein* that means to silence, to muzzle, or to stop a mouth (Rom. 3:19; Heb. 11:33). Here the verb refers first to the mouth of Paul and then to that of the Corinthians.

11. And why? Because I do not love you? God knows I do.

The conclusion to this section seems out of place, for why does Paul ask two short questions followed by a solemn affirmation? To whom does the first question refer? Not to the Corinthians, for they knew that Paul loved them dearly (2:4; 12:15b). Instead, he points to the antagonists who have slandered his name and left the impression that Paul did not love the congregation of Corinth, a slander contrary to the evidence. The specific accusations have to do with money, as is often the case in human relations. The rumor was spread that Paul's refusal to request payment for work performed was an indication that he did not care for the Corinthians. This was also patently untrue. Paul loved the people from his heart and knew that the slanderous remarks were designed to break the relationship between him and the Corinthians.

To prove his point, the apostle calls God to be his witness. If anyone in Corinth accuses Paul of an indifferent attitude, this person will have to face God, who knows that Paul is fully committed to the cause of Christ.

Greek Words, Phrases, and Constructions in 11:9–10

κατενάρκησα—the compound controls the genitive case of οὐθενός (no one). The verb is derived from κατά and ναρκᾶν (to become stiff or numb), from which we have the word *narcotics*. The verb as a compound is intensive and signifies being a burden. Paul's use of this verb here and in 12:13 may reflect his geographic background, for it was current in Cilicia and perhaps was an idiom.

καύχησις—this noun conveys not the result but the process or activity of boasting.

φραγήσεται—the future passive of the verb φράσσω (I stop) here alludes either to silencing someone's boasting or to blocking it.[39]

---

12 And I will continue to do what I am doing, so that I may take away the occasion from those who desire an occasion to be found equal to us in what they boast about. 13 For such are false apostles, deceitful workers, posing as apostles of Christ. 14 And no wonder! For Satan himself masquerades as an angel of light. 15 It is no great thing when also his servants masquerade as servants of righteousness, whose destiny will be what their deeds deserve.

---

6. False Apostles
11:12–15

Many translations begin a new paragraph at this juncture, for Paul wishes to elaborate on the last words of verse 9, "I have kept and will keep myself from

---

39. Bauer, p. 865.

being a burden to you." Also, verse 12 introduces Paul's discussion on the false apostles. And last, because of its dearth of detail, this verse is subject to many interpretations.

12. And I will continue to do what I am doing, so that I may take away the occasion from those who desire an occasion to be found equal to us in what they boast about.

a. "And I will continue to do what I am doing." Once again Paul states his determination to abide by the principle of working gratuitously in promoting Christ's gospel. But the specific purpose is to defend himself against the allegations of his accusers.

We would like to have more information at this point concerning the words spoken by the intruders and the reaction of the Corinthians. We have the text but not the explanatory footnotes, so to speak. Hence, any interpretation of this verse must rely on a measure of conjecture.

b. "So that I may take away the occasion from those who desire an occasion." Here is a direct reference to Paul's opponents, whom the apostle identifies by their strategies and schemes. He is fully aware of their tactics and thus writes that he wants "to cut off the pretext of those who wish a pretext."[40] His words are severe. He wants to eliminate any justification they may find for their actions.

What were the pretexts the interlopers used in their attempt to foil the apostle? Perhaps they claimed that they also would preach the gospel without charge and thus be exactly like Paul. But this cannot be an explanation. Paul reveals that the false apostles were exploiting and taking advantage of the Corinthians (v. 20; and see I Cor. 9:12).

Next, these false teachers could boast of their apostolic status and claim to be on the same level as the rest of the apostles. Except for Paul, apostles appointed by Jesus accepted financial support from the churches they served (I Cor. 9:14). The difficulty with this interpretation is not the payment for service but the service itself. The false teachers preached a different Jesus and a different gospel, and they presented a different spirit (v. 4). They could never be on the level of apostles appointed by Jesus.[41]

c. "Those who desire an occasion to be found equal to us in what they boast about." Part of the problem in interpreting this text lies in understanding Paul's intention. Is it Paul's desire to bring his opponents to his own level? Then they must become equal to him in persecutions, sufferings, rejection, weakness, and poverty. For his rivals, such conditions were unthinkable (vv. 21–31).

Is Paul cutting off his opponents' scheme to be equal with him and boast along with him? Yes, for Paul saw through their scheme and knew that they wanted him to depart from his self-imposed principle not to accept compensation for his work. If they would succeed in this scheme, then they could boast of

---

40. Bauer, p. 127.
41. C. K. Barrett pointedly observes, "Genuine apostleship and right doctrine were inseparable." See "ΨΕΥΔΑΠΟΣΤΟΛΟΙ (II Cor. 11.13)," in *Essays on Paul* (Philadelphia: Westminster, 1982), p. 92.

equality. Their boasting is based on fraud (compare 5:12). Their aim is to bring Paul down to their level, elevate themselves, and destroy his apostleship.

Paul's principle served him effectively in his effort to curb the impostors. With it, he could prove that his love for the Corinthians was genuine. By comparison, he could legitimately call these false apostles exploiters (v. 20).

13. For such are false apostles, deceitful workers, posing as apostles of Christ.

Paul once more (v. 12) mentions his accusers. He speaks plainly and designates them as false apostles. Earlier he had resorted to irony by labeling them as superapostles (v. 5; 12:11), but here he spells out their fraudulence in severe terminology: "false apostles, deceitful workers," and impostors.

The word *such* links this verse to the preceding passage and introduces a description of those people who desired to place themselves on the same level as the apostles. However, the descriptive adjective *false* makes equality with Paul impossible for these reasons:

1. Although someone can be a witness by giving false testimony, it is not possible to be an apostle and preach a gospel that is not the gospel (Gal. 2:6–7).
2. Apostles are appointed by Jesus, recognized by the church, and committed to the truth. False apostles are never so appointed, recognized, and committed.
3. Apostles are commissioned by Jesus to serve the entire church. Neither Jesus nor the church sent false apostles; therefore, such people lack authority to serve.

Further, these pseudo-apostles were persons of Jewish extraction and not of Gentile origin (compare Gal. 2:4; Rev. 2:2). They were Judaizers who appeared in Corinth with a perverted gospel, much the same as those who came to the churches in Galatia.[42] By rejecting Christ's gospel, they proved their falsehood by their status (false apostles) and appearance (masquerade).

In unusually blunt language, Paul identifies the false apostles as deceitful workers. Except for the phrase *evil workers* (Phil. 3:2), Paul never uses such strong language as the term *deceitful* in his epistles. With that term he disqualifies the impostors and figuratively drives them out of Corinth.

These false apostles used deceit to hide their identity. They masqueraded as apostles and were accepted as such by some who were not fully acquainted with the requirements for apostleship. Paul had to reveal the identity of these impostors. They were never apostles of Christ, but people who pretended to be for Christ.

14. And no wonder! For Satan himself masquerades as an angel of light.

Paul is not at all surprised by the disguise of these pretenders. He is forthright in his analysis and sees behind them the person of Satan, who has sent them to

---

42. Refer to Barrett, "ΨΕΥΔΑΠΟΣΤΟΛΟΙ," p. 103.

Corinth. Throughout his ministry, the apostle was fully conscious of Satan's schemes and attacks, which he had to endure from time to time (see 2:11). Indeed, he mentions that the god of this age (Satan) causes unbelievers to live in darkness by blinding them (4:4).

Satan is the archenemy who is able to transform himself into an angel of light. Darkness and light have no fellowship with one another (6:14), yet Satan appears as a light-bearer. Nowhere else but here do the Scriptures give this description of Satan. We know that Satan presented himself before God in heaven (Job 1:6), but the writer does not depict him. Only in apocryphal literature are there references to Satan changing himself into an angel of light.[43] But Paul did not have to consult this literature to learn about Satan, for he experienced firsthand the schemes of the devil.[44] He had repeated encounters with Satan, who had power to afflict him physically (12:7), to obstruct his work in the church (I Thess. 2:18), and to display "all kinds of counterfeit miracles, signs and wonders" (II Thess. 2:9).

In his well-known hymn, "A Mighty Fortress Is Our God," Martin Luther aptly describes Satan:

> The prince of darkness grim
> We tremble not for him;
> His rage we can endure,
> For lo! his doom is sure,
> One little Word shall fell him.

Satan continues to frustrate God's purposes by posing even as an angel of light. He has power to perform "great and miraculous signs" and to deceive people, "even the elect—if that were possible" (Rev. 13:13–14; Matt. 24:24). Darkness is the realm of Satan, but God dwells in unapproachable light (I Tim. 6:16). Through his Word, God dispels darkness and gives light, life, and love (I John 1:5; 2:10; 3:14).

15. It is no great thing when also his servants masquerade as servants of righteousness, whose destiny will be what their deeds deserve.

If Satan is able to masquerade as an angel of light, then Satan's servants can masquerade as servants of righteousness. This is not to say that the false apostles are also able to transform themselves into angels of light. They remain human beings, but the words they speak are as deceptive as those spoken by Satan to Eve in Paradise (Gen. 3:4). These false apostles are in Satan's employ and continuously pretend to be servants of righteousness.

The wording of this verse is the strongest denunciation yet of Paul's adversaries. Paul calls them Satan's servants. We ought not to be surprised at this denun-

---

43. Life of Adam and Eve 9:1 reads, "Then Satan was angry and transformed himself into the brightness of angels." And The Apocalypse of Moses 17:1 says, "Then Satan came in the form of an angel and sang hymns to God as the angels."

44. See the commentaries of Plummer (p. 309) and Hughes (p. 394).

ciation. Jesus did exactly the same by associating the clergy of his day with Satan (John 8:44); and John says that people who continue to live in sin are children of the devil (I John 3:8–10).

Why does Paul choose the phrase *servants of righteousness* to depict Satan's assistants? Earlier in his epistle, he wrote about the ministry of righteousness (3:9) and drew a contrast between condemnation and commendation. A person who is condemned before a tribunal faces death, but the one who is declared innocent has life. A righteous person filled with the Holy Spirit is in a right relationship with God and has been reconciled to God (5:18).[45] But this is not at all true for the false apostles who are servants of Satan and practice deception. They appear as ministers of God and call themselves apostles of Christ (v. 13), but by doing so they appropriate titles that belong to the apostles. The time has come for the Corinthians to unmask these impostors and expel them from their midst.

The end of Satan's servants will match their actions. Paul is eloquent in his brevity, for the word *end* points to the final judgment. He has no need to elaborate on this concept. He already told his readers that everyone will have to appear before the judgment seat of Christ to receive his or her just recompense (5:10).[46]

After Paul's forthright denunciation of the false apostles, the end of their stay should be in sight if the Corinthians take action. The intruders' words and deeds have become a disgrace, so that the church is now compelled to banish them.

Practical Considerations in 11:12–15

On the beach at Miletus, Paul told the Ephesian elders that he had "not hesitated to proclaim to [them] the whole will of God" (Acts 20:27). Both to the Jews and the Greeks he had proclaimed God's revelation and urged them to repent and believe in Jesus Christ. The mark of an apostle is to be a witness of Jesus' resurrection, to preach the entire account of God's truth, and to speak only the words of his Sender. That is, an apostle of Jesus Christ represents his Master and advances only the Lord's teachings, never his own. This person is worthy to bear the apostolic title that Christ conferred on him. He is like an ambassador who is the mouthpiece of his government.

Similarly, if the modern preacher fails to preach the teachings of God's revelation and substitutes his own views, he does not fulfill his calling. If he tells stories and presents a social or political discourse instead of preaching the Good News, he disobeys his Sender (compare John 20:21). The preacher has been appointed to preach the Word "in season and out of season" (II Tim. 4:2) and not to omit anything.

Some scholars suggest that we add to the Bible some of the apocryphal books that circulated in the early Christian church, for example, the Gospel of Thomas.[47] But Scripture

---

45. J. D. G. Dunn, *Baptism in the Holy Spirit*, SBT, 2d series 15 (London: SCM, 1970), p. 136.

46. I Cor. 3:17; II Cor. 5:10. See also Matt. 16:27; John 5:28–29; Rom. 2:6; 3:8; Eph. 6:8; Phil. 3:19; Col. 3:24–25; II Tim. 4:14; I Peter 1:17; Rev. 2:23; 20:12–13; 22:12.

47. Consult Robert W. Funk, Roy W. Hoover, and the Jesus Seminar, *The Five Gospels: What Did Jesus Really Say?* (New York: Macmillan, 1993). For a refutation, see Michael J. Wilkins and J. P. Moreland, eds., *Jesus Under Fire: Modern Scholarship Reinvents the Historical Jesus* (Grand Rapids: Zondervan, 1995).

itself forbids adding to or deleting anything from the Bible. Near the end of the Bible we find God's copyright, a warning for anyone who dares to tamper with his Word:

I warn everyone who hears the words of the prophecy of this book: If anyone adds anything to them, God will add to him the plagues described in this book. And if anyone takes words away from this book of prophecy, God will take away from him his share in the tree of life and in the holy city, which are described in this book.
—Revelation 22:18–19

Greek Words, Phrases, and Constructions in 11:12–15

Verses 12–13

ἵνα . . . ἵνα—the second particle depends on the preceding noun ἀφορμήν (occasion) and explains the first one.

ψευδαπόστολοι—the term appears only here in all Greek literature. Perhaps the early church coined compound nouns with the prefix ψευδ-, as in the combinations *false brothers, false teachers,* and *false Christ.*[48] The expressions *false prophets* and *false witness* have origins in the Old Testament.

Verses 14–15

ἄγγελον φωτός—the noun φωτός perhaps may be understood adjectivally: "a shining angel."[49]

εἰ καί—this is not the combination *even though;* the words should be taken separately as "if" and "also."

---

16 I repeat: let no one take me for a fool. But if you must, then accept me as a fool, so that even I may boast a little. 17 What I say in this resolve [of mine] to boasting, I do not speak on the authority of the Lord but as in foolishness. 18 Because many boast in a worldly manner, I also will boast. 19 You will gladly put up with fools, since you are so wise! 20 For you put up with anyone who enslaves you, anyone who devours your goods, anyone who takes advantage of you, anyone who thinks he is better than you, or anyone who slaps you in the face. 21 To my shame, I confess that we were too weak for that.

---

7. Foolish Talk
11:16–21a

Although Paul has shrewdly exposed his adversaries in the preceding paragraph, he has not yet come to an end. He wants to play the fool for a moment to demonstrate a decisive difference between him and his opponents. Note that these interlopers are mistreating and humiliating the Corinthians. Such behavior could never be attributed to Paul but only to the real fools whose folly has become self-evident. The false apostles boast about themselves and bully the Corinthians, but Paul admits that he is too weak for such behavior.

---

48. For an overview see Barrett, "ΨΕΥΔΑΠΟΣΤΟΛΟΙ," pp. 87–107.
49. Moule, *Idiom-Book,* p. 175.

16. I repeat: let no one take me for a fool. But if you must, then accept me as a fool, so that even I may boast a little.

a. "I repeat: let no one take me for a fool." By saying, "I repeat," Paul refers to verse 1. There he wrote about foolishness, here about being a fool. There he wished that the Corinthians would put up with his foolishness, while here he asks them to accept him in his role as a fool.[50]

In the first part of the chapter, Paul shifted attention away from his supposed foolishness. Before he could elaborate on that and fulfill his purpose, he had to warn the people of the false apostles who had come to seduce them. He told them that these so-called apostles were preaching a different Jesus and gospel and presenting a different spirit. He called them servants of Satan whose end would match their deeds.

Now he is ready to return to the words and thought of verse 1. He tells his readers that no one should regard him as a fool. But who uses this epithet against him? I suggest the possibility that the broad term *someone* alludes to the Judaizers who endeavored to undermine Paul's authority (see the commentary on 10:2).[51] The wording of Paul's command is such that no one should think of him as a fool. The readers ought to understand that he is no fool in comparison with the false teachers, whose boasts are arrogant. The apostle cannot boast like these prating people, because he always rejoices in the Lord (10:17; I Cor. 1:31).

b. "But if you must, then accept me as a fool." The conditional clause is abbreviated and implies reality; that is, some people indeed did consider him a fool. And now Paul urges them to accept him as such, an interpretation made clear by another translation: "Receive me, even if it be only as a fool."[52] Paul is saying, "Whatever you think of me, please accept me." The readers should receive him as an apostle of Jesus Christ, even though he ironically allows himself to be called a fool.

c. "So that even I may boast a little." In a preceding verse (10:8), Paul had spoken about boasting somewhat excessively about the authority that the Lord had given him. But now he intimates that after the Corinthians had listened to the boasting of the false teachers, they should give Paul equal time. Then they will discern that the bragging of these people cannot be compared to Paul's commission, life, and experiences. The current paragraph is a prelude to the catalog of sufferings he endured for the sake of Jesus Christ (vv. 21a–29).

The little boasting that Paul intends to do can be interpreted as either degree or time. In view of his aversion to saying anything about his own achievements, the temporal interpretation appears to be correct. Paul wants to imitate the Lord Jesus Christ who never boasted, but for the sake of influencing the Corinthians to better insight he momentarily adopts the character of a fool.

---

50. Consult the commentaries of Lietzmann (p. 149), Plummer (p. 313), and Windisch (p. 344).

51. Consult Grosheide, *Tweede Brief aan Korinthe*, p. 404.

52. Moule, *Idiom-Book*, p. 151. See also Aída Besançon Spencer, *Paul's Literary Style: A Stylistic and Historical Comparison of II Corinthians 11:16–12–13, Romans 8:9–39, and Philippians 3:2–4:13* (Jackson, Miss.: Evangelical Theological Society, 1984), p. 188.

17. What I say in this resolve [of mine] to boasting, I do not speak on the authority of the Lord but as in foolishness.

a. *Translation*. The first clause presents a translation problem that originates in the Greek word *hypostasis*. This term appears twice in this epistle (9:4 and here) and three times in Hebrews (1:3; 3:14; 11:1). It is variously rendered as substantial nature, essence, situation, condition, reality, or confidence.[53]Many translators choose the last interpretation and speak of Paul's self-confident boasting. But another perspective gives the matter its proper focus: the present setting refers to Paul's daring or his resolve to speak as a fool.[54] In fact, Paul has been forced by the bragging of his adversaries to come to this resolve and place himself on their level.

b. *Explanation*. This paragraph (vv. 16–21) is an introduction to the next one, a list of Paul's sufferings (vv. 21b–29). The difference is that in the first section he presents form and in the following one content.

Paul invites the Corinthians to look at him as a fool and, thus, for a few moments to accept him as such. Truly, he is out of his apostolic role when he plays the fool, but he is willing to do so to get the attention of his readers. He expects that they are able to see the role he is playing and note that his acting is only for a moment. In other words, what Paul is saying ought not to be interpreted as coming from the Lord but rather out of the circumstances into which Paul has been cast.

The phrase *the authority of the Lord* has nothing to do with whether these words of Paul are or are not inspired. They certainly are, for Paul is filled with the Spirit. Elsewhere he writes, "I have no command from the Lord" (I Cor. 7:25), but this does not mean that his words lack divine authority. Momentarily he has adopted a role that is not his own, yet with it he seeks to advance the cause of Christ.

18. Because many boast in a worldly manner, I also will boast.

This verse provides the clearest explanation of why Paul engages in boasting. He desires equality with his opponents. If they are able to boast foolishly, Paul wants to have the same privilege so that the Corinthians can observe the differences between them.

The last time the apostle wrote the term *in a worldly manner,* he referred to his rivals who had accused him of conduct that typified an unbeliever (10:2, 3). In his epistles, this term often "characterizes human behavior as a purely worldly activity and perspective."[55] It connotes sin committed by unregenerate people who live apart from God (Rom. 8:4, 5, 12, 13; II Cor. 1:17; 5:16 [twice]; 10:2, 3; 11:18; Gal. 3:3).

Does the church in Corinth expect Paul to stoop to a worldly level? He informs them that he indeed is going to do this. But if they should acquiesce to

---

53. Bauer, p. 847.

54. Harm W. Hollander, *EDNT,* 3:407. Refer to Helmut Köster, *TDNT,* 8:585.

55. Alexander Sand, *EDNT,* 3:231. The Greek κατὰ σάρκα appears twenty times in Paul's correspondence; many of them refer to physical relations, descent, and standards.

Paul's intention, they would be put to shame. And this is exactly what Paul has in mind. He wants them to see the negative influence of the intruders in their midst. His desire is to have the Corinthians comprehend that they can boast only in the Lord. Paul's boasting in a worldly manner, although classified as folly, is designed to show the Corinthians the error of their way.

19. You will gladly put up with fools, since you are so wise!

Now and then Paul expresses himself in irony so pointed that no one is able to ignore it (compare I Cor. 4:8, 10), although the first part of the verse is a statement of fact. The church in Corinth welcomed anyone, especially those who were willing to preach and teach the people. The expression *gladly* is a true description of the warm welcome newcomers received in the Corinthian congregation.

The members of the church were willing to overlook the character flaws, abusive behavior, and devious doctrine of the false apostles. They voluntarily traveled the second mile to accommodate them. When Paul writes that they gladly put up with fools, it is the fourth of five times he uses the verb *to put up with* in this chapter (vv. 1 [twice], 4, 19, 20). All the uses are in the context of tolerating foolishness in their midst. The term *fools* does not allude to Paul (v. 17) but to the intruders. They are the ones who by their words and actions demonstrate their separation from the source of wisdom and knowledge, Jesus Christ (see Col. 2:3).

The last part of the text is laced with sarcasm: "since you are so wise!" With this pointed remark, Paul wants to shame the readers so that they realize they have been misled by so-called apostles. The incongruity is that human wisdom in reality is nothing but foolishness. In brief, the Corinthians have been duped.

Paul has a subtle play on words in the Greek text that cannot be matched in English. He calls fools *aphronoi* and the wise *phronimoi,* and with these words identifies two groups of people: the false teachers and the Corinthians respectively. His choice of words is deliberate, for he wants to show a close relationship between the two. Relying on their own wisdom, the people in Corinth have made fools of themselves. They begin to perceive their folly when in the next verse Paul enumerates five steps of degradation.

20. For you put up with anyone who enslaves you, anyone who devours your goods, anyone who takes advantage of you, anyone who thinks he is better than you, or anyone who slaps you in the face.

a. *Structure.* Paul lists five clauses that in the Greek are factual, conditional statements.[56] Each of them describes what the interlopers are doing to the members of the Corinthian congregation. Further, the descriptions, which range from slavery, robbery, control, and pride to physical assault, show an increase in severity:

if anyone enslaves you,
if anyone devours your goods,

---

56. Spencer (*Paul's Literary Style*, p. 161) notes that in this epistle these conditional clauses refer almost always to Paul's opponents or their attack.

if anyone takes advantage of you,
if anyone thinks he is better than you,
if anyone slaps you in the face.

The repetition of the first two words in each clause adds emphasis and solemnity. Paul's use of the singular, "anyone," includes all those who were engaged in these reprehensible practices. The converse of these statements is true of Paul.

b. *Clauses.* "[If] anyone . . . enslaves you." The verb *to enslave* in the Greek has an intensive force that suggests being in bondage. The people in Corinth were enslaved to the impostors. Although the text provides no details, we surmise that the bondage refers to doctrine, conduct, and financial support. By contrast, Paul had come to Corinth not to be served but to serve the people in obedience to his Master (Matt. 20:28). He made himself a slave to everyone for the sake of the gospel (I Cor. 9:19).

"[If] anyone . . . devours your goods." The Greek verb *katesthein* displays intensity and means to devour or consume utterly. The false teachers ate the Corinthians out of house and home,[57] so to speak. Their conduct could be compared with that of the Pharisees, who devoured widows' houses (Mark 12:40; Luke 20:47). By contrast, Paul never became a financial burden to any member of a local church (e.g., see vv. 7, 9; 12:13–14).

"[If] anyone . . . takes advantage of you." The Corinthians discovered that the intruders were controlling them and taking away their freedom. We are not told in what respect the Corinthians were losing their freedom. But the exact opposite is the teaching of Christ's gospel: "The truth will set you free" (John 8:32).

"[If] anyone . . . thinks he is better than you." Paul's adversaries had come to Corinth with letters of self-commendation. As soon as they had been accepted, they revealed their arrogance (compare I Cor. 4:18). Conversely, Paul always followed Christ's example of meekness and gentleness (10:1).

"[If] anyone . . . slaps you in the face." Whether this clause must be interpreted literally or figuratively matters not. The point is that the behavior of these rude assailants was entirely out of place in the Corinthian church. In comparison, Paul always made known his love for and gentleness to the people (I Cor. 4:21). Also, he teaches that an overseer in the church must not be violent but gentle (I Tim. 3:3).

The Corinthians have put up with false teachers who have come to ruin them. For the people it is time to admit that they have been both wrong and wronged. Why they permitted the exploitation in their midst remains a mystery. But they must take action and rid themselves of the invaders on the one hand and of shame on the other.

21a. To my shame, I confess that we were too weak for that.

The first thing that stands out in this short sentence is Paul's spiritual care for the Corinthians. He is a leader who is exceptionally sensitive to the pastoral

---

57. Barrett, *Second Corinthians*, p. 291.

needs of his people.[58] He calls attention not to their shame, which he could have done, but to his own.

What is Paul's shame? He concedes, with some irony, that he has been conducting himself as a weakling.[59] His opponents had marked him as such (10:10; I Cor. 2:3) and, compared with them, he had been weak in courage and force. The contrast between him and his foes is stark; while he has been gentle, they have been forceful. What they have been saying about him is true: he has been a weakling.[60]

With this comparison, the readers are able to see the difference between the apostle Paul and the false apostles. They will have to decide whether to continue with their spiritual mentor or with the impostors. Paul's statement is designed to expose the divergences of true and assumed apostolicity. The point is that the people in Corinth must fully understand the grievous error of their disloyalty to Paul.

Practical Considerations in 11:20

Jesus says that in the last days false Christs and false prophets will appear. Someone will say, "'Look, here is the Christ!' or 'There he is!'" But the Lord tells us not to believe those voices (Matt. 24:23–24).

In the middle of the first century, false teachers had already entered the church to lead the Christians astray. In their respective letters, Peter and Jude write that false prophets had slipped into the church to introduce destructive heresies (II Peter 2:1–3; Jude 4). And toward the end of that century, John says that these people were antichrists who left the church because they did not belong there (I John 2:19).

Today the Christian community faces similar problems. Religious charlatans are able to gain a following of gullible men and women. These charlatans enslave people with their teaching and steal from them to live luxuriously. It is sad indeed that some Christians quickly turn away from the doctrines of the Scriptures to follow someone whose words and deeds are in conflict with those teachings. These followers are being enslaved, robbed, and cheated. Their stance has blinded them to reality and the truth. They ardently defend their acknowledged leader whom they consider their messiah. And they will continue to do so unless the law of the land intervenes, death terminates their perilous plight, or the error of their way becomes obvious to them and they repent.

Greek Words, Phrases, and Constructions in 11:16–21a

Verses 16–17

κἄν—the contraction of καὶ ἐάν introduces the protasis of a conditional sentence that expresses probability. The apodosis consists of an aorist imperative δέξασθέ με (accept me).

---

58. Refer to D. A. Carson, *From Triumphalism to Maturity* (Grand Rapids: Baker, 1984), p. 112.

59. Bauer, p. 589. See the commentaries of Furnish (pp. 497–98) and Hughes (p. 401 n. 68).

60. Martin (*II Corinthians*, p. 366) paraphrases the verse: "What a pity we are not like that—you seem to prefer bullies." But Paul concedes his weakness in a pastoral, not in a forceful, manner.

ὑποστάσει—preceded by a demonstrative pronoun and definite article (ταύτῃ τῇ), the noun requires the qualification *my resolve*.

Verse 20

The verbs in the five successive clauses are unique: two are compounds and have an intensive meaning (καταδουλοῖ = he enslaves; κατεσθίει= he devours), one is idiomatic (λαμβάνει = he does him in), one is middle (ἐπαίρεται = he puts on airs), and the last one (δέρει = he hits) can be interpreted literally or figuratively.

These clauses are introduced by the recurring phrase εἴ τις, which indicates conditionality of fact.

Verse 21a

κατὰ ἀτιμίαν—this phrase, "with respect to shame," can apply to the intruders, the Corinthians, or Paul. The last choice is preferred because of the context: the first person singular of the verb λέγω.

ὡς ὅτι—these words are translated either "as though" or "that." Translators prefer the latter.

The first person plural pronoun ἡμεῖς is used in an emphatic contrast to Paul's opponents. Also, notice the perfect tense of ἠσθενήκαμεν (we have been weak) that indicates action in the past with lasting significance for the present.

But in whatever matter anyone dares [to boast]—I am speaking foolishly—I also dare [to boast]. 22 Are they Hebrews? So am I. Are they Israelites? So am I. Are they Abraham's descendants? So am I. 23 Are they servants of Christ? (I talk like someone who is irrational.) I can surpass them: In toils much more diligently, in prisons more frequently, in beatings more severely, often facing death. 24 Five times I received from the Jews the forty lashes minus one. 25 Three times I was beaten with rods, once I was stoned, three times I suffered shipwreck, I spent a night and a day adrift at sea. 26 I have been on many journeys, in danger from rivers, in danger from robbers, in danger from my own countrymen, in danger from Gentiles, in danger in the city, in danger in the country, in danger at sea, in danger from false brothers, 27 in toil and hardship, often without sleep, in hunger and thirst, often without food, in cold and nakedness.

28 Besides these external things, there is the daily pressure on me: my concern for all the churches. 29 Who is weak, and I am not weak? Who is caused to stumble into sin, and I am not burning?

---

8. List of Sufferings
11:21b–29

After a prelude (vv. 16–21a), Paul is ready to present a résumé of experiences that he extols against his will. In fact, he has made a fool out of himself by boasting, because boasting about oneself is a violation of the biblical principle to boast only in the Lord. Even though he is speaking foolishly, his intent is to picture the painful consequences of being an apostle of Christ. And with respect to this résumé, none of his adversaries is able to match the list.

a. *Division.* Paul writes a section that can be called "the discourse of a fool." It is a catalog of his status and work for the Lord. The section 11:21b–12:10 can be divided into three parts, all of which are introduced with the concept *boast*. They are verse 21b, "I also dare to boast"; verse 30, "If I must continue to boast"; and

383

12:1, "I must continue to boast." Paul concludes his discourse by saying, "I have been a fool, but you forced me to it" (12:11).

b. *Pattern.* The catalog of circumstances, experiences, and sufferings that Paul now records he presents in segments consisting of short sentences. There are five sets of statements, of which one highlights a parenthetical remark, two a concluding remark, and one an introduction. These five sets are followed by statements on Paul's concern for the churches, personal weakness, and sin.[61]

The first set of statements has four questions with short answers and a parenthetical aside; they describe physical descent and spiritual commission. The next one features three statements on suffering, listed in an increasing order of severity, and followed by a conclusion. The third set continues with a series of four statements on suffering, succeeded by a concluding remark. The fourth is a sequence of eight descriptions of danger introduced by a comment on travel. The last set has five lines, of which three highlight double experiences and two single ordeals.

c. *Repetition.* There is some similarity and overlap with a previous list of hardships (see 6:4–10). Indeed, some of the same experiences are featured twice (e.g., beatings, imprisonment, hard work, sleeplessness, hunger [6:5]).

> *vv. 22–23a*
> Are they Hebrews? So am I.
> Are they Israelites? So am I.
> Are they Abraham's descendants? So am I.
> Are they servants of Christ?
> (I talk like someone who is irrational.)
>   I can surpass them.

> *v. 23b*
> In toils much more diligently,
> in prisons more frequently,
> in beatings more severely,
>   often facing death.

> *vv. 24–25*
> Five times I received from the Jews
>   the forty lashes minus one.
> Three times I was beaten with rods,
>   once I was stoned,
> three times I suffered shipwreck,
>   I spent a night and a day adrift at sea.

> *v. 26*
> I have been on many journeys,
> in danger from rivers,

---

61. Michael L. Barré has developed a chiastic arrangement of verses 21b–29 in which he exhibits the many similarities. See "Paul as 'Eschatological Person': A New Look at II Cor 11:29," *CBQ* 37 (1975): 500–526.

in danger from robbers,
in danger from my own countrymen,
in danger from Gentiles,
in danger in the city,
in danger in the country,
in danger at sea,
in danger from false brothers.

v. 27
In toil and hardship,
often without sleep,
in hunger and thirst,
often without food,
in cold and nakedness.

vv. 28–29
Besides these external things, there is the
daily pressure on me:
    my concern for all the churches.
    Who is weak, and I am not weak?
    Who is caused to stumble into sin,
    and I am not burning with anger?

**21b. But in whatever matter anyone dares [to boast]—I am speaking fool-
ishly—I also dare [to boast].**

First, Paul turns his attention from the Corinthians to his opponents. By writing the word *anyone,* he has in mind his adversaries, whom he had singled out
earlier with this term (see 10:7, 11; 11:16, 20). They are the Judaizers who have
commended themselves, boasted of their self-confidence, labeled Paul a fool,
and mistreated the people in Corinth.

Next, the main verb *to dare* needs a complementary infinitive in English (but
not in Greek). The general context forces the translator to supply the verb *to
boast,* which I have placed in brackets. Paul dares to meet his enemies on their
level and boast accordingly (see 10:12 for the use of "dare" and 10:13–17 for
"boast").

Third, when Paul, speaking foolishly, presents factual information (vv. 22–
29), he towers above the false apostles. And by placing these people under him,
he implies that he remains the spiritual father of the Corinthians (I Cor. 4:15).

**22. Are they Hebrews? So am I. Are they Israelites? So am I. Are they Abra-
ham's descendants? So am I. 23a. Are they servants of Christ? (I talk like someone who is irrational.) I can surpass them.**

a. "Are they Hebrews? So am I." Abram is called "the Hebrew," a well-known
appellation first recorded in Genesis 14:13. The Egyptians referred to the offspring of Jacob as Hebrews.[62] In later times, the term *Hebrews* was "deliberately

---

62. Gen. 39:14, 17; 40:15 [land of the Hebrews]; 41:12; 43:32; Exod. 1:15, 16; 2:6, 7, 13.

used as an honored name from the past" to replace the unacceptable word *Jew*.[63]

Paul called himself a Hebrew of Hebrews (Phil. 3:5) and implied that both his father and his mother shared that descent. His native tongue was Aramaic, for in Jerusalem he addressed the Jewish people in that language (Acts 21:40). Even Jesus spoke to Paul in Aramaic (Acts 26:14). And in the early Christian church, Aramaic-speaking widows were distinguished from those who spoke Greek (Acts 6:1). On the basis of Scripture passages, we conclude that the term *Hebrew* relates to many areas: history, culture, nation, and language.[64]

The opponents of Paul could claim to be Hebrews in every sense of the word. The question remains whether they came directly from Jerusalem or from somewhere in the dispersion (e.g., Paul hailed from Tarsus), although they seem to have come from the land of Israel itself. These people could boast about their unblemished descent, but so could Paul. He was born of Hebrew parents in dispersion, but in his early youth he came to Jerusalem, where he received his education.[65]

b. "Are they Israelites? So am I." The next question mentions the word *Israelite*, which means a descendant of Jacob. This patriarch wrestled with the angel, overpowered him, and received the name *Israel* (the one who wrestled with God; see Gen. 32:28). His offspring, including the Samaritans, called him their father (see John 4:12). Yet not the Samaritans but the Jews were called Israelites. And Jesus instructed his disciples not to enter a town of the Samaritans, but to go to the lost sheep of Israel (Matt. 10:5–6).

The expression *Israel* relates first to God's covenant people, who throughout the Old Testament are known as the children of Israel. Next, it refers to the land that God had promised to the patriarchs and their descendants. But the people of Israel were not bound to the land, for since the exile they have been scattered throughout the nations.[66]

Paul says that the people of Israel are recipients of the divine glory, the covenants, the law, the temple worship, and the promises (Rom. 9:4). Although they have this status, Paul adds that "not all who are descended from Israel are Israel" (Rom. 9:6). Only the faithful are considered to be sons and daughters of Israel; they are the true Israelites who will be saved (Rom. 11:1, 5, 7, 26). The adversaries gloried in the name *Israelite*, but so did Paul in a spiritual sense.

---

63. Joachim Wanke, *EDNT*, 1:369. See also Georgi, *Opponents of Paul*, p. 42; Karl Georg Kuhn, *TDNT*, 3:367–668. An inscription in the lintel from a synagogue in Corinth has the name *Hebrews*. Could this be why the expression *Jews* occurs only once in II Corinthians? Also, a letter in the epistolary of the New Testament is called the Epistle to the Hebrews instead of the Epistle to the Jews.

64. Consult Walter Gutbrod, *TDNT*, 3:388–91; compare also SB 3:526.

65. W. C. van Unnik, *Tarsus or Jerusalem: The City of Paul's Youth*, trans. George Ogg (London: Epworth, 1962), p. 44.

66. Barrett (*Second Corinthians*, p. 293) distinguishes the terms *Hebrew* and *Israelite* by making the observation that "*Hebrew* deals with it from the racial, *Israelite* from the social and religious angle." But if Paul is enumerating designations flaunted by the false apostles, we do well to refrain from developing conceptual contrasts.

c. "Are they Abraham's descendants? So am I." The third identification is even broader than the two preceding ones, Hebrews and Israelites. Among the descendants are Isaac, Ishmael, and the sons of Keturah (see Gen. 25:1–6, 12–18).

The literal expression *seed of Abraham* is common in Paul's epistles. In addition to this verse, it appears in Romans 4:13, 16, 18; 9:7; 11:1; and Galatians 3:29. Although Paul's foes used this term (compare John 8:33–39), the apostle relates the expression to Christ and all the believers in the New Testament community.[67] Paul, too, could claim to be a descendant of Abraham, but in a deeper sense than the intruders avowed.

d. "Are they servants of Christ?" This question is not on the same level as the three that precede it. Those pertained to birth and descent, this one to a divine calling. Paul does not scold the false teachers for using the title *Christ's servants*. He compares their claim to his own experiences as an apostle whom Jesus called as his chosen instrument to suffer much for his name (Acts 9:15–16).

Throughout this letter, Paul uses the word *servant* four times: "servants of a new covenant" (3:6), "servants of God" (6:4), "servants of righteousness" (11:15), and "servants of Christ" (11:23). The first two references apply to himself, but the context of the last two demands that we apply it to the false apostles.[68] The flow of the present passage prohibits an interpreter from relating the phrase to the twelve apostles in Jerusalem. Although the meaning of "servant" is equivalent to "apostle," the implication is that the interlopers had presented themselves as apostles to the people in Corinth. This is evident from Paul's earlier comments (vv. 13–15). We understand, therefore, that the expression *servants of Christ* is a self-designation of the opponents, which Paul now quotes for the sake of comparison.[69]

e. "(I talk like someone who is irrational.) I can surpass them." Paul's choice of words is striking, for he writes a word that occurs only once in the New Testament. It is stronger than his remark about speaking "in foolishness" (vv. 17, 21b). This is no longer a matter of uttering foolishness but of deliberately going counter to one's better judgment.[70]

The apostle interrupts himself with the comment that he talks irrationally. That is, Paul knows better and yet he is going to boast about his own accomplishments. Instead of saying "So am I," he says that he "can surpass" all the false apostles (compare Phil. 3:4).[71] Now he has to prove his point and enumerate his feats performed in service to Christ. But as his servant he must render all the praise and honor to his Sender and should never boast about himself. Paul intention-

---

67. Siegfried Schulz, *TDNT,* 7:545; Ulrich Kellermann, *EDNT,* 3:264.

68. Bultmann (*Second Letter,* p. 215) states that the servants of Christ are "the apostles. . . . Their right to [title and claim] is left undecided."

69. Windisch, *Der Zweite Korintherbrief,* p. 352; refer also to Georgi, *Opponents of Paul,* pp. 32–39, and John N. Collins, "Georgi's 'Envoys' in II Cor 11:23," *JBL* 93 (1974): 88–96.

70. Refer to Grosheide, *Tweede Brief aan Korinthe,* p. 412.

71. Martin (*II Corinthians,* p. 375) notes that Paul's use of the word ὑπέρ is "a snide glance at the ὑπερλίαν ἀπόσοτολοι (11:5)."

ally goes against his own principle. He does so to prove that the apostolic office is the highest rank in the churches and that only those who have been appointed by Christ are true apostles.

23b. In toils much more diligently, in prisons more frequently, in beatings more severely, often facing death.

a. "In toils much more diligently." This verse begins the second set of clauses that describe Paul's predicaments. The first clause and those that follow must be interpreted in the light of the preceding remark, "As an apostle of Christ I surpass all the false apostles." Paul has been more diligent than anyone else, so that he could well express himself with a superlative: "I am most industrious."

In his address to the Ephesian elders at Miletus, Paul declares that he had taught them publicly and from house to house. He preached to both Jews and Greeks and called them to repentance and faith in Jesus (Acts 20:20–21). Also, he began teaching students in the local synagogue at Ephesus. After his expulsion from that building, he daily lectured in the hall of Tyrannus (Acts 19:8–9). Then, night and day he constantly remembered in prayer the needs of the churches that he had founded (v. 28; Phil. 1:3–4; Col. 1:3; I Thess. 1:2–3; II Tim. 1:3). And, he wrote a number of letters to these churches and to individuals. In spiritual matters, Paul labored harder than anyone else (I Cor. 15:10). This tentmaker and leatherworker even worked diligently with his own hands to meet his personal needs and those of his companions (Acts 20:34; II Thess. 3:8). In short, Paul toiled physically and spiritually from early morning until late at night.

b. "In prisons more frequently." In the Greek, the adverb *perissoterōs* (much more) is comparative but here borders on the superlative. It occurs in the first three phrases of this verse and must be translated in harmony with the nouns that precede it. The first clause is superlative, while the second one is comparative. Luke relates only one imprisonment of Paul at this stage of his ministry, namely, the jailing of Paul and Silas at Philippi (Acts 16:23–30).

We have no further information concerning Paul's experiences, for in Acts Luke does not present biographies but a history of the church. We surmise that in the so-called silent years after his conversion and during his three missionary journeys, Paul had frequently been imprisoned. Clement of Rome mentions that the apostle had been handcuffed seven times.[72] Additional incarcerations recorded by Luke occurred after this letter was composed.

c. "In beatings more severely." Again, we lack information about how severe and how frequent these trouncings were (6:5). They may include the blows he received from hostile Jews and Gentiles. However, we are able to point to the increasing severity, which each phrase in this text reveals: toils, incarcerations, beatings.

---

72. I Clem. 5.6. After Paul composed this letter, he was imprisoned four times (in Jerusalem, in Caesarea, and twice in Rome). If we add to these four his jailing in Philippi, the phrase *more frequently* seems to be an understatement, as does Clement's total of seven.

d. "Often facing death." In Lystra Paul faced death when the Jews from Pisidian Antioch and Iconium stoned him (Acts 14:19). The frequent lashings in Jewish synagogues and beatings in Roman custody brought Paul near the edge (see the commentary on 1:8–10). Illnesses could affect Paul's health to a perilous degree. Other life-threatening events, such as a storm at sea, might be factors to consider. Proceeding from the second segment in the series to the third, the apostle lists a number of mortal perils in the next few verses.

24. Five times I received from the Jews the forty lashes minus one. 25. Three times I was beaten with rods, once I was stoned, three times I suffered shipwreck, I spent a night and a day adrift at sea.

The total number of beatings Paul received was eight: five from the Jews and three from the Romans. He also lived to tell of the experience of being stoned by the Jews. During Paul's so-called silent years and those of his three missionary journeys, he possessed phenomenal physical stamina. His endurance can only be attributed to God's grace.

a. "Five times I received from the Jews the forty lashes minus one." The scourgings that Paul endured in local synagogues were administered according to the law of Moses (Deut. 25:2–3). They resulted from his preaching the gospel of Christ to Jewish people who turned against him (Acts 13:45). The Jews accused Paul of not observing the law and of teaching Jews in the dispersion to set aside the Mosaic law. For instance, they said that Paul told these Jews not to circumcise their sons and not to observe their customs (see Acts 21:21). Paul made table fellowship with Gentiles a matter of principle and told fellow Jews to do likewise (Gal. 2:11–14). Thus, he broke ranks with those Jews who observed strict dietary rules and who consequently reported his conduct to synagogue officials, who ordered him to be flogged.

That no mistake in counting should be made, the thirty-nine lashes were counted out aloud. The number thirty-nine was determined by a division into three parts: thirteen lashes were laid upon the chest and twenty-six on the back of the guilty person.[73] In the presence of a judge, the prone victim was beaten with a whip made of calfskin. Jesus told his disciples to watch out for men who would deliver them to local councils to be flogged in synagogues (Matt. 10:17; Mark 13:9). And before his conversion Paul himself beat men and women who believed in Jesus (Acts 22:4, 19; 26:11).

b. "Three times I was beaten with rods." We know only of the beating Paul and Silas received in Philippi (Acts 16:22–23). Roman citizens were generally protected by law from being scourged (Acts 22:24–29); Cicero writes, "To bind a Roman citizen is a crime, to flog him is an abomination, to slay him is almost an act of murder; to crucify him is—what? There is no fitting word that can possibly describe so horrible a deed."[74] Paul could have relinquished the right to protec-

---

73. SB 3:527. See also Talmud *Makkoth* 3.1–9; consult Sven Gallas, "'Fünfmal vierzigweniger einen . . .' Die an Paulus vollzogenen Synagogalstrafen nach 2Kor 11,24," *ZNTW* 81 (1990): 178–91.

74. Cicero *Against Verres* 2.5.66 (LCL).

tion because of his Roman citizenship. Although he probably sought to advance the cause of the fledgling church in Philippi, his remark that he had been insulted there refers to serious injustice and injury (I Thess. 2:2). He would not have waived his right to protection three times. We know from other sources that the Porcian law to safeguard Roman citizens from corporal punishment was not always observed.[75] Hence, we conclude that in spite of Paul's citizenship he was beaten three times.

c. "Once I was stoned." The Mosaic law prescribed stoning to punish someone who had blasphemed, served other gods, or committed adultery (e.g., Lev. 24:14, 16, 23; Deut. 17:5; 22:24; John 8:2–11). The law stipulated due process by having two or three witnesses, who then were asked to throw the first stones (Deut. 17:6–7). However, due process was not followed when God's servants were stoned: Zechariah (II Chron. 24:21), Stephen (Acts 7:58–60), and Paul (Acts 14:19). Stephen was killed on the charge of blasphemy, but his trial was a mob action rather than a legal procedure. Except in the case of Paul, stoning was fatal.

d. "Three times I suffered shipwreck." The only instance of a shipwreck Luke has recorded is the one at Malta (Acts 27:39–44). But that occurred after Paul wrote this verse. Throughout his ministry, the apostle traveled frequently and extensively by ship.[76] Thus, he "was no stranger to the sea and its perils."[77] During some of these numerous voyages, he could have experienced shipwreck. Survival was deemed miraculous, because if shipwrecked sailors and passengers made it to shore, they were often killed or taken captive by the local population.

e. "I spent a night and a day adrift at sea." The Jews divided a twenty-four-hour period into night and day (see Acts 20:31). At six in the evening, the new day began and lasted until the next evening at six. This verse probably refers to one of Paul's previous experiences, rather than an additional occurrence. Clinging to debris, constantly being doused by high waves on the open sea, and being deprived of food and fresh water would test anyone's mettle. Paul's memory of that experience was indelible.[78] In fact, he writes the Greek perfect tense that describes this harrowing ordeal.

26. I have been on many journeys, in danger from rivers, in danger from robbers, in danger from my own countrymen, in danger from Gentiles, in danger in the city, in danger in the country, in danger at sea, in danger from false brothers.

This is the fourth set of short phrases, introduced by a statement on travel that is followed by eight sources of danger. Paul moves from the perils of the sea to those on the land.

---

75. Livy 10.9.4–5; Josephus *War* 2.14.9.

76. Acts 9:30; 13:4, 13; 14:26; 16:11–12; 17:14; 18:18, 21; 20:3–6, 13–14; 21:1–6; 27:1–6; 28:11–13.

77. Hughes, *Second Epistle to the Corinthians,* p. 411. Robert E. Osborne ("St. Paul's Silent Years," *JBL* 84 [1965]: 59–65) concludes that the place of the three shipwrecks remains unresolved.

78. Josephus (*Life* 3 [13–15]) relates that he suffered shipwreck on a voyage to Rome when there were six hundred persons aboard, and people had to swim all night until he and many others were rescued.

a. "I have been on many journeys." Apart from the many voyages Paul took, the distances he traveled on foot were often extraordinarily long. If a day's journey is twenty miles (thirty-two kilometers) a day (depending on road conditions and weather), then we begin to understand the extent and duration of some of Paul's travels. For example, Paul walked from Jerusalem to Ephesus (Acts 18:18–23; 19:1), which is a distance of about a thousand miles (sixteen hundred kilometers).[79] With customary stops for Sabbath rest and visits to churches along the way, Paul would have needed at least three months to complete the journey. He traveled from Philippi to Jerusalem both on foot and by ship within a seven-week period, from Easter to Pentecost, according to Luke's day-to-day travelogue in the Book of Acts.[80]

Paul spent the night in inns or homes of Christian friends, or pitched his tent in open fields. Road markers and maps assisted him in choosing the routes he had to take. However, the dangers that he faced were real and could be from both natural causes and people he encountered en route.[81]

b. "In danger from rivers, in danger from robbers." On his travels, Paul had to cross rivers which, in the spring of the year, overflowed their banks. The dangers of these swollen streams were not to be taken lightly. Moreover, even though the Romans kept their main roads safe, robbers could easily attack travelers and relieve them of their possessions. Bandits had their hideouts at the Cilician Gates, a mountain pass to the north of Tarsus, that provided access from the southern coast to the plateau of central Asia Minor.

c. "In danger from my own countrymen, in danger from Gentiles." These two clauses show contrast, as do the next three. Windisch suggests that because of an oversight in copying, the words "in danger from false brothers" have been misplaced at the end of the verse. He wants to put them here to form a sequence of three classes of people: countrymen, Gentiles, and false brothers. But supportive textual evidence is lacking and, therefore, his rearrangement is unacceptable.[82] Paul may not have thought of balancing every clause in this verse, as is clear from the preceding line: rivers and robbers have nothing in common.

Acts describes many incidents in which Paul was confronted by angry Jews and hostile Gentiles. Because of these people, he endured lashings and beatings. From them he tried to escape and frustrate their plots (e.g., see vv. 32–33; Acts 14:6; 17:10, 13–14; 20:3, 19).

d. "In danger in the city, in danger in the country, in danger at sea." These three phrases cover "the whole surface of the earth."[83] In the numerous cities Paul visited, he faced the dangers of being humiliated, dragged into court,

---

79. Consult Jerome Murphy-O'Connor, "On the Road and on the Sea with St. Paul," *Bible Review* 1 (1985): 40–41.

80. Acts 20:6, 13–16; 21:1–3, 4, 7–8, 10, 15, 17. See Simon J. Kistemaker, *Exposition of the Acts of the Apostles,* New Testament Commentary series (Grand Rapids: Baker, 1990), p. 749.

81. Refer to E. F. F. Bishop, "'Constantly on the Road,'" *EvQ* 41 (1969): 14–18.

82. Contra Windisch (p. 358).

83. Plummer, *Second Corinthians,* pp. 326–27.

beaten, and imprisoned. We have no information about the dangers he experienced in the country. He had already noted three shipwrecks and the time spent on the open sea.

e. "In danger from false brothers." The last entry is of special concern to the Corinthians, for they themselves know the devastation that the people posing as brothers have caused. Here Paul's work is at stake, which differs from attacks on his life or possessions. It is no wonder that Paul climaxes the list of eight dangers with that of the false brothers.[84]

The Greek word *pseudadelphoi* (false brothers) occurs only twice in the New Testament (here and in Gal. 2:4). The false brothers are Jewish Christians who have come to the churches Paul has founded and have proclaimed a different gospel, which is not the gospel of Jesus Christ (v. 4; Gal. 1:6–7). They exploited the Corinthians and even slapped them in the face (v. 20). If the people in Corinth were in physical danger from these intruders, did Paul also suffer bodily violence at their hands? We cannot be sure, but he clearly regarded them as dangerous. Even in the church he had founded and where he expected to find security, danger lurked.

27. In toil and hardship, often without sleep, in hunger and thirst, often without food, in cold and nakedness.

In five short clauses Paul depicts his physical condition, which, in contrast to that of the false apostles, is discomfort and poverty. However, he is enumerating facts without a trace of complaint, for he is the one who wrote:

> I know what it is to be in need, and
> I know what it is to have plenty.
> I have learned the secret of being content
> in any and every situation,
> whether well fed or hungry,
> whether living in plenty or in want.
> —Philippians 4:12

This is the fifth set of statements in Paul's catalog of incidents and sufferings. He composed five clauses, of which three highlight double experiences and two list a single affliction; the second line harmonizes with the first and the fourth with the third.[85] And the last line forms a concluding statement that features his physical appearance.

a. "In toil and hardship, often without sleep." Apparently Paul is using an idiom, because the combination *toil and hardship* occurs elsewhere (I Thess. 2:9; II Thess. 3:8). Earlier he noted that he worked much harder than any other apostle (v. 23). Now he adds that he often lacked sleep, the restorative power that energizes the body. Sleep deprivation can occur because of nocturnal la-

---

84. Consult Barrett, *Essays on Paul,* p. 88; Lietzmann, *Korinther,* p. 151.

85. One translation (NJB) fills out the fourth line by adding the word *drink:* "And often without food or drink." No textual support exists for this addition; also it breaks the harmony of the lines.

bors, worry, or vigils.[86] Not only the context but also other texts in this epistle suggest that Paul's anxiety for the churches kept him awake at night (v. 28; 2:13; 7:5).The church at Corinth remained a constant worry for him.

b. "In hunger and thirst, often without food." This is not the first time that Paul informs the Corinthians about going hungry and thirsty (I Cor. 4:11; II Cor. 6:5). He endures these deprivations for the sake of Christ, not in the sense of voluntary fasting but because of poverty. Yet he knows that he does not have to worry, because God will meet all his needs (Matt. 6:31; Phil. 4:19).

c. "In cold and nakedness." Near the end of Paul's life, he instructs Timothy to fetch the cloak that he had left behind at the home of Carpus in Troas (II Tim. 4:13). His cloak served to ward off the cold at night and to keep him warm in winter or in mountainous areas. Paul writes that he walks around in rags (I Cor. 4:11; see also Rom. 8:35) that subjected him to exposure. Nakedness should be understood as insufficient clothing that caused him to suffer from the cold. Notice that he ends the list with a reference to his physical condition and outward appearance. The comparison between him and the false apostles who lived in ease and luxury is telling.

Practical Considerations in 11:23–27

Today's travelers usually can count on comfort, speed, and security. Travel by air or road occurs with relative ease, and great distances are covered in a brief time. Competition in the travel industry improves conveniences and makes passengers content. They in turn will recommend the services received.

The differences between our travels and those of Paul are incomparable. We travel throughout the world in comparative safety, while the apostle had to endure untold hardship and face countless dangers. Traveling in a northwesterly direction, Paul always went not by sea but on land because of the adverse westerly winds. He sailed west only once, as prisoner from Caesarea to Rome. But traveling from Greece to Palestine, Paul took a ship to save considerable time and energy.

If there was one person who could have uttered a word of complaint about his travel experiences, it would have been Paul. But in all his letters and in Luke's account in Acts, he never expressed one dissonant comment about his life. Paul spent his life in the service of his Sender in total obedience and utter confidence that God would protect him from harm and supply him in all his needs. His catalog of hardships is one of the most moving paragraphs in all his epistles. After reading and rereading it, we are emotionally struck and kept from uttering even a single syllable of complaint about our own service to the Lord.

---

28. Besides these external things, there is the daily pressure on me: my concern for all the churches.

This verse and the next form the conclusion to the list of Paul's experiences and hardships. He is no longer discussing the trials that affected him physically;

---

86. Martin, *II Corinthians*, p. 380. E. F. F. Bishop, "The 'Why' of Sleepless Nights," *EvQ* 37 (1965): 29–31, thinks that Paul spent his nightly hours talking about the Messiah. Carson (*From Triumphalism to Maturity*, p. 122) attributes lack of sleep to "too many responsibilities."

he now mentions the responsibility of caring for all the churches. As an apostle, he was not in charge of one particular congregation but had the oversight over the entire church of Jesus Christ.

Paul has completed his catalog of sufferings, which in itself is a record of human endurance. Now he wants to tell the Corinthians that he carries a burden for them and the sister churches. And this burden is more important to him than all the hardships he has had to bear.

a. *Translation.* The first clause in this verse can mean either "besides everything else" (the things that have been left out) or "besides these external things." The Greek adverb *parektos* places before the translator the choice of "other things" (NKJV) or "external things" (NEB, NJB, NAB).[87] There are sound arguments for either position, but Paul makes a distinction between the condition of his body and the pressure on his mind. The preceding verse (v. 27) describes his physical condition. This passage reveals Paul's mental burden. On the basis of context, I favor the translation *external things.*

b. *Care.* The daily care for the churches weighed heavily on Paul's mind. Christians would come to him from numerous places to seek his counsel. (When Paul was imprisoned both in Caesarea and in Rome, he counseled Christians who sought his advice on matters related to doctrine and practice.) In Rome, he welcomed all who came to see him (Acts 28:30). We can well imagine the demands on his time and energy, especially when his visitors brought to his attention problem cases that needed to be resolved. Paul's involvement increased proportionately with the development of the church. His apostolic office gave him the responsibility over all the churches, as is evident from his correspondence (I Cor. 4:17; 7:17; 14:33; II Cor. 8:18). He was a father to all his spiritual children.

No one of the false apostles could claim to care for all the churches. No one could claim to care for them with prayers, letters, visits, and words of encouragement. No one could claim to love the Corinthians from the depth of his heart (2:4; 11:11; 12:15). Paul writes that he daily carried the burden of caring for all the churches. Not the intruders but Paul proved to be the caring apostle.

29. Who is weak, and I am not weak? Who is caused to stumble into sin, and I am not burning?

Just before Paul begins his discussion on his accomplishments, he writes the word *weak:* "We were too weak for that" (v. 21a). In the concluding verse of his discussion he asks, "Who is weak?" He speaks not to or about his adversaries; rather he pastorally addresses the Corinthians.[88]

a. "Who is weak, and I am not weak?" We can understand that the members of the Corinthian church looked up to Paul because of his apostolic status. But

---

87. Moffatt's translation places the first clause of verse 28 as the last clause in verse 27.

88. Contra Barré, "Paul as Eschatological Person." By rephrasing verses 21b–23a, he sees a parallel in verse 29 and applies both passages to Paul's opponents; he has to place verse 28 in parentheses to make the paragraph fit. But verses 28 and 29 form a unit that expresses Paul's pastoral concern for the church.

Paul places himself at their level and informs them that if there are any who are weak, he shares their frailty. If he were referring to physical weakness he would be uttering a falsehood, especially in view of the sufferings he endured. Instead, he has in mind spiritual weakness. The people regard him as a hero of faith who could well occupy an honorable place in the gallery of Hebrews 11. As their pastor, Paul reveals to them that he struggles with the same weaknesses they encounter. The author of the Epistle to the Hebrews describes the task of the high priest and says, "He is able to deal gently with those who are ignorant and are going astray, since he himself is subject to weakness" (5:2). A pastor may never despise the spiritual weaknesses of his people. Instead he must be filled with compassion and accommodate himself to their needs.[89] As the Suffering Servant "took up our infirmities and carried our sorrows" (Isa. 53:4; Matt. 8:17), so Paul serves the church of Jesus Christ.

b. "Who is caused to stumble into sin, and I am not burning?" The second question is also pastorally oriented. Paul uses the same Greek expression (*skandalizein*, to cause to stumble) that he used in his discussion of causing a weaker brother to fall into sin (I Cor. 8:11–13).[90] Paul does not specify the agent who causes one of the weaker members to fall into sin. The emphasis is on his pastoral task of standing next to someone who has been trapped in sin and of supplying help and spiritual encouragement.

The last clause has various translations, for burning can allude to agony (NJB), concern (NASB), distress (*Cassirer*), and indignation (NKJV, NRSV). There is no guideline to determine the precise feeling Paul wished to convey. But we assume that it included sympathy for the sinner, distress over sin, anger toward the person who caused the sin, and a desire to seek both remission and restoration.

Greek Words, Phrases, and Constructions in 11:23–27

Verse 23

ὑπὲρ ἐγώ—the preposition serves as an adverb in this short clause: "I am more." ὑπερβαλλόντως—this adverb differs from the comparative adverb περισσοτέρως (more) because it expresses the superlative idea, "to a much greater degree."[91] θανάτοις—in the plural, the noun denotes not death but possible modes of dying.

Verse 25

Three of the four verbs in this verse are aorist and convey the single action of each event. But the last one, πεποίηκα, is in the perfect to indicate Paul's vivid recollection of the experience.[92]

---

89. Calvin, *II Corinthians*, pp. 152–53.

90. Bauer suggests, "Who has any reason to take offense?" (p. 753), but this is a secondary translation.

91. Bauer, p. 840.

92. Refer to J. H. Moulton, *A Grammar of New Testament Greek*, vol. 1, *Prolegomena* (Edinburgh: Clark, 1908), p. 144.

Verses 26–27

The noun κινδύνοις (dangers) followed by prepositions and nouns must be interpreted to mean "dangers arising from."

The plural of ἀγρυπνίαις (wakings) and νηστείαις (fastings) stresses that these occurrences were involuntary.

---

30 If I must continue to boast, I will boast of the things that show my weakness. 31 The One who is praised forever, the God and Father of our Lord Jesus Christ, knows that I do not lie. 32 In Damascus, the governor under King Aretas guarded the city of the Damascenes to arrest me. 33 But through a window in the wall I was let down in a basket, and so I escaped from his hands.

---

9. Escape to Safety
11:30–33

The second segment of the so-called discourse of a fool (see the introduction to v. 21b) begins with verse 30, where Paul takes up the matter of boasting. At first glance, the verses that follow seem to show a lack of coherence. First, there is a statement on boasting (v. 30); then a doxology and an affirmation that Paul is speaking the truth (v. 31); and last, a brief account of his escape from Damascus (vv. 32–33).

But the difficulties can be explained if we understand Paul to write a postscript to his list of trials. He wants to stress a weakness. He does this by writing an introductory sentence (v. 30) to this postscript that features a unique episode; the next verse (v. 31) refers to the truthfulness of this unique experience in Damascus (vv. 32–33). Allan Menzies observes that "this incident could not have been put into the enumeration of ver[ses] 23, 24, the rhythm of which is complete without it."[93]

In short, this segment looks forward and brings to light one of the earliest incidents in Paul's apostolic ministry that reflects his weakness. Indeed, the purpose of this segment is to illustrate a weakness of Paul that was evident already in Damascus.

30. If I must continue to boast, I will boast of the things that show my weakness.
After listing a series of sufferings that followed one another in rapid succession, Paul pauses momentarily and then recalls an incident that did not fit the category of afflictions. He records an incident of weakness. With this segment he introduces a reference to boasting by writing a factual statement in the form of a conditional sentence. Even though he detests bragging about himself and his ordeals, necessity compels him to do so—but in his own way. In the first segment he boasted about the beatings he received, in the second about his defeat and shameful retreat.

Notice that Paul is going to boast about things that exhibit his weakness. The future tense points not to the catalog of misfortunes he has enumerated in the

---

93. Allan Menzies, *The Second Epistle of the Apostle Paul to the Corinthians: Introduction, Text, English Translation and Notes* (London: Macmillan, 1912), p. 89.

first segment,[94] but to the incident he plans to depict in succeeding verses. Undoubtedly there were many incidents of weakness in Paul's life, but the one concerning Damascus is sufficient.

Who would be so foolish as to mention a setback that damages one's reputation? People note their accomplishments but overlook their faults. Not so with Paul, who honestly and purposefully displays his deficiencies so that in his weakness God's power is made perfect (12:9).

Paul did not begin his apostolic career in Damascus as an eminent preacher under whose leadership the local church flourished. On the contrary, he was a firebrand who was wanted by the authorities, who escaped under cover of darkness, and who proved to be a failure. From Damascus he traveled to Jerusalem, where within two weeks his life was again in danger. Christian brothers took him to Caesarea and sent him home to Tarsus (Acts 9:28–30; Gal. 1:18). Paul was unable to lead, and his weakness was evident.

31. The One who is praised forever, the God and Father of our Lord Jesus Christ, knows that I do not lie.

The first clause is a typical Jewish saying that even in Paul's writings occurs more than once (see Rom. 1:25; 9:5; compare Luke 1:68; II Cor. 1:3). This benediction usually appears at the conclusion of a discourse, often in these words: "The Holy One, blessed be he."[95]

The second part of this verse is an invocation of God the Father of the Lord Jesus Christ. These are solemn words, for Paul calls God himself as a witness to verify that what he is going to write is true. He appeals to God whom he describes as the Father of Jesus Christ. Through Christ he also may call God his Father, and with this expanded Jewish saying he appeals to Christians of both Jewish and Gentile origin.

The invocation concerns the truth of the words that relate the apostle's escape from Damascus. Whether Paul's adversaries were acquainted with this episode cannot be verified. If they knew and slandered Paul, the reason for these words becomes clear. In the presence of God, before whom nothing is hidden, Paul avers that he speaks the truth.

Why would anyone doubt the truth of Paul's account? The boasting of his weakness is so ridiculous that his opponents may be inclined to think that he is speaking foolishly. No one boasts about failures.

32. In Damascus, the governor under King Aretas guarded the city of the Damascenes to arrest me. 33. But through a window in the wall I was let down in a basket, and so I escaped from his hands.

---

94. Some scholars think that the verse reflects what Paul has already written. See the commentaries of Furnish (p. 539), Martin (p. 383), and Windisch (p. 362). But the introduction of a new paragraph and the future tense of the verb *to boast* point forward, not backward.

95. SB 3:64, 530. In the Old Testament, the formula "Blessed be the LORD, the God of . . ." is recorded in numerous places (e.g., Gen. 9:26; I Sam. 25:32; I Kings 1:48; II Chron. 2:12). Consult Hermann W. Beyer, *TDNT,* 2:764.

In his record of Paul's escape from Damascus, Luke furnishes a number of details not found here. He notes a plot of the Jews to kill Paul. With others these Jews were watching the city gates day and night, but Paul's followers aided him in his escape under cover of darkness. They lowered him in a basket through an opening in the city wall (Acts 9:23–25).

The two accounts of Luke and Paul complement each other and fill in the broad picture. According to Luke, Paul confounded the Jews in Damascus by proving from the Scriptures that Jesus is the Christ. The breaking point came when they decided to kill the apostle, but they were unable to do so without the help of the authorities. They appealed to the governor who had been appointed by King Aretas IV. The governor ordered his guards to watch the city gates day and night to apprehend Paul; the Jews also watched these gates.

Christian friends helped Paul escaped by hiding him in a dwelling, located on the city wall, that was probably owned by one of them (compare Josh. 2:15). At night, they placed Paul in a basket and through the shutters of the house they lowered him to the ground outside the city walls. Luke uses the word *spyris,* which refers to a large hamper, while Paul writes *sarganē,* a plaited basket often used by fishermen.

Damascus had been conquered by the Roman general Pompey in 66 B.C.[96] For years, numerous Nabatean traders had formed a colony in the city. In the time of Aretas's reign, the Romans permitted the king to appoint a governor in Damascus as a representative of the Nabateans.[97] Some scholars imply that the governor's guards were guarding the gates outside the city; others insinuate that the governor was a Jew who represented the Nabateans. But the governor must have possessed authority to guard the entrances to the city. If both Jews and Nabatean guards watched the gates day and night, we would expect them to be inside the walls of Damascus.

Why would a Nabatean king instruct his governor to capture Paul? We know that Paul spent three years in Arabia (Gal. 1:17–18), which was the territory of King Aretas. If Paul can be described as an impulsive individual in those early years, we cannot picture him continuously in meditation. He probably was actively engaged in telling the Nabateans and perhaps the king himself about Jesus. His persistence could have stirred up ample ill will, so that he became a fugitive in Arabia.[98] He returned to Damascus, but there he met opposition from the Jews, who found an ally in the Nabatean governor.[99] In later years, Paul experienced the opposition of Jews elsewhere as they sought to influence local authorities to have Paul tried and punished (e.g., Acts 18:12–17).

---

96. Josephus *Antiquities* 14.29; *War* 1.127.

97. Consult Ernst A. Knauf, "Zum Ethnarchen des Aretas II Kor 11.32," *ZNTW* 74 (1983): 145–47; F. F. Bruce, "Chronological Questions in the Acts of the Apostles," *BJRUL* 68 (1986): 276.

98. Consult Seyoon Kim, *The Origin of Paul's Gospel* (Tübingen: Mohr, 1981; Grand Rapids: Eerdmans, 1982), p. 63; Jerome Murphy-O'Connor, "What Was Paul Doing in 'Arabia'?" *BibRev* 10 (1994): 46–47.

99. Windisch, *Der Zweite Korintherbrief,* p. 366.

The contrasts in Paul's life are vivid. He went to Damascus breathing murderous threats against the Lord's disciples, but he returned to Jerusalem as the Lord's disciple. He came to arrest Christians, but he was the person about to be arrested. He traveled to Damascus as a free man, but he left the city as a fugitive. And last, Paul's escape from Damascus is a contrast of his confessed weakness and God's protective power.

Hughes calls attention to succeeding verses in which Paul describes his ascent to the third heaven, to paradise (12:2–4). Paul's ascent to heaven is contrasted with his lowly descent "from a window in the Damascus wall."[100] The apostle will not boast about himself but about his own weaknesses (12:5).

Additional Comments on 11:32–33

A number of subjects need to be discussed; they range from the Nabatean kingdom, Aretas IV, and Rome, to the chronology of Paul. By discussing them we gain a better background understanding of these verses.

a. *Nabatean kingdom.* Josephus provides many descriptive details about the Nabateans, whom he calls Arabians. Their country stretched from Syria in the north to Egypt in the south, although these borders were disputed. Their capital, Petra, located south of the Dead Sea, became a center of trade routes and contributed to the commercial influence of the Nabateans.

Their first king was Aretas I, who ruled during the Maccabean uprising (II Macc. 5:8). In 96 B.C., Aretas II promised the citizens of Gaza that he would aid them in their fight against the Jews.[101] He extended his territory into Syria when the Seleucid dynasty was in disarray. His successor, Aretas III, ruled Damascus in 85 and fought against the Jews in Judea.[102] The Romans under Pompey entered Syria in 66 and then conquered Damascus. The Nabateans retreated and supported the Jews in their defense of Jerusalem against Rome. At the end of that century, Aretas IV occupied the Nabatean throne and became a powerful ruler.

b. *Aretas IV.* This king ruled from strength (9 B.C.–A.D. 40). He allied himself with the house of Herod by giving his daughter in marriage to Herod Antipas, tetrarch of Galilee and Perea (Matt. 14:1). This marriage took place prior to A.D. 14 and was designed to promote peace between Jews and Arabs. In 27, Herod Antipas went to Rome, where he met Herodias, his niece, who was married to his half-brother Philip (Luke 3:19). Herod Antipas wanted to divorce his wife and marry Herodias. But his wife heard about his plan and fled to her father, Aretas IV. The relationship between Antipas and Aretas turned ugly and war broke out. Antipas was defeated in 36, but he was protected by the Romans. Emperor Tiberius sent Vitellius, the Roman legate in Syria, to punish Aretas. But Tiberius died in office on March 16, 37, and Vitellius ceased his military campaign.

c. *Rome.* Caligula, a friend of Herod Agrippa I, became emperor in 37. Agrippa received the title of king over an area that eventually became as large as that of his grandfather Herod the Great. Instigated by Herodias, Antipas went with her to Rome in 39 to petition the emperor for a similar title. But Agrippa told Caligula that Antipas's loyalties

---

100. Hughes, *Second Epistle to the Corinthians,* p. 422.
101. Josephus *Antiquities* 13.13.3.
102. Josephus *Antiquities* 13.15.2.

to Rome were suspect. The result was that Antipas was banished and Agrippa received his tetrarchy.[103]

Did Aretas at that time have any authority over Damascus? The suggestion has been made that Emperor Caligula granted Aretas power over that city. Although there is no evidence to substantiate this conjecture, it is credible to think that Caligula permitted Aretas to appoint a governor (ethnarch) for the Nabatean people living in the greater part of Damascus. This governor would promote the trade interests of the Nabateans and make Damascus "a trade center of paramount importance," a circumstance that would favor the interests of Rome.[104] No coins bearing the images of emperors Caligula and Claudius, dating from 37 to 54, have been discovered in Damascus. The absence of Roman coins of this period may be due to the commercial interests of the Nabateans, who customarily used their own coinage.

d. *Chronology of Paul.* What does all this have to say about a possible date for Paul's flight from Damascus? We know that Aretas, who died in 40, did not earn the favor of Emperor Tiberius, Caligula's predecessor. Also, we may infer that with the accession of Caligula in 37, the political landscape changed in both Palestine and Syria. In other words, we focus attention on the last few years of the fourth decade in the first century.

In the Book of Acts we have one indisputable date that serves as an anchor. The proconsul Gallio came to Corinth in July 51 and, following Roman regulations, served there for one year (Acts 18:12). Going back into Paul's chronology, we know that Paul arrived in Corinth in the last half of 50. He had spent time in Syrian Antioch and in various places on his second missionary journey (Acts 15:35–17:33). He had been at the Jerusalem Council, presumably in 49, where the question of admitting Gentile believers into the church was settled (Acts 15:1–29).

Paul informs the Galatians that after fourteen years he visited Jerusalem (Gal. 2:1). This is fourteen years after Paul's conversion, when he was accompanied by Titus, a Gentile who was not compelled to be circumcised (Gal. 2:3).[105] If we assume that the visit of Paul and Titus to Jerusalem took place in 49, then Paul's conversion occurred in 35 at the gates of Damascus. And we date his escape from that city three years later (Gal. 1:18).

Greek Words, Phrases, and Constructions in 11:31–33

Verse 31

ὁ θεὸς καὶ πατήρ—here are two functions for one person. Also note that the phrase ὁ ὢν εὐλογητός modifies not the genitive (τοῦ κυρίου Ἰησοῦ) but the subject (God and Father) in the nominative.

Verses 32–33

ἐφρούρει—the imperfect tense indicates the continuous watch at the city gates.

---

103. Josephus *Antiquities* 18.7.1–2.

104. Philip C. Hammond, *The Nabataeans—Their History, Culture and Archaeology* (Gothenburg, Sweden: Åströms, 1973), p. 37.

105. This view admittedly overlooks the famine visit (Acts 11:30) when Barnabas and Paul visited Judea. But the presence of Titus at Jerusalem fits the Council visit that took place because numerous Gentiles were entering the church.

τὴν πόλιν Δαμασκηνῶν—the genitive case adjectivally depicts the inhabitants of the city.

διὰ τοῦ τείχους—literally "through the wall," but graphically "along the wall," where the house built into it was located.

Summary of Chapter 11

To counteract his opponents, Paul writes a discourse on boasting foolishly. Breaking his principle to boast only in the Lord, he asks his readers to put up with him and his foolishness. He uses an illustration taken from marriage. Christ is the husband of the Corinthians, who then should be pure. Would the local church fall away from Christ, much as Eve deserted God? The danger is real, because "superapostles" have entered the church and preach a different Jesus, have a different spirit, and bring a different gospel. Paul admits that he is not an orator but he has consistently taught the Corinthians the gospel of God free of charge.

Earlier Paul had written that he would not receive any remuneration for his spiritual work in Corinth. He repeats himself by saying that he preaches gratuitously so as not to be a burden to anyone, although he does receive financial aid from Macedonian churches. His boast is that he can work by being independent of the people he serves. He maintains this principle because he loves the Corinthians and because he wants to eliminate the intruders' boasts that they are Paul's equals.

Paul bluntly calls the intruders false apostles and deceitful workers. They are not apostles of Christ but agents of Satan who masquerade as servants of righteousness. They will receive judgment and condemnation.

After directly confronting his opponents, Paul resorts to setting aside his rule not to boast about himself. He calls himself a fool for doing so, but he must boast so that the Corinthians are able to see the difference between his love for them and the exploitative behavior of the intruders.

Boasting, says Paul, is done by a fool. In fact, he notes that he is talking like someone who is irrational. He begins by giving a résumé of his physical descent and spiritual commission: he is a Hebrew, an Israelite, Abraham's descendant, and Christ's servant. Then he presents a list of his sufferings, which include hard work, imprisonment, flogging, beating, being stoned, shipwrecks, and risking dangers on land and sea, in city and country. He suffered from hunger, cold, and lack of sleep. In addition, he feels his responsibility for all the churches.

Last, he boasts in things that expose his weakness. He freely mentions that as a fugitive, he was let down the wall in a fishbasket and so escaped from Damascus.

12

Apostolic Authority, *part 3*

(12:1–21)

Outline (continued)

12

1 I must continue to boast. Although nothing is gained by it, I will go on to visions and revelations of the Lord. 2 I know a man in Christ, who fourteen years ago (whether in the body or outside the body, I do not know, but the Lord knows) was caught up as far as the third heaven. 3 And I know such a man (whether in the body or outside the body, I do not know, but the Lord knows) 4 was caught up into paradise and heard words too sacred to utter and that man ought not to speak.

B. Paul's Vision and Warnings
12:1–13:10

Paul's opponents may have boasted of having received divine knowledge through visions and revelations. If this is the case, the apostle must continue to boast despite the fact that he abhors talking about his own experiences.[1] He writes about boasting only when he is forced to defend his apostolic calling. Since the time of his conversion at the gates of Damascus, Paul had received communications from the Lord through visions (Acts 16:9–10, 18:9–10; 22:17–21; 23:11; 26:19; 27:23–24; and see Gal. 2:2). These frequent communications from Jesus confirmed his close relationship with his Lord.

For this reason, Paul wishes to affirm his calling by relating to his initial readers an event that occurred prior to his ministry among them. This incident differs from the suffering he had endured for the sake of the gospel (11:23–32), for it was a moment of heavenly ecstasy. But Paul's report of this incident is so obscure that it leaves his readers with a number of unanswered questions.[2] We understand, however, that Scripture is a book primarily about creation and redemption and not about the details of the life hereafter. With Moses we say: "The secret things belong to the LORD our God, but the things revealed belong to us and to our children forever" (Deut. 29:29).

1. Revelations
12:1–4

1. I must continue to boast. Although nothing is gained by it, I will go on to visions and revelations of the Lord.

---

1. Paul features the verb *to boast* five times in this chapter (vv. 1, 5 [twice], 6, and 9). He uses neither this verb nor the noun *boast* again in the rest of this epistle.

2. Compare David E. Garland, "Paul's Apostolic Authority: The Power of Christ Sustaining Weakness," *RevExp* 86 (1989): 380.

a. "I must continue to boast." Forced to extend his boasting into a third section (see the introduction to 11:21b), Paul essentially repeats the words of 11:30. There he wrote a conditional sentence, "If I must continue to boast, I will boast of the things that show my weakness." Here he states that he must continue to boast, but he refuses to call attention to himself: the literal reading of the text is, "It is necessary to boast." In verse 9, Paul concludes his discourse on this subject by noting that boasting of his weakness reveals the power of Christ in him. In short, his boasting is designed not to promote himself but to reveal the glory of the Lord. With these words, he clearly delineates the difference between himself and his opponents.

b. "Although nothing is gained by it, I will go on to visions and revelations of the Lord." The apostle clearly states that boasting benefits no one. Because he has been forced to boast, he has made a fool of himself (v. 11). Paul is not now referring to boasting in the Lord (I Cor. 1:31; II Cor. 10:17), but to the idle bragging of his opponents. Indeed, he would have kept silent if his opponents had not forced him to speak. They oblige him to give an account of himself; if he refuses to boast of visions and revelations, they call him a fraud. So he yields to their pressure but protects himself by stating the futility of prating about spiritual experiences. For Paul, direct communications from the Lord are holy moments that are not intended for public scrutiny.

The second sentence in this verse depicts a contrast. That is, notwithstanding the futility of boasting, Paul plans to say something about visions and revelations he has received from the Lord. He points to Jesus, his Sender, who repeatedly discloses information to him.

What are these visions and revelations? First, God permits a human being to have supernatural experiences of seeing something of Jesus, angels, or heaven. Paul had a heavenly vision at his conversion near the gates of Damascus (Acts 26:19; see also the Martyrdom of Polycarp 12.3), and Peter had a vision of a sheet filled with animals coming down out of heaven (Acts 10:11–16).

Next, visions that come to a person in a trance or a dream often are experiences in which recipients receive information to guide them on their way into the immediate future. God communicates revelation through visions. A notable difference between the two is that visions are frequently introduced with a word of encouragement (e.g., "Fear not"). Revelations, by contrast, focus on aspects of the birth, ministry, suffering, death, resurrection, ascension, and return of Jesus Christ.[3] On Patmos, John had the unique experience of seeing Christ, who communicated divine revelation to show the believers. New Testament visions and revelations originate with Christ, whom Paul in this verse honors with his boasting.

2. I know a man in Christ, who fourteen years ago (whether in the body or outside the body, I do not know, but the Lord knows) was caught up as far as the third heaven.

---

3. See Geoffrey B. Wilson, *II Corinthians: A Digest of Reformed Comment* (Edinburgh and London: Banner of Truth Trust, 1973), pp. 149–50 n. 1).

In this verse and the next two, Paul relates an incident that gives him a privileged status. He has been permitted to enter the very abode of God (compare 5:1–5), where he received disclosures that he is unable to divulge. His circumstance is similar to that of individuals who died and were raised to life (for example, Lazarus). They returned from the dead but did not reveal any information about heaven. Persons who have had near-death experiences also are able to talk about temporarily leaving the body, yet they fail to relate all the details of what they saw and heard.

Paul is able to pass on to his readers the framework of his vision, but he is barred from giving them revelation about heaven. His experience, however, fortifies him for the rigors of his apostolic calling.

a. *Structure.* Verses 2, 3, and 4a display Semitic parallelism, which is especially common in the Psalms (see, e.g., Ps. 29:1–2; 96:7–9). The following list shows both repetition and elucidation.

I know a man in Christ	I know such a man
who fourteen years ago	
(whether in the body or outside the body	(whether in the body or outside the body
I do not know, but the Lord knows)	I do not know, but the Lord knows)
was caught up as far as the third heaven	was caught up into paradise
	and heard words too sacred to utter

Notice that the reference to time in the first column is not repeated in the second and that the "third heaven" is a synonym for "paradise." Also, the experience of being in or out of the physical body is known not to Paul but to the Lord. And last, Paul speaks of being caught up to heaven and hearing "words too sacred to utter and that man ought not to speak" (v. 4b).

b. *Significance.* "I know a man in Christ." At first the apostle seems to be speaking about someone else. But his words in verse 7 clearly indicate that he refers to himself. There he notes that a thorn in his flesh keeps him from being conceited about having received extraordinary revelations. He often uses the third person singular pronoun as a substitute for the first and second persons singular.[4] D. A. Carson correctly observes that the text makes no sense if Paul boasted about someone else's revelations in his own defense against the opponents.[5]

The descriptive phrase *in Christ* occurs frequently in the epistles of Paul.[6] Here it signifies that he as a believer is in close fellowship with Christ. Once again Paul ascribes glory to the Lord.

"Who fourteen years ago." If we place the date of composition for this epistle at the year 56, then Paul's rapture occurred in 42, when he was founding churches

---

4. SB 3:530–31. This phenomenon is not limited to Semitic languages but is prevalent in many cultures.

5. D. A. Carson, *From Triumphalism to Maturity* (Grand Rapids: Baker, 1984), p. 136.

6. The New Testament records seventy-five occurrences, of which seventy-two are in Paul's epistles and three in I Peter.

in Syria and Cilicia (refer to Acts 15:41; Gal. 1:21). We know nothing about the years between Paul's departure for Tarsus and his arrival in Antioch (see Acts 9:30; 11:25–26). His trance in Jerusalem cannot be identified with this event because that trance does not fit the chronology of Paul's biography (Acts 22:17).[7]

"Whether in the body or outside the body I do not know, but the Lord knows." The Jews taught that God created Adam's body and soul as one unit (Gen. 2:7), and only death can separate the two. By contrast, Greek philosophy taught a separation of body and soul; that is, the soul, which is immortal, must be set free from the body, which is evil. Paul followed Jewish thinking and saw a separation only at the time of death (5:1). But now he is not concerned about this matter and simply states that the Lord knows the answer. Note that Paul repeatedly refers to the Lord, who receives glory and honor.

"Was caught up as far as the third heaven." Being caught up implies that Paul offered no resistance. Indeed, he remained passive while God took him temporarily to heaven. Paul writes about the third heaven, and in the parallel passage calls it paradise (v. 4). But what is the meaning of "the third heaven"? Are there three levels, of which one is God's dwelling? John Albert Bengel writes, "The first heaven is that of the clouds; the second of the stars; and the third is spiritual."[8] Thus, the first relates to the atmosphere, the second to space, and the third to God's abode. The Jews, however, used the phraseology of the Scriptures that speaks of "the heavens, even the highest heavens" (Deut. 10:14; I Kings 8:27; II Chron. 2:6; 6:18; Neh. 9:6).[9]

The highest heavens are where God, the angels, and the saints dwell. The writer of Hebrews pointedly states that Christ entered these heavens to be in the sanctuary of God's presence (Heb. 4:14; 9:24; see also Eph. 4:10). Explaining the expression *third heaven,* John Calvin astutely remarks that "the number three is used as a perfect number to indicate what is highest and most complete."[10] So is the phrase *the seventh heaven* used in rabbinic circles: the numeral seven signifies perfection.[11]

---

7. Contra C. R. A. Morray-Jones, "Paradise Revisited (II Cor 12:1–12): The Jewish Mystical Background of Paul's Apostolate. Part 2: Paul's Heavenly Ascent and Its Significance," *HTR* 86 (1993): 286.

8. Refer to John Albert Bengel, *Bengel's New Testament Commentary,* trans. Charlton T. Lewis and Marvin R. Vincent, 2 vols. (Grand Rapids: Kregel, 1981), vol. 2, p. 330.

9. Philip Edgcumbe Hughes understands the Old Testament language to distinguish between the heavens (atmosphere and space) and the highest heavens (without limits of dimension and space). The first refers to the visible creation, the second to the invisible and spiritual heavens. See *Paul's Second Epistle to the Corinthians: The English Text with Introduction, Exposition and Notes,* New International Commentary on the New Testament series (Grand Rapids: Eerdmans, 1962), p. 433. Some rabbis read I Kings 8:27 differently: "heaven and the heaven of heavens." They understood the text to refer to three categories. See SB 3:531.

10. John Calvin, *The Second Epistle of Paul the Apostle to the Corinthians and the Epistles to Timothy, Titus and Philemon,* Calvin's Commentaries series, trans. T. A. Small (Grand Rapids: Eerdmans, 1964), p. 156.

11. Babylonian Talmud, *Hagigah* 12b. See Apocalypse of Moses 40:2; Testament of Levi 2:7; 18:5–6, 10; Helmut Traub, *TDNT,* 5:511.

3. And I know such a man (whether in the body or outside the body, I do not know, but the Lord knows) 4. was caught up into paradise and heard words too sacred[12] to utter and that man ought not to speak.

The repetition of verse 3 emphasizes the content of verse 2 and forms a prelude to verse 4a. But does Paul insinuate that he experienced two raptures: one to the third heaven and the other to paradise? Do these two designations refer to different locations, or are they synonyms for the same place? Even though a number of scholars argue that Paul relates two different experiences, the context favors the identification of the third heaven and paradise. First, the word *and* (v. 3) should be interpreted to mean that the following text explains the concept of "the third heaven." And, Paul gives one date (fourteen years), so the two terms refer to one event.[13]

a. *Paradise.* "Now the LORD God had planted a garden in the east, in Eden," and he "took the man and put him in the Garden of Eden" (Gen. 2:8, 15). The Septuagint translates the expression *Garden of Eden* as "paradise," a word that connotes bliss. The word *paradise,* derived from Old Persian, connotes a park encompassed by a wall. After Adam and Eve were expelled from the garden (Gen. 3:24), "paradise" occurs a few times in the Old Testament and describes a delightful place that existed before the fall into sin (e.g., Gen. 13:10; Ezek. 28:13; Joel 2:3). In the Septuagint and rabbinic literature, this word was given a religious meaning.[14]

Two references from apocryphal literature place paradise in the third heaven. One is II Enoch 8:1, "And those men took me from there, and they brought me up to the third heaven, and set me down there. Then I looked downward, and I saw Paradise." The other is II Enoch 42:3, "And I ascended to the east, into the paradise of Eden, where rest is prepared for the righteous. And it is open as far as the [third] heaven; but it is closed off from this world."[15] We assume that Paul was acquainted with the literature of his day and that he borrowed its vocabulary. If this is the case, we surmise that he regarded the term *third heaven* as a variant of "paradise" without attaching significance to the number of heavens.[16]

The New Testament features the word *paradise* three times: Luke 23:43, "Today you will be with me in paradise"; Revelation 2:7, "To him who overcomes, I

---

12. Bauer, p. 109.

13. Ralph P. Martin, *II Corinthians,* Word Biblical Commentary 40 (Waco: Word, 1986), p. 403.

14. Joachim Jeremias, *TDNT,* 5:765–66. Refer also to C. R. A. Morray-Jones, who concludes that the interior of Solomon's temple "was both a replica of its celestial counterpart and an image of the primordial and future paradise, with which the heavenly temple was closely connected if not identified." See "Paradise Revisited (II Cor 12:1–12): The Jewish Mystical Background of Paul's Apostolate. Part 1: The Jewish Sources," *HTR* 86 (1993): 206.

15. J. H. Charlesworth, ed., *The Old Testament Pseudepigrapha,* 2 vols. (Garden City, N.Y.: Doubleday, 1983). vol. 1, pp. 114, 168.

16. Andrew T. Lincoln, *Paradise Now and Not Yet: Studies in the Role of the Heavenly Dimension in Paul's Thought with Special Reference to His Eschatology,* SNTSMS 43 (Cambridge: Cambridge University Press, 1981), p. 79.

will give him the right to eat from the tree of life, which is the paradise of God"; and II Corinthians 12:4. The first two passages are eschatological and reveal that Jesus is present with the saints in paradise, namely, heaven. The third passage also locates paradise in God's presence, where Paul hears words that the Lord does not permit him to reveal. We conclude that identifying the third heaven and paradise appears to be not an inference but a correct interpretation of this passage.

b. *Prohibit.* "And [he] heard words too sacred to utter and that man ought not to speak." There are two parts to the last part of verse 4, hearing inexpressible things and a restriction on speaking them. I do not think that Paul was sworn to secrecy, as if he were privy to the mysteries of a religious cult.[17] Jesus told his opponents that he taught openly in the temple (Matt. 26:55); similarly, the apostles proclaimed their teaching everywhere to all people (e.g., Col. 1:25–27).

Paul has been caught up to heaven not to hear a doctrinal discourse but to hear heavenly sounds that he is unable to describe to others on earth. In heaven, he is in a sphere so different that it cannot be compared with what Paul has always known on earth. He is unable to portray what he has observed. Perhaps we can see some similarity in the case of a tourist who returns to his native country and tries to relate what he has seen and heard in another culture. Often he lacks the words to impart a true picture of the sights and sounds he has noticed abroad. The difference, however, is that the things Paul watched in heaven are too sacred for our human minds to comprehend and assimilate.

The text also notes a restriction: Paul was not permitted to talk about the things he had experienced. To an extent he was not alone, for both Old and New Testaments cite examples of persons who were forbidden to reveal what God had communicated to them (compare Isa. 8:16; Dan. 12:4, 9; Rev. 14:3; and contrast Rev. 22:10).[18] But the prohibition Paul received was different from that of Isaiah and Daniel, who had not had the privilege of being taken up to heaven.

Practical Considerations in 12:1–4

A pastor made his rounds in one of the hospitals in Hamilton, Ontario, Canada, and came to the bedside of a member of his church. The patient was an elderly gentleman who had been in a coma for a few days. Knowing this, the pastor feared that his visit would be ineffective because he could not be sure the patient would be aware of his presence. But as he entered the room, the patient suddenly came out of the coma, looked at the pastor, and said: "Pastor, I have just been in heaven."

---

17. Refer to F. F. Bruce, "Was Paul a Mystic?" *RTR* 34 (1975): 66–75. Also consult William Baird, "Visions, Revelation, and Ministry: Reflections on II Cor 12:1–5 and Gal 1:11–17," *JBL* 104 (1985): 651–62.

18. Consult C. K. Barrett, *The Second Epistle to the Corinthians,* Harper's New Testament Commentaries series (New York: Harper and Row, 1973), p. 311; J. D. Tabor, *Things Unutterable. Paul's Ascent to Paradise in Its Greco-Roman, Judaic, and Early Christian Contexts* (Lanham, Md.: University Press of America, 1986).

Surprised by the patient's remark, the pastor expressed his reservations by cautiously asking, "And how do you know that you were in heaven?" The man replied, "I know because I saw Jesus." Once more the pastor revealed skepticism when he inquired, "And how do you know that you saw Jesus?" The patient responded, "I could see the marks in his hands." With growing interest in the ensuing conversation, the pastor asked, "What did Jesus say to you?" The man elaborated: "Jesus said, 'Come, I have paid for you.'" Having said that, the patient breathed his last and responded to the Lord's invitation.

Now and then God permits us to see a glimpse of heaven. He lifts the curtain of heaven, as it were, so that we are able to peek and see what the Lord has in store for us.

Greek Words, Phrases, and Constructions in 12:1–4

Verse 1

καυχᾶσθαι—the textual variations for this phrase appear to be "attempts to ameliorate the style and syntax."[19] Some texts insert the particle εἰ before the infinitive to make the clause conform to the reading in 11:30. Other manuscripts substitute δέ for δεῖ, but then Paul would have written the particle δέ twice in the same context. Still others read δή in place of δεῖ, as an affirmation ("truly"). The reading adopted by translators has the support of the better manuscripts. All versions read the sentence as a declarative statement, with the exception of the Jerusalem Bible: "Must I go on boasting, though there is nothing to be gained by it?"[20]

οὐ συμφέρον—this is a periphrastic construction with the present participle and the understood verb ἐστίν. Because the negative particle modifies the periphrastic construction, it is correct to write οὐ instead of μή. Some manuscripts have the variant συμφέρει (D*) or συμφέρει μοι (D¹ H Ψ), which is the translation of the New King James Version: "It is doubtless not profitable for me."

Verse 2

πρὸ ἐτῶν δεκατεσσάρων—the use of the preposition πρό (before) is most interesting because it signifies "ago" instead of "before." Grammarians question whether the construction is a genitive of time and wonder whether a Latinism has influenced Greek speech.[21]

τὸν τοιοῦτον—the definite article and correlative adjective denote the quality of the person. The expression is repeated in verse 5, where it is in the genitive case. Both verses refer to Paul.

---

19. Bruce M. Metzger, *A Textual Commentary on the Greek New Testament* (Stuttgart and New York: United Bible Societies, 1994), p. 516.

20. Hans Windisch states that the text is corrupt (see *Der Zweite Korintherbrief*, ed. Georg Strecker [1924; reprint ed., Göttingen: Vandenhoeck und Ruprecht, 1970], p. 367). But if this were true, then countless passages would have to be labeled as such. These errors in transcription originate from faulty eyesight or hearing: the omission of the iota in δεῖ or the confusion of the same sound in δεῖ and δή. The Majority Text has the reading δή and substitutes γάρ for δέ.

21. See C. F. D. Moule, *An Idiom-Book of New Testament Greek*, 2d ed. (Cambridge: Cambridge University Press, 1960), p. 74; A. T. Robertson, *A Grammar of the Greek New Testament in the Light of Historical Research* (Nashville: Broadman, 1934), p. 622.

Verse 4

ἄρρητα ῥήματα—the adjective is a compound with the privative ἀ and the base ῥητός. It serves as a verbal adjective that expresses both passivity and impossibility: it cannot be spoken. The noun denotes the result of individual utterances.

οὐκ ἐξόν—the present neuter participle needs the understood verb *to be* for a periphrastic construction. Then the use of the negative particle οὐκ is grammatically correct.

---

5 I will boast about such a man, but I will not boast about myself, except about my weaknesses. 6 For if I should wish to boast, I would not be a fool, because I would speak the truth. But I refrain, so that no one may think of me more than what he has seen or heard from me, 7 even in the light of the extraordinary character of revelations. Therefore, so that I might not be too exalted, I was given a thorn in my flesh, a messenger of Satan, to buffet me, so that I might not be too elated. 8 I begged the Lord three times on this to remove it from me. 9 But he said to me: "My grace is sufficient for you, for [my] power is made perfect in weakness." Therefore, all the more gladly I will boast of my weaknesses, so that Christ's power may dwell in me. 10 Hence, I take delight in weaknesses, insults, hardships, persecutions, and difficulties for the sake of Christ. For when I am weak, then I am strong.

---

2. Human Weakness
12:5–10

Paragraph division at this juncture differs in Greek New Testaments and translations. Many versions introduce no new paragraph until verse 11, while other translations have a division at the beginning of verse 7. However, the Greek text does not show any punctuation at the juncture of verses 6 and 7, which indeed may be an infelicitous place to begin the next verse.

We can either combine verses 5 through 7 or begin a new segment comprising verses 5 through 10. The latter is preferred because Paul continues to speak of boasting about his weaknesses (vv. 9–10).

5. I will boast about such a man, but I will not boast about myself, except about my weaknesses.

The apostle distinguishes between the man caught up to heaven and himself. But from verse 7 we know that Paul speaks about himself in verse 5. He does so in a manner that marks a difference between the Paul who had been permitted to see the delights of heaven and the Paul who in weakness toils on earth.[22] But he refuses to boast about his visions and revelations and declines to prate about himself. Instead he glories in his weaknesses, many of which he has listed in his catalog of sufferings for the Lord (11:23–33). He reiterates his earlier remark: "If I must continue to boast, I will boast of the things that show my weakness" (11:30).

Why did the Lord grant Paul this celestial view if the apostle is unable to reveal it? The vision was designed to encourage Paul in his work for the Lord, during which he would encounter defeat, distress, and physical abuse.

---

22. Jean Héring rightly observes that there is no duality, only "a distinction between two aspects of his being." See *The Second Epistle of Saint Paul to the Corinthians,* trans. A. W. Heathcote and P. J. Allcock (London: Epworth, 1967), p. 91.

When Jesus called Paul near Damascus, he appointed him to be a witness to the Gentiles and informed him how much he would have to suffer for the name of Christ (Acts 9:15–16). Paul met defeat in Damascus and fled under cover of darkness to safety (Acts 9:25; II Cor. 11:32–33). His ministry in Jerusalem came to an abrupt end when his opponents tried to kill him and Christian friends put him aboard ship to Tarsus (Acts 9:29–30). As he established churches in the provinces of Syria and Cilicia (Acts 15:41; Gal. 1:21), he was flogged and beaten by either Jews or Gentiles (11:23–25). We suspect that he must have been discouraged. Yet during the time he spent in the provinces, God gave him the unique occasion of entering heaven for the purpose of strengthening Paul in his apostleship. He treasured the visions and revelations that continued to lift his spirit as he fulfilled his apostolic task. Indeed, of all God's servants he was most privileged.

6. For if I should wish to boast, I would not be a fool, because I would speak the truth. But I refrain, so that no one may think of me more than what he has seen or heard from me, 7a. even in the light of the extraordinary character of revelations.

a. "For if I should wish to boast, I would not be a fool, because I would speak the truth." This verse is linked to the preceding verse (v. 5), which mentions boasting twice and weaknesses once. Boasting about weaknesses runs contrary to the human psyche, which prefers to emphasize strengths.

Paul begins this verse with a conditional sentence that reveals an innate aversion. Boasting involves calling attention to himself, which he refuses to do. Earlier he said that boasting must be done in the Lord (see 10:17; I Cor. 1:31). This sentence must be understood in the context of Paul's opponents taunting him to boast about his credentials. If there should be anyone in the church who could glory in status, Paul would be the person. He had founded churches in Asia Minor, Macedonia, and Greece. He had worked much harder, had suffered more frequently, and had been exposed to more dangers than anyone else. And he had been given a celestial experience that placed him far above his co-workers and certainly above his detractors.

Far be it from Paul to glory in a position of esteem and achievement, even though he could justifiably boast (see 11:21b). But he does not wish to be a fool by bragging irrationally, a behavior that apparently characterized his adversaries. Speaking foolishly reveals the sin of lying or shading the truth. Paul, however, refuses to put himself on the level of his antagonists and to participate in their foolishness.[23] He is frank, open, reliable, and truthful in his writing. Conversely, he wants to be on the same level as his readers and thus he avoids leaving the impression of being a hero of faith. "We are familiar with the danger of thinking too highly of ourselves; it is as real a danger, though probably a less con-

---

23. This is not the first time Paul writes the words *foolishness* and *fool*. In chapters 11 and 12, he uses the first term three times (11:1, 17, 21) and the second five times (11:16 [twice], 19; 12:6, 11). In the New Testament, these two expressions are located predominantly in these two chapters.

sidered one, to be too highly thought of by others. Paul dreaded it; so does every wise man."[24]

b. "But I refrain, so that no one may think of me more than what he has seen or heard from me, even in the light of the extraordinary character of revelations." Verse 6b provides no hint that Paul is speaking to his opponents. Rather, he addresses the curiosity of his readers, who would like to learn more about his status. They know him as their spiritual father and respect him as the apostle who taught them the gospel of Christ Jesus. Now that he has given them information about his heavenly visions and revelations, he realizes that they are also filled with questions about heaven and the life hereafter.

Paul tells his readers that he does not want them to go beyond what they have heard from him and what they have seen in him. He wants the Corinthians to think of him as a spiritual brother in the Lord. They must look at Paul as a man with many flaws (compare Rom. 7:14–25), a person who had to cope with external weaknesses, hardships, and humiliations.[25] Thus, he boasts not about himself, but about his weaknesses. Paul's emphasis in this discourse remains on weaknesses that form the basis of his boast (see vv. 7, 9–10).

Additional Comments on 12:5–7a

Two Roman Catholic translations rearrange these verses. One, the New Jerusalem Bible, adds the first part of verse 7, "because of the exceptional greatness of the revelations," to verse 6. The other, the New American Bible, takes the last sentence of verse 6, "But I refrain, lest anyone think more of me than what he sees in me or hears from my lips," and makes it the first sentence of verse 7.

Translations that take verse 7a as the introductory clause of the entire verse favor the variant reading that omits the conjunction διό (therefore). This omission is supported by P[46], D, Ψ, 88, 614, and numerous translations. To retain the conjunction produces awkward grammar. Héring, therefore, asserts that it should be dropped, with the period at the conclusion of the first clause in verse 7.[26] We demur, for why would a more difficult reading have been inserted if the variant is the correct reading? The rule that the harder reading is the preferred text still stands.

Some translators reverse the Greek word order of verse 7 and begin the sentence with the second clause of this passage, "And lest I should be exalted above measure by the abundance of the revelations, a thorn in the flesh was given to me" (NKJV; see also GNB). But in these translations the conjunction διό has been deleted.

If verse 7a is part of the preceding sentence, it further explains the first clause, "But I refrain" (v. 6b). The entire sentence, which is syntactically correct, then reads: "But I refrain, so that no one may think of me more than what he has seen or heard from me, even the extraordinary character of revelations."[27] Then verse 7b begins with the inferential conjunction διό.

---

24. James Denney, *The Second Epistle to the Corinthians*, 2d ed., The Expositor's Bible series (New York: Armstrong, 1900), p. 351.

25. Consult Jules Cambier, "Le critère paulinien de l'apostolat en II Cor. 12,6s," *Bib* 43 (1962): 481–518.

26. Héring, *Second Epistle of Paul*, p. 92.

27. Refer to Victor Paul Furnish, *II Corinthians: Translated with Introduction, Notes, and Commentary*, Anchor Bible 32A (Garden City, N.Y.: Doubleday, 1984), p. 528.

One translator sees a break between verse 6 and 7 and renders the first clause of verse 7a as an independent sentence by supplying the verb *to be:* "Then there is the matchless grandeur of these revelations" (*Cassirer*). Here the Greek conjunction καί, in a somewhat forced rendering, means "then" or "therefore."

Another suggestion is to understand the first half of verse 5 to be continued in the second half of verse 6: "I will boast about such a man. But I refrain, so that no one may think of me more than what he has seen or heard from me, even the extraordinary character of revelations." If we connect these two verses, then 5b and 6a must be regarded as a parenthetical remark.[28] But such a construction in these verses is too cumbersome, for it causes an extended lapse in the discourse. Hence, this proposal must be rejected.

In conclusion, we admit that verses 5, 6, and 7a present a complicated construction, one that continues to trouble readers and translators. Nonetheless, by making verse 7a the last clause of verse 6b, we are confident that this construction of the passage conveys Paul's intent.[29]

7b. Therefore, so that I might not be too exalted, I was given a thorn in my flesh, a messenger of Satan, to buffet me, so that I might not be too elated.

a. "Therefore, so that I might not be too exalted, I was given a thorn in my flesh." This conclusive statement is introduced with the adverb *therefore.* But this word can hardly be linked to verse 6b with its specific content. Instead, the statement summarizes Paul's emphasis of boasting in his weaknesses. Pride slips surreptitiously into the human soul and rules in such a manner that a person often is unaware of its presence.

Throughout Paul's discourse on boasting, he has given the Lord glory and honor. His desire is to remain humble and to refrain from boasting about himself and his achievements. He knows that the privilege of experiencing celestial visions and revelations might result in pride. The temptation to elevate himself above his companions was real.

The Lord intervened by giving Paul a thorn in his flesh. The Greek has the term *skolops,* which means either a stake or a thorn. It will not do to think of impalement or crucifixion, because Paul always uses *stauros* when he writes about the cross. Here the word means a thorn or some other object that pierces Paul's flesh and injures him. Paul also writes the word *flesh,* which points to the frailty of his physical body. Most scholars agree that this term must be interpreted literally. That is, Paul endured physical pain.

b. "A messenger of Satan, to buffet me, so that I might not be too elated." The second part of verse 7 is designed to explain the first part. However, the difficul-

---

28. F. J. Pop, *De Tweede Brief van Paulus aan de Corinthiërs* (Nijkerk: Callenbach, 1980), p. 358. Compare Allan Menzies, *The Second Epistle of the Apostle Paul to the Corinthians: Introduction, Text, English Translation and Notes* (London: Macmillan, 1912), p. 91. See also *Moffatt*.

29. Ernest B. Allo, *Saint Paul Seconde Épître aux Corinthiens,* 2d ed. (Paris: Gabalda, 1956), p. 308; F. W. Grosheide, *De Tweede Brief van den Apostel Paulus aan de Kerk te Korinthe,* Kommentaar op het Nieuwe Testament series (Amsterdam: Van Bottenburg, 1939), p. 437; Josef Zmijewski, "Kontextbezug und Deutung von 2 Kor 12,7a. Stilistische und strukturale Erwägungen zur Lösung eines alten Problems," *BibZ* 21 (1977): 265–72.

ties in understanding Paul's remark increase with every clause. We would like to believe that the original readers of this epistle understood the meaning of these words. But the fact that Paul reveals his heavenly visit for the first time is an indication that his reference to a thorn in his flesh is also news.

Paul writes that his physical affliction is a messenger of Satan, namely, one of Satan's evil angels. By giving Paul a thorn to cause him physical discomfort, God allows Satan to send one of his angels to torment him. We are reminded of Job, who also was afflicted by Satan; indeed, God set limits for Satan, who could do only what God allowed him to do (see Job 1:12; 2:6).

The next phrase, "to buffet me," is yet more descriptive; that is, the messenger of Satan hits Paul in the face. Buffeting occurred when members of the Sanhedrin struck Jesus with their fists (Matt. 26:67; Mark 14:65). Both Paul and Peter use the word when they describe being beaten unjustly (I Cor. 4:11; I Peter 2:20).

How do we relate the "thorn in the flesh" to "a messenger of Satan," and these two phrases in turn to striking Paul in the face?

Explanations of Paul's ailment are numerous; there are at least twelve different suggestions, many of them helpful. Among the suggestions are epilepsy, hysteria, neuralgia, depression, eye problems (refer to Gal. 4:14–15), malaria, leprosy, rheumatism, a speech impediment (see 10:10; 11:6), temptation, personal enemies (compare 11:13–15), and punishment by a demon.[30] These theories are ably defended by scholars who are acquainted with both Jewish literature and Paul's life depicted in Acts and the epistles. Certainly, some conjectures are worthy of consideration. But every one meets weighty objections. Whether Paul's affliction happened to be external or internal, the outcome remains the same: our theories are mere guesses, for we do not know what ailed the apostle.

We note a contrast depicted in this verse. Paul who rises to the third heaven to see celestial light is afterward continually tormented by a messenger from the prince of darkness. Paul tells his readers that this contrast happened to keep him humble, "so that I might not be too elated." Twice in this verse (v. 7b) he writes the same clause, plainly for emphasis.

Additional Comments on 12:7b

Of the profusion of proposals we will briefly examine five explanations about Paul's affliction. Many of these proposals have had supporters throughout the centuries, but for lack of scriptural evidence they remain mere guesses.

1. *Depression.* From chapter 1 we learn that Paul was disheartened by his experiences in Asia Minor (1:8). He had encountered severe setbacks caused by persons such as Dem-

---

30. The literature on this matter is vast. I list only a few articles alphabetically arranged: Michael L. Barré, "Qumran and the 'Weakness' of Paul," *CBQ* 42 (1980): 216–27; Hermann Binder, "Die Angebliche Krankheit des Paulus," *ThZeit* 32 (1976): 1–13; Jerry W. McCant, "Paul's Thorn of Rejected Apostleship," *NTS* 34 (1988): 550–72; David M. Park, "Paul's *skolops tē sarki:* Thorn or Stake? (II Cor. xii 7)," *NovT* 22 (1980): 179–83; Jean J. Thierry, "Der Dorn im Fleische, (2 Kor. xii 7-9)," *NovT* 5 (1962): 301–10; Laurie Woods, "Opposition to a Man and His Message: Paul's 'Thorn in the Flesh'" (2 Cor 12:7)," *AusBRev* 39 (1991): 44–53.

etrius the silversmith (Acts 19:23–41). But this can hardly explain the thorn in Paul's flesh. Even though Paul experienced opposition, we have no indication that he suffered from severe depression. Instead he writes: "In every way we are afflicted, but we are not hard pressed. We are perplexed, but we are not thoroughly perplexed" (4:8). We are "sorrowful yet always rejoicing" (6:10).

2. *Poor eyesight.* Writing to the Galatians, Paul mentions that his illness was a trial to them. Yet they accepted him as an angel of God and would have done anything for him, even tearing out their eyes and giving them to him (Gal. 4:14–15). Was Paul suffering from ophthalmia?[31] Paul wrote the epistle to the Galatians in large letters (6:11), used scribes to write other letters for him (see Rom. 16:22), and had difficulty seeing the high priest Ananias at the meeting of the Sanhedrin (Acts 23:5). But we are not sure whether the Galatians' desire to give Paul their eyes must be understood literally or figuratively. This appears to be hyperbole; specifically, they would give Paul the most precious part of their physical bodies. And last, the passage speaks of an angel of God (Gal. 4:14), but not about an angel of Satan.

3. *Epilepsy.* Did Paul suffer from occasional fits of epilepsy, of which his conversion experience at the gates of Damascus is an example? An epileptic spell causes unconsciousness, which was not the case when Jesus arrested Paul near Damascus. Also, when a person is unconscious, pain is not a factor. Epilepsy does not correspond to being painfully pummeled in the face with fists. There is no evidence in either Acts or Paul's epistles that he ever suffered from this malady. And to say that Paul's illness in Galatia was epilepsy because the Galatians might have shown their contempt and disdain[32] reads something into the text (Gal. 4:14). Paul is referring not to a literal action but is using a figure of speech.

4. *Enemies.* This epistle portrays the opposition Paul had to fight continually. His opponents were indeed a source of mental agony for him. Yet we must say that an interpretation that identifies his enemies with the thorn in the flesh is inconsistent with the available evidence. We cannot imagine that Paul would pray three times to be relieved of his enemies.[33] He advises the Galatians not to cause him any trouble, "for I bear on my body the marks of Jesus" (6:17). As a servant of Christ he gladly bore the evidence of stoning, beatings, and infirmity.

5. *Demon visitation.* This theory teaches that when Paul was in heaven, his pride overwhelmed him. But he was suddenly attacked by a demon who punished him to keep him humble. Paul prayed three times to the Lord to have the attack stopped, but he was told that he had to learn his lesson and rely on the sufficiency of God's grace.[34] There are exegetical objections to this interpretation: the physical discomfort of the thorn in the flesh is not a temporary ordeal in heaven but an enduring pain on earth. Further, there is no indication in the text that Paul experienced punishment in heaven, because that is a most unlikely place for a demon to beat the apostle. And last, a thorn in the flesh was given to him not by a messenger of Satan but by the Lord, who allowed Satan's messenger to buffet Paul.[35]

---

31. Consult Patricia Nisbet, "The Thorn in the Flesh," *ExpT* 80 (1969): 126; Alan Hisey and James S. P. Beck, "Paul's 'Thorn in the Flesh': A Paragnosis," *JBR* 29 (1961): 125–29.

32. The literal translation of *ekptuō* is "I spit out," but translators prefer the secondary meaning: "I disdain."

33. Refer to A. Thacker, "Paul's thorn in the flesh," *EpworthRev* 18 (1991): 67–69.

34. See Robert M. Price, "Punished in Paradise (An Exegetical Theory on II Corinthians 12:1–10)," *JSNT* 7 (1980): 33–40.

35. For additional theories, consult Windisch, *Der Zweite Korintherbrief,* pp. 385–88.

Understanding the apostle's affliction literally is a viable approach, especially in the light of a parallel. On the Sabbath, Jesus healed a woman who had been crippled by a spirit for eighteen years. He asked the synagogue ruler, "Then should not this woman, a daughter of Abraham, whom Satan has kept bound for eighteen long years, be set free on the Sabbath day from what bound her?" (Luke 13:16). The parallel, however, breaks down when we look at the conclusion. The woman suffered for nearly two decades and was healed; Paul was not healed but was granted grace to endure the affliction.

---

8. I begged the Lord three times on this to remove it from me. 9a. But he said to me: "My grace is sufficient for you, for [my] power is made perfect in weakness."

a. "I begged the Lord three times on this to remove it from me." Paul knows that not Satan but God is in control. If Satan had his wish, he would have preferred the apostle Paul to be proud instead of humble. Writes Carson, "[Satan's] interests would be much better served if Paul were to become insufferably arrogant."[36] Then the cause of Christ would suffer irreparable damage. But this is not the case, for God watches over his servant. He curtails the power of Satan by permitting him to send only a messenger to Paul. God keeps Paul from harmful pride and on the path of humility by allowing Satan's messenger to afflict him.

Whatever Paul's physical ailment may have been, it was of long duration, as the present tense of two verbs (to buffet; to be elated) in the preceding verse seem to indicate. Three times in succession Paul appealed to Jesus to remove this affliction from him. The expression *three times* reminds us of Jesus' prayers to God in the garden of Gethsemane (Matt. 26:36–46 and parallels).[37] We do not know whether Paul uttered his petitions three times in quick succession or over a period of time. And we do not know whether Jesus answered him three times or only after the third prayer.

The difference between Jesus' prayers and those of Paul is evident. Jesus prayed to the Father, and in response an angel from heaven came to strengthen him (Luke 22:43). But Paul prayed to Jesus that the affliction caused by an angel of Satan be taken from him. A similarity is that neither Jesus nor Paul saw his request fulfilled. Jesus went to his death on the cross and Paul continued to suffer physically for the rest of his earthly life.

Furthermore, after Jesus withstood three temptations of Satan, the devil left him for a while (Luke 4:13) and returned. Paul writes that Satan prevented him again and again from visiting the church in Thessalonica (I Thess. 2:18; consider in addition I Cor. 5:5; II Cor. 11:3; I Tim. 1:20). He also knew that Satan could appear as an angel of light and use his servants to deceive God's people (11:14–

---

36. Carson, *From Triumphalism to Maturity*, p. 145.

37. Scripture often notes a threefold prayer of the saints. The Aaronic blessing consists of three parts (Num. 6:24–26); Elijah prayed three times for the son of the widow in Zarephath (I Kings 17:21); and the psalmist prayed in the evening, in the morning, and at noon (Ps. 55:17; see also Dan. 6:10). Consult SB 2:696–702; and Windisch, *Der Zweite Korintherbrief*, p. 389.

15). Paul appealed three times to the Lord to deliver him from the attacks of the evil one and received a negative response that was nevertheless satisfactory.

Does the Lord answer prayer when we in faith petition him? The answer is affirmative in light of John's statement on prayer:

> This is the confidence we have in approaching God: that if we ask anything according to his will, he hears us. And if we know that he hears us—whatever we ask—we know that we have what we asked of him.
>
> —I John 5:14–15

God's will is the principal factor in answering our prayers. God hears our petitions but fulfills them only when they are in accord with his will. He seeks to advance our spiritual well-being, which in Paul's case was humility brought about by the messenger of Satan.

Do we pray to God or to Jesus? The relationship between Father and Son is one of perfect unity in a fellowship of love, so that we can offer our prayers to God through his Son Jesus Christ. The Lord tells us to pray in his name, and he will do what we ask (John 14:14). Other examples of praying to Jesus are the last words of Stephen (Acts 7:59, 60); the acclamation "Come, O Lord" (I Cor. 16:22; Rev. 22:20); and the doxology "The grace of the Lord Jesus Christ be with your spirit" (Phil. 4:23 and parallels).[38]

b. "But he said to me: 'My grace is sufficient for you, for [my] power is made perfect in weakness.'" Paul writes the perfect tense ("he has said") to stress that the Lord's answer has abiding validity. In other words, Jesus utters a precept that is true for everybody, anywhere, and always. Although the Lord's reply is negative, it nonetheless gives Paul the assurance that Jesus supplies him in all his needs.

Hence, the first term in the Greek word order of Jesus' reply is "sufficient." This word is emphatic because of its primary position, but it also implies the absolute authority of the sovereign Lord: the provisions that he supplies are sufficient for his people. Paul himself could testify to that truth by telling the church in Philippi, "And my God will meet all your needs according to his glorious riches in Christ Jesus" (Phil. 4:19).

Jesus says, "My grace is sufficient for you." With two personal pronouns, "my" at the beginning and "you," at the end of this sentence, the balance is striking. The grace that Jesus provides encompasses kindness and goodness toward Paul. Grace proceeds from the giver to the recipient and thus describes Jesus' character, which is "full of grace and truth" (John 1:14b). Apart from the gifts of redemption, apostolic calling, and spiritual power that Paul had received, he obtained the gift of grace that consisted of poise to deal with difficulties in his life. The apostle was able to endure the pain of his affliction because of relief that the Lord extended to him. Jesus did not remove the thorn from Paul's body, but he granted relief through his all-sufficient grace.

---

38. R. G. Crawford, "Is Christ Inferior to God?" *EvQ* 43 (1971): 203–9.

Jesus' grace is revealed in his power.[39] Not Paul but Jesus receives praise and adoration, for divine power is brilliantly displayed when human weakness is noticeably evident. Calvin comments, "God's strength is made perfect only when it shines out clearly enough to win the praise that is its due."[40] The evidence of Christ's power in Paul's weakness demonstrates that not the false apostles, who boasted of their own prowess, but Paul, who boasted in the Lord, was the true apostle.

9b. Therefore, all the more gladly I will boast of my weaknesses, so that Christ's power may dwell in me.

With a concluding remark, Paul responds to and accepts Jesus' word. In the preceding context, he had mentioned the concept *weakness* a few times.[41] But now the Lord himself uses the word and Paul cheerfully repeats it.

With this response Paul reveals his inner being, for the one sentence (v. 9a) uttered by Jesus causes the apostle to be joyful in his lot. Complaints and continued pleas are a common reaction to a negative answer, but Paul does not express them. Instead Paul demonstrates gladness, because he is fully aware that divine grace will be more than sufficient for him to cope with his malady. He cheerfully endures his human frailty knowing that Christ functions within him (Gal. 2:20).

Why does Paul boast in his weaknesses? The weaker he is, the stronger the power of Christ works through him. Jesus wants to use him as a messenger who comes not in his own strength but knows his complete dependence on the Lord. In fact, the wording of the last clause in this verse is unique, for Paul literally says, "that the power of Christ may pitch a tent over me."[42] The picture is that of God descending from heaven and dwelling in the tabernacle among the people of Israel (Exod. 40:34). It is that of Jesus, who came down from heaven and dwelled, as in a tent, among his people (John 1:14).

We see indeed a picture of Paul's total submission to Christ. All the adversities that come his way he gladly acknowledges as areas in which Christ's power becomes more effective. Christians wholeheartedly pray the wording of a sixteenth-century document:

> And so, Lord,
> uphold us and make us strong
>   with the strength of your Holy Spirit,

---

39. The better manuscripts omit the possessive pronoun *my*, which "was no doubt added by copyists for the sake of perspicuity" (Metzger, *Textual Commentary*, p. 517). Translators are evenly divided on including or excluding it. I prefer to include the pronoun, but the clause "power is made perfect in weakness," which is devoid of possessives ("my" and "your"), shows balance.

40. Calvin, *II Corinthians*, p. 161.

41. See 11:30 and 12:5 for the noun *weakness* and 11:21, 29 for the verb *to be weak*.

42. Consult the commentaries of Barrett (p. 317), Calvin (pp. 161–62), Martin (p. 421), and Windisch (p. 392) on the interpretation that Christ's power descends on Paul from heaven. See also Robertson, *Grammar*, p. 602. For the view that Christ enters into the apostle horizontally, see Wilhelm Michaelis, *TDNT*, 7:386–87.

so that we may not go down to defeat
   in this spiritual struggle,
but may firmly resist our enemies
   until we finally win the complete victory.[43]

10. Hence, I take delight in weaknesses, insults, hardships, persecutions, and difficulties for the sake of Christ. For when I am weak, then I am strong.

Paul began his discussion about boasting in 11:1 and continued it through his lengthy catalog of hardships in that same chapter. After his revelation of his celestial experience, he returned to his emphasis on weaknesses (vv. 1–6), and now brings his discourse to an appropriate ending.

The repetition of the preceding passage (v. 9b) is evident:

verse 9b	*verse 10*
Therefore, all the more gladly	Hence,
I will boast of my weaknesses,	I take delight in weaknesses . . .
so that Christ's power	for the sake of Christ.
may dwell in me.	For when I am weak,
	then I am strong.

The apostle gladly accepts the weaknesses that he has to endure: "insults, hardships, persecutions, and difficulties." This is a shorter list of adversities than the one in the preceding chapter (11:23–29). For the sake of Jesus Christ, Paul joyfully accepts all these sufferings to further the gospel. He knows that he has to suffer much for the name of Jesus (Acts 9:16). But he also knows that he "can do everything through Christ who strengthens [him]" (Phil. 4:13; compare II Tim. 4:17).

The conclusion ends on a note of triumph: "For when I am weak, then I am strong." He reiterates what he wrote at the beginning of this verse, namely, that he delights in weaknesses for the sake of Christ. All things are performed through and for Christ, so that he may receive glory and honor.

Greek Words, Phrases, and Constructions in 12:6–10

Verses 6–7a

θελήσω καυχήσασθαι—the future indicative is used. It often serves as a substitute for the subjunctive. The aorist infinitive denotes single occurrence.

ἐρῶ—the future tense of εἶπον (I said), which follows in the sequence of two other verbs in the future: "I wish," and "I will be."

εἰς ἐμὲ λογίσηται—this expression, "charge to my account,"[44] is a technical term employed in the world of commerce.

τῇ ὑπερβολῇ—the dative case denotes not means but cause. Paul uses the term in 4:7, "the extraordinary power." It can also mean "exceedingly" (see 1:8; Rom. 7:13; I Cor. 12:31; Gal. 1:13).

---

43. Heidelberg Catechism, answer 127.

44. Friedrich Blass and Albert Debrunner, *A Greek Grammar of the New Testament and Other Early Christian Literature,* trans. and rev. Robert Funk (Chicago: University of Chicago Press, 1961), #145.2.

διό—some manuscripts delete this inferential conjunction. Its omission may have been caused "when copyists mistakenly began a new sentence with καὶ τῇ ὑπερβολῇ τῶν ἀποκαλύψεων, instead of taking these words with the preceding sentence."[45]

Verses 7b–8

ἵνα μὴ ὑπεραίρωμαι—is this phrase in its second occurrence an unintentional mistake of a scribe who included it? Or did Paul write it for emphasis? Although both questions are intriguing, an affirmative answer to the latter choice is preferred.

ὑπὲρ τούτου—the pronoun is in the neuter, which refers to Paul's sufferings and is broader than the masculine, which would point to either the thorn or the messenger of Satan.

Verses 9–10

τελεῖται—this is the present passive, which means that the Lord is the agent and that the process of perfecting Paul continues.

ἐπισκηνώσῃ ἐπ᾽ ἐμέ—the preposition is repeated to show direction: Christ's power descends on Paul. The compound verb features the word *tent* to reveal the Lord's intimate presence in the life of Paul.

εἰμί—the last word in the sentence is emphatic and depicts Paul's frame of mind. He is and remains strong in the Lord.

---

11 I have been a fool, but you forced me to it. Indeed you should have commended me, for in nothing am I inferior to the superapostles, even though I am nothing. 12 The signs of an apostle were worked out among you with great perseverance, by signs, wonders, and miracles. 13 In what respect, then, were you inferior to the other churches, except that I never became a burden to you? Forgive me this wrong!

14 Look, this is now the third time that I am ready to come to you, and I will not burden you. I do not want your money, but you. For the children ought not to gather treasures for their parents, but the parents for their children. 15 I would most gladly spend [everything] and be expended for you. If I love you to a greater degree, am I to be loved less? 16 Very well! [You say] that I have not been a burden to you. But, [you say] I, as a crafty fellow, took you in by deceit. 17 Did I take advantage of you through any of the men I sent to you? 18 I appealed to Titus and I sent the brother with him. Did Titus take advantage of you? Did we not conduct ourselves in the same spirit? Did we not walk in the same footsteps?

---

3. Intended Visit
12:11–18

a. Apostolic Apology
12:11–13

Throughout Paul's discourse on boasting, he has made known his aversion to talking about himself. But when the Corinthians force him to boast because they want to compare him with the so-called superapostles, Paul yields. The tone in verses 11 through 13 communicates that he does not have in mind the twelve dis-

---

45. Metzger, *Textual Commentary,* p. 516.

ciples, or to be exact Peter, James, and John (Gal. 2:9).[46] He is thinking of the ones whom he has labeled false apostles and deceitful workers (11:13).

The true apostle of Jesus Christ lives a life of complete obedience to his Lord; the false apostles are interested in filling their pockets with money extorted from the people. Also, the Lord advances the spread of the gospel by accompanying apostolic preaching with signs, wonders, and miracles (Heb. 2:4). He withheld his blessings from the false prophets, who never performed these miracles.

Paul served as apostle to all the churches, one of which was the Corinthian congregation. From others he received financial support for his work, while he offered the gospel free of charge to the Corinthians (I Cor. 9:18). If Paul had disadvantaged them in any way, he begged their indulgence.

11. I have been a fool, but you forced me to it. Indeed you should have commended me, for in nothing am I inferior to the superapostles, even though I am nothing.

a. "I have been a fool, but you forced me to it." Five times Paul writes the expression *fool* in his discourse on boasting (11:16 [twice], 19; 12:6, 11). And in every instance, he makes it known that he does not want to be a fool. Because he spoke the truth, he could not even be a fool (v. 6). Being a fool undermines the cause of Christ, brings blame on the church, and calls into question Paul's apostolicity.

The Corinthians seemed to be imperceptive to Paul's love and devotion to them; they were swayed by the false teachers and forgot about Paul's instruction. Notwithstanding his affection for them, they had without reflection forced Paul to show his apostolic credentials. That is they compelled him to boast about his own accomplishments.

Paul sensed that he had become a fool by yielding to their pressure. Although his role as fool has come to an end, his boasting continues as he lists the marks of an apostle (v. 12). In every respect he excels all other people, even if he calls himself unworthy to be an apostle (I Cor. 15:9; Eph. 3:8; I Tim. 1:15). Earlier he stated that nothing is gained by boasting (v. 1), and now he designates himself a fool for having succumbed to the constraint the people in Corinth had placed on him. Not Paul but the members of the Corinthian church should have recited the catalog of the suffering he had endured for the sake of the church and the advancement of the gospel.

b. "Indeed you should have commended me, for in nothing am I inferior to the superapostles." The Corinthians should have defended their mentor against the covert and overt attacks on him. They ought to have been mindful of the words of Solomon, "Let another praise you, and not your own mouth; someone else, and not your own lips" (Prov. 27:2). They were expected to commend Paul, for they were his epistle that everyone could read (3:2).

Already in the preceding chapter (11:5), Paul wrote about the superapostles, which in the broader context is a designation for his opponents and conveys

---

46. For other views see Martin (p. 427), Héring (pp. 77, 79), Furnish (pp. 503–4), Windisch (p. 330).

irony (11:13).[47] These people were not apostles, because they were not called and commissioned by the Lord and their works were not crowned with his blessings. They were people of a different spirit who preached another Jesus and a different gospel (11:4–5). Conversely, Paul's weakness related him intimately to Jesus, with whom he claimed affinity, for he writes that Christ was crucified in weakness (13:4). In the person of Jesus we note an overt contradiction: human weakness and God's strength.[48] And the same is true for Paul, who also is aware of divine power in the midst of human weakness (1:8–11).

c. "Even though I am nothing." Paul willingly lowers himself by saying that he is nothing and thus reveals his humility. He noted earlier that he lowered himself to elevate the Corinthians with the gospel (11:7). Others may vaunt their elevated status and exact money from the people of Corinth. Paul, however, displays his lowliness and writes that he is nothing but a recipient of God's mercy and grace (I Tim. 1:13–14). Accordingly, the Corinthians must draw their own conclusions and determine who is a true apostle of Jesus Christ.

12. The signs of an apostle were worked out among you with great perseverance, by signs, wonders, and miracles.

The requirements for apostolicity were two: having followed Jesus from the time of his baptism to his ascension and having witnessed his resurrection (Acts 1:21–22). Paul had not been a disciple of Jesus, yet near the gates of Damascus the risen Christ called him to be his apostle to the Gentiles. His calling aside, Paul had to defend his apostleship against the vicious attacks of his adversaries. They insisted that he prove he truly was an apostle.

In similar fashion Jesus was repeatedly asked by scribes, Pharisees, and Sadducees to give them a sign that proved he was the Messiah (e.g., Matt. 12:38; 16:1; John 2:18). But the Lord never satisfied their curiosity. And when the apostles began their ministry at Pentecost, the members of the Sanhedrin questioned by what power or name they healed a lame man (Acts 4:7). We see a parallel in the demand for a sign during both Jesus' ministry and that of the apostles. In Corinth, Paul had to respond to the same demand.[49]

The Corinthians should have known that Paul's credentials came from God, who gave him the power to be a competent minister of the new covenant (3:5–6). It is true that we have no record that Paul performed wonders and miracles in Corinth. However, a few months after he wrote II Corinthians, he penned his letter to the Romans and remarked that his preaching was accompanied by signs and wonders (15:19). Wherever the apostles preached the gospel, God strengthened their testimony "with signs, wonders and various miracles, and gifts of the Holy Spirit" (Heb. 2:4). For example, on his missionary journeys Paul restored a lame man (Acts 14:8–10), cast out demons, healed the sick (Acts 16:18; 19:11–

---

47. The translation of the term *superapostles* in the Syriac Peshitta, "the very highest apostles" (11:5 and 12:11), suggests irony. Compare "the very chiefest apostles" (KJV).

48. James McCloskey, "The Weakness Gospel," *BibToday* 28 (1990): 235–41.

49. Refer to Karl Heinrich Rengstorf, *TDNT,* 7:258–59.

12), and raised the dead (Acts 20:10). The power of God to heal, restore, and give life authenticated Paul's apostleship.

God disclosed Paul's genuineness to the Corinthians by performing signs, wonders, and miracles in their midst. The triad of signs, wonders, and miracles occurs elsewhere in the New Testament (see Acts 2:22; II Thess. 2:9; Heb. 2:4). By comparison, the combination *signs and wonders* is so common that it is considered a coined expression of Semitic origin.[50]

Do signs, wonders, and miracles differ? They are only aspects of the same phenomenon: a sign comprises a mark, a wonder prompts amazement, and a miracle relates divine power manifested in unique situations. Neither Jesus nor the apostles performed miracles to satisfy the public's curiosity. They performed them in response to faith or to increase faith (e.g., Matt. 8:5–10; 9:27–30; John 2:11). Nowhere in his epistles does Paul ever "write for the purpose of inducing people to believe in miracles."[51] For him, faith comes from hearing the message through the gospel of Jesus Christ (Rom. 10:17).

Paul uses the passive voice in this text, "The signs of an apostle were worked out among you," and the Greek reveals that these signs were thoroughly worked out. Indeed, everyone in Corinth was able to verify the signs of Paul's apostleship during the eighteen months of his ministry in that city (Acts 18:11).

Paul's apostolicity became increasingly visible as he continued the work of founding the church. They were performed with great perseverance, according to the writer of this epistle. We surmise that he reminisced about the opposition he had to endure from the Jews as they dragged him before Gallio's court (Acts 18:12). He also thought about his painful visit to the Corinthians (II Cor. 2:1). Throughout his ministry to these people, Paul never abandoned the church. Even after he left Corinth, he continued to care for the members of the congregation by sending them letters and emissaries.

13. In what respect, then, were you inferior to the other churches, except that I never became a burden to you? Forgive me this wrong!

a. "In what respect, then, were you inferior to the other churches?" In the preceding context Paul displayed irony (v. 11b). Again he reveals a trace of sarcasm by comparing the Corinthian church with other congregations he had founded. The people in Corinth knew that the apostle had been fair in his dealings with them and with the churches in Macedonia and Asia Minor. In reality, Paul had spent more time and energy on the Corinthian congregation than on any other church. They had precipitated many problems and had made many demands on him. Because of their problems, Paul wrote two canonical epistles that set forth divine revelation, profound theology, and practical advice for all churches throughout the ages.

---

50. Among others, Deut. 6:22; Neh. 9:10; Dan. 4:2; 6:27; Wis. 8:8; Matt. 24:24; Mark 13:22; John 4:48; Acts 4:30; 5:12; 14:3; Rom. 15:19; Heb. 2:4. See also I Clem. 51.5 and Barn. 5.8.

51. Alfred Plummer, *A Critical and Exegetical Commentary on the Second Epistle of St. Paul to the Corinthians*, International Critical Commentary series (1915; Edinburgh: Clark, 1975), p. 359.

Some scholars allege that in this text Paul berates the Corinthians for believing the false accusations his adversaries had spread. These opponents presumably had told the Christian community in Corinth that their congregation was founded by someone who was not a true apostle. Therefore, so they were told, they were inferior to all the other Christian churches.[52] However, this interpretation must be rejected, because in this epistle Paul refers only to the churches he has founded (8:1, 19, 23–24). Also, Paul does not want to boast about missionary work performed in the territories of other workers (10:16). All indications are that the apostle has in mind only the churches he himself had founded.

b. "Except that I never became a burden to you." Were the Corinthians disadvantaged as they compared themselves with the churches in Macedonia and Asia Minor? Certainly not, because Paul never charged anyone for his services. Even when Paul was in need he did not become a burden to the Corinthian congregation. On the contrary, Christian brothers from the Macedonian churches brought him monetary gifts to meet his need (11:9).

c. "Forgive me this wrong!" According to the customs of that day, teachers had to be paid for their services. If they refused to take the money, they indicated that their work was inferior and not worthy of pay. The congregation was perhaps offended by Paul's refusal, especially when they noticed that Christians from other churches brought him gifts. If I have offended you in this matter, Paul is saying, please forgive me (consult the commentary on 11:9).

Greek Words, Phrases, and Constructions in 12:11–13

Verse 11

γέγονα ἄφρων—the perfect tense of the verb γίνομαι (I become, am) indicates that although Paul was a fool only for a time, the stigma remains. The Majority Text inserts the present participle καυχώμενος (boasting) after the word *fool:* "I have become a fool in boasting" (NKJV). But the better manuscripts omit the participle.

ὤφειλον—the imperfect tense with the personal pronoun ἐγώ puts a continued burden on Paul ("I was obligated"). The Corinthians were obliged to commend Paul. When they failed to fulfill their duty, Paul himself had to show his credentials.[53]

Verses 12–13

τοῦ ἀποστόλου—the definite article refers to the whole class of apostles.[54]
κατειργάσθη—the aorist passive of the compound verb implies that God is the agent. Also, the compound denotes that the action is done thoroughly. Compare Philippians 2:12.

---

52. Hans Lietzmann, *An die Korinther I/II,* augmented by Werner G. Kümmel, Handbuch zum Neuen Testament 9 (Tübingen: Mohr, 1969), p. 158; Rudolf Bultmann, *The Second Letter to the Corinthians,* trans. Roy A. Harrisville (Minneapolis: Augsburg, 1985), p. 232; Phillipp Bachmann, *Der zweite Brief des Paulus,* Kommentar zum Neuen Testament series (Leipzig: Deichert, 1922), p. 405.

53. Consult Robert Hanna, *A Grammatical Aid to the Greek New Testament* (Grand Rapids: Baker, 1983), p. 333.

54. Robertson, *Grammar,* p. 408. Martin (*II Corinthians,* p. 425) translates the definite article as "a [true] apostle."

τί γάρ ἐστιν ὅ ἡσσώθητε—the relative pronoun ὅ is difficult to analyze and makes the clause complicated. Moule translates, "What is there in regard to which you came off worse. . . ?"[55] The verb ἡσσώθητε is the aorist of ἑσσόομαι (I am inferior to) with ὑπέρ (than) as the preposition of comparison.

b. Gratuitous Service
12:14–15

Once more Paul introduces the topic of the gratuitous service he has supplied to the Corinthian congregation (11:11). He desires that nothing stand between him and the presentation of the gospel—not even money. His life is characterized by constant readiness to serve the Lord in any situation, and in Corinth Paul spends his life for the local people.

14. Look, this is now the third time that I am ready to come to you, and I will not burden you. I do not want your money, but you. For the children ought not to gather treasures for their parents, but the parents for their children.

a. "Look, this is now the third time that I am ready to come to you, and I will not burden you." Paul begins a new paragraph and calls attention to something special, namely, his forthcoming visit to Corinth. Hence, he writes "Look!"

Paul is not saying that he has made preparations to go to Corinth and has been hindered. The epistle itself defies such an interpretation, because in 13:1 he writes that it is now his third visit to the Corinthians. Directly and indirectly he informs the people about his proposed visit (10:2; 12:20–21; 13:1, 10).

During his first visit to Corinth, he founded the church while he stayed with tentmakers Priscilla and Aquila (Acts 18:1–4). The second visit was painful, an experience he would not like to repeat (2:1). It is true that after his initial stay of eighteen months in Corinth (Acts 18:11), he had planned to visit the church twice, first by arriving there on his way to Macedonia and then by returning to the members and being sent by them to Jerusalem (1:15–16; I Cor. 16:5–7). With this arrangement, they would have benefitted twice from his intended visit. Unfortunately, his plan was never realized because of a conflict that needed attention. After Paul had taken care of the matter, he was ready to pay the Corinthians a third visit.

In the preceding chapter Paul had already told the people in Corinth that he would not become a financial burden to them. He wanted to be independent, so that no one would ever be able to say that he was bound to them in a patron-client relationship.[56] He wrote, "And in everything I have kept and will keep myself from being a burden to you" (11:9). At the same time, he had solicited money for the saints in Jerusalem. Not he but his assistants were to handle these

---

55. Moule, *Idiom-Book*, p. 131.

56. Jerome Murphy-O'Connor, *The Theology of the Second Letter to the Corinthians*, New Testament Theology series (Cambridge: Cambridge University Press, 1991), p. 97. See also Furnish, *II Corinthians*, p. 508.

gifts. He wanted to shield himself from any suspicion of using the money for personal interests (see I Cor. 16:4; II Cor. 8:20).

b. "I do not want your money, but you." Paul is not interested in financial advancement. Instead he has his mind set on the spiritual welfare of the Corinthian congregation. Even though he already had made it clear that he would not ask the members for money, he again states the matter forthrightly: "I seek not your money but your very souls." He wants to see them prosper spiritually.

c. "For the children ought not to gather treasures for their parents, but the parents for their children." The apostle borrows an illustration from family life. While children are still at home, their parents provide for them in all their material needs: food, clothing, and untold other items. At that stage in life, children do not build up the material resources of the parents. Treasures are gathered by parents for their children, who become heirs; parents rarely inherit the treasures of their children. King Solomon wisely observes, "Houses and wealth are inherited from parents" (Prov. 19:14a). An exception must be made in a case where sick or aging parents are dependent on the help of their children.[57]

Paul's illustration is meant to tell the Corinthians that they are his spiritual children and that he is their spiritual father (I Cor. 4:14–15; II Cor. 6:13; compare I Thess. 2:11). In that capacity he grants them untold spiritual riches through Jesus Christ, and they are heirs (Rom. 8:17). Hence, as children they are dependent on him and not he on them. However, as he confers on them his loving care in the setting of the household of faith, he expects that they, as obedient children, show genuine love to him. Children, then, may show their love by presenting gifts to their parents. R. C. H. Lenski aptly asks, "Since when dare a parent not accept a little present from his grateful children?"[58] Paul, however, was not looking for monetary gifts from the Philippians when they repeatedly sent him financial aid. Instead he was interested in seeing spiritual dividends flowing from his work among them (Phil. 4:16–17).

15. I would most gladly spend [everything] and be expended for you. If I love you to a greater degree, am I to be loved less?

a. "I would most gladly spend [everything] and be expended for you." In this sentence Paul stresses the pronoun *I*, which has the force of "I myself." He calls attention to himself as their spiritual father, who gives leadership and sets the tone. Next, he writes an adverb in the superlative form, "most gladly"; that is, without reservation he offers himself for the Corinthians (compare 6:11–12; 7:3; Phil. 2:17). He overlooks the faults and shortcomings of the Christians in Corinth and makes it known that he sacrifices himself for them.

The Greek has a play on words that we are able to reproduce in English: spend and be expended. We have supplied an object ("everything"), which is lacking in the Greek text, for the transitive verb *to spend*. At other places where the verb

---

57. See the commentaries of Calvin, p. 165; Windisch, pp. 399–400.

58. R. C. H. Lenski, *The Interpretation of St. Paul's First and Second Epistle to the Corinthians* (Columbus: Wartburg, 1946), p. 1315.

occurs, the object is provided (e.g., "[the woman] had spent all she had" [Mark 5:26]). Here Paul is saying that without any hesitation he would spend everything he possesses (money, resources, energy, time, and talent) on the welfare of the Corinthians. He told the Ephesian elders that he had not coveted anyone's silver, gold, or clothing; he worked with his own hands to supply his own need and the needs of his companions (Acts 20:33–34; see also I Thess. 2:9). In Corinth, Paul performed manual labor (tentmaking) to support himself, and so he released the church from any financial obligation to him. In a sense, then, Paul spent his own resources on the Corinthians.

The apostle willingly traveled the second mile for the sake of his people in Corinth. He says that he would most gladly be expended on their behalf; he would wear himself out for them. Both verbs, "spend" and "expend," control the conclusion of verse 15a, "for you." But the Greek is much more inclusive than the English; it literally reads, "for your souls,"[59] and means "for your temporal lives." The soul comprises both being and existence and is the "seat and center of life that transcends the earthly."[60] Paul is willing to sacrifice himself in the interest of providing a genuine life, that is, a full life, for the Corinthians.

b. "If I love you to a greater degree, am I to be loved less?" As Paul told the Thessalonians that he loved them so much that he shared the gospel and his life with them (I Thess. 2:8), so he told the Corinthians that he loved them dearly (11:11). As a father, he loved the members of the churches to the point of doting on them, especially the people in Corinth. Yet Paul expected reciprocal love (6:12–13) to build a healthy relationship.

There is not a trace of uncertainty in Paul's statement on love when he writes, "If I love you." This is fact, not wishful thinking. He loves the Corinthians more abundantly than other congregations. In total they have received four epistles (two canonical, a prior letter [I Cor. 5:9], and a painful letter [2:3]), two visits, and many envoys (Silas, Timothy, Apollos, and Titus). The members of that church should have responded with genuine affection and respect. The opposite, however, is true, as he receives more love from other churches than from the congregation in Corinth. Some translations treat verse 15a as a declarative sentence: "Though the more abundantly I love you, the less I am loved."[61] If we place a question mark at the end of the sentence, Paul's tone of voice becomes subdued. We concur with all the modern versions that favor the rhetorical statement.

Should Paul because of his abundant love for the people in Corinth be loved less by them? He could have demanded his rights and insisted on their reciprocal love. But he refrains from hard demands so that his love may touch the hearts and lives of the Corinthians. Love is not always reciprocated; at times it means

---

59. See NKJV, NASB, NJB, RSV, *Moffatt;* and the variations of *Cassirer* and *Phillips.*

60. Bauer, p. 893; Eduard Schweizer, *TDNT,* 9:648.

61. NKJV; see also the older translations: Martin Luther (German), Louis Segond (French), Casiodoro de Reina (Spanish), the Staten Vertaling (Dutch), and the Authorized Version (KJV).

loving the unlovable and spending money, time, and energy thanklessly. James Denney writes, "Spend and be spent, and spare not till all is gone; life itself is not too much to give that love may triumph over wrong."[62]

Greek Words, Phrases, and Constructions in 12:14–15

Verse 14

τρίτον τοῦτο—here is an accusative absolute, "this is the third time," that relates to the aorist infinitive ἐλθεῖν and not to the phrase ἑτοίμως ἔχω. In this context the verb ἔχω signifies "I am [ready]."

Verse 15

ἥδιστα—the adverb means "very gladly," and is an elative superlative (see v. 9).

ἐκδαπανηθήσομαι—the future passive of ἐκδαπανάω (I spend, exhaust) occurs once in the New Testament. As a compound it shows intensity. The agent in the passive construction is the life Paul leads. At least one translation presents this construction as a middle ("I expend myself," NIV).

περισσοτέρως—this comparative adverb is identical to the expression in 7:15 and means "especially."

εἰ—for the sake of emphasis, the Majority Text has added καί after this particle. The Western text omits the particle, but the better manuscripts retain it without the conjunction.[63]

ἀγαπῶ[ν]—most Greek editions of the New Testament have the finite verb ἀγαπῶ, but the Majority Text and the editions of Nestle-Aland[27] and United Bible Societies[4] have added a ν to make the word a present participle. We infer that this consonant has been added or deleted. But if we read it as a participle, then we must read it as if there is the verb εἰμι in a periphrastic construction: "If I am loving you more." Although the difference does not appear in translation, the participial construction is harder to explain than the finite verb and is preferred.

---

c. Scurrilous Slander
12:16–18

We surmise that Paul has received an oral report from a person who has recently come from Corinth and has informed the apostle about comments made by his adversaries in the church. Paul has now come to the point of directing a few remarks to the people who are slandering him in his absence.

16. Very well! [You say] that I have not been a burden to you. But, [you say] I, as a crafty fellow, took you in by deceit.

Gentleness has now changed to candor. The apostle must address slander that can be counteracted only by confrontation. He alludes to the words spoken by his opponents and which are believed by some members of the church. He

---

62. Denney, *Second Corinthians,* p. 366.
63. Consult Metzger, *Textual Commentary,* p. 517.

realizes that slander can change the relationship between him and the Corinthian church. Therefore, he must deal forthrightly with this evil and eradicate it.

Paul knows that an unwholesome sentiment exists in the church. He himself has received no money at all from the Corinthians, and they admit that he has not been a financial burden to them. And that is to his credit. Thus he writes the first words, "Very well!"

The next comment, introduced by the adversative *but,* exposes the sting of slander. The saying that Paul cannot be trusted has been circulating openly in Corinth. The background is that Paul, who refused to accept money for his services, has sent Titus to them with a request for a collection. The slanderers spread the rumor that under the guise of helping the poverty-stricken saints in Jerusalem, Paul and Titus are working to fill their own pockets. These doubters suspect that the money will not go to the poor but will remain with the apostle.

Paul uses the Greek term *panourgos,* which I have translated "crafty fellow." It conveys the idea of a person who is "ready to do anything" to achieve his purpose.[64] This odious expression originates not with Paul but with his opponents. They use a word that is a cognate of the one the apostle writes to describe the "craftiness" of the serpent deceiving Eve (11:3). Further, they accuse Paul of deceitfully taking in Corinthians who have put their trust in him.

17. Did I take advantage of you through any of the men I sent to you?

This is the first of four successive questions. This rhetorical question demands a negative answer from the recipients of this letter. Just as they admitted that Paul had never been a financial burden to them, so they have to state that neither he nor his envoys had ever manipulated them for their own benefit. Taking advantage of the people for one's own profit may characterize the intruders but not the apostle and his associates. Paul restates what he had written earlier,

> "We have wronged no one,
> we have corrupted no one,
> we have defrauded no one" (7:2).

The Corinthians know Titus to be a trustworthy person, one who has served them well in difficult times (see the commentary on 7:13b). They can hardly accuse him of fraud and exploitation. Neither Paul nor any one of the brothers he sent to Corinth has ever given an indication of deceit or self-interest. The apostle sent his envoys to fulfill specific mandates for the benefit of the church of Jesus Christ. Earlier, Timothy had visited them, and perhaps Apollos (I Cor. 4:17; 16:10–11, 12); both men could vouch for Paul's honesty and sincerity. The trustworthy Corinthian leaders Stephanas, Fortunatus, and Achaicus also could testify to Paul's integrity (I Cor. 16:17).

Paul writes the perfect tense of the verb *to send* to disclose that in the last few years he had commissioned a number of his associates to go to Corinth. The ef-

---

64. Bauer, p. 608.

fect of their missions is lasting, for the congregation has come to know them as men who are above reproach. If then the Corinthians acknowledge the integrity of these men, should they not also accept the one who sent them?

18. I appealed to Titus and I sent the brother with him. Did Titus take advantage of you? Did we not conduct ourselves in the same spirit? Did we not walk in the same footsteps?

a. "I appealed to Titus and I sent the brother with him." This is the first time since 8:6–8, 18–23 that Titus's name appears, now in the context of Paul's defense against slander. Titus had proven himself in the Corinthian church and had been appreciated for his honesty and trustworthiness. For this reason, Paul does not hesitate to use his co-worker's name. If the people in Corinth trusted his associate in connection with the collection for the poor in Jerusalem, then they should also respect Titus's sender, the apostle Paul.

Paul sent Titus to Corinth three times: first, to resolve the matter of the sinner who repented (2:13; 7:6, 13); next, to begin the work of collecting money for the saints in Jerusalem (8:6); and last, to complete the task of gathering the funds (8:17, 18, 22). Of these three, the first mission does not fit into the current discourse, which refers to finances. At this moment the third mission had not yet started. Note that the delegation for the third mission consists of three members: Titus, the brother who is praised by all the churches, and "our brother who has often been tested."

In 8:16–24, Paul uses the present tense (e.g., "we are sending" [vv. 18, 22]) to connote that his emissaries will leave soon for Corinth to finish the work of collecting. They will depart after Paul has completed this letter.

The second mission (8:6) harmonizes well with the present passage, for Paul writes the past tense ("I sent") and mentions only two persons, Titus and the brother.[65] (Incidentally, it is possible that the brother [8:18] is to be identified with the person mentioned in 12:18, but we lack certainty.) We conclude that Paul refers to Titus's second visit to Corinth, when he was sent there to initiate the collection (8:6).

b. "Did Titus take advantage of you? Did we not conduct ourselves in the same spirit?[66] Did we not walk in the same footsteps?" Of these three rhetorical questions, the first calls for a negative answer and the other two positive answers. The Corinthians were well acquainted with Titus and knew that he would not defraud them. They trusted Paul's associate, who testified to the apostle's veracity. And if this was so, the people would have to agree that Paul's conduct also was irreproachable. These two people are of one mind, have the same motives, and follow in each other's tracks.

---

65. Compare the commentaries of Grosheide (p. 457), Lietzmann (p. 159), Martin (pp. 447–48), Plummer (pp. 364–65), and Pop (pp. 376–77).

66. One translation has capitalized the word *spirit:* "Can you deny that he and I were following the guidance of the same Spirit and were on the same tracks?" (NJB). But Paul contrasts internal and external aspects, the human mind and human footsteps (compare 2:13).

Practical Considerations in 12:16–18

Feeling the rough edge of slander is far from pleasant for any of us. We feel that we are being robbed of our good name and reputation and that we are in bondage to disdain and derision. A natural reaction to slander is a defensive attitude, but in his writings Paul teaches us to use kindness as an antidote to slander (I Cor. 4:13).

Is not the devil our adversary who always seeks an opportunity to slander us before God (compare Zech. 3:1)? But should Christians always turn the other cheek and accept slanderous accusations as hardships that must be endured? Scripture does not teach that we must be silent rather than speak the truth. Paul defended himself against false accusations advanced by his opponents. He demonstrated to his readers his integrity, so that they in turn might defend him in his absence and prepare the way for a return visit to Corinth. Christians ought not to avoid confronting misrepresentations but in a positive manner they must uphold the truth. Theirs is the calling to be witnesses for the truth and to express it firmly.

Greek Words, Phrases, and Constructions in 12:16–18

Verse 16

ἔστω—the present imperative ("let it be so"), freely translated, means "granted" or "very well!"

ὑπάρχων—this present participle assumes the function of the verb *to be* and expresses a causal connotation: "because I am."

Verses 17–18

ἀπέσταλκα—the perfect active tense refers to Paul sending his associates on various missions to Corinth, "but he implies that there is no present harm or burden placed upon them as a result of those endeavors."[67]

τὸν ἀδελφόν—the definite article conveys the meaning *the well-known brother* and probably points to 8:18.

19 All along you are thinking that we make our own defense to you. No, before God, we are speaking as those in Christ. Indeed, dear friends, everything we do is for your edification. 20 For I am afraid that when I come, I may find you not as I wish, and that you may find me not as you wish. I fear that possibly there may be strife, jealousy, outbursts of anger, outbreaks of selfishness, slander, gossip, arrogance, and disorder. 21 I fear that again, when I come, my God may humiliate me before you, and I will mourn over many of those who have sinned earlier and have not repented of the impurity, sexual immorality, and sensuality they have committed.

4. Genuine Concerns
12:19–21

The apostle has completed his defense against the false charges disseminated by his opponents. He is finished with his indirect references to the collection for

---

67. See Hanna, *Grammatical Aid*, p. 333.

the poverty-stricken saints in Jerusalem. Now he devotes his attention to the moral lives of the Corinthians, so that when he visits them he may see a spiritual transformation. He stresses that his readers, too, must stand before God.

19. All along you are thinking that we make our own defense to you. No, before God, we are speaking as those in Christ. Indeed, dear friends, everything we do is for your edification.

a. *Textual problems.* The first sentence in this passage has a variant reading, as is evident in the translations. The Greek word *palai* (all along) is *palin* (again) in some manuscripts. Therefore, some translators have adopted the reading, "Again, do you think that we excuse ourselves to you?"[68] Adopting this reading is an easy way out of a problem. But the basic rule is that the more difficult reading is probably the correct one. In this case the harder reading is "all along," which nearly all versions have accepted.

Next, many translations present this first sentence as an interrogative (e.g., NAB, NIV, NRSV), while others see it as a declarative statement (e.g., GNB, NASB, NJB, REB, *Cassirer*).[69] In either translation, the message of the text remains the same.

And last, the Greek text has the verb *to think* in the present tense, which some versions present in the progressive perfect, "Have you been thinking all along?" (NIV). Paul communicates to the Corinthians that all the time they have been and are thinking of his defense. A direct translation of the present tense, "you think" or "you are thinking," however, makes good sense and is the choice of many translators (see GNB, NAB, NCV, *Moffatt*).[70]

b. *Personal defense.* Paul should have no need to defend himself in the presence of the Corinthians, because they themselves are living testimonies to recommend him (3:1–3). He knows, however, that they have questions concerning his defense in response to the accusations against him. Thus, he anticipates their reaction and immediately addresses their concerns. He does not have to prove his innocence, but he needs to set the record straight.

Paul sees himself as always being in the presence of God, whose all-seeing eye is ever upon him. He defends himself not in the presence of the Corinthians but in God's sight. The apostle knows that God is his Judge (compare 1:12; 2:17). Paul speaks as one who is in the fellowship of Christ; to be precise, he speaks with the authority of his Sender.

c. *Spiritual edification.* The purpose for Paul's defense is to serve the members of the church in Corinth. He writes, "Indeed, dear friends, everything we do is for your edification." The Greek expression *ta panta* is a more comprehensive term than we are able to convey with "everything" in English. He is saying that he de-

---

68. NKJV. Héring (*Second Epistle of Paul,* p. 97) adopts the reading "once more" and notes that it makes better sense.

69. Furnish (*II Corinthians,* p. 560) favors the declarative statement, "because, taken as a question, it would blunt the effect of the preceding series of questions (vv. 17, 18) to which it does not belong."

70. Robertson (*Grammar,* p. 879) writes that the progressive present "in such cases gathers up past and present time into one phrase."

votes the totality of his work to their spiritual edification. He views their spiritual life as a house that is in the process of being built. They are able to live in that house, but it is far from being completed. Paul the builder continues to advance the work performed on their spiritual dwelling (see 10:8; 13:10; Rom. 14:19; 15:2).

Whenever the apostle addresses the readers with the appellation *dear friends,* he not only speaks tenderly but also hints that he must have a painful word with them.

20. For I am afraid that when I come, I may find you not as I wish, and that you may find me not as you wish. I fear that possibly there may be strife, jealousy, outbursts of anger, outbreaks of selfishness, slander, gossip, arrogance, and disorder.

a. "For I am afraid that when I come, I may not find you as I wish, and that you may not find me as you wish." Paul expresses a measure of fear, because he knows that apart from the praise he has expressed for the church in Corinth, everything is not well. And the less pleasant aspects of life in the congregation now must be mentioned. He realizes that he will touch on sensitive matters and that his words will lead to reactionary sentiments. But he also knows that unwholesome lifestyles must be discussed in this concluding section of his discourse.

Earlier Paul experienced a painful visit and then determined not to return to the Corinthians. He is not interested in a repetition of that experience (2:1). At that time, the people humiliated him by not following his directives.

In a previous chapter, Paul had warned the Corinthians that on his arrival he would have to be bold toward some people in the congregation. He would not tolerate those who lived by worldly norms (10:2). And he told them that the words he wrote while he was absent would be turned into deeds when he was present (10:11). He feared that he would have to apply corrective discipline to recalcitrant sinners. The duplication of the word *fear* in the second part of this verse and at the beginning of the following verse underlines his anxiety. His question is whether the forthcoming meeting in Corinth will create exasperation for him and the church.

The second part of the introductory sentence exhibits a syntactical parallel that stresses the negative:

I may find you	you may find me
not as I wish	not as you wish

A father addressing his erring children implicitly expresses the hope that they will reform their ways. Even though the Corinthians had received Paul's teachings and admonitions, they neglected to heed them. With Paul's visit approaching, the apostle urges them to mind his words. If not, they will see him coming with a whip in his hand (I Cor. 4:21). For them the time has come to repent of their sins and to rededicate themselves to the Lord.

b. "I fear that possibly there may be strife, jealousy." Let no one think that the Corinthians had broken with their past and were living holy lives. Superficiality

435

was an integral part of their daily life, so that the sins of the past were those of the present. Paul inserts the word *possibly* to soften the impact of his message, but he voices apprehension that a number of sins are flourishing among them. He lists eight, which can be arranged into four pairs.

Strife and envy are the first two vices. In his first canonical epistle, after the greeting and thanksgiving, Paul rebuked the readers for the divisive spirit that has led to quarreling (I Cor. 1:11). He had even asked them to acknowledge that their strife and envy characterized them as being unspiritual and worldly people (I Cor. 3:3; see also Rom. 13:13; Gal. 5:20). Toward the end of the first century, Clement of Rome addressed a letter to the church in Corinth. In this letter the words *jealousy, envy,* and *strife* occur often,[71] an indication that these sins continued in that church. By allowing these vices to hold sway, the people in Corinth undermined the unity of the church and caused peace to vanish.

c. "Outbursts of anger, outbreaks of selfishness."[72] Only here in Paul's Corinthian correspondence do we read about "outbursts of anger" (compare Gal. 5:20; Eph. 4:31; Col. 3:8). The root of anger lies in human nature controlled by sin. Only by the power of the Spirit and through the renewing of the heart can anger be overcome.[73]

Selfishness (Greek, *eritheia*) is a vice exhibited in egoism; it creates strife in which individualism is the motivating force (Rom. 2:8). This vice can be detected in the laxity of the Corinthians toward the matter of the collection for the saints. Evidence seems to point to *eritheia* as referring to labor relations; the laborer exchanges his energy for wages and thus is interested in profits. By extension, the Corinthians cared more about their interests than about the collection.[74]

d. "Slander, gossip." These sins of the tongue can best be described as talking behind someone's back; gossip is described in Greek as whispering into someone's ear. Paul writes the plural form for both words to denote repeated instances. English usage calls for the singular of both nouns.

Both slander and gossip are transgressions of the command in the Decalogue not to utter false testimony against one's neighbor (Exod. 20:16; Deut. 5:20).

e. "Arrogance, and disorder." The Greek here also has the plural for both nouns, which we have translated in the singular. The Greek word *physiōsis* (arrogance) occurs only here in the New Testament, but it derives from the verb *physioō* (I make arrogant) and means to be puffed up or conceited. The verb appears often in I Corinthians (4:6, 18, 19; 5:2; 8:1; 13:4), which indicates that the sin of pride was not uncommon in Corinthian circles.

The term *disorder* occurs three times in the two canonical letters of Paul to Corinth (I Cor. 14:33; II Cor. 6:5; 12:20; see also Luke 21:9 and James 3:16). It refers to unruly situations that seemed to prevail in both the local church and society.

---

71. E.g., I Clem. 3.2; 4.7; 5.5; 6.4; 9.1.

72. Bauer, p. 309. Consult also Heinz Giesen, *EDNT,* 2:52.

73. Hans Schönweiss, *NIDNTT,* 1:106.

74. Friedrich Büchsel, *TDNT,* 2:660–61.

Paul takes a realistic view of the church and is fully aware that the sins he observed when he founded the congregation are still rampant. He forthrightly mentions their sins and hopes that the members will change their lifestyle from worldly behavior to godly conduct. When he arrives in Corinth, he anticipates seeing a change in the lives of the people. Yet he does not put his expectations too high, for some of the members are determined to continue their sinful way of life.

21. I fear that again, when I come, my God may humiliate me before you, and I will mourn over many of those who have sinned earlier and have not repented of the impurity, sexual immorality, and sensuality they have committed.

a. "I fear that again, when I come, my God may humiliate me before you." The repetition of words from verse 20a is obvious, although the Greek grammar gives readers a problem. The adverb *again* can be taken with the clause *when I come*, as is the case in most translations, or it can modify the main verb, "humiliate" (REB). The main verb should control the adverb. The grammatical problem can be solved, however, when we note that the adverb, because of its position at the beginning of the sentence, belongs to both the clause *when I come* and the verb *to humiliate*.[75] If we take "again" with the clause *when I come*, we do repeat wording from verse 20a. However, Paul often repeats a phrase to emphasize his message. And he adds "again" for the sake of variation.

The fear Paul expresses centers on the humiliation that was his part during his painful visit (2:1). And although that conflict had been resolved and forgiven (2:5–11), Paul has no desire to provoke another conflict that may cause him embarrassment.

What does Paul mean when he writes, "my God may humiliate me before you"? The agent who humiliates him is not the Corinthian church but God. Hence, in this matter he writes "*my* God," for his God grants him authority to strengthen the church (13:10). But God also exercises discipline. He cuts off those people who refuse to listen to him after they have been warned repeatedly. This necessary action is a source of grief and humiliation for Paul in the presence of the Corinthians. Paul serves as God's agent to enforce discipline, and so he will not spare those who continue in their sins (13:2). Earlier, the apostle told the Corinthians to expel from their midst the wicked man who committed incest (I Cor. 5:1–5, 13). Used by God for this purpose, Paul endured humiliation before the church of Corinth. He now fears that discipline may have to be administered again.

Paul is aware of the difficulties he will face upon his arrival in Corinth. We do not know what the outcome of his visit has been, but we are told that he spent

---

75. Henry Alford, *Alford's Greek Testament: An Exegetical and Critical Commentary*, 7th ed., 4 vols. (1852; reprint ed., Grand Rapids: Guardian, 1976), vol. 2, p. 718; Murray J. Harris, *2 Corinthians*, in vol. 10 of *The Expositor's Bible Commentary*, ed. Frank E. Gaebelein (Grand Rapids: Zondervan, 1976), 12 vols., p. 401; H. A. W. Meyer, *Critical and Exegetical Handbook to the Epistles to the Corinthians* (New York and London: Funk and Wagnalls, 1884), p. 693.

three winter months there (Acts 20:3) and that the church was pleased to contribute to the collection for the saints in Jerusalem (Rom. 15:26).

b. "And I will mourn over many of those who have sinned earlier and have not repented." The apostle rejoices when the church continues to grow spiritually but mourns when some members refuse to heed the teachings of the Lord. Mourning often pertains to sin that someone has committed; for example, he tells the Corinthians to be filled with grief over the incest committed by the immoral man (I Cor. 5:2). Like a parent, Paul mourns over those children who willfully go astray. He knows that unconfessed sin results in spiritual death.

The future tense, "I will mourn," indicates that Paul's sadness may not become reality if sinners repent. But if there is no sign of repentance, punishment follows. For Paul, mourning over sin is not a passive state but an active exercise of his apostolic authority. If need be, he will administer discipline, even excommunicating unrepentant sinners (13:10).[76]

Many people in Corinth have sinned but have not repented. Paul writes that "they have sinned," signifying impenitents who continue to pursue sinful lifestyles. On his painful visit to Corinth (2:1) he had warned them, and he again chastises them in this letter (13:2). Paul desires to see a genuine change of heart and a forsaking of sin. Indeed, many have turned from immorality and have been washed, sanctified, and justified (I Cor. 6:11). Throughout his correspondence with the Corinthians, he urges them to flee immorality and to purify themselves from everything that defiles body and spirit (I Cor. 6:18; II Cor. 7:1).

There is no indication in the text that Paul is thinking of persons who have recently been influenced by false apostles. He alludes to those sinners who have hardened their hearts, have lived sexually immoral lives, and have undermined decency in the life of the church.

c. "And have not repented of the impurity, sexual immorality, and sensuality they have committed." Impurity separates the sinner from worship and from God's people. The Old Testament teaches that this impurity relates to sexual processes, including adultery, rape, homosexuality, and discharges (Lev. 15:2, 16, 19, 25; 18:6–23).

In I Corinthians, Paul described sexual immorality as a sin that the Corinthians had to flee (5:1; 6:13, 18; 7:2).

The term *sensuality* in this context appears to connote sexual sins. Elsewhere in his epistles, Paul links two or three aspects of immorality (Gal. 5:19; Eph. 5:3; Col. 3:5).[77]

These sins separate the sinner from the body of the Lord Jesus Christ. Members of that body ought not to engage in the sins of sexual immorality. If they continue to indulge in them after they have been repeatedly warned, they show that they are spiritually dead.

---

76. Consult Windisch, *Der Zweite Korintherbrief,* p. 410.

77. Refer to Joseph Jensen, "Does *Porneia* Mean Fornication: A Critique of Bruce Malina," *NovT* 20 (1978): 161–84.

Greek Words, Phrases, and Constructions in 12:19–21

Verse 19

πάλαι—numerous manuscripts, the Western text, Majority Text, and translations have the reading πάλιν (again), which fits the context. But the more difficult reading in the better witnesses is the word πάλαι (all along).[78]

τῆς ὑμῶν οἰκοδομῆς—the position of the personal pronoun denotes emphasis: "your edification" (see 9:2).

Verses 20–21

οὐχ—this negative particle modifies not the verb εὕρω (I find) in the subjunctive but the verb θέλω (I wish) in the indicative.

ἔρις, ζῆλος—the better manuscripts present these two nouns in the singular. Others have the plural to conform with the succeeding nouns that are plural.

ἐλθόντος μου—"when I come." This genitive absolute construction is not quite correct grammatically because of the personal references to Paul elsewhere in the sentence.

τῶν προημαρτηκότων—the perfect active participle is a compound with the preposition προ (before). The definite article denotes a class of people and the perfect tense lasting action. However, the aorist active participle μετανοησάντων (repented) indicates single action. The two participles are controlled by one definite article signifying one group of people and two aspects.

Summary of Chapter 12

The apostle continues to boast, not for self-promotion but for God's glory. He counteracts the boasts of his opponents by saying that he has received visions and revelations from the Lord. He modestly refers to himself by talking about a man in Christ who was privileged to ascend to the third heaven, that is, paradise. There he heard things that he is not allowed to repeat. Thus, he is unable to boast about heavenly things. Instead he boasts about his weaknesses.

The celestial experience can lead to sinful pride. To keep Paul from such sin, the Lord sends a messenger of Satan to torment him with a thorn in the flesh. Three times Paul pleads with the Lord to remove this affliction. The answer he receives is that God's grace is sufficient for him, because God's power is perfected in Paul's weakness. Paul, accepting the Lord's response, exults in infirmities and other impediments.

Forced against his will to boast, Paul states that he has made a fool of himself. Not he but the recipients of his epistle should have commended him in the presence of the superapostles. Paul lists the marks of apostolicity: signs, wonders, and miracles. He also states that he has never been a burden to the readers, that he did not ask for their possessions, and that parents should gather treasures for the children. Neither he nor Titus ever took advantage of them.

---

78. See Metzger, *Textual Commentary,* p. 518.

Paul concludes by telling the readers that he has done everything to strengthen them in the knowledge that he lives in God's presence. He expresses his fear that on his arrival there may be misconceptions. He warns them to avoid the sins of strife, jealousy, anger, and selfishness. He speaks directly to those who have continued to live immorally and have not repented.

13

Apostolic Authority, *part 4*

(13:1–10)

**and
Conclusion**

(13:11–13)

Outline (continued)

13

1 This is now the third time that I am coming to you. "Every matter must be established on the testimony of two or three witnesses." 2 When I was with you the second time and now, although away from you, I forewarned and forewarn again those who sinned in the past and all the rest of them: When I return, I will not spare them. 3 Because you are demanding proof that Christ is speaking through me, [know that] he is not weak toward you but strong within you. 4 For indeed, he was crucified in weakness but lives by the power of God. For indeed, we are weak in him, but we shall live with him by the power of God to serve you.

5 Examine yourselves to see whether you are living in the faith; test yourselves. Or do you not know that Jesus Christ is within you? Unless perhaps you fail the test. 6 I hope that you will realize that we have not failed. 7 But we pray to God that you will not do anything wrong—not that we seem to have passed the test, but that you do that which is right even as if we seem to have failed. 8 For we are not able to do anything against the truth but only for the truth. 9 For we rejoice when we are weak and you are strong. And this we pray that you may be made perfect. 10 Therefore, I write these things while absent from you, so that when I am with you I will not have to act harshly on the authority that the Lord has given me for your edification and not for your destruction.

---

5. Final Warnings
13:1–10

Many commentators see not a break at the beginning of this chapter but rather a continuation of the admonitions Paul wrote in the preceding paragraph (12:19–21).[1] Even though this discourse is closely related to the previous chapter, there is an unequivocal emphasis on Paul's forthcoming visit to the congregation in Corinth. He already told the readers that he would visit them (12:14), but now he speaks judicially about verifying testimony, issuing warnings, their demand for proof of authority, and the manifestation of divine power.

a. Christ's Powerful Word
13:1–4

1. This is now the third time that I am coming to you. "Every matter must be established on the testimony of two or three witnesses."

No congregation founded by Paul received more care, advice, and visits from the apostle than the church of Corinth. Paul had stayed with the Corinthians a year and a half during his first visit (Acts 18:11). While he was in Ephesus for three years (Acts 20:31), he wrote at least three letters to Corinth; afterward he penned one from Macedonia. He embarked from Ephesus to pay the people in

---

1. See the commentaries of Bachmann, Barrett, Bultmann, Lietzmann, and Martin.

Corinth his second and painful visit (II Cor. 2:1). In Ephesus he received a letter from the Corinthian church (I Cor. 7:1), and three of its members visited him there (I Cor. 16:17). No church meant more to Paul than the troublesome community of Corinth.

Paul purposely mentions his forthcoming visit once more (12:14) to focus attention on the importance of it. Earlier he had threatened to punish the arrogant in Corinth with a whip (I Cor. 4:21); these were probably the people he rebuked on his second visit. Now he tells them that, if necessary, he will come to hold court and administer discipline. He would rather see people repent and change their ways than come and apply corrective measures. To make his point, he quotes from the law of Moses: "A matter must be established by the testimony of two or three witnesses" (Deut. 19:15).

Whenever a court brought a defendant to justice in biblical times, it rejected as insufficient evidence the testimony that came from only one witness (Num. 35:30; Deut. 17:6; I Tim. 5:19; Heb. 10:28). Protecting the innocent, a civil or an ecclesiastical judge would ask for more than one witness to bring indisputable proof of wrongdoing (Matt. 18:16).[2]

Why does Paul quote the Scriptures at this point? The most common answer comes from both ancient and modern commentators who have identified three witnesses and three visits.[3] We are unable to ascertain whether on his initial visit Paul issued warnings. Yet we know from a fragment of the missing letter that the Corinthians were not to associate with sexually immoral people (I Cor. 5:9). The emphasis is on the repetition of his warnings, which he issued at least three times. Paul admonished recalcitrant Corinthians in letters and on visits. He repeatedly warned those who indulged in sexual immorality and other sins. By writing this epistle he again warns them; if they do not listen, he will take decisive action when he returns to Corinth.[4] In addition, he will now meet those Corinthians who have been influenced by the false apostles. Should Paul have to call witnesses at a meeting in Corinth, he can summon Titus and other leaders to testify.

The connection between the ordinal numbers (second and third visits) and the cardinal numbers ("two or three witnesses") is not accidental. Throughout his letters to Corinth, Paul reveals an abundance of direct and indirect quotations from the five books of Moses,[5] the Psalms and Proverbs, and the Prophets.

---

2. SB 1:790–91.

3. Chrysostom, Theodoret, Calvin, Lietzmann, Plummer, Bachmann, Alford, Windisch, Allo, Grosheide, Pop, Wendland, Bruce, and Barrett.

4. C. K. Barrett, "Paul's Opponents in 2 Corinthians," in *Essays on Paul* (Philadelphia: Westminster, 1982), pp. 76–77; see also *The Second Epistle to the Corinthians*, Harper's New Testament Commentaries series (New York: Harper and Row, 1973), p. 333; Ralph P. Martin, *2 Corinthians*, Word Biblical Commentary 40 (Waco: Word, 1986), pp. 469–70; D. A. Carson, *From Triumphalism to Maturity* (Grand Rapids: Baker, 1984), p. 173; Victor Paul Furnish, *II Corinthians: Translated with Introduction, Notes and Commentary*, Anchor Bible 32A (Garden City, N.Y.: Doubleday, 1984), p. 575.

5. E.g., references to the Pentateuch are twelve from Genesis, twenty one from Exodus, three from Leviticus, fourteen from Numbers, and twenty from Deuteronomy.

Both Jewish and Gentile Christians memorized many of these references and quoted them proverbially. Paul makes a mental leap from the ordinal numbers *second* and *third* to the cardinal numbers *two* and *three* in the proverbial passage of Deuteronomy 19:15.[6] He communicates the meaning of this proverb, because the people knew Jesus' teaching on church discipline (Matt. 18:16). They indeed expelled a person who had committed incest (I Cor. 5:1–5). Also, all the churches were fully acquainted with the rule of requiring the testimony of two or three witnesses (I Tim. 5:19).

2. When I was with you the second time and now, although away from you, I forewarned and forewarn again those who sinned in the past and all the rest of them: When I return, I will not spare them.

The parallel Greek construction of the Greek text becomes cumbersome in translation. I have departed from Paul's original word order in which he writes three clauses, each having two components joined by the conjunction *and*. He concludes the parallel with a warning.

I have forewarned	and	I am forewarning
while present the second time	and	absent now
to those who have sinned earlier	and	to all the rest
	when I return, I will not spare	

From the parallel construction we learn that during Paul's second visit to Corinth he reproached those who sinned in the past, and during his third visit he will admonish all the others.[7] But this does not mean that he will not take to task the sexually immoral people when he meets them. Nor does the phrase *all the others* have a clearly defined meaning. Paul indicates only that since his last encounter with these stubborn sinners, he also faces people who have followed his opponents. And he encounters other people who have overlooked flagrant sin in the Corinthian community (see the commentary on 2:6). In the last verse of the preceding chapter, Paul remarks that he mourns over those who not only sinned in the past but also continue in their sin (12:21). He now uses the same verbal construction: "those who have sinned in the past." The sin of immorality strangles them.

The apostle is not interested in a confrontation. His ardent desire is that all those sinners repent and follow the Lord Jesus Christ. Then they will support and strengthen the body of Christ. But if they fail to listen and obey, Paul will not spare them when he arrives in Corinth. He reminds them of his second visit, when he reproached them. Now away from them, he forewarns them in this let-

---

6. Hendrik van Vliet, *No Single Testimony. A Study on the Adoption of the Law of Deut. 19:15 Par. into the New Testament* (Utrecht: Kemink, 1958), pp. 2, 88.

7. Refer to John Albert Bengel, *Bengel's New Testament Commentary,* trans. Charlton T. Lewis and Marvin R. Vincent, 2 vols. (Grand Rapids: Kregel, 1981), vol. 2, p. 336; Philip Edgcumbe Hughes, *Paul's Second Epistle to the Corinthians: The English Text with Introduction, Exposition and Notes,* New International Commentary on the New Testament series (Grand Rapids: Eerdmans, 1962), p. 476.

ter. Further, as he confronted them during his painful visit, so he intends to confront them upon his third visit. The verb *to spare* has no direct object in the Greek text, but the implication is that Paul does not intend to acquit unrepentant sinners. He is not addressing the entire congregation, for then we would have expected him to write the plural pronoun *you* (compare 1:23). Omitting the direct object, he asks the readers to supply it and thus he makes them conscious of the fact that they cannot ignore flagrant sin in their midst. We are not told how Paul plans to execute his threat. We surmise that his option is to excommunicate hardened sinners from the community of believers.[8] The church in Corinth had to take action and, guided by Paul, remove evil from its midst.

3. Because you are demanding proof that Christ is speaking through me, [know that] he is not weak toward you but strong within you.

a. "Because you are demanding proof that Christ is speaking through me." The last sentence in the preceding verse and this sentence are closely related. Paul states the reason that he will not spare rebellious people: the Corinthians question his apostolic authority and want proof that they hear the voice of Jesus Christ. They realize that Paul is determined to deal with hardened sinners, but before any action can take place the people in Corinth demand proof of Paul's authority.

In the previous chapter (12:12), Paul had spelled out the marks of apostolicity. They should know that he had demonstrated these marks, for they had observed the power of the Holy Spirit at work in establishing the church. Conversely, Paul was aware that his opponents had exerted their influence in the congregation and had urged the members to ask Paul to prove his apostolicity. They used the Corinthians to pose the question: "Is Christ speaking through you?"

Here then is the heart of the problem that Paul is addressing in the last four chapters of this epistle: Is Paul an ambassador for Christ? Has he brought the Corinthians the message of Christ and does he speak with divine authority? In the concluding part of his discourse, Paul states their question, which he had answered already in other settings. Thus, he concludes his discussion on tongue-speaking and prophecy by saying, "If anybody thinks he is a prophet or spiritually gifted, let him acknowledge that what I am writing to you is the Lord's command" (I Cor. 14:37; see also Rom. 15:18). And in his chapter on the resurrection, he clearly states that he is equal to Christ's apostles, even though he is the least of them (I Cor. 15:9–11). For the Corinthians, to raise the question is to answer it in the affirmative.

Paul's meekness and gentleness had confused the Corinthians, who had been awed by the forcefulness of his adversaries. They should know, however, that if they doubt that Paul is an ambassador of Jesus Christ, they are distrusting Christ himself, who has commissioned Paul. In other words, instead of facing Paul when he comes, they will meet the power of Christ.

---

8. Consult John Calvin, *The Second Epistle of Paul the Apostle to the Corinthians and the Epistles to Timothy, Titus and Philemon*, Calvin's Commentaries series, trans. T. A. Small (Grand Rapids: Eerdmans, 1964), p. 170.

b. "[Know that] he is not weak toward you but strong within you." This sentence must be interpreted by its context. Paul is not saying that by becoming followers of Christ the Corinthians now experience the Lord's power within them. Rather, by doubting Paul and the divine message he delivers, they face a powerful Christ. To restore order and administer discipline, "the Christ who spoke in Paul was not weak, but mighty."[9] As Paul told the Corinthians in his first epistle, "If anyone disregards [the command of the Lord], he is disregarded [by God]" (I Cor. 14:38, my translation).

Scripture is replete with incidents in which God acted decisively against those who opposed his word. Listed are a few examples from both the Old and New Testaments:

1. The death of Aaron's sons Nadab and Abihu (Lev. 10:1–5)
2. Miriam and Aaron doubting Moses' leadership (Num. 12:1–15)
3. The death of Korah, Dathan, and Abiram (Num. 16:1–33)
4. The excommunication of the incestuous man (I Cor. 5:1–5)
5. Falling into the hands of the living God (Heb. 10:26–31)

Through Paul, Jesus had demonstrated his power with signs, wonders, and miracles performed in their midst (12:12). The power of his word had been at work also in the hearts and lives of the people. They were like a letter from Christ written "on tablets of human hearts" (3:3). They themselves would have to acknowledge Christ's power at work in their lives. But if they doubt the evidence, the consequences for them will be severe.

4. For indeed, he was crucified in weakness but lives by the power of God. For indeed, we are weak in him, but we shall live with him by the power of God to serve you.

a. *Parallels.* This verse features two sentences with parallel messages and wording. Both are introduced with an emphatic "for indeed." The subject of the first sentence is Christ and that of the second the plural personal pronoun *we.* Both sentences have "weakness" and "weak," the verb *to live,* and the phrase *by the power of God.* Also, both sentences have two clauses separated by the adversative *but;* the second lists two phrases, "in him" and "with him," and the purpose clause, "to serve you."

b. *Contrast.* "For indeed, he was crucified in weakness but lives by the power of God." This sentence affirms a truth concerning Jesus that unbelievers ridiculed. They considered Jesus' crucifixion an evidence of weakness, for they had expected him to walk away from the cross and be immune to the power of death. Instead, Jesus permitted the shame of being nailed to a cross on which he died as an evildoer cursed by God (Deut. 21:23).

---

9. Consult James Denney, *The Second Epistle to the Corinthians,* The Expositor's Bible series, 2d ed. (New York: Armstrong, 1900), p. 376.

Paul writes the word *weakness,* but what does he mean by it? Jesus assumed the figure of a servant who in human form "humbled himself and became obedient to death—even death on a cross" (Phil. 2:8; and see II Cor. 8:9). He shared in our humanity and thus partook of our human frailty. But Jesus also had to die on the cross to fulfill God's will. Submissive to that will, "he learned obedience from what he suffered" (Heb. 5:8). God made Christ to become weak and so take upon himself our sins, "that we might become God's righteousness in him" (5:21).

Conversely, Jesus comforted grief-stricken Martha by saying, "I am the resurrection and the life" (John 11:25; see 14:6). He lives by the power of God, so that his divine power surmounted his human weakness. He rose victoriously from the grave and triumphantly lives and reigns forever. The people who scoff at Christ will meet the Judge at their appointed time and face his power (compare I Peter 4:17–18).

c. *Result.* "For indeed, we are weak in him, but we shall live with him by the power of God to serve you." This sentence continues to explain the preceding verse (v. 3) by saying that Christ's power is at work in the apostle and his associates. The numerous scars on Paul's body silently testified to the suffering he had endured in the interest of advancing Christ's gospel. He had frequently faced death when he was beaten with rods, was flogged, and was stoned. But God spared him, so that the life of Jesus might be manifested in Paul (4:10). And through this life Christ strengthened and renewed Paul in a real and intimate way. The apostle's weaknesses were counterbalanced by the evidence of Christ's power at work in him (see 12:9).[10]

What is Paul saying with the clause, "but we shall live with him by the power of God to serve you"? He speaks primarily of God's power that is at work in him not merely for personal strength and stamina but also for administering discipline to rebellious Corinthians.[11] Notice that he writes the future tense ("we shall live") to indicate that when he is among them, God's power will be evident. As he already indicated in the first few verses of this chapter, he will exercise discipline, if necessary, not in his own name but by the power of God. "The display of power such discipline presupposes will be supported by nothing less than the power of the resurrected Christ."[12] And disciplinary action in the case of the Corinthians is for their own benefit. The succeeding context indicates that the members of the church must examine and test themselves to see if they are in the faith and have Jesus Christ in their hearts (v. 5).

---

10. Consult Colin G. Kruse, *The Second Epistle to the Corinthians: An Introduction and Commentary,* Tyndale New Testament Commentaries series (Leicester: Inter-Varsity; Grand Rapids: Eerdmans, 1987), p. 219.

11. Barrett interprets verse 4b eschatologically by writing that life with Christ "belongs primarily to the future" (*Second Corinthians,* p. 337). The context of Paul's discourse, however, is not futuristic but corrective.

12. Carson, *From Triumphalism to Maturity,* p. 176.

Greek Words, Phrases, and Constructions in 13:1–4

Verse 1

τρίτον τοῦτο—this combination means "this the third [time]," which in our idiom becomes "for the third time."

ἐπὶ στόματος—the preposition with the genitive signifies "on," and the noun *mouth* relates to the testimony that proceeds from it.

δύο μαρτύρων καὶ τριῶν—in English parlance we say, "two *or* three witnesses."

Verse 2

ὡς—the particle may denote duration ("while") or concession ("although"). The concessive meaning is preferred.

νῦν—a variant Western text and the Majority Text add the verb γράφω after the adverb *now* (see KJV, NKJV). But the better manuscripts support the reading without the verb ("I write").

ἐὰν ἔλθω—the particle normally introduces a conditional clause that expresses probability. But here it has a temporal connotation: "when I come."

εἰς τὸ πάλιν—this is an idiom in which the preposition is used figuratively related to time: "again, for another visit."[13]

ὅτι—this is not the conjunction *that*. It is the recitative ὅτι, which introduces a saying and functions as a colon followed by quotation marks.

Verse 4

καὶ γάρ—note that Paul uses this combination twice to bring out a parallel of "Christ" on the one hand and "we" on the other. The Majority Text has the particle εἰ after the first combination with the translation "For though" (KJV, NKJV).

ἐξ—the preposition governing the genitive case can be either cause or source.

εἰς ὑμᾶς—the second sentence in this verse is disjointed; it is difficult to determine whether to take the last two words with either "to live" or "the power of God."[14]

b. Prayer for Perfection
13:5–10

This is the last paragraph Paul writes before he pens his final greeting and benediction in the conclusion. He casts this paragraph in the form of exhortation and prayer. Not interested in having to deal harshly with the Corinthians, Paul urges them to test their faith in Jesus Christ to see whether he is living within them. If this proves to be the case, the apostle will not have to administer discipline. Thus, his prayer for the people in Corinth is for their restoration and maturity. He ends this segment with a summary of his lengthy discourse (12:19–13:10); and he states that his authority in Christ is not for their destruction but for their edification.

---

13. C. F. D. Moule, *An Idiom-Book of New Testament Greek,* 2d ed. (Cambridge: Cambridge University Press, 1960), p. 69.

14. Consult Bruce M. Metzger, *A Textual Commentary on the Greek New Testament* (Stuttgart and New York: United Bible Societies, 1994), p. 519.

5. Examine yourselves to see whether you are living in the faith; test yourselves. Or do you not know that Jesus Christ is within you? Unless perhaps you fail the test.

a. "Examine yourselves to see whether you are living in the faith; test yourselves." Paul continues with the subject of the preceding verses (vv. 2–4): he stresses self-examination of one's spiritual life and daily conduct. The last phrase in verse 4, "to serve you," forms the bridge between the preceding and the present text.

With two imperative verbs, "examine" and "test," the apostle emphatically instructs his readers to undertake the crucial task of introspection.[15] In the Greek, moreover, the personal pronoun *yourselves* precedes both imperatives for emphasis and is part of the commands. Paul, then, turns the matter on its head with respect to the Corinthians. They questioned whether Christ speaks through him, but he tells them to examine their own hearts to see whether Christ is living within them. They desire to find out whether Paul's credentials are genuine. But Paul matches this inquiry with an injunction for them to see if their own lives are authentic. He wants the readers to clean their spiritual houses before he arrives in Corinth, so that both they and he can enjoy peaceful and edifying relations.

Paul asks whether the readers are in the faith and indicates his confidence that they indeed are believers. The expression *in the faith* appears four times in the Greek text of the New Testament epistolary (I Cor. 16:13; II Cor. 13:5; Titus 1:13; II Peter 1:5). Paul is not referring to objective faith that is rooted in doctrine but to subjective trust in Jesus Christ. He has in mind the living faith of a believer who faithfully walks in the footsteps of the Lord and communes with him in prayer.[16]

True faith is active and constantly forces Christians to test themselves to see whether Jesus Christ through the Holy Spirit lives in their hearts. True faith testifies to intimate fellowship with the Father and his Son (I John 1:3).

b. "Or do you not know that Jesus Christ is within you? Unless perhaps you fail the test." The question Paul asks the Corinthians is rhetorical, and from them he expects an affirmative answer. The first word ("or") links the question to the preceding two clauses with imperative verbs. Having obeyed the commands, the readers are now asked to respond to the query whether Jesus Christ is living within them. We may call this question "a direct appeal to the consciousness of [Paul's] readers."[17] If they know that the Lord lives and dwells within their hearts, they consequently want to exalt him, do his will, and forsake evil.

---

15. Refer to Hermann Haarbeck, *NIDNTT*, 3:810; R. C. Trench, *Synonyms of the New Testament*, ed. Robert G. Hoerber (Grand Rapids: Baker, 1989), pp. 293–95. The verbs imply that the testing will have positive results; that is, the Corinthians will pass the test.

16. Compare Jean Héring, *The Second Epistle of Saint Paul to the Corinthians*, trans. A. W. Heathcote and P. J. Allcock (London: Epworth, 1967), p. 100 n. 6.

17. Charles Hodge, *An Exposition of the Second Epistle to the Corinthians* (1891; Edinburgh: Banner of Truth, 1959), p. 306.

The phrase *Jesus Christ within you* probably is a saying that originated with Jesus, who in his farewell discourse said to his disciples, "You will realize that I am in my Father, and you are in me, and I am in you" (John 14:20). Because the words appear more than once in Paul's epistles, we surmise that this phrase was a current saying in the early Christian church. No doubt Paul cites it here as a well-known formula.[18]

Paul makes a last comment, a declarative clause that borders on a rhetorical question requiring a negative response. His emphasis in this paragraph is on testing; for the Corinthians, he poses the possibility of failing the test. He knows that they are able to pass it, yet he wants them to contemplate the consequences of failure. Failure leads to hardening of the heart, and hardening of the heart to spiritual death.

Practical Considerations in 13:5

Churches with roots in the Reformation exhort their members to prepare themselves spiritually before coming to the communion table. They follow Paul's instruction not to come to the table in an unworthy manner but to examine themselves before they eat the bread and drink of the cup. If they fail to come prepared, they invoke God's judgment upon themselves (I Cor. 11:27–29).

We should not only prepare ourselves before celebrating the Lord's Supper, but also continually test our actions, words, and inclinations (compare Gal. 6:5). Human weakness, however, often causes us to underestimate the danger of failing to test ourselves. If failure occurs, our laxity turns into backsliding. Backsliding is characterized by failing to pray, to obey the message of Scripture, to worship, and to associate with fellow believers on the Lord's Day. It is a sad commentary on the church when corporate responsibility for oversight is lacking (Heb. 3:12–13; 4:1, 11; James 5:19–20). As a consequence, countless Christians gradually drift away from the Lord and, after some time passes, they no longer have fellowship with him. Every believer must give an answer to the question whether he or she is in the faith.

If I ask the question, "What does it mean to me to be in the faith?" I answer:

> I belong to Jesus Christ in this life and in the life to come;
> I dedicate my whole being to him as his faithful servant;
> I present my heart to him promptly and sincerely;
> I oppose sin and the works of the evil one;
> I long to be eternally with Jesus.[19]

---

6. I hope that you will realize that we have not failed. 7. But we pray to God that you will not do anything wrong—not that we seem to have passed the test, but that you do that which is right even as if we seem to have failed.

---

18. Gal. 2:20; Eph. 3:17; Col. 1:27. Compare Hans Windisch, *Der Zweite Korintherbrief*, ed. Georg Strecker (1924; reprint ed., Göttingen: Vandenhoeck und Ruprecht, 1970), p. 420.

19. Consult the Heidelberg Catechism, answers 1 and 32; Rom. 10:9; I Cor. 12:27; II Cor. 5:8–9; Eph. 6:11; John Calvin's motto.

a. "I hope that you will realize that we have not failed." When the Corinthians submit themselves to self-examination and seek the fellowship of the Lord through the working of the Holy Spirit, they will acknowledge the reality of Paul's directives. Paul and his associates have passed the test and are waiting for them to do likewise. When this happens, the Corinthians and Paul with his co-workers will be one in the Lord. More, the people in Corinth will recognize Paul as a true apostle of Jesus Christ. They will acknowledge that he has sought and will continue to seek their spiritual welfare by daily remembering them in prayer.

b. "But we pray[20] to God that you will not do anything wrong." In his epistles Paul describes himself as a man of prayer. Many times he writes that he constantly remembers the people and their needs in prayer.[21] Here he prays not that either God or he will wrong the Corinthians; instead, he prays to God that the readers will refrain from doing evil and do that which is good.[22]

The apostle calls on God to come to the aid of the Corinthians. He is asking for divine help to root out both evil practices in their conduct and inappropriate words directed against Paul. He prays that God may bring about a change for the good in the hearts and lives of the Corinthians.

Paul does not have to explain what he means by doing wrong. The Corinthians know that he refers to their conduct and the influence of his opponents. Those wrongs must be removed, so that when Paul comes to Corinth the relations between him and the people will be harmonious. He wants a continuation of the amity that characterized their association before the difficulties began.

c. "Not that we seem to have passed the test, but that you do that which is right even as if we seem to have failed." This sentence is the continuation of Paul's prayer.[23] In the first two clauses the negative *not* and the adversative *but* contrast the concepts of failing and doing right. The principal motif in Paul's argument is a change for the better in the spiritual lives of the Corinthians. When changes have taken place in the people, the apostle need not resort to discipline. He states his sentiment not out of selfish motives but out of a desire to advance the Corinthians.

Paul's adversaries, however, will attack him if the Corinthians repent of their sins. They will accuse him of being mild and meek, of failing to produce evidence of his apostolicity, and of not being Christ's spokesman. In their eyes, Paul's conduct proves that he is a failure when the Corinthians listen to him. But those members of the Corinthian church who take his words to heart will have to commend his integrity and authenticity. They will know that he has not failed

---

20. The Majority Text has the singular ("I pray"; KJV, NKJV, *Moffatt, Phillips*).

21. See, e.g., Rom. 1:9–10; Phil. 1:4; I Thess. 1:2–3; II Tim. 1:3; Philem. 4.

22. Hans Lietzmann argues that God is the subject of the verb *to do,* while Werner G. Kümmel objects, saying that the Greek expression ποιεῖν κακόν (to do evil) has "you" as subject. See *An die Korinther I/II,* augmented by Werner G. Kümmel, Handbuch zum Neuen Testament 9 (Tübingen: Mohr, 1969), pp. 161, 214.

23. Martin, *2 Corinthians,* p. 481.

the test, but instead has proven to be Christ's apostle. They will also acknowledge that Paul does not come to Corinth to protect his personal integrity; he comes as their spiritual father who promotes the interests of his children.

8. For we are not able to do anything against the truth but only for the truth. 9. For we rejoice when we are weak and you are strong. And this we pray that you may be made perfect.

a. "For we are not able to do anything against the truth but only for the truth." To say that verse 8 follows verse 7 is self-evident. But the word *truth* shows that verse 8 clarifies the hypothetical situation described in the previous passage. In the present context, what is the meaning of "truth"? Paul is neither dogmatic nor poetic in mentioning truth; he is utterly practical by asking the readers to look at reality rather than appearance. The Corinthians are advised to see everything in the light of truth. Let no one think that Paul played loosely with the truth in a seemingly contradictory way (see v. 7). As an apostle and an ambassador for Christ, he must promote truth at all times. By contrast, servants of Satan, who is the father of the lie, constantly subvert truth. Not so the servants of Jesus, who said, "I am . . . the truth" (John 14:6). With every word Paul speaks or writes, he promotes truth.

Paul's zeal for the spiritual well-being of the Corinthians coincides with his zeal for the truth, which is Christ's gospel. He proclaims the Word of God, the gospel of Christ, and the message of truth. He already noted that his opponents have proclaimed another Jesus and a different gospel (11:4). Conversely, Paul is Christ's apostle and can do nothing but represent him. Should he fail to do so, he would no longer be Christ's apostle.

b. "For we rejoice when we are weak and you are strong." At first sight, Paul appears to reintroduce the subject of weakness and strength without linking it to the preceding discussion. But we see the apostle responding to the content of verse 7 with two arguments, the first one in verse 8 and the other in verse 9. Each is introduced by the word *for*. When we see the arguments in sequence, we read a continuous discourse. Verse 9, then, explains verse 7b, in which Paul writes that he desires nothing better than that the Corinthians seek to "do that which is right even as if we seem to have failed." He rejoices in the truth (compare I Cor. 13:6) when he knows that the members of the church in Corinth are strong in their faith.

The contrast of weak and strong was the subject of the preceding chapter (12:8–10). Paul is not now saying that when he is weak, he is strong in the Lord. Rather, he points to himself as weak and to the Corinthians as strong. He writes the verb *to be weak* in the present tense to describe his condition and the present tense of the verb *to be strong* with reference to the Corinthians. He also uses the personal pronouns *we* and *you* for emphasis. His weakness and their strength is a source of joy for Paul, for their strength proves that he is an apostle through whom Christ speaks (v. 3). And their spiritual strength speaks "better than his own strength would do."[24]

---

24. Barrett, "Paul's Opponents in 2 Corinthians," p. 78.

Paul minimizes himself by saying that he is weak, so that the power of the gospel may energize the people in Corinth and make them spiritually strong. When he sees the local church at work through the Spirit's power, he rejoices. Then the Christians in Corinth are strong in the truth and serve the Lord in the light of his Word. The apostle rejoices and calls himself weak because not he but God has made the people strong.

c. "And this we pray that you may be made perfect." The last sentence in this verse refers to and repeats part of verse 7. Once more Paul says that he and his co-workers pray; he even specifies the content of their petition. They pray that the Corinthians may be made perfect. The process of making someone perfect is that of restoring him or her (see Gal. 6:1). Paul alludes to the spiritual restoration and the perfection of the Corinthians, which in this earthly life will always remain a process. His request to God is that the Corinthians will mend their ways and then as the body of Christ live in conformity with the teachings of the gospel. Restoration can come only by forsaking evil practices, striving to do good, living harmoniously with fellow believers, and obeying God. Reinier Schippers succinctly observes, "The life of the saints is to correspond to the grace given, and this itself is the standard to which they are to aspire."[25]

10. Therefore, I write these things while absent from you, so that when I am with you I will not have to act harshly on the authority that the Lord has given me for your edification and not for your destruction.

a. "Therefore, I write these things while absent from you, so that when I am with you I will not have to act harshly." Now Paul comes to the conclusion of his remarks and says that he writes these things while he is still away from Corinth. Some scholars state that the expression *these things* refers to only chapters 10 through 13.[26] Others think that with this summary statement Paul has in mind the entire epistle.[27]

However, I interpret this verse in relation to the reverberating echo of an earlier comment about his coming to Corinth (12:20, 21). In that comment, Paul expresses his fear that when he comes, he will find not everything well in the church. Paul has no interest in repeating his painful experiences in Corinth (2:1) when he visits for a third time (v. 1). He now prays that the third visit may be pleasant. (For a discussion on chronology and unity of the epistle, see the Introduction.)

The apostle repeats the concepts of being absent from and present with the readers of his epistle (see 10:1–2, 11; 13:2). His comment that he is absent is linked to the hope that he soon will be in their midst. Paul informs the church in Corinth that on a forthcoming visit some Macedonians will accompany him

---

25. Reinier Schippers, *NIDNTT*, 3:350. See also Gerhard Delling, *TDNT*, 1:476.

26. See the commentaries of Windisch (pp. 424–25), Furnish (p. 574), Martin (p. 485).

27. Ernest B. Allo, *Saint Paul Seconde Épître aux Corinthiens*, 2d ed. (Paris: Gabalda, 1956), p. 341; F. W. Grosheide, *De Tweede Brief van den Apostel Paulus aan de Kerk te Korinthe*, Kommentaar op het Nieuwe Testament series (Amsterdam: Van Bottenburg, 1939), p. 484; F. J. Pop, *De Tweede Brief van Paulus aan de Corinthiërs* (Nijkerk: Callenbach, 1980), p. 397.

(9:4). He also writes that he is ready to visit that church for the third time (12:14; 13:1).

This letter is written in preparation for Paul's visit, so that on his arrival he does not have to act harshly toward the Corinthians. The Greek adverb *apotomōs* (harshly; found only here and in Titus 1:13) comes from the verb *to cut off* and here implies that Paul is ready to deal severely with the people to the point of breaking relationships with them. Expecting a favorable response to his letter, Paul hopes to avoid the kind of painful clash that was his lot during his second visit.

b. "On the authority that the Lord has given me for your edification and not for your destruction." The wording of the last part of this verse is almost identical to that of 10:8b (see the commentary). Jesus called and commissioned Paul as missionary to the Gentiles and gave him apostolic authority to do his work. The Lord gave him the power to build and to destroy, as God appointed the prophet Jeremiah to "tear down, to destroy and overthrow, to build and to plant" (Jer. 1:10; see 24:6).

Even though Paul had to apply his authority in the case of the incestuous man in Corinth (I Cor. 5:1–5; and see I Tim. 1:20), he always sought to use authority to edify the members of the church. Jesus came to seek the lost and to lead sinners to salvation. His ambassadors strive to do likewise and dedicate their ministry to edifying the followers of Christ.

Calvin says that the gospel itself possesses authority, because it is "the power of God for the salvation of everyone who believes" (Rom. 1:16).[28] This power becomes evident in the lives of those who believe and obey the gospel; but those who refuse to listen to divine instruction face spiritual bankruptcy. No one desires the tearing down of relationships, not even God (refer to Ezek. 18:23, 30–32).

Before his conversion to Christianity, Paul tore down the church. Yet he spent the rest of his life to build it up.[29] Notice, therefore, the force of the negative adverb *not* in the last part of this verse.

Greek Words, Phrases, and Constructions in 13:5–10

Verse 5

εἰ—the particle followed by the present indicative of the verb *to be* denotes certainty and factuality.

ἤ—this little particle meaning "or" should not be omitted in translations, for Paul is asking a rhetorical question that demands a positive answer.

εἰ μήτι—the combination of these two words signifies "unless perhaps" (see Luke 9:13; I Cor. 7:5).

---

28. Calvin, *II Corinthians*, pp. 175–76.
29. Compare Carl Schneider, *TDNT*, 3:413.

δοκιμάζετε—the family members of this verb are well represented in the first part of this chapter: the noun δοκιμή (proof, v. 3); the verb δοκιμάζω (I test, v. 5); the adjectives ἀδόκιμοι (failing to meet the test, vv. 5, 7) and δόκιμοι (passing the test, v. 7). Philip Edgcumbe Hughes points out that "the corresponding sequence of terms in our English version . . . is inadequate to convey the force of the original."[30]

Verse 7

μὴ . . . μηδέν—the double negative in the subordinate clause is for emphasis: "no evil at all."[31]

ποιῆσαι—this is a timeless aorist infinitive, but ποιῆτε is in the present subjunctive to express a desire for continued action.

ὡς—the particle should not be overlooked, for it conveys the meaning *like* or *as*, in the sense of appearance.

Verse 10

καθαίρεσιν—this noun, derived from the compound verb καθαιρέω (I take down), connotes the process of tearing something down. The noun is a synonym of κατάρτισιν (restoration) in verse 9.

---

11 Finally, brothers [and sisters], good-by. Mend your ways, accept encouragement, be of one mind, live in peace, and the God of love and peace will be with you. 12 Greet one another with a holy kiss. All the saints greet you.

13 The grace of our Lord Jesus Christ, and the love of God, and the fellowship of the Holy Spirit be with all of you.

V. Conclusion
13:11–13

Paul's scroll is nearly filled, so that his final remarks in verses 11 and 12 are brief and to the point. In quick succession, he writes short clauses that summarize instead of explain his commands. Also, verse 11 repeats words used earlier in the epistle and thus serves as a concise recapitulation of its message.

The change in tone between the preceding paragraph, in which Paul admonishes the readers, and the letter's pleasant conclusion is obvious. This change can readily be explained if we understand that Paul uses the last lines to express his warm affection toward the Corinthians.

11. Finally, brothers [and sisters], good-by. Mend your ways, accept encouragement, be of one mind, live in peace, and the God of love and peace will be with you.

a. "Finally, brothers [and sisters], good-by." The word *finally* is a familiar word that Paul utters at the conclusion of a discussion or a letter (compare, e.g., Phil.

---

30. Hughes, *Second Epistle to the Corinthians*, pp. 482–83 n. 178.

31. A. T. Robertson, *A Grammar of the Greek New Testament in the Light of Historical Research* (Nashville: Broadman, 1934), p. 1173; Robert Hanna, *A Grammatical Aid to the Greek New Testament* (Grand Rapids: Baker, 1983), p. 334.

3:1; I Thess. 4:1; II Thess. 3:1; II Tim. 4:8). It serves to introduce a summary and is usually followed by instructions. In this instance, Paul takes leave of his readers by addressing them as brothers. The term *brothers,* which includes the women in the church of Corinth, communicates his deep love for the recipients of his letter. Whenever he writes this designation, he voices both tender care for his readers and simple equality; he places himself on their level.

Paul's good-by has a deeper meaning than a mere word of farewell, for the Greek word *chairete* conveys a measure of joy (see Phil. 4:4; I Thess. 5:16). Throughout this epistle, Paul has demonstrated his joy in relation to the Corinthians (2:3; 6:10; 7:7, 9, 16; 13:9). Joy is one of the characteristics a sincere Christian displays even in times of hardship, oppression, sorrow, and grief. The present tense of this Greek verb indicates that the characteristic of joy must continue to be part of a Christian's life.

b. "Mend your ways, accept encouragement, be of one mind, live in peace." In verse 9 the apostle wrote about restoration and being made perfect. Once more he pens the same word, but now in a verb form that conveys encouragement to restore everything in the lives of the Corinthians and to strive for perfection. The present tense in the translation "mend your ways"[32] reveals Paul's hope that the Corinthians will begin to do so before his arrival.

The words *accept encouragement* translate the Greek verb *parakaleisthe,* which is a command in the present tense of the verb *parakalein* (to summon, encourage, appeal to, comfort). The translations of this particular verb are unusually varied: as a passive ("be comforted," NASB) or as a middle ("encourage one another," NAB, NJB, TNT). Still other renderings are "Be of good comfort" (KJV, NKJV), "Agree with one another" (NEB), "Listen to my appeal" (NIV, NRSV, *Cassirer*), "Pay attention to what I have said (CEV; see also NCV, *Moffatt*), and "Accept my encouragement" (*God's Word*).

In his epistle Paul uses the verb *parakalein* seventeen times, but only here as a command. Elsewhere he writes the verb in the imperative with the meaning *encourage!* (I Thess. 4:18; 5:11; Titus 2:6, 15). Hence, I prefer to interpret Paul's admonition as his word of encouragement to the readers.

Next, he tells the recipients of his letter to "be of one mind." This exhortation occurs often in Paul's epistles. For instance, he urges the Romans to strive for unity (12:16; 15:5) and entreats Euodia and Syntyche in Philippi to live in harmony (Phil. 4:2; see also 2:2). Thinking along the same lines of biblical teaching means unity in the Christian faith but not necessarily uniformity. The Reformers of the sixteenth century allowed for freedom in interpreting Scripture, yet they noted that the church may never waver on the cardinal doctrines of God's Word. Christians must stand united in heart and mind against the attacks of the evil one. They are told repeatedly to love one another (John 13:34; I John 2:8; II

---

32. Bauer, p. 417. Some commentators interpret the verb as a passive ("be restored," Furnish, pp. 581–82, or "be perfected," Hughes, p. 486) and then must designate God as the agent.

John 5). Also, they are unable to act by themselves, but they can rely wholly on God, who grants them his love and peace.

Last, the apostle instructs the Corinthians to live in peace. Mindful of dissension in the church, Paul follows Jesus by exhorting Christians to live at peace with everyone (Rom. 12:18; II Cor. 13:11; see Mark 9:50). It is the peace that comes from God. This is evident from the Aaronic blessing to his people: "The Lord turn his face toward you and give you peace" (Num. 6:26).

c. "And the God of love and peace will be with you." After writing five imperatives, Paul adds a clause that he introduces with the conjunction *and*. He is not writing an afterthought but a benediction with which he and others customarily conclude their letters.[33] In these writings the phrase *the God of peace* occurs, but here Paul adds the word *love*. That God is love becomes clear in the first epistle of John (I John 4:8, 16), in which the writer discusses this attribute of God. Is there any difference between the phrases *God of love* and *love of God* (v. 13 [14])? The answer is no, because both words describe one of God's characteristics. God is both the source and the giver of love.

Sinful human beings daily receive God's love and peace. God is good to all (Ps. 145:9); he makes his sun to shine on the good and the bad and rain to fall on the just and the unjust (Matt. 5:45). But when people refuse to listen to his Word and continue to live in hatred and conflict, they fail to obtain God's love and peace. Therefore, Paul's command to live in peace is followed by his blessing of God's love and peace. His directive and his blessing should be understood as cause and effect, for love creates an atmosphere of peace.

Believers know that there cannot be pure love and abiding peace apart from God. They know that God effects reconciliation between himself and sinful humanity and that appeasement produces harmony (5:19). He grants his peace to all those who want to be reconciled to him and live in unity with one another. Hodge keenly observes, "We have here the familiar Christian paradox. God's presence produces love and peace, and we must have love and peace in order to have his presence. God gives what he commands."[34]

The assurance that God's love is with the Corinthians comes in the conclusion of this brief benediction: "the God of love and peace *will be with you*." The words echo Jesus' promise at the conclusion of the Great Commission: "And surely I am with you always, to the very end of the age" (Matt. 28:20). All those who listen obediently to God are confident that they are the recipients of his love and peace. The benediction is not a vague promise for the future but a sacred guarantee of abiding validity.

12. Greet one another with a holy kiss. All the saints greet you.

Most Greek New Testaments have two sentences in this verse, and so do many translations.[35] Others divide this passage into verses 12 and 13. This means that the chapter in these translations has fourteen instead of thirteen verses. Robert

---

33. Rom. 15:33; 16:20; I Cor. 14:33; II Cor. 13:11; Phil. 4:9; I Thess. 5:23; II Thess. 3:16; and Heb. 13:20.
34. Hodge, *Second Epistle to the Corinthians,* p. 311.

Estienne in 1551 and 1555 numbered the verses of the New Testament and gave thirteen to this chapter. But in 1572, the Bishops' Bible was published with four-teen verses, and most translators have adopted its numbering.[36] I have followed the sequence given in the Greek New Testaments.

Greeting one another with a holy kiss, a practice rooted in Jewish culture, was and still is customary and expected (Rom. 16:16; I Cor. 16:20; I Thess. 5:26; I Peter 5:14). A light touch of the lips against the cheeks, both left and right, common in many societies in the Middle East and elsewhere, was a standard practice in the early church.[37] The kiss was devoid of erotic implications, for the epistolary writ-ers call this practice holy. This description points to the context in which the cus-tom occurred, namely, among the saints. It meant that the saints formed the fam-ily of God and accepted each other as brothers and sisters. The kiss signified, then, that as family these people committed themselves to promoting love, peace, and harmony in the church.[38]

The second sentence in this verse voices Paul's striving for the unity of the church. "All the saints greet you" probably refers to the Macedonian churches, whose members were vitally interested in the spiritual well-being of the Corin-thians (9:2–5; 11:9). The word *all* includes these churches and reveals harmony in the churches that Paul had founded. At the same time it implies an appeal for unity in the Corinthian congregation.

13. The grace of our Lord Jesus Christ, and the love of God, and the fellow-ship of the Holy Spirit be with all of you.

Countless pastors pronounce this benediction at the conclusion of worship services. It is the blessing of the triune God to the believers who have "come to worship and leave to serve." The prayer is that the Father, Son, and Holy Spirit may endow the worshipers with the virtues of love, grace, and fellowship to equip them for service. Because of its trinitarian formula, this is the richest benedic-tion in the entire New Testament.

The order of the trinitarian formula differs from the sequence in which the Father is first, the Son second, and the Spirit last. Here the Son precedes the Fa-ther, which indeed is unusual. Earlier in the letter Paul alludes to the Trinity in the usual order (1:21–22; compare also Rom. 1:1–4). Peter in his introduction to his first epistle mentions the Trinity in the sequence of God the Father, the Spirit, and Jesus Christ (I Peter 1:2). We can only surmise that Paul's emphasis on the Lord Jesus Christ caused him to mention the Second Person of the Trin-

---

35. Nes-Al, UBS, BF, Merk, Majority Text; but the TR and Souter have fourteen verses. English trans-lations with thirteen verses are CEV, *God's Word*, GNB, JB, NJB, NAB, NRSV, SEB; others end the chapter with verse 14.

36. Consult Furnish, *II Corinthians*, p. 583.

37. Refer to John Ellington, "Kissing in the Bible: Form and Meaning," *BibTr* 41 (1990): 409–16.

38. See the commentaries of Denney (pp. 384–85), Martin (p. 502), Grosheide (p. 486); but Pop (p. 399) expresses some reservation.

ity first. His emphasis on the phrase *our Lord Jesus Christ* is evident throughout the epistle (1:2, 3; 8:9; 11:31; 13:13).

a. "The grace of our Lord Jesus Christ." This clause occurs also in 8:9 and at the conclusion of many epistles.[39] It is a benediction formula that features the concept *grace,* which must be interpreted to mean "the whole blessing of redemption."[40] Through his ministry, death, and resurrection, Jesus Christ showered his grace upon his people by saving them from their sins (Matt. 1:21).

b. "And the love of God." The grace of Jesus Christ comes first and the love of God follows. Through God's love, Christ's grace is extended to believers to be appropriated by them. God loved the world to such a depth that he gave his one and only Son for our salvation (John 3:16; Rom. 5:8). R. C. H. Lenski asks, "If the sinner bows his head at the pierced feet of the Lord because he is overwhelmed by the grace, shall he not be utterly lost in this ocean of the love which is as great and as blessed as God himself?"[41] The answer is affirmative, for this divine love is granted only to those people who believe and thus are recipients of eternal life.

c. "And the fellowship of the Holy Spirit be with all of you." The third divine gift is fellowship, which in some translations is rendered "communion." "Fellowship" conveys the sense of close companionship that in this case pertains to the Holy Spirit dwelling in the heart of a believer. Indeed, Paul indicates that the Spirit makes the body of the believer his dwelling place or temple (I Cor. 6:19).

A question, however, is the meaning of the genitive case in the phrase *of the Holy Spirit.* Is it a subjective or an objective genitive? The two preceding clauses feature the subjective or possessive genitive, for Paul has in mind the grace that emanates from Jesus and the love that God grants us. But do we have the fellowship that originates with the Holy Spirit (the subjective genitive) or do we enter into fellowship with the Spirit (objective genitive)? Scholars have defended either interpretation at length, while others argue that both interpretations are valid. Writes Kruse, "In any case Christians can share 'objectively' in the Spirit only if the Spirit himself as subject makes that participation possible."[42]

A last remark must be made concerning the words *be with you all.* Do they apply only to the third clause or to all three clauses? In view of Paul's other benedictions (see footnote 39), we do well to link the concluding remark to every one of the three clauses. Divine grace, love, and fellowship are extended without exception to all people who have put their faith and trust in Jesus Christ.

---

39. Rom. 16:20; Gal. 6:18; Phil. 4:23; I Thess. 5:28; II Thess. 3:18. See also I Cor. 16:23.

40. Calvin, *II Corinthians,* p. 176.

41. R. C. H. Lenski, *The Interpretation of St. Paul's First and Second Epistle to the Corinthians* (Columbus: Wartburg, 1946), pp. 1340–41.

42. Kruse, *Second Corinthians,* p. 224. See Ralph P. Martin, "The Spirit in 2 Corinthians in Light of the 'Fellowship of the Holy Spirit' in 2 Corinthians 13:14," in *Eschatology and the New Testament: Essays in Honor of George Beasley-Murray,* ed. W. H. Gloer, Festschrift for G. R. Beasley-Murray (Peabody, Mass.: Hendrickson, 1988), pp. 113–28.

Greek Words, Phrases, and Constructions in 13:12–13

ἀσπάσασθε—the aorist tense of the verb *to greet* normally appears as the customary greeting at the conclusion of epistles, with the exception of III John 15, where the present imperative occurs. To greet someone is a single action, not an extended process.

τοῦ ἁγίου πνεύματος—the question of subjective or objective genitive can best be solved by accepting both.

ἀμήν—the Majority Text concludes with the word *amen*. But the better manuscripts fail to support this reading.

Subscripts are many and varied. One has the abbreviated heading "To the Corinthians B." Another adds to this heading the name *Philippi*. Still others list the place of composition and the writers: "To the Corinthians, the second epistle, from Philippi by Titus, Barnabas, and Luke." One other witness reads, "The Second Epistle to the Corinthians was written from Philippi, a city of Macedonia, by Titus and Luke" (see the KJV).[43] The shortest subscript, "To the Corinthians B," has solid manuscript support and thus appears as the title of this letter. The numerous variants are indicative of accretions and underscore our inability to affirm their veracity.

Summary of Chapter 13

Repeating himself, Paul informs the readers that he will pay them a visit for the third time. But this will be a visit to call forth testimony against those people who continue to live in sin. Paul has repeatedly warned them, and in his letter he again forewarns them to repent, so that upon his arrival in Corinth he no longer has to deal with problems. These people doubt that Paul speaks with the authority of Christ, but he will prove that he is no weakling. Through God's power living within him, he serves the people of Corinth.

Paul turns matters around by exhorting the Corinthians to examine their own hearts to see if Christ Jesus lives there. The apostle does not want to see the people fail that test, for he himself did not fail it. He pleads with them not to err but to live in the sphere of truth. His prayer is for the Corinthians to be strong and to strive for perfection. Paul writes about these matters so that when he comes to them he may find them responsive. He wants to edify them in the faith with the authority that the Lord has given him.

The letter ends with a final appeal to strive for restoration, unity, and peace. Paul exchanges customary greetings and concludes his epistle with a trinitarian benediction that stresses divine grace, love, and fellowship.

---

43. Metzger, *Textual Commentary,* p. 519.

Bibliography*

Commentaries

Alford, Henry. *Alford's Greek Testament: An Exegetical and Critical Commentary.* 7th ed. 4 vols. 1852. Reprint ed. Grand Rapids: Guardian, 1976.

Allo, Ernest B. *Saint Paul Seconde Épître aux Corinthiens.* 2d ed. Paris: Gabalda, 1956.

Bachmann, Phillipp. *Der zweite Brief des Paulus an die Korinther.* Kommentar zum Neuen Testament series. Leipzig: Deichert, 1922.

Barnett, Paul. *The Message of 2 Corinthians: Power in Weakness.* Bible Speaks Today series. Leicester and Downers Grove: InterVarsity, 1988.

Barrett, C. K. *The Second Epistle to the Corinthians.* Harper's New Testament Commentaries series. New York: Harper and Row, 1973.

———. *A Commentary on the First Epistle to the Corinthians.* London: Adam and Charles Black, 1971.

Beasley-Murray, G. R. *2 Corinthians.* In vol. 11 of the *Broadman Bible Commentary,* edited by C. J. Allen. 12 vols. Nashville: Broadman, 1971.

Bengel, John Albert. *Bengel's New Testament Commentary.* Translated by Charlton T. Lewis and Marvin R. Vincent. 2 vols. Grand Rapids: Kregel, 1981.

Bernard, J. H. *The Second Epistle to the Corinthians.* Vol. 3 of *The Expositor's Greek Testament,* edited by W. R. Nicoll. 1910. Reprint ed. Grand Rapids: Eerdmans, 1961.

Best, Ernest. *Second Corinthians.* Interpretation series. Atlanta: John Knox, 1987.

Betz, Hans Dieter. *2 Corinthians 8 and 9: A Commentary on Two Administrative Letters of the Apostle Paul.* Edited by George W. MacRae. Hermeneia: A Critical and Historical Commentary on the Bible. Philadelphia: Fortress, 1985.

Bratcher, R. G. *A Translator's Guide to Paul's Second Letter to the Corinthians.* London: United Bible Societies, 1983.

Bruce, F. F. *1 and 2 Corinthians.* New Century Bible series. London: Oliphants, 1971.

Bultmann, Rudolf. *The Second Letter to the Corinthians.* Translated by Roy A. Harrisville. Minneapolis: Augsburg, 1985.

Calvin, John. *The Second Epistle of Paul the Apostle to the Corinthians and the Epistles to Timothy, Titus and Philemon.* Translated by T. A. Small. Calvin's Commentaries series. Grand Rapids: Eerdmans, 1964.

* Consult the Index of Authors and the footnotes for referemces to the numerous books and articles in this commentary.

Bibliography

Clarke, Adam. *The Bethany Parallel Commentary on The New Testament.* Minneapolis: Bethany House, 1983.

Cranfield, C. E. B. *The Epistle to the Romans.* 2 vols. International Critical Commentary series. Edinburgh: Clark, 1979.

de Boor, Werner. *Der zweite Brief an die Korinther.* 4th ed. Wuppertaler Studienbibel. Wuppertal: Brockhaus, 1978.

Denney, James. *The Second Epistle to the Corinthians.* 2d ed. The Expositor's Bible series. New York: Armstrong, 1900.

Duduit, Michael. *Joy in Ministry: Messages from II Corinthians.* Grand Rapids: Baker, 1989.

Fallon, Francis T. *2 Corinthians.* New Testament Message series. Wilmington, Del.: Glazier, 1980.

Furnish, Victor Paul. *II Corinthians: Translated with Introduction, Notes, and Commentary.* The Anchor Bible. Vol. 32A. Garden City, N.Y.: Doubleday, 1984.

Goudge, H. L. *The Second Epistle to the Corinthians.* Westminster Commentaries series. London: Methuen, 1927.

Grosheide, F. W. *De Eerste Brief van den Apostel Paulus aan de Kerk te Korinthe.* Kommentaar op het Nieuwe Testament series. Amsterdam: Van Bottenburg, 1932.

————. *Commentary on the First Epistle to the Corinthians: The English Text with Introduction, Exposition and Notes.* New International Commentary on the New Testament series. Grand Rapids: Eerdmans, 1953.

————. *De Tweede Brief van den Apostel Paulus aan de Kerk te Korinthe.* Kommentaar op het Nieuwe Testament series. Amsterdam: Van Bottenburg, 1939.

Hanson, R. P. C. *The Second Epistle to the Corinthians.* Torch Bible Commentaries series. London: SCM, 1954.

Harris, Murray J. *2 Corinthians.* In vol. 10 of *The Expositor's Bible Commentary,* edited by Frank E. Gaebelein. 12 vols. Grand Rapids: Zondervan, 1976.

Hendriksen, William. *Exposition of Philippians.* New Testament Commentary series. Grand Rapids: Baker, 1962.

Henry, Matthew. *Acts to Revelation.* Vol. 6 of *Matthew Henry's Commentary on the Whole Bible.* 6 vols. New York: Revell, n.d.

Héring, Jean. *The Second Epistle of Saint Paul to the Corinthians.* Translated by A. W. Heathcote and P. J. Allcock. London: Epworth, 1967.

Hodge, Charles. *An Exposition of the Second Epistle to the Corinthians.* 1891. Reprint ed. Edinburgh: Banner of Truth, 1959.

Hughes, Philip E. *Paul's Second Epistle to the Corinthians: The English Text with Introduction, Exposition and Notes.* New International Commentary on the New Testament series. Grand Rapids: Eerdmans, 1962.

Kistemaker, Simon J. *Exposition of the Acts of the Apostles.* New Testament Commentary series. Grand Rapids: Baker, 1990.

————. *Exposition of the First Epistle to the Corinthians.* New Testament Commentary series. Grand Rapids: Baker, 1993.

Klauck, Hans-Josef. *II Korintherbrief.* Würzburg: Echter, 1984.

Kruse, Colin G. *The Second Epistle of Paul to the Corinthians.* Tyndale New Testament Commentaries series. Leicester: Inter-Varsity; Grand Rapids: Eerdmans, 1987.

Lenski, R. C. H. *The Interpretation of St. Paul's First and Second Epistle to the Corinthians.* Columbus: Wartburg, 1946.

Lietzmann, Hans. *An die Korinther I/II.* Handbuch zum Neuen Testament 9. Augmented by Werner G. Kümmel. Tübingen: Mohr, 1969.

Martin, Ralph P. *2 Corinthians.* Word Commentary series. Vol. 40. Waco: Word, 1986.

———. *2 Corinthians*. Word Biblical Themes. Dallas: Word, 1988.

Menzies, Allan. *The Second Epistle of the Apostle Paul to the Corinthians: Introduction, Text, English Translation and Notes*. London: Macmillan, 1912.

Meyer, H. A. W. *Critical and Exegetical Handbook to the Epistles to the Corinthians*. New York and London: Funk and Wagnalls, 1884.

Moule, H. C. G. *The Second Epistle to the Corinthians*. London: Pickering and Inglis, 1962.

Pfitzner, Victor C. *Strength in Weakness: A Commentary on 2 Corinthians*. Chi Rho Commentary. Adelaide: Lutheran Publishing House, 1992.

Plummer, Alfred. *A Critical and Exegetical Commentary on the Second Epistle of St. Paul to the Corinthians*. International Critical Commentary series. 1915. Edinburgh: Clark, 1975.

———. *The Second Epistle of Paul the Apostle to the Corinthians*. Cambridge: Cambridge University Press, 1903.

Pop, F. J. *De Tweede Brief van Paulus aan de Corinthiërs*. Nijkerk: Callenbach, 1980.

Rienecker, Fritz, und Werner de Boor. *Der zweite Brief des Paulus an die Korinther*. Wuppertal: Brockhaus, 1972.

Strachan, R. H. *The Second Epistle of Paul to the Corinthians*. Moffatt New Testament Commentary series. New York: Harper and Brothers, 1935.

Talbert, C. H. *Reading Corinthians: A Literary and Theological Commentary on 1 and 2 Corinthians*. New York: Crossroad, 1987.

Tasker, R. V. G. *The Second Epistle of Paul to the Corinthians*. Tyndale New Testament Commentaries series. Grand Rapids: Eerdmans, 1968.

Thompson, James. *The Second Letter of Paul to the Corinthians*. Austin, Tex.: R. B. Sweet Co., 1970.

Thrall, Margaret E. *A Critical and Exegetical Commentary on the Second Epistle to the Corinthians*. 2 vols. Vol. 1. International Critical Commentary series. Edinburgh: Clark, 1994.

VanGemeren, Willem A. *Psalms*. In vol. 5 of *The Expositor's Bible Commentary*, edited by Frank E. Gaebelein. 12 vols. Grand Rapids: Zondervan, 1991.

Wendland, Heinz-Dietrich. *Die Briefe an die Korinther*. 15th ed. Neue Testament Deutsch 7. Göttingen: Vandenhoeck und Ruprecht, 1980.

Wilson, Geoffrey B. *2 Corinthians: A Digest of Reformed Comment*. Edinburgh and London: Banner of Truth Trust, 1973.

Windisch, Hans. *Der Zweite Korintherbrief*. Edited by Georg Strecker. 1924. Reprint ed. Göttingen: Vandenhoeck und Ruprecht, 1970.

Studies

Badenas, Robert. *Christ the End of the Law: Romans 10:4 in Pauline Perspective*. JSNT Supplement Series 10. Sheffield: JSOT, 1985.

Barnett, Paul. *The Message of 2 Corinthians: Power in Weakness*. Leicester and Downers Grove: InterVarsity, 1988.

Barrett, C. K. *The Signs of an Apostle*. Philadelphia: Fortress, 1972.

———. "Titus." In *Neotestamentica et Semitica: Studies in Honour of Matthew Black*, edited by E. Earle Ellis and Max Wilcox. Edinburgh: Clark, 1969.

———. "Ο ΑΔΙΚΗΣΑΣ (2 Cor 7,12)." In *Verborum Veritas*, edited by Otto Böcher and Klaus Haacker. Wuppertal: Brockhaus, 1970.

———. *Essays on Paul*. Philadelphia: Westminster, 1982.

Bibliography

Bavinck, Herman. *Gereformeerde Dogmatiek.* 4 vols. Vol. 2. Kampen: Kok, 1928.

Beker, J. C. *Paul the Apostle. The Triumph of God in Life and Thought.* Edinburgh: Clark, 1980.

Belleville, Linda L. *Reflections of Glory: Paul's Polemical Use of the Moses-Doxa Tradition in 2 Corinthians 3.1–18.* JSNT Supplement Series 52. Sheffield: JSOT, 1991.

Black, D. A. *Paul, Apostle of Weakness: Astheneia and Its Cognates in the Pauline Literature.* New York: Lang, 1984.

Boettner, L. *Immortality.* Philadelphia: Presbyterian and Reformed, 1956.

Bruce, F. F. *The Acts of the Apostles: Greek Text with Introduction and Commentary.* 3d revised and enlarged edition. Grand Rapids: Eerdmans, 1990.

———. *Paul: Apostle of the Heart Set Free.* Grand Rapids: Eerdmans, 1977. U.S. edition of *Paul: Apostle of the Free Spirit.* Exeter: Paternoster, 1977.

Bultmann, Rudolf. *Exegetische Probleme des Zweiten Korintherbriefes.* Darmstadt: Wissenschaftliche Buchgesellschaft, 1963.

Carré, Henry Beach. *Paul's Doctrine of Redemption.* New York: Macmillan, 1914.

Carson, D. A. *From Triumphalism to Maturity: An Exposition of 2 Corinthians 10–13.* Grand Rapids: Baker, 1984.

Carson, D. A., Douglas J., Moo, and Leon Morris. *An Introduction to the New Testament.* Grand Rapids: Zondervan, 1992.

Cavallin, H. C. C. *Life after Death. Paul's Argument for the Resurrection of the Dead in 1 Corinthians 15.* Lund: Gleerup, 1974.

Chamblin, J. Knox. *Paul and the Self: Apostolic Teaching for Personal Wholeness.* Grand Rapids: Baker, 1993.

Charlesworth, J. H., and Jerome Murphy-O'Connor, eds. *Paul and the Dead Sea Scrolls.* New York: Crossroad, 1990.

Collange, J.-F. *Énigmes de la deuxième épître de Paul aux Corinthiens: Étude exégétique de 2 Cor. 2:14–7:4.* SNTS Monograph Series 18. New York and Cambridge: Cambridge University Press, 1972.

Cooper, John W. *Body, Soul and Life Everlasting: Biblical Anthropology and the Monism-Dualism Debate.* Grand Rapids: Eerdmans, 1989.

Crafton, Jeffrey. *The Agency of the Apostle: A Dramatistic Analysis of Paul's Responses to Conflict in 2 Corinthians.* JSNT Supplement Series 59. Sheffield: JSOT, 1991.

Cullman, Oscar. *Immortality of the Soul or Resurrection of the Dead?* London: Epworth, 1958.

Dahl, Murdoch E. *The Resurrection of the Body: A Study of I Corinthians 15.* London: SCM, 1962.

Dahl, Nils A. *Studies in Paul: Theology for the Early Christian Mission.* Minneapolis: Augsburg, 1977.

Danker, Frederick W. "Exegesis of 2 Corinthians 5:14–21." In *Interpreting 2 Corinthians 5:14–21: An Exercise in Hermeneutics,* edited by Jack P. Lewis. Studies in the Bible and Early Christianity 17. Lewiston, N.Y.: Mellen, 1989.

Deissmann, G. Adolf. *Bible Studies.* Translated by Alexander Grieve. 1923. Reprint ed. Winona Lake, Ind.: Alpha, 1979.

Dumbrell, William J. "Paul's Use of Exodus 34 in 2 Corinthians 3." In *God Who Is Rich in Mercy: Essays Presented to Dr. D. B. Knox,* edited by Peter Thomas O'Brien and David G. Peterson. Homebush West, NSW, Australia: Lancer, 1986.

Dunn, J. D. G. *Baptism in the Holy Spirit.* Studies in Biblical Theology, 2d series 15. London: SCM, 1970.

Elliot, Elisabeth. *Shadow of the Almighty.* New York: Harper and Brothers, 1958.

Bibliography

Elliot, J. K. *Studies in New Testament Language and Text: Essays in Honour of George D. Kilpatrick on the Occasion of His Sixty-fifth Birthday.* Novum Testamentum, Supplement 44. Leiden: Brill, 1976.

Ellis, E. Earle. "Paul and His Opponents." In *Prophecy and Hermeneutics in Early Christianity.* Wissenschaftliche Untersuchungen zum Neuen Testament 18. Tübingen: Mohr-Siebeck; Grand Rapids: Eerdmans, 1978.

———. *Paul and His Recent Interpreters.* Grand Rapids: Eerdmans, 1961.

Epp, Eldon Jay, and Gordon D. Fee, eds. *New Testament Textual Criticism: Its Significance for Exegesis. Essays in Honor of Bruce M. Metzger.* Oxford: Clarendon, 1981.

Fitzgerald, John T. *Cracks in an Earthen Vessel: An Examination of the Catalogues of Hardships in the Corinthian Correspondence.* SBL Dissertation Series 99. Atlanta: Scholars, 1988.

Fitzmyer, Joseph A. "Qumran and the interpolated paragraph in 2 Cor. 6:14–7:1." In *Essays on the Semitic Background of the New Testament.* London: Chapman, 1971. Reprinted from *CBQ* 23 (1961): 271–80.

Friedrich, Gerhard. "Die Gegner des Paulus im 2. Korintherbrief." In *Abraham unser Vater: Juden und Christen im Gespräch über die Bibel, Festschrift für Otto Michel zum 60.* Edited by Otto Betz, Martin Hengel, and Peter Schmidt. Leiden: Brill, 1963.

Friesen, I. I. *The Glory of the Ministry of Jesus Christ Illustrated by a Study of 2 Corinthians 2:14–3:18.* Basel: Reinhardt, 1971.

Funk, Robert W., Roy W. Hoover, and the Jesus Seminar. *The Five Gospels: The Search for the Authentic Words of Jesus.* New York: Macmillan, 1993.

Gaffin, Richard B., Jr. *The Centrality of the Resurrection: A Study in Paul's Soteriology.* Grand Rapids: Baker, 1978.

———. *Resurrection and Redemption: A Study in Paul's Soteriology.* Phillipsburg, N. J.: Presbyterian and Reformed, 1987.

Georgi, Dieter. *The Opponents of Paul in Second Corinthians.* Philadelphia: Fortress, 1986.

———. *Der Armen zu Gedenken: Die Geschichte der Kollekte des Paulus für Jerusalem.* 2d rev. and expanded ed. Neukirchen-Vluyn: Neukirchener Verlag, 1994.

———. *Remembering the Poor: The History of Paul's Collection for Jerusalem.* Nashville: Abingdon, 1992.

Gnilka, Joachim. "2 Cor 6:14–7:1 in the Light of the Qumran Texts and the Testaments of the Twelve Patriarchs." In *Paul and Qumran,* edited by Jerome Murphy-O'Connor. London: Chapman, 1968. Originally published in *Neutestamentliche Aufsätze, Festschrift Josef Schmidt zum 70,* edited by J. Blinzler, O. Kuss, and F. Mussner. Regensburg: Pustet, 1963.

Gundry, Robert H. *Sōma in Biblical Theology: With Emphasis on Pauline Anthropology.* Grand Rapids: Zondervan, Academie Books, 1987.

Gunther, John J. *St. Paul's Opponents and Their Background. A Study of Apocalyptic and Jewish Sectarian Teachings.* Novum Testamentum, Supplement 35. Leiden: Brill, 1973.

Guthrie, Donald. *New Testament Introduction.* 4th rev. ed. Leicester: Apollos; Downers Grove: InterVarsity, 1990.

Guy, H. A. *The New Testament Doctrine of the 'Last Things': A Study of Eschatology.* London: Oxford University Press, 1948.

Hafemann, Scott J. *Paul, Moses, and the History of Israel: The Letter/Spirit Contrast and the Argument from Scripture in 2 Corinthians 3.* Wissenschaftliche Untersuchungen zum Neuen Testament 81. Tübingen: Mohr [Siebeck], 1995.

———. *Suffering and the Spirit: An Exegetical Study of II Cor. 2:14–3:3 Within the Context of the Corinthian Correspondence.* Tübingen: Mohr, 1986.

467

Bibliography

Hammond, Philip C. *The Nabataeans—Their History, Culture and Archaeology.* Gothenburg, Sweden: Äströms, 1973.

Harris, Murray J. "Paul's View of Death in 2 Corinthians 5:1–10." In *New Dimensions in New Testament Study,* edited by R. N. Longenecker and M. C. Tenney. Grand Rapids: Zondervan, 1974.

———. *Raised Immortal: Resurrection and Immortality in the New Testament.* Grand Rapids: Eerdmans, 1983.

Hay, David M. "The Shaping of Theology in 2 Corinthians: Convictions, Doubts, and Warrants." In *Pauline Theology,* vol. 2, *1 and 2 Corinthians,* edited by David M. Hay. Minneapolis: Fortress, 1993.

Hermann, Ingo. *Kyrios und Pneuma: Studien zur Christologie der paulinischen Hauptbriefe.* Munich: Kösel, 1961.

Hock, Ronald F. *The Social Context of Paul's Ministry: Tentmaking and Apostleship.* Philadelphia: Fortress, 1980.

Hoekema, Anthony A. *The Bible and the Future.* Exeter: Paternoster, 1978.

Hurd, John C., Jr. *The Origin of 1 Corinthians.* Macon, Ga.: Mercer University Press, 1983.

Jervell, Jacob. *Imago Dei: Gen 1,26f im Spätjudentum, in der Gnosis und in den paulinischen Briefen.* Forschungen zur Religion und Literatur des Alten und Neuen Testaments 76. Göttingen: Vandenhoeck und Ruprecht, 1960.

Kennedy, James H. *The Second and Third Epistles of St. Paul to the Corinthians.* London: Methuen, 1900.

Kent, Homer A., Jr. *A Heart Opened Wide: Studies in II Corinthians.* Grand Rapids: Baker, 1982.

Kim, Seyoon. *The Origin of Paul's Gospel.* Tübingen: Mohr, 1981; Grand Rapids: Eerdmans, 1982.

Kline, Meredith G. *Images of the Spirit.* Grand Rapids: Baker, 1980.

Kreitzer, Larry J. *Jesus and God in Paul's Eschatology.* JSNT Supplement Series 19. Sheffield: JSOT, 1987.

Lake, Kirsopp. *The Earlier Epistles of St. Paul: Their Motive and Origin.* London: Rivington, 1911.

Lampe, G. W. H. "Church Discipline and the Interpretation of the Epistles to the Corinthians." In *Christian History and Interpretation: Studies Presented to John Knox,* edited by W. R. Farmer, C. F. D. Moule, and R. R. Niebuhr. Cambridge: Cambridge University Press, 1967.

Lang, F. G. *2 Korinther 5, 1–10 in der neueren Forschung.* Beiträge zur Geschichte der biblischen Exegese 16. Tübingen: Mohr, 1973.

Lewis, Jack P. "Exegesis of 2 Corinthians 5:14–21." In *Interpreting 2 Corinthians 5:14–21. An Exercise in Hermeneutics,* edited by Jack P. Lewis. Studies in the Bible and Early Christianity 17. Lewiston, N.Y.: Mellen, 1989.

Lincoln, A. T. *Paradise Now and Not Yet: Studies in the Role of the Heavenly Dimension in Paul's Thought with Special Reference to His Eschatology.* SNTS Monograph Series 43. Cambridge: Cambridge University Press, 1981.

Marmorstein, A. *The Old Rabbinic Doctrine of God.* 1927. New York: KTAV, 1968.

Marshall, P. *Enmity in Corinth: Social Conventions in Paul's Relations with the Corinthians.* Tübingen: Mohr, 1987.

Martin, Ralph P. "The Spirit in 2 Corinthians in Light of the 'Fellowship of the Holy Spirit' in 2 Corinthians 13:14." In *Eschatology and the New Testament, Essays in Honor of G. R. Beasley-Murray,* edited by W. H. Gloer. Peabody, Mass.: Hendrickson, 1988.

Bibliography

Mead, Richard T. "Exegesis of 2 Corinthians 5:14–21." In *Interpreting 2 Corinthians 5:14–21. An Exercise in Hermeneutics,* edited by Jack P. Lewis. Studies in the Bible and Early Christianity 17. Lewiston, N.Y.: Mellen, 1989.

Meeks, W. A. *The First Urban Christians: The Social World of the Apostle Paul.* New Haven: Yale University Press, 1983.

Metzger, Bruce M. *The Text of the New Testament: Its Transmission, Corruption, and Restoration.* New York and London: Oxford University Press, 1968.

Moore, A. L. *The Parousia in the New Testament.* Novum Testamentum, Supplement 13. Leiden: Brill, 1966.

Moule, C. F. D. "The Spirit in 2 Corinthians in Light of the 'Fellowship of the Holy Spirit' in 2 Corinthians 12:14." In *Eschatology and the New Testament, Essays in Honor of G. R. Beasley-Murray,* edited by W. H. Gloer. Peabody, Mass.: Hendrickson, 1988.

Murphy-O'Connor, Jerome. *The Theology of the Second Letter to the Corinthians.* New Testament Theology series. Cambridge: Cambridge University Press, 1991.

Nickle, Keith F. *The Collection: A Study in Paul's Strategy.* Studies in Biblical Theology 48. Naperville: Allenson, 1966.

Nickelsburg, G. W. E. *Resurrection, Immortality and Eternal Life in Intertestamental Judaism.* Cambridge: Harvard University Press, 1972.

O'Brien, Peter T. *Introductory Thanksgivings in the Letters of Paul.* Novum Testamentum, Supplement 49. Leiden: Brill, 1977.

Oostendorp, Derk W. *Another Jesus: A Gospel of Jewish-Christian Superiority in II Corinthians.* Kampen: Kok, 1967.

Pate, C. Marvin. *Adam Christology as the Exegetical and Theological Substructure of 2 Corinthians 4:7–5:21.* Lanham, Md.: University Press of America, 1991.

Pierce, Claude A. *Conscience in the New Testament.* Studies in Biblical Theology 15. Naperville: Allenson, 1955.

Ridderbos, Herman N. *Paul: An Outline of His Theology.* Translated by John Richard de Witt. Grand Rapids: Eerdmans, 1975.

Robertson, A. T. *The Glory of the Ministry: Paul's Exaltation in Preaching.* New York: Revell, 1911.

Robinson, J. A. T. *The Body: A Study in Pauline Theology.* Studies in Biblical Theology 5. London: SCM, 1952.

Schlatter, Adolf. *Paulus, der Bote Jesu: Eine Deutung Seiner Briefe an die Korinther.* Stuttgart: Calwer, 1934.

Schmithals, Walter. *Gnosticism in Corinth.* Translated by John E. Steely. Nashville: Abingdon, 1971.

———. *Paul and the Gnostics.* Translated by John E. Steely. Nashville: Abingdon, 1972.

Schoeps, H. J. *Paul. The Theology of the Apostle in the Light of Jewish Religious History.* Translated by Harold Knight. Philadelphia: Westminster, 1961.

Schreiner, Thomas R. *The Law and Its Fulfillment: A Pauline Theology of Law.* Grand Rapids: Baker, 1993.

Smith, William H., Jr. "The Function of 2 Corinthians 3:7–4:6 in Its Epistolary Content." Ph.D. dissertation, Southern Baptist Theological Seminary, 1983.

Spencer, Aída Besançon. *Paul's Literary Style: A Stylistic and Historical Comparison of II Corinthians 11:16–12:13, Romans 8:9–39, and Philippians 3:2–4:13.* Jackson, Miss.: Evangelical Theological Society, 1984.

Stephenson, A. M. G. "A Defence of the Integrity of 2 Corinthians." In *The Authorship and Integrity of the New Testament.* Theological Collections 4. London: SPCK, 1965.

————. "Partition Theories on II Corinthians." In *Studia Evangelica II.1: The New Testament Scriptures,* edited by F. L. Cross. Texte und Untersuchungen 87. Berlin: Akademie, 1964.

Stockhausen, Carol K. "Moses' Veil and the Glory of the New Testament: The Exegetical and Theological Substructure of II Corinthians 3:1–4:6." Ph.D. dissertation, Marquette University, 1984.

Sumney, Jerry L. *Identifying Paul's Opponents: The Question of Method in 2 Corinthians.* Sheffield: JSOT, 1990.

Tabor, J. D. *Things Unutterable: Paul's Ascent to Paradise in Its Greco-Roman, Judaic, and Early Christian Contexts.* Lanham, Md.: University Press of America, 1986.

Theissen, Gerd. *The Social Setting of Pauline Christianity: Essays on Corinth.* Edited and translated by John H. Schütz. Philadelphia: Fortress, 1982.

Thrall, Margaret E. "2 Corinthians 1:2: ΑΓΙΟΤΗΤΙ or ΑΠΛΟΤΗΤΙ." In *Studies in New Testament Language and Text: Essays in Honour of George D. Kilpatrick on the Occasion of his Sixty-fifth Birthday.* Novum Testamentum, Supplement 44. Leiden: Brill, 1976.

————. "'Putting On' or 'Stripping Off'" in 2 Corinthians 5:3." In *New Testament Textual Criticism: Its Significance for Exegesis, Essays in Honor of Bruce M. Metzger,* edited by Eldon Jay Epp and Gordon D. Fee. Oxford: Clarendon, 1981.

van Unnik, W. C. "Reisepläne und Amen-Sagen, Zusammenhang und Gedankenfolge in 2 Korinther 1. 15–24." In *Sparsa Collecta: The Collected Essays of W. C. van Unnik. Part 1.* Novum Testamentum, Supplement 29. Leiden: Brill, 1973.

————. "The Semitic Background of ΠΑΡΡΗΣΙΑ in the New Testament." In *Sparsa Collecta: The Collected Essays of W. C. van Unnik. Part 1.* Novum Testamentum, Supplement 30. Leiden: Brill, 1980.

————. *Tarsus or Jerusalem: The City of Paul's Youth.* Translated by George Ogg. London: Epworth, 1962.

van Vliet, Hendrik. *No Single Testimony. A Study on the Adoption of the Law of Deut. 19:15 Par. into the New Testament.* Utrecht: Kemink, 1958.

Vielhauer, Philipp. *Geschichte der urchristlichen Literatur.* Berlin and New York: de Gruyter, 1975.

Vos, Geerhardus. *Biblical Theology: Old and New Testaments.* Grand Rapids: Eerdmans, 1948.

————. *The Pauline Eschatology.* Grand Rapids: Eerdmans, 1961.

Wedderburn, A. J. M. *Baptism and Resurrection: Studies in Pauline Theology against Its Graeco-Roman Background.* Wissenschaftliche Untersuchungen zum Neuen Testament 44. Tübingen: Mohr-Siebeck, 1987.

Wenham, John. *Redating Matthew, Mark and Luke: A Fresh Assault on the Synoptic Problem.* London: Hodder and Stoughton, 1991.

White, John L. "Ancient Greek Letters." In *Greco-Roman Literature and the New Testament: Selected Forms and Genres,* edited by David E. Aune. SBL Sources for Biblical Studies 21. Atlanta: Scholars, 1988.

Whiteley, D. E. H. *The Theology of St. Paul.* Oxford: Blackwell, 1964.

Wilkins, Michael J., and J. P. Moreland, eds. *Jesus Under Fire: Modern Scholarship Reinvents the Historical Jesus.* Grand Rapids: Zondervan, 1995.

Winter, Bruce W. "Are Philo and Paul among the Sophists? A Hellenistic Jewish and a Christian Response to a First-Century Movement." Ph.D. dissertation, Macquarie University, 1988.

Witherington, Ben III. *Conflict and Community in Corinth: A Socio-Rhetorical Commentary on 1 and 2 Corinthians.* Grand Rapids: Eerdmans; Carlisle: Paternoster, 1995.

Bibliography

Wright, N. T. "On Becoming the Righteousness of God." In *Pauline Theology,* vol. 2, *1 and 2 Corinthians,* edited by David M. Hay. Minneapolis: Fortress, 1993.

Young, Frances, and David F. Ford. *Meaning and Truth in 2 Corinthians.* Biblical Foundations in Theology series. London: SPCK, 1987.

Zuntz, G. *The Text of the Epistles: A Disquisition upon the Corpus Paulinum.* London: Oxford University Press, 1953.

Zwaan, J. de. "Some Remarks on the ΓΥΜΝΟΣ in II Cor. v.3." In *Studia Paulina.* Haarlem: Bohn, 1953.

Tools

Aland, Barbara, et al. *The Greek New Testament.* 4th rev. ed. Stuttgart: Deutsche Bibelgesellschaft; United Bible Societies, 1993.

Balz, Horst, and Gerhard Schneider, eds. *Exegetical Dictionary of the New Testament.* 3 vols. Grand Rapids: Eerdmans, 1990–93.

Bauer, Walter. *A Greek-English Lexicon of the New Testament and Other Early Christian Literature.* 2d rev. and augmented ed., F. Wilbur Gingrich and Frederick W. Danker from Walter Bauer's 4th ed. Chicago and London: University of Chicago Press, 1979.

Berkhof, Louis. *Systematic Theology.* Grand Rapids: Eerdmans, 1941.

Blass, Friedrich, and Albert Debrunner. *A Greek Grammar of the New Testament and Other Early Christian Literature.* Translated and revised by Robert Funk. Chicago: University of Chicago Press, 1961.

Bromiley, G. W., ed. *The International Standard Bible Encyclopedia.* Rev. ed. 4 vols. Grand Rapids: Eerdmans, 1975–78.

Brown, Colin, ed. *New International Dictionary of New Testament Theology.* 3 vols. Grand Rapids: Zondervan; Exeter: Paternoster, 1975–78.

Burton, E. D. *Moods and Tenses of New Testament Greek.* Edinburgh: Clark, 1898.

Calvin, John. *Institutes of the Christian Religion.* Translated by Ford Lewis Battles. Edited by John T. McNeill. 2 vols. Philadelphia: Westminster, 1960.

Charlesworth, J. H., ed. *The Old Testament Pseudepigrapha.* 2 vols. Garden City, N.Y.: Doubleday, 1983.

Cicero. *The Verrine Orations.* 2 vols. Loeb Classical Library series. London: Heinemann; Cambridge: Harvard University Press, 1935.

Epstein, Isidore, ed. *The Babylonian Talmud.* Seder Mo'ed. 4 vols. London: Soncino, 1938.

———. *The Babylonian Talmud.* Seder Neziken. 4 vols. London: Soncino, 1935.

Goold, E. P., ed. *The Apostolic Fathers.* Translated by Kirsopp Lake. 2 vols. Loeb Classical Library series. Cambridge: Harvard University Press; London: Heinemann, 1976.

Guthrie, Donald. *New Testament Introduction.* 4th rev. ed. Downers Grove: InterVarsity, 1990.

Hanna, Robert. *A Grammatical Aid to the Greek New Testament.* Grand Rapids: Baker, 1983.

Hawthorne, Gerald F., and Ralph P. Martin. *Dictionary of Paul and His Letters.* Leicester and Downers Grove: InterVarsity, 1993.

Heidelberg Catechism. Grand Rapids: Board of Publications of the Christian Reformed Church, 1975.

Hendriksen, William. *Bible Survey: A Treasury of Bible Information.* Grand Rapids: Baker, 1953.

Bibliography

Hennecke, Edgar. *New Testament Apocrypha.* Edited by Wilhelm Schneemelcher. Translated by R. McL. Wilson. 2 vols. Philadelphia: Westminster, 1963–64.

Josephus, Flavius. *Antiquities.* Loeb Classical Library series. London: Heinemann; Cambridge: Harvard University Press, 1966–76.

———. *Life* and *Against Apion.* Loeb Classical Library series. London: Heinemann; Cambridge: Harvard University Press, 1966–76.

———. *Wars of the Jews.* Loeb Classical Library series. London: Heinemann; Cambridge: Harvard University Press, 1966–76.

Kittel, Gerhard, and Gerhard Friedrich, eds. *Theological Dictionary of the New Testament.* Translated by G. W. Bromiley. 10 vols. Grand Rapids: Eerdmans, 1964–76.

Kümmel, Werner Georg. *Handbuch zum Neuen Testament* 9. Tübingen: Mohr, 1969.

Ladd, George Eldon. *A Theology of the New Testament.* Edited by Donald A. Hagner. Rev. ed. Grand Rapids: Eerdmans, 1993.

Metzger, Bruce M. *A Textual Commentary on the Greek New Testament.* Stuttgart: Deutsche Bibelgesellschaft; New York: United Bible Societies, 1994.

Moule, C. F. D. *An Idiom-Book of New Testament Greek.* 2d ed. Cambridge: Cambridge University Press, 1960.

Moulton, J. H. *A Grammar of New Testament Greek.* 3d ed. Vol 1, *Prolegomena.* Edinburgh: Clark, 1908.

Moulton, J. H., and Wilbert F. Howard. *A Grammar of New Testament Greek.* Vol. 2, *Accidence and Word-Formation.* Edinburgh: Clark, 1929.

Moulton, J. H., and Nigel A. Turner. *A Grammar of New Testament Greek.* Vol. 3, *Syntax.* Edinburgh: Clark, 1963.

Nestle, E., and Kurt Aland. *Novum Testamentum Graece.* 27th ed. Stuttgart: Deutsche Bibelstiftung, 1993.

Philo. *De Virtutibus.* In vol. 8 of *Philo in Ten Volumes.* 10 vols. Loeb Classical Library series. London: Heinemann; Cambridge: Harvard University Press, 1968.

Plato. *Phaedrus.* In vol. 1 of *Plato in Twelve Volumes.* 12 vols. Loeb Classical Library series. London: Heinemann; Cambridge: Harvard University Press, 1982.

Rienecker, Fritz. *Sprachlicher Schlüssel zum Griechischen Neuen Testament.* Giessen: Brunnen-Verlag, 1970.

Robertson, A. T. *A Grammar of the Greek New Testament in the Light of Historical Research.* Nashville: Broadman, 1934.

Strack, H. L., and P. Billerbeck. *Kommentar zum Neuen Testament aus Talmud und Midrasch.* 5 vols. Munich: Beck, 1922–28.

Thrall, Margaret E. *Greek Particles in the New Testament.* Leiden: Brill; Grand Rapids: Eerdmans, 1962.

Trench, R. C. *Synonyms of the New Testament.* Edited by Robert G. Hoerber. Grand Rapids: Baker, 1989.

Young, Richard A. *Intermediate New Testament Greek: A Linguistic and Exegetical Approach.* Nashville: Broadman and Holman, 1994.

Index of Authors

Aalen, Sverre, 25–26
Achilles, Ernst, 136 n. 2
Agnew, F., 298 n. 70
Alford, Henry, 257 n. 32, 307 n. 10, 437
    n. 75, 444 n. 3
Allo, Ernest B., 10 n. 16, 14 n. 28, 187 n. 60,
    196 n. 83, 208 n. 2, 223 n. 40, 285, 291
    n. 51, 328 n. 2, 332 n. 13, 357 n. 2, 415
    n. 29, 444 n. 3, 454 n. 27
Ambrose, 292 n. 56
Anselm, 292 n. 56
Arichea, Daniel C., 155 n. 52
Augustine, 366 n. 25

Bachmann, Phillipp, 14 n. 28, 292 n. 56,
    426 n. 52, 443 n. 1, 444 n. 3
Badenas, Robert, 119 n. 49
Baird, William, 102 n. 10, 410 n. 17
Balz, Horst, 245 n. 8, 319 n. 40, 358 n. 3
Barré, Michael L., 384 n. 61, 394 n. 88, 416
    n. 30
Barrett, C. K., 4 n. 2, 6 n. 3, 27 nn. 63, 65,
    28 n. 68, 41 n. 10, 64 n. 63, 81 n. 19, 86
    n. 36, 89 n. 42, 90, 101 n. 9, 156 n. 55,
    172 n. 20, 181, 183 n. 46, 193 n. 78, 197
    n. 87, 209 n. 7, 213 n. 17, 217 n. 26, 226
    n. 48, 226 n. 50, 229 n. 59, 234 n. 71, 247
    n. 12, 258 n. 36, 291 n. 50, 294, 298
    n. 70, 318 n. 37, 337 n. 22, 340, 348 n. 50,
    350 n. 53, 360, 362 n. 12, 365 n. 21, 365
    n. 22, 373 n. 41, 374 n. 42, 377 n. 48, 381
    n. 57, 386 n. 66, 392 n. 84, 410 n. 18, 420
    n. 42, 443 n. 1, 444 nn. 3, 4, 448 n. 11,
    453 n. 24

Barth, Gerhard, 60 n. 54
Bates, W. H., 13 n. 27, 14 n. 28
Batey, Richard, 359 n. 6
Bauer, Walter, 40 n. 8, 50 n. 31, 57 n. 43, 63
    n. 61, 72 n. 7, 75 n. 10, 76 n. 12, 83 n. 26,
    89 n. 41, 101 n. 6, 103 n. 11, 109, n. 26,
    124 n. 60, 131 n. 79, 140 n. 13, 147 n. 32,
    154 n. 49, 160 n. 63, 181 n. 43, 191 n. 72,
    214 n. 19, 258 n. 34, 259 n. 37, 260
    nn. 41, 43, 262 n. 46, 280 n. 26, 307 n. 9,
    308 n. 11, 309 n. 13, 315 nn. 29, 31, 318
    n. 35, 323 n. 49, 334 n. 17, 359 n. 5, 367
    n. 28, 372 n. 39, 373 n. 40, 379 n. 53, 382
    n. 59, 395 nn. 90, 91, 409 n. 12, 429
    n. 60, 431 n. 64, 436 n. 72, 457 n. 32
Bauernfeind, Otto, 273 n. 9
Baumert, Norbert, 276 n. 18
Bavinck, Herman, 141 n. 18, 169 n. 9
Beale, G. K., 24 n. 51, 194 n. 81
Beck, James S. P., 417 n. 31
Becker, Oswald, 369 n. 32
Becker, Ulrich, 85 n. 31
Behm, Johannes, 79 n. 17, 129 n. 74, 193
    n. 78, 253 n. 24
Belleville, Linda L., 47 n. 25, 104 n. 14,
    111, 119 n. 49, 123 n. 57, 125 n. 61, 127
    n. 68, 128 n. 73
Bengel, John Albert, 44 n. 17, 150 n. 35,
    216 n. 23, 219 n. 33, 233 n. 68, 244 n. 5,
    258 n. 35, 313 n. 23, 408, 445 n. 7
Berkhof, Louis, 199 n. 90
Bernard, J. H., 160 n. 64, 193 n. 75
Berry, Ronald, 179 n. 38

Index of Scripture

Genesis

1:3—143, 145, 147
1:26–27—141
2:7—23, 158, 167, 172, 408
2:8—409
2:15—409
2:17—23, 189, 360
3:4—375
3:8—23
3:8–19—200
3:11—360
3:13—360
3:17—360
3:17–19—189
3:19—173
3:24—409
8:21—90 n. 49
9:26—397 n. 95
13:10—409
14:13—385
17:7—231
18:20—160
22:5—50
25:1–6—387
25:12–18—387
32:28—386
32:30—119
38:17—176
38:18—176
38:20—176
39:14—385 n. 62
39:17—385 n. 62
40:15—385 n. 62
41:12—385 n. 62
43:32—385 n. 62

Exodus

1:15—385 n. 62
1:16—385 n. 62
2:6—385 n. 62
2:7—385 n. 62
2:13—385 n. 62
3:4—59
3:7–10—147
4:10—107
6:7—231
16:18—289, 314 n. 27
20–23—108
20:3–5—234
20:5—358
20:16—436
20:18—111
20:23—140
23:16b—167 n. 5
23:25–31—108
24—107
24:3—22, 111
24:3–8—119
24:7—22, 111
24:12—107
25:8—231
29:18—90 n. 49
29:45—231
30:20–21—234
31:18—103, 107
31:18–32:6—22
32—110
32:9—112
32:10—111
32:15—103
32:28—109
33:3–5—112
33:7–11—167
33:20—119
34—111
34:6—216
34:9—112

34:29—107, 111
34:29–35—22, 110, 111, 112, 114, 117, 118, 119
34:30—114, 119
34:33—118
34:33–35—118
34:34—122, 123, 124, 125
34:34–35—129
34:35—114
40:34—420

Leviticus

10:1–5—447
11:44–45—232
15:2—438
15:16—438
15:19—438
15:25—438
18:6–23—438
19:2—232
19:19—227
20:7—232
23:33–36a—167 n. 5
23:39–43—167 n. 5
24:14—390
24:16—390
24:23—390
26:12—227, 231, 314 n. 27

Numbers

6:24–26—418 n. 37
6:26—458
11:25–29—113
12:1–15—447
12:3—330
14:18—216

14:21–23—111
14:24—109
16:1–33—447
16:3—39 n. 5
20:4—39 n. 5
29:12–34—167 n. 5
32:12—109
35:30—61 n. 58, 299, 444

Deuteronomy

1:36—109
5:7–9—234
5:9—358
5:20—436
6:5—227
6:12—227
6:22—425 n. 50
9:10–11—103
9:14—111
10:14—408
11:16—227
13:14—229
15:4—288
15:10—312
16:13–15—167 n. 5
17:4—229
17:5—390
17:6—61 n. 58, 299, 444
17:6–7—390
19:15—61 n. 58, 299, 314 n. 27, 444, 445
21:23—447
22:10—227
22:24—390
23:2–4—39 n. 5
23:8—39 n. 5
23:9—39 n. 5

481

Index of Scripture

Index of Scripture

485

Index of Scripture

489

Index of Scripture

3—13
3:1—305, 456
3:2—374
3:3—54, 126 n. 66, 152 n. 41
3:4—57, 105 n. 17, 387
3:5—386
3:6—257 n. 30
3:10—43, 149, 154
3:11—154, 173
3:18—74
3:19—376 n. 46
3:20–21—168, 173
3:21—23, 170, 172, 190
4:1—219
4:2—457
4:3—294, 298 n. 68
4:4—457
4:5—330
4:6—248
4:7—131
4:8—216
4:9—458 n. 33
4:12—215, 367, 392
4:13—106, 421
4:15—223, 370
4:15–18—369
4:16—370, 371
4:16–17—428
4:16–18—271
4:17—272
4:18—90 n. 49
4:19—51, 313, 393, 419
4:23—281, 419, 460 n. 39

Colossians

1:1—38 n. 1
1:2—40 n. 7
1:3—388
1:5—217
1:10—314 n. 25
1:15—141
1:15–18—194
1:16—161
1:18—189
1:20—195
1:22—154
1:23—37, 75
1:24—43, 149, 189
1:25–27—410
1:27—117, 451 n. 18

2:2—273
2:3—367, 380
2:8—369
2:11—176
2:12—154
2:15—89, 246
2:19—152 n. 41
3—13
3:1—154
3:1–2—161
3:5—309, 438
3:8—436
3:9—127
3:9–10—256
3:10—159
3:12—217
3:13—78, 358 n. 3
3:16—273
3:24–25—376 n. 46
4:3—85
4:10—293
4:11—298 n. 68
4:16—11, 55, 102, 343
4:18—37

I Thessalonians

1:1—40 n. 7
1:2–3—388, 452 n. 21
1:5—217, 218
1:6—272
1:6–8—156
1:7–8—40
1:9—103 n. 12
1:10—142
2:2—85 n. 30, 153, 369 n. 31, 390
2:3—137
2:4—152 n. 41
2:5—69 n. 1
2:6—371
2:8—369 n. 31, 429
2:8–9—85 n. 30
2:9—285 n. 30, 21, 368, 369 n. 31, 392, 429
2:10—69 n. 1
2:11—428
2:14—42, 272
2:14–15—152
2:18—247, 330, 375, 418
2:19–20—56
3:2—39, 85 n. 30, 208, 298 n. 68, 369 n. 31
3:3—42

3:3–4—272
3:5—307
3:13—235
4—166
4:1—456
4:7—234
4:9—11, 305
4:13—48 n. 26
4:13–18—165, 173
4:14—142, 151
4:15–17—168
4:17—23
4:18—457
5:1—11, 305
5:8—218 n. 30, 335
5:11—457
5:16—457
5:18—367 n. 27
5:22—295
5:23—458 n. 33
5:24—60
5:26—459
5:27—11, 55, 102, 343
5:28—281, 460 n. 39

II Thessalonians

1:2—40 n. 7
1:4—245, 272
1:8—85 n. 30
2:3—228
2:6—228
2:9—141, 375, 425
2:10—91, 139–40
2:17—314 n. 25
3:1—456
3:3—60
3:8—388, 392
3:10—289
3:13—136
3:16—458 n. 33
3:18—281, 460 n. 39

I Timothy

1:1—38 n. 1
1:5—217
1:11—156
1:13—136
1:13–14—424
1:15—423
1:16—136
1:20—418, 455
2:7—38
2:14—360
3:3—381
3:13—246

3:15—103 n. 12
4:1—219
4:10—103 n. 12
5:17—56
5:18—369
5:19—61 n. 58, 299, 444, 445
5:22—216 n. 22
6:6–8—313
6:9—283
6:15—70 n. 2
6:16—375
6:17–18—314

II Timothy

1:1—38 n. 1
1:3—388, 452 n. 21
1:11—38
1:16—132
1:18—132
2:3–4—369
2:8b–9—335
2:15—217
2:18—173
2:23—248
2:25—199 n. 89, 254
3:11—49 n. 29
3:16—289
3:17—314
4:1—180
4:2—344, 376
4:3—143
4:8—456
4:10—86 n. 34, 261
4:11—293
4:13—85, 393
4:14—376 n. 46
4:17—421

Titus

1:1—38 n. 1
1:4—61, 86 n. 34, 240 n. 7
1:13—450, 455
2:5—216 n. 22
2:6—457
2:11—199
2:12—199
2:14—314 n. 25
2:15—457
3:9—248
3:13—58 n. 47

Philemon

1—298 n. 68

Index of Scripture

19:15—226, 233 n. 68	**21:3**—231, 232	**22:7**—180	**22:18–19**—377
20:12—181	**21:5**—193	**22:10**—410	**22:20**—62 n. 60, 180,
20:12–13—376 n. 46	**21:22**—226, 233 n. 68	**22:12**—180, 376 n. 46	419

Apocrypha

I Esdras	**II Maccabees**	**8:29**—194 n. 79	**Tobit**
8:80—234 n. 69	**1:5**—194 n. 79		**4:8**—286
	5:8—399	**III Maccabees**	
II Esdras	**5:20**—194 n. 79	**2:2**—233 n. 68	**Wisdom of Solomon**
23:1—39 n. 5	**5:27**—234 n. 69	**6:2**—233 n. 68	**8:8**—425 n. 50
	7:33—194 n. 79		**9:15**—167
	8:18—233 n. 68	**Sirach**	
		17:13—111	

Old Testament Pseudepigrapha

Apocalypse of Moses	**Life of Adam and Eve**	**Testament of Joseph**	**18:5–6**—408 n. 11
17:1—375 n. 43	**9:1**—375 n. 43	**7:4**—229 n. 60	**18:12–12**—229 n. 60
40:2—408 n. 11			
	Testament of Issachar	**Testament of Judah**	*Vitae Prophetae*
Jubilees	**6:1**—229 n. 60	**25:3**—229 n. 60	**17:21**—230 n. 61
1:20—230 n. 61	**7:7**—229 n. 60		**17:9–10**—230 n. 61
15:33—230 n. 61		**Testament of Levi**	
		2:7—408 n. 11	

Dead Sea Scrolls

CD	**1QM**	**1QS**
5:18—230 n. 62	**4:2**—230 n. 62	**3:20–21**—230 n. 62
12:2—230 n. 62	**13:2**—230 n. 62	**3:23–24**—230 n. 62
	13:4—230 n. 62	

Other Jewish Writings

Hagigah	**Makkoth**	**Sanhedrin**	*Sifre Deuteronomy*
12b—408 n. 11	**3.1–9**—389 n. 73	**111b**—229 n. 59	**11.22, #48**—146 n. 28
			117—229 n. 59

Early Christian Writings

Barnabas	**5.6**—215 n. 20, 388 n. 72	**Martyrdom of Polycarp**	**11.5**—16
5.8—425 n. 50	**5.6–7**—351 n. 54	**12.3**—406	**Sibylline Oracles**
	6.4—436 n. 71	**15.2**—90	**2:167**—230 n. 61
I Clement	**7.2**—348 n. 49		
1.3—348 n. 49	**9.1**—436 n. 71	**Polycarp** *Philippians*	**II Enoch**
3.2—436 n. 71	**38.2**—319 n. 41	**1.1**—58 n. 47	**8:1**—409
4.7—436 n. 71	**41.1**—348 n. 49	**2.3**—16	**42:3**—409
5.5—436 n. 71	**48.1**—194 n. 79	**6.2**—16	
	51.5—425 n. 50		